HARDWARE AND SOFTWARE CONCEPTS IN VLSI

HARDWARE AND
SOFTWARE CONCEPTS
IN VLSI

Edited by

GUY RABBAT

Van Nostrand Reinhold Electrical/Computer Science and Engineering Series

VNR VAN NOSTRAND REINHOLD COMPANY
NEW YORK CINCINNATI TORONTO LONDON MELBOURNE

Manufactured in the United States of America

Published by Van Nostrand Reinhold Company Inc.
135 West 50th Street, New York, N.Y. 10020

Van Nostrand Reinhold Publishing
1410 Birchmount Road
Scarborough, Ontario MIP 2E7, Canada

Van Nostrand Reinhold
480 Latrobe Street
Melbourne, Victoria 3000, Australia

Van Nostrand Reinhold Company Limited
Molly Millars Lane
Wokingham, Berkshire, England

15   14   13   12   11   10   9   8   7   6   5   4   3   2   1

Library of Congress Cataloging in Publication Data
Main entry under title:

Hardware and software concepts in VLSI.

   (Van Nostrand Reinhold electrical/computer science and engineering series)
   Includes index.
1. Integrated circuits—very large scale integration.
I. Rabbat, Guy.   II. Series.
TK7874.H384   1983   621.381'73   82.17604
ISBN 0-442-22538-5

Van Nostrand Reinhold
Electrical/Computer Science and Engineering Series
Sanjit Mitra, Series Editor

HANDBOOK OF ELECTRONIC DESIGN AND ANALYSIS PROCEDURES USING PROGRAMMABLE CALCULATORS, by Bruce K. Murdock

COMPILER DESIGN AND CONSTRUCTION, by Arthur B. Pyster

SINUSOIDAL ANALYSIS AND MODELING OF WEAKLY NONLINEAR CIRCUITS, by Donald D. Weiner and John F. Spina

APPLIED MULTIDIMENSIONAL SYSTEMS THEORY, by N. K. Bose

MICROWAVE SEMICONDUCTOR ENGINEERING, by Joseph F. White

INTRODUCTION TO QUARTZ CRYSTAL UNIT DESIGN, by Virgil E. Bottom

DIGITAL IMAGE PROCESSING, by William B. Green

SOFTWARE TESTING TECHNIQUES, by Boris Beizer

LIGHT TRANSMISSION OPTICS, Second edition, by Dietrich Marcuse

REAL TIME COMPUTING, edited by Duncan Mellichamp

HARDWARE AND SOFTWARE CONCEPTS IN VLSI, edited by Guy Rabbat

To
Elfriede, Ralph, Shirley, Alice,
Victor, Jacqueline and Joseph.

Preface

The purpose of *Hardware and Software Concepts in VLSI* is to initiate the reader to the real issues facing industry today in VLSI. This book offers an integrated view of VLSI in system architecture, chip design, technologies and computer-aided design. Such topics as large-scale computer systems, hardware algorithms, microprocessors, chip architecture: PLA (programmable logic-arrays), gate-arrays and custom design, description of bipolar MOS, gallium-arsenide, Josephson technologies as well as oxidation processes and electron beam testing, computer-aided design: layout, routing, cell design, design verification and logic simulation, are covered.

This is the first book to cover VLSI from the system down to the chip design, new technologies and processes, as well as CAD in industry.

While the material in *Hardware and Software Concepts in VLSI* is presented in a particular order, it need not be read in that order. Each chapter presents material from a spectrum of subjects in integrated systems. The first group consists of Chapters 1 to 4 and covers the system architecture of VLSI; the second group is comprised of Chapters 5 to 8 and discusses chip design in VLSI; the third group of Chapters 9 to 13 presents the latest VLSI technologies, and the fourth group of Chapters 14 to 20 discusses the latest computer-aided design tools used in VLSI.

VLSI is an exciting and very dynamic field and it is hoped that this book will contribute to introducing more people to the practical aspects of VLSI, mainly as seen from industry.

GUY RABBAT

Acknowledgments

I wish to express my gratitude to the many individuals who have contributed their ideas and their support in the development of this book. In particular, I wish to thank the following:

For contributions to the text: C. V. Ramamoorthy and Y. W. Ma, University of California, Berkeley; Mark A. Scott and Kenneth C. Smith, University of Toronto; Amar Mukhopadhyay, University of Central Florida; John E. Price, Amdahl Corporation; Seiken Yano, Yasunori Ouchi, Kodo Kimura and Kenji Okada, Nippon Electric Company; David Katz, Bell Laboratories; Joseph C. Logue, Walter J. Kleinfelder, Paul Lowy, J. Randall Moulic and Wei-Wha Wu, IBM Corporation; S. M. Faris, IBM Corporation; Youssef El-Mansy, Intel Corporation; F. S. Lee, S. I. Long, R. Zucca, B. M. Welch, and G. K. Kaelin, Rockwell International; R. C. Eden, Gigabit Logic; E. Wolfgang, P. Fazekas, J. Otto and J. Crichton, Siemens Corporation; Natsuro Tsubouchi, Mitsubishi Electric Corporation; Marvin E. Daniel and Charles W. Gwyn, Sandia National Laboratories; Melvin A. Breuer, University of Southern California; H. W. Carter, United States Air Force; R. H. J. M. Otten, IBM Corporation; I. Shirakawa, Osaka University; U. Lauther, Siemens Corporation; Hajimu Mori, Tomoyuki Fujita, Masahiro Annaka, and Satoshi Goto, Nippon Electric Company; Isao Ohkura, Kaoru Okazaki, Takeshi Tokuda and Kazuhiro Sakashita, Mitsubishi Electric Corporation; Lynea A. Miller, IBM Corporation.

The support and patience of my wife Elfriede, were of great help.

Contents

1. Introduction

The continuing advance of electronic technology has been a driving force behind the evolution of computing machinery, an evolution in which the unit cost falls while the unit capability rises. The constantly evolving ratio of cost to capability requires a frequent review of the design tradeoffs to be made. This is one of the motivations of this book.

Chapter 2 by Ramamoorthy and Ma addresses the evolution of large-scale embedded computer systems by discussing the revolutionary impact of VLSI technology on computer architecture, and design methodology by which large-scale embedded computer systems can be realized much more easily.

An embedded computer system can be defined as a computer system which controls a very large hardware complex. Any real-time control system fits into this category.

The difficulties in the design of large-scale embedded computer systems fall into two categories: First, the requirement on real-time control, criticality, high performance, and fault tolerance keeps stressing the available technology to its limits. Sophisticated computer architectures, such as pipelining, interleaved memory and parallel processing, have to be used in order to satisfy the imposed requirements. These complicated architectures usually lead to a very expensive design.

Other difficulties in developing large-scale embedded computer systems are primarily caused by the largeness of the systems and the ever changing system environment.

Despite these problems, difficulties in the design of large-scale embedded computer systems have been alleviated by the rapid advances in the following two areas: First, the emergence of VLSI technology, and second, the advances in design methodologies.

Chapter 3 by Scott and Smith examines the use of bit slice microprocessors in providing a multicomputer system with dynamic reconfiguration capabilities. These capabilities allow reconfiguration, under software control, of the system hardware into a variable number of processors of different characteristics (such as word size and instruction set). There are many potential uses of such capabilities in the areas of multiprogramming, parallel processing, and fault tolerant systems. The reconfiguration capability introduces a number of issues concerning processor function modularization that do not arise in fixed architectures. The chapter examines these issues and shows potential processor modules that are realizable with current VLSI technology.

This architecture has only recently become feasible as a result of the great reduction in the ratio of cost to capability provided by VLSI bit slice microprocessor technology.

In Chapter 4, Mukhopadhyay is concerned with hardware algorithms for pattern matching and string processing for VLSI implementation. The advent of very large scale integration (VLSI) technology has stimulated renewed interest in a fundamental issue in the context of LSI: What to put into a chip? Because they have a regular geometry based on the repetition of simple cells, memory devices are natural candidates for VLSI implementation. But there is always some communication and system overhead for utilizing a pure memory device in the total system architecture. An improvement in this situation can be made if both memory and logic can be combined to build a special-purpose processor that can take over some of the specialized functions of CPU, reduce system bottlenecks and simplify the overall communication and control structure. The basic problem seems to be the identification of tasks which can be built into special-purpose VLSI chips.

In Chapter 5, by Price, factors such as speed, power, cost reliability, custom design versus off-the-shelf and degree of risk must all be considered during the decision-making process which culminates in the choice of a specific integrated circuit technology. The feature which is called "chip architecture" must also be considered because of the effect it has in areas such as system performance, design flexibility and engineering changes. Chip architecture is defined from both an essential and an existential point of view. It consists of the integrated circuit design and layout plus application-oriented features such as mask programmable versus software programmable or fused-link programmable logic function.

According to Price, the performance figure of merit for logic chips is the signal propagation delay through a gate from input to output, ranging from greater than 10ns for medium speed to less than 1ns for very high speed gates. For memory chips, the performance figure of merit is the read access time (the delay from a valid address at the input to valid data at the output). This ranges from greater than 100ns for medium speed to less than 10ns for very high speed memory.

In Chapter 6, Yano et al. demonstrate the increasing demand for new data processing systems which have higher performance, smaller system size, lower cost and higher reliability. High speed LSIs are indispensable to meet these requirements. However, they disclose many problems as the integration level is increased.

The authors have developed a low energy, high performance VLSI technology, with an average of 1000 gates and a delay of 0.9 nanoseconds per basic gate, which utilizes a transistor array masterslice and low energy CML technology with 2 level series gated structure. A CAD system supports all the design activities and will facilitate the realization of systems based on VLSI.

They have developed a low energy, high performance VLSI technology, with an average of 1000 gates and a delay of 0.9 nanoseconds per basic gate, which utilizes a transistor array masterslice and low energy CML technology with 2 level series gated structure. A CAD system supports all the design activities and will facilitate the realization of systems based on VLSI.

In Chapter 7, Katz describes gate arrays and other forms of integrated circuit chips which continue to increase their level of integration and their speed-power performance. To cope with the very large scales of integration (VLSI) on chips, effective design strategies and computer-aids for design (CAD) are emerging. Array chips, design strategies and CAD all contribute to reducing the time, cost, and risk in VLSI chip design. This chapter examines and describes: 1) design time and cost results obtained with array chips, 2) speed-power, gates and area capabilities in array chips, 3) the common design strategies used for arrays and VLSI, and 4) a CAD system for arrays and other VLSI chips. The intent is to provide some measures of current array chip capabilities and offer some observations about essential factors in computer aided design systems for VLSI chips.

In Chapter 8, Logue et al., discusses the ability of the semi-conductor industry to produce chips with higher and higher circuit densities. This has created a challenge for the product designer: to utilize this capacity and still develop chips rapidly at reasonable cost. A multi-faceted approach to VLSI design is described that significantly reduces product development time and resource from those required with existing methods. This approach is based on the use of PLA structures or macros. It consists of a hardware/software modeling technique, use of laser-personalizable PLAs for rapid modeling of PLA macros, and a method for repairing design errors (that may hide other errors) on the actual VLSI wafers with a laser tool. A two-pass VLSI design is, therefore, highly probable.

Faris in Chapter 9, traces the evolution of VLSI superconducting technologies to illustrate examples of many engineering considerations which have to be accomodated in order to exploit VLSI tools for the purpose of realizing an ultra-high performance computer. The chapter surveys different aspects of cryo-electronic technologies, and achieves the following objectives: 1) To present a general discussion of the limitations of known computer switching elements in order to justify investigating superconductive devices and the role they may play in those future ultra-high performance computers. 2) To introduce superconductive devices, logic and memory circuits emphasizing the influence of their basic properties on maintaining their promising performance. 3) To illustrate, by means of examples, the practical considerations which lead to optimum designs and perhaps stimulate invention of new devices and circuits. 4) To emphasize that in order to qualify as building blocks for ulta-high performance computers, switching devices in general must satisfy simultaneously certain physical and engineering requirements.

In Chapter 10, Mansy proposes an MOS technology and methodology for designing devices and processes for high density high performance circuits. The procedure involves scaling down device lateral and vertical dimensions and supply voltage, while increasing the substrate doping—all by the same scaling factor.

In Chapter 11, Lee and Al discuss GaAs VLSI devices and circuits. During the last few years, there has been growing interest in the use of gallium arsenide for high speed digital integrated circuits. This is due to the intrinsic advantages of the high electron mobility of this material combined with the availability of a semi-insulating substrate. Very high switching speeds, approaching those of Josephson junction devices, have been demonstrated for GaAs logic employing short channel Schottky gate MESFETs. A reproductible ion implantation technology in GaAs has recently been developed. This technology does provide MESFETs with the uniformity in pinchoff voltage required for LSI circuits. Because of these technological advances, low pinchoff voltage depletion mode MESFET logic has been able to achieve low power dissipation and high circuit density with little sacrifice in speed, thereby overcoming many of the former objections to the feasibility of GaAs LSI circuits.

In Chapter 12, Wolfgang et al. show, for the first time, all the functions of a microprocessor and how to determine their internal dynamic behavior by means of electron beam testing techniques. The 8-bit microprocessor 8085 has been chosen as a typical representative for this purpose. Chapter 12 gives an overview of the various electron beam techniques required for the investigation of microprocessors. According to Wolfgang, during the 1970s, the instrument most commonly used in laboratories for this purpose was the mechanical probe. Some laboratories additionally applied electron beam testing techniques, which they used to supplement mechanical probing. If the two techniques are compared, the electron probe if found to have a number of advantages over the mechanical probe. However, the ten-to-twenty-fold higher cost of equipment, the distinctly more complicated measuring techniques and the unavailability, until recently, of the commercial equipment for the scanning electron microscope for electron beam testing have so far been obstacles to the acceptance of this otherwise more advantageous alternative. During the 1980s, it is to be expected that electron beam testing will be introduced as a standard method for internal probing and that the mechanical probe will only remain in use as a supplementary tool.

Chapter 13, by Tsubouchi, describes oxidation as a fundamental process of silicon device technology over the last twenty years. Oxidation methods which have received increasing attention in the last few years involve the use of high pressure. High pressure oxidation is a good method for achieving an accelerated oxide growth and preparing thermal oxide at reduced temperature. Low temperature oxidation has its greatest potential impact on high density VLSI, because of the need to minimize the creation of thermally induced defects and to maintain sharp impurity profiles in small devices.

High pressure oxidation is expected to gain rapid acceptance with the commercial availability of high pressure oxidation apparatus with appropriate safety and production capability.

Daniel and Gwyn, in Chapter 14, describe a novel CAD system. As integrated circuit complexities increase, many existing computer-aided design methods must be replaced with an integrated design system to support VLSI circuit and system design. The framework for a hierarchical computer-aided design (CAD) system is described. The system supports both functional and physical design from initial specification and system synthesis to simulation, mask layout, verification, and documentation. The system is being implemented in phases on a DEC System 20 computer network and will support evolutionary changes as new technologies are developed and design strategies defined.

Breuer and Carter, in Chapter 15, review routing techniques for VLSI. The complexity of VLSI circuits creates an enormous demand for efficient and effective layout techniques. Classically, the layout process has been divided into three subproblems, namely, partitioning (assigning logic to chips), placement (physically assigning circuits to physical locations on a chip), and interconnection (connecting the pads of the circuits so that pads associated with the same signal net are electrically common and isolated from the other nets). This chapter deals with the latter problem. To help achieve goals, numerous design automation layout tools have been developed, and new ones will continue to be developed. The degree to which these tools are used is a function of the design style being employed. For polycell and masterslice layouts, automated placement and interconnection techniques have been successfully employed since the early 1970s. Most of the techniques employed are very similar to those used for PCB layout. For custom VLSI, there is a greater demand for very high circuit density. Automatic layout techniques are beginning to be used heavily.

Otten, in Chapter 16, describes a concise survey as well as an exposition of ideas about automation of layout design. In the first part, the state and position of this part of CAD is considered. The central part of this chapter is a discussion of imperatives of a layout design system suitable for VLSI. Of course, such a system has to take account of the embedding into an integrated design system. However, layout design faces two other major problems. One results from industry's ability to pack over 10,000 gate equivalents into a single chip. Besides this increase of complexity, today's micro-electronics technology has made a variety of processes—each with its own set of design rules—available for integration. Diversity has existed for a long time, but complexity raised the problem, since development of efficient systems for designing complex systems is costly and time-consuming. Layout design shares the complexity problem with any other design task. From the proliferation of different device technologies, layout design seems to suffer most heavily. The last part of this chapter is a precursory presentation of an approach striving for conformance to the imperatives of the second part.

Chapter 17 by Shirakawa reviews routing for VLSI printed circuit boards. Most of the existing routing systems are constructed of several distinctive routers, such as maze-running routers, line-search routers, and channel routers, so that a merit of one may compensate for a defect of another. A new routing scheme is described which can be applied to printed wiring boards of different wiring densities such that the number of wiring tracks permitted between two consecutive pins of an ordinary dual in line package ranges from one to four. This scheme is distinctive in that a single-row router is combined with a line-search router in such a way that the search for possible wire segments at the stage of the line search router is implemented channel by channel, with all interconnections within each channel completed later by the single-row router.

The program operates on an ACOS 77/900 computer, and has been applied to numbers of boards. Some of the implementation results are also shown to reveal how much the described scheme may attain its potentialities in the practice of layout of high density printed wiring boards.

In Chapter 18, Lauther discusses a cell based VLSI design system. The main steps in developing an integrated circuit are functional design, physical design, design verification, and simulation and generation of test and fabrication data.

Mori et al in Chapter 19 discusses the layout design problem as follows: Given a two-layer wiring board in general, components or circuit modules are mounted on the first side of the board, each with connector pins. Connection through holes are used to connect wiring patterns on different sides of the board. These through holes are called vias. Each set of pins to be electrically connected in common, called a signal net or a power line, can be connected by wiring patterns on each layer using vias. The layout problem is to decide the positions of each component and find the routing of each signal net and power line to satisfy a given specification. The ultimate layout design goal is to provide an automatic design system which will achieve complete net connectivity meeting all physical and electrical constraints.

Efficient algorithms for the placement or the routing are quite important to reduce the design time. Particularly, in Japan, both theoretical and practical approaches have been very active for the past 10 years in universities and industries.

It is considered extremely necessary to establish an integrated CAD system, which significantly reduces the total design time required to complete the board.

Ohkura et al., in the final chapter, reviews design verification and simulation techniques. Software simulation technologies are discussed which are especially devoted for the design verification of VLSI logic circuits, such as gate array LSIs and building block LSIs. An emerging and important area in CAD is called macromodeling, macrosimulation and mixed-mode simulation. Various kinds of CAD tools have made it possible not only to develop VLSI circuits in a short turnaround time, but also to execute a rigid timing design of the circuit in order to get higher performance.

2. Large Scale Computer Systems

C. V. Ramamoorthy

and

Y. W. Ma

University of California at Berkeley

INTRODUCTION

An embedded computer system can be defined as a computer system which controls a very large hardware complex. Any real-time control system fits into this category. Examples of these systems are an air-traffic control system, a large weapons system, a nuclear reactor control system, etc. Apart from the real-time control, several other characteristics and constraints may be present in such systems such as criticality, high performance, fault-tolerance, etc. In addition, these systems are generally very large. Hence, the design of embedded computer systems has appeared to be a very difficult task.

The difficulties in the design of large-scale embedded computer systems fall into two categories: First, the requirements on real-time control, criticality, high performance, and fault tolerance keep stressing the available technology to its limits. Sophisticated computer architectures, such as pipelining, interleaved memory, and parallel processing, have to be used in order to satisfy the imposed requirements. These complicated architectures usually lead to a very expensive design.

Other difficulties in developing large-scale embedded computer systems are primarily caused by the largeness of the systems. The activities of the systems are so varied and complex that they are beyond the grasp of a single individual. For example, in the ballistic missile defense systems (BMD), besides the data processing systems, there are radar and missile subsystems. Since each of these subsystems requires special expertise to design, each subsystem is usually developed and maintained by experts who have little knowledge of the other subsystems. Consequently, some final decisions on primitives (essential system characteristics) are made in one subsystem without considering the overall system requirement. For this reason, the design of large-scale embedded computer systems are usually expensive and far from optimum. Another important problem faced by the development of large-scale embedded computer systems is the ever changing system environment. When the system application changes or the technology changes, the system has to be modified to adapt to the changes. However, systems are usually designed without making provision for future evolution. Therefore, when the system evolves, changes are incorporated into the system in an ad hoc manner. As a result, the integrity of the system is undermined, and the unstructureness of the system explodes, resulting in a regenerative, highly non-linear increase in the effort and cost of system maintenance (1). In large-scale critical real time systems, such as BMD systems, another difficulty imposed on the development process is the real time constraint and the criticality of the system. These systems must perform all the required function correctly within the given time limits, otherwise a large penalty has to be paid. However, these systems cannot be tested in real operational environments. As a result, system validation has to rely mainly on analysis and simulation. Current approaches to the development of large embedded computer systems are based primarily on experience and intuition. Consequently, these systems are very expensive to design, difficult to test adequately, slow to deploy, and hard to adapt to changing requirements (2).

Despite the above problems, difficulties in the design of large-scale embedded computer systems have been alleviated by the rapid advances in the following two areas: First, the emergence of VLSI technology has promised the availability of a million switching elements on a single silicon chip by the year 1985. These powerful and inexpensive VLSI chips can be used to form computer systems that meet the requirements imposed on large-scale embedded computer systems with relatively low cost. For example, powerful distributed systems can be formed by interconnecting a large number of inexpensive VLSI-single-chip computers. The available parallelism in these systems can provide fast response time for real-time control. Moreover, by exploiting the inherent redundancy in these systems, fault tolerance can be achieved via the technique of graceful degradation. By implementing algorithms in special-purpose VLSI chips, fast execution time of the corresponding functions can be provided. Further, the large number of switching element in a VLSI chip allows the incorporation of more intelligence into different functional units, such as memory modules and I/O modules. These intelligent functional units can perform a large amount of local processing and hence can remove bottlenecks in the system. For these reasons, VLSI technology can resolve many difficulties in designing large-scale embedded computer systems.

The advances in design methodologies also provide valuable tools for developing large-scale embedded computer systems (3). By using the concepts of levels of abstraction, decomposition and partitioning, the development of embedded computer systems can proceed in a systematic manner. As a result, the complexity of developing such systems can be greatly reduced.

IMPACT OF VLSI TECHNOLOGY ON COMPUTER ARCHITECTURE

State of the Art of VLSI Technology

VLSI technology means upward of many hundreds of thousands switching devices on a single silicon chip with feature size approaching one micron. In the last two decades, integrated circuit (IC) technology has advanced from a few to tens of thousands of transistors on a single silicon chip. For the first 15 years, since the inception of ICs, the progress in making ICs in every more complex structure has moved in an exponential fashion, at the rate of doubling the number of transistors that could be placed on a single chip (with tolerable yield) every year (4). Over the last few years, this growth rate has slowed down to doubling every 18 to 24 months. The 1980 state of the art of IC technology is about 70K devices on a single chip, such as the Motorola MC 68000 or the 64K memory chip. The past history and trend of IC technology is illustrated in Figure 2-1.

The rapid advance of IC technology is made possible mainly by the improvements in fabrication technology. The improved technology has reduced the density of defects, which makes larger chips feasible. Moreover, the improvements enable the use of much smaller transistors and wires, which increases the density of circuitry. At the same time, the reduced size also results in faster and/or lower power operation.

Limitation on Integrated Circuit Technology

Although IC technology will continue to advance rapidly, there are several factors that constrain the integration level of the future silicon IC technology. These factors can be categorized into physical limits, technological limits, and complexity limits (5).

Physical limits include the velocity of light, the principle of uncertainty, entropy (irreversibility), and thermal energy. These limits determine the fundamental unsurpassable limits which present barriers to switching speed and power dissipation. Physical limits suggest an ultimate density improvement of 1000 times over that attained by todays IC technology.

Technological limits are concerned with fabrication techniques, materials constants, and electrical parameters. The constraints imposed by technological limits can usually be circumvented by using different materials, lower operating temperatures, structure changes, improved cooling techniques, etc.

Complexity limits relate to the human inability to design circuitry which involves a very large number of components. In other words, these are concep-

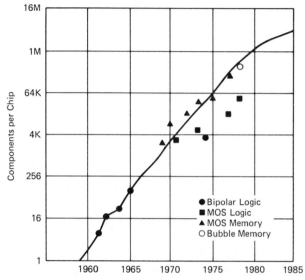

Figure 2-1. History and trend of IC technology.

tual limits. Complexity involves product definition, design engineering changes, testing, on-chip redundancy, computer-assisted design, packaging, etc. The complexity limit directly affects the design cost of VLSI chips (4). The amount of effort required for product definition, design, and layout manhours per month, starting from the first planar transistor of 1959 and projecting beyond that is shown in Figure 2-2. It can be seen that the effort explodes exponentially, doubling every two and two-thirds years. Since the cost in man-hour per month inflates at least 10 percent per year, the costs double every two years. Along with the fact that the IC density also doubles every two years, it results in a constant cost per element to define, design, and lay out complex semiconductor ICs.

In contrast with the design cost, manufacturing costs of ICs are mainly independent of device complexity. Whereas manufacturing costs have been the dominating cost and exceeded the design cost in the past, with today's high density ICs the situation is now reversing. The design cost is now becoming more important, which implies that in the future, considerable amount of effort is needed in product definition and design technology in order to surpass the limit imposed by complexity.

Practically speaking, VLSI technology is a statement about system complexity rather than transistor size or circuit performance. It stands for a technology that is capable of creating systems so complicated that the management of raw complexity overwhelms all other difficulties. The trend to increase function on a single silicon chip will continue, and despite the various limiting fac-

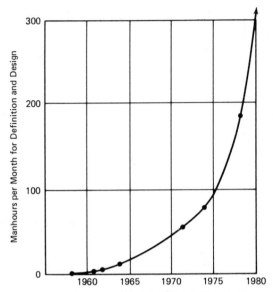

Figure 2-2. The man-hours per month for IC definition, design, and layout.

tors that constrain the growth of IC complexity, the density of transistors can at least increase an additional 400 times before the fundamental limit is reached. Ultimately, it will be the practical rather than the absolute limit that constrains the size of IC chips, and the optimal size of IC chips will be the best balance between yield and complexity.

Trends in the Use of VLSI Technology on Computer Architecture

With the large number of switching elements available in a single chip as promised by VLSI technology, the question that arises naturally is: What can we do with this technology and how can we best utilize it? Basically, there are two different architectural directions for VLSI based computers (5). The first is essentially the traditional direction that technology has been following during the last two decades, that is, putting more and more functions on a chip as well as to making the chip run faster and faster. By integrating the CPU, memory, and input/output circuitry of an older design that previously required several chips onto a single chip, the single-chip computer architecture is obtained. Since the development in the direction of designing the single-chip stand-alone computer will be plagued by the need for compatibility with prior designs, architectural progress along this direction will be relatively slow.

The other direction takes a fresh look at new technology and many recently emerged computer applications. By exploiting the advantages of VLSI technology where a complex CPU or even a full single-chip microcomputer costs only a few dollars, it becomes economical to design a system using a multiplicity of microcomputers providing more processing power than would be possible or practical using a single CPU with traditional architecture. Essentially, this direction considers the interconnection of VLSI chips, which can either be general purpose, single-chip computers or a special purpose VLSI chip, to form highly concurrent computer systems. This direction implies the exploration of many new architectural concepts and algorithm designs as well as opening up many new computer applications.

One serious drawback of VLSI technology is the limited number of pins on the chip. While VLSI chips provide an exponentially growing number of gates, the number of pins which can be accomodated remains almost constant. It has been observed experimentally that if the number of circuits on a chip is proportional to the volume of a sphere, then the number of pins that is required to serve these circuits is proportional to the surface of the sphere (6). As a result, communication becomes a very difficult design problem in the interconnection of VLSI chips. Due to the insufficient communication power and the high design cost of VLSI chips, computer systems employing VLSI technology will thus imply many architectural concepts that depart sharply from past and present practices (7, 8).

Single-Chip Computers

Motivations for Single-Chip Computers. For conventional computer systems in which the processor and memory are implemented in separate IC chips, the communication between processor and memory remains a major and difficult design problem when high bandwidth requirement is imposed on the system (9, 10). The difficulties are due to the following two factors: First, because of different loading capacities, the delay-power product of a connection residing within a single IC chip is much smaller than those interconnecting separate chips. At present, the ratio is more than two orders of magnitude and will become larger as proper scaling of MOS circuits leads to faster and smaller circuits which operate at lower power levels. Although it is possible to drive signals going through the package pins as fast as minimum size gates can drive internal signal paths by building large and power consuming driver circuits onto the chip, at present, external signals speeds are still about an order of magnitude slower due to practical tradeoffs. Hence, bringing a signal from one chip to another results in a significant performance penalty, either as increased power consumption or as exorbitant delay. Therefore, high memory bandwidth is very difficult to obtain in a conventional computer.

The second factor that limits the memory bandwidth is due to the limited number of package pins for standard semiconductor memory. As shown in Figure 2-3, a standard semiconductor memory is usually designed as a square

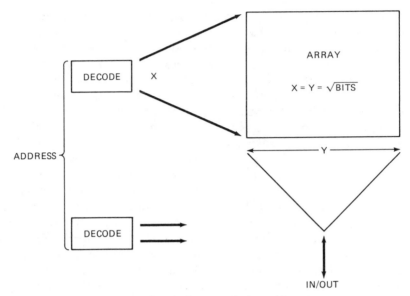

Figure 2-3. Standard memory device architecture.

matrix, since the chip area is minimized when the X and Y decodes are of the same size. The X decode is used to select one of the words, while the Y decode is used to select one of the bits in that particular word. In order to minimize the number of package pins, a "by one" organization is usually employed which leads to a severe waste of the available memory bandwidth. For example, in a 64K-bit memory device which has $X = Y = 256$, the "by one" organization has 255/256 or 99.6 percent of the available memory bandwidth unused.

In order to overcome the above difficulties, techniques such as interleaved memory, and fetching of multiple computer words at each cycle, have to be used when the required bandwidth exceeds that of a single memory module. As a result, providing high memory bandwidth usually results in a costly design. A new approach to achieve high bandwidth without incurring high cost is to integrate the processor and memory onto a single IC chip. This approach is made feasible by the increasing number of transistors on a single silicon chip. Since the data path between the processor and memory resides within a single chip, the constraints imposed on memory bandwidth in conventional computers disappear automatically. Another advantage of the single-chip computer is that the reduced number of chips and connections in the computer system also results in higher reliability. Hence, the design and development of self-contained, single-chip computer systems with processor, memory, and input/output logic all contained on a single chip of silicon is inevitable and necessary with the emergence of VLSI technology.

Features and Characteristics of Single-Chip Computers.

Design Considerations of Single-Chip Computers.   For a given typical NMOS process used in the manufacturing of single-chip computer, the manufacturing cost can be expressed as

$$\text{manufacturing cost} = K(10^{0.0243A})$$

where A = area of chip in square mils/1000 and K = constant, for a given process.

Due to the above exponential relationship between manufacturing cost and chip area, any small decreases in chip area can lead to large decreases in manufacturing cost, and vice versa. For general purpose single-chip computers which are produced in large quantities, a small reduction in manufacturing cost of a single-chip computer will result in a large cost savings in manufacturing all the required quantities. For this reason, one of the major design principles of single-chip computers is to achieve minimum chip area (10).

The area of a single chip computer can be divided into three regions: processor, memory, and buffers and bonding pads, as shown in Figure 2-4. The geometry of the buffers and pads can be thought of as a "picture frame" surrounding the CPU and memory, which is about 15–20 mils wide. Hence, the approximate area of a single chip is

$$\text{area} = (\sqrt{CPU + memory} + 40)^2$$

Since the memory area is fixed for any selected technology and quantity of memory, the CPU area is thus the only variable parameter for any design. Consequently, the CPU area has a significant influence on the resulting area and cost, and any design with smaller CPU area will be preferable to the designer.

The minimization of chip area also affects the design tradeoffs of the on-chip memory. While the bandwidth constraint on memory is relaxed for the single-

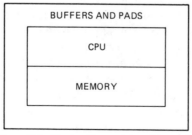

Figure 2-4. Single-chip computer chip partition.

chip computer, the design trade-off for memory bandwidth is complicated by the bus which provides the communications between the memory section and the other sections of the single-chip computer. Since the wider the bus, the more difficult it is to route—and hence the more chip area is used—in order to save chip area, the number of bits per word has to be minimized. To date, the best compromise is achieved by memory and bus widths of 8 and 16 bits. For recent products, such as Intel 8089 (11), a 20-bit register and internal bus is used.

Architecture of Single-Chip Computers.   There are two basic types of architecture for single-chip computer, namely, the "Harvard architecture" and "Von Neumann architecture". The Harvard architecture is characterized by disjoint instruction and data memories, while in Von Neumann architecture, both instruction and data reside in the same memory. The advantage of the Harvard architecture is that it provides great flexibility in word size selection since it is not necessary to have the length of instruction word as well as the various registers equal to or be a factor of the data word size. In addition, the separation of the instruction and data memories allows the overlapping of instruction and data access. For any given technology, this increased bandwidth results in higher performance over the single-chip computer based on the single memory Von Neumann architecture. The advantage of the Von Neumann architecture is that since data and instructions are intermixed in one address space, instructions can be used as data, and vice versa. To date, the Harvard architecture still provides the basic architecture for many single-chip computers. Single-chip computers based on Von Neumann architecture have started to emerge. For example, the TMS9940 (12) is based on the Von Neumann architecture. For the future single-chip computer which will be used as a general building block for highly concurrent systems than as a stand alone computer, the Von Neumann architecture will become more important.

Impact of VLSI on Single-Chip Computers.   For the last few years, self-contained, single-chip computers have been mostly used in stand-alone systems. With the high design cost of VLSI chips, the products have to be carefully designed to be of general usefulness so that large quantity will be needed and will be available at a reasonable price. In addition, since the inherent maximum speed that can be obtained from silicon integrated circuit is limited by the smallest feasible dimensions in the active constants as well as by material constants, to get more computational power from a given technology, the complexity of the system has to be increased so that more computational steps can be performed simultaneously. Due to the high design cost of a VLSI chip, sophisticated computer architecture is unsuitable for VLSI single-chip computers.

One feasible approach to achieve high computational power using VLSI technology is to employ the multiprocessor architecture. This approach has the advantage that only a small number of building blocks have to be designed. Further, the logic of these building blocks are relatively simple. Hence, the design of general purpose single-chip computers which can be used as building blocks for multiprocessor systems will become an important area for the VLSI single-chip computer.

With the large number of transistors provided in a single silicon chips, many architectural features which are only available in large computers or minicomputers can be provided in single-chip computers. Features such as large local memory, support for complex data structures, and a flexible and powerful instruction set can all be provided by the single-chip computer (9).

Large On-Chip Memory.   As increasing address spaces are provided by small computers, it has become evident that large local memory for program and data is needed in single-chip computers. For example, the Intel 8086 has a 1024K bytes memory, the Z8000 has 8192K bytes memory, and the MC 68000 has 1638K bytes memory. An attractive approach proposed in the design of X-node (13) and P1985 (9) to provide on-chip memory with high density and fast access time is to implement a memory hierarchy combined of dynamic and static RAMs. Dynamic RAM provides high density memory but its access time is relatively slow. On the other hand, static RAM provides faster access times but lower density. By using the static memory as a small cache, and the dynamic RAM as a large main memory, an on-chip memory with fast access time and high density can then be achieved.

Support of Complex Data Types and Operations.   While the traditional 8-bit microprocessor only supports simple operations on 8 and 16 bit integers, the more recent designs support a much wider variety of data types and operations. For example, the MC 68000 supports a large number of data types which include: integer, multiprecision integer, logical, Boolean, decimal, character, address, floating point and string (14). Different operations are provided to support the above data types. For the future single-chip computers, complex data structures such as arrays and structures can also be supported. The associated operations such as bound checking and address calculation of specific elements may also become cost effective when implemented by hardware.

Support of High Level Language.   The importance of high level language support has become more evident as an increasing percentage of programs developed for microprocessors are written in high level languages such as Fortran and Pascal. The advantage of using a high level language is that it can reduce the cost of coding, debugging, and maintenance. The MC 68000 supports high level languages, at both compilation time and execution time, with a clean, consistent instruction set, hardware implementation of commonly used functions such as address calculation, multiplication and division, and a set of special purpose instructions to manipulate the runtime environment of a high level language program. The language constructs which are facilitated by these special purpose instructions include array accessing, limited-precision arithmetic, looping, Boolean expression evaluation, and procedure calls. The future single-chip computer will have the capability to support a large variety of different high level languages.

Extensive Use of Microprogramming.   Due to the high complexity of VLSI chips, the lack of suitable design tools, and the difficulties in testing these chips because of the large number of transistors and small number of pins, it is necessary to have the simplest and most regular designs for VLSI based single chip computers. The most complicated part in a processor is the control circuitry. Microprogramming, which leads to a more structured, and regular design of control logic, as compared to the traditional approach to implement control which is based on carefully minimized logic functions using gates that are placed irregularly in the available space between other circuit modules, is very attractive for the implementation of control in VLSI processor.

In addition, microprogramming is also essential for testing complicated VLSI design. Since the ratio of the number of internal nodes to the number of accessible points in integrated circuits is increasing exponentially, it is impossible to test VLSI circuits by applying test patterns from outside. Hence, the use of microprogramming which enables "microdiagnostics" is very crucial for VLSI design. A further advantage of microprogramming is its flexibility and adaptability. For example, microprogramming with writable control store can support different high level languages by switching to different instruction sets.

Special-Purpose VLSI Chips

The decreasing cost of hardware has invoked the following trends in the design of special-purpose hardware modules. The first is the migration of functions from software to hardware modules in order to obtain high execution speed. Second is the distribution of intelligence into different computer systems modules, such as memory and I/O processor, in order to get better balance of system performance by removing bottlenecks in the system. Since special-purpose VLSI chips are usually produced in relatively small quantities, the design cost must be kept low in order to make the design cost-effective.

Migration of Functions—VLSI Implementation of Algorithms.   Hardware implementation of an algorithm can be executed faster than software implementation due to the inherent fast execution speed of hardware. Further, by using more hardware components, additional speed-up can be obtained. For example, using a linearly connected network of size $O(n)$, both the convolution of two n-vectors and the n-point discrete Fourier transform can be computed in O(n) units of time, rather than O(n log n) as required by the sequential Fast Fourier transform algorithm. The design cost of VLSI chips to implement algorithms can be reduced drastically if the algorithm is designed carefully in the first place (14, 15). The complexity of designing special-purpose chips is about the same as designing a high-level algorithm for the same problem if the underlying algorithm is "good" and a proper methodology which transforms the good algorithm into a final layout in a more or less mechanical way is used. Hence, for a class of problems which can be solved by good algorithms, the design of special-purpose VLSI chips to implement them becomes feasible and cost-effective.

Properties of Good VLSI Algorithms.   Algorithms that perform well on conventional random access computers are not always the best for VLSI implementation. Since VLSI has high computational power but limited communication capability, good algorithms for VLSI implementation are not necessarily those with minimal computation. Hence, the characteristics of good algorithm in the context of VLSI depart from those for conventional random access computers. On the other hand, the following three properties personify a good VLSI algorithm:

1. The implementation of the algorithm requires only a few different types of simple cells.
2. The data and control flow of the algorithm is simple and regular. This property ensures that the cells can be connected by a local and regular interconnection to form a networks, in order to minimize long distance or irregular communication.
3. The algorithm uses extensive pipelining and multiprocessing.

Algorithms with the above properties are called "systolic algorithms". The design cost of special-purpose VLSI chips for these algorithms can be kept low due to the following reasons:

1. Since most of the cells on the chip are copies of a few basic ones, only a few different, simple cells are needed to be designed and tested.
2. Regular interconnection ensures the design to be modular and extensible. Hence, a large chip can be designed by combining the designs of small chips.
3. The pipelining and multiprocessing property enables the performance requirement of a special purpose chip be met by including many identical cells on the chip.

The design cost of special purpose VLSI chip can be greatly reduced if a good algorithm is used. Hence, the most important step in the design of these chips lies on the design of the underlying algorithm. Since special-purpose

Figure 2-5. One dimensional array geometry.

chips are usually produced in small quantity, low level optimization at the circuit or layout design level which leads to minor improvements in the overall performance but drastic increase in design time may not be worthwhile.

Classification of VLSI Algorithms.   Many systolic algorithms have been designed recently. These algorithms can be classified according to the underlying geometry into: one-dimensional linear arrays, two-dimensional square arrays, trees, and shuffle-exchange networks, as shown in Figures 2-5–9 (16).

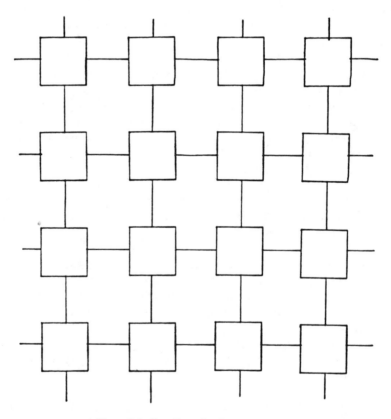

Figure 2-6. Two dimensional array geometry.

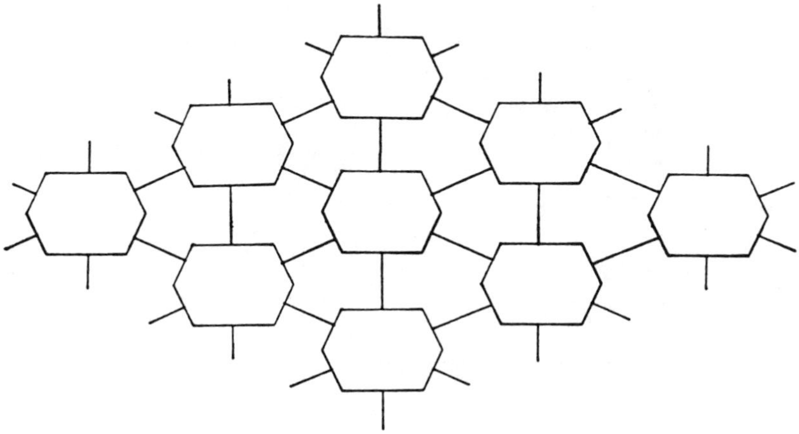

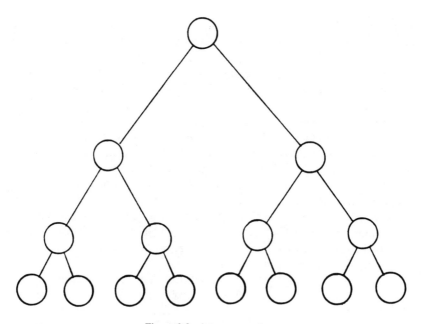

Figure 2-7. A 3 × 3 hexagonal array.

Figure 2-8. A tree geometry.

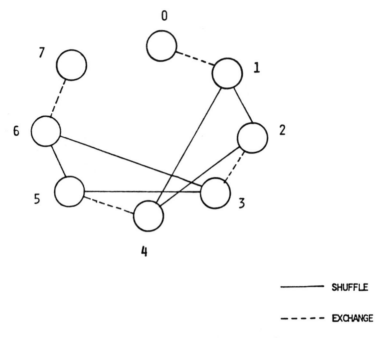

Figure 2-9. A shuffle-exchange network.

Some of the VLSI algorithms are listed in Table 2-1 according to this classification. The characteristics of each of the geometries is given in the following:

1. One-dimensional linear arrays—This is the simplest way of connecting
   cells which provides the basis for other communication geometries. The
   main characteristics of the linear array geometry is that it can be viewed
   as a pipe. Hence, it is natural for pipelined computations.
2. Two-dimensional arrays—This geometry is natural for problems involving matrices, such as graph problems defined in terms of adjacency matrices, numerical solutions to discretized partial differential equations.
3. Hexagonal arrays—This structure has the property of symmetry in three
   directions. Hence, after a binary operation is executed at a cell, the result
   and the two inputs can all be sent to the neighboring cell in a completely
   symmetric way. This type of computation eliminates a possible separate
   loading or unloading phase, which is always needed in algorithms using
   a two-dimensional array.
4. Trees—The advantage of tree structure is that the broadcasting, searching, and fan-in operations can all be executed in logarithmic-time. However, cells at high levels of the tree can easily become bottlenecks if the
   majority of communications are not confined to cells at low levels.

5. Shuffle-exchange networks—A shuffle-exchange network can be defined as follows: Let m be an integer, and the network has $n = 2^m$ nodes. Assume that nodes are named $0.1, \ldots, s^m - 1$. Let $i_m i_{m-1} \cdots i$ denote the binary representation of any integer i, for $0 \le i \le 2^m - 1$. The shuffle function can then be defined by

$$S(i_m i_{m-1} \cdots i_1) = i_{m-1} i_{m-2} \cdots i_1 i_m,$$

and the exchange function can be defined by

$$E(i_m i_{m-1} \cdots i_1) = i_m i_{m-1} \cdots i_2 \bar{i}_1.$$

The network is called a shuffle-exchange network if node i is connected to node $S(i)$ for all i, and to node $E(i)$ for all even i. By using the exchange

Table 2-1. Examples of VLSI Algorithm.

COMMUNICATION GEOMETRY	EXAMPLES
1-DIM linear arrays	Matrix-vector multiplication
	FIR Filter
	Convolution
	DFT
	Carry pipelining
	Pipeline arithmetic units
	Real-time recurrence evaluation
	Solution of triangular linear systems
	Constant-time priority queue, on-line sort
	Cartesian product
	Odd-even transposition sort
2-DIM square arrays	Dynamic programming for optimal parenthesization
	Numberical relaxation for PDE
	Merge sort
	FFT
	Graph algorithms using adjacency Matrices
2-DIM hexagonal arrays	Matrix multiplication
	Transitive closure
	LU-Decomposition by Gaussian elimination without pivoting
Trees	Searching algorithms
	Queries on nearest neighbor, rank, etc.
	NP-Complete problems
	Systolic search tree
	Parallel Function Evaluation
Shuffle-exchange networks	FFT
	Bitonic sort

and shuffle connections alternately, data at pairs of nodes with names differed by 2^i can be brought together for all $i = 0,1,\ldots m - 1$. This type of communication structure is common to many algorithms. For example, the n-point fast Fourier transform can be done O(log n) steps on the network if the processing elements can perform addition and multiplication operations. The disadvantage of the shuffle-exchange network is the low degree of regularity and modularity. Hence, this structure is not suitable for VLSI implementations. It has been shown that the network is not planar and cannot be embedded in silicon using an amount of area linearly proportional to the number of nodes (17).

Example on VLSI Algorithms.   The design of special-purpose VLSI chips to implement algorithm is illustrated by the implementation of a simple systolic priority queue (18). A priority queue can be implemented by a linear array with constant response time for the insertion, and extract minimum operations, independent of the number of elements in the priority queue, as opposed to the software implementations of a priority queue, as using some balance trees, which take O(log n) time for the above operations, where n is the number of elements in the priority queue. Each of the cells in the array has two registers A and B. The cell can access the register of its two neighbors as shown in Figure 2-10. The A registers hold elements in the queue in sorted order, with the smallest element in A, while the B registers hold elements that are being inserted into the queue. The elements of the queue are initialized to $+\infty$. The operation *insert* and *extract min* are performed at the left end of the priority queue. When elements are inserted into the priority queue, overflow elements are output at the right end. If the overflow elements are $+\infty$, no overflow has occurred. If the overflow elements are not $+\infty$, it is an indication of a real overflow.

The even and odd numbered cells pulsate alternately. At each pulse, the following operations are executed:

1. $B_i \leftarrow B_i - 1$
2. arrange the elements in A_{i-1}, A_i, and B_i so that $A_{i-1} \leq A_i \leq B_i$

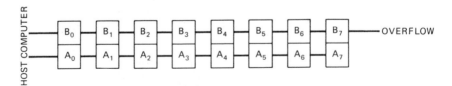

Figure 2-10. A simple priority queue.

The array pulses twice each time an operation is performed, one for the even numbered cell, and one for the odd numbered cell respectively. Cell O is a dummy cell which does not perform any operation, however, its registers can be altered by the host computer.

The operation *insert* (Q, a) is implemented by placing the value $-\infty$ in A_o, and the item a in B_o before cell 1 pulses. The element than travels to the right until it finds its proper place in the priority queue.

The *extract min* operation is implemented by loading A_o and B_o with the values $+\infty$, the minimum value can then be found in A_o. The array is ready to execute a new operation after each pair of pulsation. It is easily seen that only constant time is needed to execute the *insertion* and *extract min* operations. Because of the pipeline feature, no degradation results when many operations are requested in a row.

Distributed Intelligence in System Components. Because of the large number of switching elements in the VLSI chip, it is possible to introduce more intelligence into different components of a computer system, such as memory and I/O processor, so that the processing load on the system can be distributed more evenly among the different modules of the system, and at the same time reducing the amount of communication among the different components. One example in this area is the design of a fast cellular associative memory which expands the functions of conventional associative memory (18). Another example is the enhanced-login memory which is also an extension to associative memory aimed at the VLSI technology (19). The design of a more powerful I/O processor, such as the Intel 8089, has also been developed.

Remarks on VLSI Technology

The emergence of VLSI technology has opened many new architectural concepts which depart sharply from the design of conventional computer systems. The design of single-chip computers, special-purpose chips to implement algorithm, and more intelligent computer system modules, such as memory and I/O processors are the basic impacts of VLSI technology on computer system design. Using the general purpose or special-purpose chips as basic building blocks, very powerful but inexpensive computer systems can be designed. The low cost of these systems encourages the design of large-scale embedded computer systems which are usually special-purpose computer systems with architecture tailored to the application. However, the problem of complexity must be overcome in order to exploit the advantage of VLSI technology. Design methodology and automated design tools are needed far more urgently than ever in the generation of VLSI technology.

DESIGN METHODOLOGIES FOR LARGE-SCALE EMBEDDED COMPUTER SYSTEMS

Traditionally, the development process of large-scale computer systems consists of four successive phases: requirement and specification phase, design phase, implementation phase, and validation phase. However, due to the fact that the later an error is discovered in the development process, the more difficult and expensive it is to fix, it has become apparent that the validation process should be performed as early as possible and throughout the development process. Hence, current development methodologies for large-scale computer systems consist of only three successive phases: requirement and specification phase, design phase, and implementation phase, while the validation is performed in all these phases. Properties such as completeness, consistency, correctness, and invariance are validated at each phase. All these properties have to be satisfied at one phase before the next one can begin.

The details in each of the phases will be discussed in the following subsections. Axiomatic requirements engineering, which is a new approach to support the development of large-scale embedded computer systems by mathematical formalism will also be discussed.

Requirement and Specification Phase

In developing an embedded computer system, the objective is to design a system which satisfies users' needs. However, these needs are usually presented in a very vague and ambiguous manner. Hence, in order to achieve the objective, the requirements have to be transformed into a precise and consistent form that is verifiable and analyzable. This transformation is carried out in the requirement and specification phase. The activities in this phase are concerned with defining the functional needs, performance, and other requirements, such as trade-off criteria. The resulting specifications are used for two purposes: 1) as a problem definition for the design process, 2) as a standard against which an implementation can be validated. The success in the development of the embedded computer system greatly depends on the correct interpretation of the requirements in the specification phase. However, requirement specifications usually suffer from many problems: they are often designs rather than statements of need; they are usually incomplete and are expressed in an ambiguous language (English); they are difficult to verify and hence are often incorrect, as well as inconsistent; they are difficult to test and if one wants to modify them, it is difficult to locate and accurately modify all affected areas. The problems that arise in the requirement and specification phase will be carried through and amplified in the design of later stages. Hence, errors made in this phase are difficult and expensive to fix if not discovered early.

The magnitude and seriousness of the requirements problem can be shown by the study of Bell and Thayer (20). Traditional means to state and analyze requirements have resulted in unsatisfactory specifications. The following figures indicate the magnitude of the problem: Manual examination of two requirements specifications revealed that there were more than 50 problems in a specification document of about 48 double-spaced typewritten pages, and 972 problems in a specification containing 8248 requirements and support paragraphs (250 pages). The most frequently occurring problems are requirements that are incorrect, inconsistent, incompatible, and unclear. These account for up to 85 percent of the total.

The activities in this phase can be classified into the following components: requirement elaboration, requirement specification and attribute formulation, process definition, and requirement verification.

Requirement Elaboration. The requirement elaboration step can be considered as a problem understanding stage. The requirement engineers investigate in great detail the users' needs and then develop clear and precise requirements of the system.

Requirement Specification and Attribute Formulation. In this step, the users' original objectives are formally expressed in terms of system requirements and system attributes (2, 21). System requirements are the objectives and the constraints which the system must satisfy. Any system which meets the requirements is a candidate solution to the users' problem. Attributes, on the other hand, specify either options or evaluation criteria for qualitative comparisons of competing systems that meet the system requirements. The generation of these system requirements and attributes is the requirement specification and attribute formulation step. As pointed out previously, one of the greatest problems in requirement specifications is the misinterpretation of the original system requirements. A plausible solution is to use dual specification teams to develop the system specifications from the requirements independently as in the development of critical real-time software for nuclear power plants (22). The two specifications are then compared and discrepancies are resolved to the satisfaction of both teams. By this dual specification approach, most of the errors due to ambiguities and misinterpretations can be corrected before they can propagate into the next phase.

The system requirements can be broken down into two categories: 1) functional requirements, and 2) performance requirements. Roughly speaking, functional requirements refer to what the system is supposed to do, and performance requirements describe how well the functions defined by the functional specifications should be performed.

Functional requirements specify the input (stimulus) and the output (response) relations of the system. These input to output mappings can be expressed vigorously in mathematical formulas (23) or less formally in a specification language (24, 25). Mathematical formulation allows formal consistency and correctness proofs of the system. However, in real-world situations, the problems are usually so complex that pure mathematical formulation is impossible. For this reason, a specification language is more suitable for specifying functional requirements.

A specification language is a syntactically and semantically well defined language possibly intermixed with mathematical equations. Its whole purpose is to provide an efficient and effective medium for defining the functional requirements. Several specification languages have been developed previously (20, 24, 25). In choosing the specification language, the constructability and comprehensibility of the language must be evaluated carefully. The specification language must be able to express the functional requirements efficiently and be easily understood by the application and the requirement engineers. It must be able to specify the system requirements unambiguously and to provide capabilities of performance specifications in the case of real time systems. The language should be amenable to both static (hierarchical relationship, data definition, etc.) and dynamic (control flow and data flow) analyses. Finally, it should be backed up by a specification database management system and powerful graphical supports to provide easy and efficient accesses to the designed system.

Performance requirements specify the functional effectiveness of the system. They include the input and output rates, response time, accuracy, etc. There is essentially no notion of completeness as far as performance requirements are concerned. The requirements engineers have to work closely with the users to ensure that all the important performance aspects of the system are captured in the specifications.

Attributes, such as reliability, availability, flexibility, reconfigurability, modularity, cost, etc, represent the users' preference on the designed system. They are the evaluation criteria used to determine the characteristics that make one system better than the other, even though they both satisfy the requirements. The important issue in attribute formulation is the development of measures which can express the preferences of the users clearly and accurately. There are two popular methods to express attribute formulation, namely, utility function (26, 27) and pay-off tree (40). Utility functions is a formal approach that measures the degree of satisfaction of users in terms of the utility of the system. It has been used extensively in economics and business management. Once the utility function of a system has been formulated, the optimal system configuration can be determined by optimizing its utility. However, due to the inherent complexity in a large-scale embedded computer system, and the high interdependency of its attributes, the formulation of the utility function can be very difficult. On the other hand, the pay-off tree is a less formal approach that is being used in the development of BMD systems. In this approach, pay-off trees of system attributes are generated, together with the pay-off measure interrelationship. Since pay-off trees display clearly to the designers the tradeoffs involved in the attributes, tradeoffs decisions in later stages of the development process can then be facilitated.

Process Definition. The process definition step accepts inputs from the requirement specification and attribute formulation step and identifies major functions to be performed. First, the input stimulus and the required responses are characterized. Second, the functional requirements are decomposed into data processing requirements, communication requirements, precedence constraints, and others. Similarly, the performance requirements are decomposed into resource requirements, scheduling requirements, etc. Based on these requirements and the attributes defined previously, the information flow and the control flow of the system can be modeled and analyzed to identify the major operations to be performed and their locations of occurrence. From these analyses, the system processes required to perform the above functions can be defined. These process definitions state precisely the function of the processes, the resources required by the processes, and the interaction among the processes.

Verification of Requirements. In this step, the process specified by the process definition are verified against the original users' requirements. Since the system is developed hierarchically, the specifications of one level are the requirements of the next level. To verify the correctness of the virtual system, we only need to verify the consistency between the specifications and the requirements between consecutive levels. If an analyzable specification language is used, the consistency can be verified automatically.

Design Phase

The goal of the design phase is to start with the defined processes which are the output of the requirements and specification phase, and to come up with an implementable specification of a system that satisfies the requirement specifications, and is understandable by the implementors. The requirement specifications are user oriented while the implementation is technology oriented. The design phase therefore provides a bridge between the requirement specifications and the implementation. The end-products of this phase are functional modules with specific requirements on throughput, reliability, performance, etc. Basically, there are two different approaches to perform this required task, namely, the top-down approach and the bottom-up design approach.

The philosophy of the top-down approach is to design the system using levels of abstraction and stepwise refinements. The design process starts with the specifications defined by the requirement and specification phase, and introduces gradually more details to the specifications of the design until all the details of the specifications are produced. On the other hand, the bottom-up approach uses a trial-and-error procedure to produce the design by successive approximations. It begins with an initial design to the problem, and iteratively modifies it in order to transform it to a design which satisfies all the requirements, and is satisfactory to the users with respect to the the system attributes. The difficulties of the bottom-up approach are that the designer has to be able to guess an initial solution and to determine the necessary modifications needed to be made during the iterations. Further, it is difficult to verify that the final design satisfies all the requirements due to the ad hoc nature in the approach. On the contrary, in the top-down approach, since the design is derived directly from the requirement specifications, all the requirements should be satisfied ideally. Moreover, the verification process is greatly simplified by the hierarchy of abstractions. As a result, the top-down approach is far more superior to the bottom-up approach in designing large-scale ECS since it can reduce the complexity of the problem drastically. As a result, most of the designs of large-scale system follows the top-down approach.

In the top-down design, the design phase starts with the defined processes which are the outputs of the requirement and specification phase. Basically, the design phase requires a provision to trace the system requirements through every level of the design, and a means of assessing trade-offs at the functional level and comparing design alternatives. The major steps involved are process decomposition and partitioning, functional specification, and verification.

Decomposition and Partitioning. Since the specified system produced from the requirement and specification phase is so complex, it must be decomposed in a way such that most of the decisions can be made according to the data available within a local area of the developing system specifications. Since most of the decisions are made locally, the resulting design process will be manageable. The decomposition process can be accomplished by identifying the tightly coupled processes of system and then factoring the system into subsystems corresponding to these processes. The design of each subsystem can then be independently (or nearly so) elaborated in the remaining steps of the development process, while maintaining the inter-subsystem interactions as design invariances. The decomposition must be carried out carefully such that the following criterion are satisfied.

1. The decomposed system must be consistent, complete, unambiguous and testable.
2. The decomposed system must satisfy the correspondent requirements.
3. The decomposed system must satisfy the parametric logical specifications such that minor changes in the requirements would not require a redesign of the whole system.
4. The decomposed system must be expandable so that future growth of the system can be easily incorporated.

Partitioning is the process of grouping the subsystems or subprocesses into different sets that become the functional modules in the implementation phase. The objective of partitioning is to group the subsystems into implementable modules with a minimum amount of inter-module interactions, that is, the modules are loosely coupled. The motivation for such a partitioning is to increase modularity and testability, as well as to reduce the complexity of the interfaces and the amount of communications among subsystems. However, the problem of finding the optimal partitioning that minimizes the interaction is NP-complete. This means that the amount of time that is needed to find the optimal partitioning grows exponentially with the number of subsystems. Hence, it is very difficult as well as impractical to find the optimal partitioning and heuristics are needed to solve this problem. Good heuristic for this problem has been proposed using the max-flow min-cut technique (3).

Functional Specification.   The next major step in the design phase is functional specification of the partitioned processes. The objective of this step is to define the characteristics of the functions so as to enable optimization in the functions to processors mapping. In the functional specification, all the processes in the same partition are considered as a single function. In a manner analogous to the process specification problem, the input and output relation, the precedence constraints and the interactions among different functions are determined. In addition, the characteristics of the function are defined. These include:

1. Types of operations to be performed—matrix operations, floating point or integer operations, etc.
2. Resource requirements—storage requirement, processing power, etc.
3. Speed requirements—frequency and execution speed of the function.

The above information will be used in the implementation phase to map the processes onto the processors. An efficeint algorithm to map functions onto two processor systems has been developed by Stone (28). For the general case of n processors, the problem is NP-complete, and more research has to be done in this area to develop good heuristics.

Verification of Design.   The final step in the design phase is to verify the correctness and to evaluate the effectiveness of the design. Since the actual system has not been constructed at this stage, the way to accomplish the verification and the evaluation is to create some models for the system and to investigate the behavior of the models. The most important consideration for the applicability of any model is its credibility, since the result cannot be trusted if the model does not represent the system accurately. There are two approaches to carry out the investigation, namely, analytical modeling and simulation modeling.

In analytical modeling, the verification and evaluation are performed by solving mathematical equations and proving some mathematical properties. In order to make the analyses mathematically tractable, many simplifications on the system and assumptions on the system parameters have to be made, hence, the results obtained from the analyses may not be very useful. Further, close-form solutions cannot be found for some problems because the model is mathematically intractable. On the other hand, analytical models are easier to construct and less expensive to use than simulation models, and the results are easier to interpret.

The analytical approach is useful in the high level of the design. However, when the system gets more complicated, analytical models become difficult to use and simulations have to be used instead. Simulation models can represent the designed system in more detail, and hence more accurately. The disadvantages are that detail simulators are difficult to construct, and simulations are very expensive for complicated systems.

Implementation Phase

The implementation phase takes the functional specifications produced from the design phase and develops the system architecture. It then maps the system functions into either hardware or software modules or a combination of both. After the implementation of the system, verification and validation have to be performed to ensure that the system satisfies the specifications produced from the design phase. The validation process proceeds in a bottom-up manner. Mistakes or unfulfilled requirements found are traced back to the source of error. The system is then redesigned from that point. The major steps involved in this phase are: design or architecture, mapping of functions into software or hardware modules, and validation of the final system.

Design of Architecture.   The design of architecture for a system is greatly influenced by technologies. Today, with the low cost of hardware and advances in communication media, the distributed computer system has become the dominating architecture. The merits of distributed systems are that they provide high throughput, modularity, reliability, availability, and reconfigurability, with relatively low cost. Reconfigurability is particularly important for large-scale embedded computer systems since it can provide continuous operations to the system via graceful degradation. In addition, it can also enchance the performance of the system by dynamically reconfiguring the resources as the workload varies.

Mapping of Functions to Software, Hardware Modules.   The choice of using hardware or software to implement a particular function depends on the physical constraints of the system, the architecture chosen, and most importantly, the available technology. As the cost of hardware becomes lower, more functions can be migrated from software to hardware. Functions implemented by software are usually slow, but they are easy to modify. On the other hand, functions implemented in hardware are faster but they are not as flexible. However, the emergence of microprogramming has narrowed the gap between hardware and software, and enables many functions to be implemented with relatively high speed and low cost while retaining a high degree of flexibility. The boundary between software and hardware keeps changing as technology progresses. As we have discussed before, today, with the low cost of VLSI technology, many functions can be implemented by special purpose VLSI chips with high speed and low cost.

Validation of the Final System. In this step, the functional correctness of the resulting system is verified and validated against the specification produced from the design phase in a bottom-up approach. The individual software and hardware modules are first validated, and then the subsystems which are composed of these modules are validated. This process is performed recursively until the entire system is validated. The validation techniques are discussed in the following.

Software Modules (Program). There are three popular methods to validate programs: program proving (29, 30), program testing (31, 32), and symbolic execution (33).

Program proving is the only method that can assure that a program functions correctly. It involves proving mathematical properties in a program by mathematical formalism. Techniques in program proving include induction assertion, loop invariance, and predicate transformation. However, there are several limitations to program proving. First, it requires a tremendous amount of effort to establish the proof. It has been estimated that the proof of 100 lines of code requires about one man-month effort. Development of automated proof techniques and advances in mathematical proof techniques may alleviate this problem to some extent in the future. Second, for programs which involve parallelism, it is extremely difficult to prove the correctness of a routine if other routines can modify some of its data during execution. Third, traditional proofs of program correctness require that the program must halt. However, many software systems such as operating system and database management system, are not expected to halt. Fourth, the proof of a program is meaningful only if the assertions about the program truly represent the intended properties of the program. However, it cannot be proved that the assertions satisfy these properties. Lastly, the proofs themselves are also subject to error. In conclusion, program proving is only suitable for small, and simple software programs.

A second method for validating a program is program testing. The motivation of program testing is to provide economical and effective methods that can be applied to large-scale software systems to affirm the quality of the systems. The basic principle of program testing is to control the execution of a program with known inputs and outputs, together with internal measurement of the behavior of the program. The major steps involved are:

1. Identify a set of test data.
2. Execute the program with the chosen test data.
3. Analyze the output produced.
4. Examine the effect that the test data have on the program.

However, unless a formal proof has shown that the set of test data completely exercises the program, testing cannot prove the correctness of the program. Even for a trivial program, the set of test data that is needed to fully exercise the program is incredibly large. Hence, it is important to design test data that are likely to isolate most of the errors. One approach is to exercise all possible control paths in a program. This approach is practical for a small program, and the control paths can be identified by automated tools. For a large program, the only practical approach is to exercise all sections of code and all conditional branch possibilities. Automated tools can also be used to construct the test data. With limited amount of testing, some assurance on the reliability of the program can be obtained.

The last technique, symbolic execution, executes a program by using symbols, instead of real data objects, as input values. It is a rather recent development that combines the notions of path analysis and a limited form of program interpretation. The advantages of symbolic execution are that a single symbolic execution of a program may be equivalent to a large number of normal test runs, and by varying the amount of symbolic data and program specifications introduced, it can provide results close to a formal proof of correctness without the high cost. The importance of symbolic execution in program testing is becoming more apparent, and it is expected that symbolic execution will become the main tool to support program validation.

Hardware Modules. The techniques for hardware validation can be classifed into two categories: techniques for combinational circuits, and techniques for sequential circuits. D-algorithm and Boolean differences are popular techniques in the first categories, while open looping, and use of fault detection sequences are popular techniques for sequential circuits.

The hardware testing problem has become more difficult as more functions are implemented by VLSI (34). Since the amount of computer time needed for test generation and fault simulation is proportional to the cube power of the number of logic gates, the vast increase in density in VLSI chips makes the generation of test patterns by automated tools, and conduction of fault simulation very difficult. As a result, it is crucial to embody the idea of "design for testability" in VLSI development. The key concepts in design for testability are controllability and observability. Controllability is the ease with which a network can be "steered" through its different functions. Observability is the ease with which internal states can be examined. For sequential circuits a third concept in design for testability, predictability, is necessary. This is the ease with which the network being tested can be placed in a known state such that from this state, all the future states can be predicted. It is important to design VLSI chips that are controllable, observable, and predictable.

Some popular ad hoc techniques in design for testability are partitioning, test points, and signature analysis. Partitioning reduces the difficulties in test preparation by implementing the idea of "divide and conquer". There are two approaches in partitioning. The first one is mechanical partitioning, such as dividing a board in two. The second one is logical partitioning which isolates circuit functions by adding gates, using unused input pins, etc. Test points are concerned with how to use additional pins intelligently for testing. The idea in signature analysis is to design a circuit that can stimulate itself. The behavior of the circuit is recorded and compressed into a "signature" for analysis.

Another class of techniques in design for testability is structured design for testability. This involves more vigorous, highly structured design practices in VLSI development. The idea is to design additional circuitry in the chips in order to enchance controllability and observability.

All the techniques discussed above can be applied first to the lowest level modules, and than applied recursively to higher level subsystems. Analysis and simulation modeling can also be applied to validate the functional correctness and performance requirements. Since the entire system is available at this phase, measurement techniques can be used to ensure that performance requirements are satisfied (35). Measurements involve such steps as synthesis of benchmark, executing the benchmark in the system, and evaluation of results. Because of the hierarchical decomposition, the subsystems to be analyed are generally small and hence complexity is low.

Axiomatic Requirements Engineering (ARE)

The major activities in the requirement and specification phase, the design phase and part of the implementation phase are to define and verify the system requirements, decompose the requirements, allocate the decomposed requirements to the subsystems, and evaluate the feasibility of the decomposition and allocation of the system requirements. A systematic approach to handle these activities is called requirement engineering. The important role of requirement engineering in developing large-scale embedded computer systems has led to the emergence of axiomatic requirement engineering (ARE) which was developed for BMD systems development. Basically, ARE consists of a formal framework for requirement engineering, a set of formal techniques for the definition and development of system requirements, mathematical formalism which describes the properties of these techniques, and definitions of automated tools which support the techniques and the mathematical formalism. The goals of ARE are to identify formal methodologies to develop requirements, to support the methodologies by tools and techniques which aids the requirement specifications, and to verify and evaluate the methodologies by applying them to sample systems.

There are two approaches to developing axiomatic requirements engineering (36, 37, 38). The first approach is to derive axioms for the requirement engineering methodology from past experiences in both successful and unsuccessful system developments. These axioms can then be used to formulate theorems that state the rules for operations such as decomposition, and partitioning. The derived methodolgy will tend to lead to successful design specifications and exclude poor practices that lead to unsuccessful design. Although this approach does provide guidelines for successful design, this ad hoc approach that is based primarily on experience usually leads to a set of subjective axioms, and the lack of theoretical backgrounds make it hard to justify and support its effectiveness and correctness.

The second approach is based on general system theory. It develops the ARE by deriving methodologies deductively from the formal mathematical characterization of the definition of "systems" and its design. In this approach, the concepts of subsystem, hierarchical level, refinement, decomposition, specification, interface, etc., are all defined with mathematical formalism. Since this approach provides a mathematical framework for describing system structure and formalizes the specification of the system, the correctness and the consistency during the development of requirements can be checked by proving properties among the variables and transformations. Many difficulties in requirement engineering, such as decompositions of system functions and partitioning of performance requirements can thus be solved.

ARE can be developed by a combination of the above two approaches. Large-scale systems theory provides the algebraic structures for interrelationships among variables, while knowledge gained in experience provides insight among the transformation of the variables.

The ideas of ARE are briefly illustrated here by the formal definitions for the concepts of requirements and decomposition (39). In ARE, a system S is said to have requirements R, if $R = (X, Y, \overline{F}, P)$, where X is the domain of the input to the system, Y is the range of output of the system, $\overline{F}$ is a description of a system transformation from X to Y, and P is the range of performance indices of the system. Based on this definition, the concept and properties of decomposition can be formulated. The decomposition of system function F to F_0 can be defined formally be establishing properties like refinement, on the input, output, system parameters, performance parameter, definition of transformation, and completion conditions in F and F_0. The verification of decomposition can then be done by proving the corresponding properties. Theorems like transitivity of decomposition have also been derived from the definition of decomposition.

The limitation of ARE is that there are lots of mathematical formalisms involved, and the proof of mathematical properties may be very difficult for complex systems.

CONCLUSION

The design of embedded computer systems has appeared to be a formidable task in the past, due to the requirements and characteristics of real-time control, criticality, fault-tolerance, high performance, and largeness of the systems. Not until recently, has the design of such systems become manageable. With the emergence of VLSI technology, large-scale embedded computer systems can be realized with relatively low cost. Moreover, the advance in design methodologies also provides a systematic approach to tackle the development of such systems, and simplifies the design, implementation, validation, maintenance, and growth of large-scale embedded computer systems. Hence, the development of VLSI technology and design methodology is the driving force that makes the evolution of embedded computer systems possible.

REFERENCES

(1) Lehman, M. M., and Parr, F. N. "Program Evolution and its impact on Software Engineering." *Proceedings of the Second International Conference in Software Engineering, San Francisco* (Oct. 1976).
(2) Davis, G. G. and Vick, C. R. "The Software Development System." *Proceedings of the Second International Conference of Software Engineering* (1976)
(3) Ramamoorthy, C. V., HO, G. S. "A Design Methodology for User Oriented Computer Systems." *NCC* **78**: 953–966.
(4) Moore, G. "VLSI: Some Fundamental Challenges." *IEEE Spectrum* (April 1979).
(5) Rideout, V. Leo, "Limits to Improvement of Silicon Integrated Circuits." *Proceedings of Compcon* (1980); 2–6.
(6) Bloch, E., and Galage, D. "Component Progress: Its Effect on High Speed Computer Architecture and Machine Organization," in *High Speed Computer and Algorithm Organization* by Kuck, S., Lawrie, D., and Sameh, A. (eds.) New York: Academic, 1977.
(7) Freiman, C. V. "VLSI High Performance Processors: How Mixed the Blessing?" *Compcom* (1980): 11–14.
(8) Mead, C., Lynn, C. *Introduction to VLSI systems.* Addison Wesley, 1980.
(9) Patterson, D. A., and Sequin, C. "Design Considerations for Single-Chip Computer of the Future." *IEEE Trans. on Computers,* **c-29** No. 2 (Feb. 1980).
(10) Cragon, H. G. "The Elements of Single-Chip Microcomputer Architecture." *Computer* 27–41 (Oct 1980).
(11) El-Yat, K. A. "The Intel 8089: An Integrated I/O Processor." *Computer* 67–78 (June 1979).
(12) Bryant, J. D., and Longly, R. "TMS9940 Single Chip Microcomputer." *Proceedings on Electro* (1977).

(13) Despain, A. M., and Patterson, D. A. "X-Tree: A Tree Structured Multiprocessor Computer Architecture." *Proceedings of the Fifth Annual Symposium on Computer Architecture* (1978): 144–151.

(14) Stritter, E., and Gunter T. "A Microprocessor Architecture for a Changing World: The Motorola 68000." *Computer* 43–52 (Feb 1979).

(15) Foster, M. J., and Kung, H. T. "Design of Special-Purpose VLSI Chips: Example and Opinions." *Proceeding of the Seventh Annual Symposium of Computer Architecture* (1980): 300–307.

(16) Kung, H. T. "Let's Design Algorithms for VLSI Systems." *Proceedings of Caltech Conference of Very Large Scale Integration* (1979): 65–91.

(17) Thompson, C. D. "Area-Time Complexity for VLSI." *Eleventh Annual ACM Symposium on Theory of Computing* (May, 1979).

(18) Leiserson, C. E., "Systolic Priority Queues." *Proceedings of Caltech Conference of Very Large Scale Integration* (1979): 199–214.

(19) Denny, W. M., Buley, E. R., and Hatt, E. "Logic-Enhanced Memories: An Overview and Some Examples of Their Application to a Radar Tracking Problem." (1979), pp. 173–186.

(20) Bell, T. E., and Thayer, T. A. "Software Requirements: Are They Really a Problem?" *Proceedings of the Second International Conference of Software Engineering* (1976).

(21) Thurber, K. "Techniques for Requirements-Oriented Design." *NCC* (1977), pp. 919–929.

(22) Long, A. B., et al. "A Methodology for the Development and Validation of Critical Software for Nuclear Power Plants." *Proceedings of Compsac,* (Nov. 1977).

(23) Wymore, A. W. *System Engineering Methodology for Inter-Disciplinary Teams.* New York; Wiley-Interscience, 1976.

(24) Conn, A. P. "Specification of Reliable Large Scale Software Systems." Ph. D. Dissertation, Department of Electrical Engineering and Computer Sciences, University of California, Berkeley (1977).

(25) Ross, D. "Structured Analysis (SA): A Language for Communicating Ideas." *IEEE Trans. on Software Engineering,* **SE-3, No. 1** (Jan. 1977).

(26) Gerard, D. *Theory of Value.* New York: Wiley, 1959.

(27) Fishburn, P. C. *Decision and Value Theory.* New York: Wiley, 1964.

(28) Stone, H. S. "Multiprocessor Scheduling with the Aid of Network Flow Algorithms." *IEEE Trans. on Software Engineering,* **SE-3** No. 1 (Jan. 1977).

(29) Morgan, D. E., and Taylor, D. J. "A Survey of Method of Achieving Reliable Software." *Computer* 44–53 (Feb. 1977).

(30) Hantler, S. L., and King, J. C. "An Introduction to Proving the Correctness of Program." *Computer Surveys* (Sept. 1976).

(31) Fairley, E. "Tutorial: Static Analysis and Dynamic Testing of Computer Software." *Computer* 14–24 (April, 1978).

(32) DeMillo, R., Liption, J., and Sayward, G. "Hints on Test Selection: Help for Practicing Programmer." *Computer* 34–43 (April 1978).

(33) Daninger, J. A., and King, J. C. "Application of Symbolic Execution to Program Testing." *Computer* 51–63 (April 1978).

(34) Williams, T. W., and Parker, K. P. "Testing Logic Networks and Designing for Testability." *Computer* 9–21 (Oct. 1979).

(35) Ferrari, D. *Computer Systems Performance Evaluation.* New Jersey: Prentice-Hall, 1978.

(36) Burns, F., and Debaven, D. "Requirements Engineering: A Formal Approach." *Compcon* (Spring, 1978): 314–318.

(37) Saib, S. H., Benson, J. P., Scherer, A. D., and Parker, R. R. "Axiomatic Requirements Engineering—An Approach Based on General Systems Theory." *Compcon* (Spring, 1978): 310–313.

(38) Steding, T. L. "A Systems Theory Approach to Axiomatic Requirement Engineering." *Compcon* (Spring, 1978): 306–309.
(39) Alford, M. "Requirements for Distributed Data Processing Design." *First International Conference on Distributed Computing Systems* (1979): 1–14.
(40) Mariani, M. P. "The Use of Payoff Trees in the Distributed Data Processing Design Process." *Distributed Data Processing Technology FY 77,* Research Conference Publications (1977).
(41) Morse, S. P. Ravenel, W. B., Mazor, S., and Pohlman, W. B. "Intel Microprocessors-8008 to 8086." *Computer* 42–60 (Oct. 1980).
(42) Scharfetter, D. L. "VLSI Circuit Design: A Few Challenges for the 1980's." *Proceedings of Compcom* (1980): 7–10.

3. VLSI Microprocessors

Mark A. Scott
and
Kenneth C. Smith
University of Toronto, Canada

INTRODUCTION

The motivation for this chapter is to study the potential of a new computer architecture. This architecture has only recently become feasible as a result of the great reduction in the ratio of cost to capability provided by VLSI bit slice microprocessor technology.

Large computers generally have a computing power that is more than a single user can efficiently utilize. Thus some form of shared is customary, a multiprogramming system being the most common. By allowing the computing resources to be shared among the programs of many users, the global efficiency of usage is increased: the computing resources are not idle as often as they would be with a single user.

Since such a shared computer must meet the needs of many users, it follows that the computing environment it supports must be general purpose in nature. However this computing environment, optimized over many widely differing requirements, may not be very efficient for any one particular requirement. The overhead implied by the inefficiency of a general purpose computer at any particular task and the overhead required to support a multiprogramming system, can each become substantial portions of the total cost of computation.

Smaller computers may be used in ways which eliminate some of this overhead. For fixed computing requirements the computing resources provided can be chosen to satisfy the user's needs at optimal cost. With only a single user, the software overhead can also be kept low. In fact, with fixed computing requirements, single user utilization of a small computer can be very efficient.

However most computer users do not have fixed needs. Even a commercial installation, running only production jobs, will still run jobs with a wide range of computational requirements. Even a single task may have different degrees of utilization of the processing capability of its computer at varying stages in its execution. Consider, for example, the total task of editing and compiling a high level language program. The text editing phase does not, in most cases, require or justify the use of the resources of a large general purpose computer; however compiling a high level language program is often inordinately slow on a small machine. Thus we see that neither a small nor a large computer is optimal for all components of a common task.

This problem of providing an efficient solution to a variety of computing needs has been recognized before, and a number of attempts at solving it have been made. The general direction of these solutions has been to provide a pool of computing power, from which a user draws only a package of the size and shape appropriate to the user's computing requirements.

Until recently, computer technology did not permit other solutions to the problem. The fixed architectures of most computers do not permit effective combination of one computer with another. Yet the problem remains: the need to provide an extended range of computing power to efficiently solve a variety of problems. Apparently the solution requires a resource with a number of elements of computing power, each small enough for efficient solution of problems having low computational complexity, but also capable of providing jointly, in an efficient and effective manner, a level of computing power greater than that of any single element.

The structure of these computing elements would have to be highly flexible to allow for differing computational requirements. It is the goal of this chapter to show that such flexibility is not beyond the bounds of currently available hardware and design techniques.

Microprogramming

While the concept of microprogramming was developed with the earliest computer, it was not used to any great extent for a considerable period of time. However, more recently, its use has become very common. Both early and more recent applications of microprogramming were often for the convenience of the manufacturer, sometimes without the user of the computer even being aware of this aspect of the computer's internal structure. In this case the microprogram was generally fixed. However advances in memory technology have made dynamic microprogramming feasible, even in a real time sense. The microprogram can be changed at regular memory speeds, allowing the sophisticated user the possibility of providing the most appropriate computing environment for each task.

The Nanodata QM-1 represents a particularly interesting extension of this concept. In this machine basic aspects of the architecture (including the topology of internal bus structures) are dynamically controlled by the 'nanopro-gram'. This facility can be of considerable use to the sophisticated user. Either of the two levels of microprogramming sophistication mentioned above, that is normal microprogramming or nanoprogramming, provide some degree of flex-ibility in the processor structure.

Microprocessors

The increasing availability of low cost microprocessors has stimulated new approaches to computer architecture. Microprocessors have allowed hardware design to be controlled by the sophisticated end user. Potentially such a user can obtain a much better match of the computing environment to the user's requirements.

Early microprocessors were not greatly advanced over previous computer architectures as they were essentially fixed structure, single chip arithmetic and control units. However, more recent microprocessors have introduced increas-ingly flexible architectures. For example, the National Semiconductor IMP series, although marketed in fixed module form, was the first to introduce bit sliced arithmetic units. These arithmetic units consisted of a number of iden-tical interconnected modules or slices controlled by a common separate control unit. However the control unit was limited to a single chip with only a mask programmable ROM.

This development was followed by the Intel 3000 series which offered a more flexible design and for the first time allowed dynamic microprogramming by splitting the control functions and control memory into separate chips. More recent microprocessors have improved on this possibility: bit slice arithmetic units have progressed to being two-address devices with significant capabilities in both arithmetic (binary and decimal) and character operations. Likewise, existing microprogram control units have considerable address manipulation capabilities, providing jumps, tests, and subroutine calls within the microprogram.

As a result of this evolution it is a fact that current microprocessor hardware, while inexpensive, is sophisticated enough in all aspects (except possibly speed) to be compared with the fixed hardware of many large computers of even recent manufacture. Moreover, the bit slice approach allows the sophisticated end user a degree of flexibility in picking such characteristics as word size, instruction set, and bus structure, by which means users can more closely match computing power to computational requirements.

However, what is lacking is a truly flexible computer architecture. An archi-tecture which will provide individual computing elements (microprocessors) that can be combined in an effective manner using microprogramming and switching circuits. Such an architecture, the major focus of this chapter, per-mits a new approach to several areas of computer applications.

PROCESSOR RECONFIGURATION

Two major elements of existing families of conventional bit slice microprocessor chips are the Microprocessor Unit (MPU) and the Microprogram Control Unit (MCU). In some instances the MPU will be a single Register Arithmetic Logic Unit chip while in others it will be a number of chips such as a Register chip, an Arithmetic Logic Unit chip, and a Carry Lookahead chip. Likewise the MCU may be a single chip containing Microprogram Memory and a Microprogram Sequencer, or there may be several chips for the memory and sequencer functions.

Several MPUs are connected in a sequential fashion, as shown in Figure 3-1. An MCU is used to provide the control inputs to the MPUs. The MPU that corresponds to the most significant portion of the processor word provides the flag information that the MCU requires for microprogram decision branches. Memory and I/O connections are now shown; they will be discussed later in the chapter.

Processor Connections

The MPUs in a processor can be divided into three classes: the MPU that represents the least significant (low order) part of the processor word; the MPU that represents the most significant (high order) part of the processor word; and the other (middle) MPUs. Each MPU has several input lines (shift, carry in, some flags, etc.) from the next lower order MPU (if any), output lines (shift, carry out, some flags, etc.) to the next higher order MPU (if any), flag lines that serve as input to the MCU and control lines from the MCU. The connections of these MPU lines are shown in Table 3-1.

Table 3-1 shows that there are only a few ways that the different MPU lines can be connected, depending upon the position of the MPU in the CPU. While the table shows that the flag and control lines are connected to the MCU, it is apparent that the CPU function is not affected if there are several MCUs each having access to the same flags and running the same microprogram so that identical control line signals are produced by each MCU. These observations are used to show the basic idea of dynamic reconfiguration in Figure 3-2.

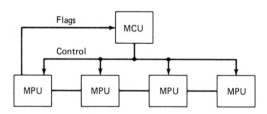

Figure 3-1. Microprocessor CPU.

Table 3-1. MPU Connections.

LINE/MPU	HIGH	MIDDLE	LOW
Input	Next lower MPU	Next lower MPU	N/C
Output	N/C	Next higher MPU	Next higher MPU
Flags	MCU	N/C	N/C
Control	MCU	MCU	MCU

In Figure 3-2 each MPU has an associated MCU and two multiplexers, one for flags and one for data. The input lines of the MPU come from the input multiplexer, which will select either the output lines of the next lower order MPU, or no connection. The output lines of the MPU go to the input multiplexer of the next higher order MPU. The flag lines to the MCU come from the flag multiplexer which will select either the flag lines from the associated MPU or the flag lines to the next higher order MCU (the outputs of its flag multiplexer). The control lines for each MPU come from its associated MCU. Note that the MPUs are connected in a circular fashion. Each MPU has a higher order (left) and a lower order (right) neighbor, with the lowest (rightmost) and the highest (leftmost) being connected.

The associated MCU and MPU and the two multiplexers can be thought of as a processor slice. As shown in Figure 3-2 each processor slice has identical components and identical connections to neighboring processor slices. If the MCUs are running identical microprograms and the two sets of four multiplexers are both set to select the A B B B inputs then the system would function exactly like the CPU shown in Figure 3-1.

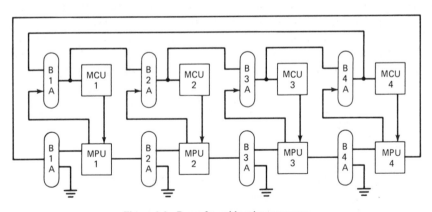

Figure 3-2. Reconfigurable microprocessor.

Table 3-2. Multiplexer Settings.

MULTIPLEXER SELECT				
1	2	3	4	CPUS
A	B	B	B	one 4 slice
A	B	A	B	two 2 slice
				one 3 slice
A	A	B	B	one 1 slice
				one 2 slice
A	A	A	B	two 1 slice
A	A	A	A	four 1 slice

However, the system shown in Figure 3-2 has a number of different configurations. By removing the constraint that the MCUs must be executing identical microprograms and changing the inputs selected by the multiplexers as shown in Table 3-2, it is possible to dynamically configure the system into a number of separate packaged CPUs, each of which is capable of operating independently.

Memory Connections

Changing the number of CPUs in the system would be of little use if the CPUs were not connected to memory in a reasonable manner. The observation must be made that while processor size is linearly proportional to the number of processor slices, the address space size is the log2 of the amount of memory. While it is difficult to limit the processor size without constraining the system, it is easy to limit the address space size since doubling the amount of memory in the system would increase the address space size by only 1 bit.

Figure 3-3 shows the CPU memory connections in a reconfigurable system. Each processor slice has a memory bus. Each associated memory is organized as a unit with the same width as the processor slice. The number of address lines on each memory bus and the size of the MAR is the address space size of the system. Each Memory Address Register (MAR) is divided into sections based upon the width of the processor slice. Each such section has an input multiplexer that can make four selections, which are: a) the current MAR value; b) the output from the associated MPU; c) the output of the corresponding multiplexer in the next lower order slice; and d) the output of the corresponding multiplexer in the next higher order slice.

If the processor size is greater than or equal to the MAR size then, when a memory operation is performed, each slice will generate its portion of the memory address. The input multiplexers for sections of the MAR that are in the same position (relative to the low order end) in the MAR as their associated slice is within the CPU will select the MPU output. If the position of the section within the MAR is higher or lower than that of the associated slice within

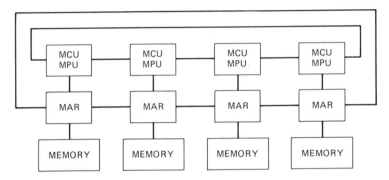

Figure 3-3. CPU memory connections.

the CPU then the multiplexers will select the output of the corresponding multiplexer in the next higher or lower order slice, respectively. This process will result in all of the MARs containing the same value (the entire memory address). Each of the slice memory buses will access the memory location that represents that portion of the entire memory word that pertains to the slice.

The operation of the system is similar if the processor size is less than the MAR size except that two or more MPU cycles must be used to output a complete memory address. Those sections of each MAR that correspond to sections of the memory address being output by the current MPU cycle are set as above. All other sections of each MAR have their input multiplexer selection as the current MAR value, so that they remain unchanged.

While it is possible to connect I/O devices to the processor slice memory buses, this does not allow sharing of the devices. A much better method is discussed later in this chapter. It uses one or more additional buses, called global I/O buses connected by bus windows to the processor slice memory buses.

Note that the method of dynamic reconfiguration described above allows systems with a large number of processor slices, to be configured into a large number of small processors or a small number of large processors, as needed. Because the connections of each processor slice are only to the two neighboring processor slices the cost of expansion is linear.

PROCESSOR SLICE DESIGN

The previous sections were intended to show the feasibility of system reconfiguration. This section will discuss solutions to a number of the more detailed problems of processor slice design that have not been discussed previously.

MicroProcessor Unit

The basic structure of a dynamically reconfigurable MPU is shown in Figure 3-4. It is similar to that of commercially available MPUs (such as the AMD

2901). There are certain differences in the signals that must be made available externally, but these do not require much additional logic and do not increase the pin count greatly.

A dynamically reconfigurable MPU requires two carry-in ports and one carry-out port. The carry-out port is connected to the flag multiplexer of the associated MCU and one carry-in port of the next higher order slice. The other carry-in port of a slice is connected to the carry flag of the associated MCU.

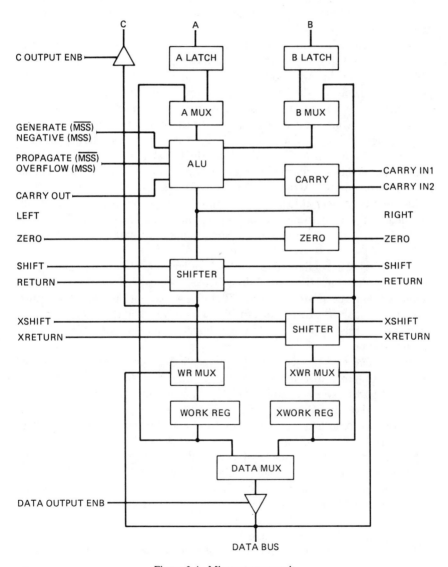

Figure 3-4. Microprocessor unit.

In an operation that requires a carry input the low order slice of a processor would select the carry flag while the other slices would select the carry-out from the next lower order slice. The carry-out from the high order slice would become the carry flag in all the MCUs of the processor.

In a static bit slice design there is normally a return line from the shift port of the highest order slice to the shift port of the lowest order slice. If the slices are used for double word shifts then two return lines are used. However, since the processor slice configurations in a reconfigurable architecture are not fixed this simple process does not work with a dynamically reconfigurable architecture.

Instead, return lines must be incorporated within the slices. In addition to the left and right shift ports there are left and right return ports. The left ports are connected to the right ports of the next higher order slice and the right ports are connected to the left ports of the next lower order slice.

All intermediate slices, when doing a shift in a particular direction, will pass values via the return ports in the opposite direction. If a left shift is being performed, then the intermediate slices will pass values from their left return port to their right return port. The value from the left shift port of the next lower order slice (which is connected to right shift port of the slice) is used as input to the internal shifter. A right shift is handled in a similar manner. Note that while there is sequential logic between the shift ports of a slice, there is only combinatorial logic between the return ports of a slice. The propagation of values on the return lines suffers only a small number of gate delays from each slice.

When a slice is configured as the high order slice of a processor then its behavior is different. If a left shift is being performed, then the value that would normally be shifted out the left shift port is sent out the right return port. If a right shift is being performed, then the value on the left shift port is ignored, and instead, the value on the right return port is used as input to the internal shifter.

When a slice is configured as the low order slice of a processor then its behavior is also different. If a left shift is being performed, then the value on the right shift port is ignored, and instead, the value on the left return port is used as input to the internal shifter. If a right shift is being performed, then the value that would normally be shifted out the right shift port is sent out the left return port.

Arithmetic, logical, circular, and even decimal shifts can be performed by the internal shifter logic. If a shift includes the carry bit then the bits shifted out the end go to the carry-out port and the internal shifter logic places the value of the carry flag (available through one of the carry-in ports) on the return line.

The dynamically reconfigurable MPU slice also has a left and right zero port. All slices except the low order slice of a processor will assert the left port if the bits within the slice are zero and if the right zero port is asserted. The low order slice is similar except that it ignores the right zero port. The value of the left zero port of the high order slice will become the zero flag in all the MCUs of the processor.

During certain complex operations the zero ports are used for different purposes, namely to transmit internal flags to all slices from either the most significant or least significant slice. For example multiply and divide operations are efficiently implemented by conditional add and shift operations that depend upon the value of the most or least significant bit of a word. When the zero ports are used in this manner then all intermediate slices merely pass values from one port to the other (the direction is determined by the operation). Depending on the operation, the most or least significant slices will actually set the appropriate value on their right or left zero ports, respectively.

If, as described above, only ripple carry was available then large processor configurations would have poor performance characteristics. However carry lookahead can easily be implemented. The system is connected using standard carry lookahead chips (74182) as if all the processor slices in the system were configured in a single processor, and the carry-out from the high order slice is connected to the carry-in to the low order slice. As described below, it does not matter that this is unlikely to be the system configuration in most cases. The Generate (G) and Propagate (P) signals from the intermediate slices of a processor are standard. The low order slice of a processor must produce a G that is the same as the carry-out and a P that is always false. Thus carry signals from adjacent slices that are not configured in the same processor will not be propagated. The G and P signals produced by the high order slice of a processor are not needed so it is possible to use the same pins to output flags, such as negative and overflow, that would go to the flag multiplexer of the associated MCU.

Table 3-3 lists all of the operations that the MPU should support. These operations allow efficient emulation of non-floating point instructions found on general purpose computers currently available. This table gives the available choices for each operator or operand on the same row. A particular operation requires selection of one operator/operand from each row. A and B represent operands generated outside the MPU (such as operands from memory or from the microprogram). In the cases in which a row is parenthesized it indicates that the choices in that row only apply if the selection in the previous row was that one directly above the parenthesized choices.

Certain common instructions such as increment and decrement are purposely omitted from the list of operations. Such instructions are subsets of the listed operations, where A or B is a constant, or A and B have the same value. The multiply and divide operations are based upon conditional add and shift loops. The provision for both binary and decimal adds and shifts allows both binary and decimal multiply and divide.

Table 3-3. MPU Operations.

Logical Operations:		
A and or B	≈A	
	xor	
	≈B	
Shift Operations:		
left	XWR	right
WR	circular	WR − XWR
logical		arithmetic
		(binary decimal)
carry		no carry
Arithmetic Operations:		
A	−A	
plus		
B	−B	
binary	decimal	
(carry no carry)		
Arithmetic Emulation Operators:		
A		
multiply	divide	
B		
binary	decimal	
(signed unsigned)		
Miscellaneous Operators:		
sign extend	parity/CRC sum	normalize

Control Bus and Registers

Most processor functions modularize easily as described above. However, those processor functions where each slice requires access to a whole processor word require a different approach. These include memory address generation, processor status (flags etc.) and instruction decoding. There must be a place to store the required information in each slice and a mechanism to pass the information between slices.

The contents of the MAR, processor status, and instruction register come from several different slices and must be communicated to all slices in the processor. This is done via the Control Bus, which has a width equal to the address space size. The left end of the control bus is connected to the right end of the control bus of the next higher order slice and the right end of the control bus is connected to the left end of the control bus of the next lower order slice. Each bus connection between adjacent slices utilizes a tri-state gate design that allows microprogram control of the direction of signal propagation between the buses. This can be either left, right, or none. The latter is used to logically sever the connection between control buses of adjacent slices that are not configured in the same processor.

The MPU has a general register file with a width that is equal to the slice width. Register addresses, supplied from the control bus or the microprogram, are used to access data from the register file. Alternatively data may come directly from the control bus, and the register file is bypassed. Outputs from the MPU would be available to both the register file and the control bus (although either of these destinations may be disabled). Alternatively one of the output ports of the general register file may be directed to the control bus and the MPU while the output from the MPU is returned to the register file.

In a general register architecture the file would contain the general registers, program counter, and other special registers. In a stack architecture the file would contain the stack pointer, the top of stack registers, program counter, and other special registers. In an accumulator architecture the file would contain the accumulators, index registers, program counter, and other special registers. Note that a slice would have only its associated segment of these registers in its general register file.

The general register file is not very appropriate for frequently used quantities such as the MAR, whose width would require several MPU cycles for access. The solution is for each slice to have a small control register file with a width equal to the address space size. This will allow the MAR to be stored in a single word. While it may not be enough to store the processor status in a single word, in most cases the processor status and instruction registers will be larger than the slice size, but not larger than the address space size, thus they would be best stored in the control register file, or instruction register in one word, it will certainly be much more efficient than using the general register file.

Each control bus line has connections to the control register file, and the general register file and the MPU of its slice. The control bus can be considered as having sections with the width of the processor slices. There are tri-state multiplexers and demultiplexers from the MPU to each of the sections of its control bus. The overall process slice organization is shown in Figure 3-5.

The control bus design performs the functions of several of the multiplexers described in the Processor Reconfiguration section. During MAR generation each MPU places its part of the memory address on the section of its control bus that is in the same position (relative to the low order end) as the slice is within the processor, and sets the left control bus port to propagate left and the right control bus port to propagate right. If a section of a control bus is in a higher position than the slice is within the processor then both control bus ports are set to propagate right, if it is lower then both ports are set to propagate left. This will result in the entire memory address propagating to each slice's control bus from which it can be loaded into the associated control register file.

When flags are produced by the high order MPU, they will be placed on a section of the control bus and the right control bus port of the high order slice and both ports of the other slices will be set to propagate right. The flags can then be loaded into the control register file of each slice.

The contents of the control register file, such as flags from the processor

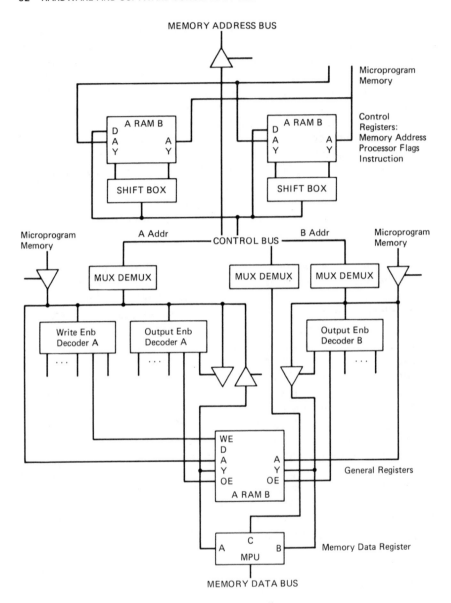

Figure 3-5. Processor slice.

status register or fields from the instruction register (e.g. op codes, register addresses, and immediate operands) must often be made available to the slice MPU. The control bus, control register file, and shift box are used to achieve this.

Microprogram Control Unit

The Microprogram Control Unit (MCU) is required to support a variety of next address generation instructions. The choices of next address may be influenced by various condition codes. The next address may be generated from the microprogram memory or from the user memory (such as during instruction decode). The MCU should provide for the repetitive execution of loops of microinstructions or single microinstructions. The number of times that a loop is executed may be controlled from the microprogram memory or from the user memory (such as during multiple bit shifts). In certain cases (such as arithmetic normalization) the execution of a loop may be terminated by a condition code. In such a case the number of times the loop was executed should be available to the MPU. Because a number of available bit slice MCUs provide suitable capabilities, the architecture of the MCU will not be discussed in detail.

Processor Integrated Circuit Chips

The processor slice MPU described above can readily be implemented on a single integrated circuit chip. The MPU chip would require 15 pins to handle the shift, return, zero, carry, and other flag values. It would require 6 to 12 control lines (depending upon how the control signals are encoded) to implement the proposed MPU operations. The MPU chip has 4 data bus connections per bit, which would require 16 pins for a 4 bit slice, or 32 pins for an 8 bit slice. Thus a 4 bit slice MPU would fit on a 48 pin chip, while an 8 bit slice MPU would require a 64 pin chip. The complexity of the chip is not beyond that of chips presently in production.

The general register file and control register files can be implemented with dual port RAM chips that are presently available. The number of chips used would depend upon the amount of register storage desired.

The tri-state gate design required for the Control Bus ports could be implemented on an MSI chip. An 8 line Control Bus section would require two sets of 8 pins for the connections (ports) to the Control Buses of adjacent slices, and one set of 8 pins for connections between the slice components and the Control Bus. Four pins for enable lines are required, to enable left or right propagation at the left and right Control Bus ports. An 8 line Control Bus section would fit on a 30 pin chip. A 32 bit Control Bus would require 4 such chips. The Control Bus ports could also be implemented with standard SSI chips.

The connections between the various components of the slice and the Control Bus requires data multiplexers and demultiplexers. The multiplexers and demultiplexers required for the set of connections between a component of the slice and the Control Bus can be implemented on a single LSI chip, a 48 pin chip would handle an 8 bit slice size and a 32 bit address space (Control Bus) size; or standard SSI chips may be used. Several different connections are made to the Control Bus. There are three connections (representing the A, B, and C operands) to the general register file and MPU. There is a connection to the control register file. A connection is also required to the Memory Address Bus. However this connection does not require multiplexing and demultiplexing, so a set of tri-state gates may be used for this connection.

The shift box could be implemented with an LSI Programmable Logic Array (PLA). A 32 bit address space (control register file) size would require a PLA with 38 inputs and 32 outputs. The input are the 32 bits of the control register file, five lines for the amount of shift and one line to select negated outputs.

The (write and output) register address decoders could be implemented on a single MSI chip. With 3 bits of address to decode, the decoders could select among 8 register chips (with 16 registers per chip this would provide 128 registers in the processor). This would require 11 pins per decoder. With two A address decoders and one B address decoder it would fit on a 36 pin chip.

Architectural Efficiency

The dynamically reconfigurable architecture is as efficient as a static bit slice design in implementing most architectural features. For example, the dynamically reconfigurable architecture allows carry lookahead to be used. If the processor slice cluster is configured so that its low order slice is at one of the carry lookahead chip boundaries then carry lookahead is performed at the same speed as it would be in a static bit slice design. If the low order slice of a processor cluster is not at a carry lookahead chip boundary then there is a possible delay of one more stage of carry lookahead than would be necessary with a static design.

A static bit slice design would have a hard wired shift return line, while the dynamically reconfigurable architecture requires $2*(n-1)$ gate delays for an n slice processor cluster. However, this delay is not large compared to the bit slice cycle time except for the largest processor clusters. For example, in a 4 slice processor cluster the delay is 10%–20% of the slice cycle time. The increase in the slice cycle time could be even smaller as part of the delay may overlap with other components of the slice cycle. A static bit slice design would have an open collector wired AND of its zero flags, while the dynamically reconfigurable architecture requires 2*(n-1) gate delays for an n slice processor cluster. The Control Bus also operates in a ripple fashion with a maximum of 2*(n-1) gate delays in an n slice processor cluster.

The flexibility provided by the dynamically reconfigurable architecture does cause some performance problems. The main area of performance degradation over a static bit slice design is in decoding the Instruction Register and the selection of the Condition Code input to the MCU. A static bit slice design can efficiently implement these functions with a Programmable Logic Array (PLA). A true dynamically reconfigurable architecture cannot use this method because the decoding and selection criteria are dependant upon the processor slice configuration, and thus must be implemented in the microprogram. If however, the processor slice configurations are restricted to a reasonable subset of all possible configurations, then it is possible to increase performance by implementing all or part of the decoding and selection criteria for all possible configurations in a PLA within the MCU of each slice.

I/O BUS ARCHITECTURE

A dynamically reconfigurable architecture creates problems in providing efficient connections between processors and shared input, output, and file storage devices. This section examines an asynchronous bus structure and associated bus window devices that solve these problems. The structure introduced equips each processor with a local bus for memory and dedicated devices, with access to one or more global shared resource buses. The structure supports processor and direct memory access device controlled data transfers, both intra- and inter-bus, as well as intra-bus interrupts and interrupt transfers between buses. This section provides details of the bus lines, the bus protocols, and the operation of the various bus windows. It examines the problem of potential deadlock, and its resolution, and the problem of equitable bus sharing in periods of high bus contention.

The bus architecture requires that the dynamically reconfigurable system have at least one global shared resource bus intended primarily for the attachment of I/O devices. This global bus handles normal data transfers and interrupts between processor buses and shared devices. In a small system this bus would also handle non processor data transfers with a device acting as bus master. In larger systems non processor data transfers could be handled by one or more additional global buses. Each processor has a local bus to which is attached the processor's local memory and any dedicated devices. Each bus, local or global, will have a number of bus windows that are used to connect two buses together. These connections are generally. made between a local processor bus and a global shared device bus. A block diagram of the bus architecture is shown in Figure 3-6.

Each processor slice has its own local bus, which consists of control lines and

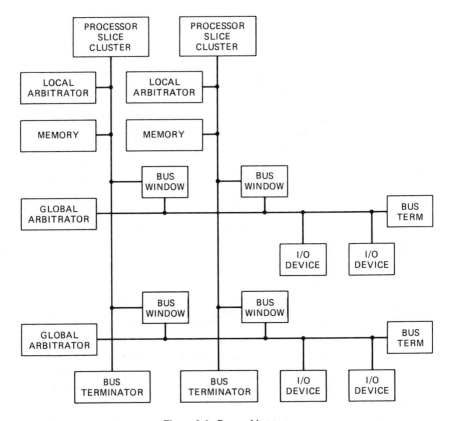

Figure 3-6. Bus architecture.

data lines equal to the number of bits in a slice. As described in detail later, when a slice is configured as part of a processor slice cluster, all the local buses of the processor slice cluster act in unison. Thus conceptually, the local buses of a processor slice cluster may be thought of as a single local bus.

The dynamically reconfigurable processor is constructed using slice chips. These physical slices provide the smallest degree of granularity available in the configuration of processor slice clusters of various sizes. It is possible, however, to organize the dynamically reconfigurable processor into logical slices composed of several physical slices, where the logical slice always operates as a whole which may not be split up. As described below, the choice of the size of logical slice has an effect upon the number of components utilized in the processor and buses. Using a logical slice size larger that the physical slice size reduces the number of components. The corresponding reduction in the flexibility of reconfiguration can be minimized by using several different logical slice sizes.

The number of components in the dynamically reconfigurable processor is a function of total processor size (slice width multiplied by number of slices) for the data related components and a function only of the number of logical slices for the control related components. For a particular system the choice of logical slice width has a limited effect upon the number of components of the processor. However, since each logical (processor) slice has its own local bus and bus window connections to global buses, the number of logical slices is the major factor in the number of components of the dynamically reconfigurable system bus architecture. For a particular system the choice of logical slice width has a major effect upon the number of components of the buses and windows. While a large number of small slices provides the maximum flexibility in reconfiguration, a smaller number of larger slices provides a considerable reduction in the number of components.

Bus Overview

The various bus lines are shown in Table 3-4. The address format supported by the various buses includes an address prefix that indicates the bus with which the address is associated. The prefix will either be a processor number

Table 3-4. Bus Lines.

Bus Lines
Address (a)
Data (d)
Master Sync
Slave Sync
Control (c)
Bus Busy
Bus Request (n)
Request Processor (m) +
Request Processor Sync +
Bus Grant (n) *
Grant Processor (m) +
Grant Sync +
Interrupt
Acknowledge
Non Processor Request
Non Processor Request Accept *
Non Processor Request Prefix (m)
Non Processor Request Prefix Sync
Non Processor Grant

(a) number of address lines
(c) number of control lines
(d) number of data lines
(m) number of prefix bits
(n) number of interrupt levels
+ Global Bus only
* Daisy Chained

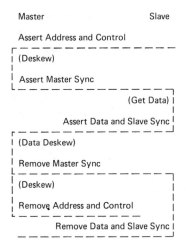

Figure 3-7. Data transfer from slave to master.

(in the case of a local bus) or a global bus number (if the address is that of a shared device). Each bus allows reference to only part of the system address space, that part which is on the bus and those parts which are on the buses that are directly connected (through a single bus window) to the bus.

Data transfers are done on a master slave basis using Master Sync and Slave Sync. These are shown in Figures 3-7 and 3-8. The Control lines specify the type of data transfer (read, write, etc.) and other characteristics. Each bus can have only a single bus master (processor or device) at any one time. The current bus master asserts the Bus Busy line, while any other device needing the bus asserts a request line.

```
Master                              Slave

Assert Address, Data, and Control
┌─ ─ ─ ─ ─ ─ ─ ─ ─ ─ ─ ─ ─ ─ ─ ─ ─
│(Deskew)
│
│Assert Master Sync
└─ ─ ─ ─ ─ ─ ─ ─ ─ ─ ─ ─ ─ ─ ─ ─ ┐
                            (Store Data) │
                                         │
                           Assert Slave Sync │
┌─ ─ ─ ─ ─ ─ ─ ─ ─ ─ ─ ─ ─ ─ ─ ─ ─ ─ ┘
│Remove Master Sync and Data
└─ ─ ─ ─ ─ ─ ─ ─ ─ ─ ─ ─ ─ ─ ─ ─ ┐
│(Deskew)                              │
│                                      │
│Remove Address and Control            │
└─ ─ ─ ─ ─ ─ ─ ─ ─ ─ ─            │
                           Remove Slave Sync │
─ ─ ─ ─ ─ ─ ─ ─ ─ ─ ─ ─ ─ ─ ─ ─ ─ ┘
```

Figure 3-8. Data transfer to slave from master.

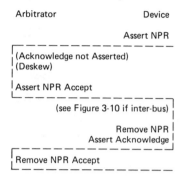

Figure 3-9. Intra-bus NPR.

Non Processor Requests

When a direct memory access device makes a data transfer it uses a non processor, cycle stealing method. The device must gain control of the bus to which it is attached, and the bus to which the destination is attached. In some cases these will be the same bus. The device begins the process of making a Non Processor Request (NPR) by the assertion of the NPR line.

The bus arbitrator will receive the assertion of NPR and if Acknowledge has not been asserted for the required deskew time, then the arbitrator may issue a NPR Accept at any time.

When a requesting device receives NPR Accept it does not immediately pass this signal on. The device may hold this signal for a set period of time, giving the device a chance to complete its request. If the device only wants control of its bus then the request is complete and the device will acknowledge, as described below and shown in Figure 3-9. If however the device wants control of both the local and global buses then the device sets the NPR Prefix lines and asserts NPR Prefix Sync, as shown in Figure 3-10.

When a window finds that NPR Prefix matches the processor or global bus

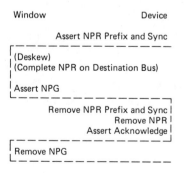

Figure 3-10. Inter-bus NPR.

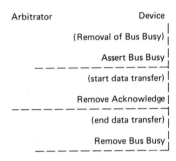

Figure 3-11. Bus master transfer.

number stored in it, and NPR Prefix Sync has been asserted for the required deskew time, then it makes a Non Processor Request on its other side. When the window has completed the request and gained control of the bus (asserted Bus Busy) it issues a Non Processor Grant (NPG) to the side prompting the request.

When a device that is holding NPR Accept receives the assertion of NPG then the request is complete, and the device clears its assertion of NPR and asserts Acknowledge.

The arbitrator receives the assertion of Acknowledge and removes the assertion of NPR Accept. If a window has issued an NPG and receives the assertion of Acknowledge it will remove its assertion of NPG. The window will continue to assert Acknowledge and Bus Busy on its other side.

A device may not remove its assertion of Acknowledge until it has seen the removal of the assertion of NPR Accept (and NPG if applicable). When the device sees the negation of Bus Busy while it is still asserting Acknowledge, it may assert Bus Busy and become the bus master as shown in Figure 3-11. The device should remove the assertion of Acknowledge shortly before it completes its transfer. If the request required acknowledgement by a bus window, this will cause the window to remove its assertion of Acknowledge on its other side. Likewise the window will remove its assertion of Bus Busy on its other side when it receives the negation of Bus Busy.

If a device has held NPR Accept for the permitted time yet has not received a NPG, then it removes its assertion of NPR Prefix Sync and the data on NPR Prefix lines, and then passes NPR Accept on to the next device. If NPR Accept has been passed on by the requesting device, before the window has issued NPG, then the window will not issue NPG and will relinquish control of the bus on its other side.

Interrupt Requests

When a device on a local bus needs to interrupt its processor it asserts the appropriate Bus Request line as shown in Figure 3-12. The arbitrator will

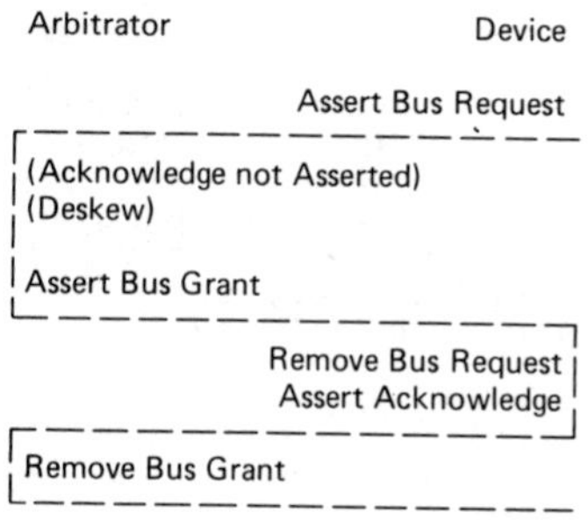

Figure 3-12. Intra-bus interrupt.

receive the assertion of this Bus Request line and if Acknowledge has not been asserted for the required deskew time, and if the processor is not currently in an interrupt sequence, then the arbitrator may issue the corresponding Bus Grant at any time.

When a requesting device receives the corresponding Bus Grant it does not pass it on. Rather it removes its assertion of Bus Request and asserts Acknowledge. When the assertion of Acknowledge is received at the arbitrator, the assertion of the Bus Grant line is removed.

Later, when the current bus master removes the assertion of Bus Busy, the requesting device asserts Bus Busy and becomes the bus master. The device is then free to do anything permitted of a bus master, but the most common action is to assert the Interrupt line which causes the next data transfer to be a vector address with which the processor can start an interrupt sequence. This is shown in Figure 3-13. The device then removes its assertion of Bus Busy.

Most devices that are used by processors will not be located on local buses, but rather will be on one of the global shared resource buses. When a device on the global bus requests an interrupt a slightly different sequence of events

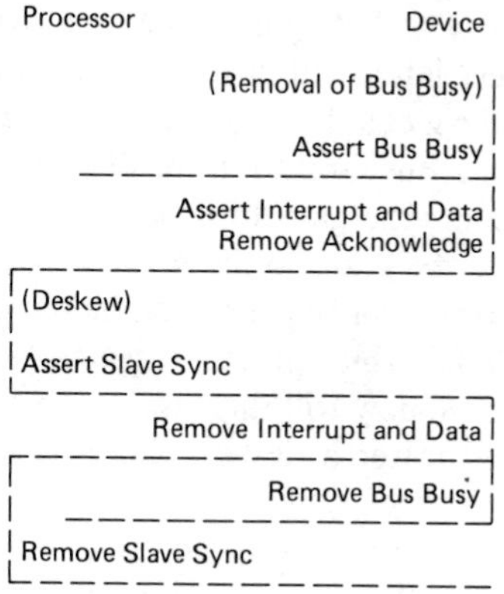

Figure 3-13. Interrupt sequence.

Figure 3-14. Inter-bus interrupt.

takes place as shown in Figure 3-14. The Request Processor lines are continually cycled through all the processor numbers, by the global bus arbitrator. When Request Processor Sync is asserted and Request Processor matches the processor number with which the device is associated, then the device asserts the appropriate Bus Request line. Each window has a Bus Request latch with inputs from the Bus Request lines of the global bus and output to the Bus Request lines of the local bus. When Request Processor matches the processor number stored in a window and Request Processor Sync is asserted then the inputs to the Bus Request latch within that window are enabled. The latch stores the requests from the global bus and transfers them to the local bus. The window may then receive a Bus Grant for one of its stored requests.

The window must become the global bus master through a Non Processor Request before it can pass the grant to the requesting device. Before releasing Acknowledge on its non processor request the window must assert Grant Sync which will prevent the global arbitrator from issuing any grants. After becoming global bus master the window will then assert the processor number on the Grant Processor lines and (after a deskew time) assert the appropriate Bus Grant line.

When a requesting device receives the corresponding Bus Grant and the Grant Processor lines match the associated processor number, then the device does not pass it on. Rather it removes its assertion of Bus Request and asserts Acknowledge.

As with a Non Processor Grant, when a window which has issued a grant receives the assertion of Acknowledge, it removes its assertion of Bus Grant and the Grant Processor lines. The window also removes its assertion of Grant Sync and Bus Busy. However the window still has Bus Busy asserted on the local bus.

A device may not remove its assertion of Acknowledge until it has seen the removal of the assertion of the applicable Bus Grant. When the assertion of Acknowledge is removed, then the window will remove its assertion of Acknowledge on its other side. When the device sees the negation of the global Bus Busy it will assert Bus Busy and start an interrupt sequence as detailed above. The interrupt sequence will be used by the appropriate window to start an interrupt sequence on the local bus. When the device removes its assertion of Bus Busy then the window will also remove its assertion of Bus Busy on its local bus side.

Data Transfers

All data transfers are done on a master slave basis. Intra-bus data transfers, such as a processor referencing its local memory, or a device that has become bus master through a request for only its associated bus, involve only the bus master and the addressed slave.

When a non local address is generated by the processor, the window that is specified by the address prefix will assert NPR on its global bus side. When the window becomes master of the global bus it will complete the data transfer on the global bus between the window and the addressed slave. The window will then release control of the global bus and complete the data transfer between the window and the bus master of the local bus (in this case the processor). Two master slave transfers are required, one on each bus. This method does not require any special processor action to check whether the address generated is local or not. The hardware will handle both: however non local references will have a longer access time. If the Control lines indicate that the data transfer is the read part of a read-modify-write cycle then the bus window will retain control of the destination global bus during the entire cycle.

When a device has become bus master through a Non Processor Request for both a local and global bus, or through an Interrupt Request from a global bus to a local bus, then the window included in the bus path will already be a bus master and will remain so until the device releases control of its bus. Data transfers through that window will proceed without delay. If the device generates any addresses that do not reference that bus window, they will be handled as described above.

These data transfer protocols have the advantage that individual references to addresses that are not on the bus on which they were generated are handled transparently. The protocols also have the advantage that during block transfers from a direct memory access device the delay in transfering data between the two buses is comparable to the delay in a single bus block transfer. The only additional delay in each data transfer operation is that there are two sets of deskew times, one for each bus. The deskew time is usually much less than other major components of a data transfer operation, such as the memory access time.

The address in a data transfer contains a prefix that specifies the processor or global bus number. In systems that have an address translation process (for virtual memory) the prefix can easily be added. If there is no virtual memory system then a very simple address translation process will suffice. The translation process maps a zero prefix into the associated processor number and leaves all other prefixes unchanged (the other prefixes should all be global bus numbers rather than processor numbers). The address translation is necessary to make programs independent of the processor they run on.

Bus Arbitration

On each local bus, the arbitrator is connected to the processor. The priority of devices on the same level is fixed by their order in the daisy chain connection of the Bus Grant or NPR Accept lines. The local arbitrator will issue a grant to any request that is made that exceeds the CPU priority level if the CPU is the bus master. If the CPU is not bus master then only Non Processor Requests will be granted and then only if the current bus master permits it (by removing its assertion of Acknowledge).

A Bus Grant or NPR Accept will arrive at the bus terminator if not acknowledged by any other device. In this event the bus terminator asserts Acknowledge and holds it as long as a Bus Grant or NPR Accept is asserted. The effect is merely to cause the arbitrator to start another arbitration sequence.

Each global bus has a separate arbitrator. The only requests arbitrated by the global arbitrator are Non Processor Requests and those only if permitted by the current bus master. The priority of devices on the same level is normally fixed as on the local bus, but to alleviate problems of equitable bus access during periods of high contention, the daisy chain order on the NPR Accept line can be made variable. This is done by substituting two lines for each daisy chain. A bus line that contains the signal from the arbitrator and a circular daisy chain line. All devices operate in the normal fashion, ignoring the bus line, and waiting for signals on the daisy chain, except for the device that is selected as head of the daisy chain. The head device takes signals from the bus line, and passes them on (if appropriate) along the daisy chain. If any signal should arrive at the head device through the daisy chain then it acts as the bus terminator.

Timeouts

The simplest form of timeout occurs on a single bus data transfer. If the address on the bus for the transfer does not match any slave address, then a Slave Sync will never be received. If a Slave Sync is not received within a set period of time, then the Master Sync and other lines asserted on the bus are removed and the data transfer is abandoned. Normally this will cause an error trap in the CPU or an error interrupt to the CPU if a device is bus master.

If a data transfer is between two buses then there can be two causes of timeouts. The first is that described above. This is the only kind of timeout that can occur if the data transfer is part of a Non Processor Request sequence. This timeout will normally cause the device to release control of the buses and initiate an error interrupt. The second kind of timeout only occurs with individual data transfers where the bus window must gain control of the destination bus. If after a set period of time the request by the bus window has not been granted then the transfer is abandoned. The processor would normally just retry the data transfer since the cause of the timeout is bus contention and is not an error. A timeout caused by bus contention cannot be differentiated, at the processor, from one caused by an invalid address but it can be differentiated by the bus window since the transfer on the destination bus can timeout only if the address is invalid. Therefore in cases where the timeout is caused by an invalid address the bus window will initiate an error interrupt.

Some bus operations require control of two buses, a local bus and a global bus. In each case the protocol followed involves gaining control of the bus associated with the initiating device or CPU, and then using the appropriate window to gain control of the other bus. This can happen during data transfers or nonprocessor requests. It can also happen with interrupt requests, but in this case the seizure of buses is always a global bus followed by a local bus. Since non processor requests and data transfers can happen in both directions (from local bus to global bus, or global bus to local bus) deadlock can occur. The bus system would deadlock if two bus operations requiring the same two buses for completion (but operating in the opposite directions) were started at approximately the same time. One operation would gain control of the global bus, while the other operation would gain control of the local bus. The first operation would then request control of the local bus, but would have to wait since the local bus was already seized (by the second operation). The second operation would be requesting control of the global bus, but would also have to wait since the global bus was already seized (by the first operation). The prevention of bus system deadlock is achieved by releasing control of the first bus seized if control of the second bus required is not granted within a set period of time. The request for the operation is left pending so that the hardware will automatically attempt to repeat the sequence, without software intervention.

In the case of interrupt requests a somewhat different situation occurs because the seizure of buses always follows a particular order, first a global bus and then a local bus. Once the global bus has been seized in this type of bus operation, the local bus required will always eventually become free, since all other operations eventually terminate successfully or timeout. Thus the interrupt request operation does not require a timeout, although the bus system will still remain deadlock free.

Processor Slice Clusters

While the previous discussion has treated processors as unitary pieces of hardware, processors are actually clusters of processor slices, and local buses are actually clusters of local buses. Each local bus that is associated with a single processor slice contains all the bus lines shown in Table 3-4. The number of data lines is that of a processor slice. The bus windows described above are duplicated for each individual local bus. The corresponding windows on adjacent local buses have two control lines running between them. Ripple Complete and Ripple Proceed. The windows also have access to the mode lines that assist with control of the processor slices, by indicating what position the slice is in within the cluster and whether a slice is the high order, intermediate, or low order slice in a cluster.

At all wait points in the protocols described above, all windows except the high order window will assert Ripple Complete to the next higher order window when the following conditions are met: the wait condition has been satisfied, and (except for the low order window) the Ripple Complete from the next lower order window is asserted, and the Ripple Proceed from the next higher order window is not asserted. Windows will not proceed with the protocol until the assertion of Ripple Complete is removed (by a momentary assertion of Ripple Proceed).

The high order window will assert Ripple Proceed to the next lower order window when the following conditions are met: the wait condition is satisfied and the Ripple Complete from the adjacent lower order window is asserted. The high order window will not proceed with the protocol until the assertion of Ripple Proceed is removed (by the removal of the assertion of the Ripple Complete input). All other windows will pass the state of Ripple Proceed from the next higher order window to the next lower order window.

All windows will have multiplexers for accessing the data lines on the global shared resource bus. Which segment of these data lines is accessed will depend upon the position of the slice in the cluster. Only the high order window will

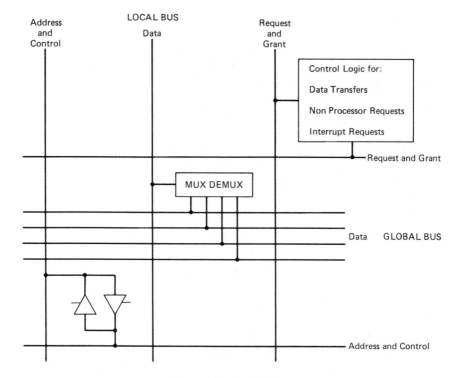

Figure 3-15. Bus window.

assert any lines other than data lines on the global shared resource bus. A bus window is shown in Figure 3-15.

Bus Integrated Circuit Chips

All control functions of a bus window processing interrupt requests, non processor requests, and data transfers in both directions, can readily be implemented on a single LSI chip. A complete bus window consists of the integrated circuit chip containing the control functions, tri-state gates to connect the address and control lines of the local and global buses, and data multiplexers and demultiplexers connecting the data lines of the local and global buses.

The control chip requires connections to the address prefix and other control lines of both the local and global buses. There must be one pin for each normal bus line and two pins for each daisy chained bus line. The total number of pins required for the bus connections is 26 plus 6 times the number of prefix bits plus 6 times the number of interrupt priority levels. There are also 4 pins required for the Ripple Complete and Proceed signals to the two adjacent processor slices. A few pins (2 to 4) are required to control the multiplexing of data between the local and global buses. These pins can also be used to input information, about the position of the slice within the cluster, to the control chip. A window supporting 3 address prefix bits and 2 interrupt priority levels would require a 64 pin chip for the control functions. A larger control chip is possible with newer integrated circuit packaging techniques.

The tri-state gates used to connect the address and control lines may be implemented on a single MSI chip, it would require 2 pins, one for the local bus and one for the global bus, for each address and control line, and 2 pins for the enable lines; or standard SSI chips may be used. The data multiplexers and demultiplexers can be implemented on a single LSI chip, a 48 pin chip would handle an 8 bit local bus and a 32 bit global bus data path; or standard SSI chips may be used.

SUMMARY

This chapter has presented a dynamically reconfigurable architecture from two different viewpoints—a detailed view of the processor organization, and a global view of the architectural configuration of a complete system.

The dynamically reconfigurable architecture described in this chapter consists of a number of slice computers arranged in a ring structure, where each slice computer has connections to its immediate neighbors on the ring. Each of these slice computers contains a processor (an arithmetic logic unit), a microprogram controller, registers, memory, and an asynchronous local bus. The bus connects memory to the processor. It also has the capability to connect I/O devices to the processor. However, most conventional I/O is done through global I/O buses that are connected to the local buses of each of the slice computers by bus windows. Viewed at this level of detail the dynamically reconfigurable architecture appears to be a typical multiprocessor system with the ability to share I/O devices. The chapter discusses the bus protocols and hardware bus windows that are necessary to support these capabilities.

Each of the slice computers in the dynamically reconfigurable architecture is capable of independent operation, since each slice computer is equipped with all of the necessary components (microprogram controller, registers, etc.). Moreover each slice computer is also equipped with connections to the adjacent slice computers on the ring. The activation of these connections allows the grouping of several slice computers into a larger packaged computer. These connections allow the information that is dependent upon the entire packaged processor (carry bits, memory addresses, etc.) to be made easily available to all parts of the packaged processor that require them.

The chapter has described the connections and processor architecture required to realize the capabilities described above. Fundamental design questions that have led to the processor architecture and its appropriate modularization of the architecture have been examined. The feasibility of implementation of the architecture with current VLSI technology is discussed and the emulation capability and potential performance of the processor architecture are also examined.

In practice the dynamically reconfigurable system described in this chapter would consist of a number of slice computers. At any instant in time the system would be configured into a number of packaged computers, each of which is composed of one or more adjacent slice computers. The system is unique in that the configuration of the packaged computers (their number and size) can be changed easily as new tasks are presented to the system.

A dynamically reconfigurable system would facilitate multiprogramming. Because each task would be on a separate packaged computer, it would incur a low software overhead. Because each processor can be tailored to task requirements, there would also be efficient hardware utilization. Packaged computers would contain the appropriate number of slice computers and the appropriate microprograms to process a task with maximum hardware efficiency. Because each task is running in an environment that is essentially uniprogramming, the complexity of the operating system is greatly reduced.

The dynamically reconfigurable architecture described in this chapter can support a variable number of packaged computers. This capability is very appropriate for parallel processing applications where each separate process can be placed on a separate processor. Processes can communicate with each other through the shared resources (such as memory) available on the global I/O buses. This architecture is particularly efficient because there is no overhead in simulating parallelism. The system is fundamentally parallel in its operation. This architecture is unique in its capability to provide true parallelism of operation on a general basis.

Fault tolerant systems constitute another area of application of the dynamically reconfigurable architecture. Faults that occur in a slice computer within such an architecture can be isolated because the system interconnections can be changed so that none of the packaged computers use the faulty slice computer. When spare slice computers are exhausted, it is possible to change the system configuration so that packaged computers of less computing capability (for example, utilizing double precision instructions on a packaged computer half the size) are used. Thus it would appear that the dynamically reconfigurable architecture has the property of extremely graceful degradation without requiring extensive hardware duplication.

In the realm of processor architecture this chapter has introduced designs of the various component modules of a dynamically reconfigurable architecture: the arithmetic logic unit, the general register file, the control register file, and the microprogram control unit. Each of these modules can be implemented with VSLI, LSI, or MSI integrated circuit chips. The interconnection of these modules through the control bus is examined. The number of interconnections necessary to provide the dynamically reconfigurable capabilities has been shown to be not large and to grow only linearly as the number of processors is increased.

This chapter has also examined the overall architecture of the dynamically reconfigurable system. Each processor is connected to its local bus which is in turn connected to a set of global I/O buses. The bus lines and devices (such as bus terminators and bus arbitrators) needed are shown. The bus window modules that connect the buses together can be implemented in a few LSI and MSI integrated circuit chips.

The dynamically reconfigurable microprocessor architecture described in this chapter, is an architecture that only recently has become feasible, as a result of the vast decrease in the cost of VLSI hardware. Architectures of this kind are expected to find application in many areas of computing, including multiprogramming, parallel processing, and fault tolerant systems.

REFERENCES

(1) Arnold, R. G. and Page, E. W. "A Hierarchical Restructurable Multimicroprocessor Architecture." *ACM Sigarch*, (Jan. 1976).
(2) Casaglia, G. F. "Nanoprogramming vs. Microprogramming." *Computer* (Jan. 1976).
(3) Davidson, S. "A Network of Dynamically Microprogrammable Machines." *ACM Sigmicro* (Dec. 1975).
(4) Davison, J. W. "The JHU Universal Host Machine II–Part I: The Machine." *The Johns Hopkins University Computer Research Report* #31.
(5) Demco, J. C. and Marsland, T. A. "Contemporary Computer Emulation on the QM-1." *IEEE Computer Society Repository* R76-142.
(6) Enslow, P. H. Jr. "Multiprocessor Organization–A Survey." *ACM Computing Surveys* (March 1977).
(7) Flynn, M. J., Neuhauser, C. J., and McClure, R. M. "EMMY—An Emulation System for User Microprogramming." *AFIPS Conference Proceedings* (1975 NCC).
(8) Heath, J. P., Cline, J., and Kennedy, J. "Dynamically Alterable Topology Distributed Data Processing Computer Architecture." *Proceedings IEEE Intl. Conf. on Circuits and Computers* (Oct. 1980).
(9) Kartashev, S. I. and Kartashev. S. P. "A Microprocessor with Modular Control as a Universal Building Block for Complex Computers." *Proceedings 3rd EURMICRO Symposium on Microprocessors and Microprogramming* (1977).
(10) Kartashev, S. I. and Kartashev. S. P. "LSI Modular Computers, Systems, and Networks." *Computer* (July 1978).
(11) Kartashev, S. I. and Kartashev. S. P. "Dynamic Architectures: Problems and Solutions." *Computer* (July 1978).
(12) Kartashev, S. I. and Kartashev. S. P. "A Multicomputer System with Dynamic Architecture." *IEEE Transactions on Computers* (Oct. 1979).
(13) Kartashev, S. I. and Kartashev. S. P. "Problems of Designing Supersystems with Dynamic Architecture." *IEEE Transactions on Computers* (Dec. 1980).
(14) Kehl, T. H., Moss, C. and Dunkel, L. "LM2—A Logic Machine Minicomputer." *Computer* (Nov. 1975).
(15) Lessor, V. R. "Direct Emulation of Control Structures by a Parallel Micro-Computer." *Stanford Linear Accelerator Center Report* #127.

(16) Lipovski, G. J. "On A Varistructured Array of Microprocessors." *IEEE Transactions on Computers* (Feb. 1977).

(17) Mallach, E. G. "Emulation Architecture." *Computer* (Aug. 1975).

(18) Neuhauser, C. J. "An Emulation Oriented, Dynamic Microprogrammable Processor, Version II." *The Johns Hopkins University Computer Research Report* #28.1.

(19) Pease, M. C. III "The Indirect Binary n-Cube Microprocessor Array." *IEEE Transactions on Computers* (May 1977).

(20) Rauscher, T. G. and Agrawala, A. K. "Developing Application Oriented Computer Architectures on General Purpose Microprogrammable Machines." *AFIPS Conference Proceedings* (1976 NCC).

(21) Rothlisberger, H. "A Standard Bus for Multiprocessor Architecture." *Proceedings 3rd ERUMICRO Symposium on Microprocessors and Microprogramming* (1977).

(22) Scott, M. A. and Smith, K. C. "A Multiple Bus Architecture." *Proceedings MIMI 80 Mini and Microcomputers Applications* (Sept. 1980).

(23) Scott, M. A. and Smith, K. C. "A Dynamically Reconfigurable Microprocessor Architecture." *Proceedings IEEE Intl. Conf. on Circuits and Computers* (Oct. 1980).

4. VLSI Hardware Algorithms

Amar Mukhopadhyay
University of Central Florida
Orlando

INTRODUCTION

The advent of very large scale integration (VLSI) technology has stimulated renewed interest in a fundamental issue raised by Moore (1) in the context of LSI: What to put into a chip? Because they have a regular geometry based on the repetition of simple cells, memory devices are natural candidates for VLSI implementation. But there is always some communication and system overhead for utilizing a pure memory device in the total system architecture. An improvement in this situation can be made if both memory and logic can be combined to build a special purpose processor that can take over some of the specialized functions of CPU, reduce system bottlenecks and simplify the overall communication and control structure. The basic problem seems to be the identification of tasks which can be built into special purpose VLSI chips.

Nonnumeric processing is one area which could benefit tremendously from VLSI. By nonnumeric processing is meant those specialized operations that are not very well suited for a classical ALU. Some examples of such operations are: string processing, sorting, merging, text and word processing, data base search and updates, graph processing, etc. The software algorithms currently used on conventional systems are not good enough to meet expected performance criteria in most applications involving large volumes of data. There is a need to develop special purpose hardware algorithms for these applications.

In developing specialized hardware for VLSI implementation, one has to remember the technological constraints. The idea is to use an algorithmic approach suitable for VLSI that reduces communication rather than computation and that is based on the replication of a basic function in space or time. Replication in space leads to cellular structure of simple cells whereas replication in time leads to parallelism or pipelining on several data streams. The need to reduce communication overhead leads to regular geometry for the cell organization. Hardware algorithms that satisfy similar criteria have been studied in the past by several authors in the context of cellular logic, iterative circuits (Hennie, (2); Minnick, (3); Mukhopadhyay and Stone, (4), logic-in-memory array (Kautz, (5)), sorting and merging networks (Batcher, (6); Knuth, (7)), pattern matching circuits (Lee and Paull, (8); Gaines and Lee, (9); Mukhopadhyay, (10)), to name a few, and recently most notably among others by Kung (11) and Kung and Leiserson (12) who named these as "systolic algorithms."

In this chapter, we will be concerned with hardware algorithms for pattern matching and string processing with particular emphasis on those that are suitable for VLSI implementation. The next few sections will present the contributions made in this area by the author and his colleagues. This will be followed by a tutorial review and a critique of other hardware algorithms for string processing reported in the literature.

The Pattern Matching Problem

The pattern matching problem consists of searching a large text stream over some finite alphabet Σ to find some or all occurrences of one or more substrings or patterns starting from specified character positions in the text stream. If the patterns are to be searched starting from any position in the text, it will be called *unanchored* mode pattern search. If the search has to be done with respect to certain specified positions in the text, the search will be called *anchored* mode pattern search. The patterns may be fully or partially specified. Let $ denote a "don't care" or "wild card" character, then the pattern A$B denotes a set of patterns viz. AAB, ABB, ACB, etc., that is any pattern that begins with A, ends with B and has a single unspecified character in the middle. The character $ will be called a "single length don't care" (SLDC) character and may appear at any place in the pattern. A special character ϕ will be used to denote the infinite set of patterns $\phi = \{\$, \$\$, \$\$\$. \ldots \}$ and will be called "multiple length don't care" (MLDC) character. A third special character ? will be used to denote either a null character or ϕ and will be called a "variable length don't care" (VLDC) character. Patterns containing any one or more of the special characters $, ϕ or ? will be called partially specified; otherwise, it will be called fully specified.

The pattern matching problem is important in many applications, such as text retrieval systems, advanced word processing systems, string processing languages like Snobol, data base management, artificial intelligence and numerical computation such as convolution and correlation.

Simple sequential algorithms for searching text typically require a worst-case run time of $0(mn)$, where m is the length of the fully specified pattern and n is the length of the text. Knuth, et. al., (13) have developed a fast sequential algorithm which reduce the run time to $O(m + n)$. Later, Boyer and Moore (14) developed an improved algorithm which has sublinear average complexity but has linear complexity at worst (15). Horspool (16) shows that this algorithm can outperform many special purpose search instructions built into some computer hardware. A generalization of the Morris-Knuth-Pratt algorithm has been proposed by Aho and Corasick (17) to deal with multiple patterns. From the point of view of implementation by hardware, none of these algorithms seem to offer a desirable, simple and regular data flow and control structure suitable for VLSI implementation. This illustrates a significant point that the most efficient sequential algorithms are not necessarily the best algorithms for VLSI implementation. Also, in dealing with massively large textual data bases, software algorithms cannot provide the needed performance (18). Furthermore, none of the algorithms discussed above handle the pattern matching problem with partially specified patterns. Fischer and Patterson (19) have shown that the linear pattern matching algorithm of Morris-Knuth-Pratt breaks down if the alphabet has "don't care" characters and they proposed a slightly worse-than-linear algorithm.

HARDWARE ALGORITHMS FOR PATTERN MATCHING

This section will present two hardward algorithms for pattern matching developed by the author (10), (20). The algorithms use an array of simple cells in which a pattern is stored, and the text to be searched is applied to this array either in serial or in parallel fashion. Each cell is primarily a comparison/storage element and generates a match signal which propagates across the array as the text is streamed through. A match signal from the last cell in the array indicates a successful pattern match.

The Basic Cells

The basic cell for serial operation is shown in Figure 4-1. The cell contains two registers holding a text character T and pattern character P (a "character" could be a bit, a 2-bit, a nibble, a byte or word combination from a finite alphabet), a comparator circuit C, a match flip-flop M, and a unit delay device Δ (a latch). The cell has a binary output f and a binary input i. The input i will also be referred to as the "anchor" or "enable" input. The equations describing the cell can be written as

$$m_{t+1} = (T = P)_t \Delta i_t$$
$$f_t = m_{t-1}$$

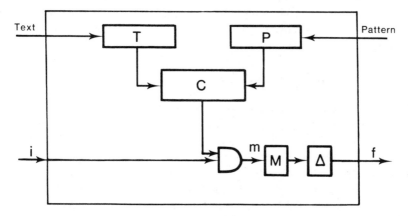

Figure 4-1. The basic cell for pattern matching with serial text input.

where m_t represents the value of the binary variable representing the match flip-flop M. The logic is clocked. The output f is 1 at a time t if the characters T and P match at time $t - 2$ with the anchor line holding a value of 1.

The basic cell for parallel text input is shown in Figure 4-2. The cell accepts the text character T directly from the bus and the equations describing its function can be written as

$$m_{t+1} = (T = P)_t \wedge i_t$$
$$f_t = m_t$$

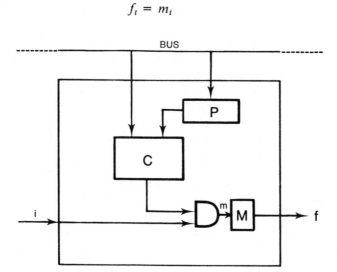

Figure 4.2. The basic cell for pattern matching with parallel text input.

The logic is clocked. The output f is 1 at time t if the input text character T and the pattern character P match at time $t - 1$ with the input i holding a value 1.

The Basic Pattern Matching Device

A cascade of basic serial cells connected, as shown in Figure 4-3, will do the basic pattern matching operation. The T registers together essentially form a shift register, and for each clock pulse the next text character is latched into the first T register. The P registers also form a shift register for loading purposes, but are static during comparison phase. Note the register T and P are connected in a fashion that allows loading of the text string and pattern string serially from left or right. It is possible to load the pattern $x_1 x_2 \ldots x_n$ from left if the characters are available in reverse order. The operation of the cascade follows these steps: load the pattern $x_1 x_2 \ldots x_n$ from right; apply text string and anchor information; observe output after lapse of $2n$ clocks since the application of the text string. If f is 1 at time $2n + s$ since the application of text string ($1 \leq s \leq l$ text l), then the pattern $x_1 x_2 \ldots x_n$ has appeared in the text beginning at position s of text provided the anchor line was "on" at time $t = s$. The "anchor" input line could be pulsed with arrival of every text character, in which case the operations will take place in the "unanchored" mode.

For parallel input of text, a cascade of basic cells connected as in Figure 4-4 will do the basic pattern matching operation. The input pattern to be matched is a string of characters $x_1 x_2 \ldots x_n$ and is placed in the registers of the cells. Each character of the text stream is applied in parallel to all the cells. If the output is 1 at time $n + s$ since the application of text string ($s \geq 1$), then the pattern $x_1 x_2 \ldots x_n$ has appeared in the text beginning position s of the text provided the anchor input was on at time $t = s$. Again, the input i to the entire cascade serves the purpose of "anchor" in the Snobol sense. If $i = 1$ at time $t = 1$, the pattern matching is anchored with respect to the beginning of the input text. If the anchoring has to be done beginning at the kth character of the input text, the input i would be pulsed to 1 at time k. In general, if the output from the kth cell $f_k (1 \leq k \leq n)$ becomes 1 at time $k + 1$, the pattern $x_1 x_2 \ldots x_k$ matches the input text. If the pattern matching is done in the unanchored mode, that is, i is pulsed at every clock time, multiple matches may take place which will be indicated by f becoming 1 a multiple number of times.

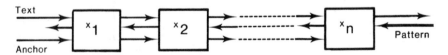

Figure 4.3. The basic pattern matching device with serial text input.

Text

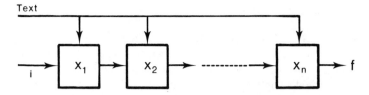

Figure 4-4. The basic pattern matching device with parallel text input.

The circuit of Figures 4-3 and 4-4 can also be looked upon as performing a functional transformation of the input bit string at the anchor line to the output bit strings f_i. This interpretation fits Gimpel's (21) definition of a pattern as a function operating on a cursor as

$$\text{(Text, Precursor Position) Pattern} = \text{(Text, Postcursor Position)}$$

Setting the anchor input to 1 provides the precursor position (notice in Snobol this will correspond to anchor position 0); the propagation of the signal indicated by f_i denotes a partial match and an advancement of the cursor position. If $f = 1$, the cursor position has advanced by n, indicating a match. As an example for the parallel text input case, if the pattern "ALPHA" is set into the cascade and an input text "ALPHALPHALALA" is applied, the values of i and f for several anchor positions are as shown in Table 4-1 for the duration of the input text. In the case of serial text input, note that the match signal propagates at half the speed of the text characters. The output f will become 1 at $t = 11$ and at $t = 15$ rather that at $t = 6$ and $t = 10$, respectively.

Table 4-1. Anchored and Unanchored Mode Operation of the Cascade: Pattern: ALPHA, Parallel Text Input: ALPHALPHALALA.

TIME →	1	2	3	4	5	6	7	8	9	10	11	12	13	14	
i	1	0	0	0	0	0	0	0	0	0	0	0	0	0	Anchored at 1
f	0	0	0	0	0	1	0	0	0	0	0	0	0	0	
i	1	1	1	1	1	1	1	1	1	1	1	1	1	1	Unanchored
f	0	0	0	0	0	1	0	0	0	1	0	0	0	0	
i	0	1	0	0	0	0	0	0	0	0	0	0	0	0	Anchored at 2
f	0	0	0	0	0	0	0	0	0	0	0	0	0	0	
i	1	0	0	0	1	0	0	0	0	0	0	0	0	0	Anchored at 1, 5
f	0	0	0	0	0	1	0	0	0	1	0	0	0	0	

Pattern Matching With "Don't Care" Characters

If the pattern has a "don't care" symbol, then the cell should essentially perform a "unit stage delay" function to propagate the match signal from the previous stage to the next stage. The cell now has a fixed length don't care flip-flop F and a variable length don't care flip-flop V. These flip-flops are connected in the form of shift registers and have to be loaded along with the pattern via the control lines from the left side of the cell. The logic diagram of the cell is shown in Figure 4-5. Note that if both the V and F flip-flops are set, the match operation is simulated for all clock times following the first appearance of 1 at the i input, which is equivalent to matching for multiple length don't care characters. For fixed length don't care operation, only the F flip-flop is set. The setting of the A flip-flops, which are also connected in the form of a shift register, will determine the anchoring. If the ith cell anchor flip-flop is set to 1 at time t, it is possible to detect the existence of the subpattern $x_i, x_{i+1}. \ldots .x_n$ in the text string beginning the text position which arrives the ith cell at time t.

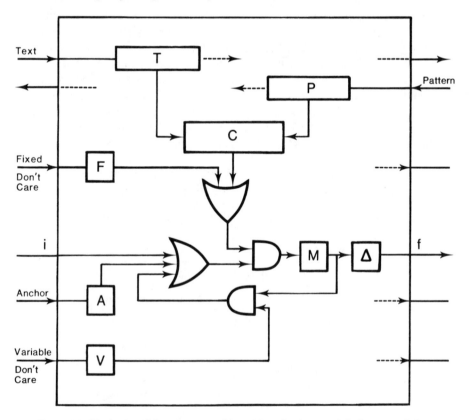

Figure 4-5. The basic cell for pattern matching with anchor input and don't care symbols.

If this substring matching has to be done in unanchored mode, the value of A has to be continuously set from clock time when the first character of the text string is at the ith cell of the cascade. The cell logic for parallel text input is essentially as shown in Figure 4-5 with the difference that the text character T comes from a bus connected to all the cells and the unit delay device Δ is absent. Any subpattern which is a suffix of the given pattern $x_1 x_2 \ldots x_n$ can be matched by properly initializing the anchor flip-flops of the cells. Simultaneous matching of several subpatterns is possible but one should apply caution in interpreting the results because $f = 1$ may imply several matches in the unanchored mode. For example, if the pattern is "abab" and the suffix subpattern is "ab," then with the text "ababab," $f = 1$ at time $t = 5$ for parallel text input will imply two matches. If the outputs from all the cells in the cascade can be observed, arbitrary matching can also be implemented. If this subpattern matching facility is to be extended to the unanchored mode, the relevant anchor inputs need to be pulsed at every clock time.

The operation of the basic pattern matching cascade is essentially the same as described earlier with simpler cells. The pattern $x_1 x_2 \ldots x_n$ is loaded along with SLDC or MLDC information encoded as bits in the F and V flip-flops and the anchor information at the A flip-flops. The text stream is applied and output of the cascade is observed for match. The idea of a simple comparator cascade without any don't care or substring matching features for the parallel text input case was also independently proposed by Copeland (22).

Let us take some examples to illustrate the ideas. The pattern to be matched is A¢A against the text stream ABABAY. Recall ¢ stands for multiple length don't care character. Tables 4-2 and 4-3 show the operation of the devices for parallel and serial text input respectively. Under each cell, two characters are shown, the top one is the text character T and the bottom one is the pattern character P. The outputs of cell 1 or the feedback input of cell 2, cell 2 and cell 3 are denoted by f_1, f_2 and f_3 respectively, of which f_3 is the match output. Note f_1 stands for the input i to the second cell or the output of the OR gate to which i is applied (see Figure 4-5). Thus if f_1 becomes 1, its value does not change throughout the operation. When $f_3 = 1$ at time 6 for parallel input (time 9 for serial input) it actually symbolizes two matches, one for the substring ABABA in the text and the other for the second occurrence of ABA starting position 3 of the text input. Smith (23) has incorporated a special machine instruction for a string processor (see later in this section) to detect all such possible beginning match positions.

The Pattern Matching Array

The pattern matching cascade of the previous section can be interpreted as an associative memory, each word of the memory being a single character. If each word contains k characters, simultaneous matching of k distinct patterns $p_1 =$

Table 4-2. Pattern Matching With Parallel Text Input: Pattern:
A¢A, Text: ABABAY.

TIME	ANCHOR	CELL 1	f_1	CELL 2	f_2	CELL 3	f_3
1	1	A	0	A	0	A	0
		A		¢		A	
2	1	B	1	B	0	B	0
		A		¢		A	
3	1	A	1	A	1	A	0
		A		¢		A	
4	1	B	1	B	1	B	1
		A		¢		A	
5	1	A	1	A	1	A	0
		A		¢		A	
6	1	Y	1	Y	1	Y	1
		A		¢		A	

$x_1 x_2 \ldots x_n$, $p_2 = y_1 y_2 \ldots y_n$, $\ldots$, $p_k = z_1 z_2 \ldots z_n$ against the input text stream is possible. If size of p_i is less than n, p_i should be placed right adjusted and the anchor flip-flop should be initialized as explained in the previous section. This corresponds to an extension of the cellular hardware in two dimensions. The output is now the logical or of the cascade outputs. If this output is 1 during the application of the input text stream, then one of the patterns p_1 $p_2 \ldots p_k$ must have occured in the input text. This corresponds to the alternation operation in Snobol which is realized by a logical OR operation in our scheme. This circuit performs the following pattern transformation

$$(\text{Text}, c)(p_1 l p_2 l \ldots l p_k) = [c_1 c_2 \ldots c_k]$$

where c is the precursor position for patterns p_i, and l denotes the alternation operation.

The circuit may be varied in many ways. The techniques for unanchored mode operation, subpattern matching, "don't care" symbols and variable anchor position, as described for a single cascade, can be extended to this two-dimensional pattern matching device. Furthermore, a simple hardware modification can achieve what might be called *selective anchoring*. Let us say that the pattern p_i is to be anchored at precursor position a_i. The k distinct pattern matching operations can then be denoted symbolically as

$$(\text{Text}, [a_1 a_2 \ldots a_k])(p_1 l p_2 l \ldots l p_k) = [c_1 c_2 \ldots c_k]$$

This can be achieved by setting the anchor flip-flops to the appropriate values within the different cascades. By incorporating additional "anchor control" logic it is possible to operate some subsets of cascades in the unanchored mode, subpattern matching mode, variable anchor position mode or a combination thereof. This could conceivably produce a rather complex pattern matching facility for future machines.

It is important to note that the difference between the unanchored and anchored mode of operation in this scheme is simply the presence or absence of a pulse at the anchor line. But this difference is tremendous in software implementation because of the sequential nature of the matching process in which each failure is to be backed up by a readjustment of the precursor position. The hardware scheme described here performs parallel computations for each possible anchor position.

Hardward for Complex String Operations

Hardware schemes to perform complex string processing operations, including most of the Snobol operations and pattern structures specified by regular expressions, have been presented by the author in earlier papers (10), (20) (Mukhopadhyay, 1978, 1980). We will present briefly some of these schemes.

Table 4-3. Pattern Matching With Serial Text Input: Pattern: A¢A, Text: ABABAY.

TIME	ANCHOR	CELL 1	f_1	CELL 2	f_2	CELL 3	f_3
1	1	A	0	–	0	–	0
		A		¢		A	
2	1	B	0	A	0	–	0
		A		¢		A	
3	1	A	1	B	0	A	0
		A		¢		A	
4	1	B	1	A	0	B	0
		A		¢		A	
5	1	A	1	B	1	A	0
		A		¢		A	
6	1	Y	1	A	1	B	0
		A		¢		A	
7	0	–	1	Y	1	A	1
		A		¢		A	
8	0	–	1	–	1	Y	0
		A		¢		A	
9	0	–	1	–	1	–	1
		A		¢		A	

If a pattern matching has to be done with respect to a contiguous word phrase, that is, patterns separated by variable number of blank symbols, two approaches are possible. For all the blank symbols, a single blank character is loaded in the *P* register and *V* is set to 1 and *F* to 0. This will hold the output *f* to 1 against arbitrary number of blank symbols between the phrases. The other alternative is to remove the blank symbols by employing a "trim" circuit as proposed by the author earlier (10). Logic similar to that used in the first approach can be used to match against a run of special symbols (span operation) or detect the end of run of special symbols (break operation). The *P* register in these cases has to be loaded with a special symbol representing the class of symbols in the span so that comparison operation is successful for any member of the class in the text stream. The *V* register has to be set to 1 and *F* to 0 as before.

The basic idea for recognizing patterns specified by regular expressions is to use feedback as in the basic cell of Figure 4-5, as well as feedforward connections for the parallel text input case. This will lead to recognition of null strings, as well as *P*, *PP*, *PPP*, etc. The idea now can be extended over a group of characters in accordance with the given regular expression structure. This corresponds to Kleene star operation (*) for regular expression (24), (25). (Copi, et. al., 1964; Kleene, 1956. The union and concatenation operations correspond to use of pattern matching cascades in parallel and in series connection, respectively. As an example, the scheme to implement a pattern structure described by a regular expression $ab^*(c + a)^*b$ is shown in Figure 4-6.

If the element *C* in the cell is enriched to perform complex operations such as the relational operations ($<$, $\leq$, $>$, $\geq$, $=$), pattern search can be carried on for relational queries in the text. The idea is sketched in Figure 4-7, where

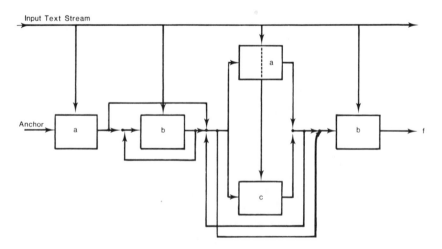

Figure 4-6. Pattern matching with regular expression.

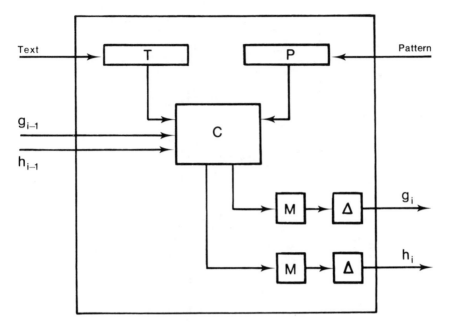

Figure 4-7. The basic cell for complex search.

the enable input, i, of the basic cell is replaced by a set of $[\log_2 k]$ inputs corresponding to functions $f_1, f_2, \ldots f_k$ (viz. f_1 could be $=$, f_2 be $\neq$, f_3 be $\geq$, f_4 be $\leq$, etc.). Let us say we are interested in $<$, $>$ and $=$ functions and encode them by a pair of bits (g_i, h_i) as (0,1), (1,0) and 1,1) respectively. The assignment $g_i = 0$, $h_i = 1$ means that including up to the ith character in the pattern, the input word has been established to be in "$<$" relationship with the resident pattern. By applying well-known logic design procedures for iterative circuits, the logic diagram for the comparator circuit C can be found. By applying a similar approach, the logic within the C network can be expanded to implement complex text retrieval queries (26), (27).

Practical Implementation

Smith (23) describes the logical design of a string processor with an instruction set which permits arithmetic, as well as pattern matching, operations. The heart of the processor is a pattern matcher which employs a cascade of eight cells. Figure 4-8 shows the basic cell for parallel text input. The text character T comes from the data bus DBUS. The line EN is the anchor input, the flip-flop M holds the output f. The cell also shows the clock, the clear pattern and the shift lines. Other symbols have meaning as previously defined. The basic cell for serial text input, as shown in Figure 4-9, looks very similar to the one

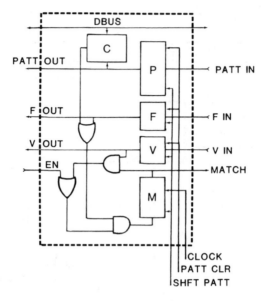

Figure 4-8. A practical implementation of the basic parallel pattern matching cell.

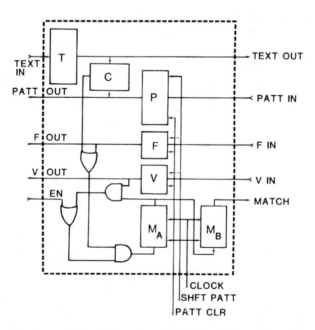

Figure 4-9. A practical implementation of the basic serial pattern matching cell.

in Figure 4-8. The result bit is latched through two flip-flops, MA and MB, in two clock cycles. The text character T moves from left to right in each clock cycle.

A schematic of the pattern matching section of the processor is shown in Figure 4-10. The register $EOSR$ may be loaded under program control to hold a character to signify the end of the text string indicated by the comparator ECOMP. The registers SLDC and MLDC can similarly be loaded under program control, and the outputs from the corresponding comparator, SCOMP and MCOMP, are used to initialize the F and V flip-flops of the cells. This design did not include anchor flip-flops for substring matching, a single anchor flip-flop ANCH determines the beginning of the pattern matching operation. The pattern is loaded left justified and the counter "left" keeps the number of characters in the pattern. The "detect" circuit detects a match output from the appropriate cell. For further details the reader is referred to Smith (23), where the detailed design of a microprogrammed sequencer, an arithmetic logic unit, the memory section, the instruction set and the control unit that integrates the subsystems together are presented. The machine has been simulated and the correctness of the hardware algorithm verified. The pattern matching algorithm without any don't care character has been analyzed and compared with a corresponding algorithm implemented on a Z-80 microprocessor. The results indicate that the machine is about twenty times as fast without even considering SLDC and MLDC and using only off-the-shelf MSI components.

Smith and Oltman (28) describe a preliminary design of 30-pin nmos serial-input pattern matching using the Mead-Conway (29) design rules. The logical limit of the chip functionality is confined to the part enclosed in dotted lines in Figure 4-10. The basic cell contains logic similar to that shown in Figure 4-9 for a single bit, repeated eight times vertically to accommodate a byte plus logic associated with shift registers, don't care logic, input/output pads. The design is now being tested for correctness and future fabrication of the chip as a prototype is planned.

A SURVEY OF OTHER ALGORITHMS

Several hardware algorithms for pattern matching have recently been reported in the literature. We will present a brief tutorial survey of these methods in this section. Some of these methods were developed in connection with searching large textual data bases and are implemented either by software or as a special-purpose device built from standard components while other methods would lead to implementation directly by special-purpose VLSI hardware. We will start our discussion with the latter class.

In a recent paper, Foster and Kung (30) describe a VLSI chip for pattern matching operation which consists of a linear array of two kinds of cells, as shown in Figure 4-11. The comparator cells (C) receive a single character of

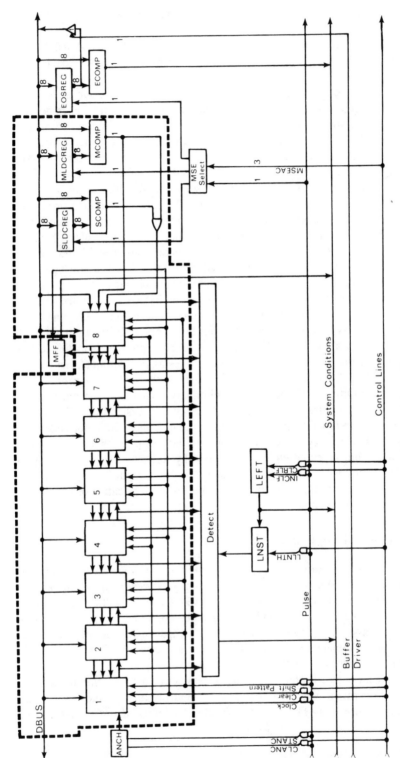

Figure 4-10. A string processor.

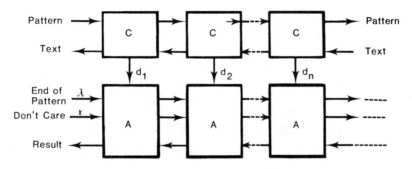

Figure 4-11. The pattern matching device of Foster and Kung.

pattern and text string, compare them to produce a match signal d, and then pass the text character to the left and the pattern character to the right. The accumulator cells (A) store a temporary result t based on the values of the "don't care" character indicator x, end of pattern marker λ and d in the following manner. Referring to the computation for the ith cell by the subscript i, if the signal λ_i is 1, t_i is set to 1 and the result bit gets the value of t_i; if $\lambda_i = 0$, then t_i is set according to the values of d_i, x_i and the previous stored value of t by the relationship

$$t_i \leftarrow t_i \Lambda(x_i \vee d_i)$$

and the result bit to the cell input passes to the output result. All characters and the binary inputs λ and x move one cell position during each beat.

The flexibility of the chip is very limited. It works only in unanchored mode, has no capability of handling MLDC, no substring matching facility and requires special control circuits to recirculate the pattern repeatedly. To handle patterns of length less than half the number of cells, the patterns have to be padded with "don't care" symbols, which is not discussed in the paper. The major advantage seems to be that the pattern need not be preloaded and no preprocessing is necessary, but only 50 percent of the hardware is in processing mode at any given time. One result bit is available every other clock period. Using nmos technology, the authors claim a speed of 250 nsec. per character.

Some of the above difficulties have been removed in a recent proposal by Foster and Kung (31). The scheme is shown in Figure 4-12. It consists of a

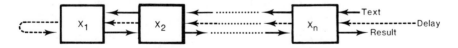

Figure 4-12. A proposed pattern matching device.

linear pipeline of cells, each of which can store a single pattern character as in the schemes proposed in the previous section. The cells are synchronized to operate on discrete beats. On each beat the text to be matched moves through the pipeline from right to left and the results of the match move from left to right. The information in both character and result streams are separated by one cell so that only half of all the cells are active on each beat. The active cell compares its stored pattern character with the text character received from its right-hand neighbor on the previous beat and then transmits the text character to its left-hand neighbor. The result bit is computed in each cell as the AND of the comparison result and the result bit it receives from its left-hand neighbor on the previous beat and transmits the result to its right-hand neighbor. The match bit of the pipeline is available on the beat after the last character is input.

Several improvements of the basic scheme are possible to make the cascade more flexible in pattern matching operations. A third input to the cascade, called the "delay" line has been suggested to carry the "anchor" information. This line carries a bit which goes through a delay element in each character cell and is sent to the left-hand neighbor of each cell on each beat. The delay line is connected back to the result input at the first cell. It is also possible to match for SLDC or MLDC by putting appropriate logic of the type discussed in the previous section and to match for multiple patterns by putting a number of cascades in two dimensional array.

Warter and Mules (32) have proposed an office automation system based on serial string searching hardware capability and a three level architecture. The first level of the hardware does the character search; the second level combines the results of the first level for substring detection including error analysis and terminal don't cares. The final level of hardware implements the logic for document match. Although no new algorithm for pattern matching is proposed, the idea of incorporating some degree of error tolerance (viz. missing or extra characters, a transposition of two characters and a simple substitution of one character for another) in the firmware and the idea of hierarchical search are novel and interesting.

A chip designed by Mead, et al., uses a straightforward algorithm, as shown in Figure 4-13. A 120-bit comparator compares the resident key loaded into a key register and the text input which is buffered into a data register. It allows the equivalent of multiple length don't care matching via the bits in a masking register and only unanchored mode operation. The match output is obtained at a common wired-NOR bus connected to an array of exclusive OR gates. The speed of the device is limited by this common wired connection which results in a large fan-in to the output NOR gate. This produces a large time delay for the comparison cycle which ultimately limits the maximum allowable data input rate. The authors report a speed in excess of 2Mhz using PMOS for the comparator and TTL for the input drivers.

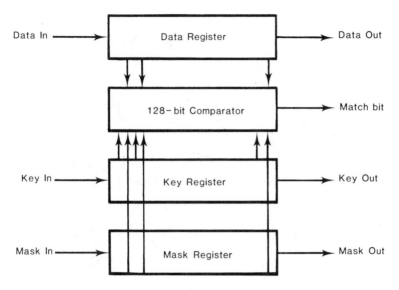

Figure 4-13. A pattern matcher by Mead, et al.

A pattern matching algorithm using a finite state automaton approach has been implemented for a text retrieval machine (33), (34), using conventional hardware viz. registers, RAM, adder, etc. The idea is based on obtaining a transition table corresponding to the given set of patterns. Bird developed an indexing scheme to encode the transition table compactly. The idea is illustrated with respect to the state diagram shown in Figure 4-14 for the set of patterns (ABC, ADE, AFG, AHI). The transitions leading to final states (6, 7, 8, 9) only are shown; all other transitions lead to the default state 0. The Bird index is shown in Table 4-4. The entries for the accepting states (6, 7, 8, 9) are all 0's. The base column entries are integers; all other entries are binary 0 or 1. A single state word is used to represent each state. State words that can be subsequently entered in one transition must be in adjacent memory words to the given state. The lowest numbered state in this group is indicated by a base address. A 1 bit is entered if the input character causes a transition to the state; otherwise, it is 0. The columns are organized alphabetically corresponding to the input alphabet Σ. The next state is computed by the following scheme: the base value of the state is added to an offset which equals one less than the number of 1's in the row for the state, beginning from the first column up to the column corresponding to the input character. If the entry in the row for this column is 0, then the machine returns to the default state. Thus, for example, if the machine in state 1 receives input F, then the base value 2 is added to offset 2 to get the next state 4. If the base value is 0, which is true for states 6, 7, 8, and 9, the state is an accepting state.

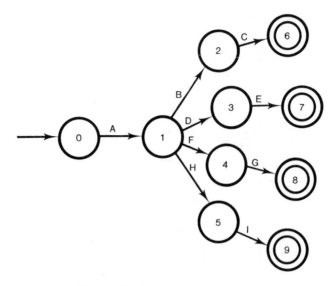

Figure 4-14. A deterministic state graph.

The Bird indexing, as explained above, works only if the directed graph of the FSA is a rooted tree. If this is not possible, another kind of state called "jump state" is added, which reads the input character but merely makes the desired transition using the base field. Obviously, one can represent any directed graph with enough jump states! Finally, if the input has a "don't care" symbol, the machine enters a special "retry" state without accepting a symbol but allowing the same symbol used in the last state to be used again.

The major advantage of the method is that it uses far less memory than a conventional FSA state table, but it may still be massive for practical size and large number of states. The method works only in anchored mode. By careful FSA design or pipelining of searches it is conceivable to operate in unanchored mode. Since the transition table is used by only one processor, default transitions for a mismatch and the restart of the machine is time consuming. Sequential states (those which are in a chain of transitions) and index states (those

Table 4-4. Bird Indexing.

STATE	BASE	A	B	C	D	E	F	G	H	I
0	1	1	0	0	0	0	0	0	0	0
1	2	0	1	0	1	0	1	0	1	0
2	6	0	0	1	0	0	0	0	0	0
3	7	0	0	0	0	1	0	0	0	0
4	8	0	0	0	0	0	0	1	0	0
5	9	0	0	0	0	0	0	0	0	1

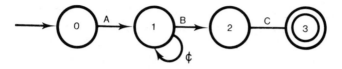

Figure 4-15. A nondeterministic state graph.

which need different base) require different amounts of processing time and cause a synchronization problem between the FSA and the disk (the text source). The method does not handle substring or MLDC; a separate FSA specially designed to handle initial and embedded MLDC was employed. The speed is limited by the fact that several steps are involved in making use of the RAM (viz. address computation, decoding, and fetch operations). Additional delays are introduced due to the addition cycle introduced in the indexing process. Quoted figures for state changes run up to 500 nsec. The construction of the FSA and the reduction of the state table suitable for Bird indexing involves nontrivial overhead in determining the overall speed of the method.

Haskin (35) improved the FSA approach by suggesting that a nondeterministic FSA state graph should be used in order to accommodate the embedded MLDC matching and that the state graph should be decomposed into smaller state graphs which are then assigned to smaller physical machines. Figure 4-15 shows a nondeterministic state graph for the pattern A¢BC. The transition from state 1 will return to itself for any character except B. If B is received, the machine will be in State 1 and 2 at the same time. Since the machine cannot be in two different states at the same time, they are recognized to be incompatible and put in different FSA. A few other criteria are also used to identify incompatibility of states: viz. if there is more than one pattern, the start states are incompatible; if two terms have a set of common characters at the beginning (viz. ABE, ABF), they could share the same start state but the transition for the last common character (viz. character B) leads to two incompatible states, etc.

The overall structure of the hardware is shown in Figure 4-16 which consists of a controller which broadcasts the text character to several character matchers (CM), one for each state simultaneously occupied by the machine. The set

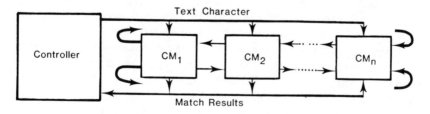

Figure 4-16. A pattern matcher based on nfsa.

of compatible states resides in one CM. A CM can be started either by a special character marking the beginning of a pattern or by being forked by a neighboring CM. Each CM contains three tables stored in RAM: a start-up table for activation of CM, the transition table within the cluster of compatible states, and a forking table which indicates at what point a forking is to take place. Each CM also has seven registers, a multiplexor, and the logic necessary to load/unload, etc. The output of each CM is sent to the controller whenever a match occurs in one of the CM's. The controller broadcasts input characters to all the CM's.

Since the character matchers are memory intensive, they should be suitable for VLSI implementation, but there is also a considerable amount of random logic in each module that offsets the memory advantage. The scheme does seem to have a large overhead since the list of patterns to be searched must be processed to produce the nondeterministic FSA and then decomposed into smaller FSA's and then loaded into the individual CM's. Each CM needs connection to a broadcast channel both for character input and for reporting match results, which increases the power requirements of the system and decreases its speed. The speed advantage over the FSA approach has yet to be established, and in terms of memory requirement the author claims about 50 percent savings over the FSA method involving about twenty-three patterns.

The idea of nondeterministic FSA's is an old concept (36). The scheme proposed by the author (10) to recognize regular expression patterns, as illustrated in Figure 4-6, is a direct implementation of a nondeterministic FSA state graph. Recently, Floyd and Ullman (37) reinvented the author's algorithm and proposed a method of implementing a nondeterministic FSA directly on a programmable logic array (PLA). A PLA consists of an AND plane which forms the product terms and an OR plane which forms sums of subsets of these terms. Unlike the conventional method of encoding n states by $[\log_2 n]$ lines, each state in the NFSA is represented by one line emanating from the OR plane. If a symbol $\lambda \epsilon \Sigma$ takes a state S_i to S_j, the output S_i from the OR plane is fed back to the AND plane to form a term λS_i for S_j. The AND plane also has lines coming directly from the primary inputs and some of the outputs from the OR plane representing final or terminal states are not fed back to the AND plane. Foster and Kung (30) improved this construction by a "chain reduction" technique which has a striking similarity with the concept of Bird indexing for encoding the transition table. Nondeterministic FSA machines for pattern matching contain long chains of states where each state has only a single output transition. If the columns in the OR plane can be ordered so that adjacent columns correspond to adjacent states in the chain, then the feedback from a state can be routed between adjacent columns, rather than between the AND and OR planes. The columns in the AND plane that correspond to these states can then be removed with some additional logic at the output of the OR plane.

Regardless of how many columns are removed, this adds a constant width to the PLA.

ACKNOWLEDGEMENT

This work has been supported by National Science Foundation Grant MCS-8005096.

REFERENCES

(1) Moore, G. "VLSI: Some fundamental challenges" in *The Coming Revolution in Applications and Design,* Rex Rice (Ed.). IEEE Computer Society Tutorial, Catalog No. EHO158-6, 1980: 107. Reprinted from *IEEE Spectrum,* April 1979.
(2) Hennie, F. C. *Iterative Arrays of Logical Circuits.* Cambridge: MIT Press, 1961.
(3) Minnick, R. C. "A Survey of Microcellular Research." *Journal of Assoc. Comp. Mach.* **14** (1967).
(4) Mukhopadhyay, A., and Stone, H. S. "Cellular Logic" in *Recent Developments in Switching Theory.* A Mukhopadhyay (ed.). New York: Academic, 1971.
(5) Kautz, W. H. "Programmable Cellular Logic," in *Recent Developments in Switching Theory,* A Mukhopadhyay (ed.). New York: Academic Press, 1971.
(6) Batcher, K. E. "Sorting Networks and Their Applications." *AFIPS Conf. Proceedings* **32**:307 (1968).
(7) Knuth, D. E. *The Art of Computer Programming, Vol. 3, Searching and Sorting.* Reading, MA: Addison-Wesley, 1973.
(8) Lee, C. Y., and Paull, M. C. "A Content Addressable Distributed Logic Memory with Applications to Information Retrieval." *Proc. IEEE* (June 1963) 924.
(9) Gaines, R. S., and Lee, C. Y. "An Improved Cell Memory." *IEEE Trans Electron, Compt.* **C-14**:72 (Jan. 1965).
(10) Mukhopadhyay, A. "Hardware Algorithms for Nonnumeric Computation." *Proc. 5th Annual Symposium on Computer Architecture.* Palo Alto, California (April 3–5, 1978) (Also, *IEEE Trans. on Computers* **C-28**(6):384–394 (June 1979).
(11) Kung, H. T. "The Structure of Parallel Algorithms," in *Advances in Computers,* Vol. 19, M. C. Yovits (ed.). New York: Academic Press, 1980.
(12) Kung, H. T., and Leiserson. "Systolic Arrays for VLSI," in *Sparse Matrix Proceedings,* T. S. Duff and C. W. Stewart (eds.). Society for Industrial and Applied Mathematics, 1979.
(13) Knuth, D. E., Morris, J. H., and Pratt, V. R. "Fast Pattern Matching in Strings." *SIAM J. Comput.* **6** No. 2 323–350 (June 1977).
(14) Boyer, R. S., and Moore, J. S. "A Fast String Searching Algorithm." *Commun. Assoc. Comput. Mach.* **20** No. 10: 762 (1977).
(15) Rivest, R. L. "On the Worst-case Behavior of String-search Algorithms." *SIAM J. Comput.* 669 (Dec. 1977).
(16) Horspool, R. N. "Practical Fast Searching in Strings." *Software—Practice and Experience* **10**:501–506 (1980).
(17) Aho, A. V., and Corasick, M. J. "Efficient String Matching Algorithm: An Aid to Bibliographic Search." *Comm. ACM* **18** No. 6:333–340 (1975).
(18) Hollaar, L. A., and Roberts, D. C. "Current Research into Specialized Processors for Text Information Retrieval," in *Proc. 4th Int. Conf. on Very Large Data Bases.* West Berlin, Germany (Sept. 13–15, 1978).

(19) Fischer, M. J., and Paterson, M. S. "String Matching and Outer Products. Massachusetts Institute of Technology, Project MAC, Technical Report 41, January 1974.

(20) Mukhopadhyay, A. "Hardware Algorithms for String Processing." *Proc. IEEE International Conference on Circuits and Computers.* New York (Oct. 1–3, 1980) 508.

(21) Gimpel, J. F. *Algorithms in SNOBOL4.* New York: Wiley-Interscience, 1976.

(22) Copeland, G. P. "A Cellular System for Non-numeric Processing." Ph.D. Dissertation, Department of Electrical Engineering, University of Florida, 1974.

(23) Smith, S. H. "A String Processing Machine." M. S. Design Project Department, Department of Computer Science, University of Central Florida, March 1981.

(24) Copi, I. R., Elgot, C. C., and Wright, J. B. "Realization of Events by Logical Nets," in *Sequential Machines,* E. F. Moore (ed.). Reading, MA: Addison-Wesley, 1964, p. 175.

(25) Kleene, S. C. "Realization of Events in Nerve Nets and Finite Automata," in *Automata Studies,* C. E. Shannon and J. McCarthy (eds.). Princeton, New Jersey: Princeton University Press, 1956.

(26) Mukhopadhyay, A. "A Backend Machine for Information Retrieval." *Proc. Conf. on Research and Development in Information Retrieval.* Cambridge, England (June 22–26, 1980).

(27) Curry, T. "TERQUL: A Text Retrieval Query Language System." M. S. Research Paper, Department of Computer Science, University of Central Florida, May 1981.

(28) Smith, G., and Oltman, D. "A Pattern Matching Device in VLSI." VLSI Class Project, Department of Computer Sciences, University of Central Florida, 1981.

(29) Mead, C. A., Pashley, R. D., Britton, L. D., Daimon, Y. T., and Sando, S. F. "128-bit Multicomparator." *IEEE J. Solid State Circuits* SC-11 No. 5:692–695 (Oct. 1976).

(30) Foster, M. J., and Kung, H. T. "The Design of Special-purpose VLSI Chips." *Computer Magazine* 13 No. 1:26–40 (Jan. 1980).

(31) Foster, M. J., and Kung, H. T. "PRA: Programmable Building Blocks for Recognizing Regular Languages in VLSI." Private communication, 1981.

(32) Warter, P. J. and Mules, D. W. "A Proposal for an Electronic File Cabinet." *MICRODELCON,* IEEE Computer Society, Long Beach, CA. (March 1979) pp. 56–63.

(33) Bird, R. M., Tu, J. C., and Worthy, R. M. "Associative/Parallel Processors for Searching Very Large Textual Data Bases." Presented at the 3rd Workshop on Computer Architecture and Nonnumeric Processing, Syracuse University, Syracuse, New York (May 17–18, 1977).

(34) Roberts, D. C. (Ed.) "A Computer System for Text Retrieval: Design Concept Development." Office of Research and Development, Central Intelligence Agency, Washington, D.C., Report RD-77-10011, 1977.

(35) Haskin, L. R. "Hardware for Searching Very Large Text Data Bases." Department of Computer Science, University of Illinois at Urbana-Champaign, Technical Report UIUCDCS-R-80-1027, (August 1980).

(36) McNaughton, R., and Yamada, H. "Regular Expressions and State Graphs for Automata." *IEEE Trans. on Computers,* 9 No. 1:39–47 (March 1960).

(37) Floyd, R. W., and Ullman, J. D. "The Compilation of Regular Expressions into Integrated Circuits." *Proc. 21st Annual Symposium on Foundations of Computer Science,* IEEE Computer Society (Oct. 1980).

5. VLSI Chip Architecture for Large Computers

John E. Price
Amdahl Corporation

INTRODUCTION

"The history of the computer industry . . . is almost solely one of technology push"(1).

The above quotation is especially true with respect to the development of integrated circuits, to the point where one of the key problems facing computer designers is how to most effectively use state-of-the-art integrated circuit technology.

Chip architecture may be defined from both an essential and an existential point of view. It consists of the integrated circuit design and layout plus application-oriented features such as mask programmable versus software programmable or fused-link programmable logic function.

This chapter first delineates the evolution of integrated circuit technology and chip architectures from the early 60s to the early 80s. Next, the potential advantages to be gained through the use of large-scale integration are described, relative to circuit design goals for large computers. Circuit and process options are considered and the choice of the optimal chip architecture and the optimal level of integration (the number of gates on a chip) is discussed in detail. The chapter ends with a look at future directions for chip architecture as the technology evolves into the realm of VLSI.

At this point, it is appropriate to define some of the terms used throughout this chapter. Table 5-1 defines the density of small-scale integration (SSI), medium-scale integration (MSI) and large-scale integration (LSI) for both logic and memory, in terms of gates per chip and bits per chip, respectively.

Table 5-1. Chip Density Definitions.

	LOGIC	MEMORY
SSI	<10 Gates	<100 Bits
MSI	10–100 Gates	100–1000 Bits
LSI	>100 Gates	>1000 Bits

Very large-scale integration (VLSI) appears to be controversial and complex in its definition, but may be summarized as:

- Greater than 1K gates per chip.
- Greater than 10K bits of static RAM.
- Greater than 40K bits of dynamic RAM.
- Less than 2μm minimum feature size.

Table 5-2 defines the performance of medium speed, high speed, and very high speed integrated circuits for logic and memory. For logic chips, the performance figure of merit is the signal propagation delay through a gate from input to output, ranging from greater than 10ns for medium speed to less than 1ns for very high speed gates.

For memory chips, the performance figure of merit is the read access time (the delay from a valid address at the input to valid data at the output). This ranges from greater than 100ns for medium speed to less than 10ns for very high speed memory.

HISTORICAL PERSPECTIVE

In this section, we look at the evolution of integrated circuits from the early 60s to the early 80s. The early 60s saw the successful introduction of small-scale integration (SSI), consisting of simple gates and latches (2). More complex functions were also implemented at that time in hybrid technology until supplanted by the appearance of medium-scale integration (MSI) in the mid-60s, consisting of integrated circuits such as counters (3), arithmetic units, reg-

Table 5-2. Chip Performance Definitions.

	LOGIC	MEMORY
Medium speed	>10 nS	>100 nS
High speed	1–10 nS	10–100 nS
Very high speed	<1 nS	<10 nS

ister arrays, etc. MSI functions were generally implemented with gate logic and laid out on the chip in a random, as opposed to cellular, structure.

During this period, the question of custom versus standard integrated circuits was revived. Earlier attempts to develop custom mask programmable and electrically programmable read-only memories (PROM's) (4) had failed because the technology was not ready. However, by the mid to late 60s, bipolar mask programmable ROM's (up to 128 bits) were introduced in order to provide the low volume user with low cost MSI. Design flexibility at low cost was also provided by means of the master-slice concept (5), in which a standard array of gates was given a custom logic function by personalizing the metal interconnections between gates.

By the end of the 60s the technology was capable of a level of integration (greater than 100 gates on a chip), at which very few standardized logic functions could be defined. Gate arrays had fallen into disfavor (due to the lack of adequate design aids for metal routing and testing), limiting custom LSI to high volume applications. High LSI design costs discriminated against the low volume user who was forced to use bipolar MSI for most of the logic design implementation. Another factor limiting more widespread use of LSI was the need to partition the logic so as to minimize the number of input and output pins per LSI chip (or maximize the gate to pin ratio) in order that standard low cost packages could be used.

However, in the early 70s, coincident select techniques and other circuit innovations (6) made possible the realization of large (1K bits and up) high speed bipolar ROM's which were rapidly put to use in a number of diverse application, including code conversion, table lookup, arithmetic logic and control logic, (especially in central processors where ROM's were required to match the logic speeds used in the processor).

This period also saw the introduction of the microprocessor, ushering in the era of low-cost computing. The full capability of LSI could now be utilized by means of software programmable functions. Medium speed applications were served by single chip MOS processors and high speed applications by bipolar bit-slice microprogrammable processor building blocks (7).

For very high speed applications, the gate array was revived. A pioneer in this approach was Amdahl Corporation, which used subnanosecond 100-gate array chips in the central processing unit (CPU) of the 470 V-Series computer systems (8).

In the latter part of the 70s, programmable logic arrays (PLA's) were introduced and used in a variety of applications. PLA and ROM performance ranged from medium to high speed, but for very high speed LSI usage was and is limited largely to gate arrays.

Recent users of very high speed gate arrays have included Control Data Corporation, 168 gates per chip (9), Hitachi Ltd, 550 gates per chip (10), IBM,

Table 5-3. Chronology of Chip Architectures from 1960 to 1980.

Very high speed			Random gate logic	Gate array Bit slice
High speed		Random gate logic	ROM Bit slice	Micro-processor PLA
Medium speed	Random gate logic	Gate array ROM	Micro-processor	

1960   1965   1970   1975   1980

←——SSI————————MSI————————LSI————————————→

1500 gates per chip (11), and Cray Research Inc., who, bucking the trend to LSI, designed a 16-gate MSI array to satisfy their system requirements (12).

Table 5-3 summarizes the evolution of chip architecture development from 1960 to 1980.

BENEFITS OF LSI

The potential benefits to be gained through the use of LSI are shown in Table 5-4. They are listed here in order of importance for large computers.

High reliability is brought about primarily by the reduction in the number of interconnections between chips. Placing more gates, and hence more interconnections, on the chip results in an inherently more reliable system due to the longer mean time to failure of on-chip interconnections compared to chip-to-chip interconnections. Additionally, mean time to repair can be minimized by use of LSI, since the fewer the number of chips in the system, the easier and faster it is to isolate a failing component and replace it.

High speed is likewise realized by the ability to put more interconnections on the chip. The capacitance of on-chip interconnections is significantly lower

Table 5-4. Potential Benefits of LSI.

- High reliability
- High speed
- Small size
- Low parts count
- Low cost

than that of off-chip interconnections, so that for a given switching current, on-chip interconnections can be switched between signal levels more rapidly than can off-chip interconnections.

Small size and low parts count are further benefits of using LSI. Together they help reduce the total number and length of interconnections between chips, with concomitant improvements in reliability and speed.

Low cost is perhaps the most notable benefit of LSI. However, in large computers the cost of LSI (not including main memory) is a small fraction of total system cost, and therefore it is of lesser importance than the previously described benefits.

CIRCUIT DESIGN GOALS

Circuit design goals for large computers are listed in Table 5-5. Maximizing speed refers to the effective speed of the circuits in the system environment. Unfortunately, raw gate delay can be a misleading figure of merit when used to assess the system performance of alternative approaches. For example, raw gate delay does not factor in the functional versatility of the gate structure, such as NOR versus AND-OR-INVERT. To be meaningful, delay should be compared between different approaches for a number of logic functions, to include latches, selectors, distributors, in addition to the more basic functions such as NOR, NAND and XOR. Additionally, drive capability (both on-chip and off-chip) of the alternative approaches must be considered. On-chip drive capability becomes a matter of increasing importance as the level of integration goes up, since the average on-chip interconnection length (and hence capacitance) will also increase as the gate density increases. Conversely, off-chip drive capability decreases in importance as the gate density increases, since more gates per chip means less (and shorter) interconnections between chips, and hence, a reduced effect of inter-chip delays on system performance.

Maximizing pins per chip facilitates partitioning the system into LSI. Additionally, case histories (13) show that large, high performance systems require more pins than lower performance systems because of the wider data path in high performance systems. Many partitioning techniques to reduce the number of pins per chip (or increase the gate to pin ratio figure of merit) have been

Table 5-5. Circuit Design Goals for
Large Computers.

- Maximize speed
- Maximize chip I/O
- Minimize power
- Minimize design time

proposed. One example claims that functional partitioning of both control and data path structures increases the gate to pin ratio by almost an order of magnitude (14).

Minimizing power is important for a number of reasons. First, it reduces the size and cost of the power supplies. Second, it reduces the cooling requirements which helps improve both reliability and cost. Third, reducing on-chip current to reduce power also improves reliability.

Minimizing design time is important to the system designer, both for the original design and also for engineering changes. Implicit in this goal are the attributes of accurate performance estimation during the design phase, zero integrated circuit design errors, and rapid turnaround time from logic design to packaged and tested chip.

CHOICE OF PROCESS TECHNOLOGY

MOS integrated circuit technology is currently superior to bipolar in terms of higher gate density (except for I^2L), lower power per gate, and higher chip yield (hence lower production cost). However, these attributes are outweighed by the higher speed of bipolar integrated circuits (15). Despite continued improvement in MOS performance, bipolar is still superior in terms of raw gate delay and output rise and fall times, both on and off-chip. The inferior drive capability of MOS results in performance which degrades far more rapidly than bipolar as the output load capacitance increases (due to higher fan-out or longer interconnect length between circuits).

This high sensitivity of MOS performance to load capacitance makes it difficult to accurately estimate path delays. Also, design changes to fan-out or interconnect length will likewise affect MOS path delays far more than bipolar.

System performance is influenced by both on-chip signal delay and signal delay between chips. Even though the higher gate density of MOS leads to fewer chips, and hence fewer chip crossings (paths between chips) in the system, the superior performance of bipolar tends to result in a total system path delay which is greater for MOS than for bipolar. This is illustrated in Figure 5-1 for the hypothetical case of on-chip gate delays of 0.5ns for bipolar and 2ns for MOS, and chip crossing delays of 2ns for bipolar and 4ns for MOS. In a large computer, the number of gate levels in a critical path will generally exceed eight, at which point it can be seen that even with three chip crossings in the critical path, the total path delay for bipolar is far less than for MOS.

CHOICE OF CIRCUIT TECHNOLOGY

The fastest bipolar circuits consist of non-saturating logic types such as emitter-coupled logic (ECL), current-mode logic (CML) and non-threshold logic (NTL). Circuit schematics of these three examples are shown in Figure 5-2.

Subnanosecond circuit delays are readily achieved with these logic forms, and they also have fairly similar gate densities.

NTL has the highest speed, with OR-AND functions, but requires extra circuitry for signal level restoration and inversion. It is best used as an adjunct to CML or ECL in situations where its superior performance can be readily utilized.

CML has the lowest power, with both OR and NOR functions, but has limited output drive compared to ECL. To avoid speed-killing saturation effects, the signal swing in CML is limited to less than half a volt. This reduces signal noise margin, making CML more difficult to design with, and requiring signal translation at the chip inputs and outputs.

ECL has high speed at medium power, with both OR and NOR functions, but more complex logic functions can be achieved with little increase in circuit complexity, delay or power, by means of series (or cascode) gating, collector-dotting, and emitter-dotting techniques (16). It is found that cascode ECL is superior to standard ECL in terms of delay and power for all but the simplest OR/NOR functions. To illustrate the functional power of cascode ECL, Figure 5-3 shows circuit schematics of a two-input exclusive-OR function implemented in both standard and cascode ECL. This vividly illustrates the advantages of cascode ECL in reducing the number of transistors and resistors, in operating with less current, and in reducing the number of delay elements in the data path.

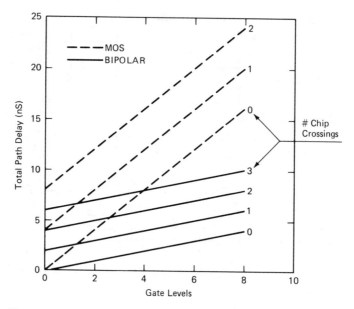

Figure 5-1. Path delay versus gate levels for MOS and bipolar technologies.

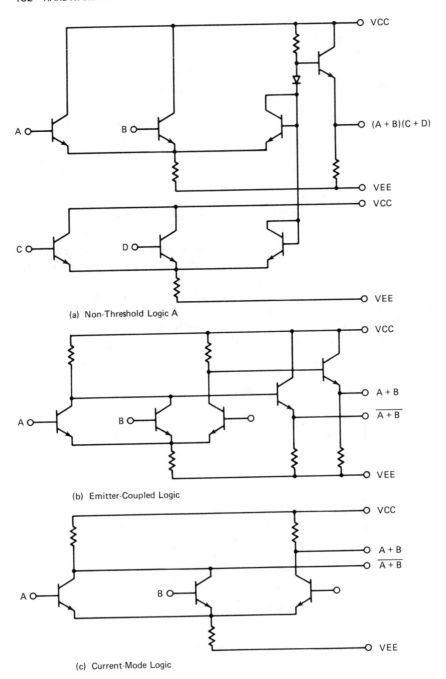

(a) Non-Threshold Logic A

(b) Emitter-Coupled Logic

(c) Current-Mode Logic

Figure 5-2. Non-Saturating logic types.

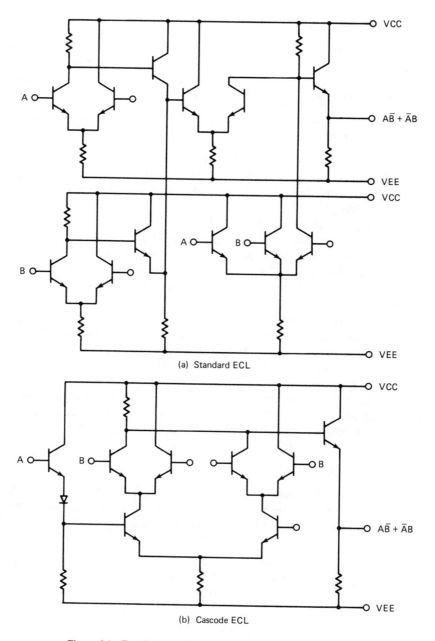

(a) Standard ECL

(b) Cascode ECL

Figure 5-3. Two-Input exclusive-Or in standard and cascode ECL.

CHOICE OF CHIP ARCHITECTURE

In this section, a number of different chip architectures are described in terms of those features which affect their suitability for use in large computers. The chip architectures are then compared against each other and an optimum chip architecture for large computers is selected.

Random Gate Logic

Some salient features of random gate logic are listed in Table 5-6. Since the chip is primarily designed for low production cost, this results in a long design and development phase in order to make the chip as small as possible and as high-yielding as possible.

When required, the chip can be designed to operate at very high speed by tailoring the design and layout of the internal circuit structures to optimize their output drive characteristics. However, use of multiple device sizes and circuit structures introduces more risk into the development process due to increased probability of error in design and increased difficulty in accurate prediction of performance.

Chip layout is often implemented manually in order to realize the smallest possible chip size, and because tailoring of the internal circuit structures is not conducive to automatic layout. This increases the probability of introducing errors into the design and hence lengthens the overall development cycle.

All of the mask levels required to fabricate the chip are designed specifically for the required chip function. Any change to the function (however minor) will usually require a completely new chip design with new layout and a new set of masks. In other words, redesign is both slow and expensive.

Microprocessor and Bit-Slice

Key features of microprocessor and bit-slice chip architecture are listed in Table 5-7. Like random gate logic, the chips are primarily designed for low production cost, resulting in a long design and development cycle.

Table 5-6. Random Gate Logic
Features.

- Low production cost
- Long design phase
- Very high speed
- Manual layout
- All mask levels unique to a specific design
- Fixed logic function

Table 5-7. Microprocessor and Bit-
Slice Features.

- Low production cost
- Long design phase
- High speed
- Manual layout
- All mask levels unique to a specific design
- Logic function defined by stored program

The chips are not normally designed to optimize performance (due to conflicts with the goal of low production cost), but ECL bit-slice chip architectures have been designed which operate in the high speed range (17, 18). It is also interesting to note that very high speed bit-slice chips are being implemented with gate array chip architectures (19) to allow design of custom additions to the bit-slice family with 12-week turnaround time.

Chip layout is usually done manually to minimize chip size and hence cost, but at the expense of a longer development cycle due to the higher probability of design iterations being required to correct layout errors.

All mask levels are unique to the specific chip design. However, the function performed by the chip is determined by a stored program resident in RAM and/or ROM chips. So-called one-chip microcomputers incorporate both RAM and ROM on the microprocessor chip itself, so that the chip function can be defined by a single mask change or by electrical programming of the ROM.

ROM and PLA

Table 5-8 lists some major attributes of ROM and PLA chip architectures. Although production cost may not be minimized, the chips offer low development cost and a fast design cycle to the user (20, 21).

High speed performance is achievable with both ROM and PLA chips. Also,

Table 5-8. ROM and PLA Features.

- Low development cost
- Short design phase
- High speed
- Automatic layout
- One mask level unique to a specific design
- Logic function defined by custom bit pattern

because of their well-defined structure, accurate performance estimation can be made during the design phase, thus minimizing the chance of being "surprised" by the actual performance of the chips.

Layout is an automated process, going directly from a truth-table or logic equation description to the bit pattern required to implement the desired logic functions. Since only one mask level is required to personalize a specific bit pattern, a very fast design cycle is readily achievable. Alternatively, with electrically programmable chips no unique masks are required to personalize the bit pattern. This results in the fastest possible turnaround time from the definition of the logic function to its realization in silicon.

Master-Slice Gate Array

Features of the master-slice gate array are listed in Table 5-9. Like the ROM and PLA chips, the gate array chip architecture is designed for low development cost and a fast design cycle to the user (22).

Very high speed is possible with ECL gate array design, and performance comes close to matching that of random gate logic. However, unlike random gate logic, the performance of gate arrays is readily and accurately estimated during the design phase, since the circuit structures available for design come from a well-defined set of functional elements.

Layout consists of defining the interconnection paths between gates on the chip, and can be accomplished either manually or by means of automatic wiring algorithms. However, if a large number of part-types are required by the user, then design automation becomes mandatory in order to keep the overall design time within reasonable bounds. Design automation is also attractive in that the same design data base used for gate interconnection can also be used for logic simulation, speed analysis, and test pattern generation.

The logic function of the gate array chip is defined by one or more layers of metal interconnections, which are the final steps in the wafer fabrication process. Thus, design turnaround time can be made reasonably fast, running around 3 to 12 weeks from when the chip logic function is defined to delivery of tested, packaged gate arrays.

Table 5-9. Master-slice Gate Array Features.

- Low development cost
- Short design phase
- Very high speed
- Automatic layout
- Only interconnect mask levels are unique to a specific design
- Logic function defined by personalized gate interconnections

Table 5-10. Comparison of Chip Architectures Against Design Goals.

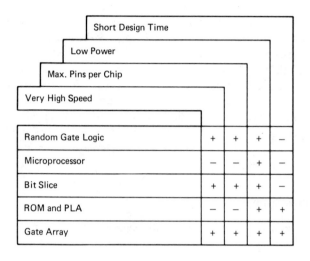

	Very High Speed	Max. Pins per Chip	Low Power	Short Design Time
Random Gate Logic	+	+	+	−
Microprocessor	−	−	+	−
Bit Slice	+	+	+	−
ROM and PLA	−	−	+	+
Gate Array	+	+	+	+

Comparison of Chip Architectures

In Table 5-10, the chip architectures just described are compared against the design goals of very high speed, maximum number of pins per chip, low power and short design time. The plus and minus signs signify either a match or a mismatch, respectively, between each chip architecture and each design goal.

Overall, the gate array chip architecture offers the best match to the circuit design goals for large computers. A variety of very high speed gate arrays have been developed to meet the design goals for large computers, and a sampling of gate array products is listed in Table 5-11.

Table 5-11. Gate Array Product Features.

MANUFACTURER	GATE DELAY (nS)	GATE POWER (mW)	GATES PER CHIP	I/O PINS
Motorola	0.8	4.4	800	60
I.B.M.	0.8	1.7	1500	94
Siemens	0.5	2.0	710	58
Hitachi	0.45	4.0	1500	108
Fairchild	0.4	4.0	2000	160

OPTIMUM LEVEL OF INTEGRATION

In the past, increasing levels of integration from SSI through MSI to LSI have been readily utilized in the design of large computers, resulting in systems with increasing levels of reliability and performance, with smaller size and at lower cost. As integrated circuit technology enters into the VLSI era, questions arise as to whether there may not be a limit to the heretofore unalloyed benefits of increasing levels of integration. For example, will system performance continue to increase with increasing density of gates per chip, or will constraints such as the ability to remove heat from the chip set an upper limit on the density of very high speed gates per chip? In this section, we examine the effect of gate density per chip on several key parameters which play an important role in the design of large computers.

Part-Type Requirements

The CPU of a large computer normally contains at least 100K gates. Partitioning this many gates into integrated circuit chips presents a number of problems.

First, the number of unique chips (or part types) required is a strong function of the level of integration (23, 24). This is illustrated in Figure 5-4 for the case of a hypothetical 200K gate CPU. At an integration level of only one gate per chip, say a two-input NOR gate, then in theory any size system could be implemented with multiple copies of this single part type. Conversely, at a level of integration equal to the size of the system (200K gates in this example),

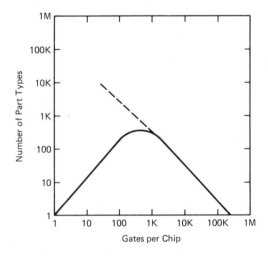

Figure 5-4. Unique chips versus gate density.

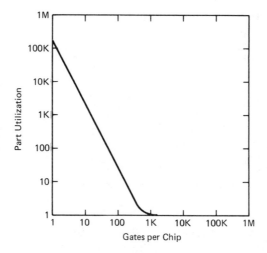

Figure 5-5. Part utilization versus gate density.

only one part type, used only once, is in theory sufficient to implement the whole system.

In between the two extremes of one gate per chip and 200K gates per chip, we see that the number of part types will, at first, increase with increasing levels of integration before peaking and then decreasing back down to a single part type. Attempts to minimize the number of part types required to implement the system, while at the same time utilizing LSI levels of gate density per chip, generally result in lower performance and/or a larger system requiring more than 200K gates.

The dashed line in Figure 5-4 shows how the maximum possible number of part types varies as a function of the gate density per chip. This is the case when each part type is used only once in the system. Typical part type utilization versus gates per chip is shown in Figure 5-5, again for the case of a 200K gate CPU. It can be seen that as gate density enters the VLSI realm, each part type is utilized only once per system. Therefore, the number of VLSI part types required is given by the number of gates per CPU divided by the number of gates per chip, e.g., for 200K gates per system and 2K gates per chip, a total of 100 part types are required. So in order to minimize design time and cost, a chip architecture must be chosen which is compatible with fast and low cost design of each part type. Although standard bit-slice architectures have been proposed for implementation of the CPU, this is not the best approach in terms of preserving uniqueness and a flexible approach to design. The master-slice gate array provides the best solution to the part number proliferation problem, either as an adjunct to the bit-slice family, or as used for total implementation of the CPU. An example of the latter approach is given

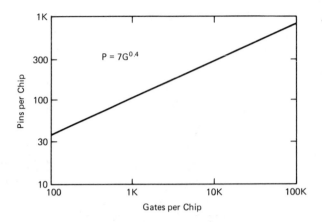

Figure 5-6. Pins versus gate density.

by the Amdahl 470 V/6 computer (25) where over 100 part types of a master-slice gate array are used to implement the 120K gate CPU.

Input/Output Pin Requirements

It appears to be intuitively obvious that increasing the number of gates per chip will, in general, require increasing the number of pins per chip. While many exceptions to this rule are found at MSI levels of gate density, nevertheless, when partitioning large systems into LSI or VLSI levels, the pressure to increase the number of pins becomes ineluctable.

However, it is found empirically that although pin requirements increase, they increase at a slower rate than the increase in gates per chip. The heuristic relationship between the number of pins and the number of gates per chip is known as Rent's rule, after E. F. Rent of IBM. Rent found that this relationship was a power law of the form $P = AG^B$, where P is the number of pins per chip, G is the number of gates per chip, and A and B are coefficients whose values depend not only on the level of integration, but also on performance requirements, e.g., if high performance is not a prime objective, then data transmission between chips can be serialized, resulting in a direct trade-off between performance and number of pins.

Figure 5-6 shows the power law relationship between pins and gates for $A = 7$ and $B = 0.4$. It is felt that this results in a realistic relationship between pins and gates at the LSI and VLSI levels, valid in terms of partitioning a large high performance system without being unduly pin-limited. Table 5-12 lists pin requirements according to this relationship, for gate densities ranging from 400 to 40,000 per chip. However, with todays packaging technology the number of pins per chip is limited to less than 200 (see Table 5-11).

Table 5-12. Pin Requirements Versus
Gates Per Chip.

Gates	400	1K	4K	10K	40K
Pins	77	111	193	279	485

Figure 5-7 shows the relationship between gates per chip and gate to pin ratio, for the same coefficients of Rent's rule as before. This shows the impact of increased gate density on increased reliability, not only due to fewer chips per system, but also because of the higher gate to pin ratio which serves to reduce the total pin count even more. The total pin count versus gate density, for a 200K gate system, is shown in Figure 5-8.

Interconnection Requirements

As the number of gates per chip increases, the number of interconnections between chips will decrease and the number of interconnections between gates within the chip will increase. Moreover, it is found that the total length of interconnections on a chip actually increases faster than the number of gates (26), resulting in the commonplace situation for LSI and VLSI of chips being metal-limited rather than device-limited, i.e., the size of the chip is determined by the space requirements for metal interconnections rather than the space requirements for devices. Hence, for a given chip technology, chip area will increase faster than the number of gates, adversely impacting yield and cost, to the point where production may be uneconomic (27).

It is also found that the average interconnection length will increase as the number of gates per chip increases. To facilitate comparison between technol-

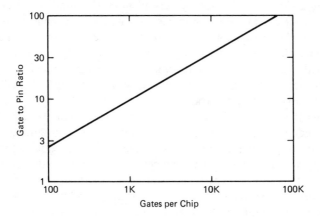

Figure 5-7. Gate to pin ratio versus gate density.

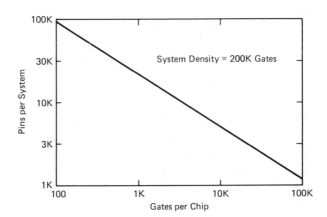

Figure 5-8. Pins per system versus gate density.

ogies, it is advantageous to define a normalized average interconnection length (L) which is simply the average interconnection length divided by the gate pitch or gate cluster (cell) pitch. Then, if P is the total number of ports in the chip requiring interconnection, there is a power law relationship between P and L given by $L = XP^Y$. Empirical data on gate arrays with numbers of ports ranging from under 300 to over 10,000 (28) indicates that the normalized average interconnection length varies as the square root of the number of ports. This is illustrated in Figure 5-9.

Prediction of average interconnection length and total interconnection length is important for a variety of reasons. First, resistive and capacitive effects are associated with interconnect length, and impact both the D.C. design and the high speed performance of the chip. Second, the ability to route the interconnections on a gate array is strongly dependent on the number of tracks available to allow the routing program to complete all the interconnections between gates. Various heuristic approaches have been developed for estimating track requirements. However, as a rule of thumb, track utilization should not exceed 50% of total available track length to guarantee a high probability of routability. Thus, knowledge of total interconnect length requirements makes it easier to design a routable gate array.

Reducing the number of ports to be interconnected will also enhance routability by reducing both the average length and the total number of interconnections. One way to reduce the number of ports without reducing the number of gates consists of grouping gates into cells which are connected internally in different ways to realize a set of SSI and MSI functions called macros (22). The gate array then becomes a macrocell array, and routability improves because of the reduction in the total number of ports which have to be interconnected. Another advantage of the macrocell array is that it allows the system designer to use standardized logic functions (macros) with well defined performance characteristics to implement the system design.

System Performance Requirements

In sections 5-4 and 5-5, the goal of optimizing system performance was discussed. It was pointed out that system performance is influenced by on-chip signal delay and off-chip signal delay. Both of these delays are functions of the level of integration.

Off-chip signal delay will decrease with increasing the level of integration, for the following reasons. First, with increased gate density the total number of chip crossings will decrease by virtue of the gate to pin relationship described earlier in this section. Second, the total number of chips in the system will decrease with increasing numbers of gates per chip, resulting in a shorter average interconnection length between chips. Therefore, off-chip signal delays will not only decrease in absolute magnitude, but will also decrease in terms of their relative contribution to overall system delay.

Conversely, on-chip signal delay will increase with increasing the level of integration. This comes about because of two factors. One is the increase in average interconnection length with increasing gate density, which results in increased load capacitance per output port and hence increased delay. The second factor is power dissipation. Considerations of reliability and cooling ability will set an upper limit on the chip power consumption. So, with a fixed amount of power per chip, the power per gate will decrease with increasing numbers of gates per chip, resulting in increased gate delay.

Since on-chip delay increases and off-chip delay decreases with increases in the level of integration, then the total system delay will be minimum for a

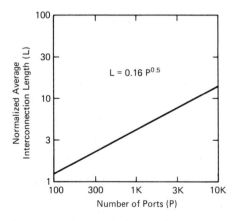

Figure 5-9. Normalized average interconnection length versus number of ports per chip.

certain level of integration. So to optimize system performance, careful consideration must be given to choosing the appropriate level of integration (29). Factors such as cooling capability, chip technology, package technology, and system architecture must all be included in the analysis of optimum level of integration. Such an analysis is obviously beyond the scope of this chapter.

FUTURE DIRECTIONS

Although gate arrays are currently the best chip architecture for large computers, this may not remain true at higher levels of integration. Routability problems will be exacerbated with more gates to interconnect, while reduction of total part numbers will lessen the need for low design cost. Possible evolutionary trends may include combinations of random gate logic, gate arrays, and PLA's, or even radically new chip architectures. Promising approaches include the PLA macro (21), and random "super-macro" logic, where investigations indicate that increasing macro gate density from 4 up to 36 results in a reduction of area per function and delay per function of 4 and 2 respectively.

If IC technology is to continue to push the computer industry, strategies must be found for the following design problems and goals:

- Better use of hierarchical design and structured design, to allow our minds to cope with the problems of large system design (30), and to facilitate a design approach which globally optimizes system performance and reliability.
- Better testing techniques, to allow rapid testing of the chips at the wafer, package, and board level, with 100% test coverage.
- Faster design and fabrication time, with a goal of 1 day turnaround time from the logic function definition of the chip to the delivery of the tested packaged part.
- Better approaches to packaging and heat dissipation, to allow from 200 to 300 pins per package and the ability to cool parts dissipating from 10 to 20 watts.

Solutions to these and other problems will permit the design of large high performance computers which fully exploit very large-scale integration, and drive up performance and reliability in an economically effective manner.

REFERENCES

(1) Bell, C. G., et al. *Computer Engineering*. Bedford, Mass.: Digital Press, 1978, Chapter 2.
(2) Kvamme, E. F., and Bieler, L. N. *Fairchild Semiconductor Integrated Circuits*. Mountain View, Calif.: Fairchild Semiconductor, 1966.
(3) Price, J. E., "An Integrated Decade Counter and Binary-Decimal Decoder." *1965 International Solid-State Circuits Conference, Digest of Technical Papers*, pp. 10–11.

(4) J. E. Price, U.S. Patent 3,191,151 (1965).

(5) Marvin, C. E. and Walker, R. M. "Customizing By Interconnection," *Electronics* 157–164 (Feb. 20, 1967).

(6) Barrett, J. C., et al. "Design Considerations For A High-Speed Bipolar Read-Only Memory." *IEEE Journal of Solid-State Circuits* SC-5 No. 5: 196–202 (Oct. 1970).

(7) Moore, G. E. "Microprocessors and Integrated Electronic Technology." *Proceedings of the IEEE* 64, No. 6: 837–841 (June, 1976).

(8) Beall, R. J. "Packaging for a Super Computer." *Proceedings IEEE INTERCON* 74 (1974).

(9) Vacca, A. A. "Considerations for High Performance LSI Applications." *COMPCON* (Spring 79): 278–284.

(10) Horikoshi, H. et al. "An Example of LSI-Oriented Logic Implementation in a Large-Scale Computer, The HITAC M-200H." *COMPCON* (Spring 80): 62–65.

(11) Blumberg, R. J. and Brenner, S. "A 1500 Gate, Random Logic, Large Scale Integrated (LSI) Masterslice." *IEEE Journal of Solid-State Circuits* SC-14 No. 5: 818–822 (Oct. 1979).

(12) Eberlein, D. D. "Custom MSI For Very High Speed Computers." *COMPCON* (Spring 79): 295–298.

(13) Russo, R. L. "On the Tradeoff Between Logic Performance and Circuit-to-Pin Ratio for LSI" *IEEE Transactions on Computers* C-21 No. 2: 147–153 (Feb. 1972).

(14) Levy, S. Y., et al. "System Utilization of Large-Scale Integration." *IEEE Transactions on Electronic Computers* EC-16 No. 5: 562–566 (Oct. 1967).

(15) Verhofstadt, P. W. J. "Evaluation of Technology Options for LSI Processing Elements." *Proceeding of the IEEE* 64 No. 6: 842–851 (June 1976).

(16) Gaskill, J. R., et al. "Modular Single-Stage Universal Logic Gate." *IEEE Journal of Solid-State Circuits,* SC-11 No. 4: 529–538 (Aug. 1976).

(17) Chu, P. "Byte-Wide Building Blocks for Microprogrammed Systems." *Fairchild Journal of Semiconductor Progress* 7 No. 4: 4–12 (July/Aug. 1979).

(18) "Scaling Down for the 80's." **Fairchild Journal of Semiconductor Progress 7** Nos. 5/6: 4–9 (Sept.–Dec. 1979).

(19) Cushman, R. H. "EDN's Seventh Annual MP/MC Chip Directory." EDN, (Nov. 5, 1980) p. 206.

(20) Patil, S. S. and Welch, T. A. "A Programmable Logic Approach for VLSI." *IEEE Transactions on Computers* C-28 No. 9: 594–601 (Sept. 1979).

(21) Golden, R. L. et al. "Design Automation and the Programmable Logic Array" *IBM Journal of Research and Development* 24 No. 1: 23–31 (Jan. 1980).

(22) Prioste, J. "Macrocell Approach Customizes Fast VLSI." *Electronic Design* 159–166 (June 7, 1980).

(23) Fubini, E. G., and Smith, M. G. "Limitations in Solid-State Technology." *IEEE Spectrum* 55–59 (May 1967).

(24) Fischer, J. L. "Programmable Components: The Shape of VLSI to Come." *Electronics* 138–142 (June 5, 1980).

(25) Wu, L. C. "VLSI and Mainframe Computers." *COMPCON* (Spring 78): 26–29.

(26) Heller, W. R. and Mikhail, W. F. "Prediction of Wiring Space Requirement for LSI." *Proceedings 14th Design Automation Workshop* (June 1977): 32–42.

(27) Keyes, R. W. "Fundamental Limits in Digital Information Processing." *Proceedings of the IEEE* 69 No. 2: 267–278 (Feb. 1981).

(28) Dansky, A. H. "Bipolar Circuit Design for VLSI Gate Arrays." *Proceedings: ICCC* (1980): 674–677.

(29) Price, J. E. "On Being the Right Size." *IEEE Design Automation Workshop* (Oct. 1981).

(30) Rowson, J. A. "A Modern Day Tower of Babel." *Lambda,* Second Quarter 4–5 (1980).

6. VLSI Masterslice Bipolar Design

Seiken Yano, Yasunori Ouchi,
Kodo Kimura, Kenji Okada.
Nippon Electric Co., Japan
Yasuo Ito
Nippon Telegraph and Telephone Public Corp., Japan

INTRODUCTION

There exists an increasing demand for new data processing systems which have higher performance, smaller system size, lower cost and higher reliability. High speed LSIs are indispensable to meet these requirements. However, they disclose many problems as their integration level is increased.

First, existing high speed circuits, such as an Emitter Coupled Logic (ECL), can meet performance objectives, but they dissipate a lot of power. When many ECL circuits are integrated in a chip, increased power dissipation necessitates the use of an expensive special cooling system. Therefore, high speed circuits with low power dissipation are desirable for LSIs. They, in turn, demand advanced bipolar processes to realize low power dissipation and high performance.

Second, as the circuits in a chip are increased by the advanced LSI technology, standard LSI products cannot satisfy the system designer's requirements in regard to their performance and functionality. Therefore, high speed system oriented LSIs are the solution to the requirement for high performance systems. These LSIs, however, require a large quantity of different types of parts and, in turn, high development cost. Moreover, the development time for these LSIs eventually occupies a large part of the system development time. Therefore, it is desirable to develop system oriented LSIs with short turn around time and a low development cost.

Many efforts have been made to achieve high performance system oriented

LSIs with a short turn around time and a low development cost. One of these approaches is the use of bipolar gate arrays or masterslices. However, existing gate arrays and masterslices have disadvantages in transistor utilization and power dissipation. To overcome these disadvantages, new masterslice LSIs have been developed which feature low energy CML (Current Mode Logic), Polysilicon Self-Aligned process, transistor array masterslice, computer aided design and application to large computers. In these LSIs, the transistor utilization efficiency and power dissipation are improved by the low energy CML with a series gated structure, collector dotting and emitter dotting.

CIRCUIT

Performance improvement for data processing systems mainly depends on advances in circuit delay time and chip integration level. Figure 6-1 shows the relation between circuit delay and chip integration level corresponding to the energy level per gate. The energy levels shown in the figure are achieved when maximum power dissipation in a chip is limited to 1 watt. For example, a small computer with 10,000 gates can be integrated in a chip, only when gates with

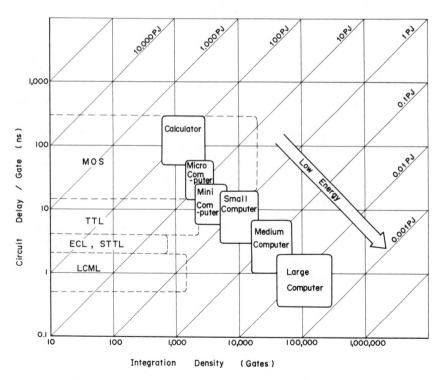

Figure 6-1. Relation between circuit delay and chip integration level.

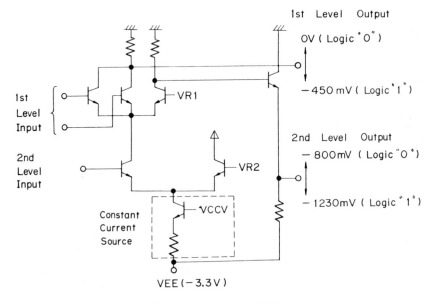

Figure 6-2. Low energy CML.

10 ns delay can be realized with 0.1 milliwatts operational power (i.e., 1 pJ). Allowable power dissipation per chip cannot be increased much more, because of cooling system limitations. Therefore, low energy circuits are required to realize very large scale integration. The low energy CML (LCML) circuit can satisfy this requirement (1-3).

The LCML circuit with 2 level series gated structure has cascade current switches between ground and a constant current source, as shown in Figure 6-2. The circuit provides two output types; the collector output and the emitter-follower output. The first voltage level, the collector output, has 450 mV logic swing from 0V (logic "0") to −450 mV (logic "1"). This small logic swing can be realized by the constant current source which minimizes the logic level variation due to the environmental change. The second voltage level, the emitter-follower output, is one diode drop of the 1st voltage level, and is restricted to internal use only. The upper and the lower current switches have the 1st and the 2nd voltage level inputs respectively.

Low Energy CML

The LCML circuit is free from transistor saturation, because of its small logic swing. The circuit power supply voltage can be reduced to −3.3 volts from the conventional −5.2 volts keeping all circuit transistors from saturation. The basic internal circuit dissipates 1 mW with a 0.9 nS delay, and the power-speed product (i.e. energy) is reduced to less than 1 pJ.

A constant current circuit, which is constructed by a transistor and a resistor, is provided for each internal and external LCML circuit to insure a sufficient noise margin for the LCML with a small logic swing. The constant current circuit is driven by a constant voltage source, VCCV, which is also integrated on chip. The circuit can minimize logic level variations due to power supply, temperature and process parameter variations.

The reference voltages, VR1 and VR2, are also generated on chip and are distributed to all circuits. A reference voltage VRI generator is constructed by a constant current source and two parallel collector resistors, and generates the middle voltage of high and low logic levels. A VRZ generator is a level shifter of reference voltage VRI. When the power supply voltage and/or temperature causes logic level change, the reference voltage CRI and VRZ are also changed to the same direction as logic level and provide a good symmetric noise immunity.

Series Gated Structure

The 2 level series gated structure has many advantages over single level current switch whose function is limited to an AND/NAND gate. By interconnecting transistors in different patterns, the circuit can be changed to many usable functions. These include exclusive OR gate, multiplexer, decoders and latches. Each circuit has one current source and, therefore, has single gate power dissipation. Propagation delay for a series gated circuit with typical fan outs and line length can be expected to be less than 2.5 nS.

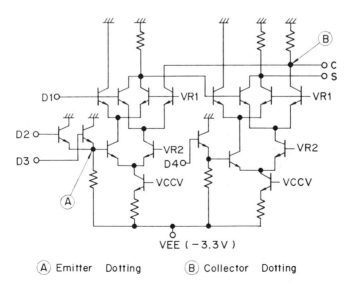

Figure 6-3. Low energy CML with series gated structure, collector dotting and emiter dotting.

By using more than one series gates, more complex functions can be easily realized, including master-slave Flip Flop (2 current sources), full adder (2 current sources) and register files. To obtain these functions with a smaller number of transistors, collector dotting and emitter dotting have been applied as well as a 2 level series gated structure. Collector dotting can be applied only when two or more collector-dotted circuits may not be switched on simultaneously. A full adder is one example of the application of these techniques (see Figure 6-3).

ADVANCED PROCESS TECHNOLOGY

It is generally understood that better LSIs require high packing density, high speed and low power. At present, the first and second requirements are mainly realized by scaling down components and interconnections. For example, in the conventional approach, fine patterns for this purpose are achieved by the electron beam exposure method. However, this method necessitates such sophisticated and expensive equipment that a new approach has been sought.

In addition, the requirement for low power demands low-power individual gates, which in turn demand high-value resistors. By the conventional method, these resistors are constructed in a single-crystalline substrate. As the degree of integration increases, they occupy a large part of the single crystalline silicon real estate. Since these resistors are electrically isolated by p-n junctions, they eventually show a large parasitic capacitance which results in an increased delay time.

Given this background, the bipolar LSI process should meet the following two conditions:

1. Small components and fine interconnections should be easily obtained without increasing process difficulty.
2. High-value resistors should be easily obtained without increasing their parasitic capacitance and chip area.

As a solution to these problems, several fabrication methods have been developed by introducing a polysilicon layer, based on conventional processes (4, 5). A new polysilicon process, called polysilicon self-aligned (PSA) process (6, 7) described in this section, features a unique application of polysilicon to a self-aligned process. This self-alignment process is realized by applying selective thermal oxidation technology for single crystalline silicon (8, 9) to a newly introduced polysilicon process. Small components and fine interconnections are easily obtained.

The polysilicon layer also provides decreased-parasitic-capacitance resistors (10, 11) which replace standard single crystalline silicon resistors. This feature in polysilicon resistors satisfies the requirement for high-value resistors for a low power individual gate without increasing the gate area and the parasitic capacitance. As a result, individual gate power dissipation is reduced without increasing delay time. In short, the PSA process has sucessfully achieved high packing density, high speed and low power.

PSA Method Concept and Fabrication Steps

The major difference between the PSA method and the conventional method lies in the processing sequence. In the conventional process, electrodes and interconnections are constructed with aluminum after the formation of all p-n junctions for transistors and resistors (Figure 6-4a). However, with the PSA method, they are constructed in a newly introduced polysilicon layer by selective thermal oxidation technology using Si_3N_4 as a mask before emitter-base junctions are formed (Figure 6-4b).

Figures 6-5a to e show cross-sectional views of these new fabrication steps. The starting material is a p-type substrate with $\sim250\Omega$/sq ion-implanted collector regions followed by diffusion or with n^+ buried layer on which a $2\mu m$, $0.2\Omega \cdot cm$ n-type epitaxial layer is deposited. After p^+ channel-stopper diffusion, the surface of this wafer is selectively oxidized to $\sim1\ \mu m$ thickness using the nitride oxide sandwich structure as a mask to oxidation, as shown in Figure 6-5a.

Then, as shown in Figure 6-5b, boron is ion implanted into the base region with an acceleration energy of 100 keV and a dose of $\sim2 \times 10^{14}\ cm^{-2}$ using photoresist as a mask.

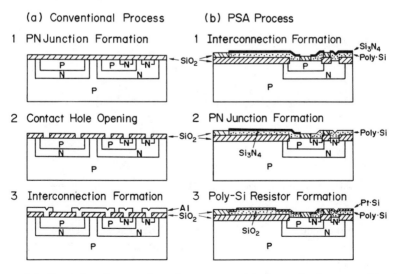

Figure 6-4. Comparison between formation processes. (a) Conventional process, (b) PSA process.

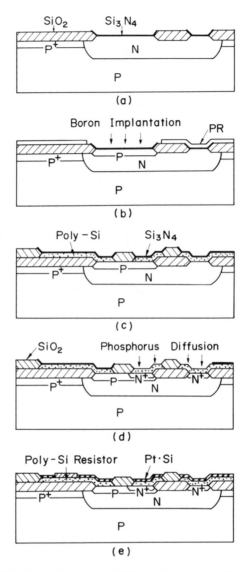

Figure 6-5. Fabrication steps for PSA transistor and polysilicon resistor.

After Si_3N_4 films are removed, the surface of the wafer is covered with non-doped CVD polysilicon to a thickness of $\sim 5000\text{Å}$. The selective thermal oxidation technology used for single crystalline silicon, as shown in Figure 6-5a, is also applied to this polysilicon layer, as shown in Figure 6-5c.

Then, as shown in Figure 6-5d, Si_3N_4 films used as a selective thermal oxidation mask for polysilicon are selectively removed, and phosphorous (n^+) is diffused through the polysilicon layer to get emitter-base junctions and n^+ collector contacts. As a result, an electrode built-in transistor with a walled emitter structure is formed. If a transistor with a low internal base resistance (R_{BB}) is required, boron (p^+) diffusion is newly added before the phosphorous (n^+) diffusion.

After the removal of the remaining Si_3N_4 films, boron (p^-) with 50 keV acceleration energy and $\sim 3.5 \times 10^{13}$ cm^{-2} dose is ion implanted into the polysilicon layer for polysilicon high-value resistor formation without using a mask, resulting in 15 kΩ/sq sheet resistivity. As shown in Figure 6-5e, the thin SiO_2 film formed in Figures 6-5c and d steps is etched off, except over the polysilicon resistors. Then the exposed polysilicon surface is alloyed with platinum into Pt-Si in a self-aligned fashion. This Pt-Si formation aims at the distinction of polysilicon resistors from polysilicon electrodes and/or interconnections and reduction in sheet resistivity for the latter elements.

Figure 6-5e shows the final schematic cross section of a typical PSA transistor and a polysilicon resistor. The emitter region is constructed by diffusion through the polysilicon electrode. The number of masking steps to obtain this PSA transistor and polysilicon resistor is the same as with the conventional process (i.e., six or seven steps). Because of the increased mask alignment ease, the PSA process is superior to the conventional process. Table 6-1 shows the PSA transistor parameters.

In the conventional process, some margin between contacts and interconnections is required. In the PSA process, however, contacts between single crystalline silicon and polysilicon electrodes are constructed in a "self-aligned fashion". Because of this, small elements can be easily obtained. This fact satisfies process condition (a) mentioned earlier.

High value polysilicon resistors, which cannot easily be used in the conventional process, are included in the PSA process. These polysilicon resistors do not occupy a single crystalline silicon area. Therefore, high-value resistors can be easily obtained without increasing their parasitic capacitance and chip area. This fact satisfies process condition (b).

A top layout view of the PSA transistor is shown in Figure 6-6. In this figure, dotted lines show the effective patterns of single crystalline silicon and polysilicon after selective thermal oxidation. Shaded areas show the effective area for emitter, base contact and collector contact. As a result, a very small transistor

Table 6-1. PSA Transistor Parameter.

Emitter junction capacitance	(C_e)	0.44 pF
Base junction capacitance	(C_b)	0.44 pF
Collector junction capacitance	(C_{cs})	0.16 pF
Cut-off frequency	(f_t)	$1 \sim 1.4$ GHz
Current gain	(h_{FE})	80

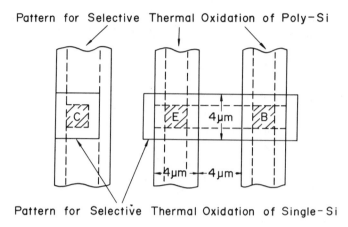

Pattern for Selective Thermal Oxidation of Poly-Si

Pattern for Selective Thermal Oxidation of Single-Si

	Effective Area
Emitter	2 x 2 μm
Base	2 x 12 μm

Figure 6-6. New transistor top layout view.

with 2 x 12 μm base regions can be easily obtained, even if conventional 4 μm design rule is applied. This is because the original photo mask pattern is uniformly shrunk by selective thermal oxidation treatment.

PSA Process Features

The following is a list of the important PSA process features.

1. In the PSA process, an electrode is directly contacted with a diffused area at the crossing point of the two masks for selective thermal oxidation of single crystalline silicon and polysilicon. As this contacting method is self-aligned and eliminates the contact-hole opening, it does not require fine patterns or accurate alignment for photomask process.
2. This process easily offers high-value polysilicon resistors which are required for the construction of low power gates. One of the most important features is that these polysilicon resistors are constructed at the same time as the interconnection formation. Unlike conventional resistors, they do not occupy any part of the single crystalline substrate. Consequently, these resistors contribute to high packing density.

3. Selective oxidation of the polysilicon layer proceeds not only downward into the layer, but also laterally. As a result, every polysilicon element, including the resistor, electrode and interconnection, becomes uniformly shrunk from the original photo-mask geometry. For example, 2 μm wide polysilicon resistors are achieved by applying conventional 4 μm photolithography.

4. No alloy spike damage appears, since emitter-base junctions are fabricated by diffusion through the polysilicon electrodes. This feature is applicable to base junctions.

MASTERSLICE

The significance of the masterslice approach has been widely recognized after gate arrays, which are one form of masterslice approaches, began to be extensively used in mainframe computers (12–16). This is because each mainframe model is manufactured in hundreds to thousands and the full custom design approach is not justifiable economically, though speed improvement would be substantial.

The masterslice approach allows high volume production during the diffusion stages with a single set of masks and the common diffusion set is customized by a variety of metal masks. This results in short turn around time and low development cost.

Layout time is also shortened by eliminating the need to design the diffusion layers for each category. Once layout is complete, it is possible to obtain sample quantities in a short time, compared to the time required for a custom design. This is mainly because wafers can be stockpiled in a completely diffused status, with first layer metal deposited. Low development cost results from shortened time and the small quantity of custom masks required.

One of these approaches uses ECL gate arrays, which have obvious advantages over full custom design circuits in regard to turn around time and development cost. However, ECL gate arrays require more current sources to realize a function than ECL custom design does, and result in high power consumption which requires a special cooling system.

The ECL masterslice approach, which utilizes the advantages of a series gated structure, has improved the efficiency of current source usage. However, existing ECL masterslices cannot take full advantage of a series gated structure because only a single voltage level is allowed for their signal transfer among functional blocks, which are the basic logical design unit of a chip and are roughly equivalent to small- or medium-scale ICs. The LSI power dissipation cannot be decreased much more, as long as a high voltage ECL is applied. Furthermore, existing ECL masterslices are constructed by cells with transistors and diffused resistors. This method has limitations in regard to transistor usage and function block layout.

Transistor Array Masterslice

New masterslice, which is constructed only by a transistor array substrate, has been developed to improve the disadvantages of existing ECL masterslices. Transistor array masterslice allows a more flexible block layout and higher resource utilization. This is because these transistors can be used as any active element in an LCML circuit and resistors can be fabricated anywhere on the polysilicon layer.

The LCML masterslice chip is 5 x 5mm in size and consists of 2 parts: an internal logic section and an external buffer section. The internal logic section

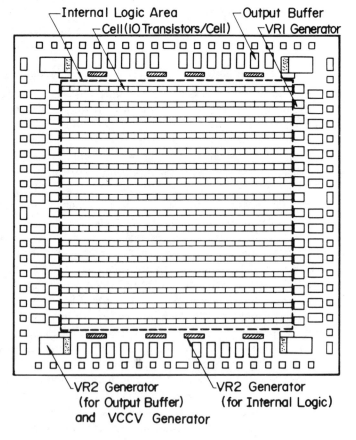

Figure 6-7. Transistor array masterslice chip.

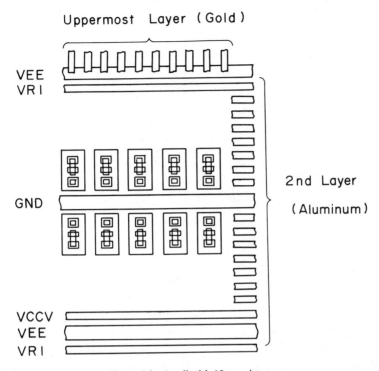

Figure 6-8. A cell with 10 transistors.

is 3.6 x 3.6 mm in size and has 384 cells arranged in a 16 by 24 matrix, as shown in Figure 6-7. Each cell contains 10 transistors of the same size, as shown in Figure 6-8. They can be used not only to construct current switches but also to construct constant current sources. This arrangement allows flexible function block layout.

Function blocks are realized by interconnecting transistors in one or more cells. For example, a full adder of 10 equivalent gates can be constructed by 17 transistors in two cells. This means that the internal logic section can contain 192 full adder blocks, which are equivalent to 1920 gates. Function block outputs are available at 1st voltage level (collector output) and optionally at 2nd voltage level (emitter-follower output). Input level shifters are also optional.

Signal transfer between function blocks is realized by using both 1st and 2nd voltage level to get the same performance and efficiency in resource utilization as with custom design circuits. For example, a 3-to-1 multiplexer, constructed with 10 transistors in one cell, has 3 data inputs at the 1st voltage level (D_0, D_1 and D_3) and 3 control inputs at the 2nd voltage level (S_0, S_1 and S_2), as shown in Figure 6-9. These second level signals are ordinarily generated as the

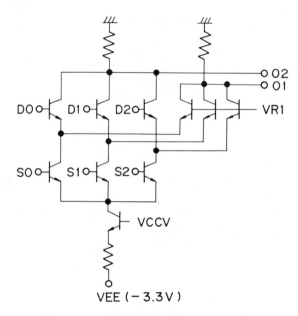

Figure 6-9. A 3-to-1 multiplexer without a decoder.

output of control logic and distributed to several similar multiplexers, depending on bit width. Therefore, compared to a conventional multiplexer with a decoder, a multiplexer without a decoder improves resource utilization efficiency and performance.

In the external buffer area, 56 output buffers, 48 reference voltage generators and 80 pads for film carrier bonding system are located. These pads include 4 pads for ground and 4 for −3.3 Volt power supply. The power distribution and pad location was carefully designed to reduce ground line voltage drop, which has direct influence on the high output level of external buffers. The external buffer circuits have 500 mV logic swing to get higher noise immunity.

The masterslice has three metallized layers; The first metal layer, deposited on the chip, is made of polysilicon, the second of aluminum, and the third of gold. Function blocks are normally realized on the polysilicon layer and sometimes with additional aluminum patterns. Inter-block signals are connected on the aluminum layer and the gold layer metallization. After function block allocation, the aluminum layer metallization, used for function blocks, is processed as pre-assigned patterns by the CAD system. The aluminum and gold metallized layers have 308 channels with 12 μm pitch and 241 channels with 15 μm pitch, respectively.

A film carrier bonding system, which features batch bonding and high reliability, is also adapted to the masterslice. Lead frames are made by photo resist etching of copper foil, which is laminated onto a 35 mm width film carrier, and by gold plating. The chips are assembled to the film carrier by thermal compression bonding between the gold pads on the chips and lead frames (See Figure 6-10). The chips with lead frames are punched off from the film carrier and assembled onto a ceramic substrate. Each chip occupies about 10 mm square of the substrate, which results in high packing density.

CAD

The CAD system is indispensable to design LSIs with short turn around time and to avoid careless mistakes. The system supports all the activities from logical design to testing the prototypes, as shown in the flow chart in Figure 6-11. These activities include logic simulation, function block allocation, 3 layer routing, delay simulation, test pattern generation and fault simulation (17–20).

Prior to designing each circuit in an LSI family, the masterslice substrate and function block design have been accomplished. A masterslice substrate consists of an array of cells, routing areas and external pads, as shown in Figure 6-7. Power supply lines are usually preassigned on the substrate.

Physical information on the masterslice is compiled into the structure library and the pattern library. Logical, physical and electrical information on the function blocks is compiled into the block libraries. These libraries are referred to by the CAD system at every stage in the chip design.

Specific items related to the series gated structure are also processed by the

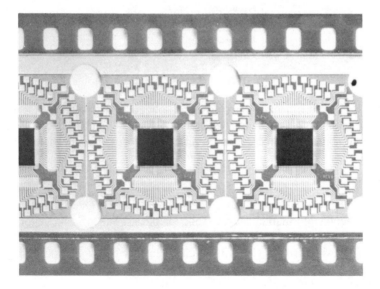

Figure 6-10. Film carrier.

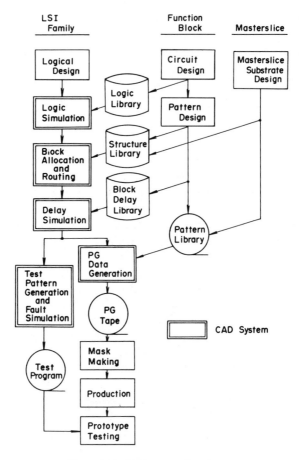

Figure 6-11. CAD system flow chart.

CAD system. They include checking signal voltage level coincidence for signal transfer among function blocks, resistor adjustment for emitter dotting and deletion of non-used output and/or input emitter follower connections.

Logic Simulation

The first step in LSI family design is logic simulation. The designer inputs interconnection information between function blocks. The logic simulator compiles the input data and detects careless mistakes, such as coding errors or logic diagram drawing errors. Then, it simulates logical behaviours according to input patterns applied to chip terminals, and detects output pattern disagreement with expected values (17).

The block logical functions are defined as macro gates, which are described by basic gates, such as AND, NAND, OR, NOR and DFF. The circuit delay times are also assigned to each of several basic gates which are used to construct a function block. Therefore, the logic simulator can also simulate the signal propagation delay in the LSIs by using function block libraries.

Layout Design

The next step is layout design, which consists of placement and routing. At this stage, based on a set of signal nets between function block terminals, the cell location for each block and the pad location for each external terminal are determined, and the wiring patterns for each net are routed.

Placement   Placement is used to assign function blocks into cell arrays on the substrate, so as to facilitate routing. The final layout design goal is to achieve 100% routing. However, it is too difficult to consider the final goal itself in the placement stage. Therefore, function blocks are allocated to minimize the total routing length of all signal nets.

Routing.   The routing procedure is divided into two stages; global routing and detailed routing. After the whole chip areas are partitioned into portions vertically and horizontally, global routing determines, for each net, portions through which the net will be routed. Global routes for all nets, being expressed as a set of portions, are obtained so that the wire density in each portion does not exceed the wire capacity for the portion. Then, the precise positions of wiring patterns are decided in the detail routing, while being constrained from the above global routes.

The detailed routing tries to find the wiring patterns for any given pair of terminals, or a pin-pair. The pin-pairs for each net are defined and ordered for routing. A line search method is adopted with a few modifications, whereby 3-layer wiring patterns can be handled.

Delay Simulation

After layout design, detail media delay, which include line delay and fanout delay for each net, is calculated by using basic delay parameters in the block delay library. The media delay and circuit delay are merged into same database. Detailed AC characteristics can be estimated by delay simulation.

A logic simulator is used for delay simulation again. In this case, the designer inputs the test patterns to activate a special delay path. Sometimes, another delay time calculation tool is used which traces all net delay without any test pattern. It calculates minimum/maximum delay and clock skew for the clock distribution net and detects race conditions between flip flops on a chip.

Test Pattern Generation and Fault Simulation

The device test patterns are generated automatically by using the scan path technique. The scan path technique is very useful for the reduction in computing time and test steps with small amounts of logic circuit increase. The test patterns used in logic simulation can be also used as device test patterns.

A fault simulator generates the comparison vector expected by input test patterns and checks fault coverage. If necessary, manual test patterns will be added to attain the detection rate design goal. Finally, the generated test patterns are converted to the device tester program.

DESIGN FOR TESTABILITY

In the LSI family development, built-in testability is important in order to test the device completely and efficiently. The scan path technique is applied to all the devices, assigning 3 special pads for testing; shift mode control, shift data input and shift data output. These preassigned pads allow the devices to be tested by the same tester, pin assignment, which results in a low cost device tester with special serial scan function limitted to these three tester pins. The technique also makes automatic test pattern generation easier. (20–22)

In the scan path technique, all the flip-flops in an LSI are connected serially and form a shift register. Each flip-flop has an input data selector, which is controlled by shift mode control input. This structure allows the flip-flops to be used as ordinary flip-flops in the normal mode and as shift registers in the test mode. In the normal mode, normal data is loaded to the flip-flop. In the shift mode, output from the previous flip-flop in the shift register chain is loaded. The output signal for each flip-flop drives both the following flip-flop and other gates.

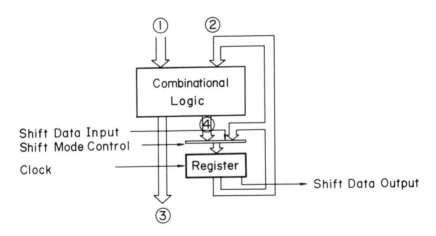

Figure 6-12. An LSI with shift path.

Table 6-2. Representative LSI design data.

TYPE	1	2	3	4	5	6	7	8	9	10	AVE.
Input pins	55	42	51	44	50	63	40	42	38	54	48
Output pins	14	30	21	24	22	9	32	29	34	18	23
Total pins (72 MAX)	69	72	72	68	72	72	72	71	72	72	71
Equivalent gates	1170	685	1244	1266	881	1088	918	742	766	1288	1005
Networks	477	447	418	447	479	535	425	431	430	353	444
Pin-Pair connections	1585	986	1060	1132	1172	1201	926	811	804	1034	1071
Fan outs/network	3.3	2.2	2.5	2.5	2.4	2.2	2.2	1.9	1.9	2.9	2.4
Cell usage (%)	98	62	94	99	81	99	86	79	72	93	87
Power dissipation (TYP. mW)	1200	1460	1410	1510	1480	1270	1530	1510	1500	1270	1410

The shift register approach enables the sequential logic circuit to be transformed to a combinational one. This is because all the states of the circuit are completely determined by the shift input data and other terminal data. After the flip-flops are set (by advancing the clock) to the new states, they can be read out by shifting out registers through the shift data output. Therefore, shift registers in the circuit can be treated as equivalent input/output terminals.

The following shows how the LSIs are tested by the scan path technique. First, test data ①, shown in Figure 6-12, is applied to input terminals under the normal mode. Second, test data ② is shifted into shift registers by changing shift mode control from the normal mode to the shift mode. Then, output terminal data ③ is compared with expected test vector. After the mode is set back to normal, output pattern ④ for combination circuits is loaded to the register by advancing a clock. The shift mode control is then set to the shift mode and each data from the shift data output is observed after each clock advance.

APPLICATION

The masterslice approach is adopted to meet the demands for system oriented LSIs. However, it is reasonable to start the development with those family members that have higher chip counts per chip type in a system and/or among systems. Therefore, the first members of the family, shown in Table 6-2, include so-called bit-slice types. They are the 4-bit slice microprogram sequencer (chip 1), the 2-byte slice error correction circuit (chip 2), the 8-bit slice timers chip 4), the 8-bit slice arithmetic-logic unit (chip 5) and the 1-bit slice register files (chip 6). The others are the imput/output interface controllers, which are expected to be used repeatedly among systems.

The representative design data for the LSI family show that they utilize 87% of masterslice cells and have 1000 equivalent gates on an average, as shown in Table 6-2. These chips contain an average of 444 networks with 2.4 fan outs,

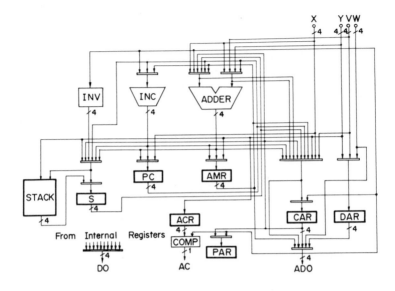

DAR : Data   Address   Register

CAR : Current   Address   Register

PAR : Previous   Address   Register

AMR : Address   Mask   Register

ACR : Address   Compare   Register

PC : Program   Counter

S : Return   Address   Register

Figure 6-13. Four bit slice sequencer.

which means that 1071 interconnections are routed on the chip. Typical power dissipation of 1.41 watts can be efficiently cooled by a forced air cooling system.

Highly successful routing rate (99% on an average) was obtained for almost all the family. Unrouted pin-pairs mainly resulted from terminal blockages, which were concerned with function block terminals beneath power supply lines. To this point, the routing algorithm should be revised so as to route pin-pairs suffering from terminal blockages in an earlier order. Peeling and rerouting of already determined routes may be an efficient way to avoid the above difficulties.

It is found that these 10 LSIs can replace about 66% of the logic-gates in a large computer. Chip counts per chip type in the system varies from 6 to 36 (average count is 12). If the number of LSI chip types is increased up to 20, more than 80% of the logic gates are expected to be replaced.

SEQ

Chip 1 in Table 6-2 is a 4 bit slice microprogram sequence controller intended for general purpose usage. The block diagram is shown in Figure 6-13. This chip has 6 input/output ports (address and data), 9-level push/pop stack, 6 address registers and address modify circuits, such as an adder, an incrementer and bit insert/mask circuits.

Two mode control inputs select two addressing modes and/or address modification modes to adapt the LSI to different circuit configurations. The LSI provides capability of conditional branching, interruption controls and repeat operations. For system trouble analysis, there is a one-level history register and an address compare function. The cycle times for address modification are 30 ns in addition mode and 14 ns in bit insertion mode. The total gate count is 1170 gate and power dissipation is 1.2W.(3) The LSI microphotograph for chip 1 is shown in Figure 6-14.

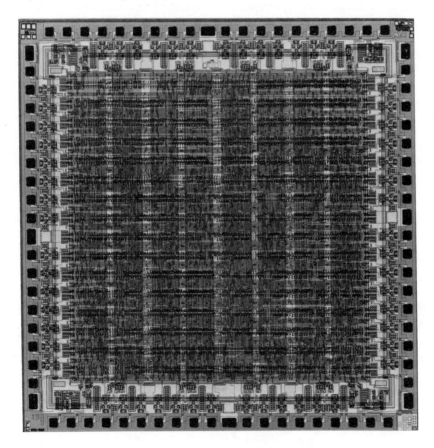

Figure 6-14. LSI microphotograph.

ECC

Chip 2 in Table 6-2 is a 2-byte slice error correction circuit (ECC), which generates and detects SEC-DED (Single Error Correct and Double Error Detect) code for memory data. This device, shown in Figure 6-15, contains a selector (SEL) for partial write, a data register (DR), a check bits and a syndrome generator (CG/SG), a syndrome decoder (SD) and a correction circuit (COR). The basic H-matrix for 2-byte data can be expandable up to 8 bytes by cascading up to 4 chips. The delay time for data correction is 25.4 ns for 4 byte data and 31.2 ns for 8 byte data. The total gate count is 685 gates and power dissipation is 1.8W, (3).

CONCLUSION

The low energy CML with -3.3 V power supply and 450 mV logic swing is adopted for a basic circuit to realize both high speed and low power. The constant current circuit, which is provided for each LCML, can minimize logic level variations due to the environmental change. The 2 level series gated structure can offer many usable functions by interconnecting, transistors in different patterns and contributes to realizing high performance.

The PSA (Polysilicon Self Aligned) process has been developed to obtain small components and fine interconnections. The polysilicon layer also provides

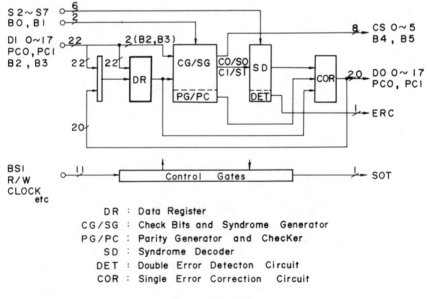

DR : Data Register
CG/SG : Check Bits and Syndrome Generator
PG/PC : Parity Generator and Checker
SD : Syndrome Decoder
DET : Double Error Detecton Circuit
COR : Single Error Correction Circuit

Figure 6-15. ECC.

high value resistors with small parasitic capacitance. The PSA process has successfully achieved high packing density, high speed and low power.

The CAD system supports all the activities from logical design to testing the prototypes. The system has improved the turn around time and avoided mistakes that would occur without the system.

The 10 representative kinds of LSIs developed on the masterslice have an average of 1000 gates and dissipate about 1.41 W. It is found that these 10 LSIs can replace 66% of large computer logic circuits. The family members will be increased to facilitate the realization of higher performance, smaller system size and better reliability.

ACKNOWLEDGMENT

The authors wish to express their thanks to people in NTT's Musashino Electrical Communication Laboratory, NEC's IC Division and NEC Computer Engineering Division, who have made many valuable suggestions and cooperated in carrying out the work.

REFERENCES

(1) Kimura, K., Shimizu, K., Shiba, H., Nakamura, T. and Yano, S. "LSI Using Low Energy, High Speed CML Circuits." *Colloque International sur les Circuits Integres Complexes* 278–287 (Dec. 1974).

(2) Akazawa, Y., Kodama, H., Sudo, T., Takahashi, T., Nakamura, T. and Kimura, K. "A High Speed 1600-Gate Bipolar LSI Processor." *ISSCC '78 Digest of Technical Paper* 208–209 (1978).

(3) Takahashi, Y., Hagiwara, N., Ito, Y., Matsuhiro, K., Nakashima, T., Nakamura, T., Yano, S. and Kimura, K. "A 1200 Gate, Subnanosecond Masterslice LSI." *Paper Tech. Group, IECE* Japan, SSD79–49, October 1979.

(4) Davies, R. D., and Meindl, J. D. "Poly I² L—A High Speed Linear Compatible Structure." *ISSCC Dig. Tech. Papers* 218–219 (Feb. 1977).

(5) Watanabe, M. "Novel Processing Technologies for High Frequency Transistors and ICs." *Proc. 3rd Int. Symp. on Silicon Materials Science and Technology* (1977): 992–1004.

(6) Okada, K. et al. "PSA—A New Approach Bipolar LSI." *IEEE J. Solid-State Circuits* SC-13 No. 5: 693–698 (Oct. 1978).

(7) Okada, K. et al. "A New Polysilicon Process for a Bipolar Device—PSA Technology." *IEEE Trans. Electron Devices* ED-26 No. 4: 385–389 (Apr. 1979).

(8) Appels, J. A. et al. "Local Oxidation of Silicon and its Application in Semiconductor-Device Technology." *Phillips Res. Rep.* 25: 118–132 (1970).

(9) Appels, J. A. and Paffen, M. M. "Local Oxidation of Silicon: New Technological Aspects." *Phillips Res. Rep.* 26: 157–165 (1971).

(10) Connel, T. R. O. et al. "A 4K Static Clocked and Non-clocked RAM Design" *ISSCC Dig. Tech. Papers* 14–15 (Feb. 1977).

(11) Mckenny, V. G. "A 5V-Only 4K Static RAM." *ISSCC Dig. Tech. Papers* 16–17 (Feb. 1977).

(12) Blood, B. "High-Speed Gate Arrays are the Building Blocks for Modern Computer Systems." *WESCON* 1 No. 3: 1–5 (1978).

(13) Hively, J. W. "Subnanosecond ECL Gate Array." *WESCON* **3** No. 3: 1–10 (1978).
(14) Offerdahl, R. E. "High Utilization of a Masterslice LSI Array." *WESCON* **3** No. 5, 1–11 (1978).
(15) Braeckelmann, W. et al. "A Masterslice LSI for Subnanosecond Random Logic." *IEEE J. Solid-State Circuits* **SC-14** No. 5: 829–832 (Oct. 1979).
(16) Blumberg, R. J. and Brenner, S. "A 1500 Gate, Random Logic, Large Scale Integrated (LSI) Masterslice." *IEEE J. Solid-State Circuits* **SC-14** No. 5: 818–822 (Oct. 1979).
(17) Kurobe, T., Nemoto, S., Shikata, Y. and Kani, K. "LSI Logic Simulation System; LOGOS2." Monograph of Technical Group on DA of Information Processing Society of Japan, DA31-2, 1977.
(18) Yoshizawa, H., Kawanishi, H., Goto, S., Kishimoto, A., Fujinami, Y. and Kani, K. "Automatic Layout Algorithms for Master Slice LSI." *Proc. 1979 ISCAS* (1979): 470–473.
(19) Goto, S. "An Efficient Algorithm for the Two-dimensional Placement Problem in Electrical Circuit Layout." *Proc. of 1979 ISCAS* (1979): 850–853.
(20) Funatsu, S., Wakatsuki, N. and Yamada, A. "Designing Digital Circuits with Easily Testable Consideration." *1978 Annual Test Conference* 98–102 (Oct. 1978).
(21) Funatsu, S., Wakatsuki, W., and Arima, T. "Test Generation Systems in Japan." *Proc. 12th Design Automation Conference* (June 1975): 114–122.
(22) Kawai, M., Funatsu, S. and Yamada, A. "Application of Shift Register Approach and its Effective Implementation." *Proc. 1980 Test Conference* (Nov. 1980): 22–25.

7. VLSI Gate Arrays and CAD Methods

David Katz
Bell Telephone Laboratories, Inc.

ARRAY CHIPS

What and Why Array Chips

A gate array chip contains an array of identical and unconnected gates or logic sites in which there are identical arrangements of transistors, diodes and resistors for forming logic functions. There are also a number of input/output gates or sites for chip to chip interconnection. Custom logic functions are realized by the interconnection pattern (metal-level masks) used on the array chip. Only the custom interconnection patterning (gate or site wiring) is required to complete the chip. The left half of Figure 7-1 illustrates an uncommitted logic array, as stocked and ready for custom interconnection. The right half of Figure 7-1 shows a completed custom logic chip on this generic array chip.

The purpose of array chips is to provide many custom codes (designs) with the shortest possible design time, lowest design cost and high confidence in a correct design outcome. Since only the selection of gates or sites and their routing (interconnection) in accord with a desired logic function are required to customize an array, the amount of design required per chip code is significantly reduced. Further, since the generic array chips are essentially predesigned, prefabricated and stocked ready for metal patterning (interconnection), the number of chip fabrication steps to complete the custom chip is reduced. Since both the amount of design and fabrication are reduced with array chips, the time, cost, and risk in custom design are correspondingly reduced.

Array chips are used almost entirely because of their short design time, low design cost, and/or low schedule risk. By their very nature, array chips require more silicon area for a given function, do not provide the highest possible levels of integration, and have significantly less design freedom when compared to full chip designs. Where high-speed, high-power logic is needed and power

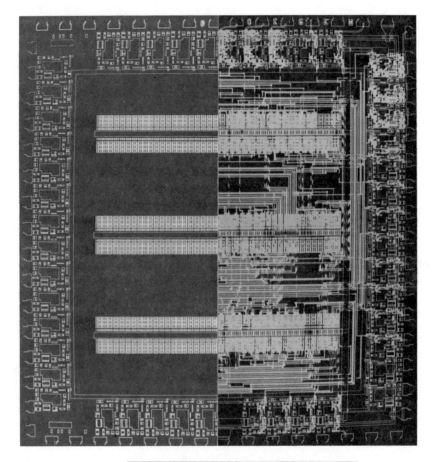

UNCOMMITTED/COMMITTED ARRAY

Figure 7-1. Graphic terminal display of a gate array chip before interconnection of gates (left half) and after interconnection (right half).

instead of chip area limits the level of integration on the chip, arrays predominate. Where the shortest design time and lowest risk are critical, arrays are often used. Where the highest level of integration possible is sought, full custom design is usually used. In most systems, both array and full custom chips are used. Both a low-power injection logic array chip and a high-power emitter-function logic array chip are described later.

The next section describes the circuits used, the speed-power products and the gate counts in bipolar array chips. Bipolar arrays are used in Bell Laboratories because the bipolar circuits best met the requirements for high speed (and high power) custom logic. The bipolar array logic chips are in the LSI and low VLSI range (200 to 2,000 gates). For higher levels of integration, the MOS technology is superior. For custom VLSI in MOS, a full custom polycell design system is used rather than gate arrays. The MOS polycell and array design systems and the CAD used are practically the same. The MOS polycell system provides good design turnaround time and high confidence in a correct outcome the first time through.

Design Time, Effort and Confidence with Arrays

Figure 7-2 shows the time used to go from a logic description to completed models with arrays. Early in 1978 the turnaround time with a 200-gate array was 14 weeks. The design and silicon processing times were about one-half that used for comparable non-array bipolar chips. Within one year, the design people drastically reduced their design time for arrays and the complete logic-to-models cycle was eleven weeks. Today, designers are using arrays with 1,000 or more gates and the interval from logic to models or production remains eleven weeks.

The three major activities in going from the logic description to array chip models or production are design, processing (masks and chip metallization), and packaging and testing. The results shown for arrays in Figure 7-2 were obtained with no change or perturbation in the design people, the design system, the mask or silicon process line or the test facilities in general use. With the array chips, models and production are synonomous. The same masks, stocked wafers, process line, packages and test programs are used for both models and for production. Clearly, large investments in special dedicated facilities for masking and processing arrays could again cut the logic-to-models time in half.

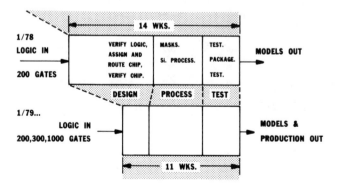

Figure 7-2. Weeks from logic description to models with array chips (with constant design people, silicon processing and test facilities).

To sum up, the design cycle results with array chips are:

- 90% confidence in a correct outcome (logic to models) within eleven weeks.
- The per code design effort or cost is one designer-month.
- The design cycle time and cost are practically independent of array size.

These are the results using general VLSI design strategies and a comprehensive set of CAD tools that are easily adapted to array, polycell and other styles of chip design. Design strategies and essential CAD for VLSI are discussed later in the sections under those headings.

Circuits, Speed-Power and Number of Gates in Bipolar Arrays

In logic chips, the primary figures of merit are the speed-power product of the gates used, the number of gates in the chip and the silicon area per gate. The lower the speed-power product, the larger the number of gates and the smaller the area, the better the chip. A measure of the progress made and current level of speed-power product, number of gates and relative silicon area of array chips used in Bell Laboratories, can be seen in Figure 7-3. This lists seven of the array chips put into use from 1977 to date. The first four are in the older junction isolated technology; the last three are in an oxide isolated technology that is in production.

For both the low power, high density injection logic (I^2L) and the higher power, higher speed logic (TTL, ECL and EFL) arrays, the number of gates

ARRAY CHIPS	MERIT FACTORS			
INTERNAL GATE CIRCUIT	INTERNAL SPEED × PWR. (PICOJOULES)	NUMBER OF GATES ON CHIP	RELATIVE CHIP AREAS	
JUNCTION ISOLATED				
1977 — I^2L	15	200	0.4	LOW POWER, HIGH DENSITY
TTL	15	320	1.0	
1980 — ECL	9	500	3.4	HIGH POWER, HIGH SPEED
EFL	3	750*	2.3	
OXIDE ISOLATED				
1979 — I^2L	6	1000	1.0	LOW POWER, HIGH DENSITY
1981 — I^2L	6	1600	1.0	
EFL	1.5	2250*	3.4	HIGH POWER, HIGH SPEED

* EQUIVALENT GATE COUNT IF ALL AVAILABLE SITES ARE 6-GATE D-FLIP FLOPS

Figure 7-3. Array chips available for use in Bell Labs.

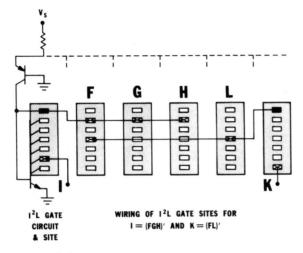

I^2L GATE CIRCUIT & SITE

WIRING OF I^2L GATE SITES FOR $I = (FGH)'$ AND $K = (FL)'$

Figure 7-4. I^2L gate circuit and wiring of gates in an array chip.

on the chip has increased by about a factor of five since 1977. In the injection logic, the speed-power product improved from 15 picojoules to 6 picojoules, due to the use of an oxide isolated technology. In the higher speed TTL and ECL arrays, a large improvement is obtained by using series-gated EFL logic (7, 8, 9,). In the junction isolated technology, the EFL circuitry reduces the effective speed-power product to 3 picojoules. In the oxide isolated technology, the EFL circuit has a speed-power product of less than 1.5 picojoules. The oxide isolated high-speed 2250-gate EFL array can operate at 1 nanosecond gate speed, has the same area as the 500-gate ECL (junction isolated) array and will use about the same total power as the ECL array. The 2250-gate EFL array was designed in a standard 4 oxide isolated technology that is already in production.

Both the EFL and I^2L arrays are in increasing use in 1981. Since the lower power I^2L array occupies 30% of the silicon area used by EFL, the I^2L array continues to be used where high speed is not required.

The injection logic (I^2L) circuit (5) used in the array is diagrammed in Figure 7-4. As shown in Figure 7-4, the I^2L "NAND" gate is a multi-output (collectors), single input (base) transistor with the emitter grounded. Base injection current for each I^2L gate is provided by a lateral PNP transistor. Wiring such gates in an array chip consists of interconnecting the appropriate collector and base contact points of the gate sites in the array. A partial wiring of some gate sites in the array. A partial wiring of some gate sites in an I^2L array is also illustrated in Figure 7-4. The main point here is that this I^2L array is gate-level logic. The chip contains a geometric arrangement of identical gates and any logic function must be constructed with the individual gates in the array. For any logic function so constructed, the function time delay will be the sum

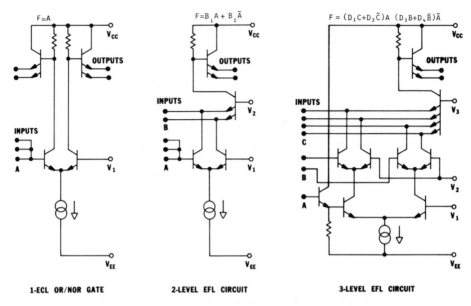

Figure 7-5. The ECL gate circuit and series-gated EFL 2-level and 3-level circuits.

of the delays of all the gates in the signal path. The total power for any function will be the sum of the powers of all the gates in the function. All this is quite different in the stacked series gated logic used in the EFL arrays.

Sites in the EFL arrays (referred to in the table in Figure 7-3) allow the construction of logic circuits that combine EFL and ECL circuits in series-gated logic stacks. Basic circuit schematics of a single level ECL gate, a two-level and a three-level ECL-EFL series gated stack are shown in Figure 7-5 (7, 8, 9).

The Boolean expressions for the current steering circuits in Figure 7-5 are:

$$
\begin{aligned}
&\text{1-ECL Gate} && F = A \\
&\text{2-Level EFL} && F = B_1A + B_2A \\
&\text{3-Level EFL} && F = (D_1C + D_2C)A + (D_3B + D_4B)A
\end{aligned}
$$

Circuits 1 and 2 use essentially the same number of transistors and resistors. Circuit 3 uses twice that of either 1 or 2. From the Boolean expressions, it is obvious that circuit 2 has much more logical power than circuit 1, the single level ECL gate. Similarly, circuit 3 has more than twice the logical power of circuit 2. Indeed, this form, and other forms, of stacked, series gated logic circuits provide significant improvements in their speed and/or power compared to single level logic like the 1-ECL circuit. Further, if each site in an array

LOGIC FUNCTION	CIRCUIT FORM	NORMALIZED TO 1-ECL GATE			NUMBER OF TRANSISTORS + RESISTORS
		DELAY	POWER × DELAY	AREA	
2:1 MUX	1-ECL	3.0	24.	5	28
	2-EFL	1.5	2.	1	6
4:1 MUX	1-ECL	3.0	42	9	52
	3-EFL	1.6	3.	2	12
8:1 MUX	1-ECL	3.0	72	17	97
	4-EFL	2.0	5	4	24

Figure 7-6. Comparison of series-gated EFL circuits with 1-ECL circuit.

contains the appropriate transistors and resistors for say the 3-level EFL circuit, then a site can contain two 1- or 2-level circuits or a 3-level circuit. Such an array would use fewer transistors and less area to realize high-level functions than would be the case in an array of single-level gates.

Stacked, series-gated logic provides a significant improvement in speed and/or power compared to single-level gate logic. Series-gated logic also uses fewer transistors and resistors (uses less silicon area) than required when these functions are realized by single-level ECL or TTL gates. The table (Figure 7-6) compares the delay-power performance and component count for the multiplex function when implemented with single-level ECL gates (1-ECL) and with two-level, three-level, and four-level EFL series-gated circuits. Similarly, significant improvements are realized for a wide range of logic functions, such as demultiplexers, flip-flops, registers, counters, and parity trees. This is described with more detail in a paper by R. J. Scavuzzo (7). This paper also points out that the series-gated EFL has performance advantages over series-gated ECL circuits.

The series-gated logic circuits in the EFL array can be used in either an ECL or a TTL environment. For the TTL environment, TTL compatible input-output is provided on the array chip. Figure 7-7 compares the series-gated EFL array logic with the low-power Schottky TTL (LSTTL) logic available in catalog parts and in gate arrays. This comparison in the delay-power plane is for six catalog MSI logic functions—2:1 MUX, 4:1 MUX, 8:1 MUX, D-Flip-Flop, 4-bit Counter, and 9-bit parity checker. These were the six most common functions (approximately 60% of the LSTTL used) in a large system that was analyzed. The EFL series-gated logic improves the power x delay product over an order of magnitude compared to both the LSTTL catalog parts and the LSTTL gate array.

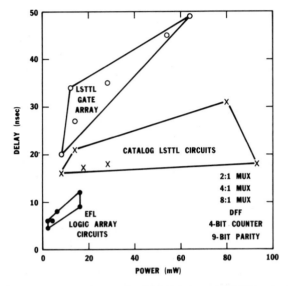

Figure 7-7.   Delay (or speed) x power for common MSI functions with LSTTL circuits and with EFL array circuits.

DESIGN STRATEGY AND CAD SYSTEM

A Design Process for VLSI

A basic design process (or strategy) used for both large gate arrays and for polycell VLSI chips is diagrammed in Figure 7-8. The heart of this design process is a library of predesigned (and hierarchical) chip parts or cells. This contains logic primitives, function cells and supercells for use by the logic designer and the chip designer. With this library, the logic designer designs and simulates his logic in terms of the high-level cells or functions in the library. The resultant high-level logic description (including test vectors) maps directly into library cell information for chip layout, for simulation, for the generation of mask information, and for the generation of a test program for an automatic test set.

Given a high-level logic description in library cell terms, the chip design or layout is reduced to the placement and routing of the called-for cells and supercells. The logic, gates, circuits, transistors and other details within the cells are invisible to the chip designer. Thus, the overwhelming mass of detailed chip design below the cell level is done once, is stored in the library, and made available to all chip designers for use in many VLSI chip designs. After chip layout, a final check is made. The chip logic is simulated with actual fan-in, fan-out, and routing on the chip taken into account.

The chip design process described (library cells, chip layout, and layout checking by logic simulation) produces large numbers of array and/or polycell chip codes with high design yield. Again, yield means correct designs that are manufacturable the first pass through the design process. With appropriate computer aids, this chip design process also produces short design intervals and low design cost.

The remaining post-layout steps (Figure 7-8) of generating the mask data, the test program for a target test set, and the manufacturing information are not design tasks. They are derived directly from the logic description, the test vectors and the chip layout. The post-layout steps are straight-forward data processing to produce specific design outputs needed for the physical processing, the testing, and the design documentation.

The central chip design process is independent of changes in silicon technology. For a new technology or a change in design rules, the new cells are first designed and verified. New cell files are created and these are put in the library as new additional cell files or as replacements for obsolete cell files. The central chip design process is unperturbed by this. The chip design process (and CAD system) can be independently and continuously improved to reduce the chip design time and cost even as the silicon technology changes. Indeed, all the design modules in this scheme can grow and improve independently of each other and of technology.

Up to this point, a modular design process or stragegy for VLSI was stressed. The view taken here is that the underlying design strategy or scheme will determine and limit the achievable performance and cost of the computer aided design system. In this design strategy, only the simulation phase (or module) is clearly synonymous with CAD or computers. For the design of many custom VLSI chips, this is probably the most necessary computer aid. Effective com-

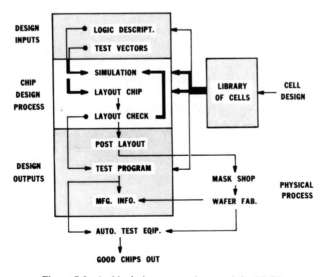

Figure 7-8. A chip design process (strategy) for VLSI.

puter aid in layout checking (including resimulation after layout) ranks a close second in necessity. Without these two aids, the probability of successfully completing a VLSI design the first time through the design process is very low. The graphical layout aids on computers are, of course, essential to reduce the labor, time and cost in this design phase. The assumption made here is that simulation and layout checking must be done by computer. However, the chip layout could, in the main, be done manually or with primitive aids, but this would be a foolhardy undertaking where many VLSI designs are needed. To the extent that array chips simplify layout, less or simpler layout aid may suffice for a high yield design process with array chips.

A CAD System for VLSI

Basically, the structure of the computer-aided design (CAD) system that has evolved in Bell Laboratories for all forms of chip design is modular and adaptive. When gate array chips increased in complexity and the demand for codes increased, no new major investment in software was required for the array chips.

The evolving CAD structure for all VLSI is a set of programs that are primarily design task oriented and comparatively independent of each other, of circuit form, and of silicon technology. The major design tasks (or functions) and the design flow in the CAD system follow from and are identical to the design strategy depicted in Figure 7-8 which was developed by the designers. They organized themselves and their work in a modular, adaptive way to cope with increasing complexity, volume of design, and the changing silicon and computer technologies. The CAD they are using reflects their strategies.

The design strategy chosen by designers for both arrays and polycell VLSI chips uses libraries of function blocks or cells. This simplifies the VLSI design task and the computational or search tasks in all phases of the design. The success of this approach is, of course, dependent on the primitives and the structural methods used in putting primitives together to form cells and in putting cells together to form chips.

From Figure 7-8, the major in-line design functions or modules, which are the major CAD functions for VLSI, are listed below.

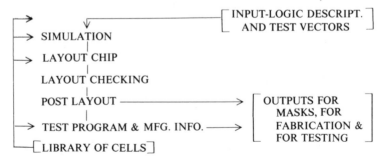

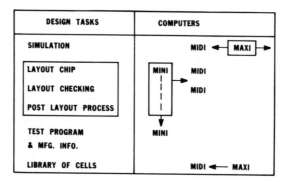

Figure 7-9. CAD programs and computer hardware for VLSI design.

These are the set of design tasks for which computer aids or programs exist and continue to grow. References (1), (3), and (6) describe several of the programs used. These major functions, which are independent modules, are also internally made up of independent submodules. Internal modularity is needed to allow for different and changing design styles. For example, any or all of the layout styles (polycell, gate array, gate-matrix and packed layout) may require some special internal submodule. Bipolar, unipolar (MOS), linear and digital circuits may also require some different treatment within a major module. However, none of these should require major new software developments in themselves (and none have).

For a VLSI design system (which involves several major CAD modules and machines), the related data bases in modules, the intermodule data flow, and the designer-CAD machine interaction need planning. The UNIX™ system (2) file handling and networking capabilities are proving valuable in multiprogram, multimachine systems. The designers workbench (4) approach appears useful here.

Of greater concern today are the kinds of computing machines and the distribution of major computer aids among machines. How the major CAD programs or functions are distributed among mini, midi, and maxi central computers is shown in Figure 7-9. The outlined layout tasks and the associated minicomputer box represent standalone minicomputer CAD developed eleven years ago for interactive chip layout. This standalone minicomputer system with interactive graphics has grown in capabilities and is still in use for a significant part of the chip layout work. Incremental growth in CAD and computers has taken place and continues in the directions shown by the arrows. The minicomputer tasks were extended downward into new postprocessors, the generation of test programs for production test sets and producing manufacturing information.

For polycell VLSI, there is a sideways movement to automatic layout on medium (MIDI) computers. The simulation programs (circuit analysis, logic and fault simulators) originally resided only on a large central maxi computer. For VLSI design new mixed-mode simulators and circuit analysis programs are going into wide use. To allow all designers adequate simulation runs with high reliability and reasonable cost, these programs are ported to medium (job dedicated) machines and to large mainframe machines such as a CRAY-1. Designing software that is easily portable (and the porting tools) increases the life cycle of the software and reduces software development and use costs.

In both programs and machines, the CAD system has grown incrementally and adaptively to meet the needs of increasing chip complexity, increasing design volume, multi-location users, organizational task partitioning and special design requirements. There are now about 100 minis, six midis, and a maxi in large use for silicon chip design at more than three locations. Increasingly, there is a need for networking for machine-to-machine data transfer. There is, of course, increased emphasis on software portability as the range of machines increases and new, more powerful, lower cost machines become available.

What Next in CAD and Computing

The new generation of 32-bit microcomputers will provide local desk or laboratory bench computing that is compatible with the larger midi and maxi machines in use for CAD. Program portability to these micros will be as good as the portability between the midi and maxi computers today. Common or compatible operating systems, compilers, languages, libraries, etc., will be available. The impact of such microcomputing in improving the performance and cost of CAD is obviously large.

With an intelligent division of CAD tasks between powerful micros and larger machines, large gains in computing aid per dollar and in human-machine system performance can be realized quite rapidly. Visualize numerous office or laboratory microcomputers, a few midis, and a maxi in a CAD system serving a large community of designers. Such a distributed computing system provides powerful, low cost, local user microcomputing power, local graphics processing and local peripherals tailored to local use and needs. Task, data, and/or job transfers from the local micros to larger machines will be virtually invisible to the users. The human user interface will be friendly, supportive, consistent and directly accessible by the users. User and computing growth will be accommodated mainly by adding local microstations. More computing power and better performance for both humans and machines will be obtained at lower cost with such a distributed computing environment and improved human-machine interaction. These are needed and rapidly becoming available.

REFERENCES

(1) Agrawal, Bose, Kozak, Nham, Pacas-Skewers "The Mixed Mode Simulator." *Proc., 17th Design Automation Conference* (June, 1980): 618.

(2) Kernigham, B. W. and Maskey, J. R., "The Unix Programming Environment," *Computer* **14** No. 4: 12–24 (April, 1981).

(3) Nagel, L. W. "SPICE 2: A Computer Program to Simulate Semiconductor Circuits." Memo No. ERLM520, U. of California, Berkeley, May, 1975.

(4) O'Neill, Savolaine, Thompson, Franke, Friedenson, Walsh, McDonald, Breiland, Evans. "Designers Workbench—Efficient and Economical Design Aids." *Proc., 16th Design Automation Conference* (1976): 399–407.

(5) Pedersen, R. A. "Integrated Injection Logic: A Bipolar LSI Technique." *Computer* 24–29 (Feb. 1976).

(6) Persky, G., Deutsch, D. N., Schweikert, D. G. "LTX—A System for the Directed Automatic Design of LSI Circuits." *Proc., Design Automation Conference* (1976): 399–407.

(7) Scavuzzo, R. J. "Digital Logic Circuit Design for Improved Power-Delay Product in LSI." *Proc., International Conference on Circuits and Computers* (Oct., 1980): 693.

(8) Skokan, Z. E. "EFL Logic Family for LSI." *Int. Solid-State Circuits Conference* (Feb. 1973) Dig. Tech. Papers, pp 162–163.

(9) Skokan, Z. E., "Emitter Function Logic—Logic Family for LSI." *J. Solid-State Circuits,* **SC-8:** 356–361 (1973).

8. Improving VLSI Design Capability

Joseph C. Logue
Walter J. Kleinfelder
Paul Lowy
J. Randal Moulic
Wei-Wha Wu
IBM Corporation

INTRODUCTION

Achieving a cost-effective VLSI (very large scale integration) chip design with a two-year design cycle requires that chip function be maximized while the time and number of iterations through the design cycle be minimized. However, as the degree of integration increases to thousands or tens of thousands of circuits per chip, it becomes more difficult to assure that the desired function is correct and that the final chip performs that function after the first or even succeeding design passes. This is especially true when the design is optimized for circuit density and performance, for example, changing the mask layout of a circuit so that it fits within a geometrical bound and still retains its electrical characteristics. This type of design is known as "custom design."

Examples of such custom chips now available are the Motorola 68000 microprocessor (1) and the Zilog Z8000 microprocessor (2). The claim has been made that today's microprocessors have from 25,000 to 70,000 transistors, which must certainly represent more than 10,000 circuits (1). The question arises as to whether the VLSI design capability of the semiconductor industry can keep pace with its technical ability to fabricate an ever increasing number of logic gates on a chip. It has been estimated that today's design cost for a VLSI chip is approximately $100 per gate (3). As our capability to put more gates on a chip increases, we must improve our design abilities, otherwise the growth of VLSI and the semiconductor industry will be seriously limited.

One technique for reducing design time at the expense of circuit density now becoming more prevalent is the master slice or gate array. Recent advances include a 5000-circuit wired chip of this type described by IBM (4) and an 1144-cell image chip supported by design automation marketed by Signetics (5). It is possible not only to reduce the design time by automated means (6), but also to decrease the manufacturing time since wafers consisting of predesigned circuits are built and stockpiled for later personalization by metal interconnections. Regardless of these advantages, it still behooves designers to guarantee correctness in order to reduce the number of manufacturing passes. Each design cycle subsequent to the first requires a debug phase to determine problems, a redesign effort, and a build phase. Only after the design is functioning well can exhaustive testing under stress conditions be performed to guarantee that the chip meets specifications. The turnaround time of the build phase varies with several factors. These include the complexity of the process, the necessity to continue to process chips already in production on the line, and process problems. In some cases, the time to process prototype parts may be as long as four months.

Based on these facts, and the need to achieve densities higher than those obtainable from a masterslice design, a technique based on the use of the PLA (programmable logic array) and known as "macro design" is utilized. This technique is one part of a multi-faceted approach to achieving successful VLSI designs and it is one of obviously many approaches that can be taken. We do not claim this to be the best approach, even though it has worked very well for us. VLSI design is a rapidly evolving body of knowledge and the approach to be described is still in an evolutionary stage.

MACRO DESIGN—PLA MACROS

Marco design is based on the observation that circuits with a high degree of logical connectivity will fit closely together when physically implemented. These aggregations of circuits are called macros. Examples of these macros, shown in Figure 8-1, are a multiplexer-register, an EXCLUSIVE-OR tree, and a most important macro—the PLA.

In PLA design, multiple logic functions are implemented in array form, analogous to the personalization of words in a READ ONLY MEMORY. PLA macros consist of 3 sections (Figure 1C):

- *Partitioning circuits*—In their simplest form these provide the true and complement functions for each input, i.e., A, $\overline{A}$ from A, and are known as 1 bit decoders.
- *AND array*—rows of AND circuits whose imputs can be selectively connected (personalized) to any combination of outputs from the partitioning circuits.
- *OR array*—columns of OR circuits whose inputs are selectively connected to any combination of outputs from the AND array.

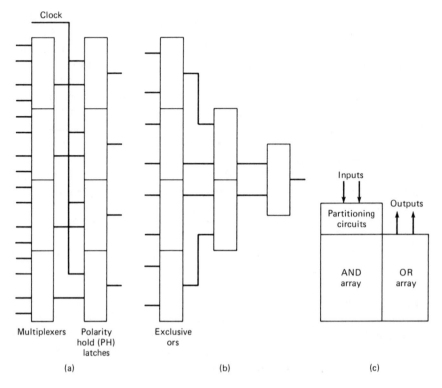

Figure 8-1. Examples of Macros:
A. Multiplexer—register macro
B. Exclusive—OR macro
C. PLA macro

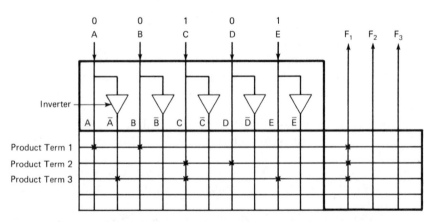

Figure 8-2. Example of a product term (Number 3) being selected.

Any function in product term canonical form, e.g., $f1 = AB + CD + \overline{A}CE$ = ... is suitable for implementation "as is" in a PLA. Each product term becomes a row within the AND array, and personalizing the OR array determines which product terms make up the function. A "match" or selection of a product term occurs when the logical state of the PLA's inputs correspond to the connection of that product term's cross-points (Figure 8-2). In FET technologies, AND and OR arrays are implemented with NOR circuits. Since PLA logic is always in canonical product term form, minimization techniques similar to the Quine-McCluskey method can be applied with computer programs.

PLA macros provide design and verification advantages which will now be discussed.

DESIGN

Generally, logic design may be defined as the transformation of a specification into logic primitives (AND, OR, INVERT, etc.), and storage elements (LATCHES, MEMORY). The objective is to obtain an accurate transformation using a minimum number of elements. This logic description is either recorded on hand-drawn diagrams and then entered into a computer data base, or entered directly into the data base graphically.

The regular structure of the PLA macro makes a tabular format convenient for specifying and recording the logic function. The format used is a matrix in which the columns are the AND-array input and the OR-array output lines of the macro, and the rows are the product terms. The logic functions of the PLA macro are defined by the following symbols:

1. In the AND array:
   I -match on a logical one.
   o -match on a logical zero.
   ● -match on either a logical one or zero (don't care state)
2. In the OR array:
   I -set output to logical one if any input product term is selected; or to logical zero if no input product terms are selected.
   ● -ignore this product term.

The AND array symbols are for input partitioning circuits which are one-bit (or one-input) decoders. Additional symbols specify partitioning circuits which are two-to-four-bit (or two-input) decoders (7) but they will not be defined here. An example of PLA logic documented in this notation is shown in Figure 8-3.

The matrix is numbered from left to right, and from top to bottom, as indicated on the top and left sides of the figure. Consider the third row. Product

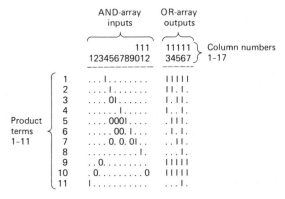

Figure 8-3. Example of PLA representation.

term 3 will be selected when column 5 is a logical zero and column 6 is a logical one. In this event, output columns 13, 15, and 16 will each be logical one conditions.

The PLA macro logic specification describes the logical functions within the macro itself. However, the interconnections of the PLAs to the other macros on the chip, and the circuit connections within the other macros, must also be specified to fully describe the logical function of the chip. This global represen-

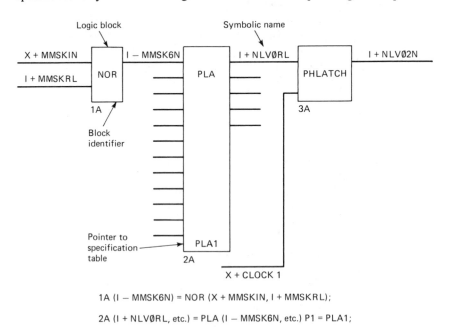

1A (I − MMSK6N) = NOR (X + MMSKIN, I + MMSKRL);

2A (I + NLVØRL, etc.) = PLA (I − MMSK6N, etc.) P1 = PLA1;

3A (I + NLVØ2N) = PHLATCH (I + NLVØRL, X + CLOCK 1);

Figure 8-4. Example of standardized logic representation.

tation of the chip uses the IBM standardized logic specification language to form a data base for documentation, simulation, test pattern generation, and checking.

In our use of the language, a primitive, a register element (latch), or a PLA macro is represented as one logic block. Each block is given a unique identification and is described by one statement. Each interconnecting net is given a symbolic name. A simplified example of this representation is shown in Figure 8-4. The PLA macro block description includes a pointer (PLA1 in the example) to the macro logic specification table (Figure 8-3). Thus, the periphery of the PLA macro is stored with the chip's logic description, and the internal logic of the PLA macro is stored separately in a table. This approach permits changes to the logical function of the macro without changing the global representation, as long as the PLA macro input and output nets remain the same.

VERIFICATION

To illustrate our verification methodology, reference will be made throughout this section to an eight-bit microprocessor chip we designed (Table 8-1).

It is the goal of verification to ensure that the chip functions exactly as intended *before* masks are created. Simulation of the chip data is a necessary but not sufficient condition for satisfying the above. For example, for the microprocessor, 320 instructions were simulated with a model derived from the logic language data. This required 12 minutes on an IBM system 370/168. But to perform exhaustive simulation, at least 1 million instructions should be run against the model and this would require over 600 CPU hours! One must also consider that many man-months of engineering time for debug and analysis would be required. Therefore, after initial design, a dual effort was undertaken

Table 8-1. Eight-Bit Microprocessor Characteristics.

Technology	n-channel MOSFET
Chip size	7.92 × 7.92 mm
Type of design	Macro
Number of instructions	65
I/O	Programmed I/O, 8 interrupt levels, memory-mapped I/O, register-mapped I/O
Storage addressability	64K bytes, extendable to 512K bytes
Performance	900-ns cycle, 6.5 μs per instruction (average)
Number of devices	12 100
Number of equivalent logic gates (2.5-way NOR circuits)	3500
Power	1.2 W
Power supplies	+5 V ± 10%, +8.5 V ± 10%
Module size	25 mm
Module pins	72

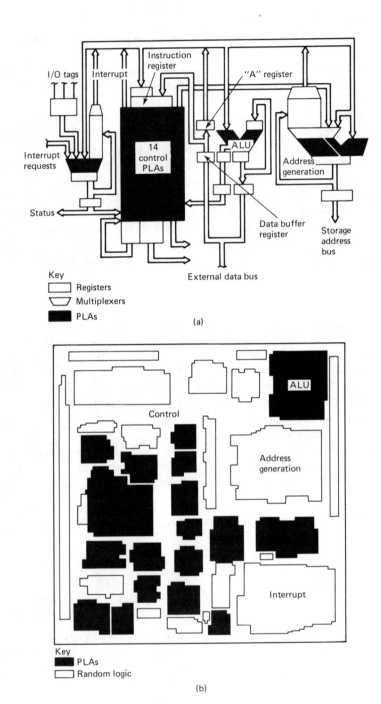

Figure 8-5. Microprocessor:
A. Logic data flow.
B. Physical macro placement.

whereby a prototype was designed and built using TTL (transistor-transistor logic) modules and field programmable PLAs, and then tested exhaustively. In parallel with this effort, the logical design of the chip in its ultimate technology (n-channel MOSFET) was entered into the computer data base using the language previously described and then a practical amount of simulation was performed. However this parallel approach created two concerns: manpower and schedule constraints would be exceeded, and the LSI data base would not faithfully reflect the prototype design.

Our solution to the first concern was to initially define functionally equivalent macros for both designs, maintain I/O correspondence along macro boundaries, and keep the designs identical to avoid duplication of design effort. The macros ranged from 50 to 500 equivalent logic gates (they are not limited by these numbers) and were either PLA or random macros. There were 19 PLA macros, which made up about one-half the circuits on the chip, including the complex "control" section (14 PLA macros). Figure 8-5a is a logic flow diagram of the microprocessor, showing macro partitioning. PLA macros are shown as shaded and random macros as unshaded. The corresponding physical outlines of these macros as they lay out on the chip are depicted in Figure 8-5b.

After the partitioning (and hence the preliminary design of the chip) had been completed, design of the prototype commenced. Most PLA macros were implemented in the prototype as field-programmable PLA modules (FPLAs) (8); see Table 8-2.

A fusible NiCr link exists at each crosspoint in the PLA. These links are opened by selectively pulsing the desired bits via circuitry on the chip. Typically, 300ma at 17 volts is required to personalize a word. The FPLA was

Table 8-2. FPLA and LPLA Characteristics.

	FPLA[a]	NEW FPLA[b]	LPLA
Inputs	16	24	34[d]
Outputs	8	16[d]	44[d]
Internal feedbacks	0	16[c]	22
Product terms	48	72	80 or 160
Array bits	1920	9216	16 320
Partitioning	1-bit	2-bit	2-bit
Maximum cycle time (input to output delay)	50 ns	200 ns	100 ns
Power dissipation	0.6 W (typical)	1.1 W (maximum)	1.85 W (maximum)
Power supply	+5 V	+5 V	+5 V

[a]Signetics 82S100
[b]NEC μPB450D
[c]JK latches
[d]Latched

personalized in the laboratory with the aid of a burn in tool or programmer (9). The tool may be operated from keyboard or tape or connected to a host computer so that the same tables used in the LSI design are used for the prototype. An FPLA module can be programmed in about 5 minutes, and each module costs about $16.

Of the 19 PLA macros, 17 mapped directly into FPLAs. The largest control PLA was implemented as seven FPLAs, and one PLA (the ALU), although functionally equivalent, was redesigned as two PLAs in series. It should be pointed out that the laser personalizable PLAs (LPLAs) and the laser tool to be described in this chapter were not available to us at this time. Had these been available, all PLAs in the LSI version would have mapped directly to the prototype design, saving modules and design time. During the debug and test of the prototype, corrections to·this part of the design were made in minutes by burning in new PLAs. Other macros were implemented with available TTL register, multiplexer, and unit logic integrated curcuit modules. These macros made up the data flow, which has similar connectivity, and therefore required fewer changes than the control section. To illustrate this point, the reader is referred back to the flow diagram in Figure 8-5a to see how an instruction is executed. The eight-bit operation field of an instruction is loaded into the instruction register and decoded with the current state of the machine by the control PLA section to generate approximately 75 signals to control the rest of the chip. On the other hand, the eight-bit (byte) data field of the instruction is merely routed from the data buffer register to the A register and then to the ALU PLA, where it is processed (e.g., during an ADD operation) to form a new byte-wide field. The registers, multiplexers (not shown), and parity-check circuits are connected similarly for each bit, and the controlling inputs of the byte multiplexers are from the control PLA section. Therefore, by design, the most complex portions of the chip are indeed the PLA macros; however, these can be changed most easily in the prototype model.

The prototype consisted of four wired cards of about 50 modules each. One engineer and one laboratory technician designed, built, and thoroughly tested the prototype in six months, expending a total of eight man-months of effort. At the completion of this effort, we were able to verify the prototype design by running in excess of six million instructions on the model in about five minutes. In addition, almost half of the 3500 circuits (the directly mapped PLA portion) had been designed and were ready for use in the LSI version.

Our second concern, ensuring that the LSI data base matched the now functional prototype, was alleviated by the following approach. First, new PLA modules for the prototype were personalized from tables in the LSI data base and tested exhaustively in the prototype to ensure that the PLA data were correct. Second, extensive simulations were run on the model derived from the LSI data base. The simulator program of the IBM Engineering design system (a collection of design-automation programs) provides a memory model which can be "loaded" with instructions that are then used as stimuli for the LSI model. One requirement to prove a design is functional and to reduce the chance that errors or redundancies exist, is to simulate enough instruction sequences so that every net switches to both logical 0 and logical 1 at least once, and that every PLA product term is selected. The simulator program has the ability to keep track of this information and thereby measure the effectiveness of simulation. Instructions were added to the memory model and simulated until every product term was selected, and every net and every I/O were pulsed at least once. In so doing, a subset of the six million instructions used to test the prototype were run against the software model. The subset consisted of 35 routines that utilized the microprocessor's instruction set in some of the many permutations possible. Each routine contained 100 instructions each requiring about five minutes apiece to run, for a total of about three hours of computer time (on an IBM 370/168 System). It was usually possible to complete all these simulations within one day. Third, a log of all changes to the prototype was kept, and the update of the LSI data base was verified. Finally, any macro which differed significantly in implementation from the prototype (such as the ALU) was exhaustively simulated by itself. Since simulation was used to verify that the computer data base matched the prototypes, the data base was suitable for automatic logical/physical checking.

The latter is the process by which mask data is compared to logic language data. Since it is normal practice to identify nets on a logic diagram with a descriptive or symbolic name as indicated in Figure 8-4, for comparison purposes the same name is placed in the mask data as a non manufacturable shape (a label). IBM has written a suite of programs (10) that recognize devices, nets and labels in the mask data and compares these with the logic data. When all devices and nets have been accounted for, the masks are sent to manufacturing.

Two engineers and one clerical specialist expended eight man-months to document and simulate the LSI design. This effort commenced two months after the start of the prototype design and lasted five months. The logic design effort (prototype plus conversion to target technology), as described in this chapter for the first-pass design of the 3500-circuit microprocessor, was completed with one and one-third man-years of effort in seven calendar months.

The results of our dual approach provided us with first pass chips from manufacturing that contained only three design defects. These design errors were attributed to omissions of logical/physical checks (an interchanged net, an incorrect circuit type, and a missing voltage connection). Fortunately, with the aid of the laser tool to be described later, we were able to break a connection on the chip and a suitable TTL patch was added to the card containing the LSI chip, so that complete chip testing could proceed. Another result was that by designing with both PLA macros and random macros (utilizing custom design techniques) better density and performance was achieved than from a "masterslice" approach. This was confirmed by a study made to compare the

Table 8-3. Results from Design Approach Comparison Study.
(Results Shown as Ratios.)

	MACRO CHIP
	MASTER SLICE CHIP
Equivalent NORs/cm^2	1.8
Average delay/circuit	0.8
Average capacitance/circuit	0.5
Average power/circuit	0.6

microprocessor designed by our group with another design using the same technology but a master slice approach. The devices in each design were totaled and the number of equivalent NOR circuits of fan-in 2.5 was calculated from the total. The results illustrated in Table 8-3, demonstrate that the macro approach afforded a 1.8 fold increase in density and a 1.7 fold reduction in power for the same or better performance over the master slice approach. One reason is that the random macros were optimized as in custom design. Secondly, the AND and OR arrays of the PLA were designed to utilize minimum technology dimensions. The choice of a PLA over an equivalent random macro was decided after the number of used crosspoints or devices was known to comprise at least 15% of the total crosspoints, based on our experience with previous designs.

The reader will note that the chip described here does not even approach the circuit densities of the most recent custom microprocessors such as the Motorolla 68000 [because the 68000 is manufactured using the more advanced technology HMOS (high-density short-channel MOS)]. HMOS circuit design techniques provide four times the speed-power product and twice the density of the standard NMOS technology (11). The question of extendability is, therefore, a valid one. One limitation of our verification approach is that the hardware model for a chip must not exceed 6 or 7 cards (about 350 modules) or it will become unwieldy. Therefore, as the target technology improves, so must the prototype technology. This has happened for the case of the PLA macros where the LPLA (to be described in the next section) has been developed. Its capability (see third column of Table 8-2) significantly exceeds that of the FPLA. Similarly, advances in off-the-shelf modules for the random macros e.g., greater function, more I/Os, and programmability, would be desirable in the future to prevent the hardware model from becoming too large. Another limitation is the possibility that because of human error, the LSI data base may not reflect precisely the same function as the prototype, despite the precautions outlined previously. We believe this risk is worth taking because of the schedule and resource savings, and therefore we recently applied our methodology to the design of a complex logic chip containing twice as many circuits as the eight-bit microprocessor and approaching the density of currently available microprocessors. In this case, the chip functioned properly when received from manufacturing with the exception of four minor logical errors which were not all discovered until the chip had been tested thoroughly in its ultimate application. Interestingly, three of the four errors were traced to a mismatch between the LSI design and the prototype. Nonetheless, the first-pass hardware was adequate for stress testing and as a result, a two-pass design was achieved.

LASER PERSONALIZATION OF PLAS

As indicated in the introduction, our design approach to VLSI has evolved over a period of time and is still evolving. At the time the eight-bit microprocessor used as the example was in development, our laser tool and the LPLA were in a very early state of development. This is why field programmable PLAs were used to implement the control circuits of the hardware simulator previously described. Today, the laser tool and the LPLA are being used to do hardware modeling with very rapid turnaround times, i.e., personalization of an entire module in 20 minutes.

The laser tool used in IBM consists of a pulsed dye laser pumped by a pulsed ultraviolet nitrogen laser, beam optics, precision x/y/z table combined with a $\theta/\emptyset 1 /\emptyset 2$ tower assembly, a TV viewer (microscope, TV camera and TV receiver), a laser energy monitor, and a control unit. The tool is driven by an IBM 5100 transportable computer (12). The dye laser produces several-nanosecond light pulses with a peak power of up to several kilowatts. These pulses are attenuated by an achromatic halfwave plate, and delivered to the optical system by a high speed electro-optic shutter. Figure 8-6 shows the schematic of the laser tool.

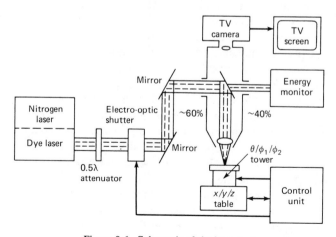

Figure 8-6. Schematic of the laser tool.

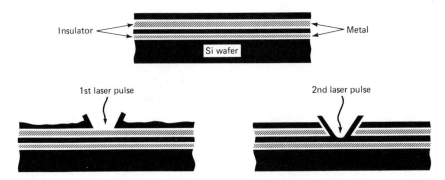

Figure 8-7. Connection of two metal layers by means of a laser beam.

A logical "1" can be personalized on a semiconductor chip by connecting a transistor to a crosspoint. This is accomplished by the welding of two overlapping layers of interconnection metalurgy at the crosspoint with a sequence of laser pulses (13, 14). A model for this connection process is shown in Figure 8-7. Only 5% of the incident laser peak power of the first pulse is typically absorbed at the upper aluminum surface. The remaining 95% is reflected.

The aluminum in the immediate area is removed primarily by vaporization (i.e., the energy of the laser is converted to thermal energy causing the aluminum to vaporize) leaving a circular opening. Surface tension of the molten metal also gives rise to a small ridge around the opening. Experiments have shown that for the 10 nanosecond pulse duration of the dye laser, 50 watts of peak power are needed to make a hole in 1.25 μm thick aluminum film.

The interlayer quartz insulator SiO2 beneath the hole is generally left unscathed by the initial laser pulse. The second laser pulse passes through the quartz unattenuated because quartz (glass) is transparent to the laser wavelength. Its energy is absorbed at the quartz-metal interface so that the aluminum at the interface becomes molten and vaporizes. The heat and pressure that is generated cause thermal stress to build in the quartz layer above, which is relieved by a localized micro-explosion, expelling the quartz through the hole in the top metal. With the sudden removal of the quartz, a pressure differential flows molten metal up the sidewalls, bridging the gap between the aluminum levels and forming a connection. The resistance of welds such as these are governed by the thickness of the metal layers and the separating quartz, i.e., the amount of metal available to form the weld and the surface area which it must cover. Equally important is the laser power which must be controlled carefully to ensure repeatable connections. Typically, a $\pm 2\%$ energy stability is called for. Figure 8-8 shows process windows for three AL/SiO2 configurations. Note that in each case an optimum input laser energy exists which will form a weld with minimum resistance. Below this power the weld is not completely formed, and at higher power levels the weld is deteriorated by vaporization. Increasing the interlayer quartz requires a greater incident laser power to make a good weld. Decreasing the thickness of the aluminum so that less metal is available to form the weld reduces the laser power needed.

For the cases shown in Figure 8-8 two laser pulses were used to form the welds. A single laser pulse regardless of incident peak power was insufficient, and typically three pulses or more damaged the underlying topology.

The LPLA used for building functional macros for modeling VLSI hardware, or for building early engineering models, consists of input latches, bit partitioning circuits, an AND array, an OR array, output latches, and off-chip drivers. The PLA can be programmed to operate as a large PLA or as two small PLAs. Table 8-2 shows the characteristics of the PLA. It performs both combinatorial and sequential logic and is equivalent to a 600-logic-gate master slice. The laser personalization technique enables us to reduce power dissipation both by programming the load resistor values to half or three-quarters maximum value, depending on the circuit loading, and by disconnecting the unused circuits on the chip. This is accomplished respectively, by welding

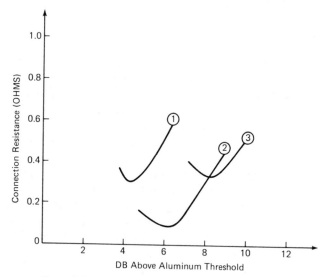

Notes: Pulse Width = Ions, AL Threshold = 15 Watts

Curve	Thickness of Total	Thickness of SIO$_2$	Thickness of Bottom AL	Dimensions in μM
1	1.05	1.4	.84	
2	1.25	1.4	.84	
3	1.25	1.8	.84	

Figure 8-8. Process windows for connection resistance versus laser power for welding different configurations of two aluminum lines.

selected resistor contact terminals and by welding current-source circuits to ground. In addition, the user has the following programmable options:

- Gated or ungated input latches.
- One—or two—bit partitioning.
- Up to a maximum of 160 product terms.
- Output latches
  —JK flip-flop
  —gated clock polarity hold
  —two way AND input polarity hold
  —exclusive OR input polarity hold.
- Off-chip drivers—
  three—state
  push—pull
  open—collector.
- Normal or inverted output.
- One or two clock design.

These features plus the 16,320 programmable sites in the array, dictate a modest chip size of 6.85 mm. The chip is solder-ball mounted to a 100-pin, 28-mm metalized ceramic substrate with a hole in the center.

In our first attempt at personalization and testing, chips were pretested on the wafer, personalized, and tested functionally. The wafer was then diced, and the chips were packaged on the module and tested. However, the yield and turnaround times of this method were unsatisfactory. To improve the situation we developed a new technique we call in-line lasering and testing (ILLT), explained below.

Pretested modules having good peripheral circuits (the unpersonalized array cannot be tested) are stockpiled to be ready for lasering and testing at the module level. Personalization patterns are processed to obtain two separate sets of data: x-y coordinates for the laser personalization step and test patterns. A high-speed link is used to transmit these data from an IBM System 370 to the IBM 5100 at the laser tool. The module is placed in a special fixture which permits the chip to be lasered through the hole in the center of the substrate while the module pins are connected to the 5100. First the X,Y coordinates position the laser to personalize the chip; then the test patterns are applied to the module while output signals are recorded and compared to the expected results stored in the 5100. The laser tool system is programmed such that if one PLA product term is in error, it either can be immediately repaired by repeating the laser pulses for that term, or deleted, by adding welds such that the product term can never be selected; e.g., personalizing all the crosspoints for that term. If a product term is deleted, the same personalization can be automatically applied to and retested at the next row of the array, so that even though the number of personalized crosspoints (and hence welds) is large, the yield will be good. This process is repeated again and again until all the product terms or rows are laser personalized and test as "good." It takes only 20 minutes to complete a module, including module-alignment time. The module yield using the ILLT technique was improved by a factor of from two to seven over our initial method. The larger the number of welds on a chip, the greater the yield improvement.

The major advantage of LPLAs is the ability to produce high-function hardware rapidly in a heavy design change environment. A disadvantage is that because of the high overhead costs of the laser equipment (space and maintenance) and relatively low throughput, LPAs are expensive. FPLAs such as those used in the microprocessor model can also be used to achieve rapid turnaround and are less costly than the LPLA. However, commercially available FPLAs do not contain the function of the LPLA, as can be seen by comparing the characteristics of a new higher functionality bipolar FLPA (15) with the LPLA (see Table 8-2). This is because FPLA technologies such as fusible link or junction punch-through require additional circuitry for personalization. In deciding which type of PLA to chose for modeling, one must therefore consider not only the cost but also by how much the increased function will simplify hardware modeling.

For the future, the laser tool can be modified to achieve smaller beam size by using a tighter optical system and a different dye to change the wavelength of the laser output. The table within the laser tool also can be improved to obtain higher resolution and accuracy by implementing a more sensitive position detector and a better mechanical structure. These improvements and thinner quartz and metal layers on the semiconductor chip would make it possible to create smaller laser welds i.e., to decrease their size from about 5-7μm to 1-2μm geometries thus providing a future laser personalization technique compatible with 1 to 2 μm mask geometries.

LASER REPAIR OF VLSI CHIPS

The laser tool for personalizing PLAs which we have described has been used to rapidly repair and modify the wiring structures of fully fabricated chips. Design alterations have been made on microprocessor, memory, and master slice logic chips without the need for totally recreating the parts with a new, corrected mask set.

As was previously described, the laser tool forms a weld between two overlying conductors separated by an insulting layer (Figure 8-7), a situation which might exist if an interconnection between layers of metal was inadvertently left out of a via personalization mask. During the development cycle of the IBM 3081 CPU, repair of this kind was made on a high-speed cache memory chip. A yield problem in early hardware was traced to a second-to-third-level metal

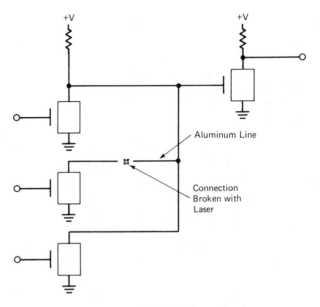

Figure 8-9. "Dot" OR circuit modification.

via which had been omitted from the mask set. In order to verify this as the problem, the conductors were "welded" in the appropriate location using the laser tool. Thus, the problem was solved in three days vs. a conventional turn-around time on the standard processing line of three months.

Selected conductor patterns can be deleted by utilizing the vaporization capability of the laser. This type of correction enabled us to proceed with the testing of the eight-bit microprocessor with the first-pass chips. Specifically, one of the inputs to a "dot" OR circuit had the wrong polarity, making it active at the wrong time. The OR circuit was deactivated by breaking an aluminum segment of this input with the laser (Figure 8-9). Additional TTL modules were next added to the card containing the chip, to perform the intended function. We were then able to run the same six million instructions that tested the model against the chip.

The deletion technique has also proved effective in diagnosing faulty IC designs. The designer can use the laser tool to "dissect" portions of the chip wiring and isolate complete sections of a chip. This was done on a masterslice chip designed as a logic level converter. In this case, the chip was mounted back-down in an empty module package and chip pads were wire bonded to module pins. The device was then powered up for electrical testing on the laser tool. While monitoring circuit outputs, the laser was used to delete aluminum interconnections, one after another, until the faulty one was uncovered. The defect proved to be a short in the chip wiring which resulted from a mask error. Usually, metal conductors are removed with a single 10-ns high-power laser pulse (100–500 W peak power) directed at the feature, generally without damage to underlying structures.

It is also possible to repair metal-to-metal via connections in which the resistance of the connection is too high due to incomplete formation of the via during processing. Vias like this can be locally sintered by using a medium-power laser pulse (20–50 W peak power). The advantage of this technique is that only the via is exposed to the high temperature, typically 300–400°C. The method was applied to a 64K (K = 1024) RAM chip during its development cycle when testing indicated high resistance paths in one portion of the chip. Several chips were corrected with the laser to provide hardware for the developers. Meanwhile, the problem was isolated to the via processing steps and solved.

One disadvantage of the vaporization and melting of metal films by the laser is that dimensions cannot usually be controlled to better than 2 or 3 μm. Rough elevated edges are frequently formed. If the deletion or weld to be made is beneath a passivation layer, that layer is frequently blown away, leaving microcracks in the surrounding area. These are fractures in the quartz of a few hundredths of a micron wide and a few microns long initially. A crack will tend to propagate across the chip, and when it passes under or above a metal line, the line distorts and breaks. The resulting chip topography is typically such that further planar processing steps are prohibited; hence, corrections must be made on completely finished devices. Another limitation of this type of correction is that a line to be deleted must be visible and not overlaid by another metallization level. Welds, on the other hand, can only be made between existing overlapping patterns. Additionally, the nature of these corrections limits their usage to short-lived development parts because the aluminum metallurgy is frequently exposed to the environment and is thus subject to corrosion. Microcracking of the dielectric layers could also present long-term stability problems. To circumvent these limitations, a series of techniques called *laser microsurgery* have been developed in which 1–2 μm geometries can be attained (16).

Laser microsurgery is the ability to focus the collimated light of the laser beam so that photosensitive materials such as photoresists are exposed in selected local areas of the wafer. In this way, new shapes on the wafer are generated. The schematic of the laser tool (Figure 8-6) shows that the system has all the basic components of an artwork generator: a computer-controlled positioning table, a focused source of ultraviolet energy (the laser), and an aperature or exposure size control. It is therefore possible to perform on-chip pattern generation, providing the circuit designer with a freedom not found in the previous weld/delete method, or for that matter, in current batch processing. The designer can define new and unique shapes on the surface of chips

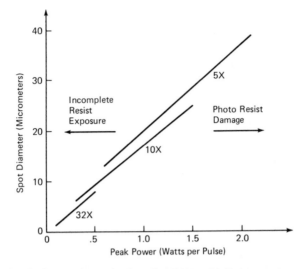

Figure 8-10. Graph of exposed spot size (in AZ - 1350J resist film) versus laser power for different lens magnification.

during any stage of processing *without* the use of a master mask by exposing a resist with the laser. By successively pulsing the laser and controlling table motion, complex patterns can be exposed.

Since the wavelength of our dye laser is 420 nm (stilbene-3 dye), it is well within the spectral sensitivity of most resits. The energy density needed to expose a film such as AZ-1350J [17] is 60 mJ/cm^2. The objective lens (Lietz 32X) of the laser tool focuses the laser beam to a 1-μm-diameter spot so that a 10-ns, 60-mW laser pulse suffices to expose the film. At low power levels (60-500 mW peak power) the diameter of the exposed spot is proportional to the incident laser power, providing an aperature capability. The spot diameter varies from about 1 to 9 μm at a rate of 70 mW per micrometer of diameter. To achieve larger spot sizes, a lower magnification lens may be used. Alternately, the incident laser peak power may be increased to insure more complete exposure as shown in Figure 8-10.

An example of the use of laser microsurgery to correct a minor defect is the unwanted short in the logic level converter chip previously cited. Once the defect had been determined (by the high-power laser deletion techniques) wafers of this design were stopped in the process cycle. Following exposure and development of the metal-pattern resist image in which the defect resided, the resist was exposed again in the region of the defect using the laser tool. This was done on each chip site of the wafer. Following development, the aluminum pattern was etched as usual, the short being removed at the same time as the rest of the excess metal. The wafer could then be further processed with passivation quartz and pad metallurgy as if no defect had ever existed. Such a change could also be made by regenerating the mask or by creating a special contact mask to expose just the defect area. A designer's choice between these alternatives would be driven by turnaround time. Layout and mask generation can take days to weeks, whereas the laser exposure can be accomplished in a matter of hours. The real-time television monitoring of the laser tool, in conjunction with the instantaneous positional readout of the x-y table, allows the designer to make *in-situ* measurements right on the TV screen, and then program the 5100 so that the laser will write the new pattern, step to the next chip, and repeat. Corrections can be made at any level of the device processing cycle, i.e., during ion implantation, diffusion, oxide, isolation, via etch, or metallization. Deletions and additions to the interconnection patterns of a chip can take place after processing is completed. The addition of conductors is accomplished by the use of a stencil or metal-lift-off process. If a metallic film is evaporated over the exposed and developed resist film, the metal in the bottom of the exposed region comes in contact with the substrate to form the conductor. Due to the vertical sidewalls of the resist image (Figure 8-11) formed by the monochromatic coherent nature of the laser, the metal is noncontinuous at the pattern edge. The photoresist is then dissolved away, removing the residual metal and leaving the conductor behind.

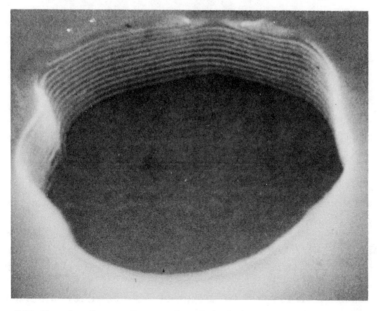

Figure 8-11. Scanning electron microscope image of laser-exposed spot in an AZ-1350J resist film.

Photoresist patterns for line additions

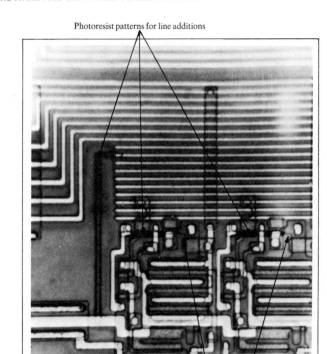

Al line deletions

(a)

Figure 8-12. A. Laser-patterned resist film for the addition of new lines. Aluminum lines have been deleted as shown.

An example of line additions to a 256K CCD memory chip with two levels of metallurgy follows. The extra metal level improves the density and performance of this type of chip by facilitating cell interconnections; however, corrections to the first level metallurgy are more difficult. Corrections were begun immediately after first level processing. Figure 8-12 (a) shows the exposed and developed resist pattern where lines are to be added. The results of the lift-off step are shown in Figure 8-12b.

A contact or via from the 1st level metal to a diffused region was omitted from the masks for this chip. By using a two-step microsurgery process, an opening in the oxide was made with one resist pattern and an etch step. A metal

Al lines added

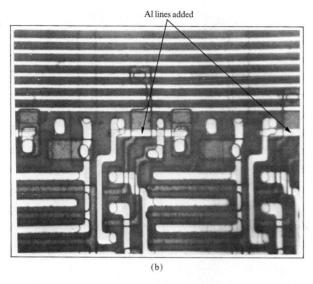

(b)

Figure 8-12. (continued)   B. New aluminum lines added to the chip by metal evaporation and lift-off.

contact and interconnection pattern was then defined with a second resist layer and the metal lift-off step. Other alterations to the first level personality included the removal of portions of lines and their subsequent rerouting by use of metal lift-off, simple deletions of unwanted lines, and the addition of an interconnection omitted on the mask. The wafer then received further processing, interlayer passivation, and second-level metal. Testing at the second level uncovered further defects on both the first and second levels of metallization. Line additions were made to the second level, and in three places, deletions for diagnostic purposes were made on buried first-level metal lines. In all, microsurgery was repeated on the same wafer thirteen separate times, with electrical testing between each step to point out new faults. After the thirteen corrections were made, all significant portions of the chip had been made operational and functionally tested. The corrections were then incorporated in a second pass of the design, which yielded totally functional parts. The corrections and the associated problem determination and testing was accomplished over a period of three months. Assuming that the corrections could also be accomplished with only three passes through the usual process steps, between 10 and 15 months would be required to obtain functional chips.

RESULTS AND CONCLUSIONS

A comparison of the PLA/laser personalization approach discussed in this chapter with an estimate of a conventional approach for the microprocessor we

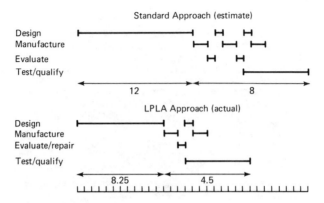

Figure 8-13. LSI productivity for the eight-bit microprocessor. The numbers refer to man-years and each division on the horizontal scale is one month. The net savings were 7.25 man-years and eight months.

have designed is shown in Figure 8-13. The result was a savings of 7.25 man-years and 8 months of processing time, and a two-pass design (excluding yield-enhancement passes). The savings reflect the use of PLA macros, the dual hardware-software modeling approach, and the ability to correct an error on the chip with the laser tool. An LPLA chip for hardware modeling can be personalized rapidly with good yields and meets present and future capacity requirements. Laser microsurgery is being used to eliminate time-consuming passes through the process line, and as a diagnostic tool to aid in the rapid isolation and definition of errors.

We conclude that the use of PLA structures, particularly in the control portion of a VLSI microprocessor improves design productivity, shortens design time, simplifies the physical design of the chip, and facilitates the implementation of design changes. The combination of a hardware simulator in conjunction with computer simulation greatly increases the probability that the VLSI chip will perform its intended function within specifications. The use of the laser tool is invaluable in correcting errors in VLSI chips. All of the above factors combine to provide operable first-pass hardware so that millions of instructions can be run to detect very subtle code sequence problems prior to final release of the masks to manufacturing. A two-pass design is therefore highly probable.

ACKNOWLEDGMENTS.

The authors gratefully acknowledge the efforts of W. D. Benedict and R. W. Bartoldus for developing the hardware modeling capability, S. E. Bello and P. W. Oman for their contributions to the design of the microprocessor, and D. A. Conrad, R. L. Golden, P. A. Latus and E. Lindbloom for their design automation programs.

The laser work described in this chapter was based on research undertaken at the IBM Yorktown Laboratory beginning in 1971. This work, summarized in references (13), (14), and (15), recognized the ability to form micron-sized connections between surfaces separated by an insulating layer. The requisite parameters for such connections, without damage to the peripheral circuitry, resulted from these early studies. Connections included Al to Si and Al to Al through SiO_2 insulating layers. Also, "opens" or disconnections were created in both Al and polysilicon lines. Modeling of the laser connection process was undertaken based on results from in-situ connection time experiments and SEM investigations of cross-sectioned connections. Finally, extensive life testing demonstrated excellent reliability for laser formed connections.

We thank W. A. Lyons for his early laser experiments, R. C. Flaker and J. P. Maslack for the design of the laser personalizable bipolar PLA, and the many individuals in the IBM Burlington and Kingston facilities who contributed to and supported this work. The contributions of A. J. Griest to laser microsurgery are much appreciated.

REFERENCES AND NOTES

(1) Stritter, Edward and Gunter, Tom. "A Microprocessor Architecture for a Changing World: The Motorola 68000." *IEEE Computer* **12, No. 2:** 43–52 (1979); Robert Sugerman, "Computers: Our 'Microuniverse' Expands." *IEEE Spectrum* **16:** 32–37 (1979).

(2) Shima, Masatoshi, "Demystifying Microprocessor Design." *IEEE Spectrum* **16:** 22–30 (1979).

(3) Robinson, Arthur L. "Are VLSI Microcircuits Too Hard to Design?" *Science* **209:** 258–262 (1980).

(4) Davis, C. M., Maley, G. A., Simmons, R. G., Stoller, H. I., Warren, R. H., and Wohr, T. E. "IBM System/370 Bipolar Gate Array Micro-Processor Chip." *Proceedings of the IEEE International Conference on Circuits and Computers* ICCC80, Port Chester, NY, (Oct. 1–3, 1980): 669–673.

(5) Signetics 8A1200 ISL gate array, Signetics Corporation, 811 East Arques Ave., P.O. Box 409, Sunnyvale, CA 94086.

(6) Feuer, M., Khokhani, K. H., and Mehta, D. A. "The Layout and Wiring of a VLSI Microprocessor." Ref. 4, loc. cit., pp. 678–679.

(7) Fleisher, H., and Maissel, L. I. "An Introduction to Array Logic." *IBM J. Res. Develop.* **19:**98 (1975).

(8) Signetics 82S100 FPLA, address as in Ref. 5.

(9) Data I/O Model X FPLA programmer, Data I/O Corporation, Commack Road, Commack, L.I., NY.

(10) Newberry, S. and Russell, P. J. "A Programmable Checking Tool for LSI." *Proceedings of IEEE England Conference,* (Sept. 1–4, 1981), report in publication.

(11) *MC68000, 16-Bit Microprocessor User's Manual.* Motorola Semiconductor Products Inc., 3501 Ed Bluestein Blvd., Austin, Texas, 78721.

(12) Feder, M. P., Smith, J. F., and Liberman, H. E. "Nitrogen-Pumped Dye Laser Tool for Fabricating LSI Connections." *Digest of Technical Papers, Conference on Laser and Electro-Optical Systems II,* San Diego, CA, (February 7–9, 1978); Optical Soc. of America, 2000 K St. NW, Washington, DC 20036.

(13) Cook, P. W., Schuster, S. E., and von Gutfeld, R. J., "Connections and Disconnections on Integrated Circuits Using Nanosecond Laser Pulses." *Appl. Phys. Lett.* **26:** 124–26 (1975).

(14) Kuhn, Lawrence, Schuster, Stanley E., Zory, Peter S. Jr., Lynch, George W., and Parrish, James T., "Experimental Study of Laser Formed Connections for LSI Wafer Personalization." *IEEE J. Solid-State Circuits* **SC-10:** 219–228 (1975).

(15) NEC uPB450D, Nippon Electric Company Ltd., Tokyo, Japan.

(16) Moulic, J. Randal and Kleinfelder, Walter J. "Direct IC Pattern Generation by Laser Writing." *1980 IEEE International Solid-State Circuits Conference ISSCC80 Digest of Technical Papers* **23:** 210–211 (1980).

(17) AZ is a registered trademark of American Hoechst Corp., Route 202-206 No., Somerville, NJ 08876. Their licensed distributer is the Shipley Corp., Newton, MA.

9. VLSI Superconducting Technologies

S. M. Faris

IBM Corporation

INTRODUCTION

The significance of VLSI has been manifestly emphasized throughout this book. High logic power, $\approx$ 10k circuits/chip, and high memory capacity, $\approx$ 1 M bits/chip, are among its promises. If these chips are packaged densely, then it is reasonable to expect, in principle at least, that faster general purpose computers would be manufactured. The performance of such computers is measured in Millions of Instructions Per Second, MIPS. For instance, IBM's newest computer, the 3081, is rated at $\approx$ 10 MIPS, which represents nearly a factor of 2 improvement over its predecessor, the 3033. These systems are based on LSI technologies. In the VLSI era, the following questions can be posed while speculating on the future of computers. 1) Can a factor of 10 or more improvement in performance be achieved? 2) What VLSI technology is likely to realize that goal? 3) Are there readily identifiable obstacles which significantly hinder that goal? While it is easy to ask these and perhaps other questions, no one possesses a crystal ball for predicting the future and providing complete answers. Computers are complex systems which are built by a large group of people trained in diverse disciplines such as physics, engineering and computer sciences. In this chapter, some of the answers are provided based on definite statements that can be made by invoking known physical laws, accepted engineering practices and ultimately considering economic realities. Tracing the evolution of Josephson computer circuits is the approach I am taking to illustrate examples of many engineering considerations which have to be accommodated in order to exploit VLSI tools for the purpose of realizing an ultra-high performance computer. This chapter is not meant to survey exhaustively every aspect of cryo-electronic technologies, rather, the main thrust is to achieve the following objectives: 1) Present a general discussion of the limitations of known computer switching elements in order to justify investigating superconductive devices and the role they may play in those future ultra-high performance computers. 2) Introduce superconductive devices, logic and memory circuits emphasizing the influence of their basic properties on maintaining their promising performance. 3) Illustrate, by means of examples, the practical considerations which lead to optimum designs and perhaps stimulate invention of new devices and circuits. 4) Emphasize that in order to qualify as building blocks for ultra-high performance computers, the switching devices in general must satisfy *simultaneously* certain physical and engineering requirements.

GENERAL REQUIREMENTS AND LIMITATIONS

The fundamental limitations of the computing process, and the future evolution of computers have been discussed by many authors (1–6). Landauer (3) focused his attention on the switching devices and the physical properties that they must possess in order to perform error-free logic operations. He recognized that in order to improve the performance of logic devices we have three choices. The first is to reduce the size of the silicon transistors. This has been pursued vigorously leading to present VLSI technologies. For instance, recently, a MOSFET with channel length of 0.3 μm and intrinsic switching speed $\approx$ 30 ps has been reported (7). The second choice is to make transistors from other semiconducting materials which have higher mobilities. This is manifested in the rapidly growing GaAs transistor effort (8, 9) which has demonstrated a switching speed of 17 ps, and further improvements are anticipated by a combination of smaller structures and lower operating temperatures (10). The third choice is to invent new transistors using novel operating principles. Landauer provided a recipe (3) for inventing new types of transistors and predicted, for example, that quasiparticles and pairs may be the ingredients in superconducting transistors which play the roles of minority and majority carriers in bipolar transistors. Recently, Gray (11) has demonstrated a small signal current gain in a superconducting device in which quasiparticles and pairs play their predicted roles. Independently, the author (12) proposed and demonstrated the QUITRON which is a transistor-like superconducting switch based on heavy injection of quasiparticles to break pairs and subsequent suppression to zero of the superconducting gap. The success of these new devices and those not yet invented hinges on whether or not they fulfill specific requirements discussed below. In his discussion of the fundamental limits of digital information processing, Keyes (6) stresses the importance of chip power dissipation, the heat removal from packages, the role interconnections play in VLSI, and the physical limitations of the devices themselves as they are scaled down in size. Realizing that semiconducting transistors are being pushed to their limits, inventing new devices may no longer be a choice; rather, it may be the only avenue left which leads to the realization of an ultra-high performance machine.

In the era during which VLSI tools exist, we may find ourselves compelled to depart from the *traditional mode,* that of building systems from existing devices, and instead adopt a *new mode,* that of specifying the system characteristics first, and then invent device and package technologies which meet those specifications. The following is an attempt to use this *new mode* to the design of a hypothetical future general purpose computer capable of 500 MIPS. This is an example used to unravel the limitations and constraints that must be accommodated by the device and package technologies we will have to invent for this system. This exercise leads to the conclusion that superconducting devices will inevitably play a significant role in future systems owing to their intrinsically low power dissipation. Although performance enhancement by means of optimized architecture is not precluded, we assume for our example that the architecture of IBM 3081 still prevails.

Computer Scientists' Requirements

Given the objective of a 500 MIPS mainframe, the computer architect (13) reveals that the Central Processing Unit, CPU, would require a cycle time τ_{cpu} $\approx$ 660 ps, assuming 3 cycles are needed to execute an instruction. He requires $\sim$ 300K logic circuits (K = 1024) each having an average delay $\tau_l \approx \frac{1}{10}\tau_{cpu}$ $\approx$ 66*ps*, and a cache capacity of 64KB (B is a byte = 8 bit) at a cycle time $\tau_c \approx \tau_{cpu}$ and an access time $\tau_{ca} \approx \frac{1}{3}\tau_{cpu} \approx 220ps$. He also computes main memory capacity of 250MB-500MB at a cycle time $\tau_M \approx 6.6$ ns.

Physical Requirements

Assuming that the cache path delay is the bottle-neck of the system, and if 50% of this delay, 330 ps, is due to the propagation of the address and data signals at $\approx$ 100 ps/cm, it is immediately obvious that we require a 3-dimensional package about 1 cm^3 which contains the cache memory chips, logic chips, and their interconnections. Since it is necessary to dissipate power in order to carry out the logic operations (1), an inevitable temperature rise, ΔT, of this package results. This has to be maintained at a tolerable level otherwise the system will either operate erratically or cease to operate altogether. Clearly devices dissipating more than 1 mW (readily available fast transistors) lead to a total power dissipation in the order of a 1000 W within our 1 cm^3 package. This poses a challenge to heat removal specialists. Cooling of actual VLSI chips by forced convection using liquids at optimum flow rates are limited to tens of watts per cm^2. Assuming that $\frac{2}{3}\tau_M \approx 4.4ns$ is the propagation delay within main memory package, and $\frac{1}{3}\tau_M \approx 2.2ns$ is the main memory chip access time, the package would have a volume $\approx$ (12 cm) (3). Realizing this with existing devices at a 1 M-bit/chip density would result in hundreds of kilo-watt power dissipation in such a small volume. Supplying this regulated power, its cost per year, and its removal from this package pose other challenges.

The circuit delay is given by: $\tau_l = \tau_d + \tau_{load}$ where, τ_d is the intrinsic switching delay of the device and τ_{load} is the delay which results when driving a useful load and depends on the fan-out number and the wire length needed. This load could be either resistive, when matched transmission lines are used, capacitive, as in the case of transistor circuits, or inductive as in the case of Josephson memory circuits. In most cases τ_{load} dominates. It is therefore clear from the above analysis that in order to realize our objective (500 MIPS), the device we need to invent must possess, simultaneously, the following physical properties: 1) ultra-fast switching speed $\approx$ 20 ps; 2) extremely low power dissipation a few μW; and 3) ultra-high density.

Engineering Requirements

While the above physical requirements are necessary, they are not sufficient. There are other engineering requirements (4) which must be fulfilled in order to guarantee the manufacturability of those memory and logic chips at a reasonable cost (yield) and error-free operation. The devices, the logic circuits and the memory cells are not identical. Their parameters vary to one degree or another as a result of imperfect line width control at the mask level, imprecise alignment between the various levels, irreproducible exposure and development of the resists, variations in the doping, material imperfections, variations in critical film thicknesses, bias variations, intrinsic noise, fluctuations in the environment, etc. The VLSI chip design is the combined effort of various people who deal with devices, circuits, process development, and characterization, and material specialists; all have the common goal of achieving high chip yield, Y_c = $(Y_{cir})(Y_{proc})$. The device and circuit properties determine Y_{cir}, where as the process related defects, shorts, opens, etc., determine Y_{proc}. The designers start with distributions of all these parameter variations and carry out statistical circuit analysis until they arrive at an optimum chip design. This process often involves many iterations, compromises, and trade-offs between performance and chip yield. Sometimes certain approaches are abandoned when insurmountable problems and inadequacies are discovered.

Certain device and circuit properties are known to the engineer to give better yields than others. Among the properties (4) which play significant roles are: devices with three terminals; high gain; inversion; non-latching; good isolation between the input and output stages; high non-linearity; high discrimination between the levels representing binary 1 and 0; high noise immunity; and the ability to standardize the levels. Figure 9-1 illustrates graphically a few of such desirable properties. The dashed region represents all possible variations in the device parameters. The inverter, Figure 9-1a, shows that the output in the 1

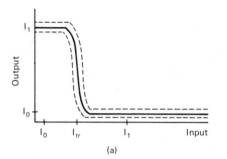   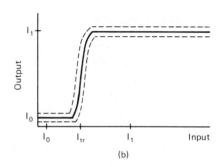

(a)   (b)

Figure 9-1. Input-output characteristic of switchable devices showing sharp non-linearity, level standardization, and parameter variation tolerance; (a) inverting; (b) non-inverting.

state I_1 remains stable as long as the input is at the zero level, I_0. In this specific case the level I_0 can vary significantly between 0 and a threshold value, I_{tr}, without affecting the stable state I_1, indicating good noise immunity and good tolerance to parameter variations. As the input exceeds the threshold, the device abruptly switches to the other stable state, I_0. From this illustration, it is clear that such a non-linear element possesses these desirable qualities: absence of hysteresis; ability to standardize levels; high discrimination ratio, $I_1/I_0 \gg 1$ and $I_{tr}/I_0 \gg 1$. Non-hysteretic devices operate in the non-latching mode which has many advantages, for example, the ability to invert. Esaki diodes (14) and Josephson junctions (28, 32, 86, 87), belong to the class of hysteretic devices which operate in the latching mode.

Non-inverting devices have the input-output characteristic shown in Figure 9-1b, i.e., the output is in the 0 state as long as the input is also in the 0 state, and it switches to the 1 state when an input larger than the threshold is applied. Devices capable of inversion have a fundamental advantage which is crucial to circuit design. They can be used to construct multi-input NOR circuits from which *all* logic and memory operations can be implemented. For example if we apply the inputs A, B, and C to a NOR circuit, we obtain the output $\overline{A + B + C}$ which upon inverting yields, $A + B + C$, the OR function. To obtain the AND function, $\overline{A}$, $\overline{B}$, *and* $\overline{C}$ are applied to the NOR circuit yielding $A.B.C$. In the latter case DeMorgan's theorem has applied, i.e., $\overline{A + B + C} = \overline{A}.\overline{B}.\overline{C}$. On the other hand, the non-inverting case, Figure 9-1b, allows construction of multi-input OR function, and with some restrictions, the AND function but is unable to implement the necessary invert function. Transistors have many of the desirable properties (4) represented by Figure 9-1a whereas Esaki diodes (14) do not. Because they lack those transistor-like properties that engineers require, Esaki diodes have not qualified as computer elements, even though they can be made faster, denser and dissipate lower power than transistors.

Economic Considerations

In addition to constraints imposed by the computer scientists, the physicists and the engineers, there are others which are dictated by the marketplace. The cost is influenced by the chip yield, the testability, the reliability, maintainability, and many more considerations which are necessary to obtain long periods of error-free operation of our hypothetical 500 MIPS machine.

The Prospects of Future Semiconducting Transistors

The performance of transistor circuits (5, 6) is measured by their power dissipation $p_l = IV$, their average delay $\tau_l = (C_d + C_L)V/2I$, and switching energy $E_l = p_l\tau_l = \frac{1}{2}(C_d + C_L)V^2$, where C_d and C_L are respectively the device and load capacitances, V is the voltage swing, and I is the device current. Miniaturization leads to improved device performance mainly as a result of reducing the capacitance since the voltage is constrained to be nearly constant by the non-linearity and noise immunity requirements (4–6), i.e., $eV/kT \gg 1$. The reduction in device area and the increase in the number of circuits lead to an increase in current density, power density and total chip power. The possible enhancement in device and circuit performance is realizable by pushing transistor technologies to their limits at the expense of power dissipation, increased device and wiring resistance, electromigration, hot electron and breakdown phenomena, punchthrough, large fluctuation in impurity concentration, and yield (6). Using submicron lithographic techniques, transistors with impressive speeds have been reported (7). For instance, silicon MOSFET with channel length of .3 μm has intrinsic switching speed of 30 ps with a power dissipation of 1.3 mW, and GaAs MESFET (8) with a channel length of .6 μm has a switching speed of 30 ps dissipating 1.9 mW at room temperature and 17 ps when cooled to 77 K. While these fast transistors will undoubtedly be found in numerous applications (9), their high power dissipation may not satisfy the one major physical requirement, i.e., low power dissipation, for our hypothetical ultra-high performance computer.

THE POTENTIAL OF SUPERCONDUCTING DEVICES

In order to break the power dissipation bottle-neck, a drastic reduction in the operating voltage must be realized. However, since our non-linearity requires that $eV/kT \gg 1$, a proportionate decrease in the operating temperature is necessary (6). Since semiconducting transistors benefit only slightly by lowering their operating temperatures below 77, our objectives might be met by turning to totally different technologies utilizing novel device concepts. It is therefore justified to seriously investigate devices based on superconducting phenomena

(16–19) which occur near the convenient temperature of 4.2K, the boiling point of liquid helium. The operating voltages would be in the mV range which is of the order of typical superconducting energy gaps. Exploiting superconductivity may be necessary to the realization of that hypothetical 500 MIPS computer because of the intrinsic low power dissipation it offers, an important prerequisite for that high performance dense package. In addition, there are other advantages in exploiting superconductivity such as: a) zero resistance eliminates power dissipation in the complex VLSI chip wiring and the interconnections within the package; b) high performance, terminated strip transmission lines having low enough dispersion to allow 10 ps pulses to propagate long distances without significant distortion (20); c) many thermally activated phenomena are frozen out, for example, alleviating the electromigration (6) problem will reflect in better reliability. We must keep in mind that the suitable superconducting devices we are going to invent must also meet those engineering requirements, for instance by possessing transistor-like properties.

Having justified the need to invent new devices for high ultra-high performance systems, in which superconductivity will play a role, the rest of this chapter deals with those engineering considerations emphasized by means of tracing the evolution of high performance logic and memory superconducting circuits based on the Josephson technology. The objective is to provoke thought, hoping to stimulate interest in the search for new devices which possess the desirable properties and avoiding those troublesome ones.

Superconductivity

Many metals and alloys become superconductors when their temperature drops below a critical value, T_c, which is 7.2K for lead, 9.2K for niobium, and 23K for Nb_3Ge. This phenomenon is characterized by perfect conductivity (21) (zero resistance) and nearly perfect diamagnetism (22) (the Meissner effect) i.e., the expulsion of magnetic field from within the superconductor. Current and fields exist only within a distance λ, which is called the penetration depth and is typically in the order of 1000Å. Another characteristic is the presence of an energy gap, Δ, separating the macroscopic ground state of the superconductor and its excited state (23). Superconductivity is destroyed if a critical current density j_c or a critical magnetic field H_c is exceeded. The parameters j_c, H_c, and Δ are temperature-dependent, having their maximum values at $T = 0$ and vanishing at $T = T_c$.

BCS theory provides a satisfactory explanation of those properties associated with superconductivity, by postulating that at low temperatures an attractive interaction exists which allows electrons of opposite spin near the Fermi level having equal and opposite momenta to condense into Cooper pairs. These correlated Cooper pairs make up the superconducting system which could be represented by a single macroscopic quantum mechanical wave function $\Psi = (n)^{1/2} \exp(i\phi)$ which obeys the Schrodinger equation, where $(n)^{1/2}$ is the Cooper pair density, and ϕ is the phase.

One manifestation of the macroscopic quantum state is flux quantization in superconducting rings. The flux which penetrates these rings has a value which is an integer multiple of the quantity $\Phi_o = h/2e$, called a fluxoid. Take the example of an applied flux Φ_a that penetrates a ring in its normal state. As this ring is cooled below its T_c, it becomes superconducting and the flux through it becomes quantized, e.g., $n\Phi_o$. If now Φ_a is turned off, those n fluxoids remain trapped indefinitely as a result of the Meissner effect, which prevents the flux from penetrating the superconducting ring so that it cannot escape. Such trapped flux is maintained by a persistent current $I_{per} = \dfrac{n\Phi_o}{L}$, circulating in the ring which has an inductance L. This phenomenon is the basis for memory applications in the cryotron (31) as well as in the Josephson technologies.

Tunneling

Tunneling is a quantum mechanical phenomenon which allows electrons to flow (tunnel) through insulating barriers. This is forbidden if the electron dynamics is treated by means of classical mechanics. The tunneling probability increases exponentially as the barrier thickness, t, is decreased (16). In Figure 9-2, a circuit is shown which consists of two superconductors S_1 and S_2, separated by t, a battery, a resistor, and an ammeter. The system S_1, S_2 and the barrier is given the name *tunnel junction*. The I-V characteristics of this junction change significantly depending on the barrier thickness and the temperature. Figure 9-2b shows that at room temperature and $t \approx 1$cm, no current is flowing. However, as t is decreased to 100Å a small current becomes measurable, and even more increase is obtained when t is further decreased to ~ 50Å. Note that these I-V curves are nearly linear when plotted in the voltage scale of 10mV, having a slope R_N which is called the normal tunnel resistance. If now the circuit is cooled below the transition temperatures, S_1 and S_2 become superconducting, developing, respectively, the gaps Δ_1 and Δ_2 and the I-V curve for $t = 50$Å becomes higly non-linear (24, 25) as shown in Figure 9-2c. The current rises sharply at $V = \Delta_1 - \Delta_2$, and at $V = \Delta_1 + \Delta_2$ which is a manifestation of the singularities in the BCS density of states (23–25). In addition to this so called quasiparticle tunneling or Giaever tunneling occurring at $V \neq 0$, Josephson predicted Cooper pair tunneling (26), which was later demonstrated by Rowell and Anderson (27). The Josephson effect shows up as a supercurrent flowing through the junction at $V = 0$ as long as the current does not exceed a critical value $I_m(H)$. Rowell (28) demonstrated that by applying a magnetic field, H, the junction can be switched between the Josephson branch, $V = 0$, and the resistive branch, $V \neq 0$.

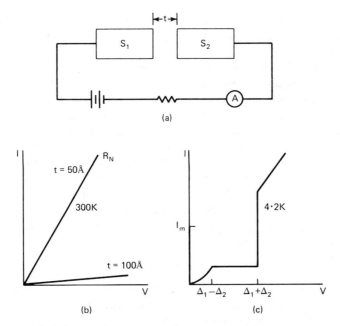

(a)

(b)

(c)

Figure 9-2.   Illustration of quantum mechanical tunneling; (a)- measuring circuit; (b)- I-V curve at $T = 300K$ for $t = 100\text{Å}$ and 50 Å; (c) I-V curve at 4.2K and $t \leq 50\text{Å}$.

DIGITAL APPLICATIONS OF SUPERCONDUCTIVITY

Cryotron Technology.   The Cryotron was the first superconducting switch used for digital applications (29–31). It is made of two superconducting films insulated from each other by a thick SiO layer (Figure 9-3a). The first film is biased by means of a gate current, I_g, below its critical current so that it remains in the $V = 0$ state. When a sufficient control current, I_c, is applied, the first film reaches its critical current and switches to its resistive state trans-

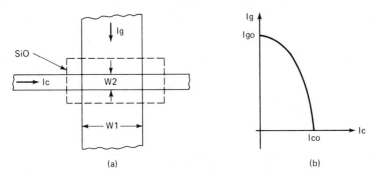

(a)   (b)

Figure 9-3.   (a)- Top view of a cryotron; (b)- switching threshold characteristic.

ferring I_g to the load. According to the switching characteristic of Figure 9-3b, the cryotron can have gain, i.e., $I_g/I_c > 1$, if the film widths are chosen such that $W_1/W_2 \gg 1$.

The cryotron thin film technology was developed and seriously considered for computer applications. Memory circuits were built using the trapped flux concept either in holes, in superconducting planes or in thin film loops containing cryotron switches. However, after nearly a decade, the promised cryotron fast switching speed did not materialize and further development of the technology was halted. Operating at cryogenic temperatures could hardly be justified then, especially at a time when the performance of transistors were improving steadily. The legacy of the cryotron technology is the introduction of integrated circuit techniques which are still with us. The most notable benefits of these techniques are: 1) the possibility of fabricating the first Josephson junctions, thus launching, with relative ease, the Josephson technology as we know it today; and 2) the successful transfer of LSI experience to benefit transistor technologies.

Josephson Technology. Subsequent to the experimental demonstration of Josephson's predictions, Rowell immediately recognized the potential for practical applications. He observed the switching action between the supercurrent state and the resistive state by means of a control magnetic field, leading him

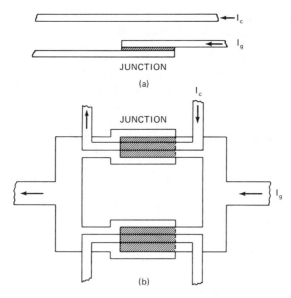

Figure 9-4. (a)- Cross section of a Josephson junction which can be switched by means of a control current I_c; (b)- a superconducting ring and two Josephson junctions form a flip-flop circuit.

to believe that tunnel junctions exhibiting the Josephson effect are suitable devices for logic operations. He was awarded a patent (32) for inventing Josephson junction logic for computer applications. Independently, and practically at the same time, Merriam (33) recognized the high speed potential of Josephson junctions and proposed the configurations shown in Figure 9-4, replacing in many already known circuits the relatively slow cryotrons with junctions while retaining the rest of the thin film cryogenic technology. In Figure 9-4b a superconducting ring is used as a memory cell; the information is represented by trapped flux which can be switched rapidly in and out of the ring by means of a control current for switching the junction in the ring. Through the AC Josephson effect, the high speed potential of Josephson junctions was verified experimentally (34) as early as 1963 when current steps at quantized voltages were induced by applying fields at microwave frequencies. Matisoo (35–37) reported sub-nanosecond switching of a flip-flop circuit similar to that proposed earlier by Merriam, Figure 9-4b. This speed coupled with the intrinsic low power dissipation renewed interest in superconducting technologies for computer applications. Ever since, the Josephson technology has been evolving at an accelerating pace (38, 39). Fairly complex memory (40–42) and logic (43–46) (97) circuits have been demonstrated. For example Figure 9-5 illustrates one of the complex fully functional circuits demonstrated so far. It is a 3-bit loop decoder (47) used with the cache memory which has a measured decoding delay of 30 ps per bit and has been demonstrated with a decoding delay as short as 20 ps per bit. This decoder incorporates a storage feature which allows the address information to be stored until decoding is initiated by means of a pulse generator. This generator produces a 1.3 mA current pulse 26 ps in duration (48). The shape of this pulse has been measured

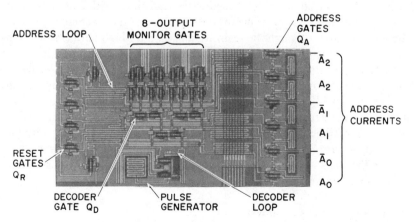

Figure 9-5. The loop decoder is one of the most complicated, fully operational circuit in the Josephson technology, after Ref. (47).

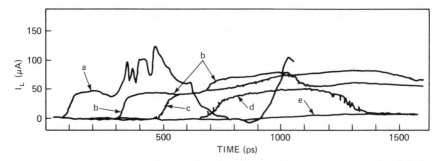

Figure 9-6. SQUID dynamics revealed in picosecond time scale by means of an ultra-high resolution. The current I_L is transferred to a matched strip line. The waveforms a-e are measured at the termination for decreasing values of the control current.

by a novel sampling technique (49–51). It has become an important tool for measuring fast signals connected with the development of Josephson circuits (53, 54). This tool has demonstrated time resolution of $\leq$ 6 ps (52) and sensitivity of $\sim 10\mu V$ (51). The time resolution is, in principle, extendible to the sub-picosecond time scale limited by the intrinsic response time (55) $\tau_i = \dfrac{\hbar}{2\Delta}$ of Josephson junctions. Figure 9-6 shows typical waveforms representing SQUID (see later section) switching dynamics measured for the first time by means of the sampling technique (51). These waveforms reveal that the internal resonances can interfere with switching and lead to a reduction in the current I_L transferred to the load R_L (see Figure 9-8a). The impact of this phenomenon is discussed below.

Greiner's invention of a process for the fabrication tunnel junctions reproducibly and the invention of superconducting lead alloys with reasonable metallurgical stability are responsible for the expansion of the Josephson computer program (59, 60). Although the realization of an ultra-high performance computer has been the primary objective, many areas dealing with non-computer applications (56) benefited from the Josephson technology research activities. Among these are the development of ultra-sensitive SQUIDs for applications in the medical field, geophysics and solid state physics (57); applying Josephson junctions in the generation, mixing, and parametric amplifications of microwaves (56), voltage standards (56); picosecond sampling (48–54); ultra-low noise temperature SIS mixers for astrophysical applications (58a); and many other applications (58b). These results show that the technology has already paid dividends in many ways and will have a lasting effect.

Josephson Junction Circuit Models

Figure 9-7 illustrates the fabrication steps (59) required for making a simple Josephson integrated circuit, Figure 9-8a, in lead-alloy junction technology.

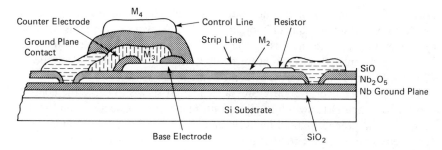

Figure 9-7. Cross-section (not to scale) revealing the Josephson fabrication needed to make the circuit in Figure 9-8a.

One starts with a silicon substrate on which a thick oxide is thermally grown and then covered with a ≈ 3000Å niobium ground plane (M_1). This is anodized to form a ≈ 350Å layer of Nb_2O_5 (I_{1A}) except for windows where a ground contact is to be made. Next, another insulating film of SiO, ≈ 1500Å, (I_{1b}) is deposited. This plays an important role in determining the electrical characteristics of the strip transmission lines. The resistor layer (R_1) made of indium-gold alloy is then deposited. Depending on its thickness it gives the required sheet resistance, e.g., 2 ohm/square. The base electrode made a 2000Å Pb-In-Au alloy (M_2) is deposited next. It is used not only to form the junction, but

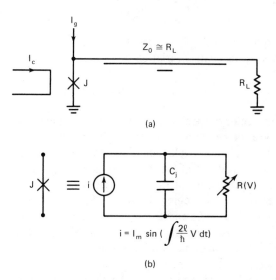

Figure 9-8(a). A simple Josephson technology circuit which consists of a Josephson device, J, a bias current I_g a control current, and a transmission line terminated with the load R_L. Applying the control causes the device to switch, transferring the waveform I_L to the load; (b) electrical model of the Josephson device.

also for wiring and making contact to the resistors. The junction area is defined by means of a window made of another 2500Å SiO layer (I_{2A}). In this window the tunnel barrier is formed using the method invented by Greiner (60). The junction is completed subsequent to the deposition of the counter-electrode, a 4000Å Pb-Bi alloy film (M_3). The control line made of 8000Å Pb-In-Au alloy (M_4) is deposited over a 5000Å SiO layer (I_3). It serves to carry the control current (the inputs) to switch the junctions, make interconnections, and make contact to the ground plane. Finally, a thick ~ 2 μm SiO passivation layer is deposited to protect the circuits. In Figure 9-8, the X is a symbol representing a single Josephson junction having the electrical equivalent circuit model in Figure 9-8b.

The tunneling barrier (Figure 9-2) is sufficiently thin (30–50Å) to allow pair current (Josephson tunneling current) to flow with zero resistance. This pair current is related to the phase difference ϕ between the superconducting electrodes by the Josephson relation:

$$I = I_m \sin \phi \qquad [9.1]$$

where I_m is the maximum current that can flow through the junction at zero voltage; this is also called the critical or threshold current. When the junction switches, a voltage is developed, which is related to ϕ by:

$$V = \frac{\Phi_0}{2\pi} \frac{d\phi}{dt} \qquad [9.2]$$

where the fluxoid $\Phi_0 = 2.07x10^{-15}$ *Vsec*. For a uniform tunnel junction with a barrier thickness t, the spatial variation of ϕ along the barrier is

$$\overline{\nabla}\phi = (2\mu_0 ed/\hbar)(\overline{H}X\overline{n}) \qquad [9.3]$$

where $\overline{n}$ is a unit vector perpendicular to the barrier and $d = \lambda_1 + \lambda_2 + t$ where λ_1 and λ_2 are the penetration depths of the two superconductors.

Equations [9.1–3] and Maxwells equations describe dynamics of the junctions and predict the sensitivity of the threshold current I_m to the magnetic field $\overline{H}$ produced by the control current I_c. The particular in-line junction geometry of Figure 9-9a leads to the switching threshold (I_m vs I_c) characteristic shown (87) in Figure 9-9b. The $I_m(I_c)$ curve draws the boundary between the $V = 0$ state (zero resistance state) and the $V \neq 0$ (resistive) state. Figure 9-9c is an I-V characteristic of the junction showing the pair tunneling branch ($V = 0$ *state*) and the single particle tunneling branch ($V \neq 0$ *state*). The latter is represented generally by a voltage dependent resistance $R_j(V)$. At the gap voltage $V_g = \dfrac{\Delta_1 + \Delta_2}{e}$ the current rises sharply and at large voltages the normal

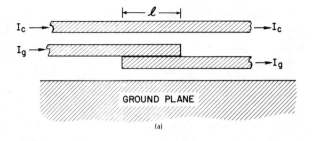

(a)

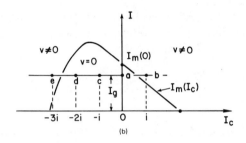

(b)

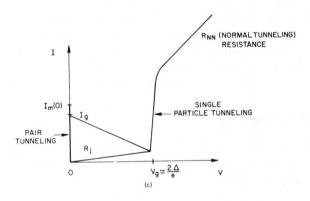

(c)

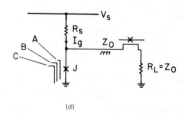

(d)

Figure 9-9. (a)- In-line gate Josephson junction configuration (87); (b)- asymmetric switching threshold characteristic $I_m(I_c)$; (c)- junction I-V characteristic; (d)- simple in-line gate logic circuit.

tunnel resistance R_{NN} is reached. For lead alloys $V_g \approx 2.8\ mV$, which is nearly 3 orders of magnitude lower than typical semiconducting gaps. In fact this accounts for the difference in power dissipation between Josephson junctions and semiconducting transistors. The junction is initially biased in the $V = 0$ state with a gate current $I_g < I_m(0)$. To switch it to the $V \neq 0$ state, the control current I_c is applied such that I_g becomes larger than $I_m(I_c)$, and according to Figure 9-9b, the $I_m(I_c)$ curve is crossed. The gate current is subsequently transferred to the load, R_L, (Figure 9c and d) where it is utilized to control other junctions in a serial fashion (serial fan-out). The load is designed such that the output voltage developed is $V_L \leq V_g$.

The tunnel barrier is responsible for the junction capacitance C_j which plays a crucial role in determining its switching characteristics. The externally supplied gate current I_g is divided according to

$$I_g = I_m \sin \phi + C_j \frac{dV}{dt} + R^{-1}V \qquad [9.4]$$

where $R = R_j(V)R_L/(R_j(V) + R_L)$. This equation together with equations [9.2] and [9.3] describe the switching dynamics of the junction. According to these equations, the capacitance determines the hyteresis, measured by the parameter (61) $\beta = 2\pi I_m R^2 C_j/\Phi_0$, which allows the junction to have its two distinct digital states. As $C_j \rightarrow 0$, the hysteresis disappears and the junction is no longer considered a switch. Present latching Josephson circuits have β ranging between 100 and 1000. There is a non-latching logic approach which requires $\beta \approx 1$ which is slow and requires tight tolerances (62, 63, 65).

Josephson Junction Properties

The following are the basic properties of Josephson devices some of which the designers can take advantage of to realize high performance and others they must design around to ensure reliability and high yield.

Switching Speed.   When the junction switches to the voltage state the switching transition is obtained using equation [9.4] as $V_L(t) = I_g R_L[1 - \exp(-t/\tau_s)]$, where $\tau_s = R_L C_j$. This assumes that the Josephson term in equation [9.4] contributes merely to an additional turn-on delay (64). For $R \approx R_L \approx V_g/I_m(0)$, the switching delay (10% to 90%) is given by $T \approx 2.4\tau_s \approx 2.4V_g C_j/I_m(0)$. At a current density $j_1 = 1000A/cm^2$, and $C_j/I_m(0) \approx 4pF/mA$, one obtains $T = 27$ ps. Switching delays of 20 ps and 9 ps have been reported respectively for 5 μm and 2.5 μm line-width technologies (47, 52).

Power Dissipation.   The power dissipated by the junction is $V_g^2/R_L \approx V_g I_m(0)$, which is presently about 1 μW and the energy is .027 fJ. This is several orders of magnitude lower than the fastest semiconductor switch.

Dispersionless Signal Transmission. Superconducting strip lines are used for signal transmission on and off the chip. These lines, which are nearly dispersionless for typical rise times ($\approx$ 10 ps), are designed to mimimize cross talk and reflections. This can be exploited in packaging ultra-high performance systems whose delays are dominated by signal propagation.

Gain. The Josephson junction is a two terminal device. Its gain is defined as I_g/I_c. When biased near its threshold, this gain can be large in principle. In practice however, it is often less than unity, because the junction is biased well below its threshold to avoid inadvertent switching by noise sources, and to accommodate parameter variations that are inevitable in the LSI environment. As shown below, arranging a plurality of junctions in inductive networks (interferometer circuits) or resistive networks (current injection circuits), a gain larger than unity is obtainable. Transformers, which are four-terminal passive elements, are used to provide isolation in Josephson circuits. The primary carries the input, I_c, which is coupled to a superconducting loop of an interferometer. In this loop (the secondary), a current is induced, adding to I_g and switching the junction as its critical current is exceeded. By having more than one control line winding, more effective gain can be realized. But such gain is always at the expense of more area, and it necessitates tight control on parameter tolerances, otherwise high chip yield would be difficult to achieve. The crucial parameters are: threshold current $L_m(I_c)$, power regulation, resistors, and junction capacitance. The threshold current variations are the most challenging ones to control at tolerances below 10%. They depend on the area variations and current density variations. The latter depend on the tunnel barrier thickness variations. Since the barrier thickness is only tens of angstroms, it has to be uniform within fractions of anagstrom as a result of the exponential thickness dependence of the tunneling probability.

Latching Property. For high $\beta \sim 100$, the junction is hysteretic. When it switches to the $V \neq 0$ state it remains latched in this state indefinitely even after the input signal has been removed. In order to reset it back to the $V = 0$ state, the gate current has to be removed, which necessitates powering the circuits with AC currents instead of DC (66a, 66b). Space has to be provided to accommodate regulating circuits such as the one shown in Figure 9-10 (66b). This circuit operates by converting the sinusoidal current I_{ac}, Figure 9-10b, into the clipped waveform I_g, Figure 9-10c, which powers logic circuits. Due to dispersion, it is not a simple task to preserve the shape of such waveforms created at room temperature and then distribute them to all logic chips at 4.2K.

The latching property restricts the time of flight of data signals transmitted from one chip and received by another. If a transmission line is electrically long such that its propagation delay is a significant fraction of the logic cycle, the

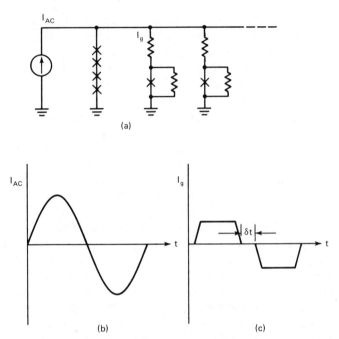

Figure 9-10. (a)- Josephson circuit converts the sinusoidal waveform in (b) to the clipped (regulated) waveform in (c) Refs. (66a) and (66b).

receiving chip may reset and be ready for the next cycle, while the received signals from the previous cycle have not had time to decay, thus causing erroneous switching. To avoid this, special receiver circuits (71–73) having polarity discrimination ability are required.

Punchthrough. This is a phenomenon (67) related to the latching property which requires the resetting of the junction by removal of the gate current. Ideally a junction already in its voltage state should reset to $V = 0$ state as soon as I_g falls below a minimum value, I_{min}, and should remain in this state as I_g, in Figure 9-10c, reverses its polarity so that the junction is ready for the next cycle. In practice, however, if dI_g/dt is high, and the dead time or dwell $\delta t \rightarrow 0$, the junction voltage lags the current, and the energy stored in C_j prevents resetting of the junction causing the junction to remain in the voltage state of the opposite polarity. This is a fault referred to as punchthrough. To prevent it, the condition $I_{min}(dI_g/dt)^{-1} \gg R_L C_j$ must be satisfied at the expense of circuit performance. Because it has a finite probability (68, 69) of occurance even for low dI_g/dt, punchthrough considerations must be taken seriously at the system level to first determine the failure rate as a function of cycle time and then design the circuits which are able to minimize the failure frequency. The punchthrough probability can be reduced drastically by ensuring that a non-zero δt always exists. To do this, special circuits have been proposed (70).

Inversion. The advantages of inversion are stressed above. In the latching mode, a Josephson device cannot invert. This constrains the Josephson technology to develop a logic family having three different circuits to implement the basic functions, AND, OR, INVERT. To get around the non-inverting characteristics, a special INVERT circuit must be used requiring a special timing signal that has to be applied after, with some safety margins, the application of the input signals to be inverted (19). The design of such a circuit requires special precautions. It is neither dense nor versatile in addition to requiring special timing pulse generators. In order to avoid it, the dual-rail scheme can be used which requires carrying both the TRUE and the COMPLEMENT of the signals from the latches (74, 75). This solution may be costly, in terms of requiring additional on and off chip wiring.

Resonance Phenomena (76–81). Josephson devices have resonant modes that are excited by the AC Josephson effect, Equations [9.1] and [9.2]. The nonlinear interaction between the Josephson junction and the resonant network leads to a current step in the time-averaged I-V characteristic at the resonance voltage V_r as shown in Figure 9-12b. As a result the junction switches to $V_r \approx$.$4mV$, instead of $V_g \approx 2.8mV$, and the output current is reduced by $V_g/V_r \approx$ 7. While in some situations resonances can be reduced (82), they still impose constraints on memory and logic circuit designers.

Flux Trapping. The superconducting ground plane may trap vortices at random locations each carrying a quantum of magnetic flux Φ_0. Since the junctions according to Equation [9.3] are known to be sensitive to magnetic flux, they are susceptible to inadvertent switching if a vortex happens to be trapped within them or even located in their vicinity. This is a source of error to be avoided at the circuit and system levels. Adequate shielding can be provided to avoid this difficulty and the results are encouraging (83, 84).

AC POWERED RANDOM LOGIC CIRCUITS

Thus far the Josephson technology has primarily concentrated on developing random logic circuits to implement the AND, OR, and special INVERT functions with considerable success. The evolution of these circuits is shown to result from attempts to accommodate the basic device properties, starting from the first in-line gate logic to the current circuits using current injection and direct coupling.

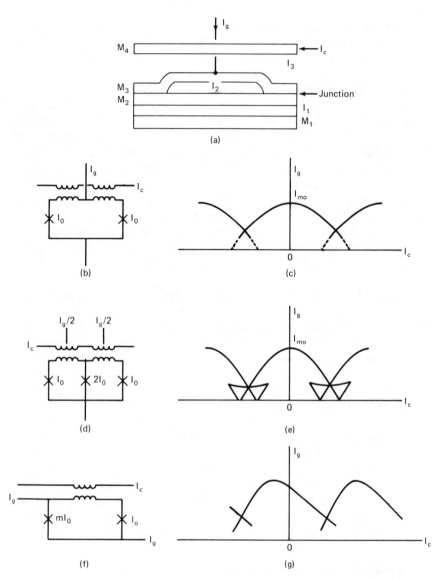

Figure 9-11. (a)- Two junction bridge interferometer cross section; (b)- model for a two junction symmetric interferometer; (c)- interference pattern of the device in (b); (d)- three junction 1-2-1 symmetric split feed interferometer; (e)- interference pattern of (d); (f)- an asymmetric two junction interferometer; (g)- interference pattern of (f).

In-Line Gate Logic

It is the simplest and densest of Josephson logic families (86). Only one in-line gate having three control lines (Figure 9-9a and d) is required to implement 3-input AND and OR functions. This takes advantage of the asymmetry in the threshold characteristic as in Figure 9-9b, obtained (87) for junction lengths l $\sim 1.5\lambda_j - l \sim 3.5\lambda_j$, where $\lambda_j = \Phi_o/2\pi\mu_o dj_1$ is the Josephson penetration depth. If the inputs, each having a current i, are applied in the positive direction, the junction functions as an OR gate. If they are applied in the negative direction, the junction functions as an AND gate. Using this approach complex functions such as adders (87b) and multipliers (43) were demonstrated. In spite of its simplicity this approach is no longer used for the following reasons: 1)- requirement of tight control of junction parameter tolerances and stringent current regulation requirements in order to accommodate three inputs; and 2)- inability to scale to lower current levels and smaller dimensions in order to reduce the capacitance and hence improve performance. The latter results from the length constraint $l \sim 1.5\lambda_j - l \sim 3.5\lambda_j$, which has to be satisfied in order to achieve the asymmetric characteristic of Figure 9-9c.

Interferometer Logic

Interferometers, also called SQUIDs, have been introduced by Zappe (63) for switching applications to alleviate the difficulties associated with in-line gate logic. They are superconducting loops made of small Josephson junctions bridged by inductors and arranged in such a way to produce any desired quantum interference pattern, the $I_m(I_c)$ characteristic. The SiO which defines the junction window in Figure 9-8a is now also used to define the loops as shown in Figure 9-11a. The loop inductance is defined by the thickness of the oxide layer, the distance between junctions, the width of the counter electrode, and the penetration depths. Three different interferometer configurations are shown in Figure 9-11. The two junction symmetric interferometer in Figure 9-11b produces the $I_m(I_c)$ pattern in Figure 9-11c; it is mostly used as a single flux quantum (SFQ) cell in main memory (41). The three junction 1-2-1 symmetric split feed interferometer shown in Figure 9-11d has the pattern depicted in Figure 9-11e. It is noted for its wide operating window and gain and is usually used for logic and cache memory write gates. The asymmetric interferometer in Figure 9-11f has the pattern in Figure 9-11g and is noted for its relatively lower resonances; it is used as cache memory sense gate and drivers (88). Interferometers as switches can be scaled to smaller current levels, thereby reducing the capacitance and improving performance. However, this can be done at the expense of density. For example, devices in 2.5 μm linewidth technology occupy an area of 50X100 $(\mu m)^2$ where a significant fraction is occupied by the loop inductance (transformer secondary). The optimum

$I_m(I_c)$ characteristic is obtained using the 1-2-1 symmetric split feed interferometer configuration having $LI_m(0)/\Phi_0 \approx 1$, which indicates that even in the case of interferometers current levels cannot be reduced indefinitely without further sacrifice in density through increasing L. Also when thermal noise considerations are taken into account, I_{m0} cannot be reduced below a minimum value dictated by satisfying the condition $\dfrac{I_m \Phi_a}{kT} \gg 1$ to ensure not only high chip yield but also low intermittent error rates (85) at the system level. Figure 9-12a shows a typical $I_m(I_c)$ characteristic of a 1-2-1 symmetric split-feed

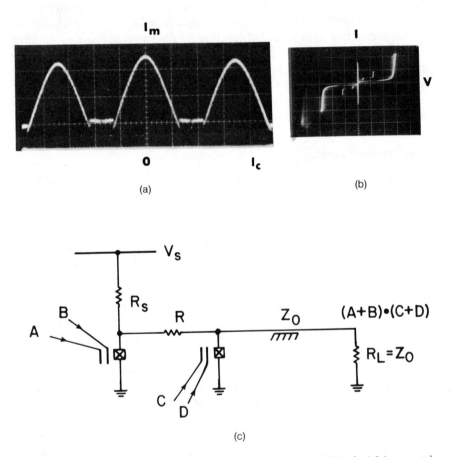

(a)

(b)

(c)

Figure 9-12. (a)- a typical measured quantum interference pattern, $I_m(I_c)$, of a 1-2-1 symmetric interferometer, vertical scale: .5 mA/div, horizontal scale: 1 mA/div; (b)- a measured I-V characteristic of an interferometer, as in (a), showing the fundamental (at .4 mV) and third harmonic of the resonance (at 1.2 mV), vertical scale: 1 mA/div, horizontal scale: 1 mV/div. (c)- interferometer logic circuit performing the function $(A + B)(C + D)$, it has no over-drive capability.

interferometer of the bridge type. Note the wide operating region, separating the $V = 0$ and $V \neq 0$ states, between the center and the side quantum lobes. By decreasing L, this operating region can be made wider at the expense of lower coupling efficiency (less gain) (47). Figure 9-12c shows the first logic circuit made with interferometers (89), the X inside the square is a symbol for an interferometer. This circuit operates on the principle that initially only the interferometer on the left carries current. Thus, in the absence of A and B, applying either C or D gives no output. However when A or B are applied the current is transferred to the device on the right which in turn switches if either C or D is present. Two such circuits are needed to implement a 3-input AND, requiring a total of 4 devices, whereas, only one junction was needed to realize the same function with in-line gate logic. Interferometers also have resonances (78–81) which impact the operability of the circuits. Figure 9-12b is an example of a measured I-V characteristic showing the fundamental and the third harmonic of the resonant frequency $\omega_r^2 = 2/LC_j$, displayed as current steps at voltages V_r and $3V_r$, where $V_r = (\Phi_0/2\pi)\omega_r$. Note that the step height at $3V_r$ is larger than $.51_m(0)$, indicating that the resonant circuit has a high Q. Unlike in-line gates, however, interferometer resonances have been damped using a planar geometrical arrangement allowing a damping resistor, R_d, to be connected across the lumped interferometer inductance (82). This unfortunately increased the turn-on delay which can be long, tens of picoseconds, if there is insufficient current over-drive. Since the circuit of Figure 9-12c does not have adequate over-drive capability (lack of gain) other circuits with more gain have been developed. Because damping of the resonances degrades markedly the circuit density, such an approach cannot be adopted for memory devices because maintaining high density is a central issue.

Current Injection Logic (CIL)

Recognizing that gain limitations impose a severe constraint on the circuit designer, the current injection amplifier shown in Figure 9-13a has been introduced (90–97). This concept provides gain by cascading stages having junctions with increasing critical currents fed by one or more current sources and an appropriate resistive network arrangement. With current injection, adequate gain has been obtained using a circuit occupying less space than that required by an interferometer. The current injection concept leads to other advantages such as absence of resonance problems, and much less susceptibility to trapped flux due to the absence of closed superconducting loops. Hybrid circuits have been introduced (90, 95, 97) combining current injection to achieve gain with magnetically switched interferometers to achieve isolation. Figure 9-13b is such a hybrid logic circuit which uses current injection switching of a single junction to carry out the AND function while the interferometers carry out the isolation as well as the OR function. The circuit operates as

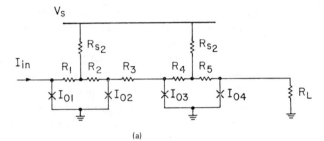

(a)

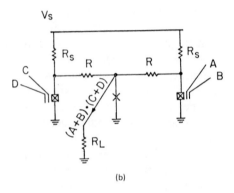

(b)

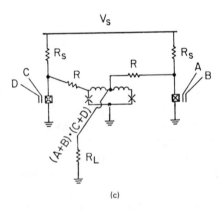

(c)

Figure 9-13. (a)- Current injection circuit providing current level gain; (b)- a hybrid circuit combining magnetically switched interferometer and switching by current injection to perform the AND function; (c)- an AND circuit identical to (b) except the center junction is replaced by an injection interferometer.

follows. Input A is applied to switch the interferometer on the right, transferring its current to the single injection junction in the center. This current alone is not sufficient to switch the single junction. However when C is applied, the interferometer on the left transfers an additional current to switch the injection junction. Subsequently, the total current is transferred to the load representing the function A AND C. Based on these concepts, a complete logic family was developed (95–97), featuring a non-linear current injection interferometer. This is shown in Figure 9-13c replacing the single junction in Figure 9-13b. Unlike, the single junction, the design of this injection interferometer is not so simple because it is subjected to several constraints (95), namely, $L_1 I_{01} = L_2 I_{02}$; $I_{01}/I_{02} = 3$; $(L_1 + L_2)I_{02} = \Phi_0$; and the damping of internal resonances. Using optimum nominal parameters, the non-linear injection interferometer should have an improved AND characteristic. In practice, however, when realistic parameter tolerances are taken into account, coupled with the above design constraints, its advantages over a simple single junction are not so obvious. These current injection logic (CIL) circuits offer a factor of 2 more gain than their predecessors thus reducing drastically the impact of the turn-on delay. This improvement is achieved by increasing the power dissipation of each circuit by a factor of 2 and reducing the density.

Direct Coupled Logic (DCL)

The damped interferometers required for isolation in CIL are the density bottle-neck. Potential candidates to replace these bulky interferometers are the isolator circuits (99–101) shown in Figure 9-14. The input is allowed to be coupled directly to this circuit, instead of magnetically, due to the presence of the junction J_1. The circuit in Figure 9-14a operates as follows (99). When the input is applied, the device Q and J_1 switch, transferring all the gate current to the load R_L. In the mean time the input current goes to ground through L and R. Here L is either a small stray inductance or it can be chosen to improve the switching dynamics. This isolator can be used to replace the interferometers in Figure 9-13b and c to obtain a direct coupled AND circuit. The key to the success of this isolator, i.e., designability with wide margins, is ensuring that J_1 will switch at all times and under all LSI conditions. This is accomplished by designing Q to have gain so that it is able to conduct much larger gate current than the critical current of J_1. The circuit in Figure 9-14b achieves this purpose (101) by means of the resistor R_2. Thus the gate current can be larger than the critical current of J_1 because it divides between R_1 and R_2. The isolator in Figure 9-14c, JAWS (100), ensures switching of J_1 by means of an additional bias source. These circuits have leakage problems due to the presence of R_1 which causes a current to be fed back to unswitched input circuits which might cause them to switch inadvertently. The leakage current is given by $I_{LK} = I_{go}(N - 1)R_1/(R_1 + R_L)$, where I_{go} is a fan out current and N is

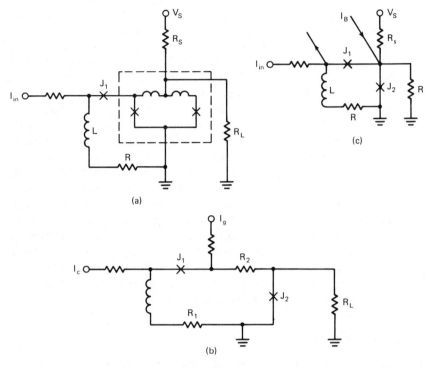

Figure 9-14. Isolating circuits for direct coupled logic.

the number of inputs to a circuit. From this it is clear that for $R_1/R_L = .125$ one obtains for the leakage current $.111\ I_{go}$ and $.444\ I_{go}$ respectively for $N = 2$ and 5. These leakage levels are not tolerable. They impose a restriction on the maximum I_{go} level allowed. The isolators of Figure 9-14a and c can minimize this problem because R_1 in this case is used only to avoid flux trapping. The isolator in Figure 9-14b, on the other hand, is constrained by maintaining a definite ratio $R_1/R_2 \approx 2$, resulting in a relatively worse leakage problem.

Thus Josephson random logic circuits have evolved to the DCL varieties which are relatively compact, and relatively immune from flux trapping and resonance problems. They have a fan-in capability which has to be limited to perhaps 3 because of still imperfect isolation (leakage). The parallel fan-out capability is restricted by the limited gain, although the situation can be improved by utilizing an amplifying buffer stage similar to that shown in Figure 9-13a.

EVOLUTION OF SUPERCONDUCTING MEMORIES

The superconducting memories which have been studied most extensively rely on trapping of quantized magnetic flux in closed superconducting loops to represent the stored binary information (106, 42). The basic storage element shown in Figure 9-15 consists of a loop having a total inductance $L_T = L_R + L_L$ and a superconducting switch S_W. This switch can be opened and closed by means of a control signal $I_x(t)$, and a current source I_y which is connected at two points splitting the loop into L_R and L_L. The storing (writing) operation is carried out in the following sequence. In the absence of $I_x(t)$, and when S_W is closed, a positive I_y is applied as in Figure 9-15a. This divides into two parts, one part, $\left(\dfrac{L_R}{L_T} \right) I_y$, flows in the left branch and the other, $\left(\dfrac{L_L}{L_T} \right) I_y$, flows in the right branch. The switch opens upon application of $I_x(t)$, transferring all I_y to the right branch, Figure 9-15b. The switch is required to possess the crucial property of closing as soon as the current through it decays below a minimum value, I_{min}, whether or not $I_x(t)$ remains. Cryotrons (29–30) and inductively shunted Josephson devices (102) satisfy this requirement. The current transfer and subsequent closing of S_W cause flux to be trapped in the loop. Next, $I_x(t)$ and then I_y are interrupted. As a result of flux conservation, a persistent, clockwise circulating current $I_{cir} = -\dfrac{L_R}{L_T} I_y$ is developed and remains

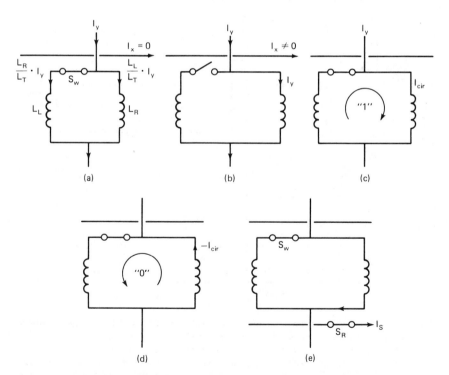

Figure 9-15. Superconducting storage element in which binary information is represented by quantized flux, trapped when the switch S_W is opened.

stored indefinitely in the loop, Figure 9-15c. This corresponds to a stored quantized flux $\Phi_s = n\Phi_o = L_T I_{cir} = -L_R I_y$. By reversing the polarity of I_y and repeating the same sequence, a counterclockwise current, $-I_{cir}$ is developed and stored as in Figure 9-15d. Of course by simply applying $I_x(t)$, S_W opens, allowing the flux to escape. Based on this, the storage of binary information, 1 and 0, can either be represented by $+I_{cir}$ and $-I_{cir}$ respectively, or by I_{cir} and O respectively. Reading is accomplished by means of a second switch, S_R, (Figure 9-15e) which is sensitive to the current or flux within the loop and is able to discriminate between levels. It is interesting to note that this storage element is the dual (103) of the single FET memory cell which relies on the charge stored in a capacitor to represent the binary information. The latter, however, has to be refreshed periodically as a result of charge leakage, whereas the flux trapped in superconducting memory cells remains indefinitely.

Current Transfer Dynamics

The first flip-flop, Figure 9-16a, using Josephson junctions was originally investigated by Matisoo (36, 37), who demonstrated the high speed potential of such a circuit. Here the current is transferred from one branch of the loop to the

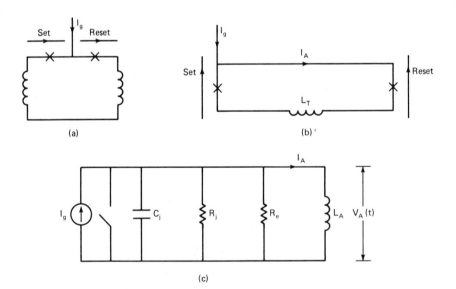

Figure 9-16. (a)- The basic flip-flop circuit; (b)- a variation of (a) which is commonly used in many Josephson memory circuits; (c)- equivalent circuit model used to investigate current transfer dynamics, current steering in loops; (d)- measured current waveform, transferred into a loop of inductance 470 pH, and compared with simulation; (e)- voltage waveform; (f)- general noninductive superconducting loop; (g)- current transfer into a sense line as in (f), (after Ref. (88).

other. This concept of current steering in loops is found in numerous memory circuits ranging from the storage elements (memory cell) to the peripheral circuits, an example of which is the array line driver circuit shown in Figure 9-16b. DC powered operation is one of the most prominent features of these circuits. It eliminates the need for on-chip regulators used for AC powered logic circuits, resulting in significant density and yield advantages. In most of these circuits, the inductance in series with the SET junction is negligible. To simplify the analysis and to obtain preliminary designs, the electrical equivalent circuit model of Figure 9-16c is found adequate. It is used to study the current transfer dynamics associated with most loops. The junction (or interferometer) is simply replaced by a switch, neglecting the non-linearity of the Josephson effect. This is justified provided that the current transfer times are much longer than the period of the Josephson oscillations. The Josephson effect is responsible for the self-resetting mechanism and for an additional turn-on delay. Self-

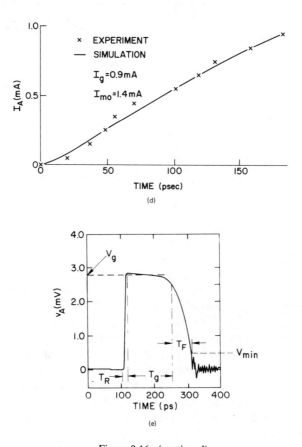

Figure 9-16. (continued)

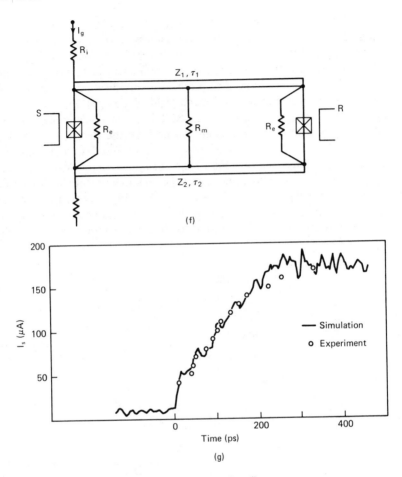

Figure 9-16. (continued)

resetting is very crucial to the operation of all circuits which employ the current steering concept in superconducting loops (36, 37, 47). Numerical simulations are usually required in order to obtain more accurate predictions of the behavior of more complicated circuits. An external resistance, R_e, is in many situations needed to optimize the dynamics and fulfill the following design objectives (102, 105, 47): 1) the instantaneous $I_A(t)/I_g$ does not exceed unity; 2) the steady state $I_A/I_g \rightarrow 1$; 3) when the RESET signal is applied, $I_A/I_g \rightarrow 0$; and 4) obtain the shortest possible transfer times. Of course, parameter variations inevitably lead to deviations from such nominal objectives. Such deviations must be minimized in order to enhance the yield.

By analyzing the dynamics (102, 105, 47), one learns that in order to obtain $I_A/I_g = 1$, the condition $\dfrac{R_T}{R_c} \approx 1.6$ must be adhered to (105), where R_T is the parallel combination of all resistances shunting the device, and $R_c = \sqrt{\dfrac{L_T}{4C_j}}$ is the critical damping resistance. In the limit of $\dfrac{I_g}{C_j\beta} \gg V_g$, the current transfer time is given by $\tau_A \approx \dfrac{L_T I_g}{V_g}$, where, $\beta = (1/L_T C_j - \alpha^2)^{1/2}$, and $\alpha = 1/2R_T C_j$. In the other limit, $\dfrac{I_g}{C_j\beta} < V_g$, $\tau_A \approx 3\sqrt{L_T C_j}$. Figure 9-16d depicts a measured waveform (47) transferred into a loop circuit similar to the one shown in Figure 9-16b. Simulating the circuit using measured parameters shows good agreement with the measured dynamical waveform. This indicates that the models used are reasonable and that short current transfer times are achievable. Here the junction switches at $t = 0$, its voltage and that of L_A rise rapidly to a peak and then begin to fall toward zero, the steady state value, as shown in Figure 9-16e. As soon as the voltage drops to the minimum level,

$$V_{min}^2 \approx I_m(I_c)\, \frac{\Phi_o}{\pi}\, C_j,$$ the device self-resets rapidly to the zero voltage state. At this point, although the average voltage is zero, rapid plasma oscillations are present and decay with a time constant, $R_T C_j$. These oscillations are negligible if the loop can be treated as a simple inductor. This situation prevails when the number of flux quanta admitted into the loop is large ~ 1000. However, the high performance cache memory necessitates the reduction of these flux quanta (105), creating many loops which can no longer be treated as simple inductors (88, 104). In this new situation the plasma oscillations play an important role and impose new constraints on the designs. For example Figure 9-16f shows a typical loop whose length spans the memory array. It consists of a forward strip line section and a return strip line section having impedances Z_1 and Z_2 and delays τ_1 and τ_2 respectively. It requires a resistor, R_m, connected in the middle, to damp out any oscillations created subsequent to self-resetting of the gates. The isolating resistors, R_i, are needed to reduce the disturbances produced by adjacent loops. The loop can be treated as a simple inductance if $\gamma = \dfrac{R_T C_j}{\tau_1 + \tau_2} > 1$. However when $\gamma < 1$, the loop can no longer be treated as a simple inductance (88, 104). In this case the switching, the self-resetting and disturb dynamics become so complicated that lengthy computer simulations are necessary to arrive at acceptable designs. The total circuit environment as well as accurate models are incorporated in those simulations.

Device resonances have a direct impact on the transfer dynamics. Switching to a resonance voltage V_r causes erratic current transfer, namely the loop current deviates significantly from nominal values. Henkels (105) has established a design criterion which makes switching into the resonances tolerable. This requires that the constraint $V_{min} > V_r$ be met with sufficient margins. The price one pays for meeting this constraint is accepting longer transfer times. The measured waveform in Figure 9-16g is an example of a sense line designed with interferometers (88) in 5 μm line width technology to obey Henkels resonance criterion. Because switching into the resonance is allowed, a factor of 3 longer delay resulted. Note also that because the line has the general configuration in Figure 9-16e oscillations are shown superimposed on the waveform produced by simulations. In high performance arrays with extremely short access times, < 300 ps, such as those required by our hypothetical 500 MIPS computer, such delay penalties are not acceptable. Using the so called holey interferometer configurations which allow damping of resonances is not an acceptable solution either for memory arrays because of a significant loss in density. Henkels has shown (88) that the situation improves if relatively dense asymmetric bridge interferometer switches (Figure 9-11a, f, g) can be used. Simulations have indicated that these devices have low fundamental resonance amplitudes that may be avoidable and there is no evidence that the harmonics will present any difficulties.

Cells for Random Access Memory (RAM) Arrays

The cells in a typical bit organized random access memory array, Figure 9-17, have to satisfy rigorous requirements, especially since the circuit yield of an LSI memory chip is given by $Y_{cir} = (1 - p)^N$, where p is the probability that a cell will not operate due to any one of several mechanisms and N is the number of cells in the array. It is therefore imperative that cell designs have wide safety margins in order for the chips to be operable according to the design objectives and manufacturable at affordable costs. As indicated in Figure 9-17, a cell can be selected for either read or write operation by energizing a column, y-line, and a row, x-line, this selected cell is located at the intersection. The other cells which are subjected to either only a selected y-line or only a selected x-line are referred to as half-selected. For example if I_{y1} and I_{x2} are energized then the cell 21 is selected, cells 11 and 22 are half-selected and cell 12 is unselected. The half select condition has been the main concern in memory cell designs. It is still the dominant factor in determining the yield in Josephson technology memories. Many cells have evolved to cope with these considerations.

Cache Memory Cell. The first Josephson technology cell, proposed by Anacker (106), consists of two in-line gates for writing and a third for sensing,

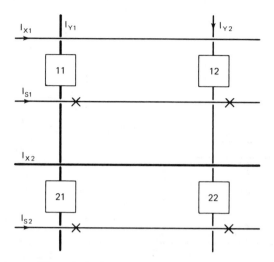

Figure 9-17. Random access memory array.

Figure 9-18a. The binary information is represented by circulating currents $\pm$ I_{cir} (Figure 9-15c and d). This cell features nondestructive read-out, and non-volatility if maintained in the cryogenic environment. Taking advantage of the switching threshold asymmetry inherent in in-line gates, Figure 9-18b, writing 1 or 0 is determined by the polarity of the x-current, while keeping y-current monopolar. Thus, each write gate switches only when it conducts a current, 21_{cir} of the same polarity as $I_x(t)$. The write gate of a half-selected cell conducts I_{cir} of the same polarity as $I_x(t)$. An acceptable design is that which prevents this from switching, e.g., maintaining the failure probability $p \gg 1$. During the read cycle, the sense gate of a selected cell reads 1 by switching to the voltage state in response to the control current 21_{cir}. It reads 0 by remaining in the zero voltage state because its control, zero in this case, is insufficient for switching. In the read half-select condition, the control of the sense gate can be $\pm I_{cir}$ and should be designed not to switch. This cell is subjected to another severe constraint, namely, it requires a special set-up cycle to write a 1 in every cell in the array before normal read/write operation is allowed. This can only be accomplished when a write gate, conducting $\dfrac{I_y}{2} = I_{cir}$, is subjected to an $I_x(t)$ current much larger than nominal, forcing the peripheral circuits to accommodate this special requirement. This operating condition is represented by the dashed trajectory shown in Figure 9-18b.

Figure 9-18c shows a denser cell requiring only a single write gate and operates in the same way as the first cell, Figure 9-18a, except for requiring y-current to be bipolar also (40). The resonances, the set-up cycle, the narrow

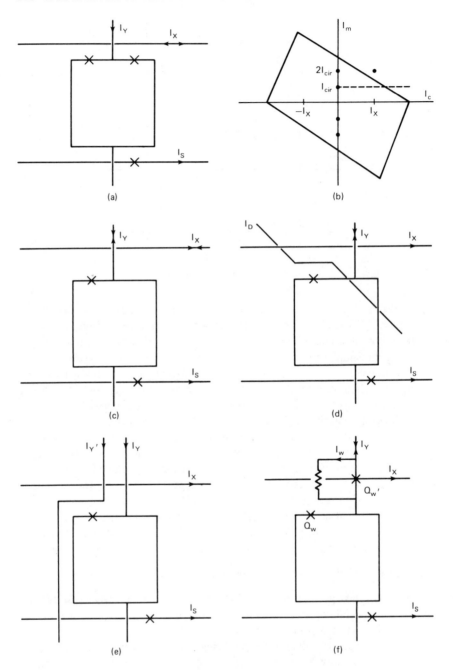

Figure 9-18. Evolution of Josephson memory cells.

margins, and the in-ability to scale to lower current levels are the reasons for abandoning these cells and adopting new approaches that incorporate interferometers (105).

Improved margins are obtained using the cell introduced by Henkels (105), Figure 9-18d. This requires triple coincidence of I_y, $I_x(t)$ and a new current running diagonally across the array to select a cell for writing. The write gate is a symmetric interferometer located in the left branch of the loop which has an inductance ⅔ of the total loop inductance. This gate is controlled by two lines, $I_x(t)$ and I_D. The y-current is required to be bipolar to produce the circulating currents $I_{cir} = \pm I_y/3$. The sense gate is controlled by the right branch of the loop. The disadvantages of this cell are: 1) added complexity and reduced density as a result of the diagonal-lines: 2) further reduction in chip density results due to the requirement of an additional decoder for the diagonal line; 3) additional logic is required to derive the diagonal address by subtracting the x from the y addresses; 4) the write operation is the bottle-neck in terms of yield because the write gate has to switch out of two different current levels, I_{cir}, during the set-up cycle, and 2 I_{cir} during normal operation; and 5) write gate has a discrimination ratio of 2 between the selected and half-selected condition. The advantage of this scheme is the high discrimination ratio of 3 during the read operation. The performance, yield and density requirements warranted the search for an alternative.

The cell shown in Figure 9-18e, invented by Wolf (107), eliminates entirely the special set-up cycle and the difficulties associated with the diagonal decoder. Its operation is based on the presence or absence of circulating current to represent the stored binary information. This immediately eliminates the requirement of a polarity switch to produce bipolar currents crucial to the operation of previous cells. The write gate requires two control currents, the $I_x(t)$ and I_y'; the latter is selected by the y-decoder. Writing a 1 in a selected cell is accomplished by coincidence of I_y and $I_x(t)$, while writing a 0 is accomplished by $I_x(t)$ and I_y'. The disadvantage of this cell is the intrinsically narrow margins attributed to a discrimination ratio of only 2 between the selected and half-selected cells both during read and write operations. Taking advantage of flux quantization, it has been demonstrated experimentally that some margin improvements are realized if one or two fluxoids are stored (108) and asymmetric sense gates are used (88).

Recently, a cell has been introduced (109) featuring wider intrinsic margins than any of the previous cells. This is realized by breaking the write half-select bottle-neck, and at the same time realizing a discrimination of 3 between select and half-select cells during the read operation. As shown in Figure 9-18f, an additional device Qw', controlled directly by $I_x(t)$, is connected in series with the storage loop. To obtain the self-resetting mode of operation, this device is shunted by a small resistance (47). Its output is a pulse, I_W, which is an AND

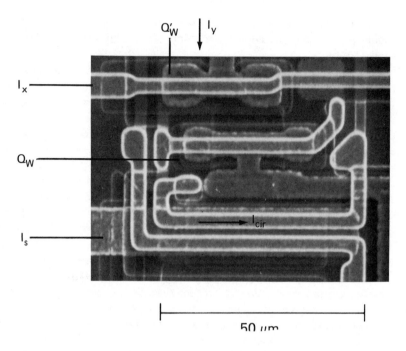

Figure 9-19. Electron-micrograph of the wide margin memory cell in Figure 9-18f.

function of $I_x(t)$ and and I_y, is used to control the write gate Q_W. Note that, unlike previous cells, $I_x(t)$ here does not control directly the write gate. Consequently, the write half select considerations are eliminated entirely. Since I_W in all non-selected cells is nominally zero, this corresponds to an infinite discrimination ratio. Because bipolar I_y can be used with this cell, a discrimination ratio of 3 is obtained during the read operation. This cell can also exploit any benefits that accrue from flux quantization when one or two fluxoids are involved. It is interesting to note that although an additional device is needed to obtain the margin improvements, the density degradation is slight. This is a result of eliminating half-select constraints, additional control lines and their returns. Using this cell requires the added complexity associated with developing a high performance polarity switch to produce bipolar y-current. The operability of this cell has been confirmed by simulations. In order to examine the complicated dynamics, these simulations involved not only the cell itself but also the y-loop which, in turn, is driven directly by means of a novel high performance polarity switch, discussed below. A preliminary design has been fabricated but not yet tested. It is displayed in Figure 9-19 to show its various components and that its density could be competitive with the Wolf cell.

The LSI viability of these cells and their extendibility to the VLSI era remain a subject of investigation. Presently under consideration is a 4k-bit fully decoded cache chip (88) having a projected access time less than 1 nsec designed in 2.5 μm all lead-alloy technology. The components of such a chip have been previously tested individually.

Main Memory. The single flux quantum memory cell (41) (SFQ) is the densest Josephson RAM cell, making it a possible candidate for main memory. It consists of a single two junction interferometer similar to that of Figure 9-11a. It is designed to have $LI_0/\Phi_0 \sim .5$ (Figure 9-20a) so that the quantum modes overlap sufficiently to create a wide operating region below the crossing point of these modes as shown in Figure 9-20b. This cell gives a clear example of trading performance for density, namely, in order to obtain very small L (which reflects the cell size), I_0 must be kept large leading to larger delays. Because, according to our discussion pertaining to current transfer dynamics, in the inductive limit, the transfer time is proportional to the current. There are critical points, P_{CL} and P_{CR} which separate the solid and dashed segments of the quantum modes. Crossing the modes below the critical points (moving across the dashed segments) causes a quantum transition i.e., admitting or expelling a flux quantum without switching to the voltage state, this is the basis for writing. Crossing above the critical points causes switching to the voltage state, which is the basis for reading. One mode of operation requires a DC current, I_B, to bias all cells at mid-point between the modes. Bipolar $I_x(t)$ and I_d (diagonal) currents are needed to determine the binary information to be stored. Half-select considerations once again necessitate the diagonal line along with an additional decoder and additional logic to compute its addresses. All these have an adverse effect on density. In addition, the low discrimination ratio of 2 affects the yield and imposes the constraint of tight tolerance require-

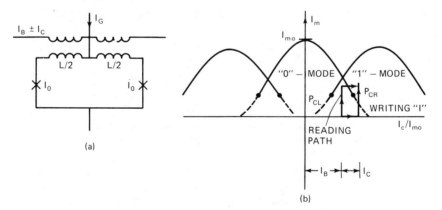

Figure 9-20. Single Flux Quantum (SFQ) memory cell to be used in main memory.

ments. To write a 1 in a selected cell, positive $I_x(t)$ and I_D are applied first then followed by I_y. This sequence results in crossing the dashed segment below the critical point, P_{CR}, causing a quantum transition to the 1 mode. Reading is accomplished by reversing the sequence, namely, applying I_y first, the $I_x(t)$ and I_D. This results in a path which crosses above the critical point, so that if the cell has a 0, switching takes place, and if it has a 1, no mode boundary crossing results. Thus, reading of this cell is destructive, requiring that a read cycle be followed by a write cycle to preserve the information. So far a cross section of a 16k-bit SFQ memory array chip has successfully been built and tested (110). It included many necessary peripheral circuits. Based on the theoretical and experimental investigation of the dynamics, it is concluded that a 15 nsec access time is possible.

Read Only Memory.   In the memory hierarchy (13, 111), the cache memory is usually small, expensive, and fast enough to keep up with the CPU, while main memory is much larger and about 10 times slower. The read only memory (ROM) is another type which also plays a vital role in computers. They are used in many applications (111) such as: code converters, look-up tables, decoders, character generators, instruction lists, PLAs, etc. ROMs generally possess several attractive features, among them are: high density, high speeds, nonvolatility, and low cost.

In a word organized m x n array, the binary address, $\log_2 m$ bits wide, is decoded to select and trigger 1 out of m word drivers. The selected word line interrogates all n memory cells located in this row. The stored information (program), m x n bits, is sensed and transmitted out, one word randomly selected in each read cycle. The program is permanently fixed during or after chip fabrication which is the reason for giving this type of memory and name read-only memory. Also because the circuits and parts of the cell associated with the writing cycle are eliminated, significant saving in real estate is realized. ROMs, therefore, are generally denser and faster than the read/write cache (111).

The circuit details of the ROM depends of course on the devices used. Figure 9-21 illustrates how a DC powered Josephson ROM (JROM) can be implemented using Josephson interferometers as the main switching elements. The array in this example consists of 4 loops in the x-direction carrying the control currents $w1$-$w4$, and 4 loops in the y-direction carrying the gate currents $y1$-$y4$. Four ROM cells (interferometers) are serially connected and form part of each y-loop. The cells programmed to switch are designated by 1. The reset pulse ensures that at the end of each read cycle the currents $y1$-$y4$ are present and $w1$-$w4$ are absent. The decoder in a subsequent read cycle selects 1 out of 4 word lines which control the cells in one row. Those cells which switch to the voltage state cause their respective y-currents to decay to zero, while the y-currents of the unswitched cell remain unchanged. Identical sense circuits are

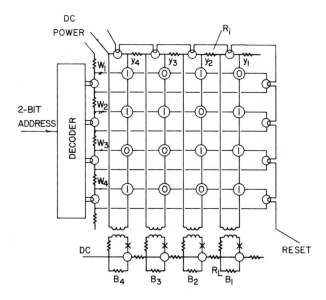

Figure 9-21. JROM array construction based on the DC powered loop concept.

transformer coupled to the y-loops. Each circuit responds to the decay of a y-current undergoing a negative transition by switching to the voltage state, transmitting an output pulse. The outputs of these circuits, B1-B4 represent the word stored in the selected address. The detailed operation of the decoder and the sense circuitry is described below.

Using interferometers as the basis for the JROM cells, several methods have been devised to program them to switch (logical 1), or keep them from switching (logical 0). The best method is that which results in a cell combining density, speed, wide operating margins and low cost. The following are descriptions of several programming methods emphasizing their possible advantages and disadvantages.

A-Control Line By-Pass (112).   Figure 9-22a shows a layout (top view) of two adjacent cells which have currents corresponding to those of the array in Figure 9-21. The two cells are identical interferometers except at the M4 level. The control line of the 0 cell by-passes the interferometer so that the current I_{w1} does not couple to it. This device has an $I_m(I_c)$ shown in Figure 9-22b indicating that it cannot switch to the $V \neq 0$ state for any value of control current. The 1 cell, on the other hand, has an $I_m(I_c)$ curve shown in Figure 9-22c and it will switch when I_{w2} is applied. The advantage of this scheme is its simplicity and its compactness. The cells can be programmed at the M4 process step, or by means of an additional mask. The latter may be preferable because it allows

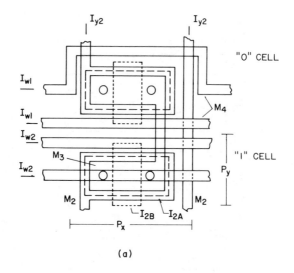

(a)

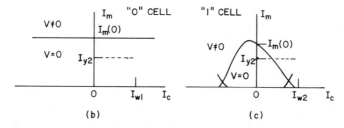

Figure 9-22. (a)- Two JROM cells programmed by means of control line by-pass; (b)- the 0 cell switching characteristic; (c)- 1 cell switching characteristic.

for the complete fabrication of a large number of chips which can be programmed at a later time. This programming method has the disadvantage of producing x loops having electrical characteristic which depend on the program, thus the dynamics are not predictable.

B-Junction Critical Current Alteration.   In this scheme (113), the 12A which defines the circular windows is eliminated to produce a 0 cell (Figure 9-23a). Thus two large area rectangular junctions are created which have large critical currents and result in the $I_m(I_c)$ curve shown in Figure 9-23b preventing the

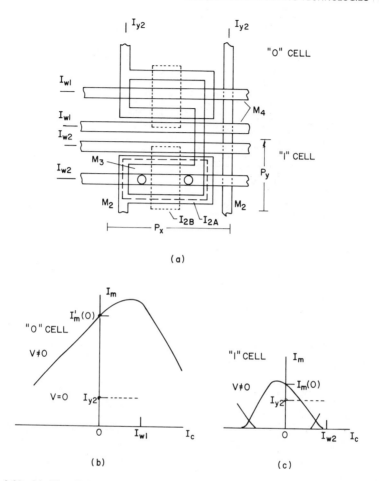

(a)

(b)   (c)

Figure 9-23. (a)- Two JROM cells programmed by means of Josephson critical current alteration, note the absence of the 12A; (b)- the 0 cell switching characteristic; (c)- the 1 cell switching
characteristic.

cell from switching at the operating control current I_{wl}. The 12A of the 1 cell
remains and defines relatively smaller junction areas and results in the $I_m(I_c)$
curve shown in Figure 9-23c. This scheme is also simple, compact and design-
able with acceptable margins. The electrical characteristics of the array are
nearly independent of the program. Its disadvantage is the programmability at
one of the early process steps instead of at the very end. Critical current alteration can be accomplished at the end of the fabrication process by shorting a
junction with a mask or a laser beam (114), or ion implantation (115). These
proposals are not as simple as the readily available 12A programming method.

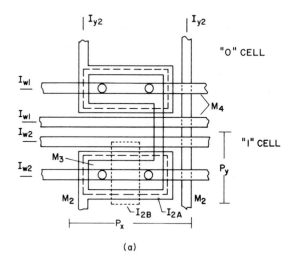

(a)

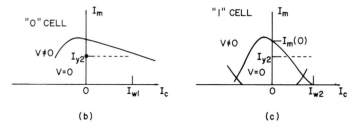

(b)   (c)

Figure 9-24. (a)- Two JROM cells programmed by means of interferometer inductance L_m alteration, note the absence of the 12B; (b)- the 0 cell switching characteristic; (c)- the 1 cell switching characteristic.

C-Interferometer Inductance Alteration.   Another method for producing 0 cells is to alter the inductance (116, 117) of the interferometers L_m for example by removing the 12B layer as shown in Figure 9-24a. This produces the interference pattern shown in Figure 9-24b which indicates that at a normal operating control currents switching does not take place. The 1 cell, on the other hand, keeps the 12B layer, resulting in the interference pattern of Figure 9-24c which allows switching at normal operating control currents. The designability of this scheme is not as simple nor as certain as the critical current alterations scheme. In order to obtain acceptable discrimination between the 1 and 0 cells, inductance variation of perhaps a factor of 3 is necessary. This impacts the cell density because the 12B length, the distance between the two circular junc-

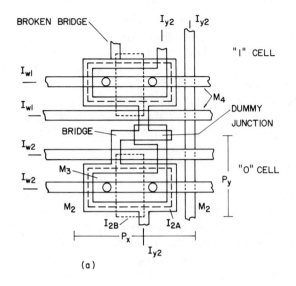

(a)

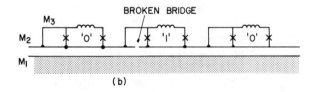

(b)

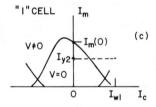

Figure 9-25. (a)- Two JROM cells programmed by means of current path alteration, by breaking the bridge; (b)- illustration of how the broken bridge renders the interferometer sensitive to
control currents; (c)- the 1 cell switching characteristic.

tions, determines I_m. Another way to alter I_m is by placing on the finished
ROM chips a fifth metal layer (118) having holes where a 1 cell is desired.
With this scheme, it may not be possible to realize acceptable discrimination
between 1 and 0.

D-Current Path Alteration.   In this scheme (119) each JROM cell is made of
an interferometer, an M2 bridge, and a shorting junction (dummy junction)
(120) as shown in Figure 9-25a and b. The path of the current I_{y2} is altered by

breaking the bridge to form a 1 cell having the interference pattern of Figure 9-25c, which can switch upon application of appropriate control currents. If the bridge remains unbroken, the cell represents a 0 because the I_{y2} flows mainly through the M2 and the voltage state is never obtained. This approach seems to be promising because it eliminates nearly all the shortcomings of the others. It has the best discrimination between the 1 and 0 cells. This is because the 0-cell does not switch for any value of control current or gate current. Thus designability is simple and high yield is possible. After the end of all fabrication steps, the program can be written by breaking the bridges by a variety of methods, such as laser beams, e-beams, or other etching means.

E-Programmable Erasable Schemes. Junction made with the semiconductors CdS or CdTe as the tunneling barrier have unique properties. When they are irradiated with light at 4.2K, their tunneling probability can be increased by up to 3 orders of magnitude (121, 122). The light causes holes to be trapped indefinitely inside the semiconducting material, which causes the average potential barrier height to decrease. Upon raising the junction temperature to approximately 70K, the trapped holes disappear. An optically programmable and erasable JROM cell has been proposed exploiting this effect (123). The cell layout would be similar to that of Figure 9-23. The 12A and 12B are present for both the 1 and 0 cells in addition to using either CdS or CdTe as the barrier material. Initially all the cells in the array are 1 cells having the interference pattern of Figure 9-23c and switch when subjected to a control current. According to a prescribed program, some of the 1 cells are turned into 0 cells by means of an optical beam. The critical currents of these cells are increased, resulting in an interference pattern similar to that of Figure 9-23b, which does not allow switching at normal control current levels. The information written by this method can be erased by simply raising the temperature of the array and rewritten later with another program.

Peripheral Circuits

The block diagram, Figure 9-26, shows the components needed to implement a fully decoded cache memory chip (88). The binary information, addresses, read/write, and data, is received by the interface circuits which amplify and then convert their current levels into short pulses. The use of pulses prevents the possibility of fault states resulting from switching both set and reset gates of the various flip-flop loops used through-out Josephson memories. The decoders use those pulses to select either the proper x, y drivers to write 1, x, y' to write a 0, or s, y to read. The sense bus collects the data from the array and sends off chip via an other interface circuit. The timing network is required to ensure that all the parts of the chip are working harmoniously and synchronized with the master clock of the CPU. Depending on the cell, a polarity switch or an additional diagonal decoder may be required.

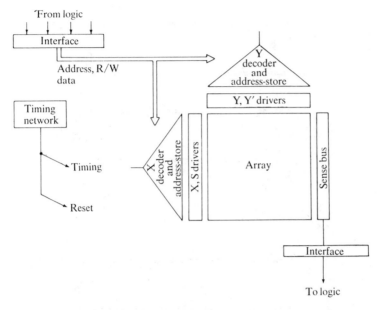

Figure 9-26. Diagram of a typical Josephson cache RAM array showing its components, after Ref. (88).

Drivers (88, 104).   The x, y, and s driver sets each consists of a number of loops connected in series by isolating, R_i, resistors and connected to a DC current source as in Figure 9-27. These drivers are selected and activated by decoders according to the address and function information. Each y-driver loop connects a column of memory cells, an x-driver loop controls the write gates in a row of memory cells, and an s-driver loop connects sense gates in a row of memory cells. The end of each s-driver loop is a transformer coupled to the sense bus. All of these loops are subjected to the same dynamic considerations discussed above in order to realize acceptable designs.

Decoders.   Originally, three decoders (40) were considered for Josephson memories. These have been supplanted by the loop decoder (47, 124) shown in Figure 9-28. Its operation is based on current steering in superconducting loops and the concept of self-resetting in resistive loops. Such a decoder has the following attractive features 1) the compactness required by memory chips; 2) fast operation; 3) wide margins; 4) automatic complement generation; and 5) address storage capability. To explain the operating principles, the 2-bit (1 out of 4) decoder example shown in Figure 9-28a is used. Applying the address 1 0 0 1 representing respectively the control currents $\overline{A}_1$, A_1, $\overline{A}_2$, and A_2, causes address loop currents I_{A_1}, and I_{A_2} to be transferred into those address loops indicated drawn by the heavy lines. The waveforms of these address currents, produced by computer simulation, are shown in Figure 9-28b. The decoder is

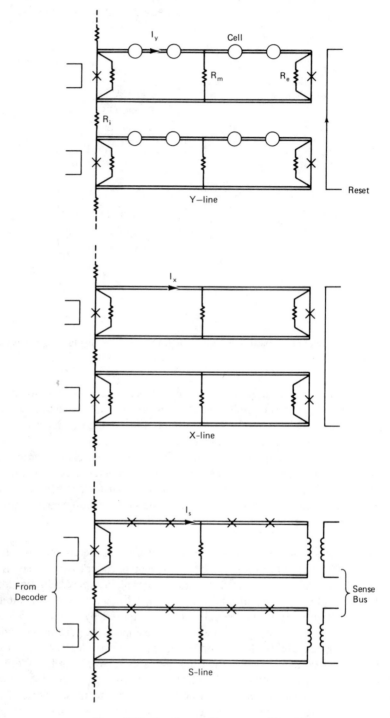

Figure 9-27. Josephson cache memory drivers.

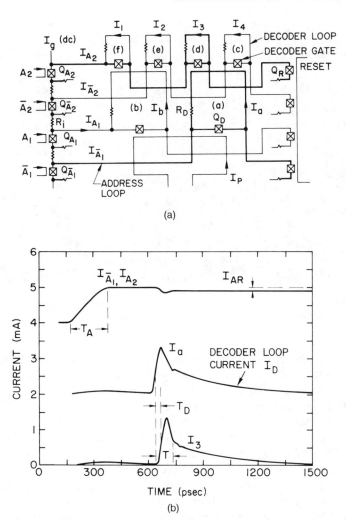

(a)

(b)

Figure 9-28. (a)- A 2-bit loop decoder, heavy lines represent current path according to the specific address 1001; (b)- address loop and decoder loop waveforms produced by computer simulation to illustrate the operation of the loop decoder example in (a), after Ref. (47).

then triggered by a pulse, I_p, which controls and switches only the device, Q_D, carrying the address current $\bar{I}\bar{A}1$ producing a current pulse, I_a in the small decoder loop a. This then switches the current carrying device in loop d, producing the desired output pulse, I_3, thus 1 out of 4 outputs is selected.

To confirm the operability of this decoder, a test vehicle was designed in 5μm lead alloy technology. This test vehicle included 3-bit decoders with and without address loops, isolated address loops to study their dynamics, trigger pulse generators, and a half of a 6-bit decoder. All these experiments operated

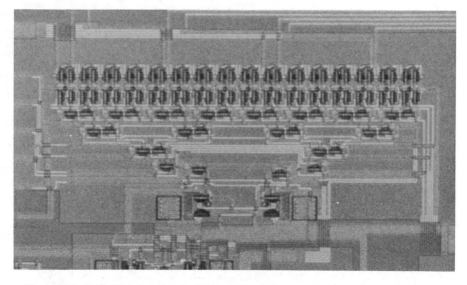

Figure 9-29. Half a 6-bit loop decoder fabricated in 5 μm lead-alloy technology, two pulse generators are used for triggering different parts, only 4 address combinations were designed to be tested.

satisfactorily. Having experimentally verified their potential, loop decoders are presently being incorporated in the high performance cache designs. Figures 9-5 and 9-29 show respectively a full 3-bit decoder and a half 6-bit decoder fabricated in 5 μm lead alloy technology. These decoders used the symmetric split-feed interferometers shown in Figure 9-30 as the main switching element, having $LI_{mo}/\Phi_o = .5$, and $I_{mo} = 1.5$ mA. The 3-bit decoder was complete with address loops and a trigger pulse generator. The full operation was verified over a wide range of bias current. The 6-bit decoder (Figure 9-29), on the other hand, did not have the address loops. It was designed to test only four address combinations supplied directly. It operated satisfactorily, indicated that complex circuitry can be designed and tested. In order to measure the decoding delay, T_d (Figure 9-28b), the experiment shown schematically in Figure 9-31 was designed and successfully implemented. It consists of 10 decoder loops connected in series and isolated dynamically by L_i and R_i. The series string is powered by a single DC source I_g. The device C of the first loop and the monitor gate B are triggered simultaneously by I_{in}. The first loop produces a pulse which triggers sequentially the remaining stages, until a pulse at the final stage is produced and used to control the monitor gate A. The measured time difference between the voltages, V_A, and V_B, produced by switching A and B gives the decoding delay of the 10 stages, Figure 9-31b. Thus the decoding delay as function of I_g is measured and compared with computer simulation predictions as displayed in Figure 9-31c.

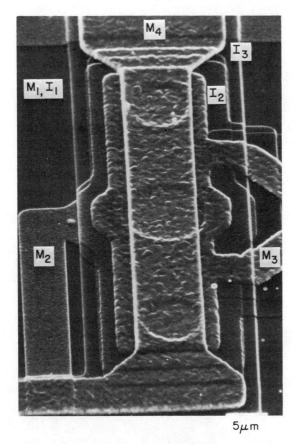

5μm

Figure 9-30. Electron-micrograph of a three junction 1-2-1 symmetric split feed interferometer used as the main switching element in the loop decoder test vehicle.

Sense Bus. During the read operation, the stored information is transferred from any randomly selected memory cell to a sense line. The sense bus collects this information from the sense lines and transmits it off the memory chip via an interface circuit. To do this the sense bus scheme shown (99) in Figure 9-32a is being considered its speed (88). It consists of a sense bus loop as long as the array itself, connecting in series edge detecting circuits (125) each of which is transformer coupled to a sense line. The operation of the sense bus is explained with the aid of the diagram in Figure 9-32b. At $t = 0$, the beginning of each CPU cycle, the control signal ϕ_s triggers device A to transfer the current I_{SB} into the large loop. When the decoder selects a sense line, the sense current, I_s, rises, causing the current I_i to be induced in one of the small loops. The polarity of this current is opposite to that of I_{SB} such that the total current through device C decreases preventing it from switching. At the same time, I_i

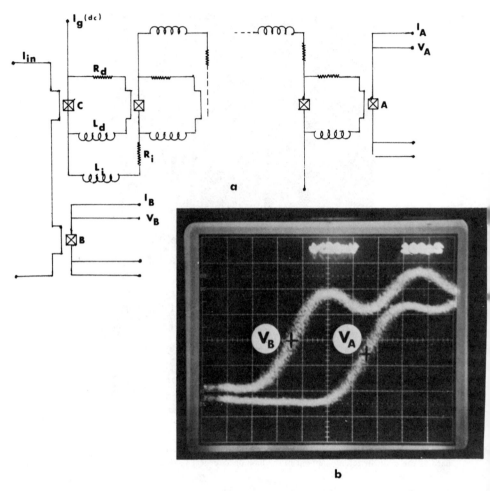

Figure 9-31. (a)- Circuit used to measure loop decoder delay; (b)- 10 stage decoding delay is the difference between the 50% points of the voltage waveforms; (c)- measured decoding delay per stage as the gate current is varied, results compare favorably with computer simulations.

rises through device B which switches upon exceeding its threshold and rapidly resets. If the selected memory cell contains a 1, its sense gate switches, causing I_s to decay to zero. This causes a current, I_i of opposite polarity to be induced in the small loop, adding to I_{SB} until C switches upon exceeding its threshold. The device B also switches and the current I_{SB} decays. The current I_D, through device A rises and causes switching of the interface device D. If the selected cell contains a 0, the sense bus is activated only at the end of the cycle when

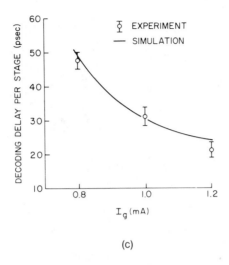

(c)

Figure 9-31 (Continued)

device D is de-activated and no signal is transmitted through the interface. The crucial circuit element which is sensitive to the decay of I_s has been fabricated (Figure 9-32c) and tested. Its operation has been tested quasistatically as shown in Figure 9-32d. The appearance of the voltage only subsequent to the removal of the I_s, confirms the sense bus principle. The dynamics of the whole sense bus has been simulated predicting that delays < 95 ps are possible.

Polarity Switch.   This circuit produces either bipolar $I_x(t)$ or bipolar I_y currents required by the SFQ memory or the wide margin cell shown in Figure 9-18f. In order to realize a high performance polarity switch, interferometers have to be used for switching. So far, the only schemes (126) that can do this are shown in Figures 9-33 and 9-34. They consist of large loops to carry the bipolar I_y current which powers many memory cells in series, and small loops which contain the switchable interferometers, T_1, Q_1, T_o, and Q_o. The circuit in Figure 9-33 operates as follows. Initially, the devices Q_1 and Q_0 carry the DC current I_p. Energizing I_1 and I_{c1} selects one polarity, while energizing I_0 and I_{c0} selects the opposite polarity. The main reason for requiring pairs of currents is to ensure wide operating margins, by maintaining the device operating current either zero or I_p, instead of the additional operating current, $2I_p$. When I_{c1} is applied, Q_1 and T_1 switch, transferring the current $\approx I_p$ to Q_0. The presence of I_1 induces a current $\approx -I_p$ which cancels the transferred current, so that only I_p instead of $2I_p$ remain flowing within Q_0. Similarly, when I_{c0} is applied, a current of opposite polarity is transferred to the loop and

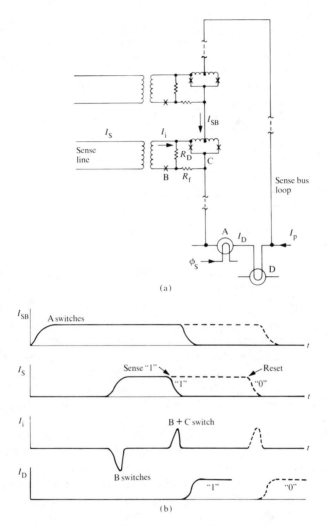

Figure 9-32. (a)- Sense bus circuit; (b)- waveforms illustrate the operating principles of the sense bus after 88; (c)- micrograph of an edge detecting circuit made in 5μm technology, after 125; (d)- quasistatic operation of the detecting circuit, after 125.

to Q_1 which is left with only I_p flowing through it as a result of the cancellation induced by the presence of I_o. In order to have the selection of one or the other polarity carried out with a single decoder, the scheme shown in Figure 9-34 may be preferable for it results in significant saving in real estate. The principles of operation of both schemes are identical. The dynamics of the latter

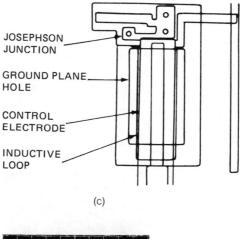

JOSEPHSON
JUNCTION

GROUND PLANE
HOLE

CONTROL
ELECTRODE

INDUCTIVE
LOOP

(c)

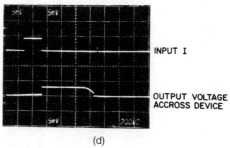

INPUT I

OUTPUT VOLTAGE
ACCROSS DEVICE

(d)

Figure 9-32 (Continued)

scheme has been simulated using 1.5 mA levels, thus demonstrating its potential viability. As illustrated in Figure 9-35, a bipolar I_y current can be produced
in a reasonably well controlled manner. The transfer time of 500 ps can be
reduced by more than a factor of 2 by lowering the operating current levels.

ALTERNATIVE DC POWERED LOGIC CONCEPTS

This section introduces two logic approaches which can be DC powered thus
relaxing some of the basic constraints associated with the latching property and
the AC power requirement. They still, however, are subject to the other limitations discussed above, and to the question of their versatility and extendibility. Although these approaches may not be as flexible as the traditional random

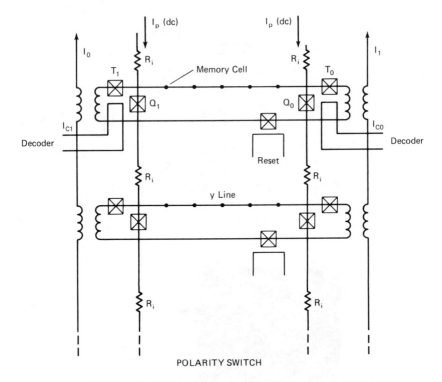

Figure 9-33. Polarity switch which uses interferometers as the basic switchable devices.

logic, the potential improvements in density, yield, and performance, may warrant their further investigation. DC power results in a significant density improvement as in the case of Josephson cache memory due to the utilization of the relatively compact bridge interferometers.

Functional Loop Logic (FLL)

It is a logic circuit (124, 127) which may be designed to perform complex functions such as adders, mutliplexors, decoders, etc. Each circuit performing a different function is to be optimized individually in order to derive whatever density, performance, and yield enhancements that may be difficult to obtain if it were made of the basic AND, OR and INVERT circuits. FLL circuits are DC powered because they use the self-resetting concept (49) which requires that the loads be either superconducting loops (inductive loads) or small enough resistors, R_s, such that the device steady state voltage is $I_g R_s \leq V_{min}$, where, $V_{min}^2 = \Phi_o I_m(0)/\pi C_j$. The full adder shown in Figure 9-36a is an example chosen to illustrate the FLL concept. It is made of 4 large superconducting

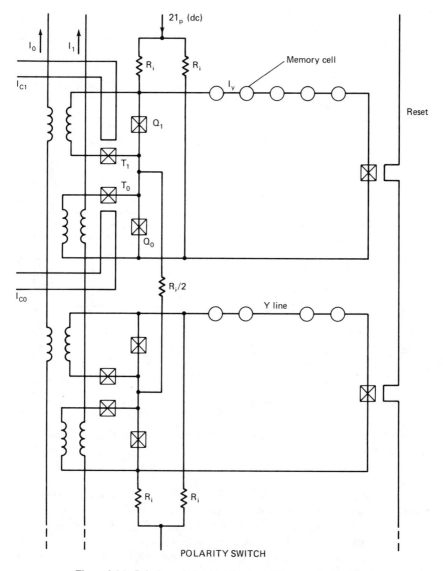

Figure 9-34. Polarity switch which is selected by a single decoder.

loops which carry the current I_A. Interferometers are located at both ends of each of these loops which can be switched when either the set, reset, X_n, and Y_n pulses are present. Each large loop has several small resistive loops in series, each of which consists of a resistor and an interferometer. The large loops perform simultaneously the function of a storage register, the inverting function

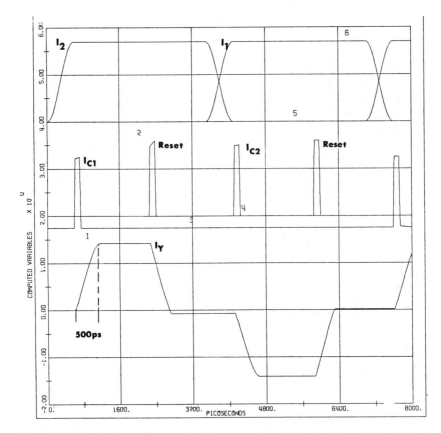

Figure 9-35. Bipolar I_y waveform produced by a polarity switch as in Figure 9-24, at 1.5 mA operating current levels.

to produce $\overline{X}_n$ *and* $\overline{Y}_n$, and play a part in the AND function. Density improvement can be achieved because only one compact bridge interferometer is needed to perform the AND function. For instance, the device in the small resistive loop 8 switches when the large loop has a current representing X_n and the control current I_{D1} is present. Loop 8 then delivers the current I_{D2}, which after it controls the output loop C_n decays to zero as the device self-resets. The output loops perform the OR function which produce finally S_n, C_n, and $\overline{C}_n$. Based on this concept a decoder satisfying the cache memory requirement has been demonstrated in 5 μm technology with a nominal decoding delay of 30 ps per stage. Operating at lower current levels higher performance can be obtained. This is borne out by the computer simulation results of Figure 9-36b. Nominal loop current transfer times of 85 ps and interstage delay of 20 ps are in principle realizable when operating at current levels of $\sim$ .35 mA.

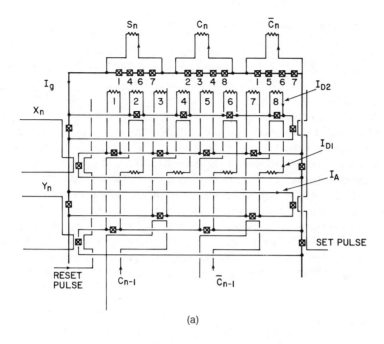

(a)

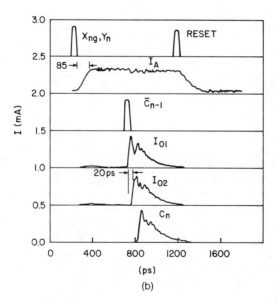

(b)

Figure 9-36. (a)- DC powered functional loop logic (FLL) circuit performing the full adder function; (b)- simulated waveforms of the FLL full adder in (a).

Josephson Programmable Logic Arrays (JPLA)

The latching and the non-inverting properties make implementation of JPLA not so straightforward as in the transistor PLA (128, 129). The combination of timing schemes and special interface circuits (130), however, help make possible the JPLA example shown in Figure 9-37. The DC powered read only memory (ROM) arrays discussed above use superconducting loops which serve many purposes: 1)- the horizontal loops are registers to store the inputs; 2)- the vertical loops store the outputs of the AND-ROM; and 3)- all the loops carry out the selection and switching of the personalized ROM cells. These cells are interferometers connected in series and make up the loops which carry the currents U_1-U_8 and W_1-W_3 when the pulse ϕ is applied. The cells personalized to switch are indicated in Figure 9-6 by the symbol, cross in a circle. For example, those cells carrying the current U_7 switch in response to $\bar{x}$, $\bar{y}$, and z, causing U_7 to decay to zero. Subsequent application of the pulse ϕ_A activates the non-inverting interface circuit A which transmits the signals B_1-B_8, reflecting the state of the AND-ROM. These, in turn, activate the OR-ROM so that the

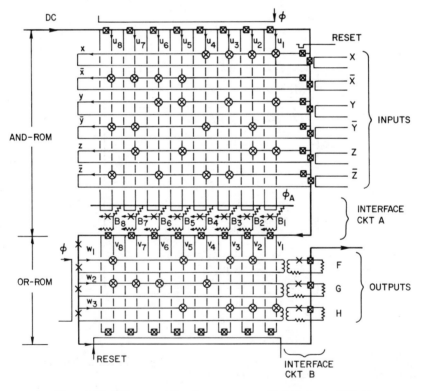

Figure 9-37. DC powered Josephson programmable logic arrays (JPLA).

currents V_1-V_8 are transferred into their respective loops and control the cells in the OR-ROM. When the personalized cells switch a combination of the currents W_1-W_3 decay to zero. The interface circuit B detects the negative current transition (125) and responds by transmitting the outputs F, G, or H. This particular example is personalized to carry out the full adder function, where, $Z = C_{n-1}$; $F = S_n$; $G = C_n$; and $H = \overline{C}_n$. Although the concepts and individual circuits used in this JPLA have been tested experimentally, no full JPLA has been tested to date.

CONCLUSION

We have taken a hypothetical ultra-high performance computer, 500 MIPS, as a vehicle to explore the limitations of existing devices, and the roles they might play in realizing this objective by exploiting VLSI tools. We found that in order to satisfy the computer architect's requirements, the basic building blocks, the switchable devices, are constrained to possess simultaneously certain properties. The physical properties are: 1) ultra-high density; 2) ultra-low power dissipation; and 3) ultra-high switching speeds. The engineering properties are: 1) high isolating ability; 2) gain; 3) high tolerance to wide parameter variations; 4) noise immunity; 5) high non-linearity; 6) ability to standardize levels; 7) high discrimination between 1 and 0 levels; 8) non-latching operation; and 9) ability to invert. Presently there is no device which combines all of these properties to realize 500 MIPS machine. Pushing transistors to their limits results in improved speed and density; however, the power dissipation will be the bottle-neck. These considerations justify investigating superconducting devices having low power dissipation potential. The superconducting device which has received much attention recently is based on the Josephson effect. Its high speed, $\sim$ 10 ps, and low switching energy, $\sim$ .001fJ, are well established; however, the Josephson technology is still evolving to accommodate other engineering considerations.

A large portion of this chapter is devoted to the impact of lacking transistor-like properties and other engineering considerations on the evolution of logic and memory circuits in Josephson integrated circuit technology. The motivation has been in part to stimulate interest in the search for new generations of cryogenic devices. Knowing in advance the desired properties to maintain, and the troublesome properties to avoid, should render the search more fruitful.

Stimulating discussions with A. Davidson, R. Matick and R. W. Keyes, are gratefully acknowledged.

REFERENCES

(1) Landauer, R. W. *IBM J. Res. Dev.* **5**:183 (1961).
(2) Keyes, R. W. and Landauer, R. *IBM J. Res. Dev.* **14**:152 (1970).

(3) Landauer, R. W. *Physics Today* **23**:22 (1970).
(4) Keyes, R. W. *IEEE Trans. Comp.* **C-26**:1017 (1974).
(5) Keyes, R. W. *IEEE J. Solid State Circuits* **SC-14**:193 (1979).
(6) Keyes, R. W. *Proc. IEEE* **69**:267 (1981).
(7) Lepselter, M. P. *IEEE Spectrum* **18**:26 (1981).
(8) Mizutani, T. et al. *Electron Lett.* **16**:815 (1980).
(9) Lee, F. S. et al. *Proc. IEEE ICCC80,* N. B. Guy Rabbat, editor, p. 696 (1980).
(10) Gaensslen, F. H. et al. *IEEE Trans. Elect. Dev.* **ED-24**:218 (1977).
(11) Gray, K. E. *Appl. Phys. Lett.* **32**:392 (1978).
(12) Faris, S. M. et al. *Bull Am. Phys. Soc.* **26**:306 (1981).
(13) Matick, R. E. *Computer Storage Systems and Technology.* New York: John Wiley and Sons, Inc., 1977.
(14) Chow, W. F. *Principles of Tunnel Diode Circuits.* New York: John Wiley and Sons Inc., 1964.
(15) Faris, S. M. *Proc. IEEE ICCC80,* N. B. Guy Rabbat, editor, p. 1196 (1980).
(16) Matisoo, J. *IEEE Tran. Magn.* **MAG-5**:848 (1969); Keyes, R. W. *IEEE Trans. Magn.* **MAG-15**:213 (1979).
(17) Tinkham, M. *Introduction to Superconductivity.* New York: McGraw-Hill Book Company, 1975.
Solymar, L. *Superconducting Tunneling and Applications* London: Chapman and Hall, 1972.
(18) Van Duzer, T. *IEEE Trans. Microwave Theory and Technique* **MTT-28**:490 (1980).
(19) Matisoo, J. *IBM J. Res. Dev.* **24**:113 (1980).
(20) Kautz, R. L. *J. Appl. Phys.* **49**:308 (1978).
(21) Onnes, H. K. *Akad. Van Wetensehappen* **14**:113 (1911).
(22) Meissner, W. and Ochsenfeld, R. *Naturwiss* **21**:787 (1933).
(23) Bardeen, J., Cooper, L. N. and Schrieffer, J. R. *Phys. Rev.* **106**:162 (1958).
(24) Giaever, I., and Megerle, K. *Phys. Rev.* **122**:1101 (1961).
(25) Giaever, I. *Phys. Rev. Lett.* **5**:464 (1960).
(26) Josephson, B. D. *Phys. Lett.* **1**:251 (1962).
(27) Anderson, P. W., and Rowell, J. M. *Phys. Rev. Lett.* **10**:230 (1963).
(28) Rowell, J. M. *Phys. Rev. Lett.* **11**:200 (1963).
(29) Buck, D. A. *Proc. IRE* **44**:482 (1956).
(30) Newhouse, V. L., Bremer, J. W. and Edwards, H. H. *Solid State Electronics* **1**:261 (1960).
(31) Crowe, J. W. *IBM J. Res. Dev.* **1**:275 (1957); Garwin, R. L. ibid, 304.
(32) Rowell, J. M. U.S. Patent 3,281,609 (Jan. 1964).
(33) Merriam, M. F. *IBM Tech. Disc. Bull.* **7**:271 (1964).
(34) Shapiro, S. *Phys. Rev. Lett.* **11**:80 (1963).
(35) Matisoo, J. *Appl. Phys. Lett.* **9**:167 (1966).
(36) Matisoo, J. *Proc. IEEE* **55**:172 (1967).
(37) Matisoo, J. *Proc. IEEE* **55**:2052 (1967).
(38) *IBM J. Res. Dev.* **24,** March 1980, special issue covering many aspects of the Josephson integrated circuit technology.
(39) *IEEE Transactions on Electron Devices* **ED-27**, October 1980, special issue on Josephson technology for computer and non-computer applications.
(40) Henkels, W. H. and Zappe, H. H. *IEEE J. Solid State Circuits* **SC-13**:591 (1978).
(41) Gueret, P., et al. *IBM J. Res. Dev.* **24**:155 (1980).
(42) Zappe, H. H. *IEEE Trans. Elect. Dev.* **ED-27**:1870 (1980).
(43) Herrell, D. J. *IEEE J. Solid State Circuits* **SC-10**:360 (1975).
(44) Fulton, T. A., et al. *IEEE Trans. Magn.* **MAG-15**:1876 (1979).

(45) Hasuo, S., et al. *IEEE J. Solid State Circuits* **SC-16**:43 (1981).
(46) Harris, R. E., et al. *Appl. Phys. Lett.* **35**:720 (1979).
(47) Faris, S. M. *IEEE J. Solid State Circuits* **SC-14**:699 (1979).
(48) S. M. Faris, U.S. Patent 4,144,465 (1979).
(49) S.M. Faris, U.S. Patent Appl. SN 06/105,674.
(50) Faris, S. M. *Appl. Phys. Lett.* **36**:1005 (1980).
(51) Faris, S. M., and Pedersen, N. F. *Proc. 16th Low Temp. Phys. Conf.* (Aug. 1981).
(52) Tuckerman, D. B. *Appl. Phys. Lett.* **36**:1008 (1980).
(53) Ketchen, M. B. *Proc. ICCC80*, N. B. Guy Rabbat, Editor, p. 874, 1980.
(54) Anderson, C. J. and Ketchen, M. B. *IEEE Trans. Magn.* **MAG-17**:595 (1981).
(55) Harris, R. E. *Phys. Rev.* **B13**:3818 (1976).
(56) *Proc. Future Trends in Superconductive Electronics.* Deaver, B. S. Jr., Falco, C. M., Harris, J. H. and Wolf, S. A. Editors. American Institute of Physics, New York, 1978; *Proc. Superconducting Quantum Interference Devices and their Applications.* Hahlbohm, H. D., and Lubbig, H. Editors. Walter de Gruyte, Berlin, 1980.
(57) Ketchen, M. B. and Voss, R. F. *Appl. Phys. Lett.* **35**:812 (1979); Voss, R. F., Laibowitz, R. B., Raider, S. I. and Clarke, J. *J. Appl. Phys.* **51**:2306 (1980).
(58a) Hamilton, C. A. *Cryogenics,* May 1980, p. 235; Richards, P. L., Shen, T. M., Harris, R. E., and Lloyd, F. L. *Appl. Phys. Lett.* **34**:347 (1979).
(58b) Laibowitz, R. B., Broers, A. N., Yeh, J. T. C., and Viggiano, J. M. *Appl. Phys. Lett.* **35**:891 (1979).
(59) Greiner, J. H., et al. *IBM J. Res. Dev.* **24**:195 (1980).
(60) Greiner, J. H., Basavaiah, S. and Ames, I. *J. Vac. Sci. Techn.* **11**:81 (1974).
(61) McCumber, D. E. *J. Appl. Phys.* **39**:3113 (1968).
(62) Gueret, P., and Baechtold, W. *IBM Research Report RZ 847,* June, 1977.
(63) Zappe, H. H. *Appl. Phys. Lett.* **27**:432 (1975).
(64) Harris, E. P. *IEEE Trans. Magn.* **MAG-15**:2031 (1979).
(65) Baechtold, W. *IEEE J. Solid State Circuits* **SC-14**:887 (1979).
(66a) F. Fang and D. J. Herrell, U.S. Patent 4,092,553.
(66b) Arnett, P. C., and Herrell, D. J. *IEEE Trans. Magn.* **MAG-15**:553 (1979).
(67) Fulton, T. A. *Appl. Phys. Lett.* **19**:311 (1971).
(68) Jewett, R. E., and Van Duzer, T. *IEEE Trans. Magn.* **MAG-17**:599 (1981).
(69) Harris, E. P., and Chang, W. H. *IEEE Trans. Magn.* **MAG-17**:603 (1981).
(70) Faris, S. M. *IBM Tech. Disc. Bull.,* to be published.
(71) Baechtold, W. *IBM Tech. Disc. Bull.* **21**:3006 (1978).
(72) Faris, S. M. *IBM Tech. Disc. Bull.* **22**:2145 (1979).
(73) Klein, M., unpublished.
(74) Davidson, A. *IEEE J. Solid State Circuits* **SC-13**:583 (1978).
(75) A. Davidson and D. J. Herrell, U.S. Patent 4,136,290.
(76) Kulik, I. O. *Sov. Phys.-Tech. Phys.* **12**:111 (1967).
(77) Werthamer, N. R., and Shapiro, S. *Phys. Rev.* **164**:523 (1967).
(78) Zappe, H. H., and Landman, B. S. *J. Appl. Phys.* **49**:344 (1978).
(79) Gueret, P. *Appl. Phys. Lett.* **35**:889 (1979).
(80) Song, Y., and Hurrell, J. P. *IEEE Trans. Magn.* **MAG-15**:428 (1979).
(81) Faris, S. M., and Valsamakis, E. A. *J. Appl. Phys.* **52**:915 (1981).
(82) Zappe, H. H., and Landman, B. S. *J. Appl. Phys.* **49**:4154 (1978).
(83) Cabrera, B. PhD Thesis, Stanford University, 1975.
(84) Bermon, S., unpublished results.
(85) Raver, N. IBM Yorktown, in preparation.
(86) Henkels, W. H. *IEEE Trans. Magn.* **MAG-10**:860 (1974).
(87a) Herrell, D. J. *IEEE Solid State Circuits* **SC-9**:277 (1974).

(87b) Herrell, D. J. *IEEE Trans. Magn.* **MAG-10**:864 (1974).
 (88) Faris, S. M., Henkels, W. H., Valsamakis, E. A., and Zappe, H. H. *IBM J. Res. Dev.* **24**:143 (1980).
 (89) Klein, M., and Herrell, D. J. *IEEE J. Solid State Circuits* **SC-13**:577 (1978).
 (90) Faris, S. M. unpublished; and *IBM Tech. Disc. Bulletin* **20**:2031 (1977).
 (91) S. M. Faris, U.S. Patent 4,274,015.
 (92) T. A. Fulton, U.S. Patent 4,051,393.
 (93) Fulton, T. A., Magerlein, J. H., and Dunkleberger, L. N. *IEEE Trans. Magn.* **MAG-13**:56 (1977).
 (94) Hebard, A. F., Pei, S. S., Dunkleberger L. N., and T. A. Fulton, *IEEE Trans. Magn.* **MAG-15**:408 (1979).
 (95) Gheewala, T. *Appl. Phys. Lett.* **33**:781 (1978).
 (96) T. Gheewala, U.S. Patent 4,177,354.
 (97) Gheewala, T. *IBM J. Res. Dev.* **24**:130 (1980).
 (98) Baechtold, W. *Proc. ICCC80,* N. B. Guy Rabbat, Editor, p. 878, 1980.
 (99) S. M. Faris, U.S. Patent 4,149,097.
(100) Fulton, T. A., Pei, S. S., and Dunkleberger, L. N., *Appl. Phys. Lett.* **34**:709.
(101) Gheewala, T., and Mukherjee, A. *IEDM Tech. Dig.,* *482,* Washington DC, 1979.
(102) Zappe H. H. *J. Appl. Phys.* **44**:1371 (1973).
(103) Davidson, A., and Beasley, M. R. *IEEE J. Solid State Circuits* **SC-14**:758 (1979).
(104) Valsamakis, E. A., and Faris, S. M. to be published.
(105) Henkels, W. H. *J. Appl. Phys.* **50**:8143 (1979).
(106) Anacker, W. *IEEE Trans. Magn.* **MAG-5**:4 (1969).
(107) Wolf, P. *IBM Tech. Disc. Bull.* **16**:214 (1973).
(108) Henkels, W. H., and Greiner, J. *IEEE J. Solid State Circuits* **SC-14**:794 (1979).
(109) S. M. Faris, U.S. Patent 4,151,605.
(110) Broom R. F., et al. *IEEE J. Solid State Circuits* **SC-14**:690 (1979).
(111) Lueke, G., Mize, J. P., and Carr, W. N. *Semiconductor Memory Design and Applications,* New York: McGraw-Hill Book Company, 1973.
(112) Hamel, H. C., and Terlep, K. D. *IBM Tech. Disc. Bull.* **17**:3349 (1975).
(113) Faris, S. M. *IBM Tech. Disc. Bull.* **20**:4197 (1978).
(114) Baechtold, W. *IBM Tech. Disc. Bull.* **21**:2536 (1978).
(115) Anacker, W. unpublished.
(116) Baechtold, W. unpublished.
(117) Gueret, P. unpublished.
(118) Chang, W. *IBM Tech. Disc. Bull.* **22**:2962 (1979).
(119) Faris, S. M., Braslau, N. *IBM Tech. Disc. Bull.* **24**:277 (1981).
(120) Kilgannon, T. J., Jr. *IBM Tech. Disc. Bull.* **24**:1107 (1981). Proposes a scheme which replaces the dummy junction with a second bridge for a possible density improvement.
(121) Giaever, I., and Zeller, H. R. *Phys. Rev.* **B-1**:4278 (1970).
(122) Barone, A., Rissman, P., and Russo, M. *Rev. Phys. Appl.* **9**:73 (1974).
(123) Faris, S. M. *IBM Tech. Disc. Bull.* **22**:4264 (1980).
(124) S. M. Faris, U.S. Patent 4,198,577.
(125) Faris, S. M., and Davidson, A. *IEEE Trans. Magn.* **MAG15**:416 (1979).
(126) S. M. Faris U.S. Patent 4,210,921.
(127) Faris, S. M. *IBM Tech. Disc. Bull.* **21**:3384 (1979).
(128) Fleisher, H., and Maissel, L. I. *IBM J. Res. Dev.* **19**:98 (1975).
(129) Logue, J., this book, chapter 18.
(130) Faris, S. M. unpublished.

10. VLSI MOS Technology

Youssef El-Mansy

INTEL Corporation

INTRODUCTION

MOS device scaling theory as presented in 1974 (1) offered a methodology of designing devices and processes for high density high performance circuits. The procedure involved scaling down device lateral and vertical dimensions and supply voltage while increasing the substrate doping, all by the same scaling factor (S). Scaled devices have higher currents, less capacitance and a power delay product that is reduced by the factor S^3. In practice, however, voltage supplies were not scaled down for various reasons such as TTL compatibility and operating margins. The power delay product could only be reduced by a factor in the range S to S^2. Nonscalability of voltages combined with shrinking of device lateral dimensions resulted in a number of effects on device characteristics that are caused by high fields. Some of these effects are related to material physical properties such as carrier velocity saturation while others could be reduced by proper process techniques such as threshold voltage geometry dependence. Shrinking the vertical dimensions enhanced the role of parasitic resistance and capacitance in affecting device currents. It also made the thickness of the inversion channel an important parameter for thin gate oxide devices.

For scaled devices, a number of factors have a major role in defining the terminal behavior of the device. Among these are:

1. Velocity saturation of mobile channel charge.
2. Source and drain ohmic and contact resistances.
3. Finite Inversion channel thickness screening.
4. Hot electron and high voltage limitations.

What makes these effects significant is that they are mostly dependent on material physical properties and as such innovations in processing techniques would not have major impact on them. An effect that is also important for small devices is the threshold voltage dependence on geometry. However, it has been the subject of numerous publications (2–9) and will not be treated here.

We start by looking at the drain current of a long channel device. Various effects are then introduced, one at a time. Finally, some results are presented and conclusions are drawn as to future scaling of MOS devices. For proper comparisons of various stages of scaled devices, *a square* device is considered throughout the analysis, an n-channel device is considered unless otherwise specified.

LONG CHANNEL DEVICE

A cross-section of the device under consideration is shown in Figure 10-1. A planar metal or silicon gate structure is assumed with rectangular geometry. Figure 10-1a defines the notation used for terminal currents and voltages. The

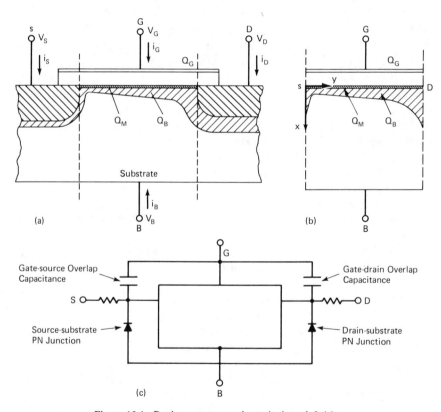

Figure 10-1. Device structure and terminology definition.

substrate is taken as the voltage reference. The intrinsic device is shown in Figure 10-1b while Figure 10-1c illustrates the parasitic components required to represent the full device.

Also indicated in the figure are three physically distinct total charges stored in the device when conditions depart from equilibrium, namely: gate charge Q_G, channel (mobile) charge Q_M and substrate (depletion charge) Q_B. Each of these charges communicates with the external circuits via a specific terminal. The device drain current results from a flow of mobile charge between source and drain terminals. The channel charge is defined by the interaction of applied voltages and structural parameters in the device. This interaction is usually multidimensional. The approach adopted here is to develop a one-dimensional model and then introduce multidimensional effects as add-on components. Such an approach is consistent with starting with a large device which is basically one-dimensional in nature and then introducing multidimensional effects pertinent to small devices.

Basic Parameters and Current

The device is treated as a one-dimensional device where the charge is generated by the gate field and moves from the source to the drain under the influence of the drain field; i.e., the vertical and lateral fields are completely decoupled. This is normally referred to as the Gradual Channel Approximation (GCA) (10). Some fundamental processing parameters are introduced using this device as the vehicle and then multidimensional effects are introduced subsequently.

Gate Flat-Band Voltage

In general, the gate and substrate materials are not the same (e.g., the gate could be aluminum while the substrate is silicon or both could be silicon with different impurity species and concentrations). This results in a work-function difference between the two materials. Also, during the device processing, charged particles are created within the gate insulator and at the substrate-insulator interface. This will cause some of the field lines originating from the gate to terminate on these charges instead of inducing a charge in the substrate. The silicon surface represents an abrupt change in the crystal regularity and leads to the creation of energy levels which are usually referred to as surface states. All of these effects are lumped into a parameter called the flat band voltage which is defined as the voltage applied to the gate to produce a *zero electric field at the insulator-substrate interface*. This parameter is defined as

$$V_{FB} = \emptyset_{MS} - \frac{Q_{ss}}{C_O} \qquad [10.1]$$

Table 10-I. Metal—SiO$_2$—Si Work Function Difference for Al and Au at 300°K.

Si IMPURITY CONCENTRATION (cm^{-3})	$\emptyset_{MS}$, eV			
	Al-SiO$_2$ n-TYPE^{2}Si	Al-SiO$_2$ p-TYPE^{2}Si	Au-SiO n-TYPE^{2}Si	Au-SiO$_2$ p-TYPE^{2}Si
10^{14}	−0.36	−0.82	0.54	0.08
10^{15}	−0.30	−0.88	0.6	0.02
10^{16}	−0.24	−0.94	0.66	−0.04
10^{17}	−0.18	−1.00	0.72	−0.1

where $\emptyset_{MS}$ is the work function difference between the gate and substrate materials. For a metal gate this function is shown in Table 10-1 for different metals and substrates (11–13). For silicon gate, $\emptyset_{MS}$ is the difference between the gate and substrate Fermi levels. The effective gate voltage is then the difference between the applied gate voltage and the flat band voltage.

Charge Components

If a voltage V_G, with respect to an arbitrary reference as shown in Figure 10-2, is applied to the gate, a space charge is induced in the substrate which contains an equal charge to that on the gate but with opposite polarity. The charge in the substrate comprises two components; a channel charge Q_m and a depletion charge Q_b as shown in Figure 10-2. The assumption is made that the channel charge exists within a sheet of zero thickness at the semiconductor

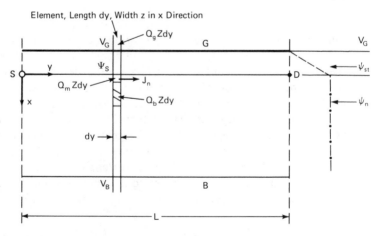

Figure 10-2. Definition of physical quantities in terms of volume element normal to silicon surface and current transport direction, on basis of gradual channel approximation.

surface. A threshold surface potential Ψ_{st} is defined for the existence of the channel (or equally for surface inversion) which is related to the channel Fermi potential $\emptyset_n$ as

$$\Psi_{st} = \emptyset_n + \emptyset_f \qquad [10.2]$$

where $\emptyset_f$ is the substrate Fermi potential. The various charge components under inversion conditions are then written as

$$Q_g = C_O(V_G - \emptyset_n - V_{FB} - 2\emptyset_f)$$
$$Q_b = C_{DE} \sqrt{\emptyset_n - V_B + 2\emptyset_f/\beta}$$

and

$$\left.\begin{array}{r} Q_m = -(Q_g + Q_b) \\ = -C_O(V_G - \emptyset_n - V_{FB} - 2\emptyset_f) \\ + C_{DE} \sqrt{(\emptyset_n - V_B + 2\emptyset_f)/\beta} \end{array}\right\} \qquad [10.3]$$

where C_O is the gate insulator capacitance per unit area, C_{DE} is the extrinsic Debye capacitance and β is the thermal voltage given by KT/q, K being the Boltzmann constant, T the absolute temperature and q the electronic charge. At the source and drain terminals, the parameter $\emptyset_n$ takes the values V_S and V_D respectively.

Gate Threshold Voltage

This is defined as the voltage applied to the gate just to cause inversion at the source end of the channel; i.e., to make the surface potential at the source end equal to Ψ_{st}. Setting $Q_m = O$ in equation [10.3] with the source voltage V_S substituted for $\emptyset_n$ and V_{GT} substituted for V_G, we obtain for the threshold voltage with respect to the source

$$V_T = V_{FB} + 2\emptyset_f + \frac{C_{DE}}{C_O} \sqrt{\frac{1}{\beta}(V_S - V_B + 2\emptyset_f)} \qquad [10.4]$$

Simplified Charge Components

In this simplified model, the thickness of depletion region below the channel is taken to be constant with distance along the channel and equal to the thickness at the source end. The charge density components are then given by

$$Q_g = C_O(V_{GF} - \emptyset_n)$$

while

$$Q_b = -C_{DE} \sqrt{\frac{1}{\beta}(V_S - V_B + 2\emptyset_f)} \qquad [10.5]$$

and

$$Q_m = -C_o(V_{GT} - \emptyset_n)$$

where

$$V_{GT} = V_G - V_T, \; V_{GF} = V_G - V_{FB} - 2\emptyset_f \qquad [10.6]$$

Drain Transport Current

The equations for the transport current can now be written

$$i_D = u_n Z Q_m \frac{d\emptyset_n}{dy} \qquad [10.7]$$

where u_n is the low field mobility, Z is the device width, Y is the direction of current flow along the channel. Integrating between the source and the drain

$$i_D = \frac{u_n Z}{L} \int_{V_S}^{V_D} Q_m \, d\emptyset_n \qquad [10.8]$$

For a square device $(Z = L)$, i_D becomes

$$i_D = u_n C_O \left[V_{GT}(V_D - V_S) - \frac{V_D^2}{2} + \frac{V_S^2}{2} \right]$$
$$= u_n C_O F(V_G, V_D, V_S) \qquad [10.9]$$

which is valid for values of V_D up to saturation. The drain saturation voltage V_{DSAT} is defined as the drain voltage V_D at which $\partial I_D / \partial V_D = 0$. In this case from [10.9] $V_{DSAT} = V_{GT}$. In the saturation region $(V_D > V_{GT})$ the transport current is then written as

$$i_D = u_n C_O(V_{GT} - V_S)^2 \qquad [10.10]$$

The current behavior as expressed by equations [10.9] and [10.10] is displayed in Figure 10-3 in both the linear $(V_D \leq V_{GT})$ and saturation $(V_D > V_{GT})$

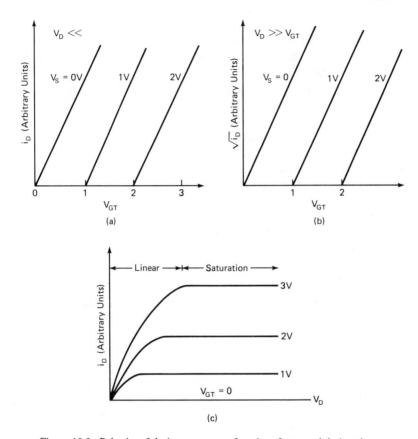

Figure 10-3. Behavior of drain current as a function of gate and drain voltages.

regions of operation. The current dependence on gate voltage shown in Figures 10-3(a) and 10-3(b) changes from a linear to square law dependence. The dependence on V_D where the linear and saturation regions of operation are pointed out is shown in Figure 10-3C.

SMALL DEVICE SIZE EFFECTS

In developing the model presented in the previous section, the gradual channel approximation was used and the solution was based on a one-dimensional electrostatic analysis. This limits the applicability of such model to device structures where such an approximation can be reasonably satisfied. As the device dimensions become smaller, the use of two-dimensional or even three-dimensional solutions becomes crucial to the proper evaluation of device parameters. Such a complete solution is only achievable by using numerical techniques and the results are not in a form suitable to gain physical insight. An alternative is to identify the important effects that result from shrinking device dimensions and to treat such effects on a one-at-a time basis. What is implied here is that these effects can be decoupled, which is, of course, an approximation.

The following mechanisms are identified as the most important in affecting the behavior of small devices:

- Velocity saturation of channel carriers.
- Source/drain parasitic resistance.
- Finite thickness of inversion layer.
- Voltage/hot electron limitation.

These mechanisms and the manner in which they affect the device parameters are now discussed. The model developed earlier is used as a vehicle throughout this development.

Carrier Velocity Saturation

As the channel length L_E is reduced, the electric field along the channel increases and the carrier velocity deviates from the linear dependence on field and finally saturates at a scatter limited value. A simple way to express such behavior is

$$u_e = \frac{u_n}{1 + \frac{u_n}{v_o} E}$$

where v_o is the scatter limited value and E is the electric field. The drain current in equation [10.9] is modified to

$$ID = u_n C_O \cdot F_v \cdot F(V_G, V_D, V_S) \qquad [10.11]$$

where

$$F_v = (1 + v_{av}/v_o)^{-1}$$

and

$$v_{av} = \frac{u_n(V_D - V_S)}{L_E}$$

As can be seen from equation [10.11], the effect of carrier velocity saturation is that the current in a square device reduces as the channel length is decreased

$(F_v < 1)$. The current also saturates at a lower drain voltage which is now given as

$$V_{DSAT} = V_S + \frac{v_o L_E}{u_n} \left\{ \sqrt{1 + \frac{2u_n(V_{GT} - V_S)}{v_o L_E}} - 1 \right\} \quad [10.12]$$

and the corresponding saturation current is (cf. to equation [10.10]).

$$I_{DSAT} = \tfrac{1}{2}u_n C_o(V_{GT} - V_S)^2 \left\{ 1 - \left(1 - \frac{v_o L_E}{u_n(V_{GT} - V_S)} \right. \right.$$

$$\left. \left. \times \left(\sqrt{1 + \frac{2u_n(V_{GT} - V_S)}{v_o L_E}} - 1 \right) \right)^2 \right\} \quad [10.13]$$

which again illustrates the effect of velocity saturation in reducing the current.

We now consider some aspects of that expression. We start by looking at the limiting conditions.

1. *Long Channel*:

$$L_E \gg \frac{u_n(V_{GT} - V_S)}{v_o}$$

For this case, the saturation voltage given by [10.12] becomes

$$V_{DSAT} = V_{GT}$$

and the saturation current in [10.6] becomes

$$I_{DSAT} = \tfrac{1}{2}u_n C_o(V_{GT} - V_S)^2$$

which are the standard long channel expressions.

2. *Very Small L_F Limit:*

$$\text{as } L_E \rightarrow 0$$
$$V_{DSAT} \rightarrow 0$$

and

$$I_{DSAT} \rightarrow I_O = C_o Z V_o(V_{GT} - V_S) \quad [10.14]$$

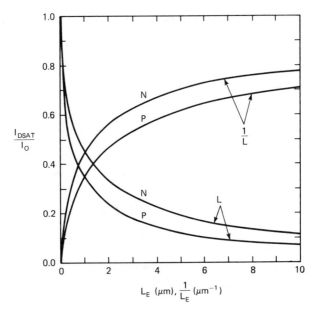

Figure 10-4. Normalized (to max. current) saturation current vs L_E for p and n channel devices.

which represents the ultimate current available in a given technology if punch-through does not pose a limitation.

3. The saturation current dependence on gate voltage changes from square law to linear dependence for very short channels. This is consistent with a change from mobility dependence to saturation velocity dependence. A plot showing the saturation current vs. channel length is shown in Figure 10-4 where the rate of increase of current as the channel length is reduced diminishes.

Source and Drain Resistance (14)

As devices are scaled down, junctions get shallower and contact openings to these junctions become smaller. Both lead to an increased parasitic resistance in series with the device. The effect of such resistance is enhanced by the fact that the intrinsic device resistance becomes smaller for scaled devices. The resistance of each of the source and drain regions can be written as

$$R_S = R_\square \frac{L_D}{L_E} + R_C = R'_\square \cdot \frac{L_D}{L_E} \qquad [10.15]$$

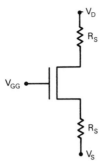

Figure 10-5. Series resistance.

where $R_\square$ and R_C are the diffusion (per square) and contact resistances respectively. It is assumed that the ratio L_D/L_E is constant as it is determined by lithographic alignment and resolution capabilities which normally track each other. For very small dimensions ($\lesssim 1\mu$m) R_C will be a dominant factor. The effect of the parasitic resistance can be incorporated in equation [10.2] to give (refer to Figure 10-5)

$$I_D = uC_O \cdot F_{vR} \cdot F(V_G, V_D, V_S) \qquad [10.16]$$

where

$$F_{vR} = \left(1 + \frac{v_{av}}{v_o} + \frac{2R_S}{R_{CH}}\right)^{-1}$$

$$R_{CH} = \left\{uC_O\left(V_G - \frac{V_D + V_S}{2}\right)\right\}^{-1}$$

The increased value of R_S reduces the current of square device as the junctions and contacts are scaled down.

Finite Inversion Layer Thickness

Experimental results (15, 16), on thin insulator devices have shown a degradation of device currents and transconductances. In those devices, the gate insulator thickness is of the same order as the inversion layer thickness. This causes the potential drop across the inversion layer to be a large portion of the applied gate to source voltage (17). A simple model to describe that effect is illustrated in Figure 10-6, where it shows that, in strong inversion, the effective gate capacitance is less than C_O and is the series combination of C_O and C_{CH}.

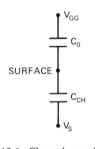

Figure 10-6. Channel capacitance.

This can be incorporated in the drain current expression by modifying the capacitance C_O by a factor F_{CH} to give

$$I_D = uC_O \cdot F_{vR} \cdot F_{CH} \cdot F(V_G, V_D, V_S) \qquad [10.17]$$

where

$$F_{CH} = \left(1 + \frac{C_O}{C_{CH}} \right)^{-1} \qquad [10.18]$$

and the final gain constant of the device is

$$K = uC_O \cdot F_{vR} \cdot F_{CH} \qquad [10.19]$$

For a device with a gate capacitance of the order of the channel capacitance (70Å nitride or 35Å oxide), this effect causes the measured current to be half of the expected value (of an equivalent device with zero inversion layer thickness).

Voltage/Hot Electron Limitations

We define the maximum usable voltage in the device as the lowest of the punchthrough, junction breakdown and latchup initiated by the substrate impact ionization current. In advanced submicron technologies junction breakdown and latchup are responsible for limiting the maximum voltage. Figure 10-7 shows the results obtained on various n- and p-channel technologies as a function of scaling factor. The n-channel device behavior is dominated by the latchup caused by substrate currents while the p-channel device is dominated by junction breakdown, Figure 10-8. This is due to the difference between holes and electrons impact ionization coefficients (18). The behavior of substrate cur-

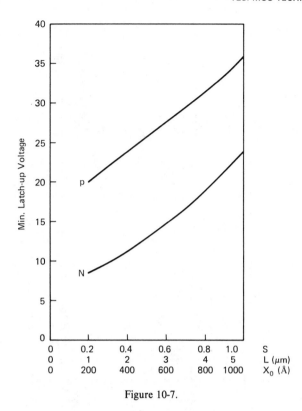

Figure 10-7.

rents as a function of scaling factor is shown in Figure 10-9 which shows consistently a three order of magnitude difference in the current. A similar argument applies for channel hot electrons that can get trapped into gate oxides and cause a long term shift in threshold voltages.

DISCUSSIONS AND CONCLUSIONS

Using an NMOS 1975 process as a reference (scaling factor S of 1) and using the relationships derived here, the data in Table 10-2 and Figure 10-10 was generated. Scaling factors of 0.7 and 0.4, applied to channel lengths, oxide thickness and junction depth, produce scaled technologies that have existed in production in 1977 and 1979 respectively. As can be seen from the data, the physical mechanism with most effect on those technologies has been velocity saturation while other mechanisms discussed here were nonsignificant. Results on technologies with scaling factors in the range 0.3 to 0.05 are also shown. The ratio of the oxide thickness to channel length has been kept constant while

P-Channel

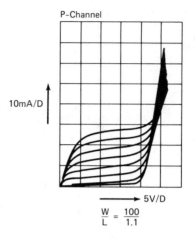

10mA/D

5V/D

$$\frac{W}{L} = \frac{100}{1.1}$$

N-Channel

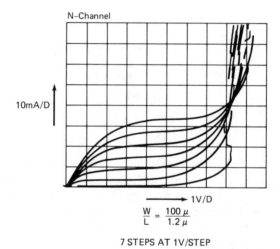

10mA/D

1V/D

$$\frac{W}{L} = \frac{100\,\mu}{1.2\,\mu}$$

7 STEPS AT 1V/STEP

Figure 10-8.

the equivalent parasitic resistance has been increased by the inverse of the scaling factor. As contact windows become smaller, contact resistance contribution becomes significant (18), and this is (as opposed to making the junctions shallower) the major factor in increasing $R'_\square$. As devices are scaled down, the current gain peaks for a device with a scaling factor of 0.2 (1 μm channel length and 200Å gate oxide). For that device, the finite inversion layer thickness and series resistance reduce the gain by about 14% and 7% respectively. Matters get worse for smaller scaling factors. By lowering the operating voltages, the

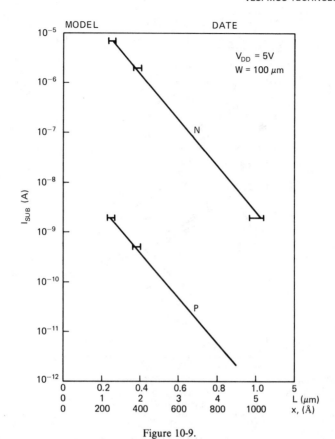

Figure 10-9.

Table 10-2. The Contribution of the Different Factors to Current Reduction in Scaled Devices (SiO$_2$, 5V)

SCALING FACTOR s	PROCESS PARAMETERS			VELOCITY SATURATION & RESISTANCE PARS			CHANNEL CAPACITY	LONG CHANNEL GAIN	SHORT CHANNEL GAIN
	X_0 (Å)	L_E (μm)	$R'_\square$ (Ω)	$\frac{\nu_{AV}}{\nu_0}$	$\frac{2R_S}{R_{CH}}$	$F_{\nu R}$	F_{CH}	$\mu C_0 \times 10^8$	$K \times 10^8$
1	1000	5	20	0.35	0.007	0.74	0.97	3.3	2.35
0.7	700	3.5	28.5	0.5	0.0015	0.66	0.95	4.7	2.96
0.4	400	2	50	0.83	0.044	0.53	0.92	8.25	4.06
0.3	300	1.5	66.7	1.17	0.078	0.44	0.9	11	4.35
0.2	200	1	100	1.75	0.175	0.34	0.86	16.5	4.8
0.1	100	0.5	200	3.5	0.7	0.19	0.75	33	4.73
0.05	50	0.25	400	7	2.8	0.09	0.6	66	3.67

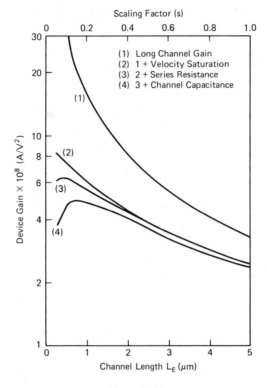

Figure 10-10.

turn around point will move to smaller channel lengths and some gain advantage can be obtained going to 0.5μm devices. For p-channel devices, the same trends are observed. Figure 10-11 illustrates the gain factor behavior for p- vs. n-channel devices which shows the peaking occurs at a slightly lower value for the p-channel. The relative performance merits and operating range of p- vs. n-channel devices have also been changing in favor of p-channel devices for the more recent technologies. Two paths will be (or are) emerging that will determine the interaction between device/technology scaling and applications:

1. For those applications where the driving force is to minimize the power-delay product and increase density, there is a strong move towards reduced operating voltages and further scaling of devices and technologies. The work horse will still remain n-channel devices to utilize its inherent speed advantage. Such reduction of operating voltages will either be achieved through a new power supply standard (to replace the 5V) or by generating a reduced supply internally on a chip still using an external 5V supply.

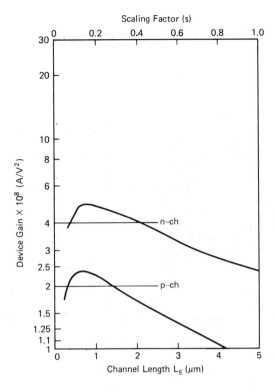

Figure 10-11.

2. For applications where the minimum signal poses the constraint, the drive for a reduced operating voltage is not as strong an issue since this is detrimental to the signal and/or the density. Usually, the minimum limit of the signal is imposed by information integrity in a noisey environment, ability to resolve, control and reproduce minimum device dimensions and device matching. To keep the operating voltage high and at the same time continue the scaling trend and performance pay-offs, p-channel devices will find an increased use. This, combined with ease of design and lower power dissipation, will make CMOS technologies a viable contendor in traditionally NMOS strongholds.

In summary, devices obtainable from technologies with an S factor in the range 0.1–0.2 are more than adequate for applications foreseen in the next decade. A need which has always been present and will even become stronger in present and future technologies is for device optimization and lower resistance interconnect layers. A minimum of two levels (probably metal) is required for the proper utilization of density and performance achievable in VLSI.

REFERENCES

(1) Dennard, R. H., et al. "Design of Ion-Implanted MOSFET's with Very Small Physical Dimensions." *Journal of Solid-State Circuits* SC-9: 256–268 (Oct. 1971).

(2) Lee, H. S. "An Analysis of the Threshold Voltage for Short-Channel IGFET's." *Solid State Electronics* 16: 1407–1417 (1973).

(3) Yau, L. D. "A Simple Theory to Predict the Threshold Voltage of Short-Channel IDFET's." *Solid-State Electronics* 17: 1059–1063 (1974).

(4) Dang, L. M. "A One-Dimensional Theory on the Effects of Diffusion Current and Carrier Velocity Saturation on E-Type IGFET Current-Voltage Characteristics." *Solid-State Electronics* 20: 781–788 (1977).

(5) Wang, P. P. "Double Boron Implant Short-Channel MOSFET." *IEEE Trans. Electron Devices* ED-24: 196–204 (March, 1977).

(6) Omura, Y., and Ohwada, K. "Threshold Voltage Theory for a Short-Channel MOSFET using a Surface-Potential Distribution Model." *Solid-State Electronics* 22: 1045–1051 (1979).

(7) Wang, P. P. "Device Characteristics of Short-Channel and Narrow-Width MOSFET's." *IEEE Trans. Electron Devices* ED-25: 779–786 (July, 1978).

(8) Sun, E., et al. "Breakdown Mechanism in Short-Channel MOS Transistors." *IEDM Tech. Digest* 478–482 (1978).

(9) Klaassen, F. "Modelling of Scaled-Down MOS Transistors." *Solid State Electronics* 23: 237 (1980).

(10) Shockley, W. "A Unipolar Field-Effect Transistor." *Proc. IRE* 40: 1365–1376 (Nov. 1952).

(11) Sze, S. M. *Physics of Semiconductor Devices.* New York: Wiley-Interscience, 1969.

(12) Grove, A. S. *Physics and Technology of Semiconductor Devices.* New York: Wiley and Sons, 1967.

(13) Cobbold, R. S. C. *Theory and Application of Field-Effect Transistors.* New York: Wiley-Interscience, 1970.

(14) Chatterjee, P. K., et al. "The Impact on Scaling Laws on the Choice of N-Channel or P-Channel for MOS VLSI." *IEEE Trans. Electron Device Letters* EDL-1: 220 (1980).

(15) Ito, T., et al. "Thermal Nitride Gate FET Technology for VLSI Devices." *Int. Solid-State Circuits Conference Digest* 74 (1980).

(16) Sodini, C. G., et al. "Charge Accumulation and Mobility in Thin-Gate MIS Devices. *IEEE Trans. Electron Devices* ED-27: 2177 (Nov. 1980).

(17) El-Mansy, Y. A., and Boothroyd, A. R. "A New Approach to the Theory and Modelling of Insulated Gate Field-Effect Transistors." *IEEE Trans. Electron Devices* ED-24: 241–253 (March, 1977).

(18) El-Mansy, Y., and Caughey, D. M. "Characterization of Silicon-on-Sapphire IGFET Transistors." *IEEE Trans. Electron Devices* ED-24: 1148–1153 (Sept. 1974).

(19) Nozawa, H., et al. "High Density CMOS Processing for a 16K-Bit RAM." *IEDM Tech. Digest* 366 (Dec. 1979).

11. VLSI Gallium Arsenide Technology*

F. S. Lee, S. I. Long, R. Zucca, B. M. Welch, G. Kaelin and
R. C. Eden

Rockwell International

INTRODUCTION

During the last few years, there has been growing interest in the use of gallium arsenide for high speed digital integrated circuits. This is due to the intrinsic advantages of the high electron mobility (1) of this material combined with the availability of a semi-insulating substrate (2). Very high switching speeds, approaching those of Josephson junction devices, have been demonstrated for GaAs logic employing short channel (L_g = 0.6 μm) Schottky gate MESFETs. Propagation delays as low as 17.5 ps at 77°K or τ_D = 30 ps at room temperature have been reported (3). Maximum clock frequencies of 5.5 GHz have also been observed on binary frequency dividers (4). However, high level integration has not yet been achieved with most of these approaches.

While future system applications of gigabit digital circuits are possible at all levels of integration, an ever expanding range of applications will be achievable as complexity increases through the LSI range and into the VLSI range. This will allow such systems as signal processors, microwave frequency synthesizers and high speed A/D converters to be built on a single chip in more efficient architectures than are currently achievable. In addition, it is desirable in high speed integrated circuits to build at the highest possible level of integration, since off-chip interfacing through packages and transmission lines introduces propagation delay, and is costly in power dissipation. Therefore, a competitive, practical and versatile GaAs IC design should provide compatibility with LSI/

*The work on D-MESFET SDFL was supported in part by the Advanced Research Projects Agency of the Department of Defense and was monitored by the Air Force Office of Scientific Research under contract F49620-77-C-0087.

VLSI density and power requirements while maintaining propagation delays at least below 200 ps/gate.

Issues common to all LSI/VLSI circuit technologies are low power, high density and extremely high process and functional yields. The depletion mode GaAs MESFET technology has long been used for the fabrication of microwave transistors. When GaAs was first considered for IC implementation, it was expected that depletion-mode (normally on) MESFET technologies were incompatible with the LSI requirements because of high power dissipation and gate areas. However, the use of low negative threshold voltage (~ -1 V) depletion-mode MESFETs can overcome these limitations if sufficient threshold voltage uniformity can be realized.

A reproducible ion implantation technology in GaAs has recently been developed. This technology does provide MESFETs with the uniformity in threshold voltage required for LSI circuits (5). Localized ion implantation also permits the use of planar instead of mesa fabrication methods. Because of these technological advances, low negative threshold voltage depletion mode MESFET logic has been able to achieve low power dissipation and high circuit density with little sacrifice in speed, thereby overcoming many of the former objections to the feasibility of GaAs LSI circuits.

A low power high speed depletion mode MESFET design, the Schottky Diode FET logic (SDFL) (6), has been developed for the fabrication of LSI/VLSI circuits. An 1008 gate GaAs IC–8 $\times$ 8 multiplier has been successfully fabricated using the SDFL approach. The design and performance of the 8 $\times$ 8 multiplier will be discussed in the last section of this chapter. The advantages of GaAs material for high speed VLSI are presented in the section of that name. Various GaAs logic designs and process techniques are then described in their respective sections. And in addition to the discussion of the multiplier, the performance of GaAs ICs for different design approaches are compared in the last section.

ADVANTAGES OF GaAs FOR HIGH SPEED VLSI

Gallium Arsenide has been utilized extensively over the last 6 years for low noise microwave amplification (7, 8). Metal-semiconductor field effect transistors (MESFETS) with 0.5 to 1.0 μm gate lengths have been available from several sources in manufacturing quantities, and the GaAs FET has replaced most competing small signal amplifier devices in the upper microwave region (8–18 GHz).

During the last 4 years, there has been a growing interest in the use of GaAs for digital integrated circuits. This is due largely to the high electron mobility and drift velocity of GaAs at room temperature and to the high resistivity ($>10^8$ Ω cm) exhibited by GaAs when compensated with Cr or other deep levels. This semi-insulating GaAs is available as a substrate which can be used for direct ion implantation of active devices. The high resistivity of the substrate is helpful in minimizing interconnect capacitance in an IC. The high mobility and drift velocity of electrons yields FETs with high f_r (current gain-bandwidth product) which is directly related to switching speed.

The f_r of a FET, $g_m/(2\pi Cgs)$, is dependent on the transconductance, g_m, which is proportional to either the electron mobility, μ_r, or the saturated drift velocity, V_s. The gate-source capacitance, C_{gs}, is approximately equal for Si and GaAs MESFETs. Theoretical predictions of the performance margin to be expected over silicon FETs (MESFET or NMOS) depend critically on which model is believed to correctly apply to a very large scale integrated circuit. The mobility model predicts about 6 times higher g_m for GaAs than silicon for equivalent device geometries (8), while the velocity saturation model implies only a factor of 1.5 to 2 difference in g_m at high electric fields (9). The mobility model certainly applies to very low negative threshold voltage devices ($V_{th} > -0.5$V) while the velocity saturation model is applicable to high negative threshold voltage (<-2 V) devices such as discrete microwave MESFETs operating as Class A amplifiers, for gate lengths of the order of 1 μm. The switching FET used for low power GaAs logic has a threshold voltage of ~ -1 V intermediate between the values that assure pure mobility and pure saturation regions. Since the device switches between on and off states, it operates in a mobility controlled region for a fraction of a cycle and in saturation for another fraction. Velocity overshoot of electrons accelerated in the high mobility conduction band central valley before they transfer to the lower mobility satellite valleys tend to increase switching speeds, the effect being more appreciable for short gate (~ 0.5 μm) devices.

In view of the complexity of the models, it becomes attractive to compare GaAs and Si FET devices in a practical manner. Figure 11-1 shows experimental curves of saturated drain current vs gate voltage at fixed drain voltage for GaAs MESFETs of 0.5 and 1.0 μm gate lengths (10), for 1.0 μm Si MESFETs (11,12) and for n-channel MOSFETs (NMOS) of 0.7 and 1.3 μm channel lengths (13,14).

All the curves in Figure 11-1 are being nearly parabolic at the origin and tend to become linear only at high gate voltage, due to current saturation. However, logic devices for VLSI circuits are or will be required to operate at moderate voltage swings (>1 V) between "off" and "on" states, where the curves are nearly parabolic. Comparing MESFETs in Figure 11-1, both the GaAs and Si devices exhibit approximate square law drain current vs gate voltage characteristics, $I_{ds} = K(V_{gs} - V_{th})^2$, but with greatly differing K values as would be predicted from a comparison of transconductance. Drain currents also differ by about a factor of six due to the higher GaAs mobility. Silicon NMOS devices outperform Si MESFETs because the gate oxide can be made quite thin (200 to 300Å), much thinner than the MESFET gate depletion region. Therefore, the capacitive coupling of the gate is larger for the MOS-

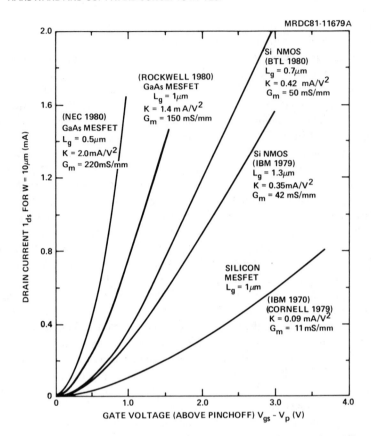

Figure 11-1. Drain current vs gate voltage (at fixed drain voltage) for a number of GaAs and Si FET devices (MESFET's and MOSFET's). The gate voltages are measured from threshold.

FET than it is for the MESFET. However, the K factor for the 0.7 μm NMOS device is still nearly 2 times smaller that the K factor for the 1.0 μm GaAs MESFET and over 3 times smaller than K for the 0.5 μm GaAs MESFET.

The ~3 times higher transconductance of GaAs FETS as compared to Si devices can be exploited to obtain higher speed, lower power dissipation or a combination of both. For higher speed, one would retain "large" voltage swings and use the higher transconductance to attain high slew rates. For low power dissipation, one would reduce the magnitude of the voltage swings and keep the currents unchanged. In general, both options are impractical, since very high currents may exceed the permitted power dissipation, and too low a voltage swing may not allow for sufficient noise margins. Therefore, the advantages arising from high device transconductance are exploited for a combination of higher speed and lower power dissipation. The balance between the two is determined, to a great extent, by the choice of logic family, with adjustments from device design. The first GaAs ICs were made with buffered FET logic (BFL), which achieved high speed ($\sim$34 ps/gate)[22] with a moderately high power dissipation ($\sim$40 mW/gate). On the contrary, direct coupled logic (DCL) using enhancement mode FETs is capable of very low power dissipation, but it suffers from difficulties in obtaining high yield due to the very low noise margins (the voltage swings are constrained to be <0.5 V). Schottky diode FET logic (SDFL) offers a good compromise. Speeds are still high ($\sim$60 ps/gate) but the power dissipation is very moderate (<1 mW/gate) and, therefore, acceptable for LSI/VLSI. The voltage swings of $\sim$1 V used in SDFL are quite compatible with the current GaAs technology capabilities. The most complex IC made with GaAs, a 1008 gate multiplier, has been fabricated using SDFL.

GaAs DIGITAL DEVICE AND IC APPROACHES

In the following section, the active switching devices most frequently used or proposed for use in GaAs integrated circuits will be briefly reviewed. The primary circuit design approaches employed for GaAs FET logic circuits will also be presented.

The Schottky barrier gate field effect transistor (MESFET) is the main active device used in GaAs ICs. Figure 11-3a shows a cross sectional diagram of a typical planar, ion-implanted MESFET fabricated by localized implantation into a semi-insulating GaAs substrate. The channel implant species, energy and dose is chosen so that the peak doping and doping profile depth (as shown in Figure 11-2) result in a device with the desired threshold (V_{th}) voltage. If the device channel is conductive at $V_{GS} = 0$, the threshold is negative and a depletion-mode (normally-on) device is obtained. The logic voltage swing can extend from $-V_{th}$ to the onset of gate conduction due to the forward biased gate-source junction. Larger logic voltage swings will produce the highest speed circuits for a given device type since higher I_{DS} per device area will be available for charging load capacitances.

If the built-in potential of the Schottky gate metal is capable of preventing current flow in the channel at $V_{GS} = 0$, an enhancement-mode (normally-off) device results. This device requires forward gate bias ($V_{GS} > 0$) to enable flow of I_{DS}. Therefore, the logic voltage swing of an enhancement-mode FET is restricted to a narrower range (V_L) (generally 0.7 V, the forward gate conduction voltage) than was the depletion-mode FET device. This restriction results in smaller I_{ds} for a given device area of an enhancement-mode FET than a depletion-mode FET, and therefore, the propagation delay is generally higher and power dissipation lower on GaAs ICs implemented with normally-off transistors.

JFET devices, using a p$^+$ gate stripe formed by selective ion implantation, have also been successfully employed in GaAs digital ICs (15). A diagram of

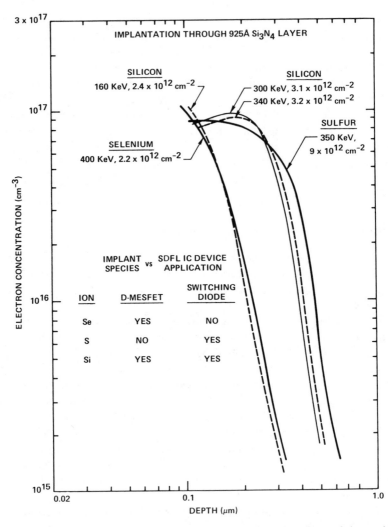

Figure 11-2. Active layer profiles (for the n-FET channel Selenium implant and the n+ high-speed switching diode sulfur implant and the Silicon implant for both the n— and n+ region.

a GaAs JFET is illustrated in Figure 11-3b. The JFET is somewhat more difficult to fabricate than a MESFET because of the additional p$^+$ implant process steps and the precise control of the p$^+$ junction depth necessary to control the threshold voltage of the device. However, sufficient control has been obtained, at least for SSI circuits (15). Gate lengths in the 1 to 2 μm range are readily achievable with optical lithography. The greater built-in potential of

MRDC81-13138

(a)

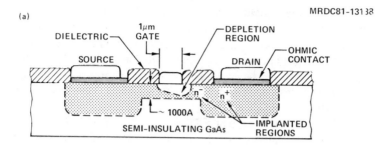

(b)

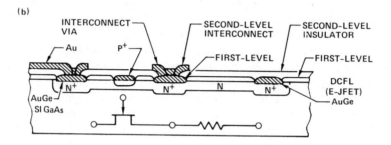

(c)

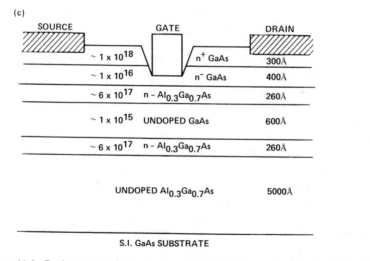

Figure 11-3. Device cross section view of (a) SDFL (b) DCFL (E-JFET) and (c) HEMT circuit.

the $p^+ - n$ junction (approximately 1.1 V) should provide a significant speed advantage for enhancement-mode JFETs over MESFETs, since $I_{ds} = K(V_{GS} - V_{th})^2$ assuming that source and gate resistances are minimized on this structure. However, the speed performance reported to date on these devices has not yet equaled the MESFET. The larger available logic voltage swing will be beneficial in increasing noise margins for normally-off JFET logic over normally-off MESFET logic.

The choice of a particular type of FET device is associated with a choice of circuit and fabrication approach. The depletion mode metal-semiconductor (Schottky barrier) FET (D-MESFET) is the most widely used device, and also the one that has given the highest performance to date. Circuits employing depletion mode MESFETs pose the least fabrication problems because Schottky barriers on GaAs are easier to fabricate than $p - n$ junctions, and the larger (typically > 1 V) logic swings associated with D-MESFET circuits avoid excessively stringent requirements for FET threshold voltage uniformity. Because any regions of the source-drain channel not under the gate are automatically strongly conducting in D-MESFETs, precise gate alignments are not required, nor are special gate recess etch processes or other means to avoid parasitic source and drain resistances necessary. The MESFET fabrication simplicity makes it considerably easier to acheive high yields than with more complex device structures. On the other hand, however, logic gates employing depletion mode active devices necessarily require some form of voltage level shifting between FET drains and gates to meet turnoff requirements, and usually require two power supplies, imposing some penalty in terms of wafer area utilization. An exception to the two power supply requirements for D-MESFET circuits is the enhancement-depletion logic approach (16) which uses -0.4 V $< V_{th} < 0.1$ MESFETs with diode level shifting in single power supply logic circuits.

Enhancement-mode MESFETs (E-MESFETs) offer circuit simplicity because the logic gates require only one power supply, but the permissible voltage swing is rather low because Schottky barrier gates on GaAs cannot be forward biased above 0.6 to 0.8 V without drawing excessive currents. A 0.5 V swing is a desirable goal for the operating range of ultra low power circuits, but very tight control is required in order to fabricate uniform, very thin active layers, so that they are totally depleted at zero gate bias voltage and yet give good device transconductance when the device is turned on. For reasonable noise margins and good dynamic performance, standard deviations of FET pinchoff voltage of the order of 25 mV should be required—a very difficult goal for GaAs FETs on LSI/VLSI compatible circuit areas.

Implementation of a MOSFET or MISFET (Metal Insulating Semiconductor FET) technology in GaAs would eliminate the logic swing limitation completely, but attaining such devices has proven difficult. Some simple ring oscillators have been fabricated with directly coupled FET logic implemented with buried channel GaAs MOSFETs with resistor loads (17). However, at this point, stable oxides have not been achieved in such circuits, so that gate threshold voltages shift with respect to the prior input signal history. This limitation has constrained the demonstration of ring oscillators and other simple circuits to operations in which the input waveform has a precisely symmetric (50% duty cycle) nature, but does not support MOSFETs in general digital circuit applications. Efforts to improve the state of GaAs oxide technology are continuing, however. The use of InP for MISFET devices may be a more promising alternative to GaAs (18).

High mobility FET devices are also being developed for use in GaAs ICs. These devices take advantage of the greatly reduced ionized impurity scattering possible at $77°K$ in a lightly doped n-GaAs channel when free carriers are introduced through a wide-gap $n^+ - Al_xGa_{1-x}As$ heterojunction as shown in Figure 11-3c. These structures have been referred to as modulation-doped FETs (19) or high electron mobility transistors (HEMT) (20), and electron mobilities of 80,000 cm^2/V-s at $77°K$ have been reported. Such FETs, fabricated with short gate lengths, should achieve high g_m and f_r with very small logic swings of only 100 mV or so. This would result in extremely low speed-power products. To utilize these devices for LSI GaAs circuits, however, an effective means of fabrication of large numbers of these transistors with nearly identical device characteristics must be developed. At the present time, a 27 stage ring oscillator with a gate delay time of 17 ps at $77°K$ has been demonstrated.

Enhancement-Mode Circuit Designs

A number of circuit designs for basic logic gate structures have been proposed or demonstrated utilizing normally-off FETs in conjunction with resistor or depletion loads and Schottky-barrier level shifting diodes. These have mainly been oriented toward use of the MESFET or JFET as the active switching devices.

The simplest circuit approach, direct-coupled FET logic, is illustrated for a 3-input (positive) NOR gate in Figure 11-4a. This circuit configuration is called directly coupled FET logic (DCFL). In this approach, a logic "0" corresponds to a voltage near zero. A logic "1" corresponds to a positive voltage capable of fully turning on the normally off FETs, a value usually limited by the onset of gate conduction in the FET; typically on the order of 0.6 V to 1.4 V depending on what technology is used (MESFET, JFET or HJFET). It has been proposed to place input FETs in series, generating the NAND function (15). However, the implementation of such design would appear impractical because the on resistance of the conducting FETs would cause larger threshold shifts than could be tolerated with the very low logic swings of E-MESFET

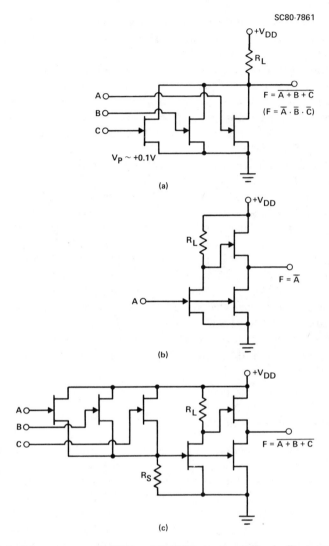

Figure 11-4. Enhancement-mode JFET or MESFET circuits. a) Simple direct-coupled FET logic (DCFL) NOR gate with resistor load. b) Pseudo-complementary buffered inverter gate. c) Combination of source-follower logic with the circuit of b) to give a buffered NOR gate. This type of approach has been extended to two-level gates as well.

logic. (It would probably work with E-JFETs or HJFETs, however, and should represent no problem with MOSFETs.)

A significant improvement to the directly coupled logic gate shown in Figure 11-4a would be to substitute for load resistor R_L, an active load current source made with a normally on (depletion mode) FET, with its gate tied to the source. Such a nonlinear load would sharpen the transfer characteristic and significantly improve the speed and speed-power products of the circuits (by perhaps a factor of 2). The fabrication of the depletion-mode active load requires a carrier concentration profile different from that of the enhancement mode devices. Although demonstration circuits using enhancement-mode devices have been fabricated using only one type of active layer, the multiple localized implantation fabrication technique used for the Schottky-diode FET logic (SDFL) approach (discussed later in this section) could be readily applied to optimize enhancement-mode circuits.

From a static point of view, the fanout capability of the directly coupled FET logic is excellent since it is determined by the very low gate leakage currents. However, from a dynamic point of view, the switching speeds are reduced by the gate capacitance loadings by a factor of approximately $1/N$ where N is the number of loading gates, as in silicon MOS. In general, the current through the resistor, R_L, or active load is kept fairly low in DCFL in order to reduce static power and improve noise margin by reducing the output "low" voltage of FET. Consequently, the output risetime under heavy fanout loading conditions is very poor. This can be greatly improved with the pseudo-complementary output buffer configuration on Figure 11-4b, at very little increase in static power dissipation, but this circuit performs only logic inversion (15). By combining the inverting buffer with a source-follower positive-OR input structure as shown in Figure 11-4c, a general multiple-input NOR gate can be achieved which has excellent fan-in and fanout drive capabilities at very modest static power levels (21). Unfortunately, this source-OR/pseudo-complementary inverter gate configuration is also quite complex, requiring 7 FETs and 2 resistors for a 4-input NOR gate, which can be expected to consume considerable chip area and have significant self capacitance.

Enhancement-Depletion Mode MESFET Logic

Because of the nonlinear, approximately square-law nature of the FET I_{ds} vs V_{gs} relationship, it is not always necessary to completely turn off the FET (i.e., make V_{gs} more negative than V_{th}) in order to obtain switching behavior.

Drain dotting of many FETs as in Figure 11-4a necessitates turning all of the FETs nearly off so that the sum of all of their drain currents is substantially less than the load current I_L (through R_L in Figure 11-4a). However, if only a single FET switches the load, it is only necessary to reduce its drain current in the off state to a value significantly smaller than I_L, while its "on" current is well above I_L. This can be achieved in depletion-mode MESFETs with reasonably small threshold voltages ($V_{th} \approx -0.4$ V) with zero or slightly positive gate-voltages, so that only a single power supply is required. For example, with $V_{th} = -0.4$ and V_{gs} (on) $= +0.7$ V, V_{gs} (off) $= +0.1$ V, we have I_{ds} (on) $= 4.84 \times I_{ds}$ (off), an ample margin for switching.

A number of circuit approaches for single supply E-D MESFET logic have been proposed and analyzed (16). Figure 11-5a shows the circuit diagram for an elemental 3-input NOR gate in the most promising of these published approaches. This uses source follower logic to obtain the positive OR function, with single diode level shifting and resistor pulldown, R_S, to drive the output inverter FET. The analysis (16) indicates proper gate operation for MESFET threshold voltages in the $-0.4 < V < +0.1$ V range, which is several times the allowable range width for E-MESFET logic and much more reasonable in terms of practical fabrication control. The supply voltage ($V_{dd} \sim 3$ V) and logic voltage swing ($V_{out} \sim 0.2$ V to 2.4 V) values used are even larger than those used in D-MESFET approaches, so that very low $P_D \tau_d$ products would not be expected. The gate output of Figure 11-5a has the same drive problems as that of Figure 11-4a, but this should be improved for heavily loaded gates with the buffer structure of Figure 11-5b. This structure is, of course, very similar (except for the two voltage shifting diodes) to the enhancement circuit of Figure 11-4c.

At the present time, demonstration circuits containing up to 15 gates have been fabricated using enhancement-mode FETs. MESFET-implemented cir-

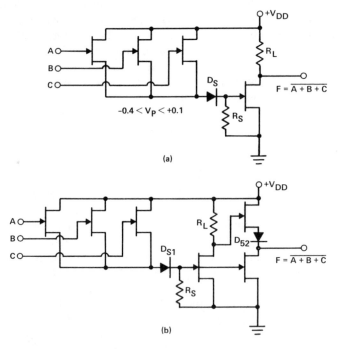

Figure 11-5. Single-supply enhancement-depletion MESFET NOR gate circuits. a) Quasi-Normally-Off 3-input NOR gate. b) 3-input NOR gate with Pseudo-complementary buffer; note similarity to Figure 11-4 (c).

cuits have exceeded the performance of JFET circuits in both speed and power even though the higher JFET logic swing should provide greater speed. Complexity of enhancement-mode circuits has probably been limited by fabrication technology and threshold uniformity. Compromise of ring oscillator and frequency divider demonstration circuits using these design approaches are made in the last section.

Depletion-Mode Logic Approaches

Buffered FET Logic (BFL) and Schottky Diode FET Logic (SDFL) gate circuit approaches have been extensively employed for depletion-mode GaAs ICs. Circuit diagrams for NOR gates formed by these two approaches are presented in Figures 11-6 and 11-7. The BFL circuit employs FETs to perform a NOR (or 2-input NAND for a dual-gate FET) function at the input. The output is driven by a source follower, with level shifting diodes to restore the required logic levels to the $+0.7$ V (high) to $-V_{th}$ (low) voltages required by the input FETs. The source-follower output driver yields a gate structure which has relatively low sensitivity, to fan-out loading and load capacitance. Also no DC output current is required to drive subsequent BFL gate inputs. Fan-in is limited for practical purposes to 3 for a NOR gate by the drain capacitances of the input transistors and the area required by these devices and 2 for the NAND gate because of voltage drop in the series FETs which results in threshold shift.

Nearly all BFL circuits reported to date have utilized relatively high negative threshold voltages (-2.5 V) and three level-shift diodes for convenience in fabrication (since epi/implant-mesa approaches provide suitable threshold control for large logic voltage swings) and have therefore exhibited high power dissipation per gate (40 mW typical). However, since fabrication methods and threshold voltage control have been improved with ion-implanted, planar approaches, there is no reason why low negative threshold (-1 V) MESFETs and two level-shift diodes should not be employed for advanced BFL gates designs. These modifications should reduce power dissipation to the 5 mW/ gate level by allowing operation at lower voltage and current levels with relatively little sacrifice in speed and could make BFL circuits a possible candidate for applications requiring lower LSI complexity (200–500 gates). Demonstration circuits with about 20 gates complexity have been reported in the literature using high negative threshold voltage BFL gates (22), however larger BFL circuits (>200 gates) using low negative threshold FETs are currently in development (23).

The SDFL circuit approach, shown in Figure 11-7 permits high speed operation comparable to the BFL approach, but results in considerable savings in area/gate (600 to 2000 μm^2) and in lower power dissipation (0.2 to 2 mW/ gate).

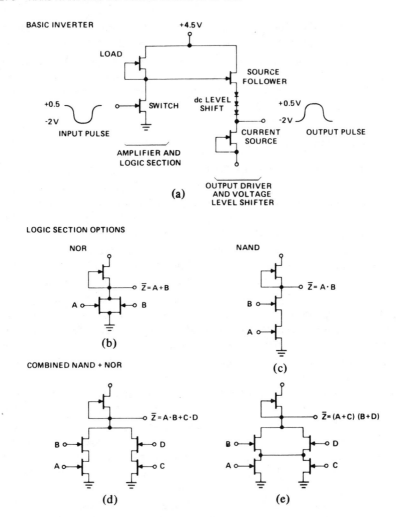

Figure 11-6. Basic circuit configurations for buffered FET logic (a) Basic inverter circuit. (b)-(e) Options for the in-put section for NOR, NAND, and combined NAND-NOR functions.

SDFL utilizes clusters of small, high performance Schottky diodes to perform the logical positive-OR function on groups of inputs which may then be further processed with the normal FET logic functions (series-NANDing, drain dotting, etc.). Figure 11-7 shows SDFL gate circuits diagrams for single, two- and three-level logic gate configurations (24). Note that the SDFL gate structure allows virtually unlimited fan-in at the first (positive-OR) logic level (SDFL circuits with up to 8-input NOR gates have been described in the literature) (25) but have the same practical restrictions to a fan-in of 2 (or possibly 3) at the second (series FET NAND) and third (drain-dot Wired-AND) levels if dynamic performance is to be maintained. This ease in implementing multilevel logic functions provides design flexibility, and saving in speed and power consumption.

The SDFL circuit approach offers large savings, not only in power, but also in circuit area, over previous D-MESFET approaches. The circuit area savings comes about because of the simplicity of the gate design and replacement of

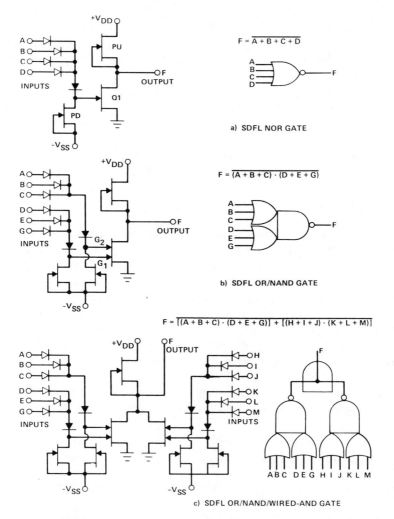

Figure 11-7. Comparison of 1-, 2- and 3-level SDFL gate configurations. All FETs are depletion-mode, typically $-1.5 < V_{th} < -0.5$ V; unshaded diodes are very small high speed switching Schottky diodes while shaded diodes are larger area, higher capacitance voltage shifting diodes.

(large) FETs with very small (typically 1 μm $\times$ 2 μm) Schottky diodes for most logic functions. The fact that the diodes are 2-terminal devices also significantly reduces the number of vias and overcrossings required in most circuits as compared to that needed when 3-terminal FETs are used as the logic elements.

The input logic diodes require a lower carrier concentration, lower sheet resistance implant than the FET channel to optimize their reverse-bias capacitance and series resistance. Thus, SDFL circuits require two separate implant steps using localized implantation into selected areas of the substrate.

Fan-out of the basic SDFL gate is limited to 3 without buffering or using wider channel widths in the driving gate. However, the propagation delay is not as sensitive to fan-out loading as the direct coupled FET logic (or NMOS) approach, since the gate-source capacitance of the switching FET is discharged by the pull-down active load instead of the preceding FET drain current when the input falls from high to low. It should be pointed out that the output node charging time depends on PU active load and C_L will depend on FO more than BFL.

The SDFL gate design has been used to fabricate circuits of LSI complexity (1000 gates). A discussion of this result can be found in Section V.

ADVANCED GaAs PROCESSING TECHNOLOGY

GaAs fabrication technologies based on both enhancement-mode (E-MESFET) and depletion-mode (D-MESFET) Field Effect Transistors have been under development for several years. Currently, the most likely candidate for achieving GaAs VLSI in the shortest time frame is the depletion-mode MESFET technology, having received the major development thrust over the past decade and having already been demonstrated at the LSI level (26). Enhancement technologies in the form of both J-FET (15) and Schottky gate E-MESFETs (3, 20) are progressing rapidly but have not been demonstrated beyond the low MSI ($\ll$100 gates) level primarily due to extremely difficult material and process requirements.

The following discussions will focus on a special D-MESFET technology—planar SDFL technology, which has already been successfully demonstrated at the LSI level.

Evolution of D-MESFET Technology

The two key disadvantages of GaAs with respect to Si, namely lack of a stable native oxide, and lack of a diffusion technology, severely restricted the early development of GaAs during the 1960s. Pressures for GaAs development came mainly from high frequency microwave system requirements, where Si could not fill the application. Initially, since ion implantation in GaAs was not yet developed, GaAs MESFETs were fabricated on epitaxial layers with mesa-defined isolated regions (shown in the left portion of Figure 11-8a). More complicated double epitaxial structures, developed later for power MESFETs, are shown in the right portion of Figure 11-8a. In order to achieve the maximum possible speed, MESFETs had to be fabricated with 1 μm gate lengths. This resolution requirement also inhibited GaAs progress during this early period since photolithography was limited to contact mask techniques resulting in marginal 1 μm resolution capability. These initial GaAs efforts employing epitaxial techniques for ultra-thin ($\sim$2000 Å) layers encountered great difficulty in achieving adequate active layer uniformity and control required for ICs applications.

Proceeding in parallel with microwave device development, GaAs ion implantation research (27) fostered the application of ion implantation for replacing epitaxial active layers (28). Subsequently, implanted layers began to be substituted for epitaxial layers, with the implant made into a high resistivity epitaxial buffer layer or directly into the semi-insulating GaAs substrate. These fabrication approaches with and without the often used recessed gate structures are shown in Figure 11-8b (22).

Simultaneous with these ion implanted material advances, more sophisticated pattern delineation techniques were becoming available. Two important advances, projection photolithography and electron beam lithography (EBL)

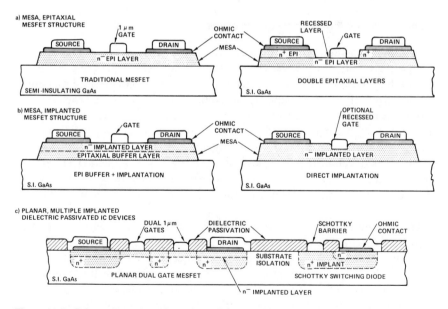

Figure 11-8. Schematic cross sections of MESFET devices showing the evolution of the GaAs technology from the simple microwave mesa-epitaxial FET to the advanced planar multiple localized implanted SDFL GaAs ICs.

have allowed GaAs MESFET devices to be routinely fabricated with 1 μm and 0.5 μm gates, respectively (29).

Instrumental in leading the Si IC industry forward to LSI was the development of planar, ion implanted, dielectric-passivated fabrication technology. Similar developments in GaAs were deemed crucial for achieving large scale integration. These concepts led the research effort for development of planar GaAs fabrication technology capable of producing the integrated circuit structures shown in Figure 11-8c (30, 31). These planar circuits are fabricated by using multiple localized ion implants directly into semi-insulating GaAs substrates. Hence, individual devices can be optimized by using different implants with the unimplanted GaAs substrate directly providing isolation between adjacent devices. This fabrication method conveniently complements the Schottky diode-FET logic (SDFL) circuit approach, since the optimization of both the MESFET and Schottky diodes requires at least two different active layers. Dielectrics in this planar process are utilized for post implantation annealing, protecting the GaAs surfaces during processing, and are an integral element of the planar multi-level interconnect structure. An example of the sophistication of this fabrication technology is illustrated in Figure 11-8c by the use of a 1 μm wide n^+ implant region placed between the dual 1 μm gates. A discussion of the key processes associated with this planar implanted SDFL IC technology follows.

Planar Localized Ion Implantation Process

The planar implantation and lithography process steps shown in Figure 11-9 comprise a totally dry (no wet chemical process steps), simple (only six mask levels), high yield process. The material processes are characterized by multiple, localized SE, S, or Si implants or combinations of implants, providing the process flexibility for optimizing various circuits. All of the dielectrics and metals are deposited using conventional processing methods including rf diode and magnetron sputtering, E-Beam evaporation and plasma enhanced CVD techniques. Resist delineation is accomplished using a 4$\times$ reduction projection aligner and all of the dielectric and metals are patterned using dry processing (reactive ion etching, plasma etching, and ion milling) and/or lift-off techniques.

The implant process steps used in this work are shown in Figure 11-9 (steps 2–5). Initially, the GaAs is coated with a thin layer of Si_3N_4 which remains on the wafer throughout all of the subsequent processing steps. The first process steps are the two localized implantations carried out through the thin Si_3N_4 layer using thick photoresist as the ion beam mask. Following the implants, additional dielectric (SiO_2) is added prior to the post implantation annealing shown in step 5.

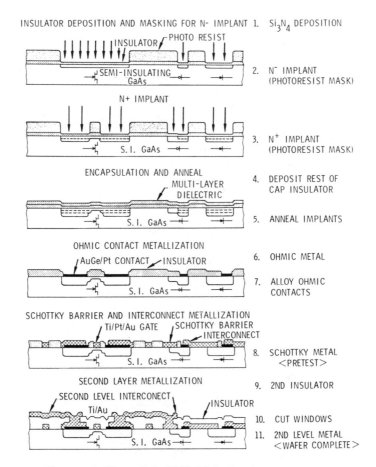

Figure 11-9. Planar GaAs SDFL fabrication steps.

Typical Se, S and Si implantation parameters and the resulting electron concentration doping profiles for the various IC implants conducted through the Si_3N_4 cap are shown in Figure 11-3. The shallow 400 keV Se or 160 KeV Si implantation profiles are peaked near the GaAs surface due to the energy absorbed in penetrating the thin Si_3N_4 layer. In contrast the 340 KeV S or Si (n^+) implants provide much deeper (~ 4000 Å) active layers than the shallow (~ 1500 Å) low threshold ($V_{th} \sim -1$ V) MESFET channel (n^-) implant. These deeper implanted layers are tailored for the high speed switching diode required in SDFL. Both n^- and n^+ implants are used for the level shifting diodes and for enhancing the doping under ohmic contact regions. As demonstrated in Figure 11-3, the appropriate choice of Si implant energy and dose results in profiles similar to the typical Se and S profiles normally used. Therefore, Si appears to be a suitable ion specie for use as a "universal" n-type implant ion in GaAs.

Initial implant specie comparison experiments have been conducted evaluating the shallow lightly-doped high resistance n^- MESFET channel layer. This active layer directly controls the threshold voltage, V_{th}, the key parameter in the optimization of power-delay product of the logic gates. The uniformity of MESFET threshold voltages for four implant species combinations is shown in Figure 11-10. As shown in this figure the n^- FET channel is implanted with either Se or Si while the n^+ ohmic contact region is implanted with either S or Si. In Figure 11-10 the average threshold voltage, $\overline{V}_{th}$, measured for 72 FETs equally distributed across the wafer lies within a narrow 0.974 to 1.184 range indicating adequate control for all the dopant variations studied. Uniformity of V_{th} is also quite good as indicated by the wafer standard deviation values ranging from a low of 68 mV (6.8%) to a high of 101 mV (9.4%). This implant optimization study has not yet singled out any obvious advantage for choosing one specie combination over another. To date, this data supports the conclusion that Se, Si and S are all viable GaAs n-type implant dopants.

Advanced Microstructure Pattern Replication Techniques

The first level metal lithography processes encompass the most crucial steps in the fabrication of planar GaAs ICs. Since GaAs ICs are designed with 1 μm features to achieve high speed, a dry pattern replication process capable of extremely high yields has been developed. This process represents a significant departure from typical microwave GaAs MESFET fabrication approaches and more closely resembles Si planar IC processing.

Common to all of the GaAs IC process steps is the delineation of the fine line resist patterns accomplished by using a Canon FPA 141 4X projection mask aligner. Pattern replication of ohmic contacts, Schottky barriers, FET gates, and first-level interconnects is accomplished using projection photolithography in conjunction with enhanced photoresist lift-off techniques.

Photoresist lift-off techniques have been commonly used in fine line (~ 1 μm) lithography applications for many years. However, when direct photoresist lift-off is used for defining metal patterns, excellent edge acuity (vertical side walls) is not always attainable and, poor lift-off process yield is commonly experienced. Therefore, in order to insure high yields from lift-off processes, enhanced lift-off techniques are commonly used (32). Typical examples of enhanced lift-off techniques are shown in the upper portion of Figure 11-11 with the plasma etched dielectric intermediate layer method used in this work

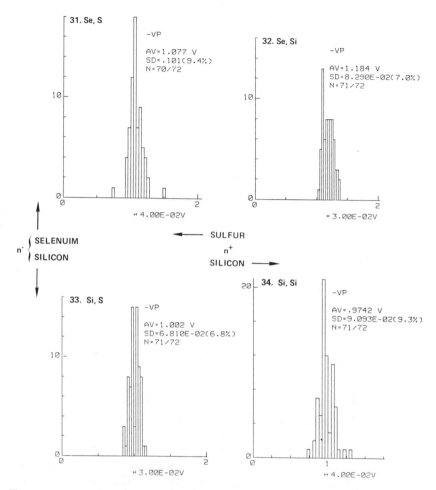

Figure 11-10. Histograms of GaAs MESFET threshold voltage uniformity for various combinations of Se, S and Si implants. Se or Si is used for the FET (n-) channel while S or Si is used under the (n+) ohmic contact regions.

shown at the bottom of Figure 11-11. The key principle used in both the multilevel or intermediate layer methods is use of evaporation shadowing. Mask structures are formed with resist ledges (multi-level techniques) or undercut resist/dielectric structures (intermediate layer) that allow convenient shadowing of the evaporated metal, thus insuring a high yield lift-off process.

The enhanced lift-off method described here was developed specifically for GaAs IC applications. This process approach takes into account the differences between processing on GaAs versus Si. For example, in this work the substrate is semi-insulating (the Si analogy would be insulating sapphire substrates in

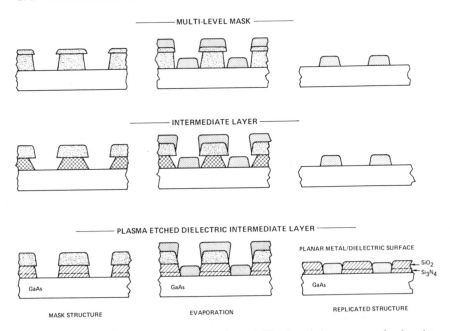

Figure 11-11. Comparison among various enhanced lift-off techniques: a. two-level resist method; b. intermediate dielectric technique; c. plasma etched dielectric intermediate layer method used in this work.

SOS technology); therefore the first level interconnects may be located directly on the substrate without the usual isolation and stray capacitance constraints associated with Si processing. Additionally, many of the commonly used freon based plasma etching techniques used for etching Si_3N_4 and SiO_2 do not etch GaAs. These unique features of GaAs motivated the development of the enhanced lift-off technique used in this work, shown in Figure 11-11. The intermediate dielectric layer is first plasma etched, then the appropriate metal is evaporated to a thickness less than or equal to the dielectric thickness. The resulting microstructure automatically provides a separation between the metal deposited in the dielectric window and the metal deposited on the top and side wall of the photoresist pattern. This structure allows solvents to easily penetrate and dissolve the photoresist. This process is easy to implement, it is very reproducible and it has high yield. The structural advantage of the intermediate layer enhanced lift-off method can be seen in the scanning electron micrograph of Figure 11-12.

Planar Multi-Level Interconnects

The planar multi-level interconnect fabrication approach is illustrated in Figure 11-13. As illustrated in the upper portion of Figure 11-13, this fabrication approach relies on maintaining a smooth metal/dielectric surface after the first level metallization steps, leading to the planar multi-level interconnect crossover structure shown. Planar crossovers greatly enhance the yield of multi-level interconnects as compared to conventional crossover structures shown in the lower portion of Figure 11-13. Also shown is the use of "filled" vias interconnecting the first level metal to the second level metal. Since there is no step coverage consideration for filled vias, higher yield, denser multi-level interconnect structures are possible.

The planar multi-level interconnect process is accomplished by fabricating the first-level metal within dielectric windows, and maintaining the metal thickness close to the dielectric thickness resulting in a smooth planar surface greatly facilitating the fabrication of complex multilayer interconnects. Figure 11-14a shows an actual cross section of the planar crossover structure resulting from these process approaches. Figure 11-14b shows a top view of a similar structure.

Planar crossovers eliminate potential crossover problems such as shorts between first- and second-level interconnects, and high-resistances or open interconnects resulting from poor step coverage. Another very important advantage is that these planar structures allow both thinner metal and dielectric films to be used resulting in less film stress, positively impacting yield and reliability. Finally, it is likely that these planar approaches have potential for extension to three levels of interconnects which will greatly impact the optimization of future complex VLSI.

PERFORMANCE OF GaAs IC

In this section, the speed power performance of various GaAs FET IC approaches will be presented and discussed. The comparison of performance will be based on measurements of ring oscillators and binary frequency dividers. In addition, the design and the performance of the most complicated GaAs IC made to date—a 1008 gate 8 × 8 multiplier will be presented.

The ring oscillators, consisting of chains of an odd number N of logic gates, provide a convenient and widely used method to evaluate propagation delay (τ_D) and dynamic switching energy ($P_D\tau_D$) for a given technology. The intrinsic gate propagation delay τ_D is related to the oscillating frequency by $\tau_D = 1/(2f N)$. The speed/power performance of ring oscillators fabricated by several GaAs IC technologies is compared in Table 11-1. It can be seen from this Table that the recent development of a 0.6 μm enhancement mode GaAs FET logic[3] fabricated by electron beam lithography (EBL) has yielded extremely low gate delay and dynamic switching energy (speed power product). A delay time as low as 17.5 ps/gate was observed at liquid nitrogen temperature. This gate delay is comparable with the highest speed obtained by the Josephson Junction logic.

For the depletion mode MESFET approach, the low threshold voltage

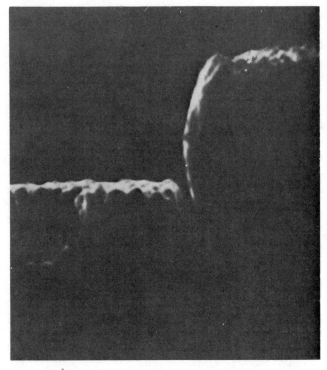

(a) BEFORE LIFT-OFF

Figure 11-12. SEM photos demonstrating the structural lift-off advantage and resulting structure of the plasma etched dielectric intermediate lift-off technique.

SDFL ring oscillators have achieved both low speed power product (40 fJ) and low gate delay time (62 ps) with a gate length of 1 μm. The depletion mode buffered FET logic also provide excellent propagation delay, but the speed power products reported to date are 20 to 40 times greater than the SDFL values. This is due to the large logic swing used (high threshold voltage) and the additional power dissipation from the buffer stage of the buffered FET logic gate. A 34 ps gate delay time was measured on a 0.5 μm FET gate BFL ring oscillator, with a speed power product of 1.4 pJ.

The ring oscillators are useful devices for the measurement of basic speed power properties of logic gates. However, in realistic sequential or combinatorial logic circuits, most of the gates are implemented with multiple inputs and with fanout of two or more. In order to more realistically evaluate the speed power performance, the performance of binary ripple frequency dividers made with several GaAs IC technologies are compared in Table 11-2. The theoretical maximum toggling frequencies listed in Table 11-2 for the binary frequency

(b) AFTER LIFT-OFF

Figure 11-12. (*continued*)

dividers are determined by the logic simulation of each circuit. It is obvious that circuit design has a strong influence on the maximum achievable clock frequency for a given GaAs FET logic. Figure 11-15 depicts the circuit diagrams of the four types of frequency dividers listed in Table 11-2.

The propagation delays determined from the dividing frequencies of all the depletion mode circuits are fairly close to those obtained from ring oscillator evaluation. This indicates that the speed of the logic gate of the depletion mode circuits is not greatly reduced by fanouts of 2 or 3. The higher toggling frequencies (also at the expense of high power) demonstrated by the HP BFL circuits and the LEP BFL circuits are primarily the consequence of the use of complementary clocked, master-slave flip flops implemented with NAND/NOR gates. This complementary clock design can also be implemented in SDFL by using the OR/NAND gate.

With enhancement mode GaAs FETs, a divide by eight frequency counter (gate length of 0.6 μm) has demonstrated a maximum clock frequency of 3.8 GHz with power dissipation of 1.2 mW/gate. This corresponds to a gate delay

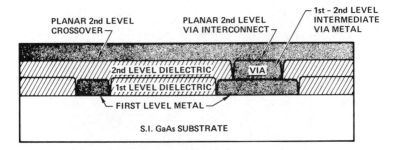

CONVENTIONAL
MULTI-LEVEL INTERCONNECT STRUCTURE

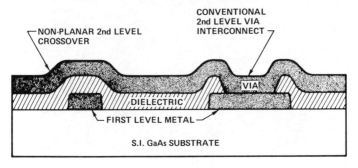

Figure 11-13. Schematic of the planar multi-level interconnect structure used in this work in comparison to conventional multi-level structures.

time of 66 ps and a speed power product of 79 fJ. This high speed and moderate power dissipation is a significant achievement. However, as described in section 3, the enhancement mode FET approach has a basic limitation on the permissible logic voltage swing, ~0.6 V, due to the onset of gate conduction. To achieve reasonable LSI/VLSI yields, further improvement in gate threshold voltage control is required. On the other hand, most of the high threshold voltage BFL depletion-mode approaches would likely be prohibited from achieving LSI/VLSI complexities due to the relatively high power dissipation required and the low packing density. To date, the most complicated GaAs IC, an 8 × 8 multiplier, was fabricated by the low power depletion-mode SDFL approach which appears to offer the best compromise between speed, power, and density.

GaAs LSI Circuit Example

In real time digital signal processing systems, multiplication is often an essential function. For example, it is a necessary operation in digital filtering and

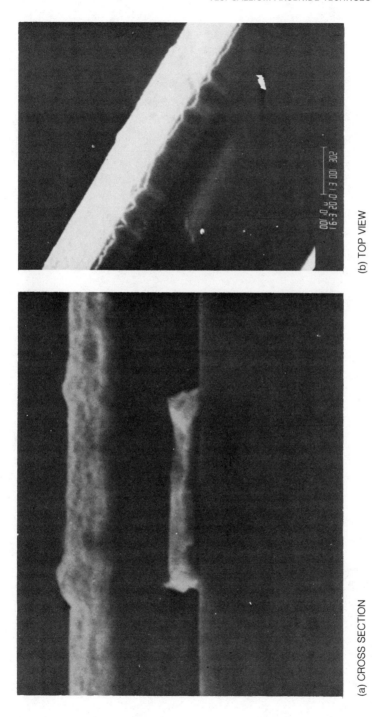

(a) CROSS SECTION

(b) TOP VIEW

Figure 11-14. SEMs of planar multi-level interconnects showing both a cross section and top views.

Table 11-1. Ring Oscillator Speed Power Performance for Several GaAs IC Technologies.

APPROACH	GATE LENGTH & GATE WIDTH (μm × μm)	PROPAGATION DELAY	SPEED POWER PRODUCT	FANIN/FANOUT
Hughes[29] DMESFET/BFL Inverter	0.5 × 50	34 ps	1.4 pJ	1/1
H.P.[22] DMESFET/BFL NOR	1 × 20	86	3.9	2/2
Thomson CSF[33] DMESFET/BFL	0.75 × 20	68	2	1/1
Rockwell[25] DMESFET/SDFL NOR	1 × 10	120	0.040	2/1
		62	0.068	2/1
FUJITSU[30] EMESFET/D-LOAD	1.2 × 20	170	0.12	1/1
FUJITSU[30] SELF ALIGN E/DCFL	1.5 × 30	50	0.287	
N.T.T[3] EMESFET/DCFL	0.6 × 20	30	0.057	1/1
		17.5*	0.616	1/1
MCD[15] EJFET/Pseudo Complementary	1.0 × 10	150	0.06	1/1
Thomson CSF[16] EMESFET/quasi-normally-off	1.0 × 35	105	0.23	
IUJITSU[42] HEMT	1.7 × 33	17.1*	0.016	1/1

*Measured at 77° K.

284

Table 11-2. GaAs IC frequency divider performance.

GaAs IC TECHNOLOGY	CIRCUIT APPROACH	THEORETICAL MAX. TOGGLE F.	MEASURED MAX. TOGGLE F.	EQUIVALENT τ_d	POWER DISSIPATION	$P_D\tau_D$
1 μm D/SDFL Rockwell	D.F.F. ÷ 2 (NOR GATE)	1/5	1.9 GHz	105 ps	2.5 mW/gate	0.26 pj
0.7 μm D/BFL[33] TCSF	D.F.F. ÷ 2	1/5 τ_D	3.0	67	40	2.68
1 μm D/BFL[36] Hughes	D.F.F. ÷ 2	1/5 τ_D	2.2	91	78	7.1
1 μm D/BFL[22] H.P.	NAND/NOR ÷ 2 COM. CLOCK	1/2 τ_D	4.5	111	40	4.4
0.6 μm D/BFL[37] LEP	NAND/NOR ÷ 2 COM. CLOCK	1/2 τ_D	5.5	91	40	3.6
0.6 μm E/DCFL[3] N.T.T.	D.F.F. ÷ 8 (NOR)	1/4 τ_D	3.8	66	1.2	0.079
1.2 μm E/DCFL[38] NEC	COMP. CLOCK ÷ 2 NOR	1/4 τ_D	2.4	100	3.9	0.39
0.7 μm D/BFL[43] LEP	DYNAMIC DIVIDER	1/2 τ_D	9	56	50	0.28

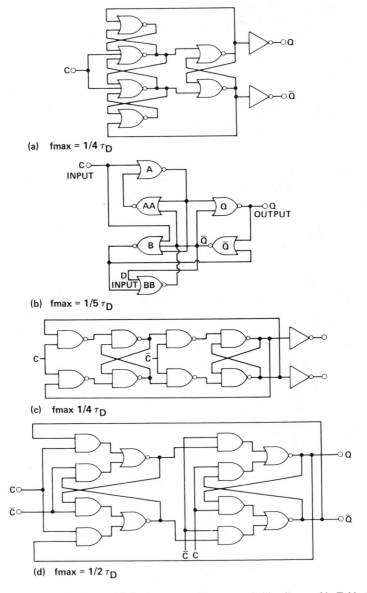

Figure 11-15. Circuit diagrams of the four types of frequency divider discussed in Table 11-2.

Fourier transform processing. In many cases, the ultimate speed and bandwidth of a digital system are determined by the multiplication process. Therefore, the successful development of a high speed multiplier can greatly enhance system performance. An 8 × 8 multiplier was chosen as a test vehicle for the evaluation of LSI/VLSI feasibility of Schottky diode FET logic (SDFL) fabricated with the process described in the previous section.

In the design of the GaAs 8 × 8 multiplier, a parallel (array) multiplication architecture was chosen because of its very modular and repetitive layout. In this approach, only two basic building blocks, a full adder and a half adder, are required to form the multiplier combinatorial array. A straight N × N parallel multiplier, without any carry look ahead or other more sophisticated architecture (such as Wallace tree), requires N(N − 2) full adders and N half adders. To obtain the 2N bit product, a maximum of (N − 1) sum delays and (N − 1) carry delays is needed. While other more complex circuits can reduce the multiply time by reducing carry delays or by recoding (39) multiplier bits to shrink the propagation path through the array, the less regular layouts resulting from these approaches would have significantly increased design time and were thus not considered for the multiplier circuit reported here.

Since the fundamental component of the multiplier is the adder cell, the speed of this cell dictates the multiply time. As shown in the block diagram of the full adder cell (Figure 11-16), this cell requires twelve NOR gates. The propagation delays for the carry and sum outputs are 1 τ_D and 3 τ_D, respectively. Adder cells with less propagation delay can be realized using two level logic gates (OR/NAND, and AND/NOR) by employing dual gate MESFETs.

To realize an 8 × 8 parallel multiplier, 48 full adders and 8 half adders were organized as in Figure 11-17 to form the 16 bit product. In addition to the array, input and output latches (D Flip-Flops) were included so that the circuit could be more readily interfaced in synchronous systems. The latches are separately clocked for inputs and outputs, and can also be disabled, or made transparent, to facilitate asynchronous testing. The implementation of this circuit required 1008 NOR gates with ~3000 FET devices (FETs and active loads), and ~3000 diodes. This level of complexity clearly qualifies this multiplier as a GaAs LSI chip and also as the *most* complex GaAs IC demonstrated to date.

The complete 8 × 8 parallel multiplier circuit measures 2.7 mm × 2.25 mm including bonding pads. A photograph of a multiplier chip is shown in Figure 11-18. Gate density, excluding pads, was about 33,000 gates/cm² for this circuit. The 8 × 8 bit multiplier chips were fabricated using the SDFL planar, directly implanted process described in Section 4. Chips were evaluated at wafer probe for functionality (at low speeds) using an automatic data acquisition system, and for high speed performance using on-chip test circuitry.

Functionality testing was carried out at two levels, evaluation of the chip

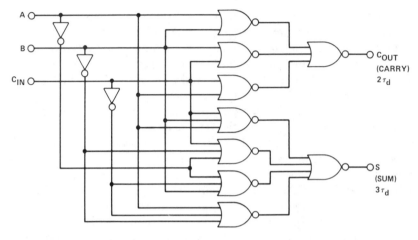

Figure 11-16. NOR implemented full adder circuit.

output response to a pulse input waveform (ripple test), and exhaustive testing of all input data combinations. The ripple test was used for prescreening chips and to study bias conditions. It consisted of performing the products 255 × 128 and 255 × 129 for the 8 × 8 multiplier where the least significant (b_0) input was driven by a pulse generator. Figure 11-19 shows the output waveform of the 8 x 8 multiplier at ripple test. The following multiplication is performed:

$$
\begin{array}{r}
A = 1\ 1\ 1\ 1\ 1\ 1\ 1\ 1 \\
B = 1\ 0\ 0\ 0\ 0\ 0\ 0\ b_0 \\
\hline
b_0 b_0 b_0 b_0 b_0 b_0 b_0 b_0 \\
1\ 1\ 1\ 1\ 1\ 1\ 1\quad 1 \\
\hline
b_0 \bar{b}_0 \bar{b}_0 \bar{b}_0 \bar{b}_0 \bar{b}_0 \bar{b}_0 \bar{b}_0 \quad \bar{b}_0 b_0 b_0 b_0 b_0 b_0 b_0 b_0
\end{array}
\qquad [11.1]
$$

Chips which passed the initial ripple test screening were subjected to a complete functionality test using a microcomputer to provide input data bits and to read the output product bits. The measured product was compared with the expected A × B, and errors were flagged to allow any design or fabrication defects to be localized.

Evaluation of the high speed performance was facilitated by the use of an on-chip feedback path which routes the complement of the most significant product bit (P_{15}) to the least significant (b_0) input bit. This connection is unstable as can be seen from the above multiplication [11.1] and results in an oscillatory condition which exercises all of the sum and carry propagation paths through the combinatorial array.

The oscillation period is determined by the time required by the signal to propagate through the loop. Since changing bit b_0 (from 1 to 0 or 0 to 1) involves the second longest delay path through the multiplier array, the delay to the most significant product bit (P_{15}) is 6 sums and 8 carries for a total of 34 τ_d. Adding the delays caused by the control gates and the latch gates when

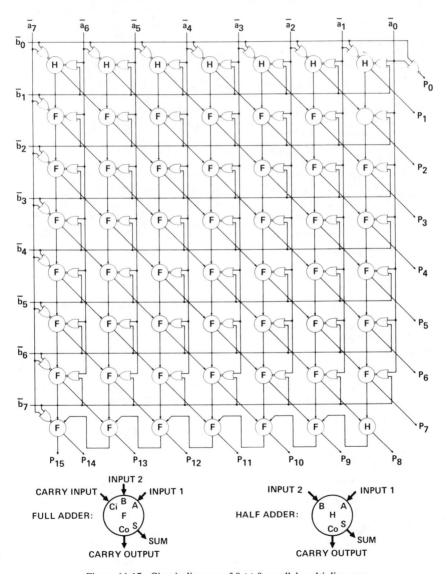

Figure 11-17. Circuit diagram of 8 $\times$ 8 parallel multiplier array.

Figure 11-18. Photomicrograph of an 8 × 8 multiplier chip. The chip including bonding pads covers a 2.5 mm × 2.25 mm area.

operating with the latches disabled or transparent, the half-period of oscillation in the test mode is 40 τ_d. An oscillation frequency of 83.1 MHz was observed, which corresponds to a propagation delay of 150 ps/gate. At this speed, a full 16 bit product would be available every 5.25 ns. This performance represents roughly an order of magnitude speed improvement over commercially available (2 μm minimum linewidth) silicon bipolar 8 bit multipliers of equivalent (array) circuit architectures (40, 41) and a 4 times improvement over the fastest silicon 8 bit multiplier employing input bit recoding and carry look ahead adders. Even faster GaAs multipliers would be expected (1.5 − 3 ns) if multiple-level logic gates, carry look-ahead and recoding schemes were applied to the logic circuit design.

Power dissipation of the multiplier circuits varied with wafer threshold voltage and bias voltages. It ranged from 0.61 W to 2.2 W. Typical circuits operated normally at V_{dd} = 2.7 V and V_{ss} = −1.5 to 2.0 V. The best propagation delay time measured is 150 ps. The typical gate delay time is ~175 ps.

The successful fabrication of the SDFL 8 × 8 multiplier brings the GaAs technology into the realm of LSI while advancing the state-of-the-art for multiplier chips. The propagation delay of 150 ps/gate observed on the 8 × 8

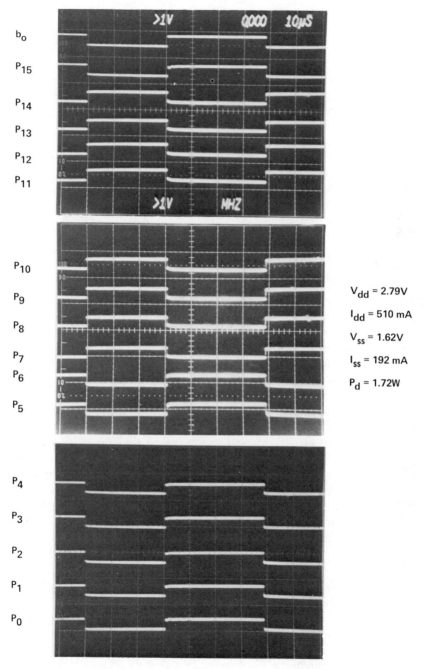

Figure 11-19. Ripple (asynchronous) test of 8 × 8 multiplier with pulse input at b_9.

multiplier is in good agreement with the results of much simpler GaAs SDFL circuits such as ring oscillators and frequency dividers.

This high speed of operation indicates that the extension of the planar SDFL circuit approach to the LSI level of complexity does not result in any significant speed degradation. The low power dissipation observed on the 8 × 8 multipliers also indicates that the SDFL approach is a suitable candidate for the VLSI range of complexity.

CONCLUSION

Advances in GaAs material, ion implantation and process technology have led to rapid progress in developing a GaAs high speed IC technology. Gate delays of ~100 psec has been routinely demonstrated by several GaAs IC technologies employing gate lengths of approximately 1 μm. Aided by processing techniques such as EBL, self aligned gate formation, etc., gate delays as low as 50 psec have also been achieved.

The outlook for the application of GaAs digital IC's is very bright. They are expected to find applications at all levels of integration, although for very high speed systems, the highest degree of integration is preferred in order to minimize the delay time between chips. At a low and medium scale integration level, GaAs IC's can be used as frequency counters for frequency synthesizer systems, as code generators in secure communications systems, as shift registers, etc. At higher levels of integration, GaAs RAM's should find application as cache memory in high speed data processing systems.

Presently, the leading technology for GaAs digital LSI circuits is the planar D-MESFET SDFL technology. In addition to the demonstrated 1008 gate 8 × 8 multiplier, several different SDFL circuits with more than 100 gates have also been successfully demonstrated. In the area of GaAs enhancement mode logic, excellent speed power performance has recently been demonstrated at a low level of integration. Further improvement in processing techniques in order to achieve the tight threshold voltage uniformity required is needed for this technology to become a major candidate for high speed LSI.

Acknowledgment

The authors are indebted to the many hard working individuals contributing to the GaAs integrated circuit programs at Rockwell. In particular, we wish to thank P. Asbeck, C. Kirkpatrick, and Y. D. Shen for their contributions in material studies, ion implantation and processing, and E. Shen and C. P. Lee for circuit design, testing, and device analysis. F. Eisen has made invaluable contributions in the development of GaAs ion implantation technology and along with F. Blum has provided, valuable guidance, and support to the development of GaAs integrated circuit technology.

REFERENCES

(1) Ruch, J. G., and Kino, G. S. "Measurements of the Velocity-Field characteristics of Gallium Arsenide." *Appl. Phys. Lett.* **10:** 40 (1967).

(2) Fairman, R. D., Chen, R. T., Oliver, J. R., and Chen, D. R. "Growth of High-Purity Semi-Insulating Bulk GaAs for Integrated-Circuit Applications." *IEEE* **ED-28:** 135 (1981) Trans. Elec. Dev.

(3) Mizutani, T., Kato, N., Ishida, S., Osafune, K., and Ohmori, M. "GaAs Gigabit Logic Circuits Using Normally-Off MESFETs." *Electronic Letters* **16:** 315–316 (April 24, 1980).

(4) Boccon-Gibod, D., Gavant, M., Rocchi, M., and Cathelin, M. "A 3.5 GHz Single-Clocked Binary Frequency Divider on GaAs." Presented at the GaAs IC Symposium, Las Vegas, November 4–6, 1980.

(5) Eden, R. C., Welch, B. M., and Zucca, R. "Planar GaAs IC Technology: Applications for Digital LSI." *IEEE J. Solid-State Circuits* **SC-13:** 419–426 (1978).

(6) Eden, R. C., Welch, B. M., and Zucca, R. "Lower Power GaAs Digital ICs Using Schottky Diode-FET Logic." *1978 Int. Solid State Circuits Conf., Digest of Tech. Papers* 68–69 (Feb. 1977).

(7) Liechti, C. A. "Microwave Field Effect Transistors." *IEEE Trans. Microwave Theory and Techn.* **MTT-24** No. 6: 279–300 (June, 1976).

(8) Higgins, J. A., Kuvas, R. L., Eisen, F. H., Chen, D. R., "Low Noise GaAs FET's Prepared by Ion Implantation." *IEEE Trans Electr. Dev.* **ED-25** No. 6:587–596 (June 1978).

(9) Eden, R. C., Welch, B. M., Zucca, R., and Long, S. I. "The Prospects for Ultrahigh Speed VLSI GaAs Digital Logic." *IEEE J. Solid State Circuits* **SC-14** No. 2:221–239 (April 1979).

(10) Data sheet for NE137 Low Noise Ku-band GaAs MESFET, Nippon Electric Co., June 1980.

(11) Roosild, S. A. private communication of silicon MESFET data from Air Force Contract F19628-70-C-0094.

(12) Barnard, J., Huang, R. S., and Frey, J. "SOS MESFET Processing Technology for Microwave Integrated Circuits." Paper 11.7 *Int. Elect. Dev. Meeting Tech. Digest* 281–283 (Dec. 1979).

(13) Dennard, R. H., Gaensslen, F. H., Walker, E. J., and Cook, P. W. "1 μm MOSFET VLSI Technology: Part II - Device Designs and Characteristics for High Performance Logic Applications." *IEEE J. Sol. State Circuits* **SC-14** No. 2:247–254 (April 1979).

(14) Suciu, P. I., Fuls E. N., and Boll, H. J. "High-Speed NMOS Circuits made with X-Ray Lithography and Reactive Sputter Etching." *IEEE Elect. Dev. Letters* **EDL-1** No. 1:10–11 (Jan. 1980).

(15) Zuleeg, R., Notthoff, J. K., and Lehovec, K. "Femtojoule High-Speed Planar GaAs E-JFET Logic," *IEEE Trans. Electron Devices* **ED-25:** 628–639 (June 1978).

(16) Bert, G., Pham Ngu, T., Nuzillat, G., and Gloanec, M. "Quasi-Normally-Off MESFET Logic for High Performance GaAs IC." *Paper 7 in Research Abstracts of the First Annual Gallium Arsenide Integrated Circuit Symposium*, Lake Tahoe, (Sept. 17, 1979).

(17) Yokoyama, N., Mimiura, T., Kusakawa, H., Suyama, K., and Fukata, M. "Low-Power High-Speed Integrated Logic with GaAs MOSFETs." *Digest of Tech. Papers, 1979 Int. Conf. on Solid State Devices*, Tokyo (Aug. 27, 1979), pp. 31–32.

(18) Messick, L. "A DC to 16 GHz Indium Phosphide MISFET." *Solid State Elect.* **23:** 551–555 (1980).

(19) Judaprawira, S., et al. "Modulation Doped MBE GaAs/n-Al$_x$Ga$_{1-x}$As MESFETS." *IEEE Elect. Dev. Lett.* **EDL-2:** 14–15 (Jan. 1981).

(20) Mimura, T., Hiyamizu, S., Fujii, T., and Nanbu, K. "A New Field-Effect Transistor with

Selectively Doped GaAs/n-Al$_x$Ga$_{1-x}$As Heterojunctions." *Japanese J. Appl. Phys. Letters* **19** No. 5:225–227 (1980).

(21) Notthoff, J. K., and Vogelsang, C. H. "Gate Design for DCFL with GaAs E-JFETs." *Paper 10 in Research Abstracts of First Annual Gallium Arsenide Integrated Circuits Symposium,* Lake Tahoe (Sept. 27, 1979).

(22) VanTuyl, R. L., Liechti, C., Lee, R. E., and Gowen, E. "GaAs MESFET Logic with 4-GHz Clock Rate." *IEEE J. Solid-State Circuits* **SC-12:** 485–496 (Oct. 1977).

(23) Liechti, C. A. private communication.

(24) Eden, R. C., Lee, F. S., Long, S. I., Welch, B. M., and Zucca, R. "Multi-Level Logic Gate Implementation in GaAs ICs using Schottky Diode-FET Logic. *1980 Int. Solid State Circuits Conf., Digest of Tech. Papers* (Feb. 1980).

(25) Long, S. I., Lee, F. S., Zucca, R., Welch, B. M., and Eden, R. C. "MSI High-Speed Low-Power GaAs ICs using Schottky Diode FET Logic." *IEEE Trans. on Microwave Theory and Techniques* **MTT-28** No. 5:466–471 (May 1980).

(26) Lee, F. S., Shen, E., Kaelin, G., Welch, B. M., Eden, R. C., and Long, S. I. "High-Speed LSI GaAs Digital Integrated Circuits." Presented at the GaAs IC Symposium, Las Vegas, Nevada (Nov. 1980).

(27) Eisen, F. E., Welch, B. M., Gamo, K., Inada, T., Mueller, H., Nicolet, M. A., and Mayer, J. W. "Sulfur, Selenium and Tellurium Implantation in GaAs." *Inst. Phys. Conf. Ser.* No. 28 (1976): Chap. 2.

(28) Welch, B. M., Eisen, F. E., and Higgins, J. A., "Gallium Arsenide Field Effect Transistors by Ion Implantation." *J. Appl. Physics* **45:** 3685 (1974).

(29) Greiling, P. T., Ozdemir, F. S., Krumm, C. F., and Lohr, B. F., Jr. "Electron Beam Fabricated GaAs integrated Circuits." *1979 IEDM Tech. Digest.*

(30) Welch, B. M., Shen, Y. D., Zucca, R., and Eden, R. C., "Planar High Yield GaAS IC Processing Techniques." *1979 IEDM Tech. Digest.*

(31) Welch, B. M., Shen, Y. D., Zucca, R., Eden, R. C., and Long, S. I. "LSI Processing Technology for Planar GaAs Integrated Circuits." *IEEE Trans. Electron Devices,* Special Issue (June, 1980).

(32) Welch, B. M., Shen Y. D., and Fleming, W. P. "Microstructure Pattern Replication for Advanced Planar GaAs LSI/VLSI." *Proceedings of Microcircuit Engineering 80,* Amsterdam (Oct. 1980).

(33) Nuzilat, G., Damay-Kavala, F., Bert, G., and Arnodo C. "Low Pinch-Off Voltage FET Logic (LPFL): LSI Oriented Logic Approach Using Quasinormally Off GaAs MESFETS." *IEEE Proc.* **127** Pt. 1, No. 5:287–296 (Oct. 1980).

(34) Suyama, K., Kusakawa, H., and Ukata, M. "Design and Performance of GaAs Normally-Off MESFET Integrated Circuits." *IEEE Transc. on Electronic Devices* **ED-27** No. 6:1092–1097 (June 1980).

(35) Yokoyama, N., Mimura, T., Fukata, M. and Ishikawa, H. "A Self-Aligned Source/Drain Planar Device for Ultrahigh Speed GaAs MESFET VLSIs." *1981 Int. Solid State Circuits Conf., Digest of Tech. Papers* (Feb. 1981).

(36) Greiling, P. T., Lundgren, R. E., Krumm, C. F., and Lohr, R. F., Jr. "Why Design Logic with GaAs and How? *MSN* 48–60 (Jan. 1980).

(37) Cathelin, M., Gawant, M., and Rocchi, M. "A 3.5 GHE Self Aligned Single-Clocked Binary Frequency Divider on GaAs." *IEEE PROC.* **127** Pt. I, No. 5 (Oct. 1980).

(38) Katano, F., Furutsuka, T., and Higashisaka, A. "High Speed Normally-Off GaAs MESFET Integrated Circuits." *Electronics Letters* **17** No. 6:236–239 (March, 1981).

(39) "2 Bit-by-4 Bit Parallel Binary Multipliers." *Supplement to the TTL Data Book,* Texas Instruments (1974).

(40) TRW MPY8HJ-1. See "Digital Processing Gets a Boost from Bipolar LSI Multipliers," *EDN Magazine* **20:** 38–43 (November 5, 1978).

(41) "Single-Chip 8 × 8 Multiplier Forms 16-bit Product in 19 nsec. *EDN Magazine* **22:** 152 (Dec. 15, 1980).

(42) Abe, M., Mimura, T., Yokoyama, N. and Ishikawa, H. "New Technology Towards GaAs LSI/VLSI for Computer Applications."presented at GaAs IC Symposium. San Diego, CA (Oct. 1981).

(43) Rocchi, Mark, "GaAs Dynamic Frequency Dividers for High Speed Applications up to 106H," Presented at GaAs IC Symposium, San Diego, CA (Oct. 1981).

12. Electron Beam Testing of VLSI Microprocessors

E. Wolfgan, P. Fazekas, J. Otto and G. Crichton,
Siemens Company, West Germany

INTRODUCTION

During the 1980s it is to be expected that electron beam testing will be introduced as a standard method for internal probing and that the mechanical probe (1-9) will only remain in use as a supplementary tool. This reversed situation has been brought about as the result of progressive miniaturization of ICs with the consequent reduction of the loading capacitance of the nodes, higher operating frequencies, higher data width of the microprocessors (the width of 32 bits would require the use of 32 mechanical probes), and the steadily increasing time between the initial design and final error free design, during which the design weaknesses are detected by internal probing.

Initial investigations with the electron probe on microprocessors were carried out in 1978 by Feuerbaum and Hernaut on the timing circuitry of a 4-bit microprocessor (10). Subsequent work has shown that a series of further functions in microprocessors can be tested with various other electron beam techniques (11, 12, 13).

The aim of this study is to show, for the first time, all the functions of a microprocessor and to determine its internal dynamic behavior by means of electron beam testing techniques. The 8-bit microprocessor 8085 has been chosen as a typical representative for this purpose (14, 15).

The next section gives an overview of the various electron beam techniques required for the investigation of microprocessors. The standard techniques have already been described in detail in the literature and are only dealt with here in so far as this is necessary for an explanation of the new techniques, viz. logic-state mapping and logic-state diagram. The third section starts off by describing the experimental setup which was used for the investigations of the microprocessor 8085. Then there is a brief explanation of the 8085 and its internal structure, as well as a description of the experimental conditions under which the 8085 was investigated. The main part of the study demonstrates how to visualize the internal instruction execution process in the individual modules. All the modules contained in the functional block diagram are dealt with here. In the fifth section an example of failure analysis is shown. The sixth and final section discusses results and limitations of the visualization of internal instruction execution, the performance of the logic-state mapping and logic-state diagram techniques, the area of application, and the future aspects of electron beam testing of microprocessors.

ELECTRON BEAM TESTING TECHNIQUES

This section describes six different techniques, four of which are well known: voltage contrast, stroboscopy, voltage measurement and sampling technique. They are only described in so far as this is necessary for an explanation of the two new techniques, logic-state mapping and logic-state diagram. Both these techniques were specially developed for the investigation of microprocessors and microcomputers.

Voltage Contrast

The voltage contrast is caused by the local electric fields above the integrated circuit (IC). The secondary electron emission induced by the primary electron beam as it scans the surface of the IC has to pass through the electric fields in order to reach the secondary electron collector. If the secondary emission is induced in regions at logic level "1" (positively polarized), the secondary electrons have to overcome a voltage barrier to be able to pass to the collector. Due to the low energy of the secondary electrons, most of them are returned to the surface of the IC. Such positive regions appear dark in the voltage contrast micrograph. If secondary electron emission is induced in regions at logic level "0" (grounded or negatively polarized), all the secondary electrons will be able to pass to the collector. These regions show up light in the voltage contrast micrograph (16, 17). An example of a voltage contrast micrograph is shown in Figure 12-8.

Stroboscopic Voltage Contrast

Dynamic signals have to be observed in the stroboscopic voltage contrast mode (18, 19, 20). In this mode, short electron pulses, a few ns in duration, are repetitively generated. In the case of microprocessors and microcomputers, the repetition frequency is the frequency of the program loop. An example can be seen in Figure 12-14a which shows a part of the instruction decoder. One interconnection is selected and shows up as a dark vertical line.

Voltage Measurement

For quantitative voltage measurements it is necessary to eliminate the influence of the local electric fields of the region surrounding the measurement point. This is best achieved by applying a strong extraction field above the specimen. The measurement concept calls for the stabilization of the voltage difference between the measurement point of the specimen and a reference electrode (21). This can be done as follows: When the voltage at the specimen changes, the secondary electrons emitted by the specimen become more or less energetic due to the different voltage differences between specimen and reference electrode. The gain or loss of energy is determined in a retarding field spectrometer, where the threshold of the retarding field is controlled by way of a feedback loop such that the original voltage difference between the specimen and the electrode is reestablished. The change in the threshold voltage then corresponds exactly to the variation of the specimen voltage. Examples are shown in Figures 12-15, 12-17c and 12-21.

Sampling Mode

In contrast to the stroboscopic mode, the phase relation between the waveform to be measured and the electron beam pulse is changed in the sampling mode. Each phase angle remains constant until a sufficient number of secondary electrons from numerous pulses have been collected. Thus the sampling frequency depends primarily on the S/N ratio or the desired voltage sensitivity (22). The combination of the voltage measurement and sampling mode techniques permits the waveform of internal nodes to be recorded. It should be noted here that in the waveform mode the electron probe is only directed towards one node.

Logic-State Mapping

This technique is based on a suggestion made by Feuerbaum (23). It is a technique which combines the stroboscopic voltage contrast with the sampling mode.

The schematic in Figure 12-1 shows how logic-state mapping evolves. The pulsed electron beam slowly scans in y-direction across the interconnections, only two of which are shown in Figure 12-1a. When the electron beam has reached the end E of the line scan, it jumps back to the beginning B, and the process commences anew.

While the pulsed electron probe on the integrated circuit always scans the

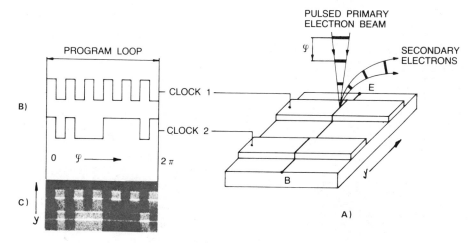

Figure 12-1. Schematic of logic-state mapping

same path B-E in the y-direction, the electron beam on the screen of the scanning electron microscope scans the screen line by line, so that a two-dimensional micrograph emerges. Simultaneously with the line feed in the y-direction, phase ϕ of the electron pulses is continuously shifted. As the phase range along the x-direction of the micrograph is freely selectable, it is possible to present either the entire program loop or selected parts of it in a logic-state mapping.

Figure 12-1b gives a schematic of the clock signals which are applied to the two interconnections, while Figure 12-1c shows the corresponding logic-state mapping, indicating the logic states "1" as dark and the logic states "0" as light bars.

Logic-State Diagram

For a comparison with the logic design, it is useful to represent the information contained in the logic-state mapping in the form of a time diagram. This can be done as follows with the electron probe (see Figure 12-2a): The pulsed electron probe jumps from one chosen interconnection (B) to another (E). Its dwell time on the interconnection is chosen in such a way that it is possible to clearly differentiate between the logic states "0" and "1". When the electron probe has reached the last interconnection (E), it jumps back to the starting point again, the phase ϕ being shifted by an adjustable discrete value. The process is repeated until the entire program loop or certain desired parts of it are measured and represented in a logic-state diagram.

Figure 12-2b again shows the clocks applied to the interconnection, while Figure 12-2c shows a logic-state diagram which has been generated with the electron probe and displayed on the screen of a conventional logic analyzer.

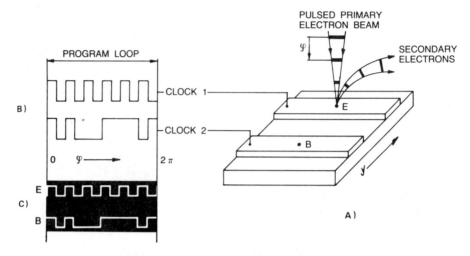

Figure 12-2. Schematic of logic-state diagram

Classification of the Electron Beam Techniques

The various electron beam techniques can be distinguished from each other in a number of ways. One way differentiates whether the electron beam is turned on, whether it is turned on and off (pulsed beam), or whether it is simultaneously pulsed and phase-shifted. These three modes of operation are identified in the left column of Figure 12-3 and depicted graphically in the middle column. One of the signals to be examined is shown in the upper portion of the middle column. The signal is divided into program loops which are continuously repeated. This cyclical repetition is absolutely essential for electron beam

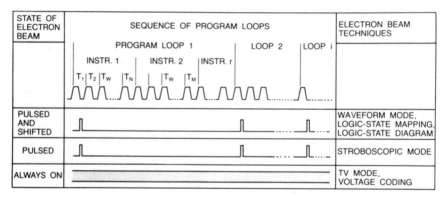

Figure 12-3. Classification of the different electron beam techniques. The program loop consists of r instructions with n or m machine states T.

techniques using a pulsed beam. The right column of Figure 12-3 gives the designations of the various techniques.

Finally the various techniques can be distinguished according to the information volume available. Operation in the TV mode gives an average contrast pattern, which is confusing because the frequencies of the various signals and the TV line frequency appear superimposed. Nevertheless it provides a good survey of whether all the function modules are properly working. Inspection in the TV mode is somewhat simpler if, for instance, the main clock is synchronized with the TV line frequency ($f_{clock} = n.f_{TV}$; n = integer). This method is known as voltage coding (2, 24). The function modules such as registers and buses can be observed particularly clearly if the microprocessor is set to the wait state T_w. In this case T_w will always appear and can be recorded in a micrograph.

The other machines states $T_1 - T_n$ can be inspected in the stroboscopic or sampling mode. These techniques afford a time resolution of ≥ 1 ns for representing all desired phase ranges of the program loop either qualitatively (stroboscopic mode, logic-state mapping, logic-state diagram) or quantitatively (waveform mode).

EXPERIMENTAL

This section first describes the experimental setup which was used for the electron beam testing of the microprocessor 8085. Then reasons for the choice of the 8085 as a typical representative are given, and its internal structure is briefly explained on the basis of a functional block diagram. The section closes with a description of the experimental conditions under which the 8085 was investigated and an indication of the reasons for the choice of the program loop.

Experimental Setup

Figures 12-4 and 12-5 show a block diagram and a photograph of the experimental setup. It consists of a modified Etec Autoscan scanning electron microscope with a large-area specimen chamber in which a printed-circuit board has been placed on the x, y stage (Figure 12-6a).

The microprocessor under test has been inserted in a socket on this board, which is implemented as a personality card for each IC to be inspected. The line drivers for the incoming signals and the signals emitted by the microprocessor are placed as close to the socket as possible. Coaxial cables, 3.5 m in length, run from the printed-circuit board, which is likewise provided with line drivers. Connected to the second circuit board through coaxial vacuum feedthroughs to a second printed-circuit board is the HP μP-Lab 5036 A which drives the device under test (Figure 12-6b). If an analysis is made on a faulty

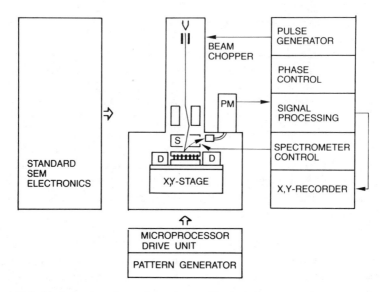

Figure 12-4. Block diagram of experimental setup. The basic instrument is a scanning electron microscope (SEM) of the Etec Autoscan type S secondary electron spectrometer, D line drivers for incoming and outgoing signals, PM photomultiplier

microprocessor, this is driven with the aid of a pattern generator, as the μP-Lab only operates with fully functional devices.

A logic analyzer (Biomation K 100) monitors the running of the program and applies the trigger to the pulse generator and phase control for the stroboscopic mode, logic state mapping and waveform mode.

Located above the microprocessor under test is the electron spectrometer for voltage measurements (21). Other important items for microprocessor inspection are a TV scanning unit, a TV monitor and a scan conversion memory (Etec Vistascan).

This setup permits the application of all electron beam techniques with the exception of the logic-state diagram, for which a sequence control (minicomputer) is additionally required. Figure 12-7 shows the block diagram of the measurement setup for the generation of a logic diagram. The excecution of the measurement is controlled by a minicomputer (Interdata 6/16). Phase control takes place via a D/A converter and a delay generator, while the positioning of the individual measurement points is carried out by means of a digital scan generator. The logic states "1" and "0" are obtained through weighting of the voltage contrast signal by means of a Schmitt trigger. The weighting values are then transferred to a shift register with the aid of a shift strobe. When all the measuring values having the same phase position are stored in the shift register, they are taken over by the logic analyzer (Biomation K 100).

Choice of the 8085 Microprocessor

The choice of the 8085 was based on the consideration that this type of microprocessor is generally well known and that it is manufactured by Siemens AG. The specimen used is a scaled-down version of the 8085, re-engineered at Siemens Research Laboratories and manufactured by Siemens Components Group.

Figure 12-8 shows a voltage contrast micrograph of the entire microprocessor 8085 and an indication of the different modules. The block diagram of the internal structure of the 8085 is shown in Figure 12-9 (14, 15). Data are transmitted on an 8-bit internal data bus, e.g. between the register array and the arithmetic unit or between the data buffer and the instruction register. The arithmetic unit consists of the A (accumulator), temporary, and flag registers and of the arithmetic logic unit. An instruction register and decoder supply information to a timing and control unit which generates both internal and external control signals. Interrupts are routed to an interrupt control unit.

Figure 12-5. Photograph of experimental setup. From left to right: standard electronics; specimen chamber and electron optical gun; pulse generator, phase control, signal processing and spectrometer control; microprocessor drive unit including pulse generators, logic analyzer, pattern generator and HP μP-Lab; TV monitor and x-y recorder.

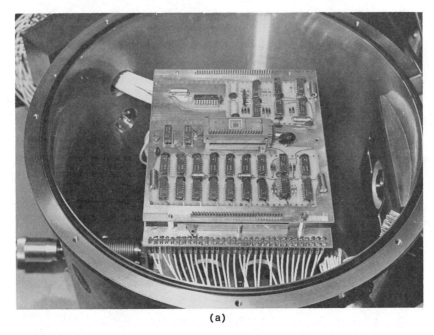

(a)

Figure 12-6. Driving of the microprocessor 8085
a) Printed circuit board with microprocessor under test (open package) and line drivers inside the vacuum chamber. b) Drive unit HP μP-Lab 5036 A.

Experimental conditions

All investigations were performed on nonpassivated devices with an accelerating voltage of 2.5 kV. It was found that the 8085 remained fully operative even after electron irradiation lasting some weeks. Only after lengthy irradiation with higher magnifications in the TV mode (unpulsed electron beam) did charging of the field oxide occur, which led to changes in the function of the microprocessor. The beam current was, in unpulsed operation, between 10^{-8} and 10^{-9} A. As a result of the relatively high duty cycles of 10^{-3} to 10^{-4} in the stroboscopic or sampling mode, this was reduced to an average of the order of one pA or less. As already mentioned in the last section, the stroboscopic and the sampling mode demand cyclic program loops, which for reasons to do with the S/N ration, should be as short as possible. The program chosen for the investigations in the next section is particularly well suited for studying the speed of the carry operation. This is important because the carry operation generally involves a speed restriction in microprocessors and microcomputers.

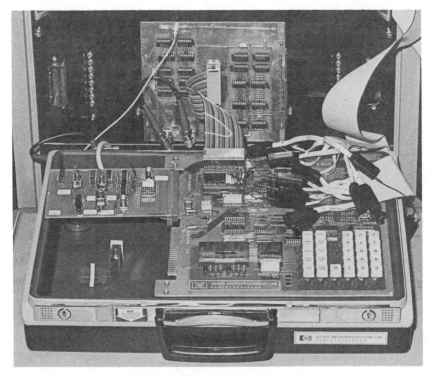

Figure 12-6(b).

Address	Instruction	Opcode	
0800	MVI B	06	
0801		FF	
0802	MVI A	3E	
0803		01	program
0804	CMC	3F	loop
0805	ADD B	80	
0806	JMP	C3	
0807		02	
0808		08	

The program runs as follows: First the value FFH (H means the hexadecimal code) is loaded into register B and the value 01H into register A (accumulator). Addition of both values is done bit by bit with the ADD B instruction. First an intermediate result of FEH appears at the output of the ALU (arith-

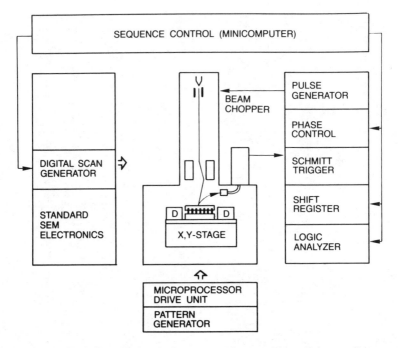

Figure 12-7. Block diagram of measurement setup for generating a logic-state diagram.

metic and logic unit), which is then modified by the ripple-through carry (CY). The final result is 00H with CY = 1. In order to retain the same value for CY in the program loop, CY is always reset by the instruction complement carry (CMC) to 0. The fourth instruction is the jump instruction (JMP) for loop back to MVI A.

VISUALIZATION OF INSTRUCTION EXECUTION

In this section all the modules contained in the functional block diagram of the 8085 (Figure 12-9) are investigated and discussed. The sequence in which the modules are dealt with is not arbitrary but rather is determined by the chronological order of events in an opcode fetch cycle (14). All the techniques described earlier are applied, the most suitable technique being chosen on the basis of the problem posed.

Timing and Control

At the start of each machine cycle M, the type of machine cycle is established in the timing and control unit. To this end, the microprocessor transmits three status signals externally (S_1, S_0, $10/M$), while a series of internal signals are generated which establish the types of the machine cycles M and of the machine states T. The internal timing is controlled by two nonoverlapping clock signals $\emptyset_1$ and $\emptyset_2$, of which only $\emptyset_1$ is led to the outside as CLK signal. Figure 12-10 shows the logic-state diagram of seven internal timing signals: the clock signals $\emptyset_1$ and $\emptyset_2$ and the machine cycle signals $\overline{M}_1$ to $\overline{M}_5$, which control the execution of the different instructions in the program loop. As no instruction is longer than three machine cycles, $\overline{M}_4$ and $\overline{M}_5$ are always high. The control signals for the machine states T can of course also be represented in the same way.

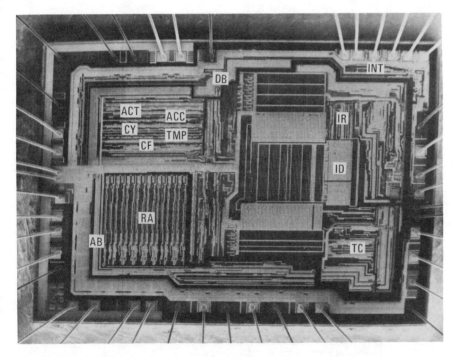

Figure 12-8. Voltage contrast micrograph of a nonpassivated microprocessor 8085. ACT temporary accumulator register, ACT accumulator register, CY carry stages, TMP temporary register, CF condition flags, DB internal data bus, AB internal address bus, RA register array, INT interrupt, IR instruction register, ID instruction decoder, TC timing and control.

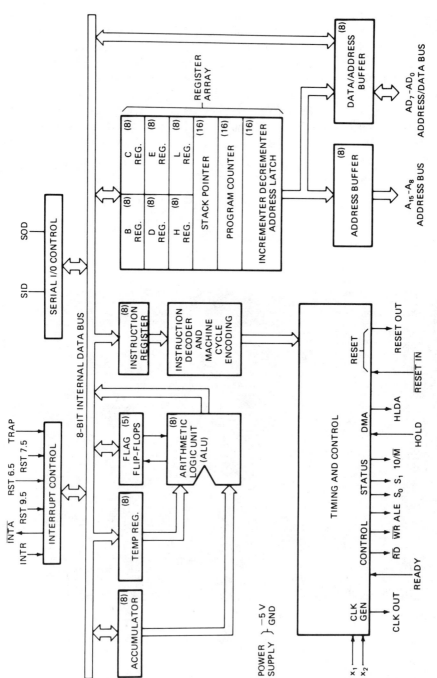

Figure 12-9. 8085 funtional block diagram (15).

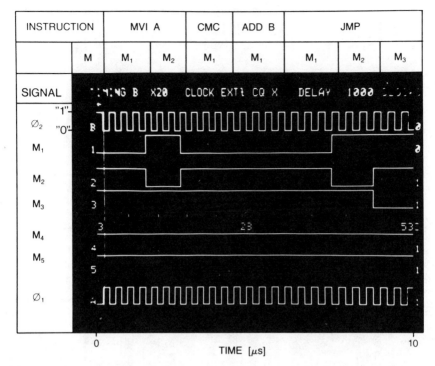

Figure 12-10. Logic-state diagram of seven internal clock signals $\emptyset_1$, $\emptyset_2$, M_1–M_5. Only $\emptyset_1$ can be measured externally as CLK signal.

Internal Address Bus

Also at the start of each machine cycle M a 16-bit address is emitted. The eight low-order bits A_0 to A_7 of the internal address bus and the signal clock $\emptyset_1$ are represented in the logic-state mapping of Figure 12-11. It is not difficult to see that the low-order addresses 02 through 08 appear on the internal address bus, always commencing with $\emptyset_2$ of the last machine state T of the previous machine cycle.

Internal Data Bus

The internal data bus interconnects the majority of the individual modules (see Figure 12-9), and serves to transmit data, e.g. between data buffer and registers or between the individual registers. The logic-state mapping and the logic-state diagram in Figure 12-12a and b show what happens on the internal data bus during the execution of the program loop. For easier time reference the

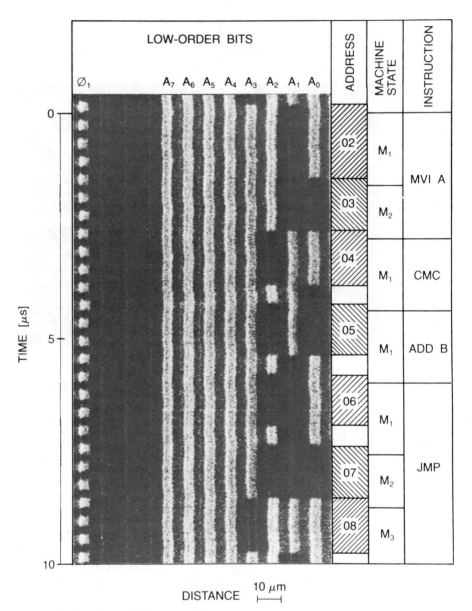

Figure 12-11. Logic-state mapping of the internal address bus (low-order addresses A_0–A_7) showing the addresses 02–08 of the program loop.

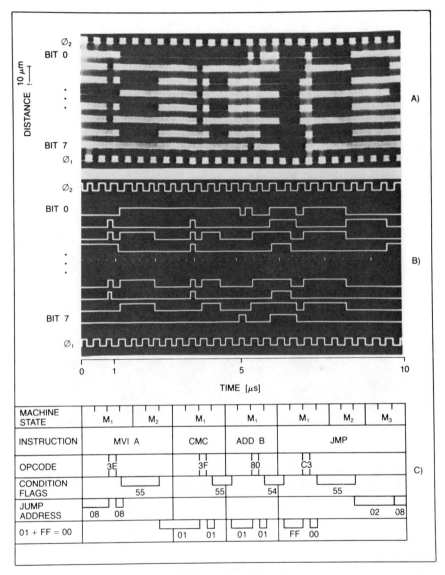

Figure 12-12. Internal data bus.

clock signals $\emptyset_1$ and $\emptyset_2$ are also mapped. In Figure 12-12c the logic states shown in Figures 12-12a and b are given in hexadecimal code and sorted according to the type of data: instruction opcode, condition flags, jump address and the operands A and B along with the result of the ADD instruction (01 + FF = 00).

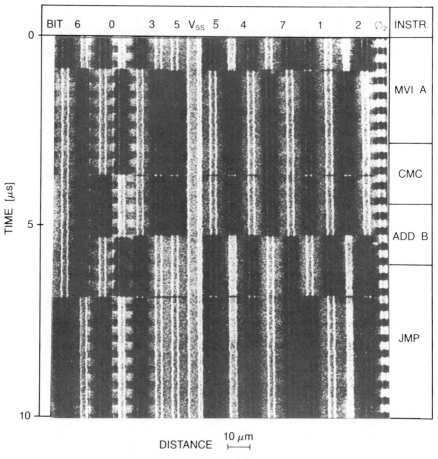

Figure 12-13. Logic-state mapping of instruction register measured at the interconnections between the instruction register and the instruction decoder. The spikes at some interconnections do not influence the correct execution of the instructions.

Instruction Register

After the opcode has been transferred onto the internal data bus from the data buffer, it is stored in the instruction register. Figure 12-13 shows the logic-state mapping of the interconnections between the instruction register and the instruction decoder. Eighteen interconnections can be recognized in the mapping viz. the eight bits and the eight associated inverts plus one supply line and the clock signal $\emptyset_2$. The contents of the register change during each $M_1 T_3 \emptyset_1$ and then remain unchanged until the next opcode fetch machine cycle.

Instruction Decoder

The instruction decoder is for decoding the 8-bit opcode in a programmable logic array. Figure 12-14 shows the first decoder field, in which one control line out of 48 is selected at a time. Figure 12-14a is a stroboscopic voltage contrast micrograph showing the selection of the JMP instruction. Also drawn into this figure is the position of the line scan, with which the logic-state mapping of the

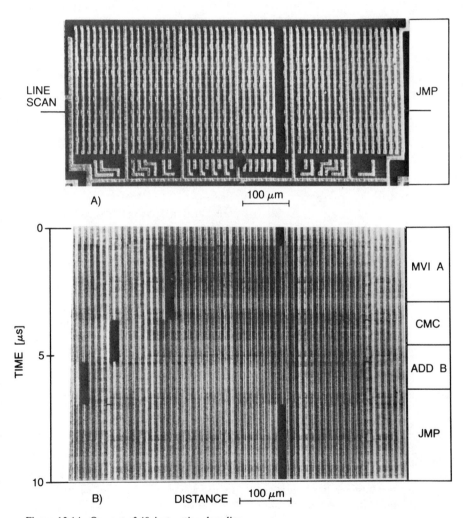

Figure 12-14. One-out-of-48 instruction decoding
a) Stroboscopic voltage contrast micrograph shows decoding of JMP instruction (dark interconnection)
b) Logic-state mapping of the entire program loop with four instructions.

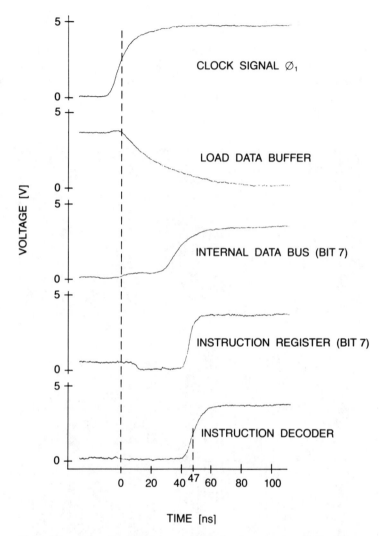

Figure 12-15. Time delay (47 ns) of data transmission between data buffer and instruction decoder measured using the waveform mode.

entire program loop was generated (see Figure 12-14b). The speed of data transmission from the data buffer along the internal data bus into the instruction register and the decoder is shown by the waveforms in Figure 12-15. The overall delay time, counting from clock signal $\emptyset_1$, is approximately 47 ns.

Accumulator and Temporary Register

Figure 12-12c shows when the operands A = 01 and B = FF appear on the internal data bus and when they disappear. Before the arithmetic or logic operations can be executed in the ALU (arithmetic and logic unit), the operands have to be loaded into the accumulator (ACC) and temporary register (TMP). The accumulator has an auxiliary register, the temporary accumulator register (ACT), into which the contents of the ACC register are transferred before being logically combined with the TMP register. Three logic-state mappings of registers ACT, TMP and ACC are presented in Figure 12-16. Operand A is transferred into the ACT register with JMP: $M_1T_1\emptyset_2$, operand B into the TMP register with JMP: $M_1T_2\emptyset_1$. Following this the ADD instruction is executed; its results appear in the ACC register with JMP: $M_1T_3\emptyset_2$ and is then tranferred onto the internal data bus, where it remains during $\emptyset_2$ (see Figure 12-12). Besides the operands A and B the JMP addresses 02 and 08 are also stored in the TMP register.

Arithmetic and Logic Unit (ALU)

It is now possible to investigate the execution of the ADD instruction more closely. The two operands A and B contained in the registers ACT and TMP

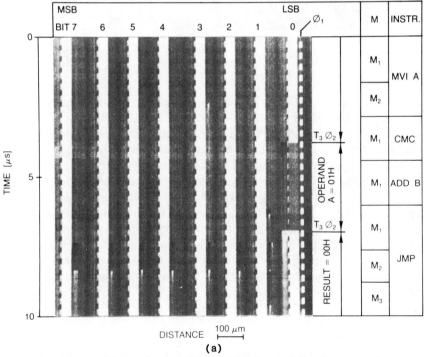

(a)

Figure 12-16. Content of registers in the arithmetic unit during the program loop.
a) Accumulator register (ACC)
b) Temporary accumulator register (ACT)
c) Temporary register (TMP).

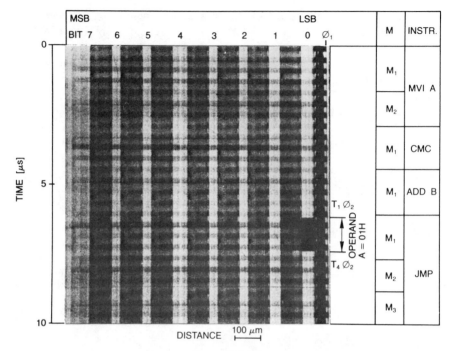

Figure 12-16(b)

were both chosen so that a carry occurs: 01H + FFH = 00H + carry. Figure 12-17 shows eight carry stages, CY0 through CY7. The first stage, CY0, presets the carry operation (JMP: $M_1T_1\emptyset_2$). At instant $T_2\emptyset_1$ (addition of A to B) all 8 bit pairs are added simultaneously, followed by the correction in the form of a ripple-through carry. Figure 12-17a shows the eight carry stages in a logic-state mapping. Since the entire program loop is represented, the ripple-through carry operation cannot be dissolved. That is why the time scale has been extended in Figure 12-17b; it is now easy to see that the individual stages switch with a time delay. The entire ripple-through carry is finished after approximately 20 ns, which corresponds to a propagation delay of approximately 3 ns per stage. Figure 12-17c shows the waveforms measured at six of the stages, but on another, faster device. The overall propagation delay here is only 15 ns.

Condition Flags

There are five condition flags associated with the execution of instructions on the 8085 (14): carry (bit 0), parity (bit 1), auxiliary carry (bit 4), zero (bit 6) and sign (bit 7). As far as our program loop is concerned, the condition flags of the instruction MVI A and JMP are not affected. Instruction CMC affects

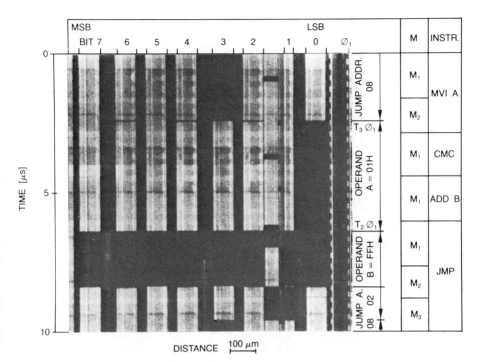

Figure 12-16(c)

only the carry, while instruction ADD B affects all five condition flags. The condition flags for our arithmetic operation 01H + FFH = 00H are:

Carry	1	because it is a carry out of most significant bit (MSB)
Parity	1	sum of the bits of the result is zero
Auxiliary carry	1	ADD causes a carry out of bit 3 into bit 4
Zero	1	result of ADD instruction is zero
Sign	0	the MSB is not 1

The condition flags are thus 55H for the ADD B instruction. The CMC instruction influences the carry flag, i.e. it becomes 0 and thus causes the condition flags to change to 54H. The flags with each $M_1T_4\emptyset_1$ on the internal data bus (see Figure 12-12).

Register Array

The flip-flops in the register array of the 8085 are covered with oxide and are therefore not readily visible in voltage contrast. Scanning the electron beam

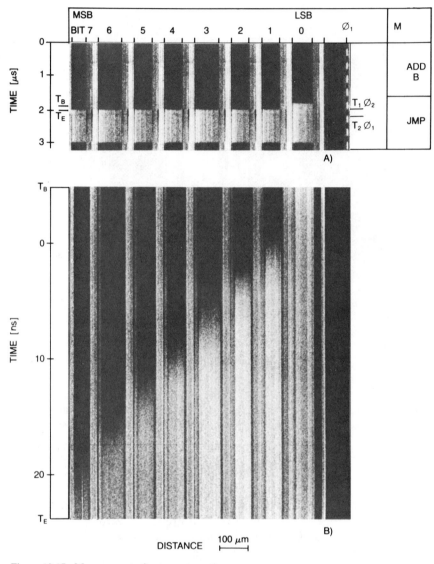

Figure 12-17. Measurement of carry propagation.
a) Logic-state mapping shows preset of carry propagation at bit 0 (JMP: $T_1 \varnothing_2$ = change from dark to light). Start of the ripple through carry operation occurs at bit 1 ($T_2 \varnothing_1$).
b) Visualization of the ripple through carry using an extended time scale for logic-state mapping (phase range $t_a - t_b$).
c) Waveform measurements at six carry stages CY1–CY6.

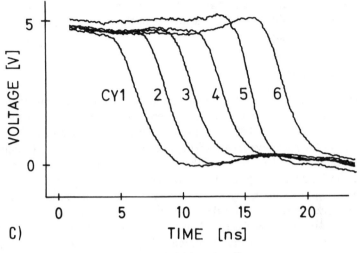

Figure 12-17 (*continued*)

with 2.5 keV primary energy charges the oxide positively until impinging and emitted electrons attain equilibrium. If the logic state of the node now changes from "1" to "0" under the oxide, then the oxide is recharged at this position and it shows up light. Further scanning re-establishes equilibrium and the voltage contrast disappears. To achieve mapping of the register contents despite this, a special program has to be selected: a particular bit pattern and the pattern FF are entered alternately into the registers. It can be seen from the stroboscopic voltage micrograph in Figure 12-18, although not very clearly, that the registers B, H and D are loaded with the contents 66H, 99H and 66H.

Interrupt

To represent the interrupt operation, the standard program loop was interrupted via the pin RSI 6.5 during instruction MVI A. The interrupt causes the internal execution of RESTART (14), whereby the program counter is pushed on the stack and a JMP instruction to the RESTART address (0034) is carried out. At this address our microprocessor drive unit, the μP-Lab, provides for a JMP to the address 0AFC at which the interrupt program commences. In order to keep the program loop as short as possible, only instructions EI (enable interrupt) and RET (return) are executed. RET effects pop of the stack and continuation of the main program loop.

  Figure 12-19 shows the logic-state mapping of the internal data bus of an interrupted program loop containing eight instructions with a total of 61 clocks shown beside the logic state diagram is its interpretation in graphic form, split into six columns: opcode, condition flags, jump address, return address, restart address and the operands A and B together with the result of the ADD operation (01 + FF = 00). The precise sequence of the interrupt operation can be gathered from the mapping.

FAILURE ANALYSIS

The previous section showed the application of the electron beam technique on a fully functional 8085 microprocessor. There will now be a demonstration of a failure analysis by means of an example. In this particular case, an error was generated by the excessive length of the access time of the external memory. The consequences in the interior of the 8085 were to be elucidated, for which purpose the instruction register was investigated more closely. Figure 12-20 shows two logic-state mappings and their analysis for the interconnections that link the instruction register with the instruction decoder. For clarity only 4 bits (and the inverts) of the 8 bits are shown. The correct instruction sequence— INR A, DCR A, JMP— is shown in Figure 12-20a, while Figure 12-20b indicates that the three original instructions have turned into two at 5.9 MHz, the first being instruction MVI A (move immediately to accumulator) and the second the unchanged JMP. This is due to a change of bit 1. The timing and length of the sequence of instruction cycles may be seen from the internal clock pulse 0, which appears in each case at the lower edge of the micrograph.

It is now evident why the microprocessor no longer functions properly: a wrong instruction has been processed. Figure 12-20 provides a clue to the cause. When instructions are changed, spikes appear which show up as light or dark stripes over the interconnections (Figure 12-20c). Since only the spike over bit 1 of the instruction register led to the change of the instruction, it is only necessary to trace bit 1 further. This is best accomplist ed in the waveform mode.

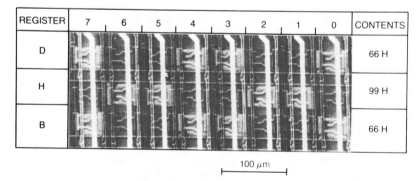

Figure 12-18. Stroboscopic voltage contrast micrograph showing the content of registers B, H and D. The nodes are buried under an oxide layer.

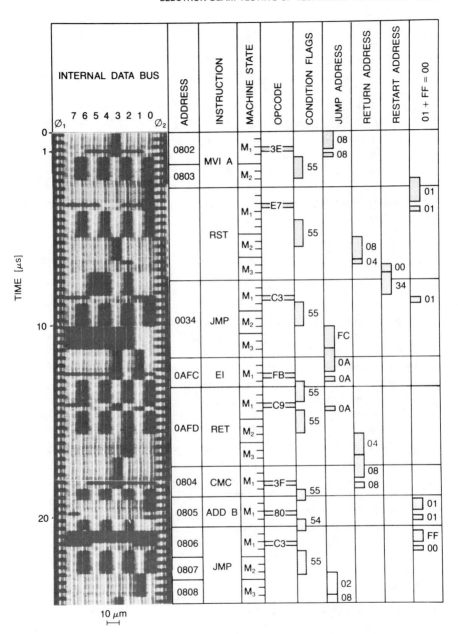

Figure 12-19. Logic-state mapping of internal data bus showing an interrupt operation within the program loop. The notations of the logic states, which are arranged in six columns, are given in hexadecimal code.

Figure 12-21a–j shows the information stored in the instruction register, the internal data bus and the address/data buffer together with two control signals at two different frequencies, 5.5 MHz and 5.9 MHz. The waveforms a, b, c disclose that a binary "0" has been written from the internal data bus into the instruction register. The spike on the internal data bus (c) has no influence on the information stored in the instruction register ("0"), whereas in (h) the spike is accepted by the instruction register as a binary "1" thereby causing the instruction INR A to be altered to MVI A.

It still remains to be explained why the spike appears on the internal data bus. The answer may be found with the aid of Figure 12-21d, e and i, j: the instruction appears too late at the address/data buffer so that the control signals Load Internal Data Bus (d, i) transfer the previous information to the internal data bus 1.

DISCUSSION

Results

Using a fully functional 8085 microprocessor, we have demonstrated that all the logical functions, such as e.g. the instruction execution, can be visualized almost everywhere on the microprocessor with the aid of electron beam techniques. These investigations were limited to the upper level metallization. An exception here is the register array, where the individual cells in which the information is stored are coated with oxide. But even here it is possible to test how the selected cells are loaded, although quantitative measurements through oxide are impracticable.

The electron beam techniques are particularly well suited for determining the speed of execution. Microprocessor speed limits can thus be localized, provided that a critical sequence of instructions was chosen.

It is important for the circuit analysis that different device parameters such as supply voltage, temperature and clock frequency can be varied during the investigation with the electron beam techniques, for only then is it possible to determine the working range of a microprocessor.

Limitations

The following requirements have to be met:

- Low acceleration voltages (typically 2.5 kV) must be chosen for the primary electron beam in order to avoid radiation damage. This means that only nonpassivated microprocessors can be investigated.

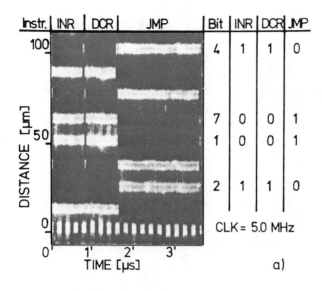

a)

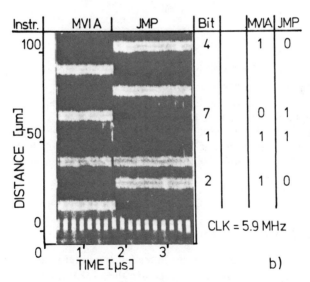

b)

Figure 12-20. Logic-state mappings showing the content of the instruction register
a) Correct instruction execution of INR, DCR, JMP at 5.0 MHz
b) Due to a change of bit 1 from "0" to "1" another instruction, MVI A, is executed at 5.9 MHz
c) Logic-state mapping of bit 1 shows a spike at 5.0 MHz which causes a change of the logic-state of bit 1 at higher frequencies (5.9 MHz).

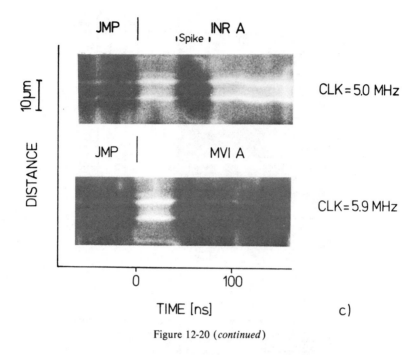

Figure 12-20 (*continued*)

- The chips should preferably be mounted in open packages so as to allow the use of all the described electron beam techniques. For on-wafer investigations only qualitative techniques, including logic-state mapping and logic state diagram can be chosen.
- Finally, the microprocessor must be operated with cyclical program loops, which should be as short as possible in order to assure the best possible S/N ratio. These requirements confine imaging and measuring to the top metallization plane.

Logic-State Mapping and Diagram

The importance of the logic analyzer in testing computer systems with a large data width is beyond dispute today. We have shown that it is now also possible to obtain logic-state mapping and logic-state diagrams inside integrated circuits with the aid of the electron probe. The number of measurement points is limited not by the electron probe, but by the logic analyzer used; in our case it is 16. The time resolution of the setup depends on the width of the electron pulses. Pulse widths of 1 ns are presently attainable with our experimental setup, which means that a logic analyzer of 1 GHz can be implemented, but only for program loops. The time taken to record the logic-state mapping in

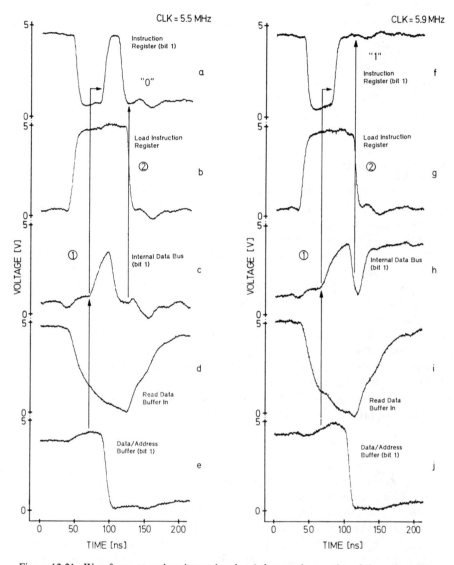

Figure 12-21. Waveforms at various internal nodes. 1 denotes the creation of the spike on the internal data bus and within the instruction register. 2 shows the transfer of data from the data bus into the instruction register.

Figure 12-12b was 100 s. We consider it possible to record the corresponding logic-state diagram in less than ⅒ s, as it covers only the relevant measurement values. In general, it is true to say that the larger the data width becomes, the more importance will attach to the two techniques of logic-state mapping and logic-state diagram.

Other Microprocessors and Microcomputers

Apart from the 8085, we have also investigated a whole series of other microprocessors and microcomputers. It was found in each case that all the functions could be checked, if only indirectly at times.

The problem with microcomputers is how to apply suitable test patterns. However, that is not a problem peculiar to electron beam testing as it applies to any electrical testing and failure analysis of microcomputers.

Area of Application

The areas of application of the various electron beam techniques can now be described and, for clarity, shown in a graphic form. Figure 12-22 shows electron beam testing during the design production and application phases of ICs. The percentage shown of electron beam testing (hatched areas) of the total analysis and test effort is only a rough estimate and refers to the time consumption and not to the number of tested ICs.

It will be noted that electron beam techniques are totally unsuitable for mass inspection, and that for two reasons: one is the inspection requirements (open package with nonpassivated chips); the other, the slow testing speed, which does not stand a comparison with that of computerized testing systems. The most favorable area of application for electron beam techniques is in the design verification phase where a newly developed IC has to be tested. For highly complex VLSI circuits, electron beam testing provides a very good empirical method for comparison with computer simultation. Also, it should be noted that no additional chip is required for electron beam testing.

Future Aspects

If we consider third and fourth-generation microprocessors (e.g. 8086 and the new 32-bit microprocessors), it is possible to divide the problems that can be identified for electron beam testing into two groups: those concerning the geometrical dimensions, and those concerning the electrical design.

Two things should be borne in mind with regard to the geometry: the smaller the width of the structure, the more difficult it is to focus and position the beam on the interconnections. The more layers there are, the fewer nodes can be measured in the upper metallization level.

In the first case, the electron-optical column has to be improved, e.g. by employing LaB_6 or field emission guns, as has been done to some extent in other laboratories. In the second case, only the designer himself can ensure that the nodes remain accessible to internal probing. For even the theoretically feasible measuring through oxide becomes problematic at spacings of ≤ 2 μm, partly because the electron beam can cause a short circuit between the adjacent inter-

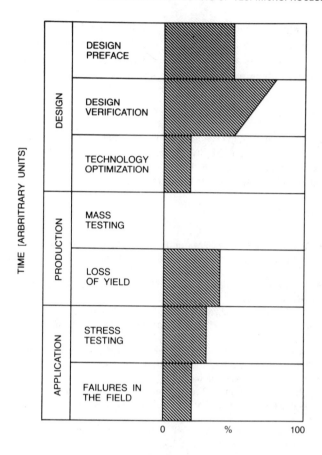

PERCENTAGE SHARE OF ELECTRON BEAM
TESTING (HATCHED AREAS) OF THE TOTAL
ANALYSIS AND TEST EFFORT.

Figure 12-22. Areas of application of electron beam techniques during design, production and application phases. The hatched areas indicate where it is useful to apply electron beam techniques as an analytical tool.

connections in the upper level and partly because the signal can be considerably distorted by the local electric fields of the upper interconnections. (Vias could be located outside of crossover regions to provide access to lower levels by the electron beam).

As far as the electrical design is concerned, there could be problems if asynchronous signals occur. Our stroboscopic and sampling techniques demand strictly synchronous processes which recur regularly. Since we do not yet have any experience with asynchronous processes, however, we can only surmise about the attendant problems and their solution. Should analog signals come up processing inside the microprocessors, e.g. application of sense amplifiers on buses, good experience is already available with DRAMS /8/ so that there is every prospect of determining such signals with an accuracy of ± 10 mV.

Acknowledgment:

The authors wish to thank Dr. U Schwabe for providing the microprocessors, Dr. H.-P. Feuerbaum, Dr. Horninger, Mr. G. Grassl, Dr. Pfleiderer and Dr. Zibert for valuable suggestions and discussion, Dr. Fuchs and Dr. Rebstock for encouragement and supporting the work, and Mrs. Reidt for doing the photographic work.

REFERENCES

(1) Everhart, T. E., Wells, O. C., and Matta, R. K. "Evaluation of Passivated Integrated Circuits Using the Scanning Electron Microscope." *J. Electrochem. Soc.* **111**: 929–936 (1964).

(2) Crosthwait D. L., and Ivey, F. W. "Voltage Constrast Methods for Semiconductor Device Failure Analysis." *SEM/1974*, pp. 935–940.

(3) Piwczyk, B., Siu, W. "Specialized Scanning Electron Microscopy Voltage Contrast Techniques for LSI Failure Analysis." *Proc. 12th Ann. Reliability Physics Symp.* (1974): 49–53

(4) Gonzales, A. J., and Powell, M. W. "Internal Waveform Measurements of the MOS Three-Transistor, Dynamic RAM Using SEM Stroboscopic Techniques." in *Proc. Int. Electron Devices Meet.* (Washington, DC, Dec. 1975): 119–122.

(5) Wolfgang, E., Otto, J., Kantz, D., and Lindner, R. "Stroboscopic Voltage Contrast of Dynamic 4096 bit MOS RAMs: Failure Analysis and Function Testing." *SEM/1976*, pp. 625–631.

(6) Child, M. R., Ranansinghe, D. W., and White, D. "Dynamic inspection of Wage Scale Integrated Curcuits." *Microelectronics* **7**: 45-48 (1976).

(7) Touw, T. R., Herman, P. A., and Lukianoff, G. V. "Practical Techniques for Application of Voltage Contrast to Diagnosis of Integrated Circuits," *SEM/1977*, pp. 177–182.

(8) Wolfgang E., Lindner, R., Fazekas, P., and Feuerbaum, H. P. "Electron Beam Testing of VLSI Circuits." *IEEE J. Solid-State Circ.* **SC-14**: 471–481 (1979).

(9) Fujioka H., Nakamae, K., and Ura, K. "Function Testing of Bipolar IC's and LSI's with the Stroboscopic Scanning Electron Microscope." *IEEE J. Solid-State-Circ.* **SC-15**: 177–183 (1980).

(10) Feuerbaum, H.-P and Hernaut, K. "Application of Electron Beam Measurement Techniques for Verifying Computer Simulations at Large Scale IC." *SCM/1978*, pp. 795–800.

(11) Crichton, G., et al. "Visualisation of the Function of a Microcomputer IC Using a Scanning Electron Microscope." *Proceedings of the Technical Sessions, IMMM 79*, Geneva, 19.-21.6.79, Organized by Kiver Communications S.S., Surbiton, Surrey, England, pp 9–14.

(12) Wolfgang, E., Fazekas, P., Otto, J., and Crichton, G. "Internal Testing of Microprocessor Chips Using Electron Beam Techniques." *Proceedings of IEEE International Conference on Circuits and Computers 1980* (1980): 548–551.

(13) Crichton, G., Fazekas, P., and Wolfgang, E. "Electron Beam Testing of Microprocessors", *Digest of Papers 1980 IEEE Test Conference*, pp. 444–449 (1980).

(14) MCS-80/85 Family User's Manual, Intel Corporation (1979).

(15) Wiatrowski, C. A., and House, C. H. *Logic Circuits and Microcomputer Systems*. New York: McGraw-Hill Book Company, pp. 247–303 (1980).
(16) Feuerbaum, H. P., and Kubalek, E. "Qualitative and Quantitative Voltage Measurement on Integrated Circuits." *Beitr. Elektronen-mikroskip Direktabb. Oberfl.* **8:** 469–480 (1975).
(17) Gopinath, A., et al. "Voltage Contrast: A review," *SEM/1978*, pp. 375–380.
(18) Plows, G. S., and Nixon, W. C. "Stroboscopic Scanning Electron Microscopy." *J. Phys. E.: Sci. Instrum.* **11:** 595–600 (1968).
(19) Gopinath, A., and Hill, M. S. "Some Aspects of the Stroboscopic Mode: A Review." *SEM/ 1974*, pp. 235–242.
(20) Balk, L. J., Feuerbaum, H. P., Kubalek, E., and Menzel, E. "Quantitative Voltage Contrast at High Frequencies in the SEM." *SEM/1976*, **1:** 614–624.
(21) Feuerbaum, H. P., "VLSI Testing Using the Electron Probe." *SEM/1979* pp. 285–296 (1979).
(22) Gopinath, A. "Estimate of Minimum Measurable Voltage in the SEM," *J. Phys. E: Sci. Instrum.* **10:** 911–913 (1977).
(23) Feuerbaum, H. P., "Beiträge zu Fortschritten in der Elektronenstrahlmeßtechnik", *Beitr. elektronenmikroskopischer Direktabbildung.* **11:** 67–71 (1978).
(24) Lukianoff, G. V., and Touw, T. R. "Voltage Coding: Temporal Versus Spatial Frequencies." *SEM/1975*, pp. 465–471.

13. VLSI Oxidation Technology

Natsuro Tsubouchi

LSI Research and Development Laboratory
Mitsubishi Electric Corporation
Itami, Japan

INTRODUCTION

Oxidation has been a fundamental process of silicon device technology for over twenty years. However, the current activity of research on oxidation physics and chemistry shows that the technology is not complete for modern LSI manufacturing process. An oxidation method which has received increasing attention over the last few years involves the use of high pressure. High pressure oxidation is a good method for achieving an accelerated oxide growth and preparing thermal oxide at reduced temperature. Low temperature oxidation has its greatest potential impact on high density VLSI because of the need to minimize the creation of thermally induced defects and to maintain sharp impurity profiles in small devices.

While high pressure oxidation was expected to be useful for LSI process, it did not gain rapid acceptance for lack of an adequate high pressure oxidation apparatus with appropriate safety and production capability. However, some apparatus suited to high-volume production has been made commercially available recently (1, 2, 3). One of the apparatus is shown in Figure 13-1. The schematic diagram of the cross section is shown in Figure 13-2. The apparatus consists mainly of an outer stainless steel pressure chamber surrounding a conventional furnace. A quartz tube, to be heated up to an appropriate temperature, is inserted into the furnace. The wafers are thermally oxidized by hydrogen and oxygen pyrogenic method at high pressure.

This system operates up to 10 atm and 1100°C and has a load capacity of 150 4″-diameter wafers. At present, commercially available high pressure systems are offered with up to 25 atm and up to 1100°C. Pyrogenic steam and

Figure 13-1. A photograph of the high pressure oxidation apparatus.

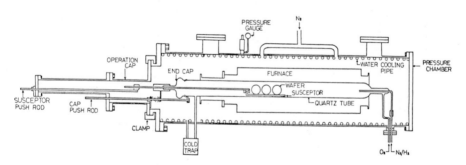

Figure 13-2. A schematical view of the high pressure steam oxidation apparatus.

dry O_2 are the oxidants for a typical oxidation. In some systems, HC1 oxidation can be performed at high pressure.

Sequence and safety controls are performed with a microcomputer. Safety controls include prevention of excess H_2, overpressure of gases, overheating, and overtemperature. These oxidation systems are being incorporated into mass production processing of MOS and bipolar LSI circuits.

HIGH PRESSURE OXIDATION OF SILICON

Oxidation of silicon at atmospheric pressure is well known, and follows a linear/parabolic relationship (4). Some reports about high pressure oxidation indicate a linear dependence of the oxidation rate on the oxidation time (5). However, recent studies of the oxidation characteristics clarify that the linear/parabolic relationship holds good under high pressure conditions (6).

Figure 13-3 shows the oxide thickness dependence on the oxidation pressure and time as a parameter of oxidation temperature. In this case, oxidation of silicon wafers was carried out in pyrogenic steam generated by the H_2 and O_2 reaction. The partial pressure of H_2O is given by

$$^{P}H^{2}O = \frac{2F_{H2}}{2F_{O2} + F_{H2}} \cdot P \qquad [13.1]$$

where F_{H2} is the flow rate of H_2 gas, F_{O2} is the flow rate of O_2 gas and P is the absolute pressure in the quartz tube. The oxidation pressure shown in Figure 13-3 is calculated from equation [13.1]. This figure indicates the linear/para-

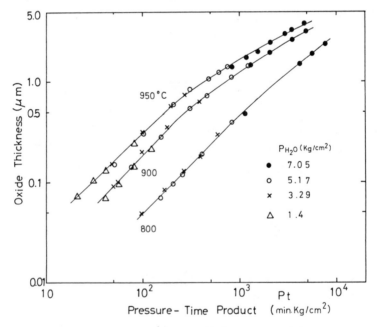

Figure 13-3. Oxide thickness dependence on the oxidation pressure and time as a parameter of oxidation temperature.

Table 13-1. Oxidation Constants as a Function of Oxidation Temperature.

CONST. TEMPERATURE	A (μm)	B $\left(\dfrac{\mu m^2}{Kg/cm^2 \cdot min}\right)$	$\dfrac{B}{A}$ $\left(\dfrac{\mu m}{Kg/cm^2 \cdot min}\right)$
950°C	0.5	3.5×10^{-3}	7×10^{-3}
900°C	0.64	2.44×10^{-3}	3.81×10^{-8}
800°C	3.2	$1.74 \times 10/^{-3}$	0.54×10^{-3}

bolic dependence on oxidation pressure and time product. The following equation is given for the high pressure oxidation of silicon.

$$X_0^2 + AX_0 = B\,P\,t \qquad\qquad [13.2]$$

where X_0 is oxide thickness, P is oxidation pressure, t is oxidation time, A and B are constants. From Figure 13-3, we get values for A and B shown in Table 13-1. The temperature dependence of the constants B and B/A are shown in Figures 13-4 and 13-5. It is seen that this dependence is exponential with acti-

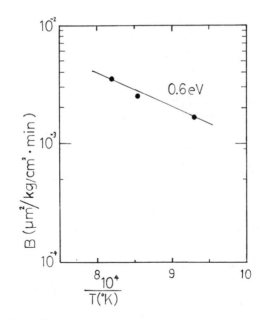

Figure 13-4. The oxidation constant B as a function of the temperature.

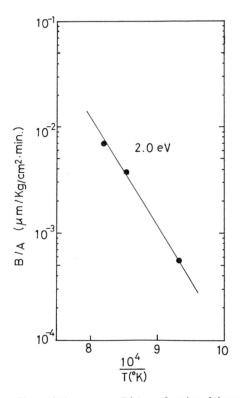

Figure 13-5. The oxidation constant B/A as a function of the temperature.

vation energies of 0.6 ev and 2.0 ev for B and B/A respectively. This activation energies are very close to those for normal pressure oxidation. From these results, it can be concluded that high pressure oxidation of silicon under steam ambient proceeds by the same mechanism as at normal pressure. The activation energy for B corresponds to the diffusion energy of water through silicon dioxide. The energy for B/A corresponds to the bond-breaking energy of silicon.

Under high pressure, the oxidation time can be reduced in inverse proportion to oxidation pressure.

Suppression of Oxidation-Induced Stacking Fault

Thermal oxidation of silicon at high temperature for a long time is known to result in oxidation-induced stacking faults (which is called OSF) in the silicon surface layer. The presence of OSF is known to have detrimental effects on the device performance characteristics such as excessive junction leakage, excess noise, video defects in CCD and so on. There has been an increasing interest in development of an oxidation method which does not generate OSF. HCl and TCE oxidations were found to be effective in eliminating or reducing the generation of OSF.

OSF is also known to depend on the oxidation time, temperature, and oxide thickness. Thick silicon oxide is required to be grown in a variety of integrated circuits such as field oxide in MOS LSI, isolation oxide in Bipolar LSI and so on. The thick oxide usually generates large OSF. However, high pressure oxidation can suppress the generation of OSF because of the shorter times and lower temperatures involved (6).

Figure 13-6 shows the length of OSF as a function of oxide thickness for high pressure oxidation and conventional wet O_2 oxidation. Solid lines indicate

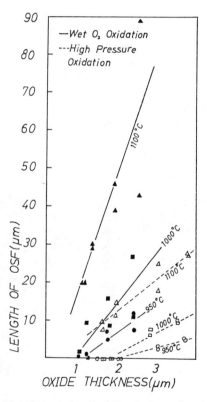

Figure 13-6. The length of oxidation-induced stacking fault as a function of oxide thickness for high pressure oxidation and conventional wet O_2 oxidation.

high pressure oxidation data and broken lines show wet O_2 oxidation at normal pressure. The length OSF formed during high pressure oxidation can be reduced significantly for the same temperature and oxide thickness when compared with atmospheric oxidation.

The length of OSF is known to be described by the following equation in atmospheric oxidation (7),

$$L = At^n \exp\left(-\frac{Q}{kT}\right) \qquad [13.3]$$

where t is oxidation time, T is oxidation temperature, A, n, Q and k are constants. This equation is reported to hold true for OSF formed under high pressure oxidation as well[7]. The constants A, n and Q are almost equal for both oxidations. The reduction of oxidation time under high pressure results in smaller length of OSF.

There is a considerable variation from wafer to wafer in the observed density of OSF, which depends strongly upon the quality of starting materials. To eliminate these wafer to wafer variations, one wafer was cut into two parts, one of which was thermally oxidized using a high pressure oxidation system and the other using a conventional oxidation system. Figure 13-7 shows a typical example of the patterns formed on each half of the same n-type silicon wafer. The sample shown on the right side was oxidized in a conventional wet oxygen ambient at 1050°C for 500 minutes. The left half was oxidized at high pressure of 6.6 kg/cm² and at 1050°C for 60 minutes. The oxide thickness for both oxidations were approximately 1.6 μm.

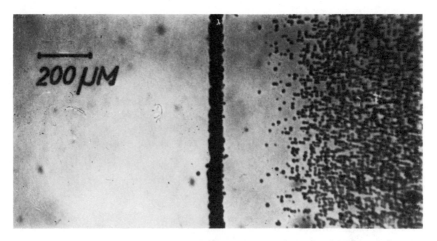

Figure 13-7. A microphotograph of etched patterns of oxidation induced stacking faults formed during high pressure oxidation (left half) and conventional wet O_2 oxidation (right half).

Selective Oxidation of Silicon

Selective oxidation of silicon, by the use of a silicon nitride film as a mask is one of the basic process technologies in VLSI. The conventional atmospheric oxidation process has been performed at high temperatures for extended times in order to grow thick selective oxide. On the other hand, the high pressure oxidation can reduce the oxidation time and temperature for similar oxide thicknesses. In applying the high pressure process to the selective oxidation of silicon, the masking resistance of the silicon nitride film is important. Furthermore, the control of the lateral oxidation, by which the silicon substrate to be protected is oxidized, is also of interest to define the selective oxidation process for fabricating VLSI.

Figure 13-8 shows the thickness of oxide formed on the silicon nitride film as a function of oxidation time and temperature.

Figure 13-9 shows the parameters associated with selective oxidation of silicon. In this figure, X and Y are respectively parallel and perpendicular to the surface of silicon. Maximum lateral oxide thickness is labelled B. The slope profile from (O, Yo) to (B, O) was investigated. The edge height of the masking nitride from the origin (O, O) is labelled H.

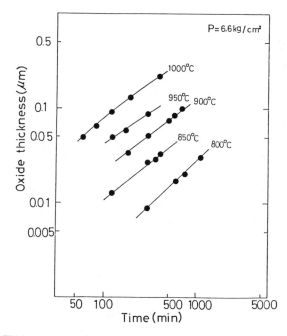

Figure 13-8. Thickness of oxide formed on the silicon nitride film as a function of oxidation time and temperature.

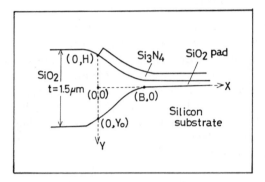

Figure 13-9. Schematic view of the cross section of the selective oxidation structure.

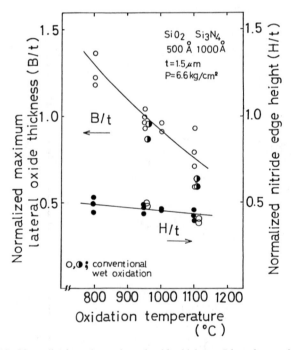

Figure 13-10. Normalized maximum lateral oxide thickness B/t and normalized nitride edge height H/t as a function of oxidation temperature at the pressure of 6.6 kg/cm².

Figure 13-10 shows a normalized maximum lateral oxide thickness B/t and a normalized nitride edge height as a function of oxidation temperature at a pressure of 6.6 kg/cm^2. Further, in this figure, the values obtained from the experiments performed by the conventional atmospheric wet oxidation are plotted here as a comparison. As can be seen from this figure, the maximum lateral oxide thickness decreases rapidly with increasing oxidation temperature and B/t becomes larger than 1.0 at oxidation temperatures lower than 950°C, that is, the lateral oxidation rate is larger than the vertical oxidation rate. Further, there is little difference in lateral oxide thickness between the values obtained from the atmospheric oxidation and high pressure oxidation. So, we can apply the high pressure oxidation to the selective oxidation of silicon using silicon nitride as a mask as well as atmospheric oxidation.

The Application of High Pressure Oxidation to Bipolar LSI

Oxide isolation, combined with shallow implanted junctions, has been helpful in achieving high speed bipolar devices. However, the long oxidation time causes redistribution of impurities from the buried collector, which results in the increase of base-collector *capacitance* C_{TCO}. We have applied high pressure oxidation to the isolation of high speed E_{CL} devices and verified the advantage of this technique in device performance.

Figure 13-11 shows the redistribution of arsenic of the buried collector measured by the spreading resistance method. In this case, the expitaxial layer was 1.8μm thick. Arsenic in the buried collector migrates toward the surface during conventional oxidation. The impurity diffusion is considerably suppressed by the high pressure oxidation.

The redistribution of boron in the field region is shown in Figure 13-12. Owing to a shorter oxidation time during high pressure growth, the boron distribution was somewhat steeper, and a slightly higher maximum concentration was obtained at the same implanation dose.

The parasitic capacitances of oxide isolated transistors are shown in Figure 13-13. C_{TC} is reduced by introducing the high pressure oxidation and is kept constant with the field doping. Collector-substrate capacitance C_{TSO} is strongly related to the field doping and the value is slightly higher in the high pressure oxidation than the conventional one at the same implantation dose. Emitter-base capacitance C_{TEO} has no dependence on the boron field dope.

The capacitance values and transistor parameters are summarized in Table 13-2. Comparing the two oxidation methods, significant improvements in device breakdown voltage and parasitic capacitance were achieved with high pressure oxidation.

The propagation delay time of three ECL gates is plotted as a function of

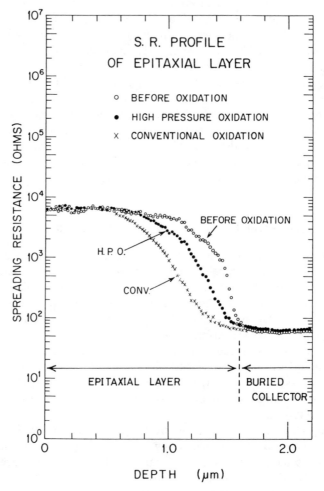

Figure 13-11. Redistribution of arsenic of the buried collector measured by the spreading resistance method.

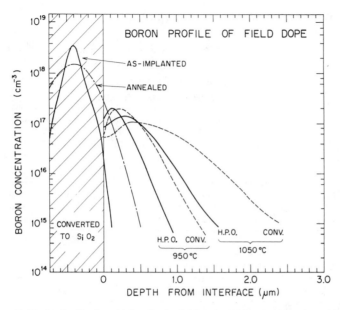

Figure 13-12. Redistribution of boron in the field region during high pressure oxidation.

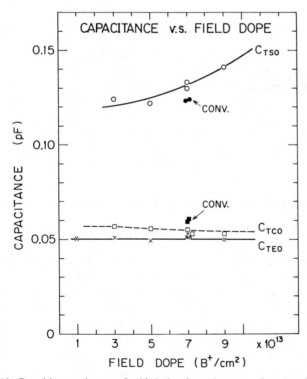

Figure 13-13. Parasitic capacitances of oxide isolated transistors as a function of field dope.

Table 13-2. Comparison of Transistor Characteristics
Fabricated by Using High Pressure and Conventional
Atmospheric Oxidations.
Typical Transistor Characteristics

	HIGH PRESSURE OXIDATION	CONVENTIONAL OXIDATION
Emitter size	$3 \times 3 \ \mu m^2$	
h_{FE}	$\backsim 100$	
BV_{CEO}	11.5 v	8 v
BV_{CBO}	29 v	23 v
C_{TCO}	0.05 pF	0.06 pF
C_{TEO}	0.05 pF	0.05 pF
$G_{TSO}{}^{(*)}$	0.12 pF	0.12 pF

$^{(*)}C_{TSO}$ of H.P.O. and Conventional transistors was measured with each optimum B^+ field dope.

field dope in Figure 13-14. It can be seen from this figure that the delay time is improved by the high pressure method. Because of the smaller broadening of the boron profile during the isolation oxidation, the optimum implant dose for field areas by the high pressure oxidation is slightly less than that of the conventional oxidation. Therefore, it is more practical to compare the delay time values between the field dope at $9 \times 10^{13}/cm^2$ in the high pressure oxidation and $1.1 \times 10^{14}/cm^2$ in the conventional oxidation, because these two conditions gave the same isolation breakdown voltages. Assuming those field doses, the delay time is slightly improved, and the values of C_{TS} are comparable between the two oxidation methods (see table 13-2).

The Application of High Pressure Oxidation to the Fabrication of MOS LSI

High Pressure Oxidation of Field and Gate in MOS Transistors. The influence of the selective oxidation temperature on the dielectric breakdown probability of the thin gate oxide grown after selective oxidation was examined. The experimental results were obtained from MOS capacitors with Al electrodes by use of the voltage ramping method. Selective oxidation of (100) oriented silicon wafers was performed, with the use of a masking silicon nitride film, at 850–1050°C, using the high pressure oxidation at a steam pressure of 5.6 kg/cm^2 and the conventional wet O_2 oxidation respectively. This gate oxide film was 500 Å thick and grown by conventional HC1 oxidation at 1050°C.

Figure 13-15 shows the dielectric breakdown probability of thin gate oxide

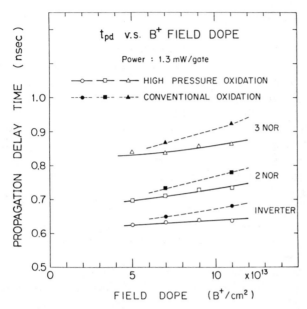

Figure 13-14. Comparison of propagation delay time of ECL gates (3-Input NOR, 2-Input NOR, Inverter) between high and atmospheric pressure oxidation.

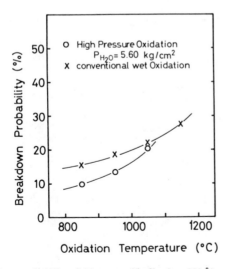

Figure 13-15. Breakdown probability of thin gate oxide film (tox-500Å) as a function of selective oxidation temperature.

film as a function of the selective oxidation temperature. The probability decreased with decreasing oxidation temperature and the high pressure selective oxidation reduced the breakdown probability in comparison with the conventional oxidation. It was reported that high temperature selective oxidation process often produced a thin layer of silicon nitride, so-called "white ribbon" (8, 9) and the masking nitride film resulted in damage to the substrate after high temperature heat treatment (10). It seems likely that the high pressure oxidation process reduces both the damage on the substrate and "white ribbon" and, therefore, improves the breakdown characteristics of the gate oxide grown by subsequent oxidation.

The effect of oxidation temperature on threshold voltage of a field transistor was investigated. The test chip was designed and fabricated using n-channel silicon gate technology including the selective oxidation of silicon and the double poly-silicon structure. A thick field oxide film of 7500 Å was grown by the high pressure oxidaton at 5.6 kg/cm^2, and conventional oxidation. As a channel stopper, the boron does of 3×10^{13}/cm^2 was implanted at 50 kev. As shown in Figure 13-16, the high pressure oxidation process results in a higher threshold voltage than the conventional oxidation process. This is because the boron

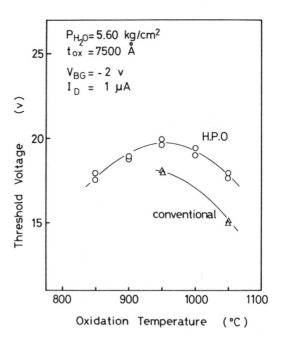

Figure 13-16. Field threshold voltage vs. selective oxidation temperature.

diffusion into the substrate during conventional oxidation is large and the surface concentration is much less than by high pressure oxidation. This phenomenon was confirmed from the boron depth profile by IMA analysis. The threshold voltage in the high pressure oxidation process was found to have a maximum value around 950°C. The boron diffusivity in silicon is small at temperatures below 950°C and the silicon containing high dope boron at the surface is converted into the field oxide.

In Figure 13-17, the oxidation pressure dependence of the threshold voltage is shown. The oxidation temperature was 950°C. Oxidation time increases with decreasing oxidation pressure. Therefore, the surface boron concentration is reduced.

As reported in previous work (11), the field oxidation in high pressure steam resulted in the improvement of the refresh time of MOS dynamic RAMs.

The thin silicon gate oxide film was grown by high pressure oxidation of the silicon substrate at the temperature between 700°C and 850°C under steam pressure of 5.6 kg/cm². The film thickness was about 380 Å and pure Al gate electrodes were formed with an area of 2 mm × 2 mm. The typical distribution of a dielectric breakdown strength for the thin gate oxide film is shown in Figure 13-18.

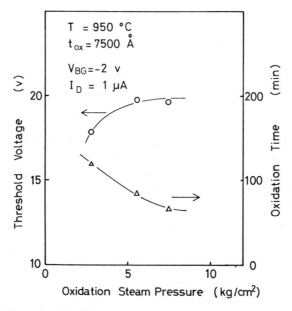

Figure 13-17. Field threshold voltage vs. oxidation steam pressure.

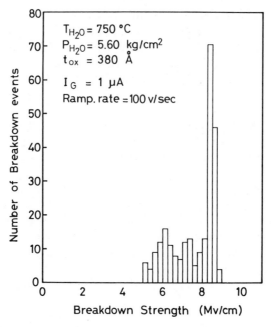

Figure 13-18. Distribution of dielectric breakdown strength of thin oxide film formed by high pressure oxidation.

The thin oxide film formed at low temperature and high pressure has almost the same dielectric breakdown strength as compared with the thin oxide film grown by use of a conventional dry O_2 oxidation at 1050°C (12). The high pressure oxidation could be applied to the formation of the thin gate oxide of MOS LSI.

MOS LSI with Double Polysilicon Layers.   In this section, we report that the accelerated growth of the silicon dioxide on the phosphorous-doped polysilicon film in high pressure steam, at a low oxidation temperature, provides a simple method to gain a thick intermediate insulator for MOS LSI with double polysilicon layers.

In this study, phosphorous-doped polysilicon films were deposited on thermally oxidized silicon substrates by the chemical vapor deposition method using the SiH_4 and PH_3 gases at 610°C in the thickness range from 4000 Å to 5000 Å. The phosphorous concentration of these films was examined by fluorescence X-ray analysis and found to be 0.8–1.2 mole percent for silicon atoms.

Figure 13-19 shows the oxidation characteristics of these films in high pressure steam in comparison with the lightly doped silicon substrate. High pres-

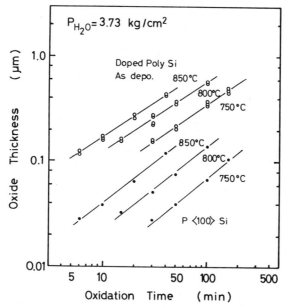

Figure 13-19. Oxidation characteristics of doped poly silicon film and single silicon.

sure oxidation was performed in a steam pressure of 3.73 kg/cm^2 between 750°C and 850°C. It can be seen that the doped polysilicon can be oxidized about 3 to 5 times as fast as the silicon substrate.

As shown in Figure 13-20, the thickness ratio of the thick oxide film on a doped polysilicon layer to the thin oxide film on a substrate increases with decreasing oxidation temperature. Moreover, it is seen from Figure 13-21 that this thickness ratio increases at the higher oxidation pressure.

To utilize this characteristic, the high pressure oxidation method was applied to the second gate oxide formation in the 64 K-bit MOS RAM device. The gate oxide thickness was 500 Å. The oxidation was carried out at 800°C and 850°C, respectively.

Figure 13-22 shows a SEM photograph of the cross section of a double polysilicon structure by conventional oxidation at 950°C. It can be seen that the thickness of the intermediate insulator by the high pressure oxidation at 800°C is 2400 Å and much larger than that of conventional oxidation (1300 Å). As shown in Figure 13-23, the rupture voltage for the oxidation at 800°C was larger than that at 850°C, due to the thick intermediate insulator. As a result, lower temperature oxidation in the high pressure steam could improve the electrical performance of MOS LSI.

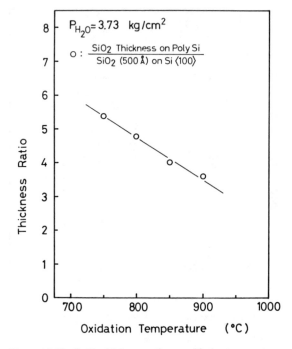

Figure 13-20. Oxide thickness ratio vs. oxidation temperature.

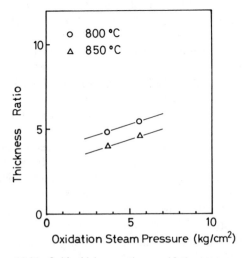

Figure 13-21. Oxide thickness ratio vs. oxidation steam pressure.

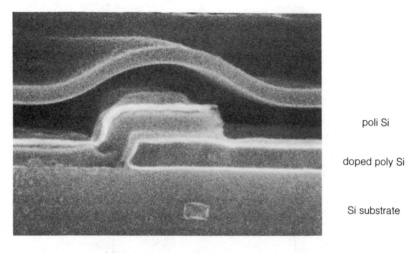

poli Si

doped poly Si

Si substrate

(a) conventional oxidation

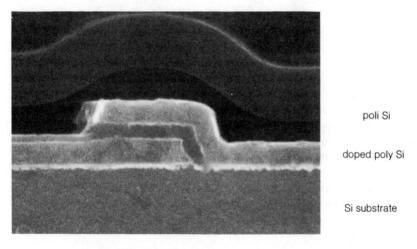

poli Si

doped poly Si

Si substrate

(b) high pressure oxidation

Figure 13-22. Cross sectional view of SEM photographs of double poly silicon layer structure: (a) conventional oxidation, (b) high pressure oxidation.

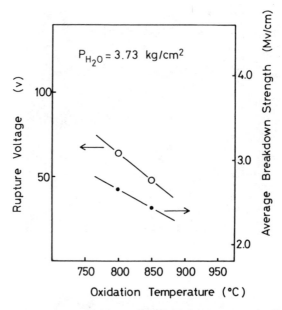

Figure 13-23. Rupture voltage of intermediate oxide between two poly silicon layers.

CONCLUSION

High pressure oxidation has not only supplemented the conventional temperature and time variables for silicon oxidation but also resulted in the improvement in device performances. The application of high pressure oxidation has been extended to various device fabrication processes. ECL and MOS RAMs are finding advantages from high pressure oxidation. We can look forward to exciting activities in applications to VLSI during the new few years.

REFERENCES

(1) Tsubouchi, N., Miyoshi, H., Nishimoto, A., Abe, H. and Satoh, R. "High Pressure Steam Apparatus for Oxidation of Silicon." *Japan J. Appl. Phys.* **16:** 1055–1056 (1977).
(2) Champagne, R., Tool, M., "High-Pressure Pyrogenic Oxidation in the Production Environment." *Solid State Technol.* **20:** 61–63 (1977).
(3) Katz, L. E., and Howells, B. F., "Low Temperature, High Pressure Steam Oxidation of Silicon." *J. Electrochem. Soc.* **126:** 1822–1824 (1979).
(4) Deal, B. E. and Grove, A. S. "General Relationship for the Thermal Oxidation of Silicon." *J. Appl. Phys.* **36:** 3770–3778 (1965).
(5) Ligenza, J. R. "Oxidation of Silicon by High-Pressure Steam." *J. Electrochem. Soc.* **109:** 73–76 (1962).
(6) Tsubouchi, N., Miyoshi, H. and Abe, H. "Suppression of oxidation-induced stacking fault

formation in silicon by high pressure steam oxidation." *Japan J. Appl. Phys.* Suppl. 17-1, 223-228 (1978).

(7) Murarka, S. P. and Quintana, G. "Oxidation-induced Stacking Faults in N-And P-Type (100) Silicon." *J. Appl. Phys.* **48**: 46-51 (1977).

(8) Kooi, E., Lierop, J. G., and Appels, J. A. "Formation of Silicon Nitride at a Si-SiO$_2$ Interface During Local Oxidation of Silicon and During Heat-treatment of Oxidized Silicon in NH$_3$ Gas." *J. Electrochem. Soc.* **123**: 1117-1120 (1976).

(9) Shankoff, T. A., Sheng, T. T., Haszko, S. E., Marcus, R. E., and Smith, T. E. "Bird's Beak Configuration and Elimination of Gate Oxide Thinning Produced During Selective Oxidation." *J. Electrochem. Soc.* **127**: 216-222 (1980).

(10) Isomae, S., Tamaki, Y., Yajima, A., Nanba, M., and Maki, M., "Dislocation Generation at Si$_3$N$_4$ Film Edges on Silicon Substrate and Visco-elastic Behavior of SiO$_2$ Films." *J. Electrochem. Soc.* **126**: 1014-1018 (1979).

(11) Tsoubouchi, N., Miyoshi, H., Abe, H., and Enomoto, T. "The Application of the High Pressure Oxidation Process to the Fabrication of MOS LSI." *IEEE Trans. Electron Devices* **ED-26**: 618-622 (1979).

(12) Osburn, C. M. and Chou, N. J. "Accelerated Dielectric Breakdown of Silicon Dioxide Films." *J. Electrochem. Soc.* **120**: 1377-1384 (1973).

14. VLSI CAD Systems

M. E. Daniel

and

C. W. Gwyn

Sandia National Laboratories

INTRODUCTION

Computer-aided design (CAD), as used in this paper, refers to a collection of software tools integrated into a system to provide the integrated circuit designer with step-by-step design assistance during each phase of the design. Although many decisions are made by the software during the design process, important decisions are the designer's responsibility. The computer aids or tools simply provide the designer with a rapid and orderly method for consolidating and evaluating design ideas and relieve the designer of the numerous routine and mechanistic design steps.

Background

CAD had its genesis in the use of a digital computer to solve a set of equations describing an electrical circuit for the transient and steady state circuit behavior. Since detailed models were used to represent circuit elements such as resistors, capacitors, inductors, diodes, and transistors, the mathematical representation could be used to accurately predict circuit waveforms for both analog and digital circuits. As the emphasis increased in digital circuit design, higher level abstract logic representations were used to calculate the circuit response. Logic or gate-level simulation was employed to numerically solve the equivalent Boolean equations to predict circuit operation.

Early computer aids for the layout of integrated circuit masks used interactive graphic systems. These interactive graphic systems provided a method for manually capturing the design by recording coordinate information analogous to a fast pencil and eraser technique and methods for superimposing mask layers, scaling, enlarging, contrasting, and reviewing the results.

The early use of CAD for physical design verification consisted of performing simple design rule checks for width and spacing violations on mask artwork files. Functional integrity was verified through circuit simulations.

The computer aids used for IC design have evolved from the early beginning noted above to support limited complexity integrated circuit designs. However, as the complexity of IC designs continues to increase, new aids and design philosophies must be developed.

Initial Sandia Design Aids

Although a limited circuit analysis capability was used at Sandia during the late 1960s and early 1970s, a decision was made in 1973 to establish a complete computer aided design capability for integrated circuits. The initial development plan required obtaining basic programs from universities and private industry wherever possible to provide a basic capability and supplementing these programs with in-house developed programs. For example, the Spice (1) circuit analysis code was obtained from the University of California at Berkeley, and a standard cell layout code for metal gate cells was obtained from RCA. Since Sandia had previously developed a simple logic analysis program, this work was accelerated to provide a gate-level simulation capability. Software was developed to postprocess the mask layout data to pattern generator formats for mask generation and plot file information for the Xynetics plotter. A software package was purchased and installed on an existing interactive graphics system with a Vector General CRT display. In addition, translator routines were written to convert design information data formats as required to minimize the manual data translation and to require the design information to be entered once in the system.

The above process is oversimplified, since a substantial commitment of staff was required to: 1) understand the acquired software and debug and correct errors, 2) perform modifications to support the software on Control Data computers, 3) identify and develop required translator software, and 4) develop additional design aids. These problems represented a large manpower investment, since most of the programs were not documented, had evolved over many years with several authors, used nonstandard FORTRAN, and were unstructured, making modifications difficult.

Although the initial design aids provided a valuable capability for simple metal gate CMOS custom integrated circuit design, many deficiencies were identified. These deficiencies, coupled with the need to support new technologies with smaller design rules (and thus higher circuit complexities), new design styles, and changing design objectives, required a new approach in the development of aids for integrated circuit design.

CAD System Requirements

Several general objectives have been identified, based on deficiencies in the above programs. The new aids must 1) be user oriented, 2) use modular software, 3) be evolutionary to meet changing design needs, and 4) be integrated into a complete design system rather than exist as an independent collection of disjoint tools.

New computer aids must be incorporated into a complete computer-aided design system satisfying a number of requirements. The system must support a hierarchical design sequence to assist the designer in specifying a system from initial concept to detailed implementation while generating complete documentation for fabrication or manufacturing.

For electronic system design, the CAD system should support the use of commercial and custom circuits. The CAD system should support individual IC design and utilize a hierarchical element library containing elements from discrete devices to very-large-scale integrated circuits (single elements to tens of thousands of devices).

Computer aids must support both functional and physical design. Functional design aids include synthesis, verification, simulation, and testing at architecture, system, logic, circuit, device, and process levels. Physical design aids support partitioning, layout, and topological analysis at all design levels. Functionality, testability, and physical design must be considered in parallel throughout the design process.

All CAD software must be as technology independent as possible and support various levels of designer sophistication from inexperienced first-time users to state-of-the-art system designers. To meet these goals, the interaction between individual programs, data base, and design engineer must be through a single, consistent interface. This interface will support monitoring the progress of a design, supplying options at any stage in the design process, and assist in the design documentation and maintenance process.

A system design language—or Hardware Description Language (HDL)—must be available for describing all levels of system behavior and structure. Organized in a hierarchical manner, the language should support functional and physical descriptions and the relationships among entities. To meet the requirements for understanding and precision, the HDL should be divided into two components—a graphical user interface and a formal system interface consisting of highly structured languages suitable for automatic processing.

During top-down design, synthesis aids must facilitate the addition of sufficient detail to generate a complete system description. Design verification software monitors internal consistency and completeness of system specifications. Final system specifications should be retained in a dynamic data base providing files in the proper format for input to each of the design aids and for documentation.

A complete CAD system satisfying the above requirements has been designed and implementation is in progress. The system description is divided into three major sections. The hierarchical design flow and concept of top-down design with bottom-up implementation is described in the first section. The second section contains an outline of requirements for specific computer aids. The final section describes the implementation philosophy, computer hardware, and present software development status.

HIERARCHICAL DESIGN

The CAD system supports a number of functions at each level in the design hierarchy. Design proceeds in a top-down fashion; i.e. a functional description is partitioned into progressively smaller functional blocks or circuits until the entire system is described in terms of well-defined modules or primitives. The design is then implemented by interconnecting the modules, simulating the larger assembly, and performing the detailed layout. This sequence continues, addressing both functional and physical problems at each level until the system is complete.

Architecture, the top level of the design hierarchy, contains elements for a broad functional system description, requirements for interfacing units specifying performance and compatibility, and methods for partitioning the system into major functional blocks such as processors, memory, and I/O. The architectural specification can be expanded at the system level to generate a more detailed description consisting of subsystem blocks or functions, which maybe further refined at the register transfer level.

At the logic level, system functions are defined as interconnections of fundamental gates or modules. Logic modules can be further decomposed into circuit primitives (e.g., transistors, resistors, capacitors). Finally in order to construct circuit elements and determine their behavior, the physical implementation and process technology is being considered.

To support a variety of technologies in a hierarchical design structure, a data base consisting of a library of elements of varying sophistication must be maintained. A distinct library must exist for each of the technologies used. Typically, the hierarchical library will contain circuits and subcircuits at various levels of complexity: VLSI, LSI, MSI, SSI, circuit primitives and/or discrete devices, defined in Table 14-1.

Electronic system design using computer aids can be divided into four major design sections: 1) partitioning and IC design planning, module design, 3) subcircuit design, and 4) completion of individual IC design. A design flow diagram is shown in Figure 14-1.

Design proceeds in a top-down structured sequence with bottom-up detailed implementation. The CAD system will support designs with circuit complexi-

Table 14-1. The Hierarchical Library.

COMPLEXITY	EXAMPLES
VLSI ($\sim 10^5$ devices)	Microcomputers, crytographic circuits, ROMs, RAMs
LSI ($\sim 10^4$ devices)	Microprocessors, A/D & D/A converters, ALUs, FFT circuits, ROMs, RAMs
MSI ($\sim 10^3$ devices)	Adders, complex gates, multiplexers, ROMs, RAMs
SSI (~ 100 devices)	AND, OR, NAND, NOR gates, buffers, memory cells
Primitive elements	Transistors, resistors, capacitors

ties ranging from small-scale (SSI), medium-scale (MSI), large scale (LSI), through very large-scale (VLSI) integration.

The complete CAD system for IC design will include a number of computer programs. These aids can be categorized as follows: design specification and partitioning, system and circuit synthesis, system partitioning, simulation at various levels, IC mask layout, design verification, testability evaluation, test sequence generation, data base, and design documentation.

SPECIFIC COMPUTER AIDS REQUIREMENTS

In addition to a number of specific computer programs for supporting a hierarchical design, an extensive data base and support software for monitoring the design flow and communication are required. Requirements for specified programs and interfaces are outlined below.

Design Executive

Currently, most design automation programs exist as independent entities with idiosyncratic user interfaces and incompatible I/O structures. A Design Executive can provide a single consistent interface between a user and the complete set of computer aids available on the CAD system.

The Design Executive supports the complex CAD system structure by mediating interactions between the user and the system, the system and the data base, and the user and the data base. The executive system user interface supports comprehensive "HELP" capabilities, the HDL, and a logically-integrated command language. Documentation describing the system and the CAD codes is maintained by the Design Executive in a hierarchical configuration. User access to this documentation structure is facilitated by the intelligent intervention of the Design Executive.

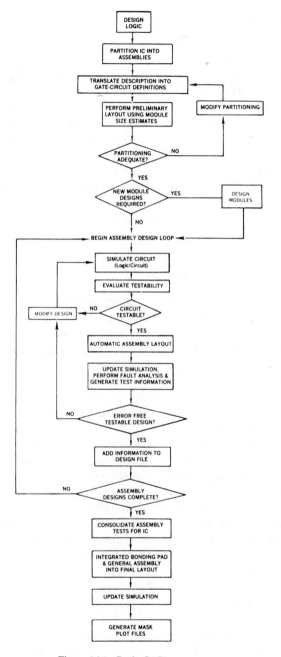

Figure 14-1. Basic CAD sequence.

HDL—Design Specification

The structure and behavior of a digital system must be described in various ways at many levels to completely characterize a design. Existing languages such as ISP (2), DDL (3), SDL (4), etc., are usually associated with specific computer programs that describe architecture, system behavior, system structure, logical structure, circuit structure, logical behavior, or physical structure. These languages lack the generality required to support VLSI design, since most are applicable to one level of design and a particular design style and are not integrated into a complete design system.

Ultimately, a new HDL must be used to describe all levels of system behavior and structure, including normal and faulty electrical, logical, and functional behavior as well as physical structure. Organized in a hierarchical manner, the HDL should allow the description of functional and physical entities, relationships among entities, and decomposition of higher to lower-level entities.

Synthesis and Functional Verification

Functional synthesis begins at the architecture level with a description of the overall behavior of a large system and interaction with the environment. As synthesis proceeds, more structural detail is added at system, logic, and circuit levels in the form of interconnection structures. Concurrently, with the addition of structural detail, behavior specifications are refined at successively lower levels: subsystem, logic, and circuit.

As behavioral and structural specifications are developed at each level of the design hierarchy, formal verification must ensure internal and interlevel consistency and completeness.

During synthesis, the actual behavior of the system will be forced to match the specifications. To effect the match, models are required for computational algorithms and interpreters, and procedures for mapping one into the other. A synthesis task should be preceded by a statement of intent. The intended behavior should be formalized and associated with a measure by which success can be evaluated. Models must be expressible in a computer form in order to manage complexity with an interactive computer support system, permit the separation of structure from associated behavior, and support direct fabrication of the synthesized system

Simulation

Simulation, or dynamic design verification, is the process of calculating the behavior of a system modeled on a digital computer within an environment specified by the designer. The objective of simulation is to verify that the system will perform correctly in an operational environment.

During top-down design, a system is successively simulated at more detailed levels of the design hierarchy: architecture, system, logic, circuit, device, and process. Ideally, simulation should be multi-level; i.e., programs should model larger circuits at a less detailed level with the capability of simultaneously simulating subcircuits more exactly. This concept complements the hierarchical design implementation. In a hierarchical simulator, the basic elements are more complex than simple modules or gates. Models formulated for entire ICs include gate, function, and transistor models; parts of a system are simulated in great detail while other parts are simulated abstractly. Models are written in high-level languages, with models for MSI or LSI chips only slightly more complex than the model for a simple NAND gate. Thus a system containing many thousands of devices or gates can be reduced to a few hundred hierarchical models, making it feasible to simulate entire VLSI systems.

Testability

Testing is the process of verifying that a system is operating properly. Because of the increased complexity of VLSI circuits, the difficulty of testing is substantially increased. To ensure that a circuit can be tested, design-for-testability techniques must be used throughout the design process.

Approaches to design-for-testability fall into two major categories: testable design styles and testability measure analysis. The use of a testable design style guarantees that testing and generating tests for a circuit will not be impossibly difficult. Testability measure analysis computes the difficulty of controlling and observing each internal node from primary input or observing a node from an output pad. This information is used in the design process to locate potential circuit testing problems and provide feedback about the effect of circuit modifications on testability.

In developing a test sequence, knowing that a good test exists is not the same as knowing the test. Deriving a test is the task of the test sequence generation phase. Given a digital circuit and a set of possible faults, a series of input signals (vectors) is generated that will force any faulty circuit to behave differently from the fault-free circuit. The test sequences depend not only upon the intended function of the circuit but also upon the fault set assumed. Test sequence generation must proceed concurrently with hierarchical design process.

Physical Design Aids

Physical design aids include tools to partition, place, and interconnect circuit components and verification tools to ensure the synthesis has been performed properly. To provide an optimum system, physical design must be considered in parallel with functional design and testability.

Partitioning programs operate on both functional and physical entities. Partitioning techniques must function in both the initial design and detailed implementation phases. During top-down design, partitioning aids are needed for hierarchical decomposition. During bottom-up implementation, partitions are modified based on lower-level implementations.

In addition to optimizing a circuit element assignment based on size and external pin connections, parameters such as circuit speed, power dissipation, and functional groupings must be considered. The partitioning aids must be capable of optimizing any of these quantities as a function of the others.

Symbolic Layout provides a shorthand method for manually sketching a circuit layout using specified symbols to represent various types of transistors and interconnections. The designer is not concerned with the geometric design rules. Symbolic layouts are postprocessed using computer aids, which expand all symbols and interconnects based on the geometric design rules for the specified technology to provide mask artwork files. In addition to converting symbols to actual geometries, many symbolic layout codes perform various degrees of compaction and device relocation to optimize the physical layout.

Physical Layout involves positioning and interconnecting electrical components. In hierarchical design, the concept of a component is generalized. Components may range in complexity from primitive transistors and fundamental gates to microprocessors that can be combined to form a microcomputer.

Hierarchical layout is applicable to a wide range of physical design levels. At the highest design level, the shape of LSI components may be adjusted and combined to form a VLSI circuit. At the lower design levels, the same algorithms may be used to combine gates into registers or transistors into gates.

Topological Analysis

Because of the high costs and long lead times involved in the fabrication of ICs, it is important to verify the correctness of a circuit design before manufacture. Verification tools must ensure the correct physical mask layout, functional operation, and assure the electrical characteristics are within specified tolerances.

Topological analysis tools can be used to verify correctness of physical layout data by examining the artwork data and the circuit inputs and outputs. Design-rule checking codes perform geometrical, logical, and topological operations on artwork data and compare the results with design rules for the specified technology. Connectivity and electrical parameter data can be extracted from artwork data and a detailed circuit reconstructed including parasitic electrical components. This reconstructed circuit can be used in performing an accurate functional and timing analysis.

Circuit Design Documentation

After a circuit or system design has been completed, the design can be documented by collecting information from the data base generated during the design process. Design documentation includes information for fabricating the IC as well as information for archiving the completed design to support later modifications. Computer aids should collect manufacturing and archival information and generate appropriate files, specifications, and reports.

Data Base

In general, the distinction between programs and data is that programs are active, data is passive (i.e., programs operate on data). The necessity for supporting the initial design, design changes, and providing software transportability dictates consistency in data handling procedures and mechanisms. Therefore, an efficient data base is vital for coordinating the various functions.

Diverse CAD programs can access design data in many ways. At one extreme, the data for each program is accessible to only that program. All operations are performed sequentially, and common data is repeated in each module. Each program interfaces with only one or two others, operates on data received from the previous program, and generates data to be used by the succeeding module. This approach has typically been used in developing design systems, since commercially-available data base management software is too general and requires excessive computer memory and access time to be used in CAD systems.

As systems become more complex, it is imperative that an overall data base be established and maintained to ensure consistency in design and to eliminate duplication of information. The data base must be designed in a flexible and modular fashion to provide upward compatibility with computer hardware and the evolving CAD software. Modularity is important in a network environment where various portions of the data base may reside at more than one computer node. In addition to the actual data used by CAD programs, the data base should contain all necessary information to properly document elements being designed.

SANDIA CAD SYSTEM IMPLEMENTATION

A CAD System meeting the criteria outlined above is being implemented in phases at Sandia National Laboratories to provide design capability—for LSI circuits initially—with evolutionary expansion and enhancement as required to support VLSI designs.

The design procedures consist of 1) identifying critical aids in the design process based on user needs, 2) acquiring existing software when available and subsequently modifying it to meet system and user needs, 3) developing new aids with appropriate expansion capabilities to support hierarchical design, and 4) integration of all aids into the design system framework. A block diagram outlining the present system implementation is shown in Figure 14-2. The solid blocks represent areas where design support is presently available and the dashed blocks indicate work in progress. Brief descriptions of the hardware and software are given below.

Hardware

The software is supported on a dedicated DECSystem 20 computer system containing 1 million words of fast memory, 160 million words of disk files, and two 9-track 800/1600 BPI, 75 ips tape drives. Two Applicon 860 interactive graphics systems and a Versatec 36 inch electrostatic plotter are connected to the DECSystem 20. A VAX 11/780 computer containing 4 megabytes of main

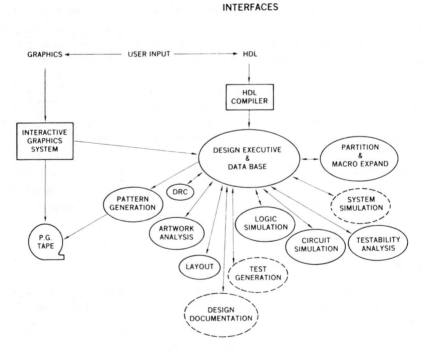

Figure 14-2. Sandia hierarchical CAD system. (Courtesy Sandia National Laboratories)

memory, 323 megabytes of disk files, two 9-track 800/1600 BPI, 125 ips tape drives is interfaced in a network configuration to provide additional computing capability. Communication among the computers and the Applicon Systems is supported by DECnet. Both dial-up and direct-wired access to the system provide support for alphanumeric and graphics terminals.

Design Software

A Universal HDL (UHDL) is being developed in essentially three stages consisting of 1) language formation by phase concatenation, 2) redundancy removal, and 3) consolidation and rewrite of the compound language. During the first step, the SDL (4) language (a PASCAL-like description) is used to describe system structure. Other languages are appended in phrase form to describe functional behavior. After gaining experience with the composite languages and after the deficiencies and required enhancements have been identified, a language for the initial UHDL will be written. Continuous refinement and enhancement of the UHDL will be required to meet design and documentation needs.

Translation from UHDL descriptions to the required formats for simulation, layout, and verification programs is performed by the Design Executive. The Design Executive also manages the data flow between the Data Base files (outlined below) and each of the design aids.

Logic-level design consists of defining, in complete detail, all components (gates, cells, modules, etc.) and interconnections required to implement a specified function. The SALOGS (5) (SAndia LOGic Simulator) code performs true-value 4-state logic simulation (true, false, undefined, and high impedance) and 8-state timing simulation (four states plus transition to each of the four states) as well as states-applied, gate activity analysis, and fault simulation. SALOGS is used for dynamic design verification, test-sequence evaluation, and fault coverage calculation.

Although crude timing simulation is accomplished in SALOGS using delay elements and transition states, more exact timing simulation is possible with MOTIS-C (6) and SIMPIL (7) for MOS and I^2L circuits, respectively. These programs use tables to describe active devices in a circuit instead of models with complex equations. Both programs provide more accurate analysis than logic simulators and run more efficiently than circuit simulation codes such as SPICE.

A more exact circuit analysis is obtained by using circuit simulation programs such as SPICE (1). SANCA (SANdia Circuit Analysis Program) is an enhanced, quasi-interactive version of SPICE containing model information for specific Sandia technologies and output plot routines. This program simulates MOS and bipolar circuits including analog and digital circuits by numerically solving the network equations to calculate the desired voltages and currents.

The cost of increased accuracy (over timing simulation) is a decrease in both execution speed and circuit size that can be analyzed. Model libraries for circuit analysis are maintained to reflect varying levels of accuracy and different modeling philosophies. Circuit models based on device physics, empirical behavior, and hybrid approaches are all used in the circuit simulation environment. A topological analysis code (CMAT) (8) automatically generates circuit schematic information (parasitic resistances, capacitances, diodes, and transistors) from layout descriptions which is fed back to the circuit level.

Physical mask layout is performed using the SICLOPS (9), (10) (Sandia IC Layout Optimization System) and SLOOP (11) (Standard-cell LayOut Optimization Program) programs to automatically place and interconnect generalized circuit elements. Two different forms of mask layout are used. A hierarchical mask layout system has been developed and used for specific designs. This hierarchical approach relies on the use of SICLOPS to perform an automatic layout of an integrated circuit using rectangular-shaped blocks. The blocks must be rectangular and can be of arbitrary size and aspect ratio. Blocks are automatically placed in an optimum configuration and complete interconnection is performed. Each of the blocks can contain nested subblocks to any depth to provide a hierarchical layout.

SLOOP is used for more conventional layout using standard cells placed in rows with interconnection between cell rows in routing channels. In addition to designing larger blocks used by the SICLOPS program, the program supports chip layouts containing only standard cell rows. The basic program can be used in an interactive mode to optimize the design, will perform 100 percent completion of all interconnections by expanding the chip size as required to complete interconnections, contains hierarchical interfaces for use with the SICLOPS code, and supports multiport gates or cells.

Hierarchical layout is applicable to a wide range of design levels. At one extreme, LSI circuit layouts can be combined to form a VLSI circuit. At the other extreme, the same algorithms can be used to combine gates into registers based on a standard cell layout.

The LOGMASC (LOGical MASK Checking) (12) program is a tool for design rule checking of IC mask design. It produces Boolean logic combinations of mask levels and is based on extensive pattern recognition techniques. The program is general, provides essentially all design rule checks which can be performed manually, and provides pattern identification and extensive topological and geometrical information concerning the interrelationships of entities in the file. False errors are minimized by selectively applying design rule checks based on the circuit use of each particular pattern being checked. Many of the algorithms can be used to solve other mask analysis problems in addition to the design rule checks.

During the circuit mask design process, transistor current or voltage gains, resistance, and capacitance values are scaled and converted to area definitions based on the nominal circuit parameter values used for circuit analysis. The actual sizes of the circuit elements and devices are adjusted to fit layout constraints based on minimum spacing, relative element partitioning, and size requirements. The circuit defined by the mask layout may be quite different than the original circuit schematic. For example, the interconnection distances between transistors introduce resistances and capacitances into the circuit which were not included in the initial circuit simulation. Additional parasitic transistors and diodes can be unintentionally introduced into the circuit which can cause improper operation. The CMAT (8) (Circuit MAsk Translator) program operates on circuit mask plot files, using pattern recognition to recognize and transcribe the mask areas into the circuit elements. CMAT employs the basic Boolean operation algorithms contained in LOGMASC and performs the required scaling operations to obtain circuit element values.

SCOAP (13) (Sandia Controllability Observability Analysis Program) is used to evaluate the testability of a circuit after the basic design has been completed. This analysis is performed prior to layout and is based on a simple analysis of the logic interconnectivity. The SCOAP program calculates the ease or difficulty of setting an internal node from a primary input to a zero or one and the difficulty of observing a logic value at any internal node from a primary output. The zero and one values for controllability may be different depending upon the exact circuitry and interconnection of the logic gates. For nodes having very high values for controllability or observability, changes are usually required in the logic circuitry to reduce the controllability and observability numbers. This reduction is required, since the numbers are proportional to the testing difficulty. For nodes with high controllability/observability measures, additional input or output tests points or signal multiplexing may be required to set logic gates or observe node logic values to achieve circuit testability. At present, structured design for testability such as the LSSD (14) approach is not required; however, since the designer is responsible for designing a testable circuit, techniques equivalent to the LSSD approach may be used in the design based on the testability analysis information.

The testability analysis program is used for both combinational and sequential circuits. Combinational measures basically relate to the number of different line assignments or input assignments which must be made to set an internal node to a given value. For sequential circuits, the measures relate to the number of clock cycles or time frames required to propagate a specified logic value from an input pad to a node or from a specific node to an output terminal.

Data Base

Because of the initial need for integrating loosely related CAD software and evolving design system specifications, a data-file base has been developed. The Sandia CAD data structure (15) is in the form of a "deciduous tree"; that is, one that can lose its leaves. This structure is a two-dimensional network with several restrictions. In one dimension, the data structure forms a shallow tree one level deep. That is, any number of data types can be associated with a given node, but they may not be broken down further. In the other dimension, the structure is a network of nodes and subnodes to any depth. The leaves on the tree are the equivalent of small sequential files of data which can be retrieved by the user application code. This data file approach forces the designer to conform to a hierarchical structure while maintaining the freedom to store test files, documentation, etc., in the same file.

SUMMARY AND FUTURE PLANS

Although a basic computer-aided LSI design capability has been established and is used by design engineers, the system is continuously evolving as new capabilities and enhancements are added to the system. The modular programs and data structures, as well as the flexibility designed into the overall system framework, tend to minimize the cost for system modification as requirements change. In addition to continuous enhancement of existing programs, new aids for design synthesis, hierarchical simulation, symbolic layout, and test sequence generation will be developed. A continuing emphasis is placed on integrating the CAD software into a complete design system.

REFERENCES

(1) Cohen, E. *Program Reference for SPICE 2* Memorandum No. ERL-M592, Electronics Research Laboratory, University of California at Berkeley (June 1976).

(2) Barbacci, M. R., et al. *The ISPS Computer Description Language.* Technical Report, Dept. of Computer Science, Carnegie-Mellon University (March 1978).

(3) Corey, W. E., et al. *An Introduction to the DDL-p Language.* Technical Report No. 163, Computer Systems Laboratory, Stanford University (March 1979).

(4) vanCleemput, W. M. *A Structural Design Language for Computer-Aided Design of Digital Systems.* Technical Report No. 136, Digital Systems Laboratory, Stanford University (April 1977).

(5) Acken, J. M., and Shauffer, J. D. "Logic Circuit Simulation." *IEEE Circuits and Systems Magazine* 1 No. 2: 3–12 (June 1979).

(6) Fan, S. P. et al. "MOTIS-C: A New Circuit Simulator for MOS LSI Circuits." *Proc. IEEE 1977 International Symposium on Circuits and Systems.* pp. 700–703 (April 1977).

(7) Boyle, G. R. *Simulation of Integrated Injection Logic* Memorandum No. UCB/ERL M78/13, Electronics Research Laboratory, University of California at Berkeley (March 1978).

(8) Preas, B. T., et. al. "Automatic Circuit Analysis Based on Mask Information." *Proc. 13th Design Automation Conference* (June 1976).

(9) Preas B. T., and vanCleemput, W. M. "Placement Algorithms for Arbitrarily Shaped Blocks." *Proc. 16th Design Automation Conference* (June 1979).

(10) Preas B. T., and vanCleemput, W. M. "Routing Algorithms for Hierarchical IC Layout." *Proc. International Symposium on Circuits and Systems* (July 1979).

(11) *SLOOP (Standard Cell Layout Optimization Program), User and Program Manual,* in preparation, Sandia Laboratories.

(12) Lindsay B. W., and Preas, B. T. "Design Rule Checking and Analysis of IC Mask Designs." *Proc. 13th Design Automation Conference* (June 1976).

(13) Goldstein, L. H. *Controllability/Observability Analysis of Digital Circuits* Sandia Laboratories, Albuquerque, New Mexico, SAND78-1895 (November 1978).

(14) Eichelberger E. B., and Williams, T. W. "A Logic Design Structure for LSI Testability." *Journal of Design Automation and Fault Tolerant Computing* 2 No. 2: 165–178 (May 1978).

(15) Stauffer, J. D. *A Data File Base for CAD* Sandia National Laboratories, Albuquerque, New Mexico, SAND80-1999, manuscript in preparation.

15. VLSI Routing

M. A. Breuer
University of Southern California

H. W. Carter
United States Air Force

INTRODUCTION

The complexity of LSI and VLSI circuits creates an enormous demand for efficient and effective layout techniques. Classically the layout process has been divided into three subproblems, namely partitioning (assigning logic to chips), placement (physically assigning circuits to physical locations on a chip), and interconnection (connecting the pads of the circuits so that pads associated with the same signal net are electrically common and isolated from the other nets). This chapter deals with the latter problem.

To help achieve our goals, numerous design automation layout tools have been developed, and new ones will continue to be developed.

The degree to which these tools are used is a function of the design style being employed. For polycell and masterslice layouts, automated placement and interconnection techniques have been successfully employed since the early 1970s. Most of the techniques employed are very similar to those used for PCB layout.

For custom LSI, where there is a greater demand for very high circuit density, automatic layout techniques are just beginning to be used.

This chapter consists of two parts. In Part I a survey of some of the better known techniques and algorithms used for automating the interconnection of LSI circuit chips is presented. Part II deals with a new routing technique based upon a graph model of the carrier geometry. For additional survey material on this subject see (1-4). Part II has been written as a self contained section, with some repetition of definitions presented in Part I. This was done so that the reader familiar with automated interconnection techniques could skip Part I and go directly to Part II.

PART I
SURVEY OF AUTOMATED INTERCONNECTION TECHNIQUES

BASIC CONCEPTS AND DEFINITIONS

A signal net consists of a set of fixed points. A chip contains a set of such signal nets. The interconnection problem consists of finding paths in the chip so that 1) each net is made electrically common, and 2) all nets are electrically isolated from each other.

There are several important parameters and constraints associated with the physical and geometric aspects of these interconnections, some of which will now be informally defined.

A layer is a fabrication plane of a chip used for interconnections. In some technologies, interconnections are restricted to a single "metal" layer, while in others two or more layers are used. For single layer technologies it is sometimes possible for one wire to cross another one by going under it using some other medium, such as polysilicon or diffusion.

For multi-layer carriers, connections between layers is made by using a via or contact. In this chapter an interconnection will often be referred to as a wire or path, and a terminal, pad, pin and via as a point. Wires have minimum widths and a minimum spacing exists between wires. For simplicity some of the electrical aspects related to the geometric and physical properties of wires, such as signal reflection, crosstalk and delay will be ignored.

The main reason the interconnection problem is difficult to solve is due to space. Each layer of a carrier has a fixed wire capacity. Once a certain percentage of this capacity is taken, it becomes extremely difficult to synthesize a path between two arbitrary points. The relationship between interconnectability and available space is discussed in (5).

The interconnection problem can be subdivided into the following four subproblems, namely wire segment generation, ordering, layering and routing. This chapter is primarily concerned with routing, namely finding a path for interconnecting two points, a point to a wire, or a wire to a wire. Prior to discussing the routing problem, these other three problems will first be briefly reviewed.

Wire Segment Generation

Most routing algorithms deal with the problem of connecting two entities, such as two points or a point and a wire. Hence, given an n point net, the net is usually first divided into $(n-1)$ wire segments, each of which connects two points. This can be done in several ways. The first is to chain the n points, i.e., to find a permutation p of the signal points $1, 2, \ldots, n$ so that

$$\sum_{i=1}^{n-1} d_p (i), p(i + 1) \text{ is minimum, where } p (i) \text{ is the } i^{th} \text{ point in the permutation}$$

and $d_p (i), p(i+1)$ is the distance between point $p(i)$ and $p(i+1)^n$. Unfortunately this problem is equivalent to the traveling salesperson problem and is NP complete.

The second most common technique used for wire segment generation is to construct a minimal spanning tree (6), which can be done in time no worse than O (n^2). The third technique, which is also NP complete, is to form a Steiner tree (7). These three concepts are illustrated in Figure 15-1.

Note that wire segments are used only to define pairs of points to be connected. The actual path taken is usually not the one defined by the wire segment, and in fact the pair of points may end up being connected indirectly, e.g., both being connected to a common via.

Wire segment generation is also useful in predicting wire demand or density prior to routing. For example, consider the routing grid and two points A and B to be connected, as shown in Figure 15-2. Assume at most one wire can be assigned to each grid segment. Two minimal length rectilinear paths are shown by the heavy lines. In general, for X columns and Y rows, there are $\binom{X+Y}{X}$ minimal length paths between A and B. From this result the probability that a given grid segment will be used in a minimal length path can be computed

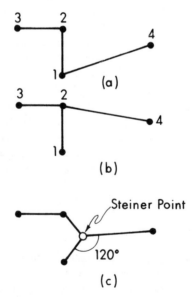

Figure 15-1. Wire segment generation. (a) Minimum chain connection. (b) Minimum spanning tree. (c) Steiner tree.

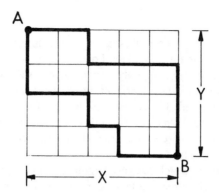

Figure 15-2. Two minimal length paths between A and B.

assuming each path is equally likely. Given all the wire segments, one can now determine a density map indicating the relative a priori demand on each grid segment of a carrier available for routing. Such a map can be used to influence the decision making process of determining the routing of points A and B.

Ordering

Wires are usually routed sequentially, hence wire segments must be put into some order prior to routing. There are two common types of ordering schemes employed, referred to as static and dynamic ordering. A static ordering scheme determines an a priori sequence in which to process the wire segments. Ordering appears to be much more important for single layer routing that for multi-layer routing. Though no clear cut "best" ordering procedure has yet been found, a good "rule of thumb" is to order wire segments in increasing order of $v = \Delta x + \alpha \Delta y$, where Δx (Δy) is the length of the $x(y)$ projection of the wire segment, and α is the "skew" parameter and is dependent on the carrier geometry. This criterion encourages shorter connections to be considered first, as well as horizontal and vertical lines to precede lines of the same length which are not horizontal or vertical.

Dynamic ordering deals with selecting the next wire segment to be routed based upon the results of routing the previous wire segments. As an example, consider a partially routed net, and a point p in the net, which is not yet connected to another point, and which is the closest to some point q (pad or via) in the given partially connected net. The points p and q define the next wire segment to be processed. It is generally believed that dynamic ordering produces better results than static ordering but requires considerably more computation time. Some results on ordering procedures have been reported by Abel (8), (9).

Layering

Layering deals with the process of assigning wire segments to layers. Layering is not required for single layer carriers. For two layer carriers, preferred direction layers are usually used, i.e., only horizontal wires are routed on one layer and vertical wires on the other. Horizontal and vertical segments can be interconnected by using a via. Hence a wire segment for a net is automatically "layered" when routed. When the two layers do not have the same electrical properties, after routing, wire segments can be reassigned to the preferred layer as long as no shorts occur.

Multi-layer carriers, which are just beginning to be produced, can be processed either as a series of single layer carriers, or as pairs of preferred layer carriers. The major problem with preferred layer routing is the need for vias, though it appears to produce higher interconnection densities than those achieved by using two non-preferred layers.

ROUTING

Routing is concerned with finding paths between points in a signal net. Routing algorithms fall into four categories, namely maze routers, line routers, channel routers, and graph routers. In this chapter only the first three of these categories will be discussed. Part II deals with one form of a graph router.

Maze Routers

One model of the routing environment is shown in Figure 15-3a. Here a grid system is shown, where at most one signal wire can be placed in each cell.

The grid is scaled so that the center to center distances for the wires meets the constraints imposed by the technology ground rules. In Figure 15-3b, the layout is redrawn to indicate cells which contain wires, referred to as blockages, by cross-hatched cells.

Assuming it is desired to find a path from A to B, it can be seen that this problem corresponds to that of finding a path through a maze. The most well known procedure for solving this problem is due to Lee (10). The Lee algorithm can find a minimal cost path in a maze between two points, if such a path exists. Cost can be quite general, and can depend on such factors as length, density, and turns. The algorithm consists of a labeling process, where a cell is assigned a label $i + 1$ if it is unlabeled, not blocked, and adjacent to a cell labeled i. Referring to Figure 15-3b, and starting with cell A containing the label 0, the labels shown are obtained. This process terminates when cell B is labeled. To find a path, one need only retrace from B to A, going from a cell having a label $i + 1$ to one having a label i.

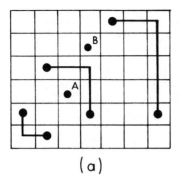

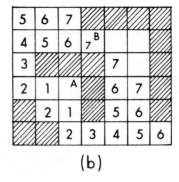

(a)

(b)

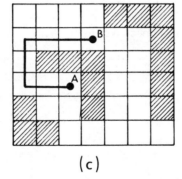

(c)

Figure 15-3. Maze routing. (a) Original layout on a grid. (b) Lee algorithm computation. (c) Path A-B.

The Lee algorithm is an extremely effective tool and is universally used. In order to reduce storage demand, Akers (11) has shown that instead of the labeling sequence 1,2,3,4,5, ... , one can use the sequence 1,1,2,2,1,1,2,2, ... Hence only a few bits per cell are necessary, independent of the size of the grid system.

The Lee algorithm has time complexity $O(m^2)$, where m is the minimum length distance between the two points to be connected. Several techniques exist for attempting to speed up this process. One is to put a constraining window around the points A and B, and not allow the labels to extend past this window. Another is to label the cells, starting from both A and B. This can reduce computation by about 50%. Finally, one can modify this technique by expanding in the direction of rows and columns, rather than radially outward in the shape of a diamond as occurs for the procedure described, when no blockages exist.

Note that the Lee algorithm can be easily modified to process two or more layers. In addition one can restrict the path generated for two layer carriers to be a preferred direction route. These enhancements can be achieved by assigning costs or weights to the cells, a few of which are listed below:

C_D^{ij} —cost of using cell i, j. This cost could
    be a function of density.
C_P^k —this is the cost of moving one cell in the
    preferred direction on layer k.
C_N^k —this is the cost of moving one cell in the
    nonpreferred direction on layer k.
C_V —this is the cost of a via, i.e., of going
    from one layer to another.

In Figure 15-4 cell a and three of its neighbors, b, c, and d are shown. Let C_D (b) = 3, C_D (c) = C_D (d) = 2, C_P^l = 1, C_N^l = 3, and C_V = 15. The label of a cell α is denoted by L_α. The labels for cells b, c and d are computed below, where L_a = 15.

$$L_b = L_a + C_P^l + C_D \text{(b)} = 15 + 1 + 3 = 19$$
$$L_c = L_a + C_N^l + C_D \text{(c)} = 15 + 3 + 2 = 20$$
$$L_d = L_a + C_V + C_D \text{(d)} = 15 + 5 + 2 = 22$$

As process geometries tend toward 1μ and switching speeds increase, parasitic influences on electrical performance become very important. Interconnect envi-

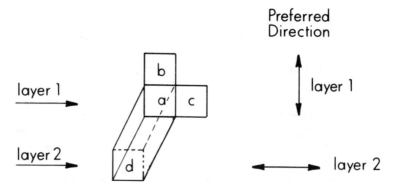

Figure 15-4. Lee cell label computation.

ronments of candidate routes should be examined for impact on electrical performance. Factors such as contact resistance, crossover capacitance, and parallel conductor coupling capacitance should and can be considered in VLSI routing costs functions.

To accomplish some of these goals, the concepts of costs previously discussed can be used, though some extensions are required. For example, during the labeling phase, the value of a label can be increased if the cell being processed is above or below a previously routed wire. Also labels can be increased if the sequence of cells being labelled are adjacent to a wire. Other constraints on path selection can also be implemented. For example, to avoid signal reflection, fan-out can be restricted to occur only at signal source terminals.

Two main drawbacks with the Lee algorithm are its relatively large demands for computer storage and computation time. To alleviate these problems researchers have looked for other techniques for routing. Two of these will be discussed in the next sections. Before concluding, however, it should be mentioned that in order to reduce computation time researchers have considered embedding the Lee algorithm into hardware, such as VLSI chip (12). This implementation of the algorithm now has a time complexity of only $O(m)$.

Line Routers

Line routers are path construction algorithms which do not employ a grid system. Paths consist of an alternating sequence of horizontal and vertical line segments on a single layer. Each segment is represented by a 3-tuple, e.g., a horizontal wire segment is represented by (x_1, y_1, x_2) where (x_1, y_1) is the coordinate of the leftmost point on the wire, and x_2 is the x-coordinate of the rightmost point. Horizontal and vertical wire segments are normally stored in a well structured manner, such as sorted as to their y-coordinate value, and then by their x_1 value. In addition, a fast procedure exists for checking as to whether two line segments intersect. Paths are found by constructing a sequence of connected line segments starting from the two points A and B to be interconnected. When a segment of one of the sequences intersects a segment in the other sequence, a path is created.

The best known line routing procedure is due to Hightower (13), and will now be briefly explained. Lines are allowed to come within "one unit" of each other, where this unit is the minimum spacing between wires. The procedure may not find a minimal length path between A and B, and in some cases may not even find a path even though one exists.

The Hightower algorithm consists of two escape procedures, a main procedure which calls these procedures, and several refinement procedures. A few basic definitions are required before the procedures can be explained. A *cover* of a point p is a line segment α such that a perpendicular to α passes through p. A *horizontal cover* of p is a cover in the horizontal direction such that no other cover of p is between it and p. A *horizontal escape line* is a horizontal line segment through p bounded by the vertical covers of p. An *escape point e* is a point on the horizontal escape line of p which is not covered by at least one horizontal cover of p or any other horizontal line segment between p and the cover. The *object point* is the escape point currently being processed, and the *target point* is the point to be reached from the object point. In the previous definitions, the word "horizontal" can be replaced by "vertical" to generate the remaining definitions required.

These concepts are illustrated with reference to the line segments shown in Figure 15-5. Here the covers of point p are b, c, d, h, i, g; the horizontal covers are c, h, and the vertical covers are $g, d; m$ and k are the vertical and horizontal escape lines, respectively, for $p; e_1, e_2, e_4$ are vertical escape points, e_3 is not; e_5 and e_6 are horizontal escape points, e_7 is not.

The general concepts of Hightower's line router are now briefly illustrated with reference to Figure 15-6. Assume it is desired to connect points A and B given the existing line segments (blockages) a, b, c, d and e, as well as the four outside boundary walls. First the escape lines α_0 and α_1 through object point A are constructed (see Figure 15-6a). Notice that there is no escape point along α_0. Along α_1 point t_2, which is one unit below the bottom edge of line a is an escape point (for A with respect to line a). Next consider point B, and in a

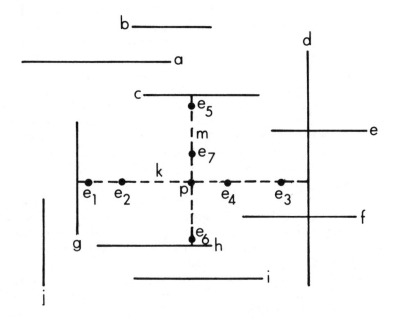

Figure 15-5. Illustration of definitions.

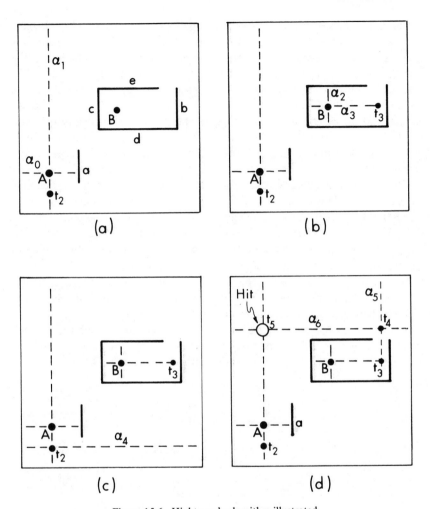

Figure 15-6. Hightower's algorithm illustrated.

similar fashion find escape point t_3 (for B with respect to e). (See Figure 15-6b.) Next, returning to escape point t_2, escape line α_4 is constructed (see Figure 15-6c). There is no escape point on α_4 since the horizontal covers of t_2 are the top and bottom boundaries. Thus, returning to t_3 and constructing the escape line α_5, the escape point t_4 for t_3 with respect to line segment c is identified (see Figure 15-6d). Continuing, construct escape line α_6 which intersects escape line α_1 at t_5, and hence a path exists, namely the one defined by the point sequence A, t_5, t_4, t_3, B. Notice that t_2 is not a point on this path.

The actual procedure employs two escape processes. A pictorial version of escape process I is shown in Figure 15-7. Here points e_2 and e_3 are found to be valid escape points around line a; there are no valid escape points around line b or c, and e_5 and e_6 are found to be valid escape points around line d. The algorithm uses the first escape point found—it never backtracks to use others.

Figure 15-8 illustrates escape process II, which is used if escape process I cannot find an escape point. In this case the procedure cyclically processes points, each one unit apart along an escape line through p, starting from a horizontal cover and moving toward p. Through each point an escape line is constructed. Then an escape point is sought along this line using escape process I. If one is found the process is completed, otherwise another point is tried until all points coincide with p, in which case no escape from p is found.

Referring to Figure 15-8, first construct the escape lines α_0 and α_1, and note that no escape point can be found using escape process 1. Next construct escape line α_2 through r_1' and again note that no escape point can be found. Finally, constructing escape line α_3 through r_2' creates escape point e.

The escape processes oscillate between escaping from a point on a path from A and escaping from a point on a path from B. If any escape line associated with a path starting from A intersects one associated with B, the process terminates. A path has been found and several refinement procedures are then evoked to improve the "shape" of the path. One refinement is to delete all escape points not on the corners of the path from A to B. Other refinement

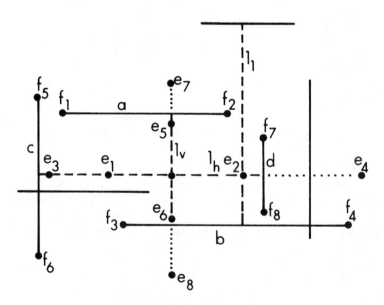

Figure 15-7. Escape process I.

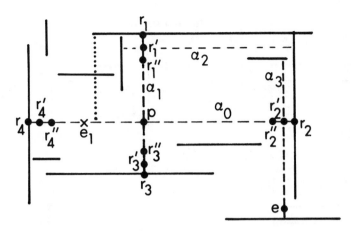

Figure 15-8. Escape process II.

techniques shorten the path from *A* to *B,* and are illustrated in Figure 15-9. In Figure 15-9a it can be seen that a perpendicular to segment (p_2, p_3) intersects the segment (p_4, p_5), which is part of the same path, hence the path can be shortened. In Figure 15-9b the extension of the line segment (p_4, p_5) intersects (p_1, p_2), hence again the path can be shortened.

In summary, this technique is a very effective and efficient procedure for finding a path between two points on a plane given blockages. If this process fails to find a path, one can always resort to the more enumerative Lee algorithm in order to see if this procedure will find a path. The line router discussed has been successfully used in several LSI DA systems, most notably in the one discussed by Mattison (14).

Channel Routing

There are several problems with the routing techniques previously discussed. One is that they deal primarily with finding a specific path between two objects, when the actual goal is to route all nets. Secondly, the nets are routed sequentially, where the path for wire segment i takes into account wire segments previously routed, but is typically not influenced by those segments which are not yet wired. Ideally it would be desirable if all wire segments were routed simultaneously.

Channel routing is an attempt to produce a smart router, i.e., one where some aspect of a path is influenced by all or some of the other wire segments. This is accomplished by partitioning the routing process into two parts, the first called global or channel routing, the second called track assignment.

Cellular routing (15) is a forerunner of channel routing, and includes some

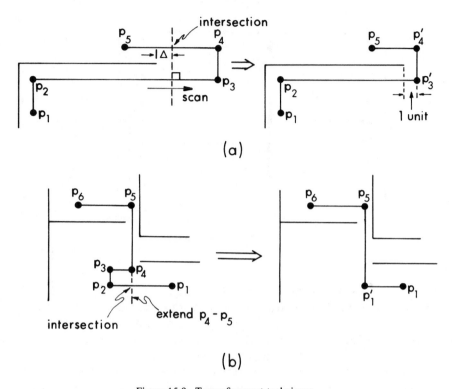

Figure 15-9. Two refinement techniques.

of the concepts discussed above. This type of router was designed for use on carriers having a regular array of points, as shown in Figure 15-10a. The cell model used to represent an array of four points, represented as diamonds, is shown in Figure 15-10b. The interior edges of these diamonds and the space between them form an octagon having sides labeled 1,2, . . . , 8. The even numbered sides and the two diagonals are associated with a channel capacity C_i. The channel capacity of a line is the wire density or number of tracks (wires) that can perpendicularly cross this line.

In Figure 15-10c a cell having four wires in its interior is illustrated. A wire segment going through an octagon is represented by a 4-tuple $\alpha_i = (S_1, P_1, S_2, P_2)$, where S_1 (S_2) is the side the wire enters (exits) and P_1 and P_2 are the relative position of this wire along the corresponding side. A wire between two points can be defined by a sequence of wire segment descriptors $(\alpha_1, \alpha_2, \ldots, \alpha_n)$. In Figure 15-10c wire segment C would be defined by the descriptor $\alpha = (8, 1, 4, 3)$. Note that with respect to a point X on the perimeter of the octagon, each wire segment divides the perimeter into two sections—one reachable (R) from X, the other unreachable. Figure 10c shows the resulting reachable parts of the perimeter for a wire entering at X, given the wire segments A, B, C, D.

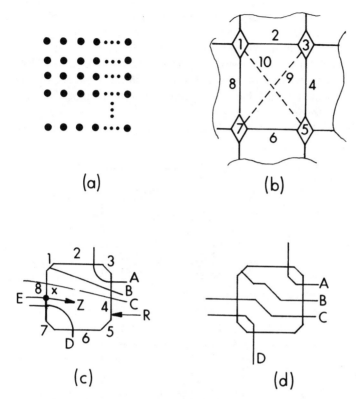

Figure 15-10. Cellular routing models. (a) Regular array of pads. (b) Cellular model. (c) Cell with assigned wires. (d) Cell with wires assigned to tracks.

The concept of reachability also includes channel capacity. For example, if the channel capacity $C_4 = 3$, then no portion of side 4 is reachable from X.

Given this model, one can now do a Lee type expansion process and label cells. For example, if the cell to the left of the cell Z shown in Figure 15-10c has the label k, then cell Z can be assigned the label $k + 1$, and the cells to the right of and below cell Z can be assigned the label $k + 2$. The cell above cell Z would not be assigned a label since it it not reachable from X. Assume $C_i = 4$ for $i = 2, 4, 6, 8$. Then using the grid system discussed in the section on Maze Routers, the interior of Z would contain $4 \times 4 = 16$ "Lee" cells. Hence the labeling process using this model is considerably faster than that when a fine grid system is used.

Once the cells are labeled a path can be easily constructed and the corresponding wire segment descriptors created. Once paths for all wires have been determined, tracks can be easily assigned. Figure 15-10d shows the result of track assignment for the wires shown in Figure 15-10c.

It is thus seen that cellular routing is a two pass routing system which uses octagons as the basic model of the carrier plane. In channel routing this model of the routable area of the carrier is generalized. An open area of a carrier is defined in which horizontal or vertical wires can exist as a channel. The channel capacity is the number of parallel tracks within the channel. A horizontal (vertical) channel normally has a top (left) and bottom (right) barrier along which signal points exist.

In Figure 15-11a a carrier containing four macro cells of logic as well as

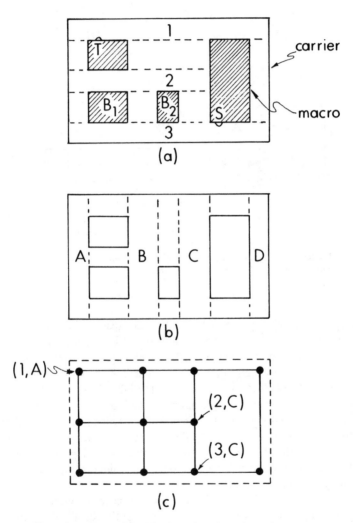

Figure 15-11. Channel routing models. (a) Floor plan of macros and horizontal channels. (b) Vertical channels. (c) Channel graph.

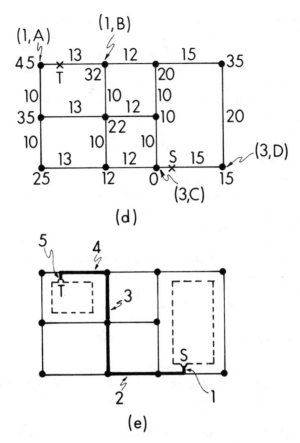

Figure 15-11. Channel routing models (*Continued*). (d) Distances from node (3, C). (e) Path from S to T in channel graph.

three horizontal channels 1, 2, 3 is shown. Each macro cell is assumed to have points around its perimeter. Clearly the spacing between objects determines the channel capacity. In Figure 15-11b four vertical channels *A, B, C, D* are shown. From these channels a channel graph can be constructed whose nodes consist of the intersection of a horizontal and vertical channel, and whose edges represent channels between nodes. Figure 15-11c represents the channel graph for this example.

Assume it is desired to connect the two points labeled *S* and *T,* shown in Figure 15-11a. To do this first label the channel graph, as shown in Figure 15-11d. The length of each channel is shown next to its corresponding edge. Starting at node (3, *C*), which is nearest to the point *S,* label the nodes with their distance from this node. This can be done using a Lee type procedure, e.g., first go to the adjacent neighbors of (3, *C*) and label these nodes. For example, node

(2, C) gets the label of node (3, C), namely 0, plus its distance from (3, C), namely 10. Given these labels and the coordinates of S and T, it is easy to find a minimal length path from S to T. One such path is illustrated in Figure 15-11e and consists of five wire segments, stubs 1 and 5, and segments 2, 3 and 4 which are assigned to channels 3, B, and 1 respectively.

Channel graphs can be constructed for custom, polycell and masterslice layouts. For the latter, they are usually very regular, for the former they can be quite irregular.

Once a path has been established for all wire segments, and the segments of each path have been assigned to channels, global wiring has been completed and track assignment may begin.

Track assignment can be done in a number of ways, depending on the objective function. One objective is to minimize the number of tracks required in each channel. This is useful in custom and polycell layouts where the area of the chip is to be minimized. Let W be a set of wire segments assigned to a horizontal channel. Each segment is assumed to have a left and right coordinate. To assign these segments to a minimal number of tracks a greedy algorithm can be used which, surprisingly, gives an optimal result (16).
Algorithm T: Left edge algorithm for track assignment.

1. Sort the edges in W based upon the value of the coordinate of their left edge.
2. Assign the first wire to the first track and delete this wire from W.
3. Find the first wire in W so that its left edge is to the right of the last wire selected. Assign this wire to the track being processed and delete this wire from W.
4. Repeat step 3 until no wire can be assigned, at which time return to step 2 and begin assigning wires to the next track.

This algorithm is illustrated in Figure 15-12, where the wires have been sorted based upon the coordinate value of their left edge. One of the optimal track assignments is indicated in Figure 15-12b.

To complete the routing, stubs must be routed and horizontal and vertical segments must be connected. A two layer routing environment is assumed. Figure 15-13 indicates how stubs can be routed, as well as how the use of a "dogleg" (17), which allows for a wire segment to be broken into subsegments, can also lead to even a further reduction in channel density. The wire ends A, B, C, D represent pseudo points, i.e., these points are to be connected to wires in the vertical channel shown. The top edges of the vertical wires assigned to this channel and to be connected to these wires now have a well defined upper coordinate value.

Once all wires have been assigned to tracks, reassignment to layers can be made. For example, if only one metal layer exists, then wires in the vertical

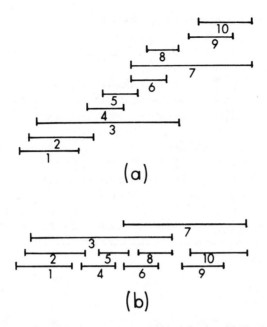

(a)

(b)

Figure 15-12. (a) Original wire segments sorted by left edge. (b) Track assignment.

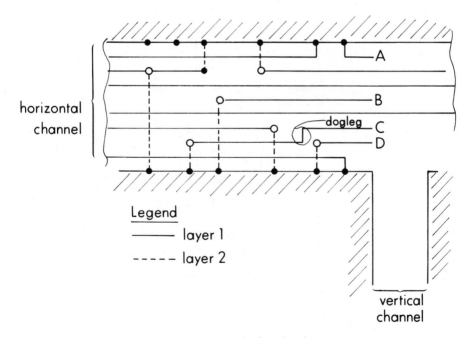

Figure 15-13. An example of track assignment.

and horizontal channels are assigned to metal layers, and stubs and some wire subsegments where channels intersect are assigned to a second layer when necessary to avoid shorts. This concept is illustrated in Figure 15-14.

Another similar channel routing problem which has been extensively studied is the single and double row routing problem, which consists of one or two rows of points and an assignment of signals to these points. It is desired to interconnect points having common signal names, again minimizing track requirements. References (18-24) deal with this class of problem.

An example of this type of problem is shown in Figure 15-11a. Interconnecting points along the right edge of block B_1 and the left edge of block B_2 is a two row problem, to be solved in channel B. Interconnecting points along the left edge of B_1 is a single row problem to be solved in channel A.

These types of configurations constitute the primary routing problems found in polycell layouts.

Summary and Conclusions

Numerous routing schemes have been developed to automate the interconnection process for LSI chips. While several routing schemes were originally devel-

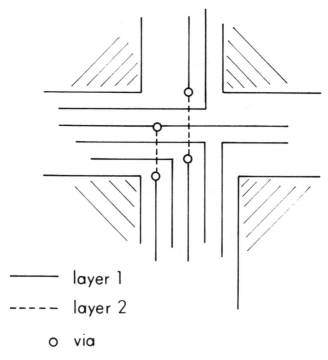

——— layer 1

- - - - - layer 2

o   via

Figure 15-14. Routed channel intersection.

oped for PCBs, such as the Lee algorithm and the cellular router, they have also been found to be applicable to LSI chips. In addition, special algorithms have been developed for LSI chips which deal with certain key aspects of the chip, such as channel size. The Lee algorithm is usually the back-up strategy used to find a path when all other techniques fail. The line router is relatively fast, but like the Lee algorithm ignores the global aspects of the problem. Channel routing using a channel graph is applicable to most routing schemes and appears to offer the best prospects for achieving high quality automatic routing.

When attempting to route a VLSI chip containing tens of thousands of circuits, some form of data management involving partitioning is necessary. One approach is to employ the strategies of top-down chip planning and bottom-up cell design. Bottom-up cell design attempts to tie together a logic design and a physical layout. Once a physical cell has been created, it can be henceforth processed by modeling it using a bounding box together with the I/O terminals for the cell. Cells can be combined in a hierarchical manner to form larger cell structures. The top-down aspect of design can be used to first position cells so that they are near to other cells to which they are to be connected, and secondly, assign the relative ordering and physical positions to cell I/O terminals so they are aligned as close as possible to those of other terminals to which they are to be connected. Clearly several iterations between cell design and chip planning are required before a clean interface between cells is achieved.

Another scheme used to manage the enormity of the routing problem is that of "bundling". This concept deals with identifying categories of wires, such as data buses, address lines, clock lines and control lines. Special algorithms can then be used for the various categories. For example, a data bus can be "bundled" as a single wire and routed between its sources and destinations. This corresponds to a channel assignment process. The unbundling of the wire occurs during track assignment.

PART II
A NEW-GRAPH ORIENTED ROUTING ALGORITHM

INTRODUCTION

The approach to routing presented here is based on channel routing methods, and has the potential to circumvent several limitations that many existing routing methods possess. The approach proposed here is to model the carrier as a weighted graph. Then, using one of several minimum-length path procedures, find optimal paths in the graph. The path represents a route for an interconnection on the carrier. Optimality may be defined in terms of several different cost functions.

Only a very special routing configuration, called a unidirectional point configuration, will be discussed. This problem has been previously studied by So (25) and Kuh et al. (18), who have shown that a large class of routing problems can be reduced to the problem considered here.

A simple example is shown in Figure 15-15. Here it is assumed that points to be interconnected lie along rows and columns and that a channel type algorithm is used to make a first pass at the routing process. In Figure 15-15 the partial results of the first pass process are shown. Here the connection between points A and A' have been made by assigning a wire segment in horizontal channel 1 between point A and via a, a segment in vertical channel 4 between vias a and a', and finally a segment between a' and A'. At the end of this process there are numerous pairs of points to be interconnected, e.g., A-a, a-a', a'-A', B-B', etc. These pairs of points can be sorted into groups, where each group consists of all pairs of points associated with the same line (row or column) of points. Such a line of points is referred to as a unidirectional point line.

The problem which will be considered in the next few sections is the inter-

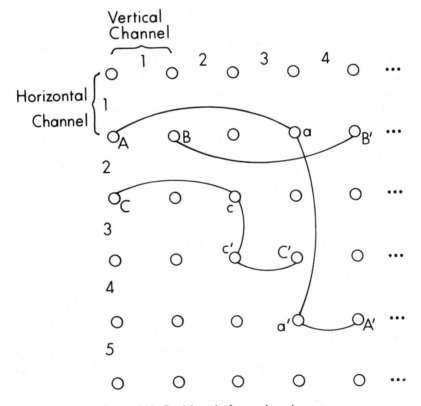

Figure 15-15. Partial results from a channel router.

connection of a given set of points along a unidirectional point line, using a single layer for routing, so that no two paths intersect. The pairs of points along a line will be routed row by row, and column by column. Two models are explored. The first called *unconstrained* routing, is where the routing space is a continuum. The second model assumes tracks exist, but wires may be moved to route new interconnections. This is called *floating-track constrained* routing.

A FORMAL DEFINITION OF THE PROBLEM

Let $A = \{a_1, a_2, \ldots, a_m\}$ be an ordered set of points lying on a horizontal straight line, called the *point line*, with end points a_1 and a_m. Assume a_i is to the left of a_{i+1}. The elements of A are called *original* points. Let $Q = \{q_1, q_2, \ldots, q_r\}$ be a set of pseudo points, where q_i represents the intersection of a routed path and the point line. Let $P = \{p_1, p_2, \ldots, p_n\} = A \cup Q$, where $n = m+r$, $A \cap Q = \phi$, and where the p_i's are just a relabling of the a_j's and q_k's. (See Figure 15-16.) The space along the point line between each adjacent point p_i and p_{i+1} is called an *interval* u_i and consists of the semi-closed interval $[p_i, p_{i+1}]$. The last interval u_n consists of only the point p_n.

A *unidirectional configuration D* (or simply, *configuration*) consists of a point set P and two areas adjacent to and on opposite sides of the point line. These areas are called *streets*, and they contain the paths in D which interconnect points in P. The upper street is denoted by S^+, and the lower street by S^-. Paths are routed in horizontal and vertical *tracks* in the streets. A *path* contains zero or more pseudo-points and two original points as its end points, and does not intersect any other path. A *feasible path* is a path which has not yet been assigned to tracks. A *routed path* is a path which lies entirely within tracks.

In routing, no "T" connections are allowed, and at most two connections can be made to a point, one from above and one from below.

Interval u_i is said to be accessible to interval u_j ($i \neq j$) if a path exists from u_i to u_j in a given street.

A *segment* (p_i, p_j) is a subpath which contains no points between p_i and p_j. Assume the location of p_i is α_i, where $\alpha_i < \alpha_{i+1}$ for all i. A *canonical segment* is a feasible segment (p_i, p_j) such that there exists no interval u_k accessible to interval u_i or u_j, where $\alpha_i < \alpha_k < \alpha_j$.

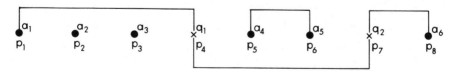

Figure 15-16. A configuration showing points and pseudo points.

Channels are rectangular areas of the unidirectional configuration bounded by routed paths, the point line, or the edge of the configuration. There are two types of channels, as illustrated in Figure 15-17, namely section channels which run horizontally, and switching channels which run vertically. A point is said to be singly covered if it is the end point of only one segment. p_i is doubly covered if it is attached to two segments.

Referring to Figure 15-17, point p_2 is said to be singly covered in street S^+. Pseudo points are always doubly covered. Point p_6 is uncovered.

The unidirectional routing problem is one of determining a feasible path between two given points $N = (p_i, p_j)$ in a routed configuration D which satisfies some cost function, and then assigning that path to appropriate tracks in D thus forming a routed path.

In practice a large set of pairs of points $\{N_1, N_2, \ldots, N_k\}$ to be interconnected is given. These points are defined over the original set of points A, and are obtained from the channel routing process referred to earlier. Assume the pairs of points N_j have been ordered and are processed sequentially.

Previous work on this problem has been reported by Kuh et al. (18) and Ting et al. (19). The work to be presented here differs from Ting's in several aspects, namely optimal results with respect to the given objective functions are

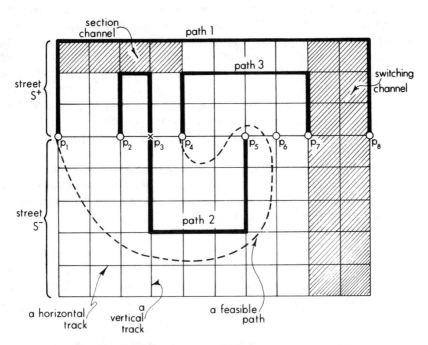

Figure 15-17. An example configuration showing streets, tracks, channels and paths.

obtained; multi-point nets are allowed; a path is found if one exists; and arbitrary street capacities are assumed.

To obtain these results. a graph G, called an *access graph* is employed which reflects the availability of tracks between points and takes into consideration all previously routed paths. The solution steps for routing a net N in D are:

1. Given D, generate G.
2. Obtain a path in G meeting the desired cost function. This path represents a feasible path for N in D.
3. Assign the feasible path to tracks thus obtaining a routed path for N in D. This produces a new configuration D^*.

The Access Graph.   A graphical model of a routed configuration D used in the solution of the problem of unidirectional routing is now presented. The nodes of the graph represent intervals, and the arcs represent section and switching channels in D.

Let D be a routed configuration with n points. Let G be an *access graph G* $= (V, E)$ associated with D, where V is a set of $2n$ nodes and E is a set of unidirected arcs defined on the nodes in V. The node set V consists of two mutually exclusive subsets V^+ and V^- each consisting of n nodes. A node v_i^+ in V^+ represents the S^+ street side of the interval u_i while a node v_i^- in V^- represents the S^- street side of interval u_i.

The set E consists of two types of arcs, namely section arcs and switching arcs. Let x be one of the two symbols $\{-, +\}$. A *section arc* $(v_i^x v_j^x)$ exists between two nodes v_i^x and v_j^x $(i \neq j)$ where v_i^x and v_j^x are in V^x if interval u_i is accessible to interval u_j and there exists no interval u_k between points p_i and p_j such that interval u_k is accessible to intervals u_i or u_j in street S^x. Thus arc (v_i^x, v_j^x) represents a canonical section channel between intervals u_i and u_j in D. Each section arc in G is labeled as (x, B), where B is a set of values reflecting characteristics of the associated channel in D, such as the length of the channel, the number of routes to be moved, etc.

A *switching arc* $(v_i^x, v_i^{\bar{x}})$ exists between every two nodes v_i^x and $v_i^{\bar{x}}$ where v_i^x ϵ V^x and $v_i^{\bar{x}}$ ϵ V_x ($\bar{x}$ is equal to $+$ if x is equal to $-$ and vice versa), if a new switch can be routed between points p_i and p_{i+1} in D. v_i^x and $v_i^{\bar{x}}$ represent the same interval u_i. An exception occurs for interval u_i, since point p_{n+i} does not exist, and by definition no paths may be routed to the right of point p_n. Thus no switching arc exists between nodes v_n^x and $v_n^{\bar{x}}$. A switching arc $(v_i^x, v_i^{\bar{x}})$ represents a switching channel in interval u_i. A switching arc is labeled (w, B), where B is a set of values similar to those for section arcs.

To clarify the definition of the access graph consider the configuration D shown in Figure 15-18. Assume there are sufficient unassigned tracks where necessary. The length of each interval is assumed to be 1 unit with the exception of intervals 5 and 6 which are each ½ unit long. Point p_6 is a pseudo-point.

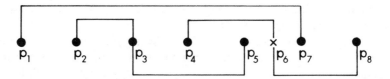

Figure 15-18. An example configuration D.

Assume only the lengths of paths are of interest. Then the label on each arc is the pair (x, δ) if the arc is a section arc, or $(w, 1)$ if the arc is a switching arc, where x is "+" or "−", δ is the length of the section channel, and the length of each switch has been arbitrarily defined to be 1 unit. All of the section channels in configuration D are listed in Table 15-1. The channels identified by an asterisk are not canonical. In this table the left point p_j of an interval u_j is used to represent that interval.

The access graph G for the configuration shown in Figure 15-18 is shown in Figure 15-19. Each canonical channel listed in Table 15-1 is reflected as an arc in G as are the seven switching arcs possible for this example (there is no switching arc for interval p_8). The length of each section arc (p_i, p_j) is $|\alpha_j - \alpha_i|$, and it is assumed all channels have width greater than zero.

The utility of the access graph is evident by picking any two nodes, say nodes 1^- and 5^+, and determining a path between them in G. Consider path $(1^-, 2^-, 5^-, 5^+)$ in Figure 15-19. This corresponds to a feasible section in configuration D from point p_1 to interval u_5 in the lower street and a switch in interval u_5. The feasible path is completed by two links, one at point p_1 and the other at point p_5, and a short section from point p_5 to interval u_5. The sum of the lengths of the arcs in the chosen path is 5 units which is also the length of the feasible path in D.

There is another path between nodes 1^- and 5^+, namely $(1^-, 1^+, 3^+, 3^-, 4^-,$

Table 15-1 All Section Channels in the Configuration shown in Figure 15-18.

STREET S^+	STREET S^-
(p_1, p_3)	(p_1, p_2)
*(p_1, p_6)	*(p_1, p_5)
(p_3, p_6)	*(p_1, p_8)
(p_7, p_8)	(p_2, p_5)
(p_4, p_5)	*(p_2, p_8)
	*(p_5, p_8)
	(p_3, p_4)
	(p_6, p_7)

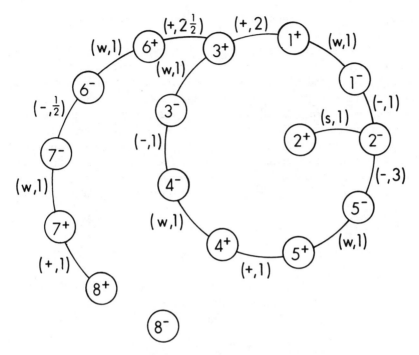

Figure 15-19. The access graph G for the configuration shown in Figure 15-18.

4^+, 5^+). The length of this path is 7 units. If shortest paths are to be routed in D, then the path of length 5 units is chosen as the desired one.

In the next sections the steps required to route nets given configurations will be briefly described.

One key tool is that of finding paths in G. This is done using the least-cost path algorithm due to Dijkstra (26) which operates in time $O(l \log n)$ for a graph with l edges and n nodes, and with a small number of edges connected to any given node in the graph. The arcs in G are labeled according to which of the various criteria is to be minimized, namely length or perturbation, which refers to the number of wires which must be moved to make room for a new wire.

UNCONSTRAINED UNIDIRECTIONAL ROUTING

For this problem it is desired to route N given D, where there are no constraints on track accessibility. Furthermore, wire length should be minimized. To accomplish this, the access graph per Algorithm 1 below is first constructed. It executes in linear time (27).

Algorithm 1. Construction of the unconstrained access graph G from a configuration D.

Method: The line of configuration points is scanned twice, from left to right, once for street S^+ and a second time for street S^-. During each scan, successive adjacent points p_i and p_{i+1} are examined with respect to routed path coverings and the directions of the paths covering them. Appropriate action is taken (via the table used in step 4) based upon which of the nine possible adjacent point configurations shown in Table 15-2 is applicable. Algorithm steps 5 to 8 perform stack and graph operations such that at the conclusion of the second point scan, the entire access graph is constructed. The procedure operates on one stack, S, which contains indices of points p_j in D. Define point p_{n+1} to be an uncovered imaginary point lying just to the right of point p_n on the point line in D.

Table 15-2. Table of all Adjacent
Point Configurations on Two Adjacent
Points.

Configuration	p_i	p_{i+1}
1	●	●
2	⌐●	●
3	●	⌐●
4	●	●⌐
5	⌐●	●⌐
6	⌐●	⌐●
7	●⌐	●
8	●⌐	⌐●
9	●⌐	●⌐

Procedure:

Step 1. (initialization) $x \leftarrow$ "+", clear stack S., and construct the $2n$ nodes $1^+, 2^+, \ldots, n^+, 1^-, 2^-, \ldots, n^-$ in G.

Step 2. (switching arcs) For $i = 1, 2, \ldots, n-1$, construct an arc between nodes i^+ and i^-, and label it ("w",1).

Step 3. $i \leftarrow$ o. Push i onto stack S. (Even though there is no point p_0 in D, this dummy item is needed in S to ensure correct processing of the end points in D.)

Step 4. (main loop) Let the top item in stack S be j. $i \leftarrow i+1$. Consider points p_i and p_{i+1} in D. Select the applicable case from Table 15-3 and branch to the particular step as directed.

Step 5. Pop stack S to get j. If $j \neq 0$ then construct an arc in G between nodes i^x and j^x and label it $(x, \alpha_i - a_j)$. Push i onto stack S and go to step 8.

Step 6. Push i onto stack S and go to step 8.

Step 7. Pop S to get j. Construct an arc in G between nodes i^x and j^x and label it $(x, \alpha_i - \alpha_j)$. Go to step 8.

Step 8. (end of main loop) If $i \neq n$ then go to step 4.

Step 9. If $x =$ "+" then $x \leftarrow$ "−", $s \leftarrow \emptyset$, and go to step 3. Otherwise, exit procedure.□

Once the access graph is constructed, the minimal length path from p_i to p_j as defined by N is determined. The resulting feasible path is then mapped into a routed path. Since wires are essentially "infinitely thin" in this model, track availability is not a problem.

As an example of unconstrained unidirectional routing, consider the routed configuration D in Figure 15-20, and assume it is desired to find the minimum

Table 15-3. The Adjacent Point Configuration Jump Table for Algorithm 1.

| | | | IF: | | |
ADJACENT POINT CONFIGURATION (TABLE 15-2)	p_i is COVERED IN S^x	p_{i+1} is COVERED IN S^x	p_i is LEFT POINT OF SEGMENT	p_{i+1} is LEFT POINT OF SEGMENT	GO TO STEP
1	no	no	—	—	5
2	yes	no	no	—	5
3	no	yes	—	yes	5
4	no	yes	—	no	7
5	yes	yes	no	no	7
6	yes	yes	no	yes	5
7	yes	no	yes	—	6
8	yes	yes	yes	yes	6
9	yes	yes	yes	no	8

length path for net $N = (p_3, p_5)$. First, the access graph representing D is generated. The resulting graph is shown in Figure 15-21. Each point in D is assumed to be separated by two units of length. Next, a minimum-length path is found in G between nodes 3^- and 5^+ as shown by the heavy arcs.

The configuration containing N is shown in Figure 15-22. Note that a pseudo-point was added between points p_1 and p_2.

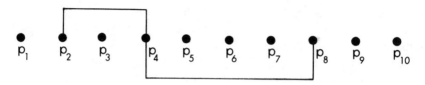

Figure 15-20. A configuration illustrating the minimum length routing of net $N = (p_3, p_5)$.

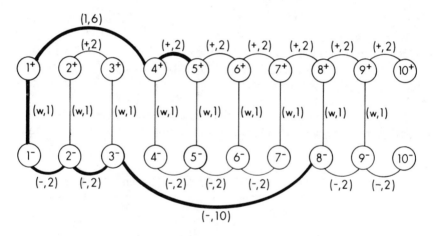

Figure 15-21. The access graph for the configuration shown in Figure 15-20.

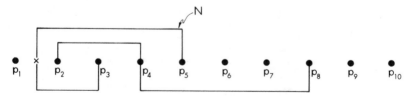

Figure 15-22. The final configuration containing the minimum-length routed path for net N.

FLOATING-TRACK UNIDIRECTIONAL ROUTING

For the case of floating-track unidirectional routing, feasible paths are assigned to tracks and are allowed to be reassigned to new tracks in order to open up space for the routing of future nets. This form of routing employs a density function which essentially keeps a record of track utilization in the streets. Given a vertical line through a configuration, the street density associated with this line is the number of routed paths which cross this line in a given street. Lines are usually drawn through configuration points. The maximum street density over the length of a feasible canonical section is one item in the label associated with an arc in the access graph. Another item is λ, the number of routed sections that must be moved to accommodate the feasible sections represented by the arc. Using these labels, one can easily find either minimum length or minimum perturbation path.

Algorithm 2 is a procedure for generating the access graph used for floating-track routing. It operates in quadratic time.

Algorithm 2. Construction of the floating-track access graph G for a configuration D.

Method: This algorithm is similar to Algorithm 1. Let ψ be a channel whose left end is at interval u_j. Then the stack contains elements of the form (j, ρ, t, λ) where ρ represents the maximum segment density of a feasible segment routed in ψ, t is the track occupied by the outer routed section bounding the channel, and λ is the number of sections which must be moved to permit a feasible canonical section to be routed in ψ. Again define point p_{n+1} to be an uncovered imaginary point lying just to the right of point p_n on the point line in D.

Procedure:

Step 1. (initialization) $x \leftarrow$ "$+$", clear stack s, and construct the $2n$ nodes $1^+, 2^+, \ldots, n^+, 1^-, 2^-, \ldots, n^-$.

Step 2. (switching arcs) For each point p_i, i $= 1, 2, \ldots, n$, if p_i is a unidirectional points and the number ϕ of pseudo-points in the unidirectional interval with p_i as its left point is less than the switching track capacity T^w, then construct an arc between nodes i^+ and i^- and label it $(w, 1, \phi, \alpha_i, 0)$. If p_i is a pseudo-point, let it be in unidirectional interval u. If the number ϕ of pseudo-points (including p_i) in u is less than the switching track capacity T^w then construct an arc between nodes i^+ and i^- and label it $(w, 1, \phi, \alpha_i\ 0)$.

Step 3. $i \leftarrow 0$ and Push $(0, 0, T^x + 1, 0)$ onto stack S.

Step 4. (main loop) $i \leftarrow i + 1$. Let the top item in stack S be (j, ρ, t, λ). Consider points p_i and p_{i+1} in D. Select the applicable case from Table 15-4 and branch to the step indicated. (In steps 5 through 7, let t_i be the track occupied by the routed segment whose end-point is i. If no such routed segment exists, set $t_i = 0$.)

Table 15-4. The Adjacent Point Configuration Jump Table for
Algorithm 2.

ADJACENT POINT CONFIGURATION (TABLE 15-2)	p_i is COVERED IN S^x	p_{i+1} is COVERED IN S^x	IF p_i is LEFT POINT IN SEGMENT	p_{i+1} is LEFT POINT IN SEGMENT	GO TO STEP
1	no	no	—	—	5
2	yes	no	no	—	5
3	no	yes	—	yes	5
4	no	yes	—	no	7
5	yes	yes	no	no	7
6	yes	yes	no	yes	5
7	yes	no	yes	—	6
8	yes	yes	yes	yes	6
9	yes	yes	yes	no	8

Step 5. Pop S to get (j, ρ, t, λ). If $t < T^x$ and $j \neq 0$, then construct an arc (i, j) in G and label it $(x, \alpha_i - \alpha_j, \rho, t, \beta)$. If $(t - t_i) = 1$ then $\beta \leftarrow \lambda$, otherwise $\beta \leftarrow 0$. Push (depth (S), t, λ) onto S. Go to step 9.

Step 6. Let (j, ρ, t, λ) be the top element in stack S. Push $(i, 0, t_i, \beta)$ onto S, and for every element in S set the second field to max $(\alpha$, depth $(S) - 1)$, where α is the current value of this field. If $(t - t_i) = 1$ then $\beta \leftarrow \lambda + 1$.

Step 7. Pop S to get (j, ρ, t, λ). If $t < T^x$ and $j \neq 0$ then construct an arc (i, j) and label it $(x, \alpha_i - \alpha_j, \rho, t, \beta)$. If $(t - t_i) = 1$ then $\beta \leftarrow \lambda$, otherwise $\beta \leftarrow 0$. Go to step 9.

Step 8. For every element in stack S, set the second field either to itself or to the depth of S, whichever is greater.

Step 9. (end of main loop) If $i \neq n$, then go to step 4.

Step 10. If $x = $ "$+$", then $x \leftarrow $ "$-$", $S \leftarrow \phi$, and go to step 3.

Using the floating-track access graph, minimum length paths may be found as for the unconstrained case. Presented here is another path function, called minimum perturbation routing, where the objective when attempting to route a new net is to move the minimum number of already routed interconnections. New segments are assigned to the innermost available track. Thus, when previously routed sections must be moved to create a free track for a feasible section, it is only necessary to move outer routed sections. Algorithm 3 is a modified Dijkstra's procedure for finding a minimum perturbation path in G.

Algorithm 3: Dijkstra's minimum-cost path procedure modified to find a minimum-perturbation path from node u_0 to node x in G.

Method: Let S_i be a proper subset of V, the node set of G, such that $u_0 \epsilon S_i$, and let $\overline{S}_i$ be the subset of V which consists of all nodes not in $S.$. Let V contain η nodes. The basic idea is to construct an increasing sequence $S_0, S_1, \ldots, S_{\eta-1}$ of subsets of V in such a way that, at the end of stage i, minimum-perturbation paths from u_0 to all nodes in S_i are known. Define a label l (u_i) for each node u_i, where l (u_i) will be a number of routed segments perturbed by routing the feasible path represented by the minimum-perturbation path from u_0 to u_i when the algorithm has processed set S_i. Define a node label $\mu(u_i)$ which is used by the algorithm to keep a correct record of the number of perturbed sections required by the minimum-perturbation path containing node u_i. PRED (u_i) points to the next node adjacent to u_i in the path beginning at x and ending at u_0.

Procedure:

Step 1. $l(u_0) \leftarrow 0$, PRED $(u_0) \leftarrow u_0$, l $(v) \leftarrow \infty$ for all $v \, \epsilon \, G$ and $v \neq u_0$, and $S_0 = \{u_0\}$.

Step 2. For each node v in $\overline{S}_i$:

(a) if arc $(u_i,$ PRED $(u_i))$ is not the same type as arc (u_i, v) go to part (b) of this step. If λ $(u_i,$ PRED $(u_i)) \geq \lambda$ (u_i, v) and if $l(u_i) < l$ (v) then set PRED $(v) = u_i$ and replace l (v) by l (u_i). If λ $(u_i,$ PRED $(u_i)) < \lambda$ (u_i, v) and if μ $(u_i) + \lambda$ $(u_i, v) < l$ (v) then set PRED $(v) = u_i$ and replace l (v) by $\mu(u_i) + \lambda$ (u_i, v). Go to part (c) of this step.

(b) if l $(u_i) + \lambda$ $(u_i, v) < l$ (v), PRED $(v) \leftarrow u_i$, $\mu(v) \leftarrow l$ (u_i) and l $(v) \leftarrow (l$ $(u_i) + \lambda$ $(u_i, v))$.

(c) compute min $\{ l$ $(y)\}$ and let u_{i+1} denote a node v for which the minimum is attained. $S_{i+1} \leftarrow S_i \, U \{u_{i+1}\}$.

Step 3. If $i = \eta-1$, exit procedure since no path exists between u_0 and x. If $u_{i+1} \neq x$, $i \leftarrow i+1$ and go to step 2. If $u_{u+1} = x$, exit procedure since a minimum-perturbation path has been found between u_0 and x.

After a minimum-perturbation path has been obtained, assign it to tracks using Algorithm 4. The algorithm operates in linear time.

Algorithm 4. Minimum-perturbation path track assignment.

Method: This simple procedure sequentially scans the minimum-perturbation feasible path P in D, moving routed sections one track further away from the point line as necessary and routing the feasible sections. Track assignments for switches are not considered since their assignment is straightforward.

Procedure:

Step 1. Let the label of an arc in G be $(x, \delta, \rho, t, \lambda)$. Let the arcs in path P be numbered sequentially in numerical order, $i \leftarrow 0$, $\overline{\lambda} \leftarrow 0$, $\overline{t} \leftarrow 0$.

Step 2. $i \leftarrow i+1$. If arc i is a switching arc, go to step 3, otherwise $\overline{\lambda} \leftarrow$ max $(\overline{\lambda}, \lambda_i)$, $\overline{t} \leftarrow$ max $(\overline{t}, t_i)$ and go to step 4.

Step 3. Move the $\overline{\lambda}$ routed paths (with the inner-most path in track $\overline{t}$) in D covering the point p, which is the left point of the switching interval, one track further away from the point line. Route the feasible segment in track $\overline{t}$ (or track 1 if $\overline{t} = 0$), $\overline{\lambda} \leftarrow \overline{t} \leftarrow 0$. Go to step 2.

Step 4. If all arcs in the path have been examined, exit the procedure since net N has been routed. Otherwise, return to step 2 to examine the next arc in path P.

As an example of floating-track routing, consider the configuration D in Figure 15-23, and assume it is desired to route an interconnection $N = (p_1, P_{13})$. The access graph G shown in Figure 15-24 is generated using Algorithm 2. Then Dijkstra's algorithm modified for finding minimum perturbation paths (Algorithm 3) is used to find a path in G. This path is shown as heavy arcs in

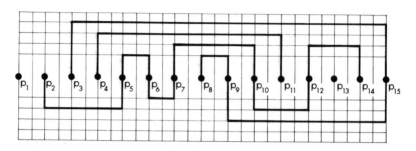

Figure 15-23. Configuration D.

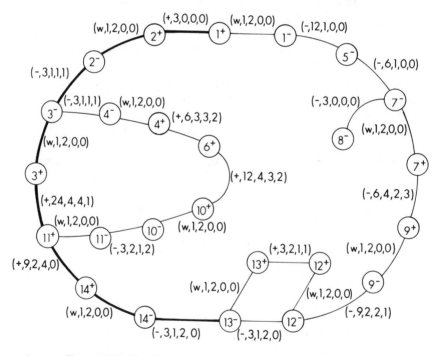

Figure 15-24. The floating-track access graph G for configuration D.

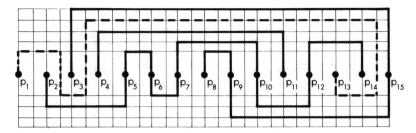

Figure 15-25. The final routed configuration. The dashed line is the newly routed interconnection $N = (p_1, p_{13})$.

G. Finally, tracks in D are assigned to sections of the path to complete the routing of N in D. Figure 15-25 shows the final configuration.

EXPERIMENTAL RESULTS

A computer program implementing algorithms presented here was written to empirically investigate unidirectional routing. Twenty four routing problems were analyzed to determine the expected completion rate of the routing program. Each problem was run three times, once for each objective (i.e., unconstrained, floating-track with minimum length routes, and floating-track with minimum perturbation routes). The nets in each problem were randomly selected and ordered with respect to length or placement on the net list. The distribution of the net lengths for all problems was exponential with more shorter nets than longer nets. In all cases 100% routing completion was obtained and all routes met their cost objectives.

Another set of inputs was used to investigate the expected running times of the algorithms as implemented via computer programs. Fifteen problem sets were analyzed. Each problem set consisted of three configurations with 0.25n, 0.50n, and 0.75n routed segments, where n is the number of points in the configuration. Configuration sizes with 20, 50 and 80 points were examined. The routed segments were arranged in random locations within the configurations. Up to 30 (but not less than 20) randomly chosen interconnections were each individually routed in each configuration, and the computer execution time of the subroutines implementing the access graph construction, minimum path determination, and track assignment algorithms was obtained for each configuration. Furthermore, the entire process was repeated for each routing goal (i.e., unconstrained minimum length, floating-track minimum length, and floating-track minimum perturbation). For all routing goals, the access graph construction procedure time was a linear function of the number of points or the configuration density (i.e., the ratio of the number of routed segments to

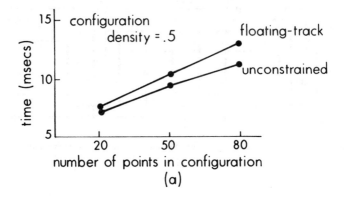

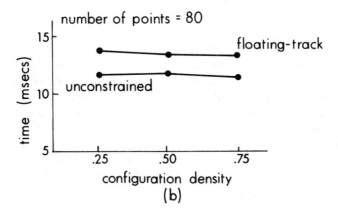

Figure 15-26. Execution times for graph construction. (a) Number of points in the configuration. (b) Configuration density.

the number of points in the configuration) as shown in Figure 15-26. In these and subsequent plots, all execution times are for a CDC-7600 computer.

As shown in Figure 15-27, the execution times for the minimum path procedures is essentially linear for the minimum length path goal, and quadratic for the minimum perturbation path goal. The family of curves in each plot are for two different path lengths: 10 arcs, and 20 arcs.

Track assignment is only applicable to floating-track routing and its associated computation time is a linear function of both configuration density and the number of points in the configuration. The floating-track assignment subroutine ran exceedingly fast; maximum time observed was 8 msec.

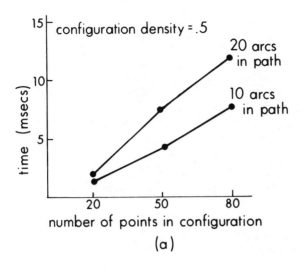

(a)

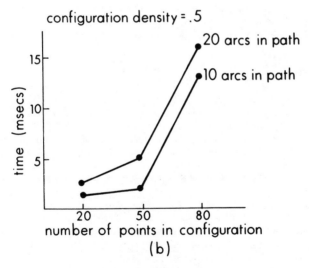

(b)

Figure 15-27. Execution times for minimum path determination. (a) Minimum length. (b) Minimum perturbation.

CONCLUSIONS

In Part II of this chapter a new and powerful model for representing the interconnection problem, namely an access graph has been introduced. This graph can be constructed in linear time from a routed configuration. Using a minimal cost algorithm for processing graphs a path can be found which minimizes one of several objectives, such as length or perturbations. This path can then be mapped back into the configuration and represents an optimal path between two points in the configuration. The ability to move previously routed paths (perturbation) makes this form of router a very powerful tool. This latter attribute is not found in most of the classical routing algorithms.

It should be noted, however, that these routing results, as well as those of most other algorithms, are dependent on the order in which nets are processed and hence are not globally optimal. In fact, when such sequential routing algorithms fail to find a path for a net, a path may sometimes be found when a different ordering is used.

ACKNOWLEDGMENTS

This work was supported in part by the National Science Foundation under Grant No. ECS-8005957, and under a VHSIC Phase 3 contract No. DAAK 20-80-C-0278, administered by the Department of the Army, Fort Monmouth, New Jersey.

REFERENCES

(1) Breuer, M. A. "Recent Developments in Design Automation" *Computer*, 23–35 (1972).

(2) Akers, S. Routing in *Design Automation of Digital Systems: Theory and Techniques* (M. A. Breuer, ed.), New York: Prentice-Hall, (1972)

(3) Hightower, D. W. "The Interconnection Problem: a Tutorial." *Computer* 7: 18–32 (1974).

(4) Nakahara, H. "Computer-aided Interconnection Routing: General Survey of the State-of-the-art." *Networks* 2: 167–183 (1972)

(5) Agrawal, P. "On the Probability of Success in a Routing Process. *Proc. IEEE* 64: 1624–1625 (1976).

(6) Loberman, H. and Weinberger, A. "Formal Procedures for Connecting Terminals with a Minimum Total Wire Length." *J. ACM* 4: 428–437 (1957).

(7) Gilbert, E. N. and Pollak, H. O. "Steiner Minimal Trees." *SIAM J. Math* 16: 1–29 (1968).

(8) Abel, L. "On the Automated Layout of Multi-layer Planar Wiring and a Related Graph Coloring Problem." Coordinated Science Laboratory Report No. R-546, University of Illinois, January 1972.

(9) Abel, L. C. "On the Ordering of Connections for Automatic Wire Routing." *IEEE Trans. on Computers* C-21: 1227–1233 (1972).

(10) Lee, C. Y. "An Algorithm for Path Connections and its Applications." *IRE Trans. on Elect. Computers* EC-10: 346–365 (1961).

(11) Akers, S. B., Jr. "A Modification of Lee's Path Connection Algorithm." *IEEE Trans. on Elect. Computers* EC-16: 97–98 (1967).

(12) Breuer, M. A. and Shamsa, K. "A Hardware Router." *J. Digital Systems* 4: 393–408 (1980).

(13) Hightower, D. W. "A Solution to Line Routing Problems on the Continuous Plane." *Proc. 6th Design Automation Workshop* (June 8–12, 1969): 1–24.

(14) Mattison, R. "A High Quality Low Cost Router for MOS/LSI." *Proc. 9th Design Automation Worshiop* (1972): 94–103.

(15) Hitchcock, R. B. "Cellular Wiring and the Cellular Modeling Technique." *Proc. 6th Design Automation Workshop* (1969).

(16) Hashimoto, A. and Stevens, J. "Wire Routing by Optimizing Channel Assignment Within Large Apertures." *Proc. 8th Design Automation Workshop* (1971): 155–169.

(17) Deutsch, D. N. "A Dogleg Channel Router.' ' *Proc. 13th Design Automation Conference* (1976): 425–433.

(18) Kuh, E. S., Kashiwahara, T. and Fujisawa, T. "On Optimum Single-row Routing." *IEEE Trans. Circuits and Systems* CAS-26: 361–368, 1979.

(19) Ting, B. Kuh, E. S. and Shirakawa, I. "The Multilayer Routing Problem: Algorithms and Necessary and Sufficient Conditions for the Single-row Single-layer Case." *IEEE Trans. on Circuits and Systems* CAS-23: 768–778 (1976).

(20) Tsukiyama, S., Kuh, E. S., and Shirakawa, I." An Algorithm for Single-row Routing with Prescribed Street Congestions." *IEEE Trans. on Circuits and Systems* CAS-27: 765–771 (1980).

(21) Raghavan, R. and Sahni, S. "Single Row Routing." Computer Science Department Technical Report 80–22, University of Minnesota, Minneapolis.

(22) Yoshimura, T. and Kuh, E. S. "Efficient Algorithms for Channel Routing." Electronic Research Laboratory Memo No. UCB/ERL M80/43, College of Engineering, University of California, Berkeley.

(23) Kawamoto, T. and Kajitani, Y. "The Minimum Width Routing of the 2-row 2-layer Polycell Layout." *Proc. 16th Design Automation Conference* (1979): 290–296.

(24) Kanada, H., Okazaki, K., Tachibana, M., Kato, R., and Murai, S. "Channel-order Router—a New Routing Technique for a Masterslice LSI." *J. Digital Systems* 4: 427–442. (1980).

(25) So, H. "Some Theoretical Results on the Routing of Multilayer Printed Wiring Boards." *Proc. IEEE Int'l. Symp. on Circuits and Systems,* (1974): 296–302.

(26) Dijkstra, E. W. "A Note on Two problems in Connection With Graphs." *Numerische Mathematik 1,* 269–271 (1959).

(27) Carter, H. W. *Optimized Unidirectional Routing.* Ph.D. dissertation, Department of Electrical Engineering, University of Southern California, January 1980.

(28) Van Cleemput, W., Linders, J. "An Improved Graph Theoretic Model for the Circuit Layout Problem." *Proc. 11th Design Automation Workshop* (1974): 82–90.

16. VLSI Layout

R. M. J. M. Otten,
IBM Corporation, New York

This chapter is a concise survey as well as an exposition of ideas about automation of layout design. In the first part the state and position of this part of CAD is considered. The central theme of this chapter is a discussion of imperatives of a layout design system suitable for VLSI. The last section is a precursory presentation of an approach that strives for conformance to the imperatives of the second section.

COMPUTER AIDED LAYOUT DESIGN

A *layout* of a system is any set of data that uniquely specifies the masks necessary for integrating the system. The layout tasks addressed in this chapter are those in which components or subsystems of fixed or variable shape have to be arranged within a given or as small as possible geometrical figure, and to be interconnected by a network of conducting paths embedded in one or more layers while giving due consideration to technological, electronic and economic constraints.

ITS CONTEXT

Data Base Considerations

The evolution of silicon technology over the past decade has been so rapid that the development of computer aids could not maintain pace with it. Existing design methods cannot cope with the presently feasible scales of integration. Many CAD-tools are outdated and some projects for developing new ones were already obsolete before completion. Layout in particular seems to be destined to cause a bottleneck in the design cycle. The Intel 8086 microprocessor, for example, required thirteen manyears merely for layout design (1). Yet it cannot be regarded as an isolated problem. Anyone in VLSI design must endorse Brooks' assertion that conceptual integrity is the most important consideration in system design (2). From the first conception to the last test, the design must be guided by well-coordinated ideas which take into account the effects a decision has on all future design tasks. During the design process the design is to be stored as data on computers. So the integrity of a design is in fact the integrity of its data base. Thoughts connected with data base design should precede the program design for individual design stages. Questions like: "What data is needed, when is it needed, by which program?" should be answered. The answers will lead to a tentative data base configuration.

Design automation data can be divided into two types: design data and library data. The division is not based on a difference in logical or physical representation, but on how the data is utilized. *Library data* is utilized in a "read-only mode" by the program subsystems. The data is not changed during a design. It is accessed by pointer references, and program subsystems may copy pertinent parts of the library. Library data can also be divided into two types: data stored in the master library and data stored in the user library. The *master library* is built, maintained and updated by a group of authorized people and protected against alterations by users. Many designs may reference data of this type. It typically represents standard components, complete with their simulation models and mask geometry. The *user library* contains data entered by the user and specific for his own design, for example, a layout structure defined by the user. *Design data* is the set of data that describes the actual state of the design. This set can also be divided into two classes: design data available to all program subsystems and design data exclusively pertaining to

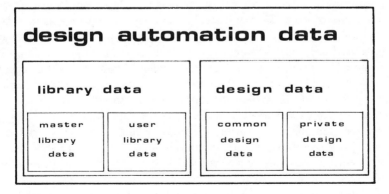

Figure 16-1. Interpretive division of data in a design automation data base.

one particular program subsystem. The two classes are called *common design data* and *private design data* respectively (Figure 16-1).

Circuit topology data is a typical example of common design data. It defines how modules—generic name for components and subsystems—are interconnected. These data are reflected in a structure known as the *potential graph* (3). It is bipartite graph in which every module is represented by a *c-vertex,* and every signal (in layout literature "every net") is represented by a *t-vertex.* An edge indicates that a module represented by the incident c-vertex, and the signal represented by the incident t-vertex, have a pin in common. For now a *pin* can be seen as merely a mechanism relating modules to signals and the reverse.

The notion of an incidence structure (4) or hypergraph (5) is apparent if the structure is introduced in the following way. With each module a set of pins is associated. The set of electrically common pins is called a signal. So, consider the first set as a point, the signals as blocks, and the pins as flags. However, only a cumbersome concept is introduced this way, without a single advantage over the formulation in terms of conventional graphs.

Every program subsystem in an automated design system will utilize the portion of the data base that represents the structure of the potential graph. However, each will replace the modules by different models. The simulator will use a functional model adequate for its level of analysis. The layout design program needs geometries of masks.

The division of design automation data into the above defined classes induces a standard data flow for the program subsystems in the system (Figure 16-2). A subsystem interacts heavily with its private data base. It is profitable that the program has direct access to this data base. So, if possible, it will reside in primary storage devices while the concerned program subsystem is active. The data in the private data base is structured according to efficiency considerations derived from the specific task of the subsystem. This is not the case for the other classes of data. For any design of considerable size they have to be on secondary storage. Program subsystems extract required data from those data bases and, if necessary, restructure it and store it into their private data bases. After appropriate decisions are taken the common data base might be updated.

Up to now, full automation of all design tasks has been unsuccessful or even impossible. Most CAD systems therefore allow extensive human intervention. In that case users should be provided with the capability of restricting and delegating read and write access to the design data base. This blurs the distinction between the user library and the design data base and raises the problem of protection against concurrent and inconsistent updates. Integration of CAD tools is to a great extent hampered by these updating and protection requirements. Additionally, capabilities to display the data in a convenient way to users should be provided.

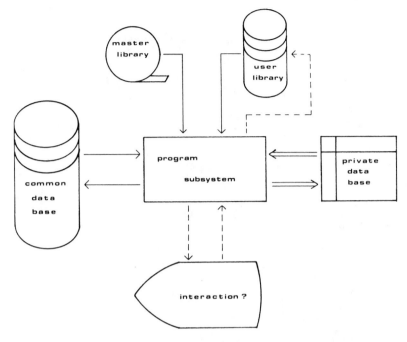

Figure 16-2. Masterplan of a data base configuration for program subsystems.

The comparison between a design system and a multi-story building has been presented at a symposium. The individual subsystems occupied a 'design' floor together with their private data base and, possibly, their interaction facilities. Communications with the common data base and the libraries, placed in the basement, were envisioned as elevators. Specification and supply could be localized on the main floor.

The symbols in the figure do not prescribe hardware; they only indicate relative accessibility.

The Design Cycle

Figure 16-3 is an oversimplification (not an idealization) of the design of an integrated circuit. Automation of the integral design leads to numerous interface problems due to the enormous quantities of design data and design constraints. It stresses the need for a well-considered common data base. The consideration for the structure of this data base is to be derived from the design decisions to be taken and the requirement of efficient and reliable storing and retrieving relevant data.

Specification answers the problem of getting design data into the data base of the automation system. Graphical means have become more and more popular, but with the increase of complexity textual forms might surpass graphical

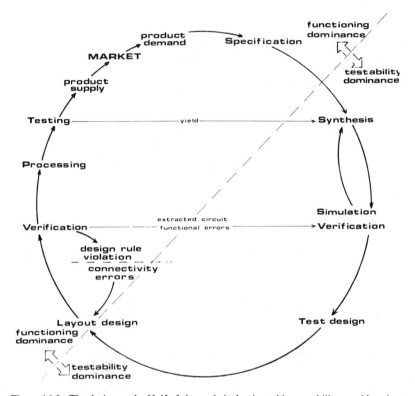

Figure 16-3. The design cycle. Half of the cycle is dominated by testability considerations.

specification in many automation activities. Attention has to be paid to the constraints forced upon the prospective user. His reluctance to use new tools has often been the insuperable problem of a CAD system.

Automatic synthesis is even not yet in its infancy. It only exists for very specific structures like PLA's. Nevertheless, the problem gets attention at some—mostly academic—places. It will certainly get more attention in the future as the problem of producing correct designs is going to dominate all other cost factors.

Single-level simulation systems have gradually found acceptance among circuit designers in the seventies, but in the same decade their inherent limits were incurred. For complex circuits, simulation at several levels is absolutely necessary, preferably simultaneously. Mixed-level simulation programs were the first answer to this need. However, more encouraging is the recent emergence of a transparent-level simulator which has a common approach to all levels while using a uniform data base (6).

When the design is functionally specified down to the lowest level and the prediction of its operation and performance is satisfactory, the physical geometries have to be developed. This task is the topic of this chapter. The state-of-the-art will be briefly described in the next section.

Actual testing is separated from the other stages of the design cycle by the fabrication of the wafer. Current philosophies concerning testing inevitably lead to the conviction that testing should conceptually be related to the earlier parts of the design cycle. 'Design with testing in mind' is the accepted apothegm reflecting this conviction. The inability to develop a test method in line with this principle made testability to the most immediate problem of complex integrated circuit design.

The major activities in test design method development have been concerned with the gate-level. Those gate-level techniques are not attractive for large scale designs. For LSI circuits it is difficult to obtain suitable specifications, and when available, fault simulation and test generation programs turn out to be very expensive, and result in excessive test application times. Trends in logical design pose additional problems for which existing techniques are not adequate. Constraining the designer by testable design rule enforcement, such as the successful level sensitive scan design approach, only delays the awareness of the fact that present-day gate-level software cannot handle the immense volume of data to be processed, often demands impracticable modeling, and has a poor adaptability to technological evolution. More future seems to be in behavioral-level testing when a top-down design approach is adopted. With this technique, testability analysis can be started at an early point in the design cycle. The volume of detail is often considerably reduced, the models are easy to prepare and to some degree independent of detailed realization, and not sensitive to technological changes. However, there is a lack of timing details. The break-through might finally be brought about by technological progress. Recently improved electron-beam techniques for the inspection of integrated circuits enhanced the observability of the design (7). Now it is possible to measure voltages at any point on the chip under test. Comparing response patterns extracted by these measurements with stored patterns of a standard model gives information about the presence of faults.

The impact of methods for increasing testability on layout design is not known. Of course, level sensitive scan design will increase the needed chip area, and the scan paths and shift lines will disturb the structure of the functional design. Layout techniques making use of such structure are degraded by these constraints, but not outdone. Electron-beam measurement might also affect the layout design stage, but probably any extra requirement can be hidden in a conventional set of design rules without forcing a mutation in the methodology.

Checking layouts by an automatic layout verification system (Figure 16-4) disencumbers people of the so-called eyeball hours, in which detailed computer-drawn plots (100 to 1000 times larger than the size of the actual circuit)

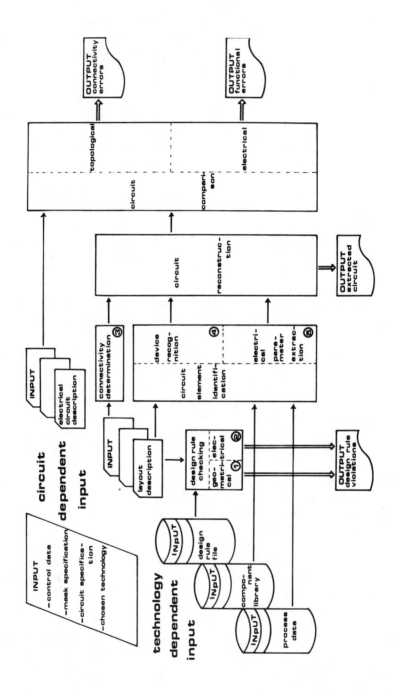

are meticulously scrutinized to check for conformance to design rules. Some of these systems also extract electrical parameters (parasitics in particular) and verify whether the circuit behavior may still be expected to correspond to the intended behavior. The most heavily used automated aid in this class is the geometrical design rule checker. It measures certain geometrical relationships and checks by comparison whether and where the design rules of the concerned technology are violated. It is an indispensable tool when the layout of complex circuits is manually or interactively designed. However, existing programs have a number of serious drawbacks. First, high average time and storage complexity. Second, many spurious errors are indicated. Third, no program is yet capable of accommodating all design rules. Besides, the performance of existing algorithms is highly dependent on a restriction to orthogonal geometries which is presently not a bad trade-off, but with the advent of regular structures such as hexagonal arrays and technologies with more than two metallization layers current verification software is outdated. The other parts of a complete verification system are still in their infancy, and for custom design almost absent. Yet, it is of utmost importance that the artwork information is correct before offering it to the production department. Two answers are promising, both avoiding layout verification. One of them is symbolic layout combined with automatic compaction techniques. The other is complete automation of the layout design task.

PRESENT STATE

Initially, many of the computer aids developed for printed circuit boards were adapted for integrated circuit layout systems. This can be seen in many present-day designs where digitizers supporting manual design and placement-routing decompositions are still prevalent. In this section, several approaches are characterized in an order of ascending degree of automation. In the second

---

Figure 16-4. IC-layout verification.
1. Geometrical design rule checkers determine conformance to layout rules such as minimum distances, tolerances, and overlap.
2. Electrical rule checkers search for illegal structures, such as crossing power lines, ground connections of individual components, cross-unders in power lines.
3. Connectivity checks trace the layout to determine which pins are connected to the same 'potential tree', to compare the result against an independent connection list.
4. Device recognition programs try to recognize components from the artwork features.
5. Electrical parameter extraction aims at determining of component parameters, load capacitances, coupling capacitances and many other parasitic elements introduced with the construction of the mask.

part of the paper some aspects of these approaches will be discussed in more detail.

Manual Design with Digitizer Support

Problems in drawing highly precise artwork completely by hand made designers pass to digitizing techniques. A digitizer is a large back-lit drawing board which is connected to a minicomputer. Coordinates of each point the designer indicates on the board, by means of a cursor or digitizing pen, can be read into the computer on command. With a plotter, artwork of the desired quality can be generated.

Often the configuration is combined with a cathode-ray-tube terminal. Beside data entry, on-line error correction is possible with such a system. However, the decision about "what goes where" is still with the designer. No particular layout style is forced upon the designer if a style-dependent checking algorithm is absent. Widely used systems in this class are CALMA and APPLICON.

Symbolic Layout Design

The earliest symbolic design systems substitute a set of symbols for the mask features. The designer manipulates these symbols while observing a few simple rules for placement on a coarse grid. Though the designer still decides, the design is considerably faster at the cost of some restrictions on the layout style. Batch programming is feasible with these computer aids (8).

With the coming of the dynamic color graphic display, symbolic layout design evolved from an aid with rather incommodious alpha-numeric characters to one of the most promising approaches. The experience and cleverness of the designer is used for developing layout topologies, since his task is only to obtain a relative placement and interconnection of symbols without detailed knowledge of design rules. An automatic program is capable of performing geometry transformation such as compaction and interconnection bending ("jogs"). The automatic program guarantees conformance to design rules which makes a design rule checker superfluous (9).

Masterslice Approach

A masterslice is a wafer processed up to the metalization layers. Each chip from such a wafer is identical as far as the kind and position of modules is concerned. Customization is only achieved through interconnection geometries. Computer aids in this approach are therefore allocation and routing programs. Full wiring completion is seldom automatically achieved and chances become very small when more than 80% of the gates on a chip are utilized.

Standard-cell

Functional cells of gate and register level are designed to conform to a common cell height and pin distribution, which often leads to non-optimal area utilization. These cells are to be placed in rows and interconnected through the intervening routing channels. The goal of placement as well as routing is to keep the channel widths as small as possible.

In principle, no human interaction is required in layout design systems based on the standard cell approach. Simple designer intervention, however, appreciably enhances the placement techniques. With up to 500 cells, standard cell programs perform very well, especially when design time dominates other cost factors such as yield, signal delay and power requirements. Its success was manifest for MOS-technology. The construction and maintenance of an up-to-date cell library has proven to be a significant overhead (10).

Array Layouts

Automatic generation of regular array structures, such as programmable regular arrays from a functional specification such as a switching function, is straightforward. To obtain high densities and small layouts, functional minimization and decomposition techniques are applied. Though layout considerations are important, they are translated into terms consistent with these techniques, and therefore they are specific for the method of functional realization.

Building Blocks

There have been several attempts to solve the layout problem stated at the beginning of this chapter completely automatically. Starting from a functional circuit specification, a layout has to be generated without any human intervention. Some of the projects with such objectives have been successfully completed, but acceptance in a production environment has not been reported. Besides, many results of these projects are of value only for some technologies.

More complex systems demand more restrictions on the shape of the modules to be placed. Most current approaches restrict the shape to rectangles. One class of these approaches is referred to as the building-block method (11). The blocks are functional units with a predesigned layout within rectangular boundaries. The interior of a block is usually very efficiently packed, and the sizes and aspect ratios, therefore, are quite varied. Placement of these blocks in a rectangular area leaves many irregularly shaped areas unutilized. Consequently, building-block approaches often yield sparse layouts. Most programs of the building-block type separate placement and routing which even more degrades the area utilization.

Other Computer Aids

Many subtasks of certain layout styles have been developed. One of the most important aids, certainly for symbolic layout, but also in many other approaches, is compaction. The intention of compaction algorithms is to squeeze layouts to reduce the amount of 'dead area'.

Wirability prediction programs have been developed for master slice layouts (12). Similar programs for other layout styles will become important in the future, because the area consumption by interconnections grows very fast with the increase of complexity. As early as possible during the design, estimation of local wiring areas is important. Since not much is known in that stage, the programs will be probabilistic in nature. As more information becomes available, the estimations have to be revised to guide placement decisions with as much information as possible.

The classical serial decomposition of the layout design task has three parts: partitioning, placement and routing. The latter two have received much attention in the literature.

Placement algorithms receive a definite treatment in (13). The first routers were mainly versions of a breadth-first search algorithm on a grid (14). They work on a one-connection-at-a-time basis. If there are solutions in a particular stage, the shortest among them will be found. However, look-ahead to avoid unnecessary blocking of future connections is difficult to implement. Later, many other grid routers were published, sometimes with quite original solutions like determining the area to be etched instead of the area to be covered by metal and amoebic movements to establish the routes. Those algorithms, however, only perform efficiently in labyrinth-like situations. For VLSI circuits, storage complexity will inhibit application. Also gridfree routers have been developed. Especially successful is the line search router (15), which is considerably faster than 'wave front routers'. However, there is no guarantee for finding a path even if it exists, but it can be modified to abolish this defect. The algorithm works with two sequences of escape points from which horizontal and vertical line probes are started. The first two points are the pins to be interconnected. When probes of different sequences intersect the search is ended, and the route is reconstructed with the line segments between the escape points.

Though the line search router is also used for LSI circuits (16), the most successful routers for complex circuits are channel routers. The problem is decomposed into independent routing problems in small rectangular areas with pins on two opposite sides. The routes consist of vertical and horizontal pieces to be realized in at least two different layers. The subtasks are reduced to easy combinatorial problems that can be rapidly solved without heavy memory requirements. The nets have to interconnect certain pins on the sides and may create points on two other sides to leave the channel area.

The first channel router (17) has been labeled as the unconstrained left-edge algorithm. The wire segments are considered to be intervals [L,R] and a partial ordering is defined over the set of intervals ($[L_1, R_1] < [L_2, R_2] \leftrightarrow R_1 < L_2$). Each actual track is subsequently filled with unplaced interval having the lowest L greater than the preceding R. If no interval satisfies those conditions, a new track is initiated until all intervals are assigned to a track. If pins are restricted to grid coordinates and contacts are never exactly opposite, the algorithm gives an optimal solution. Invalidating this condition introduces constraints on the track assignment which might be cyclic. These cycles have to be broken, for example, by manipulating pin positions. Optimal solutions have been published (18), but these branch-and bound techniques are very time-consuming. More freedom is created by allowing nets to be realized in more than one track. This led to trunkdivision and 'dogleg' algorithms (10).

STRUCTURED LAYOUT DESIGN

It has been noted before that the situation in VLSI design is to ascertain extent comparable with the software crisis of the late sixties. From this period of confusion, structured programming emerged as a systematic process for mastering complexity. It is therefore expedient to examine the principles of structured programming and evaluate their relevance to layout design. The results of such an examination are interwoven in the following discussion.

THE INEVITABLE HIERARCHY

There is a conjecture that complex systems evolve far more quickly if they are of hierarchic nature than non-hierarchic systems of comparable size, and that aspects of complex systems that are not hierarchic even elude human understanding and observation. Both in nature and in science many instances support this conjecture (19). VLSI systems will be just new examples of systems exhibiting hierarchic structure whether they evolve from stable intermediate forms (e.g. a single-chip microcomputer which combines a number of functions that previously occupied separate chips) or by a practicable design discipline (still to be developed, but certainly top-down organized).

A hierarchic system or *hierarchy* is a system composed of interrelated subsystems, each of the latter being hierarchic in structure, until some lowest level of elementary subsystems is reached. The systems in a hierarchy are called *modules*. A hierarchy can be represented by a directed tree. Each vertex in this tree represents a module. An arrow points from a module to its direct subsystems *(submodules)*. The incoming arrow of a module refers to its unique *supermodule*. The root represents the whole system. The elementary subsystems are represented by the leaves of the tree. In several approaches to layout design the submodules of the whole system play a distinct role. In order to aid memory when this set of modules recurs, these modules are related to the rather eccentric Figure 16-5 by naming them *cardinal modules.* The set of cardinal modules covers the whole system. None of the other layers in the hierarchy must have this property.

The hierarchy to be expected in VLSI systems is a functional hierarchy. The modules in this hierarchy realize partial functions of the system. These functions again are specified in terms of partial functions to be performed by lower modules except for the elementary modules. Thus, two kinds of modules are distinguished on the basis of this hierarchy: *cells,* units that are not divided into submodules, and *compounds,* units composed of submodules. Cells are the only technology dependent units of the system as far as their realization on the chip is concerned. The layout of certain cells is stored in a library, because of their frequent appearance. The layout of a cell may also be defined by the user. For both kinds of cells, *master cells* and *user cells* respectively, the layout is to be fetched intact from the place where it is stored, and inserted into the layout of a system. They are called *inset cells* to set them apart from *blank cells* of which the layout is to be determined by special technology dependent algorithms.

The functional hierarchy is to be supplied by the design system or by the designer. In the latter case the designer is constrained to make the inherent hierarchy explicit. Everybody in computer aided design knows how difficult it is to manage the introduction of a system with new constraints on the designer. When a complete system is delivered by the designer without an explicit hierarchy, it has to be partitioned on the basis of what seem to be reasonable criteria.

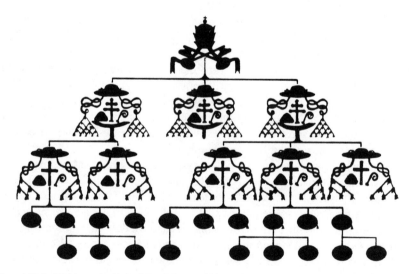

Figure 16-5. The etymological origin of the word hierarchy as an aid to memory when the notion 'cardinal modules' turns up.

Partitioning is one of the classical problems in the physical realization of a system and it never was satisfactorily solved for systems for which it is needed most, namely large scale systems. When the system is complex, partitioning is a very complex task. The problems start with the selection of the criteria. The most important consideration in decomposing a design is high block independence. Partitioning should therefore be organized in such a way that the relationships among blocks are minimized and the relationships among the elements of an individual block are maximized. In other words blocks should have a high internal strength and a low mutual coupling. The classical measure of block dependence in layout design is connectivity. It suffices for an after-the-fact judgement of the partitioning result. What is needed, however, is a guideline for producing an acceptable solution.

A partitioning method in use for building block approaches is min-cut placement (20). The acceptance can be explained by the principle of deferring detailed considerations as long as possible and the combination of partitioning and global placement. For each step, a set of modules is partitioned into two blocks such that the number of signals common to both blocks is minimal. For this partitioning, a modification of the Kernighan-Lin-algorithm (21) is applied. This algorithm starts from an initial two-block partition, and improves this partition by interchanging the pair of elements which reduces the number of common signals most. This is repeated until all elements of one block have been involved in an interchange. The best intermediate result is taken. This gives a new two-block partition with which the procedure can be repeated. Possible modifications are concerned with excluding elements from the interchange operations, and taking module areas into account.

The Structural Restraint

In structured programming there exists the discipline to restrict control flow constructs to the Jacopini-structures (22). These structures are theoretically sufficient and ensure a straightforward mapping between the computational process and the program evoking it (23). Is there a similar rule concerning the structure of layouts which is as beneficial to layout design as the structuring principle is to programming? In the past many restrictions have been proposed with different degrees of success. Building blocks, standard cell, and bristle blocks are famed examples.

In the building blocks approach, the only restriction is that the structure consists of abutting rectangles. These rectangles must give room to a given set of layout problems with fixed shape. This problem has been translated to several mathematical models in order to apply known solution techniques. These translations mostly use a certain digraph representation of dissected rectangles (24). The name polar graph for these diagrams has found acceptance in layout design literature.

A *polar graph* is an acyclic diagraph with exactly one source and one sink which has a plane representation with the source and the sink on the same face boundary.

A rectangle partitioned into subrectangles, called a *rectangle dissection,* consists of two sets of parallel line segments, H and V. Any segment in H is perpendicular to any segment in V. To construct a polar graph associated with a rectangle dissection take either H or V as the set of vertices and connect two vertices if the corresponding segments contain sides of the same subrectangle. So, there is a one-one correspondence between subrectangles and arcs. The direction of the arcs must be consistent with position of the corresponding rectangle relative to the line segment (Figure 16-6).

Four, generally different, polar graphs are associated with each rectangle dissection. When taking H as the set of vertices, the polar graphs are the same except for a reversal of all arc orientations. The same holds when case V is taken. The polar graphs with H-vertices are said to be the dual of the polar graphs with V-vertices.

When length and width of the subrectangles are assigned to the corresponding arcs, a polar graph contains the same information as the rectangle dissection. These lengths and widths satisfy the Kirchhoff laws of network theory. This observation is the key to many applications of this model in layout design. By formulating all other constraints as linear inequalities, the Kirchhoff equations and these inequalities form the simplex-tableau for minimizing the perimeter of the chip as a good approximation when the chip is kept from becoming very oblong (3).

The modules to be placed have different, but fixed rectangular shapes, and

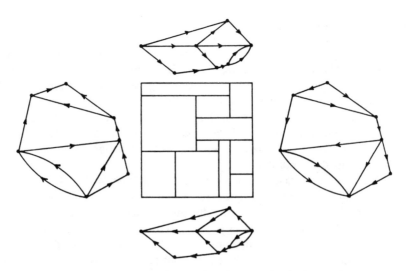

Figure 16-6. A partitioned rectangle and its associated polar graphs.

if there is a method to obtain a suitable polar graph, the problem of minimizing the chip area can be formulated as a mixed-integer 0-1 linear optimization problem (25). In the CALCOS system this formulation has been applied to LSI layout, where the polar graph is obtained by a min-cut technique with alternately horizontal and vertical lines (16).

In the layout style called *standard cell* or *polycell,* the majority of the design rules are hidden in cells stored in the cell library. The cells have a rectangular outline. Two opposite sides of each cell have to be consistent with very strict rules: the same length and fixed pin positions for the nets common to all cells. By locating a cell alongside any other cell the corresponding pins are automatically interconnected. By arranging cells in parallel rows, straight power, ground and clock lines are thus realized in each row. All other pins of a cell have to be located at the other sides. If both sides are used, cells are placed in single rows. If only one side contains individual pins, cells are placed 'back-to-back' in double rows. Between the rows there are domains not occupied by cells. These domains are called *street channels.* By the arrangement of cells in rows as described, all pins except those belonging to the common lines are facing a channel. These channels are used for realizing interconnections between pins. A net connecting pins at various locations may lie entirely within a single channel or interconnect more than one channel. *Avenue channels* perpendicular to the ones intervening the cell rows mostly contain the interconnections between the channels and between the common lines of each row. In order to avoid long interconnections, *feed-through cells* are sometimes employed.

The actual layout stages of a standard cell design (10) are:

1. Partitioning of the cells into rows by a crude global clustering algorithm or by a two dimensional placement, consisting of a candidate cell selection on connectivity basis, an initial placement trying to minimize the total net length, and an iterative exchanging of cells to improve the placement taking into account net length, row capacity, etc.
2. Determining the sequence of cells within a row. The sequence of the cells influences the net length and the density of the channel. The local density of a channel is the number of interconnections that have to intersect the cross-section perpendicular to the cell rows at that spot. The *channel density* is the maximum value attained by the local density anywhere along the channel. From the channel density, a lower bound on the channel width required to contain the associated interconnections can be derived. The major task of this stage and the next one is to minimize the necessary channel width.
3. Placement of the cells within a row. This is a rather straightforward task when the sequence of cells is known. However, the freedom left can be used to facilitate the tasks in the later stages of the design, in particular solving pin position conflicts.

4. Net decomposition and assignment of subnets to channels. Nets with pins in more than one channel have to be decomposed in order to route the channels one by one. Besides subnets in the channels containing the concerned pins, interconnections between these subnets have to be made. The avenue channels can be used if *street pin-outs* are created. In order to avoid very long interconnections, interchannel feed-throughs often can be established either by using electrically equivalent pins on opposite sides of a cell or by inserting feed-through cells into a row.

5. Analysis of pin positions. By fixing the positions and orientations of the cells, and thus the pin positions along the street channels *latitudinal constraints* are introduced when two nets enter the channel from opposite sides in the same interconnection layer and at exactly or almost the same logitudinal coordinate. If longitudinal parts of a net are to be realized by only one straight *trunk,* cyclic constraints on the position of trunks may occur. Some conflict situations can be eliminated by adjusting pin positions. If not all constraint cycles can be broken, the remaining problems must be solved by the router by slackening the straight trunk requirement ('trunkdivision', 'doglegging').

6. Routing of the street channels. For each channel, pin positions on both sides are known, and a net list is available. the *net list* contains the nets. A *net* is a set of pins that must be interconnected. Some nets may also have a street pin-out at one or both ends of the channel. The number of interconnection layers and the clearances are imposed by the technology. In order to simplify the router task, the routing on a particular level mostly occurs in only one direction, either longitudinal or latitudinal. Under these constraints the router has to route all of the nets successsully in the minimum possible area.

7. Routing of the avenue channels. After the routing of the street channels, the position of the street pin-outs is known. Since the position of the other pins on the sides of an avenue channel were predetermined, all relevant pin positions are known. The net list is also available, thus the routing of the avenue channels can be performed by the same algorithm as the routing of the street channels.

Standard cell (Figure 16-7) is the most successful layout design automation of the seventies. It is capable of always achieving a layout with all connections completed and all local design rules obeyed, but it also allows a high degree of user control. The success of the method probably can be explained by its hiding of all design rules in the predefined cells except the clearances of the wiring. Thus it reduces the design task to one optimization: minimize the width of the individual channels.

The bristle blocks system (Figure 16-8) imposes a generic layout scheme at the cost of a restriction to processor chips with communication across data-

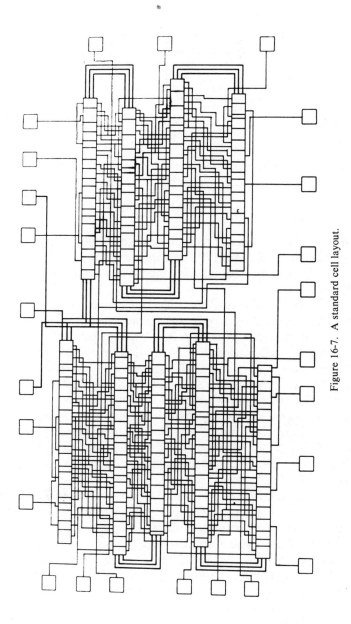

Figure 16-7. A standard cell layout.

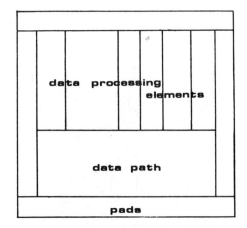

Figure 16-8. The format of a bristle block chip.

busses. For this limited class of circuits, however, the system rapidly delivers a compact layout. The cells in the library have a certain flexibility that allows 'pitch matching' for simlifying interconnections between the data processing elements (26).

Building blocks, standard cell, bristle blocks and many other standard form layout methods share the rectangular shape requirement, and there is no evidence that it was the limiting factor for the complexity the method can handle. Allowing arbitrary cell boundaries will certainly complicate layout design. Beside the rectangular form of the cells, another well-structuring principle is expedient as can be learned from careful examination of existing layout styles. This principle only allows layout structures which can be obtained by an operation called *slicing.* A single application of this operation divides a rectangle into smaller rectangles by parallel lines. The operation can be applied to each of the resulting rectangles, *slices,* but with lines perpendicular to the preceding set of dividing lines. Slicing can be repeated to any depth, alternating the orientation of the dividing lines.

Slicing configurations can be represented by a rooted tree (Figure 16-9). To describe this tree, the genealogical terminology is adopted. The whole rectangle is represented by the common ancestor. Each slicing corresponds with a parent and his children. These children are ordered according to the relative position of the associated subslices. Leaves represent slices to which no further slicing is applied. The structure tree represents the *genealogy* of the structure. Topologically a slicing structure is fixed by its genealogy. However, absolute coordinates may be generated later.

That the slicing concept yields a simple data structure is not surprising after the introduction of the genealogy tree. The genealogy tree is an ordered tree and consequently it naturally corresponds with a binary tree. In order to facilitate the traversal of the tree in both directions, references to parents should

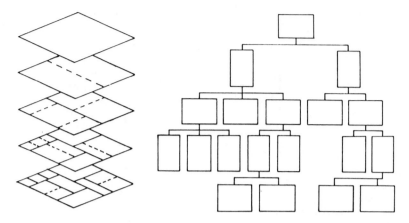

Figure 16-9. Slicing levels.

be added. This leads to a triply linked tree where each vertex has, beside a pointer to the data of the corresponding slice, a pointer to its primogenitive, a pointer to the next sibling, and a pointer to its parent.

Another principle of structured programming is that a clear notation should support the logical design. Graphical representations have always been considered to be the apt form of communicating layout data. For VLSI systems, textual forms are expected to be more efficient (27). A layout structure satisfying the slicing principle has a natural textual form, using a kind of block structure known in some programming languages (Figure 16-10).

Both a sliced layout and a hierarchic system can be represented by rooted trees. It is tempting to identify the genealogy tree of the layout structure with the hierarchy tree of a given functional hierarchy. However, this will most likely result in a structure clash, because the functional hierarchy is not primarily based on layout considerations such as area, deformation, position, orientation, and ease of wiring. Only functional strength and connectivity are often correlated. Yet it is the functional hierarchy which is most easily supplied by the designer. So it seems to be expedient to accept the functional hierarchy as a starting point, and to modify the ensuing decomposition on the basis of criteria more directly related to layout. This modified decomposition should be suitable to be mapped onto a slicing configuration. This mapping will assign a slice to each module in the hierarchy. Slices, however, will be assigned to groups of modules that do not constitute a supermodule in the given hierarchy. In order to obtain uniformity in treatment and description, the class of compounds is extended by considering these groups as modules. These newly formed modules are called *program compounds*. The compounds that are present in the functional hierarchy are called *user compounds*. By this extension a one-to-one correspondence between slices and modules is established.

Although slicing has some clear-cut advantages (not yet all mentioned), the

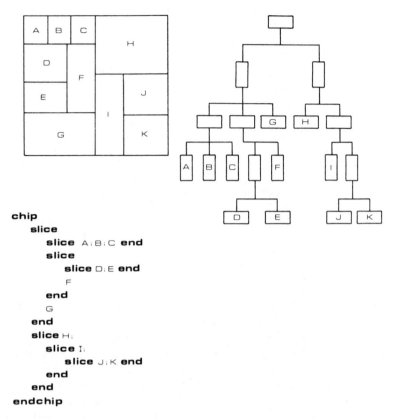

```
chip
    slice
        slice A;B;C end
        slice
            slice D;E end
            F
        end
        G
    end
    slice H;
        slice I;
            slice J;K end
        end
    end
endchip
```

Figure 16-10. A slicing configuration, its structure tree and its textual form.

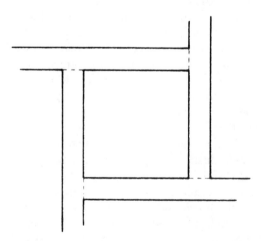

Figure 16-11. A configuration essentially excluded by the slicing principle.

question about the price paid for giving up the generality of building blocks must be answered. The answer is twofold. First, the restriction imposed by the slicing principle is not very detrimental. Most manual designs are compatible with slicing, and some trials will readily show the range of the concept. Second, there are no cycles in the precedence constraints for the wiring areas as there generally are in building blocks (28). Moreover, in slicing structures, at least one set of permissible sequences can be characterized by one simple condition: the wiring areas of a slice must be routed after the wiring areas of its child slices has been routed. It is easy to prove that dissection rectangles satisfy the slicing principle if their polar graphs are series-parallel graphs.

Wiring space management

Even a glimpse at a number of chips of different complexity reveals the problem of the wiring space inflation. A lower bound on the wiring space is the total interconnect length times a constant imposed by technology (minimum line width + minimum spacing). It has been experimentally established that the total interconnect length is growing exponentially with the number of devices (29). Progress in technology cannot overcome this effect. Of course, more interconnection layers, tricks for distributing the supply voltage, flashing the clock signal onto the chip with light, and such amendments will only partially offset the problem. Only a new design methodology can change the tendency. In many logic designs, for example, complex functions can be implemented in very regular patterns. In that case the increase in space required for interconnection and logic is kept close to linear.

Outside the regular patterns, the wiring is an extra area consumer and should be treated as such. For that reason, a new class of modules can be created. Their place is in between any pair of slices. Since they are not to be decomposed into submodules, they form a subset of the class of cells. To distinguish between the cells already present in the hierarchy and the newly created cells, they are called *function cells* and *junction cells* respectively. This completes the classification of modules (Figure 16-12).

For each module, area has to be reserved. However, it is impossible to assess the wiring space before any information concerning the placement of modules is available. Topological data, such as a genealogy, makes area prediction feasible. As more information becomes available, the estimates have to be revised.

Stochastic models for estimating wiring demand did not get much attention in literature. For master-slice circuits, a probabilistic model for wiring has been developed in order to predict wirability (12). That approach is not suited for estimating the local wiring demand in a slicing configuration in an early stage of the design. An attempt to model interconnections in custom integrated circuits has been published (30). It starts from a building block configuration. The rectangle partitioned into rectangles is viewed as a planar representation

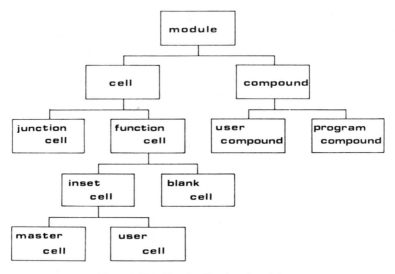

Figure 16-12. The classification of modules.

of the *channel graph*. It is assumed that pins are distributed over the edges of the graph according to a Poisson function, that interconnection paths are minimum distance paths along the edges of the channel graph while choosing between feasible minimum distance paths occurs with equal probability, and that interconnections have random lengths with an exponential distribution. Under these assumptions, the local and maximum density on an edge of the channel graph can be estimated.

The occupation of junction cells by interconnections must be carefully controlled, to check the disproportionate growth of the wiring space. Two guidelines, both having a parallel in programming, are gainful in this respect.

The first one can be compared with the desirability of scope minimization in programming (31). Its translation into the layout environment is something like "keep wires as local as possible". The scope of a net can be reflected in the textual form suggested a few paragraphs earlier.

> **slice external:** $<$ list of inherited nets $>$
> **internal:** $<$ list of local nets $>$
> $<$ slice body $>$
> **end**

The pins interconnected by a certain net belong to function cells. The minimal subtree of the genealogy containing these function cells has as its vertices 'slices' with the concerned net in their lists. Only the common ancestor has the net declared as internal. Outside this minimal subtree, only junction cells might contain a part of that net (Figure 16-13).

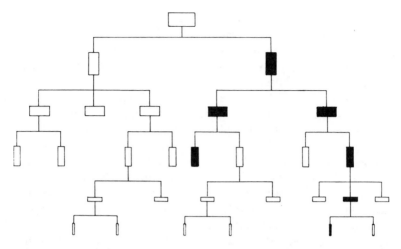

Figure 16-13. Apart from junction cells, only slices in the minimal subtree of the concerned function cells are involved. However, even the junction cell of the common ancestor might contain the net.

The other area-saving principle is pitch-matching. It consists of adjusting the pin position such that the interconnections can be made by crossing the channel without using a track (Figure 16-14). In programming, it is comparable with reducing the interface complexity by using a suitable data structure common to the blocks.

THE FLEXIBILITY IMPERATIVE

The development of a structured program is a sequence of refinement steps that terminates when all instruction are expressed in terms of the concerned programming language (32). The whole point of programming by stepwise refinement can also be seen as delaying design decisions. This avoids committing the design prematurely to specific implementation ideas and increases the ease with which modifications can subsequently be made.

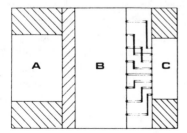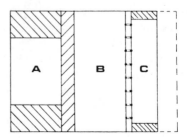

Figure 16-14. Stretching sometimes reduces the total area of its parent slice.

This postponement of design decisions is also of fundamental importance in layout design. Premature decisions lead to inefficient use of silicon area. Layout systems based on the building blocks approach manipulate rigid boxes and always end with a very low layout density, because of this a priori decision on the shapes of the modules.

The layout of a module may be realized in differently shaped areas if only the cells covered by the module and their mutual interconnections are accommodated. Of course, not all modules have the same degree of flexibility. Inset cells, for example, have fixed shapes. A layout system can only assign position and orientation to them. At the other extreme, large portions of random logic have a lot of freedom as far as their circumscription is concerned. This flexibility must be used by a layout system to compensate for differences in wiring space estimation, to allow for cell stretching in order to adjust the pin positions, and to obtain high packing densities.

In this respect, layout design can be regarded as a gradual stiffening of modules, in which the modules get shape, position, orientation and pin positions. The moments of the stiffening step depend on the kind of module.

Although flexibility of modules has to be enforced, preferable shapes also exist for modules with a high degree of flexibility. Deviations from these favored shapes can be measured in order to steer the stiffening process. The steering parameters or *deformations* are measured with formulas that depend on the type of the module. Inset cells have to fit in the assigned domains. If not, high deformations have to result. Other modules, with high flexibility, should have lower penalties for deformation. Square shapes are preferable for these modules. Adjustments to modules requiring big areas affect the final result stronger than modules with low area consumption. This should also be expressed in the deformation value.

GENERALITY DESIRABLE

Developing layout design software is a costly affair. Considering the existing variety in technological processes and the rapid changes in fabrication methods, the need for largely general approaches becomes apparent. Sooner or later, however, the differences between the various sets of design rules will take their toll. Whether it is possible to keep the divergence concentrated in small parts of the program is an open question. The leaves of the genealogy tree, i.e. the cells of the system, are of course most heavily dependent on technology. Particularly the blank cells have to be filled by technology dependent algorithms. Though the complexity of the concerned problems is quite low, one may still ask which algorithms have to be used. For neither an established theory for automatic layout design nor a set of approved algorithms is available. The main reason is that for this scale of problems, manual and interactive methods were preferred.

The most successful approach with a considerable degree of automation is the standard cell technique. As a first step towards more general layout methods, one may ask whether other technologies allow for layout design along similar lines. Although the number of interconnection layers was expected to be the most stringent condition, a program similar to standard cell has been implemented for a single-layer technology (33). Beside the potential graph, the algorithms in that program work upon a two dimensional *array of boxes* ('rectangular grid'). A *box* stands for a square unit-surface. The size of such a box depends on the components of the concerned circuit. It must be chosen such that each component can be efficiently fit in a number of these boxes. This number is called the *component size*. Boxes are arranged in rows and columns. Boxes in the first and the last columns and rows form the *border* of the array. Boxes are *adjacent* if they have a side in common.

To emphasize the parallelism, the decomposition is kept similar to the one of standard cell systems given earlier in the structural restraint section.

1. Partitioning of components in c-levels. Because of its bipartiteness, the vertices of the potential graph can be partitioned such that no block in that partition contains c-vertices as well as t-vertices. Edges connect only vertices of different blocks in such a partition. Some of these partitions have the property that blocks have one-edge-connections to at most two blocks. Assuming that the graph is connected and that at least one block does not have one-edge connections to two different blocks, it is possible to order the blocks linearly such that only pairs of consecutive blocks have edges between each other. In that case, the blocks are called *levels* and they are ordered by *level numbers*. A partitioning into levels is easily obtained: select any subset consisting either of c-vertices or of t-vertices for the first block; each next block consists of the vertices not yet selected and connected by one edge to an already established block. This way of obtaining levels is often too rigid to be practical. Replacement of an edge by a chain of edges with *pseudo-c-vertices* and extra t-vertices is allowed if the bipartiteness of the graph is preserved. These extensions and the choice of the first block can be used to get bonding pads in the chip border and to control the *c-level-claims,* i.e the minimal area required to contain all components represented in the concerned level. Level claims are also measured in the number of boxes. For reasons to be explained, level claims have to be odd, but apart from that not greater than necessary. Accordingly, the level claim for a certain level is obtained by summing up the component sizes of all c-vertices in that level, and in case the result is even, increasing it by one. The extra box is the size of an extra c-vertex called the *parity vertex*. In order to determine the number of rows and columns, the level claims are added together. The result is a lower bound on the number of boxes. In determining the array dimensions several

rules are taken into account: small chip area, restrictions on length-width ratio and others. Furthermore, the number of columns have to be even and less than the level claim of all levels except the first one and the last one. Together with the oddness of the level claims, the last requirement facilitates the placement procedure without appreciably affecting the quality of the layout.

2. Ordering of the c-vertices within a level. This ordering may be established

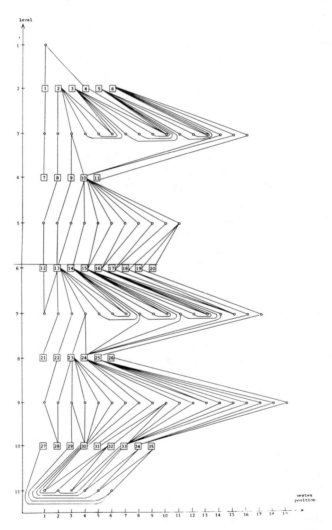

Figure 16-15. The level representation of a planarized potential graph. Vertex positions and level numbers are chosen to be consecutive integers.

under different criteria such as short total interconnection length, small number of crossings, and narrow wiring channels. If only one interconnection layer is available, a planarization process is required. A suitable planarization algorithm is the "cascade method," (3) since it produces simultaneously an ordering of the vertices in the levels. The obtained orderings are recorded by *vertex positions.* In order to facilitate the discussion, the *level representation of a graph* (LRG) has been introduced. The vertex position—if assigned—and the level number are considered as an abscissa and an ordinate respectively. Edges are represented by curves between the points assigned to its vertices by their vertex positions and level numbers. If the graph has been planarized these curves must be disjoint. Parity vertices obtain a greater vertex position than any other vertex in the level.

3. Placement of the components. The task of the placement algorithm is to establish a relation between the c-vertices and the array of boxes. On the basis of the graph, the level number, the vertex positions and the component sizes, strips of boxes will be assigned to c-levels and connected sets of boxes in these strips will be assigned to c-vertices.

Strip assignment: A strip is a set of lexicographically consecutive boxes. They have exactly as many boxes as the respective level claim requires. Provided that components with sizes greater than two have flexible geometry, every component can be represented in the strip of its level by a connected set of boxes having the correct size. If the strips are ordered according to the associated level numbers, the strip assignment must be such that the lexicographical ordering of the boxes is a refinement of the strip ordering. This method of assigning strips causes interconnections to be needed only between components in the same or in successive strips. Only pseudo-c-vertices make interconnections between non-adjacent strips possible.

Box assignment: In order to preserve the ordering of c-vertices in their levels, boxes in a strip are ordered columnwise, traversing the columns alternately up and down. In case the level number is odd, the first column is traversed top-down; if the level number is even, the first column is traversed bottom-up. Thus the ordering of c-vertices in the levels is reflected in the placement of components in a strip. Since the level claims—except possibly the first and the last one—are greater than the number of columns, components represented by c-vertices with the extreme vertex positions of the level are placed in the border of the array. If the level claims of the extreme levels are less than or equal to the number of columns, all the c-vertices of these levels are assigned to border boxes. Because of the odd-and-even conditions, a connected set of boxes (a *component domain*) is assigned to each component. The truth of this assertion is immediately clear after observing that possible jumps in the horizontal strip boundaries occur alternately after an odd and an even numbered column. As a result of this procedure, the c-level is supplied with the required number of boxes folded up to fit in the width of the array. The component domains of a c-level thus obtain a meanderlike structure (Figure 16-16).

4. Determination of the downsets and upsets. The corresponding step in standard cell methods, net decomposition, is considerably more complex than this step, because much of the work has been done already in generating an LRG. The procedure follows from the definitions. The *downset*

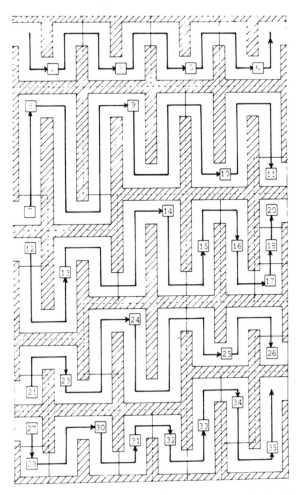

Figure 16-16. Assignment of component domains to the components. The shaded areas have no other function than emphasizing the meander which is obtained by folding the c-level. The arrows indicate the ordering of the boxes in the strips.

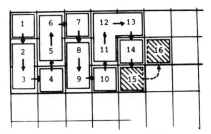

Figure 16-17. If the odd-and-even conditions are not observed, components might get domains which are not connected.

of a c-vertex is the set of t-vertices in a level with a lower number and connected with that c-vertex via an edge. The t-vertices in a higher level that are connected with a c-vertex via an edge make its *upset*.

5. Transet analysis. Let us consider a homeomorphic mapping from the plane in which the LRG is onto the plane of the array of boxes which maps the LRG within the boundary of the array and the c-vertices on points in the associated components domains. The images of c-vertices in adjacent component domains are thought to be connected with the boundary by the shortest possible line segments. The images of these line segments under the inverse of the mentioned homeomorphic mapping are called *transcurves*. With each pair of c-vertices having a claim to interconnection by a transcurve and with each c-vertex demanding a connecting transcurve to the image of the array boundary, a so-called transet is associated. A *transet* is defined as the set of t-vertices of which the t-stars (a *t-star* is a t-vertex with its incident edges) have to intersect the concerned transcurve irrespective of the chosen mapping. Three kinds of transets are distinguished. *Insets* are transets associated with c-vertices of the same level. *Intersets* belong to c-vertices from different levels. *Exsets* are transets involving the array boundary. Transets can be easily derived from the LRG. The whole procedure determining the transets comes to forming two subsets of the concerned c-levels and examining the t-vertices of the concerned t-level on having edges to vertices of both subsets (Figure 16-18). To enhance uniformity in the procedures to follow, downsets and upsets are also called transets. In the single layer case, all these sets must be ordered. The ordering is automatically obtained by a systematical search for the elements of these sets. The system must be based on the sequence in which edges leave c-levels.

6. Routing of the horizontal channels. Wiring is restricted to *channels* between strips and some folds of the meanders. Only pseudo-c-vertices make deviations from this rule possible. *Horizontal channels* strictly follow the dividing line between the strips which will be their centerlines.

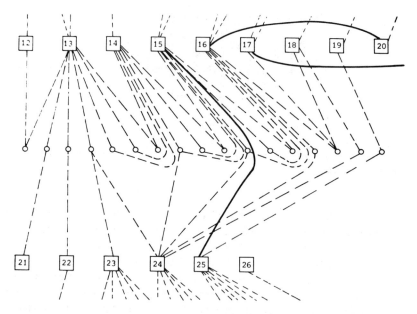

Figure 16-18. Three transcurves (full lines) are shown. Notice that the t-stars that are intersected by these transcurves cannot be avoided. These transcurves give rise to three different kinds of transets: the inset (16,20), the interset (15,25) and the exset (17). The subsets which have to be examined are (17, 18, 19) and (12, 13, 14, 15) for the inset (16,20) (16, 17, 18, 19, 20, 26) and (24, 23, 22, 21, 12, 13, 14) for the interset (15,25) and (18, 29, 20) and (12, 13, 14, 15, 16) for the exset (17).

They extend from border to border without any break. In the formation of the channel, transets play a crucial role, because of the relation between their cardinality and the required channel capacity. If the transets are ordered sets—as for example in the single layer case—there is also a direct relation between these orderings and the sequence in which the interconnections are entering the channel and the relative positions of the wires in the channel. The consequence of being able to determine the required channel capacity and the pin sequence a priori is that one is no longer dependent on pathfinding algorithms liable to fail completion because of mutual blocking. Having found the pin sequence by juxtaposition of the respective transets, coordinates have to be assigned to the pins in accordance with that sequence. In absence of a more specific rule, one may uniformly distribute the pins over channel segments reserved for connections leaving the contiguous component domain (upsets or downsets) or for connections entering the channel between two adjacent components domains (insets). Often there are specific rules, for example, imposed by the layout of the individual components or necessary to avoid loop constraints. Anyway, the relevant information for the router is a set of longitudinal *pin coordinates*, a specification of the pin position relative to the channel, and the t-vertex involved. The procedure for tracing the interconnections loosely adapts the idea of Lass' aperture (34). Here an *aperture* is a channel segment between two consecutive pin coordinates. The procedure completes all parts of interconnection nets that will fall into the range of the actual aperture before stepping to the next pin coordinate. The ordered sets of nets entering the rear side and exiting the front side are called the *old* and the *new buffer* respectively. Each net in the old buffer corresponds with a single point at the rear side of the aperture. The points in question are called *potential points*. They are distributed over the channel width. To each net in the new buffer, a potential point at the front side is assigned. Potential points are the terminal points of interconnection segments to be completed within the aperture. If the same net is contained in both buffers, the corresponding potential points will be connected. It is important to notice that the new buffer can be easily obtained from the old one, since differences are restricted to the outmost nets due to the entering or the termination of nets in the channel. New buffers are formed by duplicating the nets which have to be extended and by prefixing or postfixing eventual new nets. The procedure for assigning strips (stage 3) allows for one jump in a horizontal channel. Such a jump dose not cause serious difficulties. The channel is divided into parts by a 45° cut at the place of a jump and one part is shifted over one grid unit. Corresponding nets are connected by vertical paths.

7. Routing of the vertical channels. Apart from some slight divergences, vertical channels are formed in the same way as horizontal channels. They follow the vertical grid lines of the array. When they meet a horizontal channel, all the nets of the vertical channel are terminated (the new buffer does not become an old one). At the other side, nets have to be entered to form an old buffer from which the channel formation is continued.

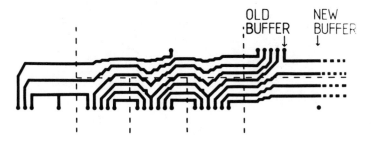

Figure 16-19. Formation of a channel.

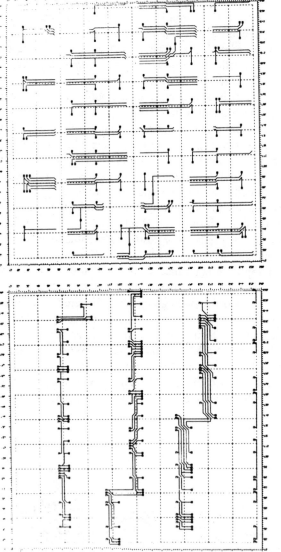

Figure 16-20. Results of the two routing phases.

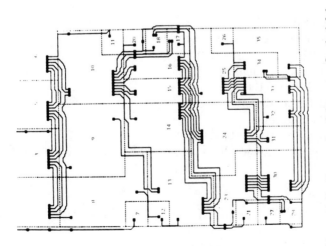

Figure 16-21. Two results of the router. On the left hand side is the completion of the example used throughout the description of the program. On the right hand side is the combination of the two results of figure 16-20.

THE GENEALOGICAL APPROACH

In the Automatic System Design Group of the Eindhoven University of Technology, a project has been initiated to implement a system conformal to the imperatives of structured layout design. The first results were published in 1980 (35). The operating principles of this system, called SAGA, will be presented in this part of the chapter.

OUTLINE OF THE SAGA SYSTEM

The core of the SAGA can be divided into three successive parts that can be distinguished mainly on the basis of the way they treat the structure tree. The last part does not affect the structure tree, the first two parts do extend the structure tree, but in an entirely different manner. The three parts are called GENEALOGIZE, PROCREATE, and INTERRELATE, because of an analogy with composing a saga (Figure 16-22).

In the other sections the main lines of the system are sketched. The position of individual procedures is here indicated in an informal program description.

SAGA (hierarchy, {module characterization})
   procedure INSETFIT (slice)
      begin for each 'child' inset cell do assign predescribed dimensions; adjust slice width to widest child slice; fit other slices with minimum overall disturbance
     end
   procedure PERMUTE (slice)
      order child slices to reduce the width to be expected:
   procedure REFLECT (inset cell)
      find optimal orientation;
   procedure IMPROVE (slice)
     begin INSETFIT
      for child slices do
        begin PERMUTE (child slice)
          for each 'grandchild' inset cell do REFLECT ('grandchild' inset cell)
     end
     PERMUTE (slice)
     for each 'child' inset cell do REFLECT ('child' inset cell)
     end
   procedure DATASCRAPE (structure)
      collect as much information as possible (pin positions of the inset cells

("FETCH"), assign net to the junction cells, assign sets of pins to slice sides, call a "FILL" routine with correct technology and style dependent features to establish the layout of the blank cells);

procedure EXPAND (structure, {modules})
    expand structure with a slice;

procedure MERGE (user compound)
    minimize deformation by merging child slices into program compounds;

procedure ROUTER (junction cell, technology, style)
    determine the contents by the appropriate algorithm;

procedure ASSEMBLE (slice)
  begin compact;
    determine relative coordinates of child slices
  end

procedure GENEALOGIZE ({modules})
  begin select a germ module;
    assign a slice to the germ module;
    structure: = assigned slice;
  while structure expansible do
    begin EXPAND (structure, {unplaced cardinal modules});
      IMPROVE (new slice)
    end
    DATASCRAPE (structure)
  end

procedure PROCREATE (structure tree, {user compounds})
  begin while user compound leaves exist do
    begin take a user compound
      represented by a leaf;
      MERGE (user compound);
      IMPROVE (new slice);
      DATASCRAPE (new slice)
    end
  end

procedure INTERRELATE (structure tree)
  begin while common ancestor not visited do
    begin select a node with all children
      except junction cells processed;
      for each 'child' junction cell of
        the associated slice do
      ROUTER ('child' junction cell);
      ASSEMBLE (associated slice)
    end
  end

a)   Giuliano (1453-1478)

b)

Piero il Gottoso
(1418-1469)

Lorenzo il Magnifico   Giuliano
(1449-1492)   (1453-1478)

Pietro lo   Giovanni   Giuliano
Sfortunato   (Leo X)   of Nemours
(1471-1503)   (1475-1521)   (1478-1516)

c)

Cosimo, Pater Patriae (1389-1464)

Piero il Gottoso   Giovanni
(1418-1469)   (1421-1463)

Lorenzo il Magnifico   Giuliano
(1449-1492)   (1453-1478)

Pietro lo   Giovanni   Giuliano
Sfortunato   (Leo X)   of Nemours
(1471-1503)   (1475-1521)   (1478-1516)

d)

Giovanni di Bicci de'Medici
(1360-1429)

Cosimo, Pater Patriae   Lorenzo
(1389-1464)   (1394-1440)

Piero il Gottoso   Giovanni   Pierfrancesco
(1418-1469)   (1421-1463)   (1431-1477)

Lorenzo il Magnifico   Giuliano
(1449-1492)   (1453-1478)

Pietro lo   Giovanni   Giuliano
Sfortunato   (Leo X)   of Nemours
(1471-1503)   (1475-1521)   (1478-1516)

e)

Giovanni di Bicci de'Medici
(1360-1429)

Cosimo, Pater Patriae   Lorenzo
(1389-1464)   (1394-1440)

Piero il Gottoso   Giovanni   Pierfrancesco
(1418-1469)   (1421-1463)   (1431-1477)

Lorenzo   Giuliano   Lorenzo   Giovanni
il Magnifico   (1453-1478)   il Popolano   il Popolano
(1449-1492)   (1463-1503)   (1467-1498)

Pietro lo   Giovanni   Giuliano   Pierfrancesco   Averardo   Vincenzo
Sfortunato   (Leo X)   of Nemours
(1471-1503)   (1475-1521)   (1478-1516)   (1486-1525)

Figure 16-22. The name and the terminology is chosen, because the procedure can be nicely compared with preparations a writer of a saga, a historical novel about a family, might make. His starting point is a number of historical facts he wants to fit in his own pattern. Since such a comparison also enhances comprehension of the program's operation, an example is given. The corresponding terms of the description in the text are given. The corresponding terms of the description in the text are given between brackets.

a) In the example, the Medici family is chosen as the subject of the saga. The writer has chosen Giuliano, the only brother of Lorenzo il Magnifico as the central character (germ module).

b) In order to find the family relations, he needs a family tree in which all legitimate male adult Medici that lived before or during the life of Giuliano, are represented. He starts with constructing this family tree (structure tree) by finding all brothers of Giuliano with their children ordered according to their age (relative position). Giuliano had only one brother, Lorenzo, who was 4 years his senior and left 3 sons.

c) Then the writer passes on to the father, Piero il Gottoso, who is treated in the same manner. However, this Medici member had only one brother, Giovanni, whose only child died before

<u>begin</u> data preparation;
   GENEALOGIZE ({principal modules});
   PROCREATE (partial genealogy, {user compounds});
   INTERRELATE (genealogy);
   data collection
<u>end</u>

DATA PREPARATION

Beside some auxiliary data derived from design rules and designer requirements the input for the SAGA-system consists of the (functional) hierarchy of
the system to be integrated and the initial characterization of the modules represented in the hierarchy. With these data the program starts building up a
module data base. This module data base will at any moment contain the
actual characterization of each module. This characterization consists of:

1. The *identification part:* In this part some fixed information is encoded
   such as name in the input file, type of the module, and place in the hierarchy. Some variant data may be added such as flexibility class (discussed later) and level in the structure tree.
2. The *graphical part:* This part either contains a pointer indicating where

---

←

reaching adulthood (so Giovanni is a leaf in the family tree which corresponds to a slice assigned
to a cell).

  d) The father of Piero il Gottoso was the famous Cosimo, theFather of the State. His younger
brother Lorenzo begot only one son, Pierfrancesco. (In the structure tree the counterpart of an
only-begotten son is an extra change of slicing direction). With this extension of the tree the
'genealogical phase' comes to an end, because the father of Cosimo and Lorenzo is the oldest
Medici of whom precise facts are known. (The structure is not expansible). He is to be the common ancestor of the characters in the saga.

  e) Though lack of factual background prevents the writer from continuing tracing ancestors,
he still is capable of extending the tree by finding children and grand-children of family members
represented by leaves in the partial tree (user compounds). Pierfrancesco for example had two
sons, of which the elder, Lorenzo il Popolano, had three sons. In one step of the 'procreative
phase' the generations are thus extended. (In the slicing configuration the corresponding cutting
line is first vertical, because Pierfrancesco was the only son of Lorenzo).

Figure 16-22. Four steps in the genealogical phase and one in the procreative phase are illustrated. It is important for comprehending the operation of the program to note which generations
are involved in each step, and when the two phases come to an end. The genealogical phase stops
when the common ancestor is found (the structure is not expansible, i.e. the whole system is
covered). The procreative phase continues until all potential parents are investigated (until all
leaves represent slices assigned to cells). In the third phase the writer has to fill in the details of
the lives and interrelations of his characters with different degrees of freedom depending on the
historical facts known about them.

the layout of the module is stored or a pointer referring to the data from which the layout is to be derived and by which algorithm.

3. The *form vector:* The components of this vector are the parameters in calculating the deformation and position cost of the module in a certain realization. The cost formula depends on the type of the module.

4. The *flexibility part:* Data subjected to the stiffening process such as dimensions and orientation (preliminary or definitive) and pin information (net to which the pin belongs, side of the rectangle in which the module is to be realized, pin position) is referred to by pointers contained in this part.

What data have to be immediately entered into the module data base depends on the type of the module. For master cells, the input file contains a reference to the master library, where the layout, the form vector, and the list of external nets with the associated relative pin positions are stored. For user cells these data must be contained in the input file itself, and routed to the user library. A pointer indicating its place in the user library should be stored in the pertaining parts of the module characterization. The form vector, the list of external nets, and the data for technology and style dependent algorithms that have to determine the internal layout of blank cells, should be in the input file for all other function cells. Again pointers should be sent to the module data base, the bulk is to be stored in the user library. For user compounds, the form vector should be evaluated from the form vectors of its submodules and some empirical provision for the area of junction cells.

The entire module data base resides in the common data base of the design system. Parts of it are from time to time copied in the private data base and an updated version might be sent back.

GENEALOGIZE

GENEALOGIZE only works on the set of cardinal modules. It selects one cardinal module that is going to be the *germ module.* This single slice is the first of a sequence of *expansible structures.* The expansion is performed by selecting a group of cardinal modules on the basis of a heuristic drop-out pro-

---

Figure 16-23. GENEALOGIZE starts with selecting a germ module among the cardinal modules, B in the figure. EXPAND starts with joining a slice containing all unplaced cardinal modules. Since the width of this slice is fixed by the side of the actual structure, the height has to be adjusted such that these modules and the estimated junction cells can be accommodated. For each individual module its deformation and its connectivity to the expansible structure is determined. These values and the components of the form vector are the arguments for the contribution of a module to the cost associated with the proposed structure. Next, the module with the highest contribution is removed, C in the figure. Now, the calculations are performed for a slice

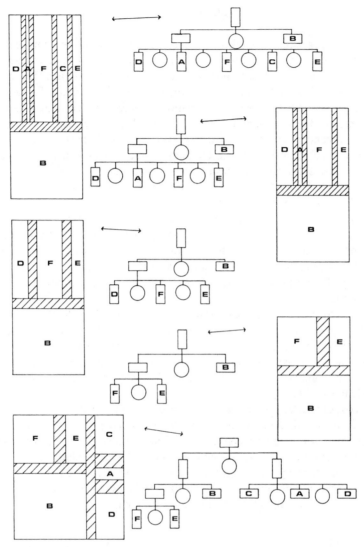

with all unplaced cardinal modules except the one removed. If the total cost and at least one individual contribution are lower than in the preceding structure the process is continued, otherwise the preceding structure is accepted for that side of the expansible structure. In the figure the process is continued until only one module was proposed for joining the expansible structure. Apparently, either the total cost or the individual contribution of that module increased, so the structure with two cardinal modules, E and F, is accepted. The entire process is repeated for all sides of the expansible structure, and the result with the lowest total cost is accepted as the new structure which is immediately improved. If this new structure is expansible the EXPAND procedure is applied to it, otherwise GENEALOGIZE is completed by extracting new data from the final structure. To prevent excessive deformation in the last steps of GENEALOGIZE, the total cost of the preceding slice is added to that of the actual new slice and compared with the lowest first proposal (thus, with all unplaced cardinal modules) of EXPAND in the preceding step. If the latter is lower that proposal is still accepted.

445

cedure. The heuristic is based on the cost calculated with the components of the form vector. It measures in a weighted manner the deformation these modules will incur and the connectivity with the expansible structure. To perform deformation calculations, the width of the interjacent junction cells has to be estimated even with the sparse information available in this stage. The inexactitudes have to be compensated by the flexibility of the modules. The contribution of connectivity plays a role in preventing interconnection lengths from unnecessary inflation, but also in choosing a side of attachment by discriminating the four sides. Each expansion, therefore, tries all sides of the expansible structure, and chooses the one allowing the lowest cost. The selected group will form a program compound if it consists of more than one cardinal module.

In Figure 16-23, two successive expansions are illustrated. With each expansion a slice is assigned to the selected group. This new slice is immediately subjected to some improvements concerning its dimensions in order to fit in inset cells, the sequence of child slices in order to minimize the maximally needed width, and the orientation of inset cells in order to simplify future wiring patterns.

The structure is no longer expansible if it contains all cardinal modules. Of such a structure, as much data is extracted as possible in that stage of the construction. The contents of the inset cells are therefore fetched from the libraries, nets are assigned to junction cells, pins are distributed over the four sides of their modules, and blank cells are filled by special technology and style dependent algorithms.

GENEALOGIZE can be seen as an automatic chip-planning method. The decisions are dominated by form considerations. However, interconnections play a dominant role in area consumption. The justification of this choice must come from practice. If interconnections should dominate the decision steps, another chip-planning algorithm must be developed. It should derive and take into account length of routes, ease of wiring, area consumption, etc. The advantages of slicing are still valid and should be retained.

PROCREATE

PROCREATE is directing all action to user compounds represented by leaves in the partial genealogy tree. As GENEALOGIZE, this procedure also estab-

---→

Figure 16-24. In PROCREATE, user compounds are optimized by establishing new program compounds such that the sum of all individual deformations is reduced. This optimization is performed for each user compound by the MERGE procedure. It starts by assigning a slice to each submodule of the concerned user compound. The widths of the junction cells are again estimated by probabilistic techniques. Next, the dimensions of the slices are calculated, and the deformations associated with these dimensions are determined. Summation of these deformations gives the total cost of the proposed slice. The pair of child slices having the highest contribution

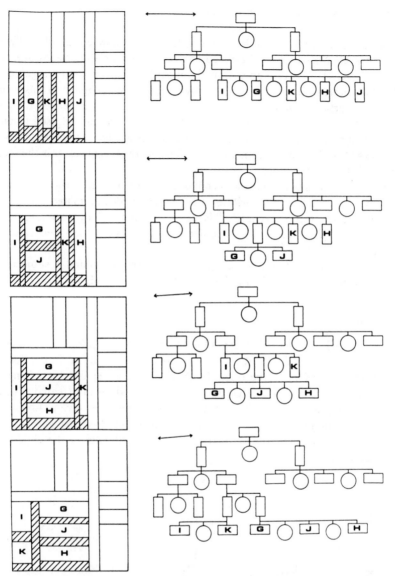

to this sum is combined to form a program compound. This is a new proposal for the slice to be assigned to the user compound. The same calculations are repeated for this newly proposed slice. If the cost is lower than for the preceding slice proposal a new program compound is formed in the same manner. If the cost was not reduced the preceding slice configuration is accepted. In the figure, the five submodules are initially assigned to child slices. G and J. apparently, have the highest deformation, and consequently have to be combined into one child slice. This new child slice and H have the highest deformations in the new configuration. So, they are combined. Now, I and K are the candidates to be merged which yields the last configuration in the figure. Combining the final child slices does not reduce the cost which means that the user compound gets a slice with two child slices containing I and K, and G, J and H, respectively.

lishes program compounds, but the constraints are now essentially different. Whereas GENEALOGIZE utilized the fact that chip dimensions are quite free, PROCREATE attempts to fit the modules in given contours guided by the deformations the modules incur. However, the area assigned to a user compound is partially based on area estimations. If less area is needed than was expected, an amount of spare area results. Spare area can be used to offset extra area demands of child slices. If more area is needed than expected, extra area has to be demanded from ancestors. The nearer this ancestor is the sooner the disturbance is nullified.

The dimensions of a slice and its child slices have to satisfy the equations in Figure 16-24. By giving the widths of the junction cells estimated values, only one degree of freedom is left. This can be eliminated by constraining the dimensions of the slice, for example fixing one of them or the aspect ratio to a feasible value.

The final slice configuration assigned to the user compound is subjected to similar improvements and data determination as in GENEALOGIZE.

INTERRELATE

GENEALOGIZE and PROCREATE establish the genealogy of the system once and for all. INTERRELATE has to assemble the layout in the bottom-up fashion. Slices are to be treated one by one in a sequence satisfying the condition that no slice is treated before all its child slices are treated. Visiting a node during the bottom-up traversal of the genealogy tree means: finding the contents of all junctions cells of the corresponding slice and subsequently squeezing the slice longitudinally. The relative coordinates of the child slices are recorded.

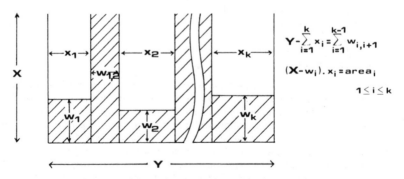

$$Y - \sum_{i=1}^{k} x_i = \sum_{i=1}^{k-1} w_{i,i+1}$$

$$(X - w_i) \cdot x_i = area_i$$

$$1 \leq i \leq k$$

Figure 16-25. A slice and its associated set of equations (no variable is negative).

STIFFENING OF MODULES

One of the imperatives of structured layout design is the flexibility of the modules. During the design process the modules are subjected to a stiffening process. in SAGA a module can be in six different flexibility classes (Figure 16-26). In which class a module is depends on how much data have been acquired, particularly on what is known about the distribution of the pins, the dimensions and the position (Figure 16-27). At the end of the design, all modules should be in the lowest class.

FLEXIBILITY CLASS		SPECIFICATION
V	a	$\dot{P}$
	b	$\ddot{P}\,\dot{x}\,\dot{y}$
IV		$\dot{P}\,\dot{x}\,\dot{y}$
III	a	$\dot{P}\,x\,y$
	b	$P\,xy$
III	b	$\overline{P}\,\dot{x}\,\dot{y}$
II	a	$\overline{P}\,x\,y$
	b	$P\,\dot{x}\,\dot{y}$
I		$P\,x\,y$
∅		$P\,x\,y\,T$

$\dot{x},\dot{y}$ provisional width, length of the module

x,y final width, length of the module

$\ddot{P}$ partial list of external nets of the module

$\dot{P}$ complete list of external nets of the module

$\overline{P}$ list of external nets distributed over the four sides of the module

P As $\overline{P}$, but with partial or complete sequence constraints

T module position

Figure 16-26. The flexibility classes of the modules.

ROUTINE	INSET CELLS	BLANK CELLS	JUNCTION CELLS	USER COMPOUNDS
EXPAND	V— IV	V— IV	— V	V— IV
MERGE	V— IV	V— IV	— V	V— IV
INSETFIT	IV—III	—	—	—
REFLECT	III— II	—	—	—
FETCH	II— I	—	—	—
DATASCRAPE	—	IV—III	V—II	IV—III
FILL	—	III— I	—	—
ROUTER	—	—	II— I	—
ASSEMBLE	I— 0	I— 0	I— 0	III— 0

Figure 16-27. Flexibility transitions.

REFERENCES

The subject 'Automatic Layout Design' was introduced into the group 'Automatic System Design of Eindhoven University of Technology by its initiator, Prof. dr. Jochen A. G. Jess. From the beginning the group aimed at full automation of the layout design task. Much study of literature, great effort in achieving this ambitious goal, and several good results can be recorded. Many scientists and students conduced to the philosophy set forth here. Major contributions are due to Dr. Marinus C. van Lier and Antoni A. Szepieniec. More authors than mentioned in the following list had an influence on the development of that philosophy.

(1) Lattin, W. "VLSI Design Methodology, The Problem of the 80's for Microprocessor Design." *16th Design Automation Conf. Proc.* (1979):548–549.

(2) Brooks, F. P. *The Mythical Man-Month.* Reading, Mass.: Addison-Wesley PC 1975.

(3) Otten, R. H. J. M., van Lier, M. C. "Layout Design for Bipolar Integrated Circuits." Eindhoven: Ph.-D.-thesis Eindhoven University of Technology, (1976).

(4) Dembowski, P. *Finite Geometries.* Berlin: Springer-Verlag (1968).

(5) Berge, C. *Graphes et hypergraphes.* Paris: Dunod, 1970.

(6) Bokhoven, W. M. G. van, "Piecewise-Linear Modelling and Analysis." Eindhoven: Ph.-D.-thesis Eindhoven University of Technology (1981).

(7) Wolfgang, E., Lindler, R., Fazekas, P., Feuerbaum, H. P. "Electron Beam Testing of VLSI circuits." *IEEE J. of Solid-State Circuits* SC-14: 471–481 (1979).

(8) Gibson, D., Nance, S. "SLIC. Symbolic Layout of Integrated Circuits. *13th Design Automation Conf. Proc.* (1976): 434–440.

(9) Hseuh, M.-Y. *Symbolic Layout and Compaction of Integrated Circuits.* Berkeley, California, Master Thesis, University of California, 1979.

(10) Persky, G., Deutsch, D. H., Schweikert, D. G. "LTX. A Minicomputer-Based System for Automated LSI Layout." *J of Design Automation and Fault Tolerand Computing* 217–255 (1977).

(11) Kani, K., Kawanishi, H., Kishimoto, A. "ROBIN. A Building Block LSI Routing Program" *Proc. IEEE ISCAS76* (1976): 658–661.

(12) Heller, W. R., Mikhail, W., Donath, W. "Prediction of Wiring Space Requirements for LS." *Journ. of Design Automation and Fault Tolerant Computing* 2 nr.2: 117–144 (1978).

(13) Hanan, M., Kurtzberg, J. M. "Placement Techniques." Chapter 5 in *Design Automation of Digital Systems* (Breuer, M. A., ed). Englewood Cliffs, New Jersey: Prentice-Hall, 1972.

(14) Lee, C. Y. "An Algorithm for Path-Connections and its Applications." *IEEE Trans. on Elec. Comp.* 10: 346–365 (1961).

(15) Hightower, D. "A Solution to the Routing Problems on the Continuous Plane." *6th Design Automation Conf. Proc.* (1969): 1–24.

(16) Lauther, U. "A Min-Cut Placement Algorithm for General Cell Assemblies Based on a Graph Representation." *J. of Design Automation and Fault Tolerant Computing* (1980).

(17) Hashimoto, A., Stevens, J. "Wire-Routing by Optimizing Channel-Assignment Within Large Apertures." *8th Design Automation Conf. Proc.* (1971): 155–169.

(18) Kernighan, B. W., Schweikert, D., Persky, G. "An Optimum Channel-Routing Algorithm for Polycell Layouts of Integrated Circuits." *10th Design Automation Conf. Proc.* (1973): 50–59.

(19) Simon. H. "The Architecture of Complexity." *Proc. of the American Philosophical Society* (1962): 467–482.

(20) Günther, T. "Die Räumliche Anordnung von Einheiten mit Wechselbeziehungen." *Elektron. Daten verarb.*, No. 6: 209–212 (1969).

(21) Kernighan, B. W., Lin, S. "An Efficient Heuristic Procedure for Partitioning of Electrical Circuits." *Bell Syst. Techn. J.* **49**: 291–308 (1970).

(22) Böhm, C., Jacopini, A. "Flow Diagrams, Turing Machines, and Languages With Only Two Formation Rules." *Comm. of the ACM* **9** No. 5: 335–371 (May, 1966).

(23) Dahl, O. J., Dijkstra, E. W., Hoare, C. A. R. *Structured Programming.* London: Academic Press (1972).

(24) Brooks, R. L., Smith, C. A. B., Stone, A. H., Tutte, W. T. "The Dissection of Rectangles into Squares." *Duke Math. Journal* **7**: 312–340 (1940).

(25) Zibert, K. "Ein Beitrag zum Rechnergestützten Topologischen Entwurf von Hybrid-Schaltungen." München: Technische Universität München, 1974.

(26) Johannsen, D. "Bristle Blocks: A Silicon Compiler." *16th Design Automation Conf. Proc.* (1979): 310–313.

(27) Gray. J. P. *Structured Design Notes.* Pasadena: Caltech (1980).

(28) Kawanishi, H., Goto, S., Oyamada, T., Kato, H., Kani, K. "A Routing Method of Building Block LSI." *7th Asilomar Conf. on Circuits and Systems Proc.* (1973): 119–123.

(29) Hightower, D. "Can CAD Meet the VLSI Design Problems of the 80's." *Automation Conf. Proc.* (1979): 552–553.

(30) Gamal. A.el. "Statistical Models for Wiring for VLSI." Proc. ICCC80: (1980): 77–79.

(31) Wulf, W., Shaw, M. "Global Variables Considered Harmful" *Sigplan Notices* 28–33 (1973).

(32) Wirth, N. "Program Development by Stepwise Refinement." *Comm. of the ACM* **14** No. 4: 221–227 (1971).

(33) Otten, R. H. J. M., Szepieniec, A. A. "Graph-oriented Approach to the Layout Problem." *Proc. IEEE ISCAS80:* (1980): 956–959.

(35) Szepieniec, A. A., Otten, R. H. J. M. "The Genealogical Approach to the Layout Problem." *17th Design Automation Conf. Proc.* (1980): 535–542.

17. Routing for High Density Printed Wiring Boards

Boards

Isao Shirakawa
Osaka University, Japan

INTRODUCTION

Most existing routing systems are constructed of several distinctive routers, such as maze-running routers (1-3), line-search routers (4-6) or channel routers (7), (8), so that a merit of one may compensate for a defect of another. While wiring densities of *printed wiring boards,* henceforth abbreviated to *PWBs,* are specified such that the *between-pins capacity* (that is, the number of wiring tracks permitted between two consecutive pins of an ordinary dual-in-line package) is limited to one, and the positions of *vias* (plated-through holes to be used for interconnection between layers) are floating, routing systems based on these conventional routers have been able to contribute much to reducing the time and cost incurred in laying out wire patterns on these PWBs. However, recent advances in technology of microelectronics have changed the design rule for PWBs in such a way that the between-pins capacity of wiring tracks can be raised up to two or more. When the specifications for a PWB are to undergo such a change, conventional routers such as maze-running routers and line-search routers, are confronted with various difficulties. As is pointed out by Doreau and Abel (9), the deficiency common to them is that they lack 'topological fluidity' (that is, the capability to defer detailed wire patterns until all interconnections have been considered). Especially as to line-search routers, which are executed track by track and have been incorporated into most of existing routing systems so as to perform the greater part of interconnections on a PWB, this deficiency is fatal when the between-pins capacity of wiring tracks is specified to be two or more. Thus in the case of high density wiring, a number of routing concepts and approaches proposed by (9)(21) may have to be incorporated in any shape.

Motivated by this, we have constructed a routing system which is distinctive mainly in that the single-row router considered in (18) is employed in conjunction with a line-search router in such a fashion that the search for wire segments in the line-search router is implemented channel by channel, with all interconnections within each channel completed later by the single-row router.

In this chapter the routing system is described, stressing mainly the algorithm and implementation. For purpose of clarity, necessary terminologies and concepts associated with the single-row router are given in the Preliminaries section and the Single-Row Router section. Routing algorithms in the line-search router combined with the single-row router and in the maze-running router are given in the following two sections. System overview and implementation are outlined in the sections on System Configuration and Implementation Results.

PRELIMINARIES

In the assembly of digital systems, multilayer PWBs are used very often to provide necessary interconnections among circuit modules. A great number of routing approaches and concepts have been proposed and extensively developed.

Most of the routing systems running in practice are constructed of several distinctive routers such that one is executed first, followed by the second working on the failures, followed by the third working on the failures of the first two, and so on (see, for example, (19-21). These routers are classified into two categories: The first consists of those which are devised to find a route whenever one exists. Maze-running routers (1,3) are typical of this category. A main drawback of these routers is that they are time consuming and require much memory space. The second consists of routers which have originated from those in the first category and try to compensate for defects in them by being less general and more efficient. Line-search routers (4,6) are typical of this category. A main drawback of these routers is that they can not always find a route even if one exists. and hence they are executed at earlier stages of the whole routing process. Usually they complete 85% or more of the interconnection requirements.

Recent advances in the technology of microelectronics enables us to produce high density PWBs for which the between-pins capacity of wiring tracks is permitted to be specified up to three (or four in the near future), and the amount of production for PWBs of between-pins capacity two or three is increasing rapidly. Noting that the between-pins capacity of a PWB is raised from one to two, three, or four, the number of cells per unit area increases by 2.25, 4, or 6.25 times, respectively. In such a high density environment there arise problems in turn, especially associated with routers in the second category which are intended to perform the greater part of the interconnection requirements. These problems are:

1. Each router which used to be fast can be no longer efficient, and moreover will not be expected to maintain such wirability as attained so far.
2. As is assumed by Doreau and Abel (9) and Foster (20), the fixed-via constraint (that is, the positions of vias are fixed on a grid) is to be set up physically and strategically, and hence each router should be revised so as to deal with this constraint.

To cope with these problems, a variety of sophisticated routing approaches have been attempted in practice (9,20). Motivated by this, we have constructed another routing scheme in which the single-row router of (18) is employed in conjunction with the line-search router of (6) in such a fashion that the line-search router first allocates nets defined on pins and/or vias within each channel, and then the single-row router realizes all nets within each channel. In what follows we first touch on this routing scheme.

The smallest unit to describe wire patterns on each layer of a PWB is a *track* on which wire segments are allocated. Given a PWB, let us provide horizontal and vertical tracks on the working area of each layer according to specifications of the density imposed on the board, and denote by a *cell* a square region at the intersection of horizontal track and a vertical one, as shown in Figure 17-1. In order that a line-search router can be combined with a single-row router, and that the fixed-via strategy can be taken, let us introduce another unit, called a *channel*, which consists of $k_u + k_w + 1$ tracks such that

1. each channel contains the upper and lower streets composed of k_u and k_w tracks, respectively, as illustrated in Figure 17-1 where the case of $k_u = 2$ and $k_w = 1$ is shown, on which portions of wire segments except vias are permitted to be generated, and
2. each channel contains exactly one track between the upper and lower streets, on which vias and pins are permitted to be placed.

Denote by a *block* a square region at the intersection of a horizontal channel and a vertical channel. Thus, it follows that there is one and only one cell in a block at which a via or pin can be located, as can be seen from Figure 17-1. It should be noted that channels described here consisting of $k_u + k_w + 1$ tracks are introduced so as to be modelled for PWBs of between-pin capacity $k_u + k_w$.

According to the approach of employing a line-search router in conjunction with a single-row router, each time a new net is to be assigned to a channel in the line-search router, it is necessary to check if this net together with all those so far assigned to the channel are realizable by the single-row router in the

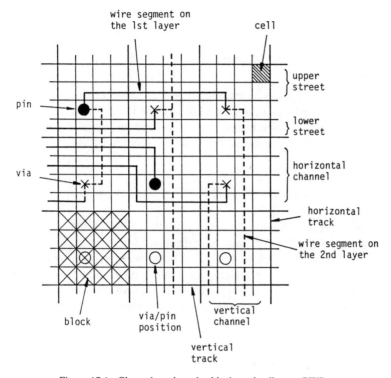

Figure 17-1. Channels and tracks; blocks and cells on a PWB.

upper and lower streets of prescribed k_u and k_w tracks, respectively, Hence, in this approach of central importance is a necessary and sufficient condition for realizability of single-row routing with prescribed upper and lower street capacities k_u and k_w, respectively. Thus in advance of describing the routing scheme, we outline a set of necessary and sufficient conditions derived in (18) in the following.

SINGLE-ROW ROUTER

The single-row routing approach, first introduced by So (15), has the promise to become one of the fundamental routing methods and is attracting a great deal of interest in terms of its applications not only to large scale backboard wiring (15,16), but also to circuit card wiring (9,18,22,23).

A specific development has been accomplished on this approach recently. Necessary and sufficient conditions for optimum single-row routing have been obtained (17,18). Thus optimum single-row routing can be employed in conjunction with the line-search router.

Figure 17-2. A set of nodes on a straight line R.

Consider a set of r nodes on a straight line R as shown in Figure 17-2, where each node corresponds to a pin or via. Given a net list $L = \{N_1, N_2, \ldots, N_n\}$, the interconnection of each net N_i is to be realized by means of a set of horizontal and vertical line segments. For example, given a net list

$$L = \{N_1, N_2, N_3, N_4\}; \qquad\qquad [17.1]$$
$$N_1 = \{1,4,7\}, \ N_2 = \{2,9\}, \ N_3 = \{3,5\}, \ N_4 = \{6,8\}$$

as shown in Figure 17-3(a), the interconnection for each net is realized as shown in Figure 17-3(b). This way of realization for a given net list L is called *single-row routine* (15), where upward and downward zigzagging is allowed, but not forward and backward zigzagging. In this realization, the space above (below) R is designated as the *upper (lower) street,* and the number of tracks available in the upper (lower) street is called the *upper (lower) street capacity.*

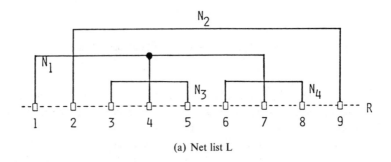

(a) Net list L

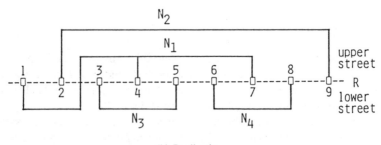

(b) Realization

Figure 17-3. A net list L and a realization by single-row routing.

Thus in this example, net list L of equation [17.1] can be realized with upper and lower street capacities two and one, respectively.

Associated with an ordered sequence $s = (N_{i_1}, N_{i_2}, \ldots, N_{i_n})$ of a net list $L = \{N_1, N_2, \ldots, N_n\}$, the *interval graphical representation* is defined (17). For example, given a net list L of equation [17.1] consider a sequence $s = (N_2, N_1, N_3, N_4)$, then the interval graphical representation associated with this s is depicted as in Figure 17-4, where each line segment represents the interval convered by a net, and they are arranged according to the order in s. Nodes which pertain to a net are marked as shown. Obviously, there are $n!$ ordered sequences for a net list of n nets, and hence there are a total of $n!$ interval graphical representations. In an interval graphical representation, let us define the *reference line* (17) as the continuous line segments which connect the nodes in succession from left to right. For example, in Figure 17-4 the reference line for the interval graphical representation associated with $s = (N_2, N_1, N_3, N_4)$ is shown by broken lines. Now, let us stretch out the reference line and map into a straight line R. Associated with this topological mapping, let each interval line be transformed into a path composed of horizontal and vertical line segments, as illustrated in Figure 17-3b, where the portions above and below the reference line are mapped into paths in the upper and lower streets, respectively. As readily seen, this topological mapping yields a realization of a given net list. Thus for each interval graphical representation, there corresponds a unique realization.

Given an interval graphical representation, let us draw a vertical line at node i, and define the *cut number* (16) $c(i)$ of i as the number of interval lines cut by the vertical line drawn at i, ignoring the one to which i belongs. Then put

$$q_M \triangleq \max_i c(i) \qquad [17.2]$$

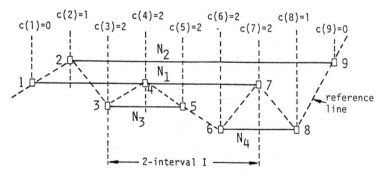

Figure 17-4. Interval graphical representation associated with $s = (N_2, N_1, N_3, N_4)$.

Given a net list L defined on R, let $I = [i,j]$ $(i \leq j)$ indicate a closed interval on R between nodes i and j, and let an interval $I = [i, j]$ such that $c(k) \geq h$ for all k on I and $c(i - 1) = c(j + 1) = h - 1$, be referred to as an h-*interval* (16). For example, for net list L of equation [17.1], $I = (3,7)$ is a 2-interval, as illustrated in Figure 17-4.

For any interval $I = [i,j]$, let $\overline{L}(I)$ denote a set of nets which nave no node on I, but have two nodes a and b such that $a < i$ and $j < b$, and let $L(I)$ indicate the union of $\overline{L}(I)$ and a set of nets having nodes on I. For example, for 2-interval $I = [3,7]$, $\overline{L}(I) = \{N_2\}$ and $L(I) = \{N_1, N_2, N_3, N_4\}$.

With the use of these notations, the realizability of single-row routing with prescribed upper and lower street capacities k_u and k_w is described without loss of generality under the following assumptions:

1. every net of a given net list contains at least two nodes.
2. every node belongs to a net.
3. any net does not contain a pair of consecutive nodes i and $i + 1$.

With respect to 3 some explanation is necessary: If any net N_k contains a pair of consecutive nodes i and $i + 1$, then delete node $i + 1$ from N_k and seek a realization. After that we can complete the realization by connecting i and $i + 1$ by means of a straight line segment on R, without changing the upper and lower street capacities.

REALIZABILITY CONDITIONS (18): A net list L is realizable by single-row routing with prescribed upper and lower street capacities k_u and k_w, if and only if

CASE I $(k_u = 1$ and $k_w = 0$ or $k_u = 0$ and $k_w = 1)$:

$$q_M = 0 \qquad [17.3]$$

CASE II $(k_u = k_w = 1)$:

$$q_M \leq 1 \qquad [17.4]$$

CASE III $(k_u = 2$ and $k_w = 1$ or $k_u = 1$ and $k_w = 2)$:

$$1° \ q_M \leq 2 \qquad [17.5]$$

$2°$ for any 2-interval I,
$$|\overline{L}(I)| = 1 \qquad [17.6]$$

$3°$ there do not exist any two consecutive
intervals I^1 and I^2 such that

$$|L(I^1) \cap L(I^2)| = 2 \text{ and } \overline{L}(I^1) \neq \overline{L}(I^2) \qquad [17.7]$$

CASE IV $(k_u = k_w = 2)$:

$1°\ q_M \leq 3,$
$2°$ for any 3-interval I, $|\overline{L}(I)| = 2$
$3°$ there do not exist any two consecutive 3-intervals I^1

$$|L(I^1) \cap L(I^2)| = 3 \text{ and } \overline{L}(I^1) \neq \overline{L}(I^2) \qquad [17.10]$$

Two efficient algorithms for Cases III and IV have been derived (18). Given a net list L, they detect its realizability, and if L is realizable, then they seek an ordered sequence s of the nets in L associated with which L is realized, in at most $0(n \cdot r)$ time, where n and r denote the numbers of nets and nodes, respectively. For example, application of the algorithm for Case III to a net list L of Figure 17-5a detects realizability in the affirmative and yields a sequence $s = (N_1, N_5, N_2, N_3, N_4, N_7, N_6)$, associated with which L is realized as shown in Figure 17-5b; on the other hand, application of the algorithm for

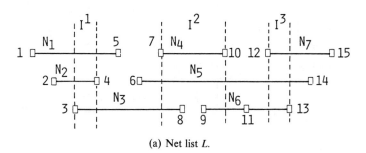

(a) Net list L.

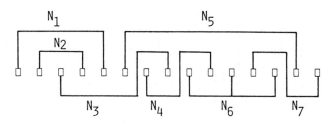

(b) Realization associated with $s = (N_1, N_5, N_2, N_3, N_4, N_7, N_6,)$.

Figure 17-5. An example of realization with $k_u = 2$ and $k_w = 1$.

Case IV to a net list L of Figure 17-6(a) detects realizability in the affirmative and yields a sequence $s = (N_8, N_5, N_1, N_7, N_9, N_{10}, N_6, N_3, N_4, N_2)$, associated with which L is realized as shown in Figure 17-6 (b).

LINE-SEARCH ROUTER COMBINED WITH SINGLE-ROW ROUTER

For the sake of simplicity, let us assume that the PWBs to be considered henceforth are of two layers; the first layer is for use of horizontal wire segments and the second one for vertical wire segments.

We first define several terminologies necessary for describing a new routing scheme which is composed of a line-search router in conjunction with a single-row router.

Given a vertical (horizontal) channel segment $\overline{PQ}$ $(\overline{ST})$ between two blocks $P = (a, y_1)$ and $Q = (a, y_2)$ with $y_1 < y_2$ $(S = (x_1, b)$ and $T = (x_2, b)$ with $x_1 < x_2)$, if each block on vertical (horizontal) channel segment $\overline{PQ}$ $(\overline{ST})$ is covered by less than $k_u + k_w$ nets in the net list of those which have been

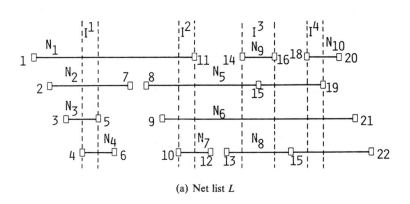

(a) Net list L

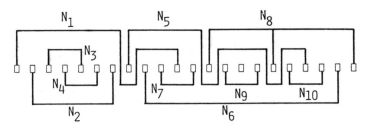

(b) Realization associated with $s = (N_8,N_5,N_1,N_7,N_9,N_{10},N_6,N_3,N_4,N_2)$.

Figure 17-6. An example of realization with $k_u = k_w = 2$.

allocated on the vertical (horizontal) channel at $x = a$ ($y = b$), then segment $\overline{PQ}$ ($\overline{ST}$) is referred to as a *feasible v-channel* (*h-channel*) segment.

Associated with a block $P = (x, y)$, let us designate a maximal feasible v- or h-channel segment passing P as a *v- or h-channel segment of level 0* with respect to P, denoted by $S_0^v(P)$ or $S_0^h(P)$, respectively. Recursively, let us define a *v- or h-channel segment of level k* ($k \geq 1$) with respect to P, denoted by $S_k^v(P)$ or $S_k^h(P)$, to be a maximal feasible v- or h-channel segment passing a block on $S_{k-1}^h(P)$ or $S_{k-1}^v(P)$, respectively, for which the cell for via position is not occupied. For example, in Figure 17-7 several v- and h-channel segments of level 0 through 2 with respect to two blocks P_a and P_b are illustrated.

Using these terminologies, a line-search router combined with a single-row router in our routing system is outlined as follows: Let a pair of pins P_a and P_b

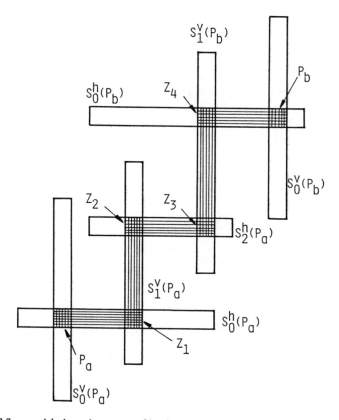

Figure 17-7. v- and h-channel segments of levels 0, 1, and 2 with respect to P_a and P_b, on which a channel path between P_a and P_b composed of feasible channel segments $\overline{P_a Z_1}$, $\overline{Z_1 Z_2}$, $\overline{Z_2 Z_3}$, $\overline{Z_3 Z_4}$, and $\overline{Z_4 P_b}$ is found.

be required to be interconnected, and let $P_a = (x_a, y_a)$ and $P_b = (x_b, y_b)$ be blocks for which the cells for via/pin position are occupied by P_a and P_b, respectively. The router tries to seek a channel path between blocks P_a and P_b defined on a set of v- or h-channel segments of levels 0, 1, and so on, which are expanded with respect to P_a and P_b. Suppose that a path is found between P_a and P_b, which consists of feasible channel $\overline{P_a Z_1} = \overline{Z_0 Z_1}, \overline{Z_1 Z_2}, \ldots ,$ $\overline{Z_{l-1} Z_l} = \overline{Z_{l-1} P_b}$. Then through the use of the realizability condition, a check is conducted for each such segment $\overline{Z_{i-1} Z_i}$ as to whether or not a new net $\{ z_{i-1}, z_i \}$ (where z_k denotes the cell for via/pin position in block Z_k, and henceforth such a notation will be used unless otherwise stated) can be realizable together with all those in the net list so far allocated to the same channel. If all these new nets turn out to be realizable, then each of them is added to the corresponding net list.

In what follows, we describe an outline of the algorithm of this routing scheme, where for the sake of simplicity, the discussion is limited to the interconnection of two specified cells p_a and p_b located in blocks P_a and P_b, respectively.

First of all, two unit operations are defined as shown in Figures 17-8 and 17-9, which join the line-search router and the single-row router.

Through the use of these unit operations of INTERSECT and TARGET, an outline of the line-search router adopted in our routing system is described as shown in Figure 17-10.

procedure INTERSECT(P,Q,SP,SQ):
<u>begin</u>
    if feasible channel segments SP and SQ passing P and Q, respectively, intersect at a block Z in which the cell for via/pin position is not occupied <u>then</u>
        <u>begin</u>
            <u>comment</u> let p, q, and z be the cells for via/pin position in blocks P, Q, and Z, respectively;
check if new nets $\{p,z\}$ and $\{z,q\}$ are both realizable together with all those in the net lists so far allocated tothe corresponding channels;
            <u>if</u> both of them are realizable <u>then</u> <u>return</u> "true"
                <u>else</u> <u>return</u> "false"
        <u>end</u>
        <u>else</u> <u>return</u> "false"
    <u>end</u> INTERSECT;

Figure 17-8. Procedure INTERSECT.

procedure TARGET(P,S,i):
begin
    let S be a specified v- or h-channel segment of some level with respect to P_a;
    let P be a specified block on S;
    let $i \epsilon \{v,h\}$;
    define $\bar{i}$ such that $\bar{i} = v$ (or h) if and only if $i = h$ (or v);
    for each block Q on $S_0^i(P_b)$ such that a new net $\{p_b,q\}$ is realizable together with all those in the net list allocated to the i-channel passing P_b do
    begin
        seek$S_1^i(P_b)$ passing block Q;
        if INTERSECT($P,Q,S,S_1^i(P_b)$) is true then return "true"
    end;
    return "false"
end TARGET;

Figure 17-9. Procedure TARGET.

procedure LINE SEARCH(P_a,P_b,n):
begin
    let $n(\geq 3)$ be the upper bound to the number of channel segments to be specified for interconnection of P_a and P_b;
    $i \leftarrow 1$;
    if INTERSECT($P_a,P_b,S_0^h(P_a),S_0^v(P_b)$) is true then
        begin comment let Z be a block at which $S_0^h(P_a)$ and $S_0^v(P_b)$ intersect;
            add nets $\{p_a,z\}$ and $\{z,p_b\}$ to the net lists for the corresponding channels;
            return "true"
        end;
    if INTERSECT($P_a,P_b,S_0^v(P_a), S_0^h(P_b)$) is true then
        begin comment let Z be a block at which $S_0^v(P_a)$ and $S_0^h(P_b)$ intersect;
            add nets $\{p_a,z\}$ and $\{z,p_b\}$ to the corresponding net lists;
            return "true"
        end;
    if TARGET($P_a,S_0^h(P_a)h$) is true then
        begin comment let Z_1 and Z_2 be blocks at which $S_0^v(P_a)$ and $S_1^h(P_b)$;
and
        $S_1^v(P_b)$ and $S_0^h(P_b)$ intersect, respectively;
        add nets $\{p_a,z_1\}$, $\{z_1,z_2\}$, and $\{z_2,p_b\}$ to the corresponding net lists;
        return "true"
    end;

Figure 17-10. Procedure LINE-SEARCH.

if $TARGET(P_a, S_0^v(P_a), v)$ is true then
   begin comment let Z_1 and Z_2 be blocks at which $S_0^v(P_a)$ and $S_0^v(P_b)$;

and

     $S_1^h(P_b)$ and $S_0^v(P_b)$ intersect, respectively;
     add nets $\{p_a, z_1\}$, $\{z_1, z_2\}$, and $\{z_2, p_b\}$ to the corresponding net lists;
     return "true"
   end;
while $i + 2 \leq n$ do
   begin
     for each block P on $S_i^v(P_a)$ such that new nets $\{p_a, z_1\}$, $\{z_1, z_2\}$, ... ,
     $\{z_{i-1}, p\}$ (when $i = 1$, let $z_0 \triangleq p_a$ and $z_1 \triangleq p$) on channel segments of levels
     $0, 1, \ldots, i - 1$ with respect to P_a, respectively, are realizable
     together with all those in the net lists so far allocated to the corre-
     sponding channels do
       if $TARGET(P, \overline{S_i^v}(P_a), v)$ is true then
         begin comment let Z_{i+1} and Z_{i+2} be blocks at which $S_i^v(P_a)$ and
         $S_1^h(P_b)$; and $S_1^h(P_b)$ and $S_0^v(P_b)$ intersect, respectively;
         add nets $\{p_a, z_1\}$, $\{z_1, z_2\}$, ... , $\{z_{i-1}, p\}$, $\{p, z_{i+1}\}$,
         $\{z_{i+1}, z_{i+2}\}$, and $\{z_{i+2}, p_b\}$ to the corresponding
         net lists;
         return "true"
       end;
     for each block P on $S_i^v(P_a)$ such that new nets $\{p_a, z_1\}$, $\{z_1, z_2\}$, ... ,
     $\{z_{i-1}, p\}$ (when $i = 1$, let $z_0 \triangleq p_a$ and $z_1 \triangleq p$) on channel segments of levels
     $0, 1, \ldots, i - 1$ with respect to P_a, respectively, are realizable
     together with all those in the net lists so far allocated to the corre-
     sponding channels do
       if $TARGET(P, \overline{S_i^v}(P_a), v)$ is true then
         begin comment let Z_{i+1} and Z_{i+2} be blocks at which $S_i^v(P_a)$ and
         $S_1^h(P_b)$; and $S_1^h(P_b)$ and $S_0^v(P_b)$ intersect, respectively;
         add nets $\{p_a, z_1\}$, $\{z_1, z_2\}$, ... , $\{z_{i-1}, p\}$, $\{p, z_{i+1}\}$,
         $\{z_{i+1}, z_{i+2}\}$, and $\{z_{i+2}, p_b\}$ to the corresponding
         net lists;
         return "true"
       end;
     $i \leftarrow i + 1$
   end;
   return "false"
end LINE SEARCH;

Figure 17-10 cont.

MAZE-RUNNING ROUTER

Recently a depth-first search technique has been introduced into a maze-running router so as to avoid unnecessary scan of cells (3,24). Based on this, the router employed in our system is constructed.

To implement this router, we provide flags $TH(z)$, $C(z)$, and $S(z)$ for each cell z, which are to furnish the following information:

TH-flag:

$TH(z) = 1$ indicates that a via or pin is forbidden at z.

$TH(z) = 0$ indicates that it is permitted.

C-flag:

$C(z) = 1$ indicates that z has been already scanned.

$C(z) = 0$ indicates that z has not yet been scanned.

S-flag: This flag indicates whether or not z is the start cell, the target cell, or a forbidden cell for routing, and also instructs the direction to be taken at z for backtracking from the target cell to the start cell after the target cell is reached by expansion.

$S(z) = 0$ indicates to move to the other layer through the use of a via.

$S(z) = 1$ indicates to move to the adjacent cell on the left of z.

$S(z) = 2$ indicates to move to the adjacent cell on the right of z.

$S(z) = 3$ indicates to move to the adjacent cell above z.

$S(z) = 4$ indicates to move to the adjacent cell below z.

$S(z) = 5$ indicates that z is the start cell.

$S(z) = 6$ indicates that z is the target cell.

$S(z) = 7$ indicates that z is forbidden for routing.

Assuming that TH, C, and S flags are specified for all cells on a PWB, the maze-running router adopted in our routing system can be briefly described as in Figure 17-11, where for two cells v and w, let $d(v, w)$ denote the rectilinear distance between v and w.

```
procedure MAZE RUNNING(s,t):
begin
        S(s) ← 5;
        S(t) ← 6;
        initialize two stacks P_STACK and N_STACK to empty;
        u ← s;
        VISIT(u)
end MAZE  RUNNING;
procedure VISIT(u):
```

Figure 17-11. Procedure MAZE-RUNNING.

```
begin
    C(u) ← 1;
    if S(u) = 6 then a wiring route from s to t is found, which can be
        identified by tracing backward from t to s by means of Father(·);
    for each adjacent cell v of u such that C(v) = 0 and S(v) ≠ 7 do
        if d(v,t) + 1 = d(u,t) then
            add an ordered pair (v,S_uv) onto the top of P_STACK;
            comment let S_uv denote an S flag value to indicate to move from u
                to v
        else
            add (v,S_uv) onto the top of N_STACK;
A: while P_STACK is not empty do
        begin
            repeat
                delete (y,S_xy) from the top of P__STACK;
                comment let S_xy denote an S flag value to indicate to move from
                    x to y
            until C(y) = 0;
            Father (y) ← x;
            VISIT (y)
        end;
    if N_STACK is empty then no wiring route exists from s to t;
    P_STACK ← N_STACK;
    make N_STACK empty;
    goto A
end VISIT;
```

Figure 17-11 cont.

SYSTEM CONFIGURATION

As has been insisted a number of times, our routing system is constructed so as to deal with PWBs of different densities such that a user can specify the between-pins capacity to be one through four. Several variations are introduced in applying the line-search router coupled with the single-row router and the maze-running router. In what follows, implementation aspects of the routing scheme are outlined.

[A] *Line-Search Router*

In order that a conventional line-search router can be available, the following mode is provided.

MODE 0: This mode of the line-search router is implemented on the assumption that each channel consists only of a single track and positions of vias are floating, although some constraints can be imposed on their relative locations according to specifications. Thus this mode can be applied to PWBs for which the floating-via strategy is available and the between-pins capacity should be set to one.

[B] *Line-Search Router* + *Single-Row Router*

There are four modes in the line-search router coupled with the single-row router. These are classified according to between-pins capacities to be specified for PWBs.

MODE 1: This mode assumes that either of the upper street capacity k_u and the lower street capacity k_w is one and the other is zero. Thus this mode is supposed to be applied to PWBs with specification that the between-pins capacity is one and the fixed-via strategy should be taken.

MODE 2: This mode assumes that $k_u = k_w = 1$, and hence it is supposed to be applied to PWBs for which the between-pins capacity is specified as two and the fixed-via strategy should be taken.

MODE 3: This mode assumes that $k_u = 2$ and $k_w = 1$, or $k_u = 1$ and $k_w = 2$, and hence is supposed to be applied to PWBs for which the between-pins capacity is specified as three and the fixed-via strategy should be taken.

MODE 4: This mode assumes that $k_u = k_w = 2$ and is supposed to be applied to PWBs for which the between-pins capacity is specified as four and the fixed-via strategy should be taken.

[C] *Maze-Running Router*

In the application of conventional maze-running routers, there may possibly occur a case where a fairly long vertical (or horizontal) wire segment is generated on the layer principally for horizontal (or vertical) use, and this vertical (or horizontal) wire segment may prevent a number of horizontal (or vertical) wire segments to cross it from being generated later on. In order to avoid such a situation, the following four modes are introduced. These are classified as:

1. Either all horizontal and vertical wire segments are limited to be generated only in horizontal and vertical channels on the first and second layers, respectively, or such a restriction is not imposed on generating wire segments on the first or second layer.

2. Fixed-via strategy is to be taken or not. *MODE A:* This mode assumes that all horizontal and vertical wire segments are limited to be generated only in horizontal and vertical channels on the first and second layers, respectively, and the floating-via strategy is available.

   MODE B: This also assumes that all horizontal and vertical wire segments are limited to be generated only in horizontal and vertical channels on the first and second layers, respectively, but the fixed-via strategy is to be taken.

MODE C: This mode assumes that any such restriction as in Modes A and B is not imposed on generating wire segments on the first or second layer, and that the floating-via strategy is available.

MODE D: This also assumes that no restriction is imposed on generating wire segments on the first or second layer, but that the fixed-via strategy should be taken.

[D] *Net Ordering*

At any stage of routing process, a set of cells which constitute a maximal inter-connected part of a net N_i is referred to as a *subnet* of N_i, and each pair of subnets of N_i is designated as a *from-to* of N_i, with its distance defined to be the shortest rectilinear distance between two cells on different subnets.

According to our benchmark tests on a number of net ordering schemes, this routing system adopts a policy to select a from-to of the shortest distance of all the remaining from-tos at any stage of the line-search router and the maze-running router.

[E] *Flowchart of Routing Process*

The modes of routing procedures stated in [A]-[C] and the net ordering scheme in [D] are incorporated into our routing system, and a general flow-chart of the whole routing process is shown in Figure 17-12. It should be noted here that Modes C and D of the maze-running router is to be applied after Modes A and B are implemented, respectively.

IMPLEMENTATION RESULTS

Described procedures have been programmed in FORTRAN (a part of the maze-running router in an assembler) and run on an ACOS 77/900 computer. In this section, implementation results of the routing system are outlined.

To implement the routing system, a number of facilities are incorporated to improve wirability of the system, on which we first touch in the following.

Framing: Since the line-search router tries to find a wiring route on a set of as few channel segments as possible, it is often observed that the router generates a wiring route running an unnecessarily long detour. Thus in this routing phase, to preclude such a redundant wire generation, a framing facility is provided which limits the search area of the router according to specifications.

Let a route between two blocks $P_a = (x_a, y_a)$ and $P_b = (x_b, y_b)$ be sought by the router, then the framing is set so that the search can be limited to a rectangular region including the so-called *minimum distance rectangular* (MDR) for P_a and P_b, that is, the minimal rectangle which surrounds P_a and P_b. The size and location of this rectangular region are determined according to those of the MDR. Suppose that the center of the MDR is located in the

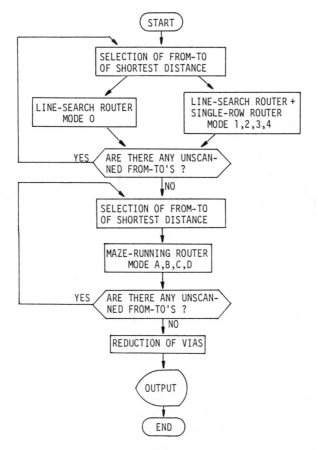

Figure 17-12. A general flowchart of routing process.

lower left-hand quarter of the center of the board, then the rectangular region is specified as illustrated in Figure 17-13, where

$$X_1 = x_a - (\alpha\Delta x + \beta\Delta y) - H, \qquad Y_1 = y_q - (\alpha\Delta y + \beta\Delta x) - H$$
$$X_2 = x_b + \gamma(\alpha\Delta x + \beta\Delta y) + H, \qquad Y_2 = y_b + \gamma(\alpha\Delta y + \beta\Delta x) + H$$

in case the center of the MDR is located in any other quarter of the board center, the rectangular region is similarly determined. According to our benchmark tests, a combination of parameter values of $\alpha = 0.7$, $\beta = 0.2$, $\gamma = 0.3$, and $H = 5$ surpasses others in wiring performance.

Specification for Line-Search Router: There are a number of ways in apply-

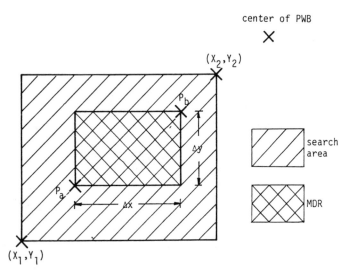

Figure 17-13. An example of MDR and search area.

ing the line-search router which may affect wirability of the system. The wiring performance of the system is observed to be fairly sensitive to the following factors

1. To what number the parameter n (the upper bound to the number of channel segments to be used) of the line-search router may well be raised.
2. Whether or not a restriction is imposed on wire pattern generation such that the router is executed for all from-tos first by setting $n = 3$, then for the failures by setting $n = 4$, and so on.
3. Whether or not a search direction, as illustrated in Figure 17-14, is adopted in expanding feasible channel segments such that the one closest to an edge of the board among all channel segments of the same level should be generated with top priority, as described in (25).

According to our benchmark tests on (1), the ratio of from-tos realized with $n = 6$ or more to all those realized by the line-search router is less than 3%, and moreover there are a number of PWBs for which the total wiring performance (that is, the performance after the maze-running router terminates) obtained by setting $n = 6$ is less than that obtained by setting $n = 5$. Thus the line-search router with $n = 5$ is mostly expected to attain the highest wiring performance, and henceforth we implement the line-search router by setting $n = 5$.

As to (2), the total wiring performance with such a restriction imposed on wire pattern generation in the line-search phase has shown a downward ten-

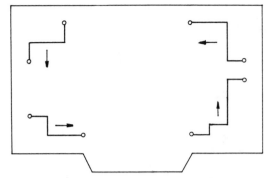

Figure 17-14. Search direction for possible wire segments.

dency against the one without it. Thus the line-search router is to be executed without such a restriction.

Considering the fact that due to the centralization of wiring routes, isolated pins which failed to be interconnected occur mostly around the center of a PWB, any sort of facilities to preclude such centralization should be attempted. A search direction facility as stated in 3 forms a part of such an attempt, and can be expected to contribute much to improving wirability. Thus such a search direction facility is to be employed in the line-search router.

In what follows, we show a part of the implementation results of this routing system.

Tables 17-1 through 17-4 show the results obtained for four PWBs, where

1. T_1, T_2, and T_3 are processing times such that
   T_1; spent by the line-search router,
   T_2; spent by the single-row router,
   T_3; spent by the maze-running router,
2. *W.P.* indicates the *wiring performance* defined by

$$\frac{\text{the number of interconnected from-tos}}{\text{the number of from-gos to be interconnected}} \times 100 \ (\%)$$

3. *C.U.R.* denotes the *cell utilization ratio* defined by

$$\left(1 - \frac{\text{the number of unused cells after implementation}}{\text{the number of unused cells before implementation}}\right) \times 100 \ (\%)$$

It should be added that Mode 0 of the line-search router skips the single-row router, and T_2 in this mode indicates the time spent only by data manipulation necessary for the maze-running router to succeed the line-search router.

Table 17-1. Implementation Results for a PWB of Size 239mm × 178mm with 253 Nets and 398 From-tos on 946 Pins.

| | LINE-SEARCH ROUTER + SINGLE-ROW ROUTER | | MAZE-RUNNING ROUTER | | | | | | |
MODE	T_1/T_2 (SEC.)	W.P. (%)	MODE	T_3 (SEC.)	W.P. (%)	TOTAL W.P. (%)	TOTAL CPU TIME (SEC.) $T_1 + T_2 + T_3$	# VIAS	C.U.R. (%)
0	112.7/1.9	99.3	A + C	1.3	0.5	99.8	115.9	444	33.5
1	64.7/11.1	97.2	B + D	6.5	2.3	99.5	72.3	513	35.0
2	44.6/9.9	99.3	B + D	1.4	0.2	99.5	55.9	402	20.2
3	43.1/10.2	100				100	53.3	405	15.1
4	41.4/8.8	100				100	50.2	382	11.9

Table 17-2. Implementation Results for a PWB of Size 318mm × 188mm with 307 Nets and 601 From-tos on 1,581 Pins.

	LINE-SEARCH ROUTER + SINGLE-ROW ROUTER		MAZE-RUNNING ROUTER			TOTAL W.P (%)	TOTAL CPU TIME (SEC.) $T_1 + T_2 + T_3$	# VIAS	C.U.R. (%)
MODE	T_1/T_2 (SEC.)	W.P. (%)	MODE	T_3 (SEC.)	W.P. (%)				
0	267.9/2.5	89.2	A + C	289.8	3.7	92.9	560.2	812	42.6
1	193.8/19.6	85.7	B + D	287.4	4.8	90.5	498.6	899	43.3
2	217.1/19.6	97.2	B + D	314.4	0.8	98.0	551.1	765	27.9
3	98.2/20.0	100				100	118.2	698	21.7
4	71.1/18.8	100				100	89.9	648	16.9

Table 17-3. Implementation Results for a PWB of Size 280mm × 203mm with 517 Nets and 1,142 From-tos on 3,668 Pins.

	LINE-SEARCH ROUTER + SINGLE-ROW ROUTER		MAZE-RUNNING ROUTER			TOTAL W.P. (%)	TOTAL CPU TIME (SEC.) $T_1 + T_2 + T_3$	# VIAS	C.U.R. (%)
MODE	T_1/T_2 (SEC.)	W.P. (%)	MODE	T_3 (SEC.)	W.P. (%)				
0	643.0/4.5	82.2	A + C	199.3	3.4	85.6	846.8	1,212	50.7
1	362.7/33.5	77.5	B + D	297.3	5.8	83.3	693.9	1,285	51.3
2	408.3/41.0	94.3	B + D	544.2	2.5	96.8	993.5	1,468	43.9
3	261.1/43.7	99.5	B + D	29.6	0.0	99.5	334.4	1,185	34.1
4	251.1/41.2	100				100	292.3	1,094	26.6

Table 17-4. Implementation Results for a PWB of Size 183mm $\times$ 274mm with 481 Nets and 911 From-tos on 2,179 Pins.

MODE	LINE-SEARCH ROUTER + SINGLE-ROW ROUTER		MAZE-RUNNING ROUTER			TOTAL W.P. (%)	TOTAL CPU TIME (SEC.) $T_1 + T_2 + T_3$	# VIAS	C.U.R. (%)
	T_1/T_2 (SEC.)	W.P. (%)	MODE	T_3 (SEC.)	W.P. (%)				
0	505.1/3.3	72.2	A + C	294.9	5.2	77.4	903.3	1,037	50.6
1	333.6/21.1	66.4	B + D	484.5	6.5	72.9	839.2	1,003	50.1
2	436.2/29.0	85.2	B + D	1,175.9	3.4	88.6	1,641.1	1,326	45.5
3	446.8/33.6	94.6	B + D	599.1	3.2	97.8	1,079.5	1,379	42.6
4	161.1/34.8	100				100	195.9	1,080	33.6

As can be seen from the tables, the wiring performance of Mode 0 is slightly better than that of Mode 1, and therefore one might have an impression that the line-search router by itself is superior to such a combination of the line-search and single-row routers as described earlier in the Line-Search Router Section. However, this tendency is naturally to be expected, considering that Mode 1 is implemented under the fixed-via constraint, whereas Mode 0 is run in an environment free from such a severe constraint. Moreover, it should be noted that application of Mode 0 to PWBs of a between-pins capacity of two or more may have not only to require a considerable modification to cope with the fixed-via constraint, but to suffer the loss of 'topological fluidity'.

It is observed from these implementation results that wirability of this routing system tends to rise rapidly as the between-pins capacity increases, and that there is not much difference among processing times spent in Modes 1 through 4, although the total numbers of cells on a PWB in Modes 2, 3, and 4 are 2.25, 4, and 6.25 times as many as that in Mode 1, respectively.

Figure 17-15 shows the final wire patterns obtained for the PWB of Table 17-4 by applying Modes 3, B and D, where the scale indicates the number of tracks.

CONCLUSION

We have described a new routing system which is distinctive in that a single-row router is implemented in conjunction with a line-search router. On employing a single-row routing scheme, we are inevitably confronted with a difficulty proper to it, which is the *via assignment problem* (26). However, such a difficulty has been overcome by coupling it with a line-search router, which carries out not only route finding but via assignment, at the same time.

Although in this system a number of improvements are still to be made, samples of implementation results reveal that the system demonstrates high wirability especially for PWBs of between-pins capacity two or more. Thus it has enormous potentialities to be of use in the practice of layout of high density PWBs. Development is continuing on more sophisticated routing, placement, and layering algorithms (27,29).

Acknowledgment:

The author would like to express his appreciation to his students, S. Asahara, M. Odani, and Y. Ogura, who have developed the programs in this system. Without their invaluable assistance this system could not be realized. He also would like to thank I. Nishioka and T. Chiba, Sharp Corp., N. Yoshida and K. Kawakita, Nippon Electric Co., Ltd., and H. Hamamura, Fujitsu Ltd., for their valuable cooperation of providing numbers of PWB examples, and Prof. H. Ozaki, Osaka University, for his continuous encouragement.

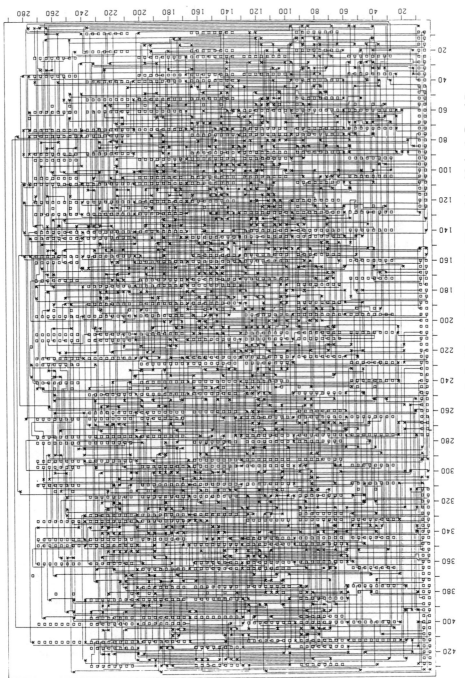

Figure 17-15. The final wire patterns obtained for the PWB of Table 4 by applying Modes 3, B, and D.

This work was supported in part by the Grant in Aid for Scientific Research of the Ministry of Education, Science, and Culture of Japan under Grant: Cooperative Research (A) 435013 (1979, 1980).

REFERENCES

(1) Lee, C. Y. "An Algorithm for Path Connections and its Applications." *IRE Trans. Electronic Comput.* **EC:10:** 346–365 (1961).

(2) Geyer, J. M. "Connection Routing Algorithm for Printed Circuit Boards." *IEEE Trans. Circuit Theory* **CT-18:** 95–100 (1971).

(3) Rubin, R. "The Lee Path Connection Algorithm." *IEEE Trans. Computers* **C-23:** 907–914 (1974).

(4) Mikami, K. and Tabuchi, K. "A Computer Program for Optimal Routing of Printed Circuit Connection." *Proc. IFIP Congress* (1968): 1475–1478.

(5) Hightower, D. W., "A Solution to Line Routing Problems on the Continuous Plane." *Proc. 6th Design Automation Workshop* (1969): 1–24.

(6) Yamamura, H., Shirakawa, I., and Ozaki, H. "A Line-search Method for the Route Connecting Problem on 2-layer Printed Circuit Boards." *Trans. IECE* **57-A:** 671–678 (1974) (in Japanese).

(7) Hashimoto, A. and Stevens, J. "Wire Routing by Optimizing Channel Assignment Within Large Apertures." *Proc. 8th Design Automation Workshop* (1971): 155–169.

(8) Kelley, M. F. and Smith, R. J., Jr. "An Optimizing Path Printed Circuit Board Router." *Proc. 10th Asilomar Conf. Circuits, Systems, and Computers* (1976): 425–430.

(9) Dereau, M. T. and Abel, L. C. "A Topologically Based Non-minimum Distance Routing Algorithm." *Proc. 15th Design Automation Conf.* (1978): 92–99.

(10) Foster, J. C. "A Router for Multilayer Printed Writing Backplanes." *Proc. 10th Design Automation Workshop* (1973): 44–49.

(11) Kernighan, B. W., Schweikert, D. G., and Persky, G. "An Optimum Channel-routing Algorithm for Polycell Layouts of Integrated Circuits." *Proc. 10th Design Automation Workshop* (1973): 50–59.

(12) Slemaker, C. S., Mosteller, R. C., Leyking, L. W., and Livitsanos, A. G. "A Programmable Printed-wiring Router." *Proc. 11th Design Automation Workshop.* 314–321 (1974).

(13) Fisher, R. S. "A Multi-pass, Multi-algorithm Approach to PCB Routing." *Proc. 15th Design Automation Conf.* (1978): 82–91.

(14) Lass, S. E. "An Automated Printed Circuit Routing with a Stepping Aperture." *Comm. of ACM.* (1969): 262–265.

(15) So, H. C. "Some Theoretical Results on the Routing of Multilayer Printed Wiring Boards." *Proc. IEEE ISCAS* (1974): 296–303.

(16) Ting. B. S., Kuh, E. S., and Shirakawa, I. "The Multilayer Routing Problem: Algorithms and Necessary and Sufficient Conditions for the Single-row Single-layer Case." *IEEE Trans. Circuits and Systems* **CAS-23:** 768-778 (1976).

(17) Kuh, E. S., Kashiwabara, T., and Fujisawa, T. "On Optimum Single-row Routing." *IEEE Trans. Circuits and Systems* **CAS-26:** 361–368 (1979).

(18) Tsukiyama, S., Kuh, E. S., and Shirakawa, I. "An Algorithm for Single-row Routing with Prescribed Street Congestions." *IEEE Trans. Circuits and Systems* **CAS-27:** 765–771 (1980).

(19) Nishioka, I., Kurimoto, T., Nishida, H., Shirakawa, I., and Ozaki, H. "A Minicomputerized Layout System for Two-layer Printed Wiring Boards." *Proc. 14th Design Automation Conf.* (1977): 1–11.

(20) Foster, J. C. "A Lookahead Router for Multilayer Printed Wiring Boards." *Proc. 16th Design Automation Conf.* (1979): 486–492.

(21) Dysart, L. and Koifman, M. "An Application of Branch and Bound Method to Automatic Printed Circuit Board Routing." *Proc. 16th Design Automation Conf.* (1979): 494–499.

(22) Asahara, S., Odani, M., Ogura, Y., Shirakawa, I., and Ozaki, H. "A Routing System Based on Single-row Routing for High Density Printed Wiring Boards." *Proc. ICCC* (1980): 290–294.

(23) ———— "A Routing System Based on a Single-row Router and its Wirability." *Internat'l J. Circuit Theory and Applications,* forthcoming.

(24) Hadlock, F. O. "A Shortest Path Algorithm for Grid Graphs." *Networks* **7**: 323–334 (1977).

(25) Nishioka, I, Kurimoto, T., Nishida, H., Yamamoto, S., Chiba, T., Fujioka, T., and Uchino, M. "An Automatic Routing System for High Density Multilayer Printed Wiring Boards." *Proc. 17th Design Automation Conf.* (1980): 520–527.

(26) Tsukiyama, S., Shirakawa, I., and Asahara, S. "An Algorithm for the Via Assignment Problem in Multilayer Backboard Wiring." *IEEE Trans. Circuits and Systems* **CAS-26:** 369–377 (1979).

(27) Asahara, S., Ogura, Y., Odani, M., Shirakawa, I., and Ozaki, H. "An Analysis of the Wiring Performance of an Automatic Routing System." *IECE Mono. CAS 80-128* (1981) (in Japanese).

(28) Tani, S. "An Analysis of Placement Performances of a Routing System." *Master Thesis, Osaka University* (1981) (in Japanese).

(29) Tsukiyama, S., Kuh, E. S., and Shirakawa, I. "On the Layering Problem of Multilayer PWB Wiring." *Proc. 18th Design Automation Conf.* (1981): 738–745.

18. Cell Based VLSI Design System

U. Lauther

Siemens Company, West Germany

INTRODUCTION

The main steps in developing an integrated circuit are functional design, physical design and generation of test and fabrication data.

Functional design starts from a specification of the intended behaviour of the circuit and results in a schematic, i.e. specifications about which components are to be used and in which way these components are to be interconnected. Design verification (simulation on various levels such as register transfer level, gate level, circuit level) will be used to make sure that the designed network exhibits the intended behaviour.

The next step—physical design—deals with the physical implementation of the circuitry on the wafer. For each component, the device geometry has to be found and then the components have to be placed and interconnected using as little silicon area as possible. Placement and routing are closely coupled problems: The quality of placement has a heavy impact on routability and the space used for wires determines the final positions of the components. This interdependence of placement and routing renders the layout problem hard not only for the human designer but also for computer programs.

Physical design also has to be verified to make sure that design rules are adhered to (design rule check) and that the circuit implemented is consistent with the functional specification (connectivity check).

In a final step, the data collected during functional and physical design are used to generate control information for mask making or for direct electron beam exposure of the wafer and for testing.

One reason for computer application in the development of integrated circuits is the vast amount of data to be handled during the design cycle. Other reasons are reliability, cost reduction and faster turn around of the design and redesign process. Consistency of all design effort, which is crucial for the success of the design effort, can be achieved only by computer utilization. For this purpose, one aims at integrated design systems which are composed of functional design, physical design and generation of test and fabrication data, grouped around a central data base (1,2). For those development steps which are not (yet) fully automated, at least the results are automatically checked. The central data base helps to guarantee consistency of all design data and avoids the tedious and error-prone multiple data entry of conventional unintegrated design aids.

One block of such an integrated design system will be discussed in the following sections: Physical design at the cell level, including placement, routing and connectivity checking. But first let us have a look at various cell concepts for IC layout.

CELL CONCEPTS

As mentioned above, the input to the physical design step is the schematic (i.e. a list of components and nets). The output consists of the position and orientation for each component and the geometry of wires and vias which connect them. The term "component" has to be understood in the wider sense described below. In the functional design step, a top down approach is usually applied. The architecture of the system is composed of a few big blocks (functions) which are decomposed into subblocks (subfunctions) on the next lower level of the hierarchy. By stepwise refinement, finally the transistor level is reached, just as in software design a function is refined down to the statement level.

It suggests itself to map the functional blocks of a certain design level into layout blocks (cells) in physical design. These cells are the "components" to be handled by placement and routing.

Designing at the cell level offers a lot of advantages:

- The layout of a cell is worked out once and used repeatedly in the same circuit; this results in a high degree of regularity of the layout which in turn lowers design time and verification expense.
- Cells which have been shown to work error free in one circuit can be used without new expense in other projects.
- The number of elements one has to deal with in placement and routing is by one or more orders of magnitude lower than in a transistor level approach; it is this reduction of complexity which makes automation of the design process feasible.
- Design automation helps to keep design costs and turn around time low and to achieve an error free design.
- Finally, the use of cell concepts leads to a clearly structured design: Details in the implementation of a function are hidden in the cell; local signals can be kept local.

The rapid increase in complexity of integrated circuits not only leads to ever increasing development costs but makes it hard to achieve an errorfree design at all; we therefore believe that a structured design style (3) supported by powerful design aids is a must in the near future.

Of course, there are potential drawbacks in the use of cell based methods; the main one is that the silicon area needed for the circuit usually is larger than in a hand tailored design on transistor level. How significant this increase in area is, depends on the cell concept employed.

There are basically three different cell concepts: Masterslice, standard cell and general cell concept. In masterslice layouts, all cells usually have the same size. These cells are placed on a matrix of predefined slots. We will not go into details since the approach is discussed elsewhere in this book.

The standard cell approach (typical programs are LTX (4) at BELL Labs, and AVESTA (5) at SIEMENS) gives a bit more freedom to the designer: Cells may have different size, but one dimension of the cells is fixed to allow for an arrangement in rows. Cell terminals are restricted to one (sometimes two) cell edges(s). Typically two rows of cells share a common routing channel towards which the cell terminals are oriented. In this placement scheme highly efficient channel routing algorithms can be applied (6,7).

The advantage of masterslice and standard cell concepts is that they lend themselves easily to automatic placement and routing; a drawback is to be seen in the difficulty of mapping functional blocks of widely varying complexity into cells of fixed or only slightly variable size. Applying the general cell concept, these problems are avoided; functional blocks are mapped to rectangular cells of any size and shape.

There is one more advantage of this method: A complete cell based design can be conceived as *one* cell. Therefore, this design style can be applied in a hierarchical way for very large circuits. In the hierarchical use of the method, sub-blocks may also be composed of standard cells arranged into rows.

In the following sections we will present a package of programs dedicated to this cell based structured design style: The SIEMENS CALCOS system which was developed for *c*omputer *a*ided *l*ayout of *c*ell *o*riented *s*ystems.

PLACEMENT

The goal of placement is to arrange the cells in a way that the interconnections can be routed and that the overall chip area is minimal.

Today's standard MOS processes usually allow for only one metal layer which has to be used not only for intercell wiring but also for cell internal connections. Therefore, the cell area typically is blocked for intercell wiring. Routing has to be done in routing channels between cells, and placement has to provide sufficient space for this purpose.

Due to the widely varying cell size, assignment to fixed locations or placement in rows is not appropriate. What is needed is a placement method which is capable of handling freely floating cells.

Most of the known placement methods can be classified into two groups: Bottom up and top down placement. Bottom up placement starts with one cell (the seed). In each cycle of the algorithm a new, not yet placed element is selected and an optimal place (relative to a figure of merit) is calculated for the element. Usually this constructive phase is followed by an iterative phase which tries to improve the solution by interchange of elements. There is a variety of algorithms of this type which differ in the selection strategy and in the figure of merit applied (usually estimated wire length) (8,9). All of these methods are sensitive to the selection of the startpoint. Another drawback is, at least in the constructive phase, the very local optimization strategy.

To overcome these drawbacks, we use a top down approach to placement. Here placement is achieved by a repeated (recursive) partitioning of the cell set controlled by the min-cut principle (10-12).

Placement of general rectangular cells poses a second problem: an efficient data structure is needed for the description and manipulation of a set of non-overlapping rectangles in the plane. We use polar graphs as a data structure for this purpose. (A polar graph is a directed graph without cycles containing one source and one sink.) Here the cell arrangement is represented by a dual pair of planar acyclic graphs. Each edge in the graph corresponds to a cell, each node represents a borderline shared by two or more cells. Calculation of longest paths in the graphs (the edge weights correspond to cell dimensions) yields all cell positions (13,14).

CALCOS was the first program to combine these two concepts just described, mini-cut controlled top down placement and polar graph representation (15). In the following paragraphs, we will outline these placement methods.

Initial Placement

When the placement program starts, the set of all cells is represented as one square the area of which is equal to the sum of cell areas and the (estimated) interconnection area. In a concurrent representation, the set of cells is represented by a dual pair of graphs consisting of one edge each (Figure 18-1a, b).

The set of cells is now partitioned into two subsets of approximately equal size in such a way that the number of nets incident to cells in different subsets is a minimum. This partitioning divides the initial square into two rectangles representing the two subsets; in the concurrent graph representation, the partitioning is expressed by splitting of the primal (dual) edge into two parallel (serial) edges (see Figure 18-1d).

The same algorithm is then applied recursively to the resulting subsets (with changing cutdirection). It terminates when each subset contains exactly one cell (Figure 18-1c-h).

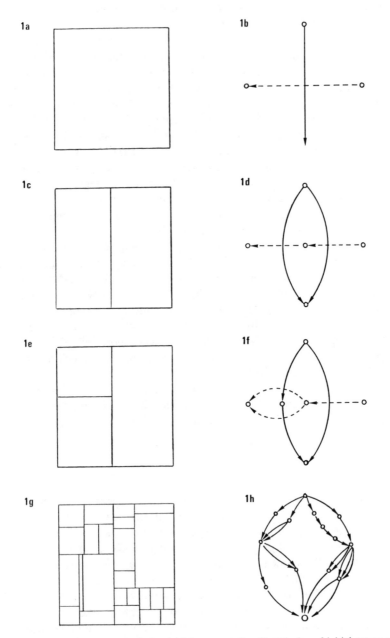

Figure 18-1. Sequence of states during initial segmentation. Partitioning of initial square and corresponding graph structure.

The initial floorplan of the layout generated by this method represents the cells with their true area (plus estimated share of wiring area) but not with their true shape. To take the cell shapes into account, the edges of the graphs are labeled with the height (width) of the corresponding cell in the primal (dual) graph. Calculation of longest paths in the two graphs then yields the coordinates of all cells (Figure 18-2a). This calculation is a very fast operation taking 0 (N) steps for N cells.

Placement Compaction

Introduction of true cell shapes may result in a lot of dead area. The underlying graph representation allows for relatively simple algorithms which reduce the amount of this unused space. Figure 18-2b shows the layout after rotational optimization. Some cells have been rotated by 90 degrees resulting in a slightly smaller floorplan. This step does not affect the initial cutlines.

A further reduction is achieved by a procedure called "squeezing" which trys to cut the longest paths in the two graphs by local changes of the graphs topology. This implies that some of the original cutlines are broken. The result of this step is shown in Figure 18-3a. Now most of the spare space has vanished.

Interactive Placement Manipulation

The polar graph representation can also be used for the implementation of powerful interactive manipulation aids. Using a CRT, cells can be rotated,

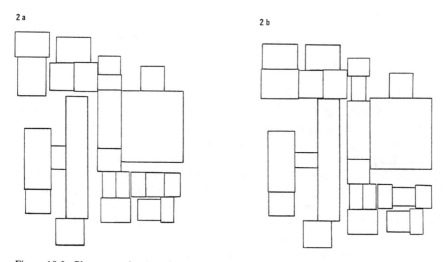

2 a

2 b

Figure 18-2. Placement after introduction of true cell shapes and after rotational optimization.

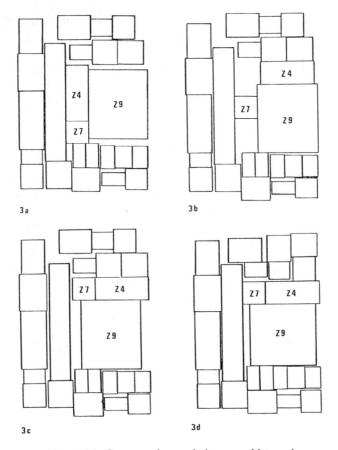

Figure 18-3. Sequence of states during manual interaction.

removed from the cell formation and inserted again at another location. Unlike usual practice in conventional graphic systems, the set of all cells is immediately rearranged when one cell has been moved.

For this purpose, all user requests (rotate, interchange, delete and reinsert) are transformed into equivalent modifications of the underlying polar graph structure; then the longest paths are recalculated yielding new cell positions.

In Figure 18-3 we can observe two such operations: First cell Z4 is inserted above Z9 with simultaneous rotation (3b), then Z7 is moved to the left side of Z4 (3c). Next, the SQUEEZE-command is executed resulting in a rearrangement of cells in the top part of the chip plan (3d).

ROUTING

Routing is done is two stages. In the first pass, global routine, we determine for each net the channels it has to run through and for each channel, the width needed to accommodate the pertinent nets. In the second pass, detailed routing, the exact position of path segments and vias has to be found for each net.

Global Routing

In global routing, the chip is modeled by a network of channels and channel junctions. For this purpose, each node of the two placement graphs is mapped into a series of channel segments which represent the space between two adjacent cells. If cells may be crossed by wires (in a two metal layer technology), then additional channel segments with limited capacity are introduced. Other special segments are used to model electrically equivalent cell terminals.

When the channel model is built, for each net the channel segments to be used are determined by shortest route calculations on the channel graph. These calculations are controlled by a cost function on the channels taking into account geometrical length, channel capacity and current "crowdedness" of the channel. For each channel, we keep track of the nets running through. This information is used to estimate the required channel width and subsequently— by feeding this information back into the placement graphs—to determine the final cell positions.

Detailed Routing

In comparable systems (16) for cell based layout, a channel router is applied for detailed routing. For a number of reasons, we decided to employ a more general line search method:

- Since signal nets and power supply lines are mixed in the routing channels we need the capability to deal with different line widths.
- "Large" vias are hard to handle in a channel router.
- A line search router, due to its net by net approach, is better suited for the inclusion of user interaction. In a final phase we want to mix editing of the layout and automatic routing—just as automatic and user controlled placement are intermixed.

Using a general line search (or more exactly, rectangle probe router), we need a simple method to transfer the information accumulated during global routing to the detailed routing pass. For this purpose, we create special obstacles which initially block all the routing channels. Whenever we attempt to route a net, we first remove those obstacles blocking the channels which had been assigned to this net during global routing. By this method the space in which a connection is searched for is greatly reduced and the performance of the router is improved. Figure 18-4 shows the arrangement of cells (crosshatched) and channel blockers (in dotted lines with diagonals) at the beginning of detailed routing. Figure 18-5a shows a small window before routine of net S46 is attempted. The relevant channel blockers are already removed.

In Figure 18-5b, routing is in progress; two path extensions have already met and the valid part of the path has been marked. In Figure 18-5c the third pin of the net has been connected and Figure 18-5d shows the final situation after completion of this net. Inspecting the series of pictures we can observe another feature of the router: To prevent blocking of cell terminals by other nets, these are protected by small pinblockers until the pertinent net is tackled. Pinblockers which are crossed by a wire are dynamically moved to preserve the protection of the pin. By this simple trick we achieve an effective look-ahead behaviour of the router. To do this automatic movement of pinblockers, and of course

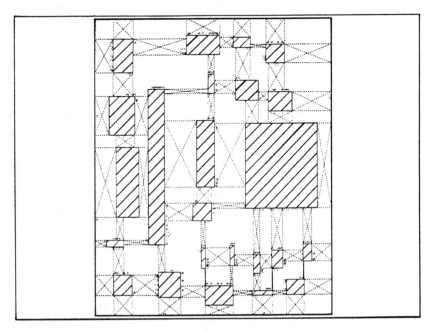

Figure 18-4. Arrangement of cells at the beginning of the detailed routing pass.

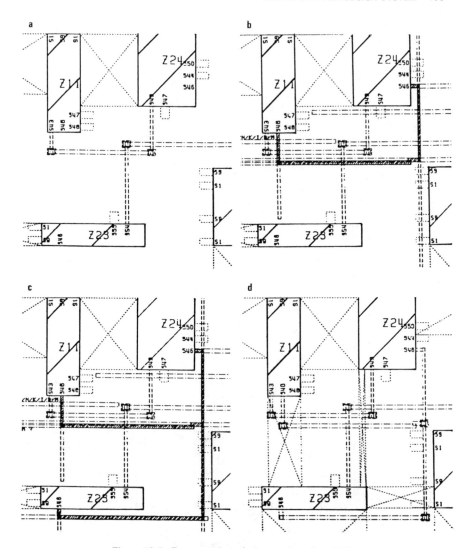

Figure 18-5. Four snapshots during routing of net S46.

for expansion of escapelines, we need an efficient data structure providing fast access to all stored items (wires, vias, blockers, . . .) on a region search basis. We use 4-dimensional, inhomogeneous binary search trees for this purpose. Details of the structure can be found in (17).

Figure 18-6 shows the total chip layout after completion of routing.

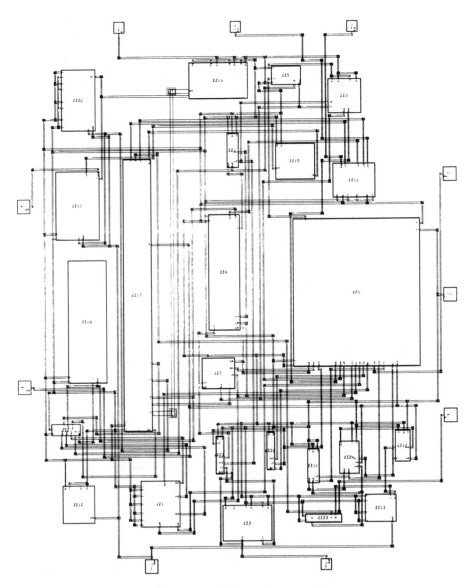

Figure 18-6. Final layout of the circuit.

Open Problems

There are two open problems with our approach to routing:

- The router uses mostly one layer for horizontal, the other for vertical wires. In many current MOS technologies one of the two layers has a high priority; power supply lines should be routed totally in metal.
- Other than in channel routing, the cell positions are fixed when detailed routing starts. Therefore, we have to overestimate the channel widths in global routing to achieve a low rate of unconnected pins. By this procedure, we waste some silicon real estate which could be saved by a second compaction pass after routing. This is a difficult problem, but it seems to be solvable (18).

DESIGN VERIFICATION

The cell level approach to physical design allows for simple and fast methods for connectivity checking. A connectivity audit is needed if manual modifications of the layout (for instance by editing at a CRT) are permitted without online checking of all actions.

The connectivity audit program extracts the connectivity information from the layout and compares these data with the intended connectivity of the circuit as expressed in the schematic. The extraction program handles all cells as black boxes; only their interface to the outer world (position and layer of cell terminals) is known to the program. Due to this technique, the amount of layout data to be handled is greatly reduced and only a minimum of technological knowledge has to be incorporated into the program.

To simplify the problem of component and pin binding, we use naming conventions: Cell types are to be referred to in the schematic and in the layout description by the same name and, in addition, individual cell instances are to be flagged with their individual names in the layout. When the layout description (which has a CIF-like macrostructure) is expanded, the program looks for the macronames which are known from the schematic and substitutes for these cell macros the pertinent black box descriptions. The black box description merely contains the set of cell terminals and the cell outline. Individual cell names are provided as text figures on the layout file and are associated to the proper instance of the cell outline by comparison of their coordinates. Connectivity analysis then groups the sets of cell terminals which are connected into nets (actual connectivity).

Whenever two terminals are in the same net as a result of this step, but in different nets in the schematic, we have found a short circuit. If the opposite is true, then we have found an open circuit.

A more detailed report on the methods used for connectivity extraction and comparison was made in (19). The program not only serves for connectivity checking, but also calculates net capacitances and delays which are fed into a central database for subsequent simulation of the circuit.

IMPLEMENTATION AND RESULTS

The set of programs discussed here was implemented in PASCAL and FORTRAN on a SIEMENS 7.760 mainframe which has a speed of about 1 MOPS, a time sharing operating system and virtual memory.

For the circuit which was used as an example throughout this discussion, we have compiled below a table of data describing the circuit and the runtime of various program steps.

Number of cells	24
pads	10
nets	53
from-tos	156
unconnects	0

Time [sec, cpu] for	
Input processing	2
Placement	8
Global routing	5
Detailed routing	32
Connectivity check	5
Total	52

It is easy to see that runtime is not at all a limiting factor. This is valid also for larger circuits. When circuits become very large, the set of programs will be applied in a hierarchical way thus avoiding any problems with computer resources.

Figure 18-7 shows an overview of the design systems components and their interaction.

ACKNOWLEDGEMENTS

To my colleagues L. Hachigk, B. Koch and W. Peine who did a big share of the programming and testing work.

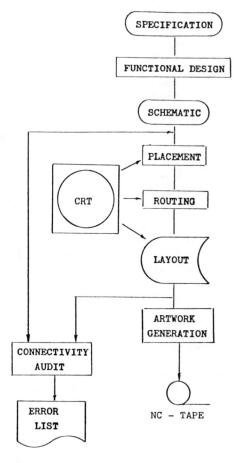

Figure 18-7. Overview of the CALCOS System.

REFERENCES

(1) Smith, Robert J. II. "Physical Design Automation." V-R Information Systems Inc.
(2) Lauther, U.. "Simple but Fast Algorithms for Connectivity Extraction and Comparison in Cell Based VLSI Designs." *Proc. ECCTD'80,* Warsaw, Poland (1980): 508–514.
(3) Mead, C., Conway, L. *Introduction to VLSI Systems.* Addison-Wesley (1979.
(4) Persky, G., Deutsch, D. N., Schweikert, D. G. "LTX—A Minicomputer Based System for Automated LSI Layout." *J. Design Aut. & Fault Tol. Comp.* I No. 3: 217–256 (May 1977).
(5) Koller, K. W., Lauther, U. "The Siemens-AVESTA-System for Computer-Aided Design

of MOS-Standard Cell Circuits." *Proc. 14th Design Automation Conf; New Orleans* (1977): 153–157.

(6) Kernighan, B. W., Schweikert, D. G., Persky, G. "An Optimum Channel-Routing Algorithm for Polycell Layouts of Integrated Circiuts." *Proc. 10th Design Automation Workshop* 50–59 (1973).

(7) Yoshimura, T., Kuh, E. S.: "Efficient Algorithms For Channel Routing." To be published.

(8) Hanan, M., Wolff, P. K., Agule, B. J. "A Study of Placement Technique." *Design Automation & Fault-Tol. Comp.* I No. 1: 28–61 (1976).

(9) Preas, B. T., Gwyn, C. W. "Methods for Hierarchical Automatic Layout of Custom LSI Circuit Mask." *Proc. 15th Design Automation Conf; Las Vegas* (June 1978).

(10) Günther, Th. "Die Räumliche Anordnung von Einheiten mit Wechselbeziehungen." *Elektronsiche Datenverarbeitung* No. 6: 209–212 (1969).

(11) Breuer, M. A. "A Class of Min-Cut Placement Algorithms." *Proc. 14th Design Automation Conf; New Orelans* (1977): 284–290.

(12) Breuer, M. A. "Min-Cut Placement." *J. Design Auto. & Fault Tol. Comp;* I No. 4: 343–362. (Oct. 1977).

(13) Brooks, R. L., Smith, C. A. B., Stone, A. H., Tutte, W. T. "The Dissection of Rectangles into Squares." *Duke Math. J.* 312–340 (1940).

(14) Ohtsuki, T., Sugiyama, N., Kawanishi, H. "An Optimization Technique for Integrated Circuit Layout Design." *Proc. ICCST-Kyoto* (Sept. 1970): 67–68.

(15) Lauther, U. "A Min-Cut Placement Algorithm for General Cell Assemblies Based on a Graph Representation." *Proc. 16th Design Automation Conf; San Diego* (1979): 1–10.

(16) Preas, B. T., van Cleemput, W. M. "Routing Algorithms for Hierarchical IC Layout." *Proc. 1979 ISCAS,* (1979): 482–485.

(17) Lauther, U. "A Data Structure for Gridless Routing." *Proc. 17th Design Automation Conf; Minneapolis* (1980): 603–609.

(18) Aurbach, R. "Oral Presentation of the Methods Used in FLOSS." *Design Automation Workshop, East Lansing, Michigan* (Oct. 1979).

(19) Lauther, U. "Simple but Fast Algorithm for Connectivity Extraction and Comparison in Cell Based VLSI Designs." *Proc. ECCTD'80, Warsaw, Poland* (1980): 508–514.

19. Advanced Interactive Layout Design System for Printed Wiring Boards

Hajimu Mori, Tomoyuki Fujita, Masahiro Annaka, Satoshi Goto
Nippon Electric Co., Japan

and

Tatsuo Ohtsuki
Waseda University, Japan

INTRODUCTION

Recent advances in microelectronics technology require high density packaging techniques for printed wiring boards of large scale digital cirucits and systems. As the printed wiring density on circuit boards increases, it is increasingly difficult for human beings to design the layout manually. Furthermore, the design time required to complete boards must be significantly shorter for electric industries in order to economically succeed in developing new equipment. Thus, a large amount of effort has been devoted to assist the designer with the layout problem.

The layout design problem is defined as follows: Given a two-layer wiring board in general, components or cirucit modules are mounted on the first side of the board, each with connector pins. Connection through-holes are used to connect wiring patterns on different layers of the board. These through holes are called vias. Each set of pins to be electrically connected in common, called a signal net or a power line, can be connected by wiring patterns on each layer using vias. The layout problem is to decide the positions of each component and find the routing of each signal net and power line to satisfy a given specification. The ultimate layout design goal is to provide an automatic design system which will achieve complete net connectivity meeting all physical and electrical constraints.

Efficient algorithms for the placement or the routing are quite important to reduce the design time. Many have been devised (1). Particularly in Japan, both theoretical and practical approaches have been very active for the past 10 years in universities and industries. See references (2–5) for the placement problem, and (6–17) for the routing problem, which were published by Japanese researchers. From the computational complexity point of view, these problems are considered to be hard combinatorial problems in the sense that the computation time required to obtain the real optimum solution increases in exponential order when the problem size, i.e., number of components or signal nets, increases. Hence, algorithms based on heuristic rationales have been employed. Although those heuristic algorithms have been improved year by year, they never have given or will never give a real optimum solution for the complete net connectivity in practical applications.

The layout design success is measured by the total time (cost) required to complete the board design. Therefore, for instance, an automatic router with higher percentage connectivity cannot be a better one than the others if it takes more design time to complete the rest of the unconnected net. In the manual layout design process, a large portion of the design time is spent on checking and error correction. Thus, it is considered extremely necessary to establish an integrated CAD system, which significantly reduces the total design time required to complete the board.

To cope with this problem, several approaches have been proposed, including commercially available systems (18). The history of the CAD systems is as follows.

First Generation CAD System

The overwhelming bulk of the layout design work has been handled through batch design systems for a period of many years. When 100% routing is not achieved by an automatic router or placer, which happens in almost all cases, the designer must examine the wiring patterns carefully on the plotted sheet to modify or create patterns for complete net connectivity. He makes up his drawing manually with necessary modifications and runs the computer in batch mode to modify the wiring patterns. The designer has to run a check program to determine whether the routing pattern is valid or not, from the standpoint of obeying design rules and net list verification. This procedure would normally be repeated several times until the checking program came up with no violations. This is time consuming and error prone, since the modification programs as well as the check programs are run repeatedly in batch mode.

Second Generation CAD System

The first part is identical to that for the first generation. However, a graphic display unit can be connected to the computer and actual geometry of the layout can be displayed. If algorithmic programs yield an unacceptable or incomplete result, the generated data can be transmitted to the graphic display station for further completion. The designer can modify that picture, visually check the geometry, and delete or add information—a process called "Computer Aided Editing." Unlike the first generation, the modification is accomplished quickly on the graphic display by the computer aided editing. This saves a great deal of manual design for wiring pattern modifications. However, since the actual geometry of its layout is manipulated manually, a check program must be run to find whether the routing pattern is valid or not in the meaning of physical design rules and net list verification. This automatic check program is used repeatedly in batch mode with the large computer, thus it is also time consuming.

Third Generation CAD System

During this past decade, the capabilities of manually controlled interactive graphics, with the designer playing an active real-time role, have been effectively integrated with true design automation technique. These techniques include automated routing or placement and design rule checking with real-time interactive graphics. All of those techniques are implemented on the same computer, usually a mega-minicomputer, realizing the significant on-line automated capabilities with real-time interactive graphics. However, the automatic functions and interactive functions are not fully integrated in the system. The automatic programs can never be interrupted freely at any moment by the designer who wants then to insert his opinion into the process in progress, interactively. And, at the end of the routing phase, a check program must be run to check the validity of the design rules applied. Furthermore, in the case of failing in 100% routing, the designer must examine the exact wiring patterns carefully on the graphic display or the plotted sheet before he successfully changes the existing patterns, which is identical to that for first or second generation CAD system. This is also time consuming.

New Generation CAD System

Though the third generation CAD system reduces the layout design time to some extent, its successful operation is fully dependent on the human being's ability. To cope with this problem, a new approach has been proposed and tried.

See Table 19-1, where important differences are described for the four generations of CAD systems. Most of the existing systems, including commercially available systems, are considered to belong to the third generation and some are in the new generation (5, 13, 19–24).

Table 19-1. Important Differences in Four Generations of CAD Systems.

	1ST GENERATION	2ND GENERATION	3RD GENERATION	NEW GENERATION
Computer	Large computer	Large computer and mini computer	Mega-mini-computer	Super-mini-computer
Graphic display	None	Storage	Storage or refresh	Refresh
Process mode	Batch	Batch and on-line	On-line	On-line
System integration	Automatic functions only	Automatic and Interactive functions are completely separate.	Automatic and Interactive functions are completely separate or partially integrated.	Automatic and Interactive functions are fully integrated.
Algorithmic programs (Router or placer)	One typical program is provided.	One typical program is provided.	Several programs are provided. The running sequence is restricted.	Several programs are provided. Any sequence or combinations can be freely selected.
Wiring pattern editing	On the plotted sheet	On the graphic display with geometric patterns	On the graphic display with symbolic patterns	On the graphic display with human being's guidance.
Finding the blockage for the unconnected net	Manual	Manual	Manual	Automatic
Check program	Batch	Batch	On-line dynamic check or at the end of routing phase	Not necessary (Always guarantee the design rule)

BRAIN SYSTEM

The BRAIN system has been developed and practically used in Nippon Electric Co., aiming at a new generation CAD system. It operates on the NEC/MS super minicomputer with 4M byte memory and beam-directed refresh display. The system is a stand-alone CAD system which allows the designer to create or modify wiring patterns freely on the refresh CRT. The automatic and interactive functions are completely integrated in the system, where the optimum exploitation of human intelligence and the computer's high speed processing can be realized.

The BRAIN system has several features over the former generation CAD systems. The following are particular ones.

1. The automatic and interactive functions are fully integrated.

    The designer can stop an automatic router at any moment while running, and can try another router or enter into interactive mode freely. After interactive editing, the designer can start any router immediately.
2. Several automatic programs are provided with different kinds of algorithms.

    Any sequence or combinations of automatic routers can be freely selected, and the designer can choose a suitable router to meet his requirement strategy.
3. The designer need not input the geometric or symbolic wiring patterns in an exact way. It is sufficient to input a rough sketch of the wiring patterns as a guide.

    The interactive router devised in the BRAIN system will find the exact wiring pattern by following the designer's rough sketch pattern. Therefore, error free wiring patterns are always guaranteed without any redundancy for any interactive editing.
4. Blocking factors and signal nets or pins are pictorially shown on the graphic display when a signal net cannot be connected by a router.

    By watching the blocking marks shown on the display, the designer at once can identify a candidate to be deleted or modified for the complete connection of the current signal net.

In the following sections, the BRAIN system hardware and software configurations are described in some detail.

HARDWARE CONFIGURATION

The BRAIN system hardware configuration is shown in Figure 19-1 and its picture in Figure 19-2.

The system operates on NEC/MS super minicomputer, which has up to 4M byte memory capacity and 58M byte disk storage capacity, coupled with 21-

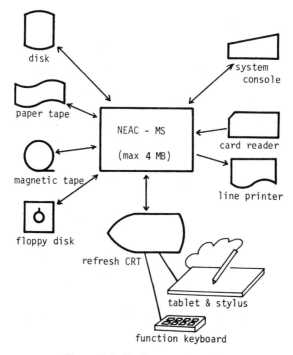

Figure 19-1. Hardware configuration.

Figure 19-2. BRAIN system.

inch beam-directed refresh graphic display. The display terminal includes a graphics tablet and a function control keyboard with 2048 by 2048 point address space. In addition, the system is equipped with a card reader, paper tape reader/puncher, magnetic tape unit, floppy disk unit and a console typewriter unit.

The BRAIN system, where highly intelligent interactive functions and automatic functions are realized, calls for a powerful minicomputer and a refresh graphic display. The NEC/MS minicomputer with extended memory and addressing capabilities remarkably speeds up the computation time for automatic programs. Furthermore, the super minicomputer simplifies the development of application software.

The refresh graphics have established dynamic and flexible interactive operations with quick response time. Any line, character or object can be deleted, rotated, dragged, dimmed, blinked or scaled instantaneously without re-creating the entire picture.

DESIGN FLOW AND DATABASES

The layout design process in the BRAIN system can be divided into 6 phases: library maintenance, input data processing, module placement, power line routing, signal net wiring and output data generation. Each phase runs on the library database and the design database, which play control roles in the system. The design flow diagram is shown in Figure 19-3. Usually, descriptions on components and boards are registered in the library database in advance. The library database organizes many kinds of data used in common. Circuits to be laid out on each board are specified in input data. The input data is compiled into the design database with its detailed descriptions on the library database. After the completion of design database generation, the designer can proceed with module placement using automatic or interactive mode. Once the placement design is completed, the power line routing starts to connect all of the power pins with respect to their pertinent requirements. Following the power line routing, the layout design is ready for signal net wiring. The wiring may then be accomplished by computer programs intermixes with interactive actions. With the layout design results, the output generation subsystem can prepare many types of documentations.

Library Data Maintenance. Component data or board data are used in common to make up various kinds of printed wiring boards. Those data are created or updated in the library database, in advance, for designing circuit boards, and are referred to at the circuit design stage.

The component data includes:

● Component shape.
● Pin (location, voltage, drill size).

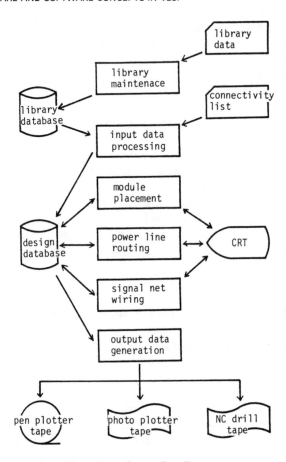

Figure 19-3. System flow diagram.

- Routing block-off area.
- Artwork data.

The board data includes:

- Board shape.
- Edge connector.
- Prohibited area.
- Preassigned power line.

They are described on punched cards or the digitizer's output tapes. A successful checking on their logical or physical validity allows creating or updating the library database.

Input Data Processing. The input processor requires design data for each printed wiring board layout, and automatically retrieves detail specifications from the library database. Circuit connections, design rules and preassigned data are described in the design data. With the input processing completion, the skeleton for the layout design is built up. While designing a printed wiring board, the design database plays the role of linking the following processes.

The circuit connections are described on a net-by-net basis. A net is simply a string of component pins or edge connectors which should be electrically common.

Design rules are as follows:

- Number of layers.
- Number of tracks between pins.
- Minimum conductor spacing.
- Signal line width.
- Power line width.

Preassigned data includes:

- Allocated component position.
- Macro grid size for component placement.
- Power line routes.

Layout Design Phase. Module placement, power line routing and signal net wiring are performed at the layout design phases, which are carried out in automatic and interactive modes. They get instructions from the design database and the results are stored into the design database. Each phase is described in detail in the following sections.

Output Data Generation Phase. Once a printed wiring board layout is completed, this system provides many forms of documentation through the design database, where the component location and wiring patterns are stored.

The following manufacturing documents are produced by interactive operations.

- Pen plotter tape
  —assembly drawings.
- Photo plotter tape
  —PWB artwork
  —solder masks
  —silk screen mask.
- NC drill tape.

Capabilities.   The BRAIN system allows the designing of a large scale PWB with complicated design rule. Table 19-2 shows current BRAIN system capabilities.

PLACEMENT

In the placement phase, the board locations of individual components should be decided to facilitate the power line routing and signal net wiring. The final layout goal is to achieve 100% routing. However, it is too difficult to consider the final goal itself in the placement phase. Until now, the usual goal has been to minimize the total routing length or the maximum density, and a number of placement algorithms have been proposed (1–4). Those placement algorithms work quite well when components to be placed are modular and component positions are restricted to predefined slots on the board.

Through accumulated experience, it has been learned that manual placement gives much better results than automatic programs in almost all cases for the component placement problems when components are in various sizes and shapes. Therefore, the authors' approach is a combination of automatic algorithms and interactive ones. Automatic programs produce initial placement, then the designer improves the placement manually on the CRT. The system provides several interactive commands, which give the designer suitable information and the ability to use the CRT in finding the optimum component placement. The automatic placement program is restricted to modular ICs and LSIs. Other discrete components, such as resistors or capacitors, are excluded from running automatic programs. After executing the automatic placement program, unplaced components are manually positioned by the designer on the CRT.

Slots on the board, where modular components are to be placed, are represented by points on an x-y coordinate system. This coordinate is called "macro grid." The designer gives it with the component orientation before running the

Table 19-2. BRAIN Capabilities.

No. of layers	2 or 4
Grid size	500,000 grid cross points
No. of signal nets	1200
No. of components	1000
No. of pins per signal net	128
No. of pins per component	200
No. of power voltage values	8
Components with off-grid pins	: possible (automatically connected by routers)
Components with preassigned wires	: possible
No. of tracks between pins	: 1, 2, 3

automatic placement program. The objective function is adopted to minimize the expected total routing length. For this kind of placement problem, one of the authors has developed an efficient algorithm (4). Figure 19-4 shows the automatic placement result.

The designer may try to improve the automatic placement result by using the interactive functions on the CRT. The BRAIN system provides the following interactive functions.

1. The designer can easily indicate the desired location of unplaced component successively on the CRT, using a stylus pen. When locating a component, the system indicates the optimal component position on the CRT, which is designated by "GRAV," as shown in Figure 19-4. The "GRAV" point is a component position where the total routing length associated with the component is minimum when the other components remain fixed in place. The designer can also give operations such as move, rotate, align or exchange, for already placed components.

2. The designer can identify power pins for components, considering each voltage value, so as to place components with the same power requirements in such a manner as to facilitate power line routing.

3. The system indicates, by blinking on the CRT, which component occupies the worst position, the second worst position and so forth. The component in the worst position is a component whose movement would contribute most to reducing the total wire length among all components.

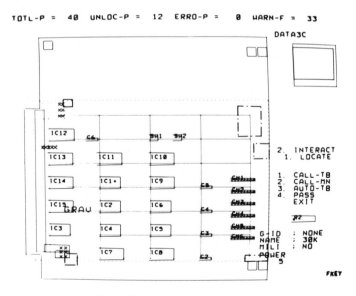

Figure 19-4. Automatic placement.

4. Besides the indication of "GRAV" point, a visual aid of displaying signal net connections is provided. Figure 19-5 shows "rubber-band" connection lines of components selected by the designer. This information helps the designer to find the optimal placement for the components.
5. The validity of any component placement is checked at any time by the system. The validity check includes:

- Component overlapping.
- Minimum conductor spacing.
- Voltage conflict.

Functions of commands in the placement phase are summarized in Table 19-3.

POWER LINE ROUTING

Power line routing is quite different from signal net wiring, in the sense that the number of pins connected in the line is much greater than that of a signal net. Furthermore, power lines have various widths. Therefore, power line routing cannot be treated in the same way as signal net wiring.

Power line routing is one of the features in the BRAIN system. In the conventional layout CAD system, power lines are preassigned or designed totally manually on the CRT, or treated as signal nets.

The power pins are identified with the same voltage, based on either the

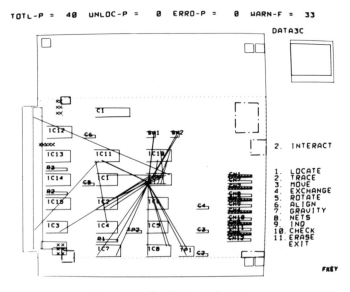

Figure 19-5. Signal net requirement.

Table 19-3. Placement Commands.

1. AUTO	Automatic placement
2. INTERACT	Interactive placement
1. LOCATE	Place an unlocated component
2. TRACE	Bring an already placed component with stylus pen
3. MOVE	Move the position of a placed component
4. EXCHANGE	Exchange the locations of two components
5. ROTATE	Rotate a component
6. ALIGN	Align components along X-axis or Y-axis
7. GRAVITY	Indicate the gravity point of a component
8. NETS	Indicate signal net connections for components
9. INQ	Blink components with the worst position, second worst position and so on
10. CHECK	Check the placement validity
11. ERASE	Erase unnecessary drawings on the CRT
3. SAVE	Save the current placement state data

library database or input data. The BRAIN system merges the power pins with the same voltage in the library and the input data. This system can identify 8 different voltage value pins.

The system can deal with the following two cases:

1. Assign power lines and signal net on different layers.
2. Assign power lines on the same layers with signal nets.

For both cases, interactive commands are provided to design power lines easily on the CRT.

In the former case, ground and power supply layers are treated independently from signal layers. Usually, one whole layer is for ground plane, and another layer is for power supply. The power plane is divided into several domains corresponding to each voltage value. In other words, power pins with the same voltage value have to be in the same domain and separated from the other domains with different voltage values. To produce these domains, the designer has to divide the whole domain by a sequence of lines, which are called insulation lines. The system provides the commands for generating, adding and deleting insulation lines. By using these commands, the designer can form domains on the CRT. Figure 19-6 shows an example, where "⊠," "⊀" and "△" represent +5V, −5V and ground pins, respectively.

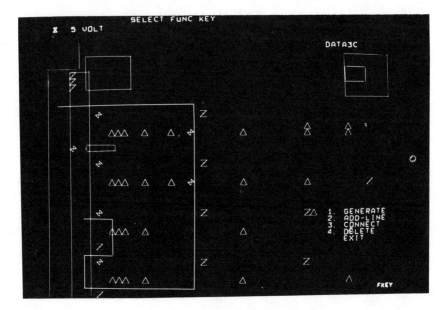

Figure 19-6. Insulation line.

In the latter case, power lines and signal lines are on the same layer. In general, power line width is larger than signal line width and not unique on the board. Furthermore there are many more pins to be connected. Therefore, it is almost impossible to design power lines in a fully automatic way. The BRAIN system offers interactive and automatic functions in the following way. Three different kinds of power lines, called categories A, B and C power lines, are introduced.

Category A power lines: Preassigned power lines. They are defined as a set of rectangles and vias. Any rectangle size is allowed.

Category B power lines: Trunk lines. The width has to be unique on the board and is given by the input data. The layout design is accomplished on the CRT interactively, where the designer commands—generate, add, delete and connectivity check—are provided.

Category C power lines: Branch lines which connect power pins to category A or category B power lines. This is done by automatic routing program. The width of the lines is specified uniquely by the input data.

In general, the design proceeds in the following way. Power lines on the edge connectors or with large width are given category A power lines. They are usually decided upon in advance for the component placement. Then, the designer interactively gives category B power line routing along the power pins neighborhoods. Connections, between component power pins and categories A or B power lines, are accomplished automatically. Figure 19-7 shows an example.

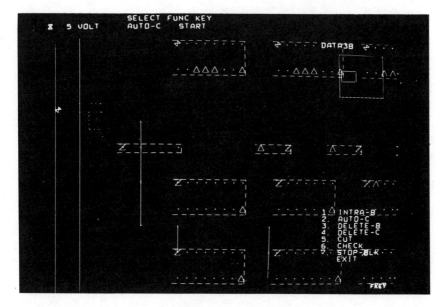

Figure 19-7. Power lines.

The system also offers commands to point out unconnected power pins by blinking on the CRT.

Functions of each interactive command are summarized in Tables 19-4 and 19-5.

Each command is executed by pushing the button of the function keyboard corresponding to the number of commands shown on the CRT.

SIGNAL NET WIRING

The wiring design goal is to achieve complete net connectivity meeting all physical and electrical constraints. It is almost impossible for automatic routers to accomplish 100% wiring without man-machine interaction. The BRAIN system integrates automatic and interactive functions, where the optimum exploitation of human intelligence and the computer's high speed processing can be realized. This enables effectively reducing the design time to accomplish 100% wiring.

Table 19-4. Power Line Routing Commands.
(Power Lines and Signal Nets Are in Different Layers)

1. GENERATE	Generate insulation line
2. ADD	Add insulation line
3. CONNECT	Connect two unconnected insulation lines by an insulation line
4. DELETE	Delete insulation lines

Table 19-5. Power Line Routing Commands.
(Power Lines and Signal Nets Are in the Same Layers)

1. GENERATE	Generate category B power lines
2. AUTO-C	Automatic layout for category C power lines.
3. DELETE-B	Delete category B power lines
4. DELETE-C	Delete category C power lines
5. CUT	Cut off unnecessary parts of category B power lines
6. CHECK	Indicate unconnected power pins

Fundamental Techniques

Signal net wiring is performed through either automatic routers or interactive routers. All of these routers run on the same wiring data structure with "bit map" board data. Therefore any router, automatic or interactive, can start immediately, one after another.

Automatic Wiring. The BRAIN system provides several kinds of automatic routers; Pattern router, DFS (Depth First Search) router and BFS (Breadth First Search) router. Each router has its own characteristic pertinent to finding a particular wiring path. Any sequence or combinations on several automatic routers can be freely selected and the designer can stop an automatic router at any moment while running. Then, the designer can try another router or enter into interactive mode freely. After interactive operations, the designer can start any router immediately. By repeating this start and stop operation for the routers, the designer can choose a suitable router to meet his requirement strategy, based on his intelligence, not mechanical "try again" procedure.

Interactive Router. The interactive router is a path finding program following the designer's rough sketch of wiring pattern. At a stage in connecting a signal net on the graphic display, the designer indicates a series of points as a rough sketch of the wiring pattern. According to this rough sketch, the interactive router will try to find a connecting path meeting all physical and electrical constraints. The two parameters are specified to the interactive router, layer number and extra search width.

The layer number specifies a board layer for a connecting path. In the case of a two layer board problem, this layer number is 0, 1 or 2. The number 1 or 2 corresponds to its board layer. The number 0 indicates no specification being given in regard to the board layer. In other words, the interactive router will decide which layer number, 1 or 2, should be used, instead of the designer's specification.

The extra search width defines a search area with extended width. Within this defined area, the interactive router tries to find a connecting path.

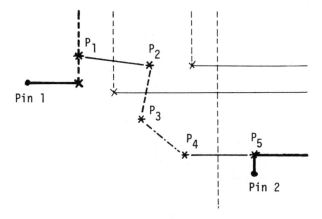

Figure 19-8. Designer's rough sketch.

Figure 19-8 shows an example of a designer's rough sketch of wiring pattern. Five points P_1, P_2, ... , P_5 are given in this order to connect Pin 1 and Pin 2. Layer 1 is specified between P_1 and P_2, or P_4 and P_5 as shown by solid lines. Layer 2 is between P_2 and P_3, and no layer number is specified between P_3 and P_4, which are shown by a dotted line and a chain line, respectively.

A rectangle is generated in such a way as to enclose P_1 and P_2 with extra search width W. For the other consecutive points, 3 rectangles are generated, as shown in Figure 19-9.

The interactive router will try to find a connecting path between Pin 1 and Pin 2 within these 4 rectangles by setting the value W. In a particular case for $W = 0$, a connecting path which passes through only specified points is obtained, if one exists. In this case, the interactive router checks the validity of the designer's detailed wiring pattern dynamically.

The interactive router releases the designer from the burden of inputting detailed wiring patterns in an exact way, which is time consuming and error prone.

Boundary Marks.   In the case of failing to find a connecting path, the BRAIN system displays boundary marks on the graphic display. A boundary mark means that, at the corresponding positions, all paths connecting a pair of pins are blocked by other signal nets or prohibited areas.

In graph theory, for any given two nodes denoted by S and T, a set of nodes which every path from S to T has to pass through is called S-T separator (25). A boundary is an S-T separator on the grid graph corresponding to the board.

Without removing a signal net indicated by the boundary marks, the blocked signal net cannot be connected. By watching the boundary marks shown on the

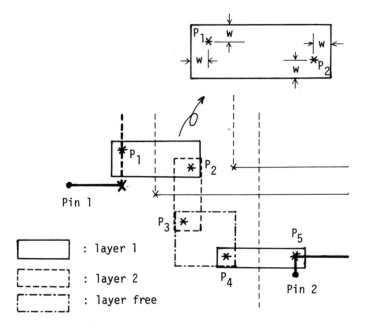

Figure 19-9. Search area.

display, the designer at once identifies a candidate for signal net wiring patterns to be deleted or modified. Therefore, these boundary marks give the designer a valuable guide to complete a signal net connection. In the existing CAD system, the designer has to waste a lot of time in finding blocking signal nets to be modified by visually checking the geometric wiring patterns on the plotted sheet.

Wiring Commands

The BRAIN system provides the following interactive functions. The wiring commands are mainly composed of automatic and interactive modes. Each one of them can be stopped at any moment while running, and can be started freely (See Table 19-6).

AUTO: executes automatic routing programs, which consist of three kinds of routers; PATTERN, DFS and BFS routers.

PATTERN: a high speed router which finds a connection path with prescribed wiring patterns. The prescribed wiring patterns as I, L and Z categories. The I category wiring pattern is a pattern without using any via hole. The L category is accomplished by using only one via hole and the Z category is accomplished by two via holes. The PATTERN router tries to find a connection path in such simple wiring patterns, without searching for complicated

Table 19-6. Wiring Commands.

AUTO	Enter the automatic wiring mode
PATTERN	Execute Pattern router
DFS	Execute DFS router
BFS	Exectue BFS router
INTERACT	Enter the interactive wiring mode
RUN	Execute a router porgram as far as possible until no connecting path can be found
CONNECT	Find a wiring path by following the designer's rough sketch of wiring pattern
MODIFY	Modify an existing wiring pattern
DELETE	Delete a part of wiring pattern
SELECT	Select a specified pin pair for connection
PASS	Change a pin pair order
SLANT	Slant a line
LOCUS	Display a wiring path candidate
PIN PAIR	Display unconnected pin pairs
VIA ELIM	Execute via elimination
SAVE	Save a current wiring result
RESTART	Restart from a specified wiring result

patterns. Therefore, the PATTERN router can be executed in a quick manner, although the wiring performance is not high. The wiring rate, calculated by the number of connected nets versus to the number of all nets, is generally 50 ~ 70%.

DFS: a router that finds a connecting path based on a depth first search algorithm (26). It is fast and efficient for up to 80 ~ 90% of the routes on the board.

The BFS: a router that is based on the classical Lee's algorithm, executing the breadth first search (27). It has two distinctive modes. One is to restrict wiring patterns to "X-Y rule," and the other one is not. The X-Y rule is a wiring assignment rule to layout vertical and horizontal wiring segments on layer 1 and layer 2, respectively. In most cases, the BFS router achieves 95 ~ 98% routing completion.

INTERACT: executes interactive editing programs to connect, modify or delete the signal net wiring.

RUN: a type of maze router. It attempts to find successive connecting paths extending as far as possible until it is stopped by reaching a dead end. In the case of failing to find connecting paths, the RUN router stops and displays boundary marks on the display.

CONNECT: an interactive router mentioned in this section. The designer's rough wiring pattern sketch is enough as a guide to use to complete the connections.

MODIFY: modify a part of wiring patterns. The same technique as that of CONNECT is adopted to find a connecting path between two points on the modified patterns.

DELETE: delete a specified part of wiring patterns. The designer indicates a point on the wiring pattern displayed on the graphics by using the stylus pen. The wiring part to be deleted is calculated automatically, corresponding to the indicated point. This part is called a "wiring block" and is discussed in the following section. It is the minimal portion of wiring patterns whose end point is either a pin or a branch point (See Figure 19-10). Unneccessary dangling or end free wiring segments are never generated, since the DELETE command restricts delete operations on such particular wiring segments.

SELECT or PASS: allows the designer to specify pin pairs or change their order for connections.

SLANT: generates slant lines with modifying wiring patterns.

LOCUS: displays a candidate for connecting paths from a pin to the specified point on the boundary marks. This candidate helps the designer to choose a suitable path for his wiring strategy.

As an aid to the designer's strategy, PIN PAIR command displays all unconnected pin pairs remaining at the current wiring result.

VIA ELIM: attempts to eliminate unnecessary via holes from the current wiring result. This is important in the sense that a large number of via holes, if carried through the final board, would increase the cost and decrease the reliability of the boards.

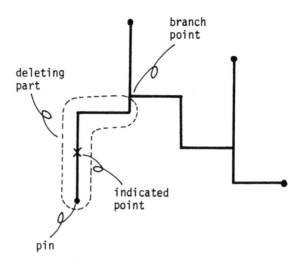

Figure 19-10. Deleting part.

SAVE or RESTART: is used to save several kinds of wiring results and restart from a specified one. This gives the designer a splendid design aid, when he wants to attack the wiring problem from the standpoint of various different layout strategies. Up to 10 wiring results can be saved and any one of them can be restarted for wiring.

As an example picture, a designer's rough sketch showing wiring patterns and the resulting pattern obtained by executing the CONNECT command are shown in Figure 19-11 and Figure 19-12, respectively. Figure 19-13 is an example of boundary marks where triangular marks "△" are displayed as the boundaries.

Specific Features

The BRAIN wiring system has several features over the existing CAD systems. The specific features are described in the following:

1. Several automatic routers are provided with different kinds of algorithms. PATTERN, DFS and BFS routers are provided in the current version.

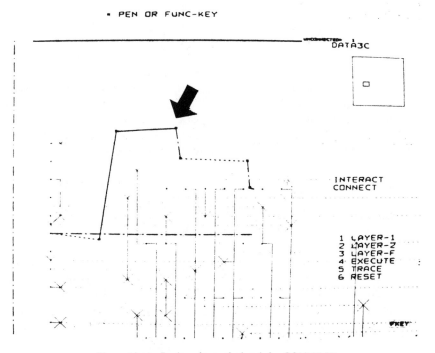

Figure 19-11. Designer's rough sketch for CONNECT.

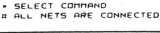

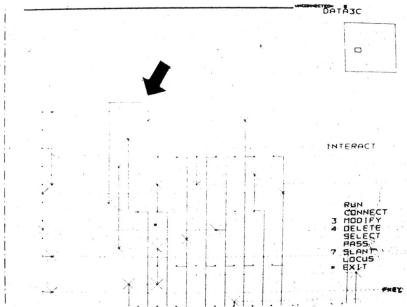

Figure 19-12. Wiring pattern result by CONNECT.

Those routers can be executed or stopped at any moment and any execution sequence is possible.

2. The automatic and interactive functions are fully integrated. The AUTO command and the INTERACT command can be switched from one to another at any moment. This switch action is performed only by pushing a "function key" button.

3. The designer need not input the geometric or symbolic wiring pattern in an exact way. It is sufficient to input a rough sketch of the wiring patterns as a guide. This function is realized in the CONNECT or MODIFY command with the interactive router, which guarantees the wiring patterns physically and electrically.

4. Blocking factors, signal nets or pins, are pictorially shown on the graphic display when a signal net cannot be connected. The boundary marks realize this function and give the designer a valuable guide to complete the connection. The designer only checks a small portion of the wiring patterns, instead of all the patterns, in order to modify the existing patterns, since the crucial wiring patterns are always on the boundary marks.

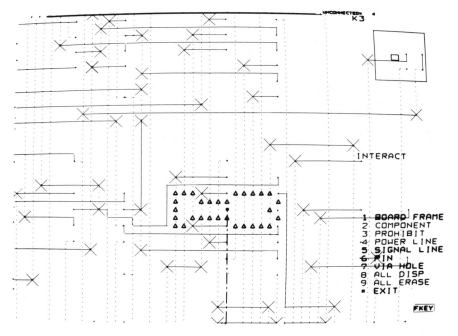

Figure 19-13. Boundary marks.

FEATURES ON IMPLEMENTATION

In the case of batch mode routing, no particular data structure is necessary for wiring patterns. However, interactive editing operations such as deletion, addition or modification, requires manipulating the wiring pattern data by some structure, so as to prevent generating unnecessary dangling lines or loops (24).

In the BRAIN system, by introducing the graph theoretical approach, called a pedigree graph, it is possible to implement the interactive operations easily without generating any dangling lines.

A signal net with n pins is segregated into n-1 pairs of pins (pin pairs) and wiring proceeds on a pin pair by pin pair basis. A wiring pattern corresponding to a pin pair is called a wiring block. One generation of a wiring block combines another two wiring blocks or isolated pins together.

Parent-child relationship is defined among those wiring blocks. Assume that wiring block A has already been generated. Then, wiring block B is generated. If wiring block B connects a point on wiring block A and some other point, then A is called a parent of B.

A pedigree graph is defined as follows. A node in a pedigree graph represents a wiring block. If wiring block A is a parent of wiring block B, then a directed arc exists from node A to node B (see Figure 19-14).

At the wiring phase beginning, pedigree graphs are constructed in simple ways for each signal net. The pedigree graph, corresponding to a signal net with 4 pins, has a star structure as shown in Figure 19-15.

First, Pin 1 and Pin 2 are assumed to be connected by wiring block A. Then, the pedigree graph is transformed to that of Figure 19-16, where there exist three connected components. Next, Pin 3 and Pin 4 are connected by wiring block B, which results in two connected components (Figure 19-17).

Then, wiring block A and wiring block B are connected by wiring block C

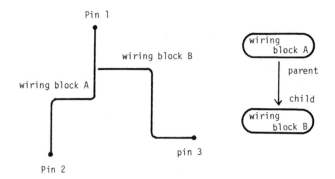

Figure 19-14. Wiring block.

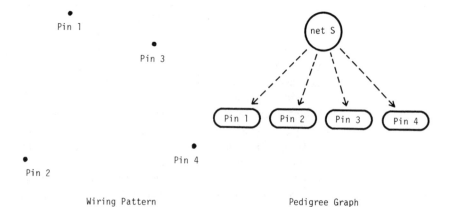

Wiring Pattern   Pedigree Graph

Figure 19-15. Initial state.

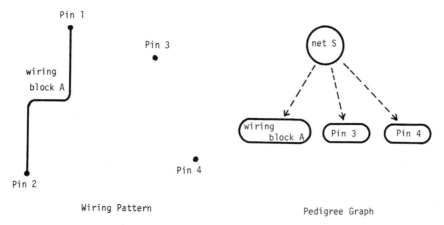

Wiring Pattern   Pedigree Graph

Figure 19-16. One pin pair is connected.

and the wiring of this net is completed. Both A and B are parents of C (Figure 19-18).

When the designer selects DELETE command and indicates a point on the pattern, the deleting part is calculated (Figure 19-10). The deleting part is the minimal portion of the wiring pattern, including the indicated point whose end points are either pins or branch points. In this example, a point is indicated on wiring block A. Then, the pedigree graph is transformed to that of Figure 19-19. If the designer O.K.'s the action, deletion is as shown in Figure 19-20. It

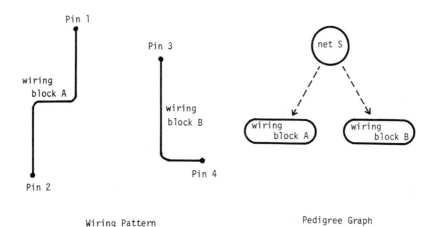

Wiring Pattern   Pedigree Graph

Figure 19-17. Two pin pairs are connected.

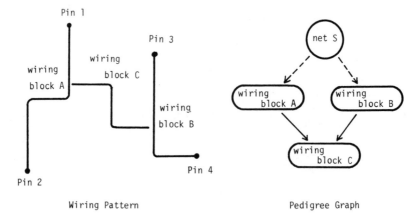

Wiring Pattern   Pedigree Graph

Figure 19-18. Connection is completed.

should be noted that a deleting wiring block is always a leaf of the pedigree graph.

Operations on wiring patterns, such as deletion, modification and addition, are actually reduced to manipulating this pedigree graph. This enables not only having a quick response time for commands, but also permits making best use of programming time.

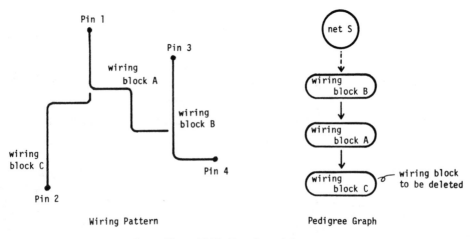

Wiring Pattern   Pedigree Graph

Figure 19-19. Transformed data.

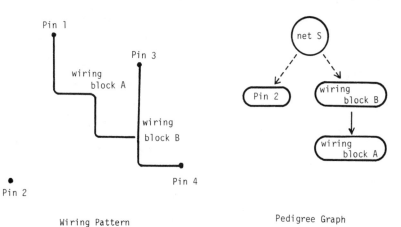

Wiring Pattern   Pedigree Graph

Figure 19-20. Deletion is completed.

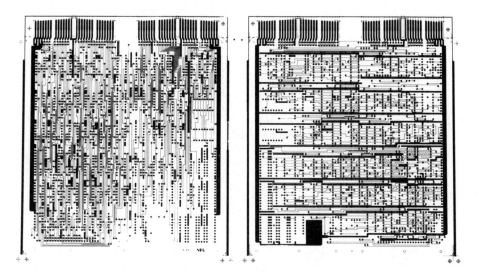

Figure 19-21. Layout example designed by BRAIN system.

CONCLUSION

This paper has presented an interactive layout design system for printed wiring
boards: BRAIN. The BRAIN system fully integrates the automatic and interactive functions and realizes an optimum exploitation of human intelligence
and the computer's high speed processing. This system has been in practical
use and contributing greatly to reducing design time and cost.

Continued development is now under way on more efficient automatic algorithms and highly interactive functions.

ACKNOWLEDGEMENT

The authors would like to thank Prof. I. Shirakawa of Osaka University, Dr. T. Mikami, Mr. T. Seki and Mr. K. Hasegawa of Nippon Electric Co. for their valuable suggestions and encouragement. Finally, they are greatly indebted to Mr. M. Odani, Mr. Y. Ogura, Mr. O. Sekikawa, Miss K. Mitsumoto and BRAIN development group members for their invaluable assistance in making programs.

REFERENCES

(1) Breuer, M. A., ed., *Design Automation of Digital Systems Volume 1*. Prentice Hall, Inc., (1972).
(2) Goto, S., Cederbaum, I. and Ting, B. S. "Sub-optimum Solution of the Backboard Ordering with Channel Capacity Constraint." *IEEE Trans. on Circuits Syst.* **CAS-24**:645–652 (Nov. 1977).
(3) Goto, S. and Kuh, E. S., "An Approach to the Two-Dimensional Placement Problem in Circuit Layout." *IEEE Trans. on Circuits Syst.* **CAS-25**:208–214 (April 1978).
(4) Goto, S., "An Efficient Algorithm for the Two-Dimensional Placement Problem in Electrical Circuit Layout." *IEEE Trans. on Circuits Syst.* **CAS-28** No. 1: 12–18 (Jan. 1981).
(5) Nishioka, I., Kurimoto, T., Yamamoto, S., Shirakawa, I, and Ozaki, H. "An Approach to Gate Assignment and Module Placement for Printed Wiring Boards." *Proc. of 15th Design Automation Conference* (1978):60–69.
(6) Mikami, K. and Tabuchi, K. "A Computer Program for Optimal Routing for Printed Circuit Conductor." *IFIP Congress* **68**:1475–1478 (1968).
(7) Hashimoto, A. and Stevens, J. "Wire Routing by Optimizing Channel Assignment within Large Aperture." *Proc. of 8th Design Automation Workshop* (1971).
(8) Yamamura, H., Shirakawa, I. and Ozaki, H. "A Line-search Method for the Route Connecting Problem on 2-layer Printed Circuit Boards." *IECE Trans.* **57-A**:671–678 (1974) (in Japanese).
(9) Chiba, T., Shirakawa, I. and Ozaki, H. "A Maze-running Method for the Route-connection on a Two-layer Printed Circuit Boards." *IECE Trans.* **59-A**:247–253 (1976) (in Japanese).
(10) Ting, B. S., Kuh, E. S. and Shirakawa, I. "The Multilayer Routing Problem: Algorithms and Necessary and Sufficient Conditions for the Single Row Single-layer Case." *IEEE Trans. on Circuits and Syst.* **CAS-23**:768–778 (1976).
(11) Nishioka, I., Kurimoto, T. and Nishida, H. "A Minicomputerized Automatic Layout System for Two-layer Printed Wiring Boards." *Proc. of 14th Design Automation Conference* (1977): 1–11.
(12) Kuh, E. S., Kashiwabara, T. and Fujisawa, T. "On Optimum Single-now Routing." *IEEE Trans. on Circuits and Syst.* **CAS-26**:361–368 (1979).
(13) Tada, F., Yoshimura, K., Kagata, T. and Shirakawa, T. "A Fast Maze Router with Iterative Use of Variable Search Space Restriction." *Proc. of 17th Design Automation Conference* (1980): 250–254.

(14) Nishioka, I., et al. "An Automatic Routing System for High Density Multilayer Printed Wiring Boards. *Proc. of 17th Design Automation Conference* (1980): 520–527.

(15) Kajitani, Y. "On Via Hole Minimization of Routing on a 2-Layer Board." *ICCC 80* (1980) 295–298.

(16) Asahara, S., Odani, M., Ogura, Y., Shirakawa, I. and Ozaki, H. "A Routing System Based on Single-row Routing for High Density Printed Wiring Boards. *ICCC 80* (1980) 290–294.

(17) Tsukiyama, S., Kuh, E. S. and Shirakawa, I. "An Algorithm for Single-Row Routing with Prescribed Street Congestions." *IEEE Trans. on Circuits Syst.* **CAS-26**:369–377 (1979).

(18) Vhiestra, J. "An Overview of Computer Aided Printed Circuit Board Design in an Electronic Industry." *Computer in Industry* **1**:41–58 (1979).

(19) Welt, M. J. "NOMAD: A Printed Wiring Board Layout System." *Proc. of the 12th Design Automation Conference* (1975):152–161.

(20) Bedard, K., Fournier, S., Shastry, B. and Stockburger, U. "A Production PCB Layout System on a Minicomputer." *Proc. of 14th Design Automation Conference* (1977):168–171.

(21) Stevens, K. R., van Cleemput, W. M., Bennett, T. C. and Hupp, J. A. "Implementation of an Interactive Printed Circuit Design System." *Proc. of 15th Design Automation Conference* (1978):74–81.

(22) Villers, P. "A Minicomputer Based Interactive Graphics System as Used for Electronic Design and Automation." *Proc. of 15th Design Automation Conference* (1978):446–453.

(23) Johnson, D. R. "PC Board Layout Techniques. *Proc of the 16th Design Automation Conference* (1979):337–343.

(24) Habra, R. R. "Interactive Graphic Wiring." *Proc. of International Conference on Interactive Techniques in Computer Aided Design* (1978):317–320.

(25) Ore, O. "Theory of Graphs." *American Mathematical Society* (1962).

(26) Soukup, J. "Fast Maze Router." *Proc. of 15th Design Automation Conference* (1978):100–102.

(27) Geyer, G. M. "Connection Routing Algorithm for Printed Circuit Boards." *IEEE Trans. on Circuit Theory* **CT-18** No. 1:95–100 (Jan. 1971).

20. VLSI Design Verification and Logic Simulation

Isao Ohkura, Kaoru Okazaki, Takeshi Tokuda and
Kazuhiro Sakashita
Mitsubishi Electric Corporation, Japan

INTRODUCTION

The scale and performance of logic systems especially in the computer field
have been improved by advancing VLSI design and fabrication technologies.
Various kinds of CAD tools have made it possible not only to develop VLSI
circuits in a short turn around time but also to execute a rigid timing design
of the circuit in order to get higher performance. Design verification in each
design step of logic systems has particularly become an important technology
in the VLSI design process. Hardware and software simulations are effective
to verify a designed system. The latter has extensively been used for the verification because of the following merits:

1. It enables us easily to know whether the intended functions of the VLSI
   circuit will be attained by the present design or not.
2. It makes it possible to simulate the timing relation of the circuit exactly
   by taking the active device parameters and loading conditions into
   account.
3. It enables us to evaluate the electrical characteristics under the fluctuations of fabrication parameters and operation conditions.

At first, the present design verification technologies will be reviewed in relation to the design flow in the next section. Secondly, a new logic simulation will
be discussed which will treat an exact rise/fall delay time of logic gates with
an ED (enhancement-depletion) MOS configuration. Transmission gate plays

an important role to improve the performance of MOS logic circuits. An exact delay logic simulation for the transmission gate will be discussed in the final section.

VLSI DESIGN VERIFICATION

VLSI Design Flow and Verification Technology

Delay time of each logic element constructing a VLSI circuit is affected much more by both the input waveform and the loading conditions than an equivalent logic system constructed of standard SSI and MSI parts. Therefore, each logic element of the VLSI circuit is unfixed in the delay properties until the physical layout is finally fixed. A hierarchical layout design method, that is a block-oriented design, minimizes the fluctuation of delay properties in a functional logic block at the physical layout design. This allows rigid timing design and is effective to attain high performance in a VLSI circuit. Figure 20-1 shows a typical design flow for custom logic VLSI circuits, especially in the case of standard cell approaches. In a more severe design example, some feedback

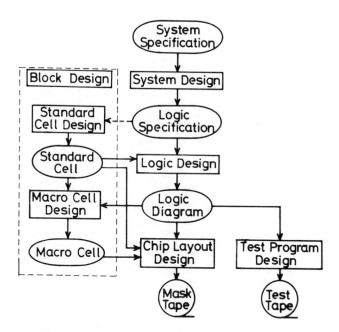

Figure 20-1. A typical design flow for VLSI logic circuits.

loops would exist, and iterative designs or specification refinements would be needed (1). The design flow is constructed by two essential processes:

1. Top-down process which breaks a high level specification down to low level.
2. Bottom-up process which constructs a high level physical block by low level blocks and standard gates.

The design procedure is roughly divided into five steps as shown in the figure. In each design step, various kinds of software simulations are performed under the different description levels to confirm the correctness of the design.

System design is used to embody the system architecture based on the specification. The architecture is verified by various levels of system simulations (2, 3, 4) with the progress of the design:

1. System Level or Processor-Memory-Switch (PMS) Level.
2. Programming Level or Instruction Level.
3. Register Transfer Level or Micro-Instruction Level.

If the system is very large, it is divided into plural VLSI chips under the consideration of delay time, power dissipation, chip size, pin numbers and so on.

Logic design consists of clarifying the gate level logic diagram based on the system architecture. The logic elements for the design are standard cells which contains standard gates (NOR, NAND, AND-OR-NOT, F/F, etc.) and functional blocks (ROM, RAM, PLA, etc.). Some other circuits may be added to improve the testability of the VLSI chip in case of the necessity. Logic simulations (5, 6) are carried out for the design verification. A functional level logic simulation (7, 8) is practical for large macro blocks or the whole VLSI chip, and gate level logic simulation (9, 10) is available for relatively small functional blocks. The delay time specification of each gate is also determined in this design step. The load drivability (or gate size) is selected by considering the delay specification and the loading condition imagined from the fan-out of the gate.

Block design consists of preparing or constructing logic elements which will be used for logic design and chip layout design of the system. The logic element group may be classified into two types of logic blocks, that is, standard cells and macro cells. The former contains standard gates and functional blocks described above. The latter contains widely used (or high performance) logic blocks constructed by standard cells (or if necessity, by manual design) according to the logic diagram. The gate size is selected by considering the delay specification and real loading conditions. The latter also includes high level macro blocks which are hierarchically constructed by low level blocks. For more difficult block designs, these macros are iteratively designed or the logic diagrams are sometimes modified mainly because of the daily specification. From these viewpoints, the design step assumes a bottom-up aspect. According to the design level, various kinds of verifications are executed.

1. Device level: The fluctuation of the electrical characteristics caused by the fabrication condition are sometimes evaluated by a two or three dimensional device simulation (11, 12, 13).
2. Circuit level: The DC, AC characteristics of designed blocks are estimated by a circuit simulation (14, 15) or a timing simulation (16, 17).
3. Gate level or Logic level: The functional operations of macro blocks are simulated by a logic simulation and the timing relations are also by an exact delay logic simulation (18) or a timing simulation.

Chip layout design consists of building the VLSI chip physically by the placement and routing of logic blocks prepared in the block design. The design verification is carried out for the confirmation of timing relations in the VLSI circuit. Hazardous conditions are detected by a delay simulation based on the physical layout information. In the case of a VLSI logic circuit, an exact delay logic simulation based on the real loading conditions is more practical than a circuit simulation or a timing simulation because the circuit complexity is very large. According to the simulation results, the gate size mainly of inter-block drivers which has been set in the block design will be modified to attain the system specification.

Test program design consists of preparing a program to test the VLSI chip for its intended performance. The program usually includes DC, AC and logic function test items. The logic function test sequence is most difficult to prepare because a sequence is desired which will detect all gate faults perfectly. The input test sequence is evaluated by a fault simulation (6, 19). The output test sequence for a given input sequence is generated by a logic simulator.

Logic Simulation

Simulators used for design verification are attempting to accurately predict both normal and abnormal behaviour of physical devices. The abnormal behaviour includes potential spikes, hazards, critical and non-critical races, etc. In order to detect these timing errors, it is essential that the gap between the simulation models and the physical circuits is reduced as much as possible in timing properties. In this section, briefly discussed are the delay modeling and the multiple value modeling implemented in present day simulators developed for logic and design verification.

Delay Modeling. The first delay model implemented in the event-driven simulators (20, 9, 10) is a nominal delay model. In the model, a single delay value t is assigned to each kind of logic element. Some devices, however, have different signal rise and fall times due to various electrical parameters such as input waveforms and load capacitances. Such devices can be modeled by assigning two delays of t_{pHL} for a transition from 1 to 0 and t_{pLH} for a transition from 0 to 1. The model is referred to as a rise/fall delay model, which closely approximates the timing properties for many device technologies. The pulse width modulation due to different rise/fall delay can be simulated by the model. This model, however, requires special event-handling of logic transitions in the treatment of pulses which are narrower than the difference in delay times. Let's consider an example in Figure 20-2 which shows a circuit with $t_{pLH} = 5$ and $t_{pHL} = 2$. If a negative pulse with a width of 2 is imposed on the input, the abnormal situation occurs. That is, the output change caused by the first input change occurs later than that by the later input change. To model this behaviour correctly, in most of the present simulators, the events will be canceled. From more pessimistic aspects, the output would be assigned to be an unpredictable value or an error state.

The more precise modeling of delay is called a delay ambiguity model or a min/max delay model (21). Commercially available logic circuits, SSIs and MSIs, operate with a propagation delay somewhat between a minimum value t_{pdm} and a maximum value t_{pdM}. These delays define an ambiguity region of duration $t_{pdM} - t_{pdm'}$ and the gate signal changes the value sometime within

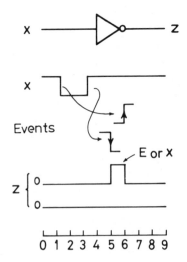

Figure 20-2. Input and output timing diagrams for a pulsed input with a width of less than the difference in delay times.

this region. In logic simulation, the ambiguity region propagates through the elements in an additive fashion. That is, each element contributes its own ambiguity in the switching times as the signal change propagates through the element. Thus, the region at the output node widens compared with that at the input. Therefore, the model results in overly pessimistic behaviour or worst-case behaviour. The delay amibiguity model can be incorporated into the nominal delay model and the rise/fall delay model.

Other methods proposed for the delay ambiguity modeling are the Monte Carlo simulation (6) where all combinations of delays can be considered and the probability model (22) where the delay distribution is approximated by Gaussian curve. However, for elements in VLSI circuits, these delay ambiguity models may not be essential since the elements in the VLSI will be fabricated simultaneously under the same process.

Another circuit delay which should be considered is an inertial delay. To switch a logic gate, some minimum energy is required. In the inertial delay model (6), this minimum energy is modeled as a minimum pulse width required to switch the logic gate. Unlike the preceding types of delay, the inertial delay should be modeled at inputs to the elements and thus a complex event manipulation such as unscheduling of a scheduled output is required. In most of the present simulators, the inertial delay is usually handled by a high frequency rejection procedure (21) which filters out any output pulse with width less than the inertial delay. Figure 20-3 shows the input/output timing diagrams of an inverter for various delay models.

Delay modeling for complex functional elements is more complicated, such as in flip-flops and MSI devices. Macroscopic modeling (23) has been proposed on the timing relations to the element, in addition to the preceding delay models. The model includes set-up/hold time, minimum pulse width of the clock, set and reset signals, variable path delay depending on logic operations, and other factors.

Multiple Value Modeling.   A two value (0, 1) simulation model is not sufficient in the design verification environment. The first major drawback of this simulation model is in the initialization of the circuit to be simulated. Since only two values exist, all signals would be initially set to 0 or 1 and thus the consistent setting of signal value is required, because for example the output value of an inverter must be inversion of the input value. Another drawback is that the abnormal states due to spikes, hazards and races cannot be generated and the effect of these states cannot be propagated. Because these drawbacks are rather severe in design verification, most of the existing simulators employ at least a three value model.

The nominal or rise/fall delay models use three or four values. Three values are 0, 1 and X, where X is the unpredictable or unknown state (5). Four values are 0, 1, X and E, where X is the initial unknown state and E is the unpre-

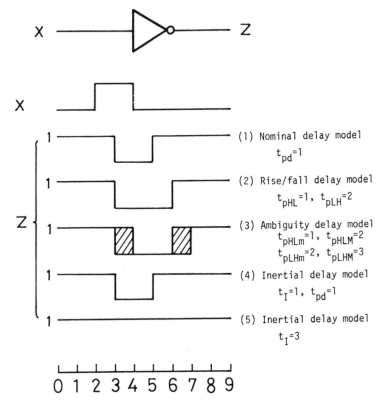

Figure 20-3. Input and output timing diagrams of an inverter for various delay models.

dictable state due to spikes, hazards and races. The delay ambiguity model requires two additional values of U (signal rising) and D (signal falling) representing the ambiguity states (21). Furthermore, some special values have been introduced for generating the states of special logic elements such as a tri-state device and a transmission gate. A value Z is introduced to represent a high impedance state for the tri-state device and dynamic states $\tilde{0}$, $\tilde{1}$ have been proposed for special MOS devices such as a transmission gate and a bus (30).

To model the physical circuits accurately, more logic values would be required, and it would drastically slow down the simulation speed. Therefore, the selection of logic values should be dependent on the purpose of the simulation. For example, in order to verify the logical correctness of a design, a nominal or unit delay simulation with four values (0, 1, X, Z) may be first employed. Once the logical correctness has been established, a rise/fall delay simulation with five values $(0, 1, X, E, Z)$ or a min/max delay simulation with eight values $(0, 1, X, E, U, D, Z, T)$ are used to test the timing properties of the circuit. In this case, T represents the transitions to and from Z. In this second step, most of the recent integrated CAD systems for VLSI circuits provide the techniques that translate the LSI connection path properties based on the chip layout into the delay values in logic simulation.

A NEW EXACT DELAY LOGIC SIMULATION FOR ED MOS LOGIC GATE

Although circuit simulators and timing simulators are able to analyze not only the delay time but also the transition time, the circuit scale is practically limited to less than a few hundred gates in the case of the former, or to less than a few thousand gates in the latter. Logic simulators, on the other hand, are available for a circuit with up to ten thousand gates. Although these simulators can handle several kinds of delay times, the delay models are still insufficient for the analysis of race and hazard in a circuit. For example, the min/max delay simulation for delay ambiguity is able to treat the delay fluctuation of the logic gate. It is, therefore, useful for the race and hazard detection of the systems constructed by commercially available logic circuits (SSI or MSI) which are produced separately at different conditions. On the other hand, the gate delay time in an LSI circuit is largely affected by the input waveform and load capacitance of the gate (24, 25), and it is sufficient to consider a parallel shift for the delay time fluctuation. Therefore, precise modeling of the rise/fall delay is an important problem for a VLSI logic simulation.

In this section, the delay time of n-channel enhancement-depletion (ED) MOS gates will be precisely analyzed and the result will be applied to a new logic simulator that is able to treat exact delay times depending upon both the input waveform and the load capacitance.

Device Structure and Delay Time Definition

Device. Figure 20-4 shows an ED MOS inverter chain discussed in this section. The enhancement transistor $Q1_n$ and the depletion transistor $Q2_n$ are a driver and a load element of the "n"th gate, respectively. The current drivability of a transistor is in proportion to W/L, where W and L are the channel width and channel length of the transistor. Usually, in custom logic LSIs by standard cell approaches, the channel width of a transistor is varied according to the demanded value of delay time. The conductance ratio β_R of each gate in a LSI circuit is assumed to be a fixed value in order to attain the same DC transfer characteristic and noise immunity. C_n is the load capacitance normalized by the gate size. For example, when the transistor size (W/L) of the concerned gate is two times larger than that of the standard gate, the normalized

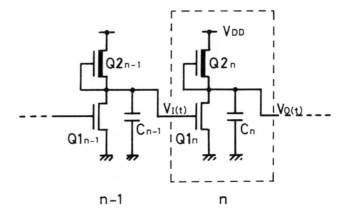

Figure 20-4. Enhancement-Depletion (ED) MOS inverter chain.

capacitance C_n is a half of the real value of the load capacitance. By this normalization, any gates in the chain are reduced to the normalized gates with fixed device dimensions. Therefore, the gate delay analysis discussed below is carried out for a standard gate size with various load capacitances. V_{DD}, $V_I(t)$ and $V_O(t)$ are the supplied voltage, input node voltage and output node voltage, respectively. Figure 20-5 shows the current-voltage characteristics of the driver transistor $Q1$ and the load transistor $Q2$. Figure 20-6 shows the DC transfer

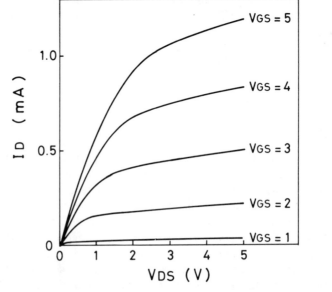

Figure 20-5. I_D-V_D characteristics of (a) driver transistor and (b) load transistor in the *n-ch.* ED MOS inverter.

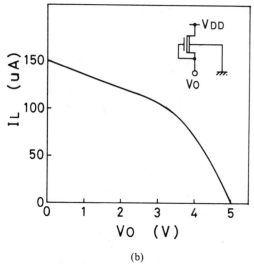

(b)

Figure 20-5. (*continued*)

characteristics of the inverter. The high level of the output node is equal to V_{DD} (5V) in the ED MOS configuration. V_L and V_{PP} are the output low level (0.2V) and the amplitude of voltage swing (4.8V), respectively. V_T is the threshold voltage of this inverter (1.75V) at which the output voltage coincides with the input voltage in the DC transfer characteristic.

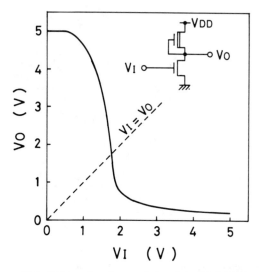

Figure 20-6. DC transfer characteristics of the ED MOS inverter.

Definition of Delay Time and Transition Time. The waveforms of the input and output nodes are illustrated in Figure 20-7. The delay times t_{pLH} and t_{pHL} are defined by the intervals of two times at which the input and the output voltages become equal to the threshold voltage V_T, respectively. The rise time t_r and the fall time t_f are defined by the time duration in which the input or the output node voltage swings between $0.1 V_{PP}$ and $0.9 V_{PP}$. With this definition, the delay times become always positive for any values of the load capacitance C_n and the input transition time t_{rI} or t_{fI}.

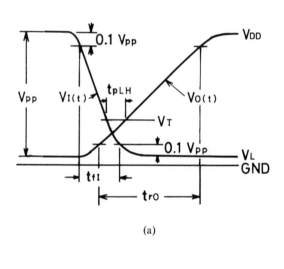

(a)

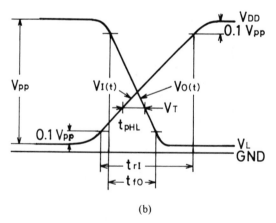

(b)

Figure 20-7. Input and output waveforms in the ED MOs inverter. (a) Input node voltage falls to the low level, (b) input node voltage rises to the high level.

Gate Delay Analysis and Theoretical Consideration

Results of Circuit Analysis.   Figure 20-8a shows the analytical result of a circuit simulation when the input node falls to the low level. Various input waveforms are obtained by changing the load capacitance C_{n-1} of the preceding gate. The delay time t_{pLH} and the output rise time t_{rO} are approximately fixed values, which depend only on the load capacitance C_n of the "n"th gate and not on the input waveform.

Figure 20-8b shows the delay times t_{pHL} and the fall times t_{fO} of the gate with a load capacitance C_n for various input rise times t_{rI}. They are largely affected by t_{rI}, and also by C_n. Here, the rise time t_{rI} is given as a function of

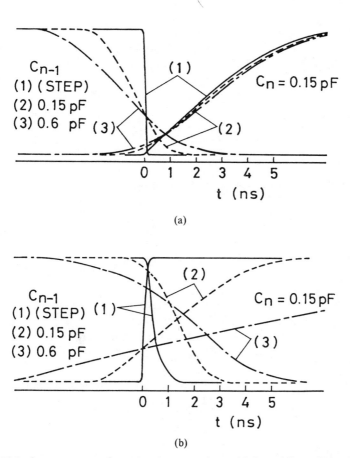

(a)

(b)

Figure 20-8. Output responses for various input waveforms. (a) Input falls to the low level, (b) input rises to the high level.

the load capacitance of the "$n-1$"th gate as suggested in Figure 20-8a. t_{pHL} and t_{fo} are, consequently, determined by the function of the two load capacitances C_n and C_{n-1}. t_{pLH} and t_{pHL} are plotted in Figure 20-9 as a function of the ratio of two capacitances C_n and C_{n-1}. The dependence of delay time on input waveform and load capacitance are confirmed in this figure as predicted in Figure 20-8.

Theoretical Consideration.   Since the delay time t_{pLH} and the rise time t_{ro} are scarcely affected by the input waveform as shown in Figure 20-8a, they are able to be represented by the case resulting from an input node step function:

$$V_I(t) = \begin{cases} V_{DD} \text{ at } t < 0 & \text{[20.1]} \\ V_L \text{ at } t \geq 0 & \text{[20.2]} \end{cases}$$

Under the approximation of the load current to be a constant value I_{LO}, the output voltage $V_O(t)$ is calculated as follows (26).

$$C_n \frac{dV_O(t)}{dt} = I_{LO} \qquad\qquad \text{[20.3]}$$

$$V_O(t) = V_L + \frac{I_{LO}}{C_n} t \qquad\qquad \text{[20.4]}$$

From equation [20.4], t_{pLH} and t_{ro} are given by

$$t_{pLH} = \frac{Cn}{I_{LO}} (V_T - V_L) \qquad\qquad \text{[20.5]}$$

$$t_{ro} = 0.8 \frac{Cn}{I_{LO}} (V_{DD} - V_L) \qquad\qquad \text{[20.6]}$$

When the input voltage rises to the high level V_{DD}, the delay time t_{pHL} and the fall time t_{fo} are significantly affected by the input waveform as shown in Figure 20-8b. The input waveform is able to be approximated by the linear ramp function as is shown in equation [20.4],

$$V_I(t) = V_L \text{ at } t < 0 \qquad\qquad \text{[20.7]}$$

$$V_I(t) = V_L + \frac{0.8(V_{DD} - V_L)}{t_{rl}} t \text{ at } 0 \leq t < \frac{'rl}{0.8} \qquad\qquad \text{[20.8]}$$

$$V_I(t) = V_{DD} \text{ at } t \geq \frac{'rl}{0.8} \qquad\qquad \text{[20.9]}$$

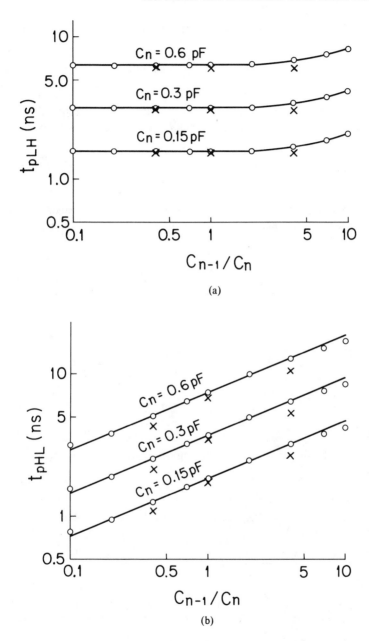

Figure 20-9. Delay times (a) t_{pLH} and (b) t_{pHL} for various capacitive load conditions. The solid lines are the results of circuit simulation and the marks X are the calculated values by equations [20.5] and [20.14].

where the input rise time t_{rl} is derived from equation [20.6] and is given by

$$t_{rl} = 0.8 \frac{C_{n-1}}{I_{LO}} (V_{DD} - V_L) \qquad [20.10]$$

At the discharge of the load capacitance C_n, the driver current $I_D(t)$ plays a more dominant role than the load current $I_L(t)$ and is approximated by

$$I_D(t) = \frac{\beta D}{2} (V_I(t) - V_{TD})^2 \qquad [20.11]$$

where β_D and V_{TD} are the conductance constant and the threshold voltage of the driver device $Q1_n$. The output node voltage $V_O(t)$ is approximately calculated by

$$-C_n \frac{dV_O(t)}{dt} = I_D(t) \qquad [20.12]$$

and then

$$C_n(V_{DD} - V_O(t)) = \frac{I_{DO}}{3} \left(\frac{0.8}{t_{rl}} \right)^2 \left(\frac{V_{DD} - V_L}{V_{DD} - V_{TD}} \right)^2$$
$$x \left(t - \frac{t_{rl}(V_{TD} - V_L)}{0.8(V_{DD} - V_L)} \right)^3 \qquad [20.13]$$

where I_{DO} is the driver saturation current at the drain voltage of V_{DD}. From equation [20.13], t_{pHL} and t_{fo} are given by

$$t_{pHL} = \sqrt[3]{\frac{3C_n(V_{DD} - V_T)}{I_{DO}} \left[\frac{C_{n-1}(V_{DD} - V_{TD})}{I_{LO}} \right]^2}$$
$$- \frac{V_T - V_{TD}}{I_{LO}} C_{n-1} \qquad [20.14]$$

$$t_{fo} = 0.5 \sqrt[3]{\frac{3C_n(V_{DD} - V_T)}{I_{DO}} \left[\frac{C_{n-1}(V_{DD} - V_{TD})}{I_{LO}} \right]^2} \qquad [20.15]$$

t_{pLH} and t_{pHL} calculated by equations [20.5] and [20.14] are plotted in Figure 20-9. They are in good agreement with the results of the circuit simulation.

Gate Modeling in Logic Simulation

Setting up the Model.   Consider a gate level simulation with rise/fall delay. In the case of a multiple-input gate, such as 2- or 3-input NOR gate, each input node has a different capacitance. Therefore, the value of fall mode delay t_{pHL} of the gate changes depending upon which input node is logically active, as discussed in the last section. This implies that the gate model should have different values of t_{pHL} and t_{pLH} corresponding to each input node, which is compared with a single set of delay times (t_{pHL}, t_{pLH}) in a conventional simulator.

A gate is normally evaluated by two basic operations; a delay operation causing the signal delay and a functional operation to give the output value. There are two possible ways to set up gate models as shown in Figure 20-10.

1. Input-side delay model

This model applies the delay operation to all of its inputs initially, and then performs the functional operation to yield the output. Thus,

$$z = F(D(x_1, x_2, \ldots x_n)) \qquad\qquad [20.16]$$
$$= F(D_1(x_1), D_2(x_2), \ldots D_n(x_n))$$

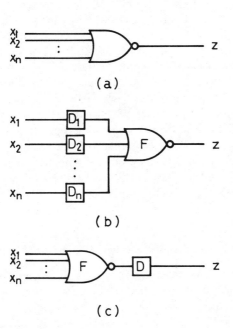

Figure 20-10. Gate modeling for ED MOS logic gate. (a) n-input NOR gate, (b) input-side delay model, (c) output-side delay model.

where $(x_1, x_2, \ldots x_n)$ are the input signals and z is the output. F is the functional operation and D is the delay operation of the gate, respectively. The delay operation for the usual NOR gate is as follows.

$$D_j = \begin{cases} t_{pHLj} \text{ for } x_j = 0/1 & [20.17] \\ t_{pLHj} \text{ for } x_j = 1/0 & [20.18] \end{cases}$$

2. Output-side delay model

This model performs the functional operation first and then the delay operation follows, in contrast with the input-side delay model. Thus,

$$z = D(F(x_1, x_2, \ldots x_n)) \qquad [20.19]$$

In the delay operation for this model, the delay value should be chosen in accordance with the logically active input to yield the output value. Furthermore, when plural input nodes cause the change of the output at the same time, minimum or maximum delay value should be selected for t_{pHL} or t_{pLH}, respectively. Thus the delay value is expressed as follows.

$$D = \begin{cases} \text{Min } (t_{pHLj}(x_j = 0/1)) & \text{for } z = 1/0 & [20.20] \\ \text{Max } (t_{pLHj}(x_j = 1/0)) & \text{for } z = 0/1 & [20.21] \end{cases}$$

Comparison of Two Models in Timing Analysis. The two models exhibit different behaviours when the input nodes change simultaneously as is illustrated in Figure 20-11. In the output-side delay model, the functional operation is performed first, and this results in the output of the gate being always 0. In the input-side delay model, the delay operation is performed first, which results in x_2 changing after x_1. Since the functional operation is performed for this new input condition, the spike is produced. On the other hand, no spike is observed in the circuit analysis under the hazardous condition. This implies that the input-side delay model is overly-pessimistic in timing analysis.

AN EXACT DELAY LOGIC SIMULATION FOR TRANSMISSION GATE

Transmission gate is effective for improving a VLSI chip complexity because the device is a logic element constructed with a single transistor. Also the power dissipation of the chip is reduced by use of the device because it doesn't dissipate DC power itself. When the gate is non-conductive, it easily realizes the high impedance state. Because of these advantages, an MOS circuit design fully utilizing the transmission gate is needed for development of high performance VLSI circuits.

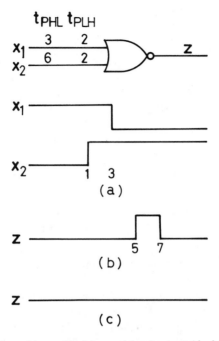

Figure 20-11. Comparison of input-side delay model and output-side delay model. (a) 2-input NOR gate and the input signals, (b) output of the input-side delay model, (c) output of the output-side delay model.

However, the delay time of the gate is difficult to analyze because it is not determined only by the input waveform and loading conditions, unlike the Boolean gate discussed in the last section. The delay time should be analyzed in the network which includes the transmission gate and the preceding gate, that is to say a driving gate. Therefore, up to now, the delay analysis has been carried out by a circuit simulation or a timing simulation or sometimes by a mixed mode simulation (27, 28). In a logic simulation which is available for large scale circuits, the delay has been modeled either over a limited range of operating conditions (29) or it has been modeled too roughly for a rigid timing design.

In this section, the delay time of a transmission gate is precisely analyzed by a circuit simulation, and then the gate modeling for an exact delay logic simulation is discussed briefly.

Transmission Gate in MOS Logic Circuit

Figure 20-12 shows an MOS circuit with a transmission gate and a driving gate which is discussed in this section. The operation modes of the transmission

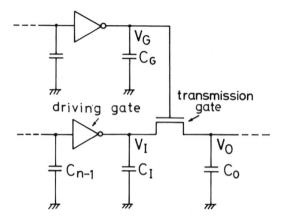

Figure 20-12. Configuration for transmission gate.

gate are generally classified into two different modes according to the timing relation in MOS circuits.

Synchronous mode corresponds to the use for the timing synchronization of the circuits, namely for latch, F/F, and register. In this mode, the data-input node of the transmission gate is pre-set to the high or low level before the gate control signal (high level) will arrive. The delay times t_{pLH}^{DG} and t_{pHL}^{DG} of the driving gate and t_{pLH}^{TG} and t_{pHL}^{TG} of the transmission gate are defined at the threshold voltage V_T as discussed in the last section. Here, t_{pLH}^{TG} and t_{pHL}^{TG} mean the delay times of the data-output signal against the gate control signal.

Asynchronous mode is found in the un-clocked selector use for the purpose of high speed data transfer. In this mode, the gate control signal is pre-set to the high level, before the data-input signal will arrive to the transmission gate. The delay times t_{pLH}^{DG}, t_{pHL}^{DG}, t_{pLH}^{TG} and t_{pHL}^{TG} are also defined at the threshold volt-age V_T as in the synchronous mode. t_{pLH}^{TG} and t_{pHL}^{TG} mean the delay times of the data-output signal against the data-input signal, contrary to the synchronous mode.

For the high speed data transfer, it is necessary that the transistor size of the transmission gate should be selected comparable or larger in comparison with that of the driver transistor in the driving gate. Therefore, the delay analysis in the next section is carried out for the case when the transmission gate size is selected to be equal to the driver transistor size. C_I and C_O in Figure 20-12 are the data-input node and data-output node capacitances normalized by the driving gate size as discussed earlier in the section on Device Structure.

Analytical Results by Circuit Simulation

Synchronous Mode. Figures 20-13 and 20-14 show the results of circuit simulation when the data-input node voltage is pre-set to the high level (V_{DD}). The

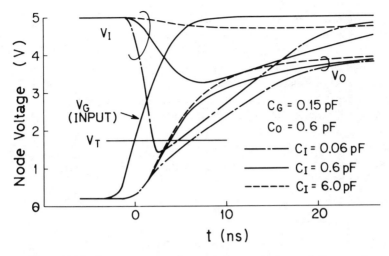

Figure 20-13. Output responses of transmission gate in the synchronous mode.

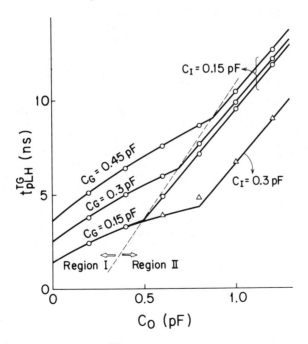

Figure 20-14. Delay time t_{pLH}^{TG} of transmission gate in the synchronous mode.

output waveform is largely affected by the value of C_I, as shown in Figure 20-13, because of the charge flow from the input to output node. In the case of the smaller C_I, the input voltage temporarily becomes lower than the threshold voltage V_T, and the output node voltage rises up gradually with the input node voltage. The relation between the delay time t_{pLH}^{TG} and C_O are classified into two regions depending upon both C_I and C_G as shown in Figure 20-14.

Region I: The delay time t_{pLH}^{TG} is almost independent of C_I and is given as a function of C_G and C_O. In this region, t_{pLH}^{TG} is mainly determined by the charging process from C_I to C_O through the transmission gate. According to a circuit analysis, the delay time is approximated by the case when the data-input node voltage is fixed to V_{DD}.

$$t_{pLH}^{TG} = f_{SH}(C_G, C_O) \qquad [20.22]$$

Region II: The delay time t_{pLH}^{TG} depends on the charging capability of load transistor in the driving gate. It is given as a function of C_G, C_I and C_O.

$$t_{pLH}^{TG} = f_{SH}(C_G, C_I, C_O) \qquad [20.23]$$

The boundary of these two regions is illustrated in Figure 20-15. The boundary lines are approximated as a linear relation of C_G and C_O.

The circuit design to set the transmission gate into Region I is effective for

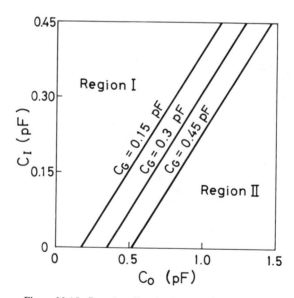

Figure 20-15. Boundary lines in the synchronous mode.

getting high speed operation. In the case of the transmission gate connected to a bus line, the operating condition is mainly in Region I because C_I, which is the bus line capacitance, is much larger than C_O.

Figures 20-16 and 20-17 show the results of a circuit simulation when the data-input node voltage is pre-set to the low level (V_{OL}). The on-resistance of the transmission gate and also of the driver transistor in the driving gate are lower than that of the load transistor in the driving gate. Therefore, the delay time t_{pHL}^{TG} is independent of C_I and is given as a function of C_G and C_O.

$$t_{pHL}^{TG} = f_{SL}(C_G, C_O) \qquad [20.24]$$

Asynchronous Mode We have seen that the results of the delay time of the driving gate t_{pLH}^{DG} and also of the transmission gate t_{pLH}^{TG} are almost independent of the input waveform for the driving gate. Figure 20-18 shows the results of circuit simulation when the input node of the driving gate falls to the low level with a constant fall time ($C_{n-1} = 0.15\text{pF}$). Because of the charge flow from the output node of the transmission gate, t_{pLH}^{DG} depends primarily on C_O, and it is consequently given as a function of C_I and C_O.

$$t_{pLH}^{DG} = f_{AH}(C_I, C_O) \qquad [20.25]$$

f_{AH} is able to be approximated as a linear function of C_I and C_O. On the other hand, the delay time t_{pLH}^{TG} is mainly determined by the on-resistance of the

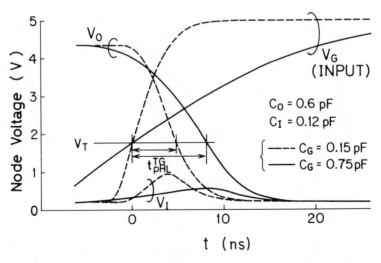

Figure 20-16. Output responses of transmission gate in the synchronous mode.

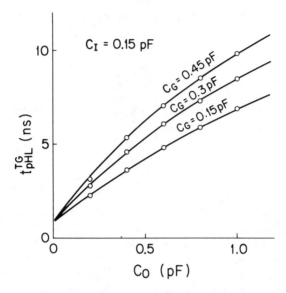

Figure 20-17. Delay time t_{pHL}^{TG} of transmission gate in the synchronous mode.

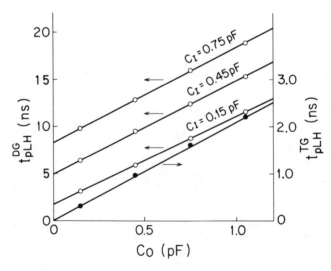

Figure 20-18. Delay times t_{pLH}^{DG} of driving gate and t_{pLH}^{TG} of transmission gate in the asynchronous mode.

transmission gate and C_O, and is independent of C_I.

$$t_{pLH}^{TG} = f_{AH}(C_O) \tag{20.26}$$

It is predicted from the results of the earlier section on Device Structure that the delay time t_{pHL}^{DG} is significantly affected by the input waveform. From the results of the circuit simulation with different values of c_{n-1}, it is found that t_{pHL}^{DG} depends on C_{n-1} but t_{pHL}^{TG} does not depend on C_{n-1}. Figure 20-19 shows the result of the analysis when $C_{n-1} = 0.15\text{pF}$. The dependence of t_{pHL}^{DG} on C_O shows almost the same tendency for different values of C_I as in Figure 20-18. Then, t_{pHL}^{DG} is given as a function of C_I, C_O and C_{n-1}.

$$t_{pHL}^{DG} = f_{AL}(C_I, C_O, C_{n-1}) \tag{20.27}$$

On the other hand, t_{pHL}^{TG} is given as a function of only C_O, as in the case of a falling input.

$$t_{pHL}^{TG} = f_{AL}(C_O) \tag{20.28}$$

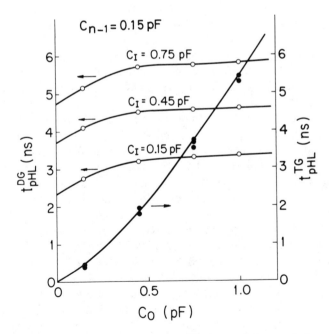

Figure 20-19. Delay times t_{pHL}^{DG} of driving gate and t_{pHL}^{TG} of transmission gate in the asynchronous mode.

Gate Modeling in Logic Simulation

The transmission gate has two different operational modes, synchronous and asynchronous. In the synchronous mode, the output transition is caused by the control-input, whereas the output transition is caused by the data-input in the asynchronous mode. Therefore, in logic simulation, the delay assignment should be done by finding which input mode causes the transition of the output. The situation is the same as in delay modeling for the ED gate in the section on Gate Modeling. The delay of the transmission gate, $D(TG)$, is expressed as follows.

$$D(TG) = \begin{array}{l} t_{pLH} \text{ (by equations [20.22] and [20.23] for } x_1 = 0/1 \text{ and } x_2 = 1 \\ t_{pHL} \text{ (by equation [20.24] for } x_1 = 0/1 \text{ and } x_2 = 0 \\ t_{pLH} \text{ (by equation [20.26] for } x_1 = 1 \text{ and } x_2 = 0/1 \\ t_{pHL} \text{ (by equation [20.28] for } x_1 \text{ and } x_2 = 1/0 \end{array}$$

where x_1 and x_2 are the control-input and data-input, respectively.

On the other hand, a problem exists on the delay assignment of the ED gate (a driving gate) feeding the data input to the transmission gate. The loading condition of the driving gate varies according to whether the control-input of the succeeding transmission gate is active (asynchronous mode) or inactive (synchronous mode). This means that the delay assignment of the driving gate cannot be determined only by the condition of its own inputs. When the driving gate and the transmission gate are individually modeled as primitive elements in a logic simulator, the driving gate requires an additional procedure, which examines the state of the succeeding transmission gate, in the delay evaluation unlike other logic gates.

In order to eliminate this additional undesired procedure, the driving gate and the transmission gate have been effectively combined into one primitive element. Figure 20-20 shows two examples of models for a circuit which contain an inverter and a transmission gate. The model (a) in the figure is a 2-input primitive element. This type of model is simple and is often used in a functional logic block into one primitive. In the model, the delay D_1 is a sum of $D(TG)$ and $D(DG)$, and D_2 is $D(DG)$. Here, $D(DG)$ is the delay of the driving gate and has the synchronous- and asynchronous-mode delays which are expressed in the same manner as equations [20.20] and [20.21]. The actual delay values of D_1 and D_2 are selected corresponding to the input condition of x_1 and x_2. For example, if x_1 is high and x_2 changes the state, the delay values which are in the asynchronous mode are taken. However, since the delay of the driving gate is not considered in processing the functional operation of the primitive, the timing of the signal transition at the inputs of the transmission gate is not correctly simulated in the case where the two inputs change states at nearly the same times. To correctly simulate the situation, the output change

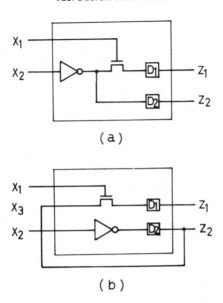

Figure 20-20. Gate modeling for transmission gate and driving gate.

of the driving gate should be treated as an event which propagates to the transmission gate. The model b makes this possible in a uniform event handling method where the events are only the output transitions of the primitive elements. The model is a 3-input and 2-output primitive element. The interconnection of these logic gates is made externally between the output z_2 and the additional third input x_3. Here, $D_1 = D(TG)$ and $D_2 = D(DG)$. D_2 is determined by the input condition of x_1 and x_2 like the model a, whereas D_1 is determined by the input condition of x_1 and x_3. These two models are easily implemented into a conventional event-driven simulator, except that the delay assignment procedure examines which input node causes the transition of the output.

CONCLUSION

The propagation delay time of the Enhancement-Depletion (ED) MOS logic gate is precisely analyzed under the consideration of input waveform and loading conditions. According to the circuit analysis and a theoretical consideration, the delay time t_{pLH} for a rising input voltage is approximately given as a function of the output capacitance of only the gate concerned. On the other hand, the delay time t_{pHL} for falling input voltage is affected by not only the input capacitance but also the input waveform which is approximately given as a function of the output capacitance of the preceding gate. t_{pHL} is consequently determined by the two output capacitances, and this allows the easy implementation of the delay model into a logic simulator. An exact delay logic simulation is attained by considering the delay components, corresponding to each input node, at the output side of the logic element.

The delay time of transmission gate is also analyzed by circuit simulation. The operations are divided into two modes: synchronous mode and asynchronous mode. In the asynchronous mode, the delay time of the preceding gate, that is a driving gate, is extremely affected by the output capacitance of the transmission gate. To simulate this phenomenon correctly, models are proposed which treat these two logic elements as one primitive element in a logic simulator. In like manner for ED MOS logic gates, the models are able to be processed in the conventional event-driven method except when the delay assignment is dependent on which input node causes the output transition.

ACKNOWLEDGEMENT

The authors wish to thank Drs. H. Oka, Y. Gamoh, Y. Horiba, T. Yahara and T. Enomoto for their encouragements and useful discussions.

REFERENCES

(1) vanCleemput, W. M. "Hierarchical Design for VLSI: Problems and Advantages." Technical Note No. 150, March 1979.
(2) Chen, R. C., and Coffman, J. E. "MULTI-SIM, A Dynamic Multi-Level Simulator." *Proc. of 15th Design Automation Conf.* (1978):386–391.
(3) Tokoro, M., et al. "A Module Level Simulation Technique for Systems Composed of LSI's and MSI's." *Proc. of 15th Design Automation Conf.* (1978):418–427.
(4) Efron, R., and Gordon, G. "General Purpose Digital Simulation and Example of its Applications." *IBM System Journal* 3:22–34 (1964).
(5) Szygenda, S. A., and Thompson, E. W. "Digital Logic Simulation in a Time-based, Table-driven Environment-Part 1, Design Verification," *Computer,* 8:24–36 (March 1975).
(6) Breuer, M. A., and Friedman, A. D. "Diagnosis and Reliable Design of Digital Systems." Computer Science Press, Woodland Hills, Cal. (1976), pp. 174–254.
(7) Chappell, S. G. et al. "Functional Simulation in the Lamp System." *Proc. of 13th Design Automation Conf.* 1976:42–47.
(8) Sasaki, T., et al. "MIXS: A Mixed Level Simulator for Large Digital System Logic Verification." *Proc. of 17th Design Automation Conf.* June 1980:626–633.
(9) Szygenda, S. A. "TEGAS2-Anatomy of a General Purpose Test Generation and Simulation System for Digital Logic." *Proc. of 9th ACM-IEEE Design Automation Workshop,* (June 1972).
(10) Wilcox, P., and Rombeek, H. "F/logic—An Interactive Fault and Logic Simulation for Digital Circuits." *Proc of 13th Design Automation Conf.* (1976):68–73.
(11) Barron, M. B. "Computer Aided Analysis of Insulated Gate Field-effect Transistors." Stanford Electronic Laboratories, Rep. No. 5501-1, Stanford, California, (1969).
(12) Toyabe, T., et al. "A Numerical Model of Avalanche Breakdown in MOSFET's." *IEEE Trans. on Electron Dev.* **ED-25**:825–832 (1978).

(13) Kotani, N., and Kawazu, S. "Computer Analysis of Punch-Through in MOSFET's." *Solid-State Electron.* **22**:63–70 (1979).

(14) Nagel, L. W. "SPLICE 2: A Computer Program to Simulate Semiconductor Circuits." Univ. of Calif., Berkeley, ERL Memo ERL-M520 (May 1975).

(15) ———, *ASTAP General Information Manual,* IBM Corp., Mechanicsburg, PA.

(16) Rabbat, N. B., et al. "A Computer Modeling Approach for LSI Digital Structures." *IEEE Trans. Electron Devices* **ED-22** (Aug. 1975).

(17) Chawla, B. R., et al. "MOTIS-An MOS Timing Simulator." *IEEE Trans. on Circuit and System* **CAS-22**:901–910 (Dec. 1975).

(18) Ohkura, I., Okazaki K., and Horiba, Y. "A New Exact Delay Logic Simulation for ED MOS LSI." *IEEE ICCC 1980*: 953–956 (Oct. 1980).

(19) Szygenda, S. A., and Thompson, E. W. "Digital Logic Simulation in a Time-based Table-driven Environment—Part 2, Parallel Fault Simulation." *Computer* **6**:38–49 (Mar. 1975).

(20) Ulrich, E. G. "Time-sequenced Logical Simulation Based on Circuit Delay and Selective Tracing of Active Network Paths." *Proc. of 1965 ACM National Conf.* (1965):437–448.

(21) Jea, Y. H., and Szygenda, S. A. "Mappings and Algorithms for Gate Modeling in a Digital Simulation Environment." *IEEE Trans. on Circuit and System* **CAS-26** No. 5:304–315 (1979).

(22) Magnhagen, B. "Practical Experiences from Signal Probability Simulation of Digital Designs." *Proc. of 14th Design Automation Conf.* (1977):216–219.

(23) Evans, D. J. "Accurate Simulation of Flip-Flop Timing Characteristics," *Proc. of 15th Design Automation Conf.* (June 1978), pp. 398–404.

(24) Bening, L. C. "Simulation of High Speed Computer Logic." *1969 Design Automation Workshop Procs.*, pp. 103–112.

(25) Koehler, D. "Computer Modeling of Logic Modules Under Consideration of Delay and Waveshaping." *Proc. IEEE* July (1969):1294–1296.

(26) Hayashi, Y., et al. "Design Theory of ED-MOS-IC." *Trans. IECI Japan* **55-C** No. 7:337–343 (1972).

(27) Newton, A. R., and Pederson, D. O. "A Simulation Program with Large-scale Integrated Circuit Emphasis." *Proc. of 17th Design Automation Conf.* (June 1980):618–625.

(28) Agrawal, V. D., Bose, A. K., Kozak, P., Nham, H. N., and Pacas-Skewes, E. "A Mixed-mode Simulator." *Proc. of 17th Design Automation Conf.* (1980):618–625.

(29) Nahm, H. N., and Bose, A. K. "A Multiple Delay Simulation for MOS LSI Circuits." *Proc. of 17th Design Automation Conf.* (1980):610–617.

(30) Watanabe, J., Miura, J., Kurachi, T., and Suetsugu, I. "Seven Value Logic Simulation for MOS LSI Circuits." *ICCC'80* (1980):941–943.

Index